SON OF THE RETURN OF MOVIE OUTLAW
By Mike Watt

Additional Material by
Ally Melling
Dr. Rhonda Baughman
Mike Haushalter
Terry Thome
Bill Watt

Introduction by Scooter McCrae

Happy Cloud Publishing
www.happycloudpictures.com

CREDITS

Some material herein previously appeared in different forms in Film Threat.com, Sirens of Cinma Magazine, Femme Fatales Magazine, and/or Movie Outlaw Blogspot.

Unless otherwise credited, DVD cover designs and Poster Art are copyright the respective holders and are reproduced here in the spirit of publicity.

PICTURE CREDITS
20th Century Fox, A-Pix Entertainment, Academy Home Entertainment, ACME-TV, Allarts / Elsevier-Vendex, Allied Artists Pictures, Alternative Cinema, American International Pictures, Anchor Bay Entertainment, Aquarius Releasing, Ardustry Home Entertainment, Artisan Entertainment, Atlantic Releasing Corporation, AVCO Embassy Pictures, Black Hill, Braveworld, Buena Vista International Spain, CBS/Fox Video, CiBy 2000 / El Deseo, Cinecom Pictures, Cinecrest, Cinefear, Cinépix Film Properties Inc., Colorama Features, Columbia Broadcasting System (CBS), Comworld Pictures, Commonwealth United Entertainment, Concorde Pictures, Dark Sky Films, Destination Films, EMI Films, Empire Video, EuropaCorp, EuroVideo, Far West Films, Film House Bas Celik, Film Workshop, First Look International, Frederick S. Clarke Publishing, Frontier Amusements, Greycat Films, Hobo Film Enterprises, Hollywoodmade, Howco Productions Inc., Icon Home Entertainment, Karl-Lorimar Home Video (KLV-TV), Key Video, Koch Media, Legacy Releasing Corporation, Lorimar Productions, Majestic Films International, MCA, Media Distribution Partners, Metropolitan Filmexport, MGM-EMI, MGM/UA Home Entertainment, Miramax Films, Missing in Action (MIA), National Broadcasting Company (NBC), New Horizons Home Video, Nordisk Film, Optimum Releasing, Orion Pictures, Paragon Video Productions, Paramount Home Video, Paul Entertainment, Phase 4 Films, Polo Pictures Entertainment, PolyGram Video, Precision Video, Random Media, RCA/Columbia Pictures Home Video, Reel One Entertainment, RKO Radio Pictures, RLJ Entertainment, Samuel Goldwyn Films, Santelmo Entertainment, Satori, Senator Film Verleih GmbH, Shout! Factory, Sony Pictures Home Entertainment, Synapse Films, Trust Film Sales, Tse Tse Fly Productions, United Artists Corporation, Universal Pictures, Vestron Video, Victorian Film, Warner Brothers Pictures, Warner Home Video
Any omissions will be corrected in future editions.

LIBRARY OF CONGRESS CATALOGUING-IN-PUBLICATION DATA
Watt, Mike
Son of the Return of Movie Outlaw / Mike Watt ; foreword by Scooter McCrae
p. cm. Includes index.
ISBN-13: 978-1537550091
ISBN-10: 1537550098
©2016 Mike Watt. All rights reserved

Front cover: Ryan Hose

Manufactured in the United States of America
Happy Cloud Publishing
Pittsburgh, PA
www.happycloudpictures.com

ACKNOWLEDGEMENTS

Special thanks to Alex Williams; Allan Tuskes; Ally Melling; Andras Jones; Autumn Cook, Dave Brown, Joe Krysinski, Ryan Hose; Betty P. Thomas; Bill Moseley; Bob Langer; Brinke Stevens; Carl Daft; Carolyn Haushalter; Carolyn Haushalter; Charles Swenson; Charlie Deitch, Pgh City Paper; Chris Gore; Chris Gore; Danny Draven; David DeCoteau; David Gregory; David Kerkes; Don May, Jr.; Dr. Rhonda Baughman; Eric Stanze; Frank Henenlotter; Gabe Bartalos; Garrett Gilchrist; Greg Ketter; Heather Drain; Jason Pankoke; John Skipp; Jonathan Maberry; Justin Wingenfeld; Ken and Pam Kish, Tom Brunner, Thomas Berdinski, Pete Chiarella, Douglas Waltz, and all of the Cinema Wastelanders; Leslie Easterbrook; Linnea Quigley; Lisa Morton; Marina Girard-Muttelet; Mark Bell; Mark Bell; Mel Damski; Michael Gingold; Michael Gingold; Mike Prosser; Mike Raso; Nicole Mikuzis; Paige K. Davis; Paul Scrabo; Peter Greenaway; Phil Hall; Ralph and Liz Bakshi; Ray Bacorn; Rian Johnson; Rich Dalzotto, Sandy Stulfire, Michelle Linhart, Horror Realm; The Hollywood Theatre; Richard Harlan Smith; Robert Kurtzman, Stephen Sayadian; Steve Railsback; Suzy McCoppin; Terry Thome; Tom Bugaj; April, Bill, and Mary Watt.

And, as always and forever, Amy.

Front cover images: Le Bossu (courtesy Philippe de Broca), The Sinful Dwarf and What? (courtesy Severin Films), Sorority Babes in the Slimeball Bowl-O-Rama (courtesy Full Moon Pictures), Heavy Traffic (courtesy Liz and Ralph Bakshi), Tommy Biondo in Scrapbook (courtesy Eric Stanze), Skinned Deep (courtesy Gabe Bartalos), Graham Chapman as Yellowbeard (courtesy Mel Damski), Down and Dirty Duck (courtesy Charles Swenson).

Back cover images (Top to bottom): The Sinful Dwarf (courtesy Severin Films), Le Bossu (courtesy Philippe de Broca), Skinned Deep (courtesy Gabe Bartalos), Heavy Traffic (courtesy Liz and Ralph Bakshi).

UPDATES TO PREVIOUS EDITIONS

As the world continues to turn and the world hunger for entertainment grows ravenous, the following films, previously reported upon in previous editions, have been raised up by benevolent benefactors and finally released to home video:

Baby of Macon (1993)—Film4 Library DVD.

Butcher, Baker, Nightmare Maker (1980)—Code Red DVD. Loaded with extras.

Fearless Frank (1967)—MGM Limited Edition Collection DVD-R. Movie only.

Fedora (1978)—Olive Films DVD

Figures in a Landscape (1970) Kino-Lorber Blu-Ray

Je t'aime, je t'aime (1968)—Kino-Lorber Blu-Ray

Skidoo (1968)—Olive Films Blu Ray

Sonny Boy (1989)—Shout! Factory Blu-Ray. An astonishing release and one I never expected to see in my lifetime. Beautiful transfer and a new commentary from the director!

The World's Greatest Sinner (1962)—Absolute Films *DVD-R.* Movie Only, transferred from what looks to be a master tape.

Twice Upon a Time (1983)—Warner Archive Collection. Beautiful transfer featuring both the John Korty-approved version as well as the "adult audio" shown on HBO. Also boasts a commentary from Korty, astonishing the world!

PREFORWARDUCTION

A few months into 2016, I had an interesting discussion with what became quite a number of online and print movie critics. The crux of the argument was that all entertainment journalists should be completely objective when it came to film reviews. "Personal opinion should have nothing to do with film reviewing." That struck me as not only high-minded but actually impossible. All reviews are reflections of personal taste. That we critics consider ourselves arbiters of taste, perhaps, should be left on the cutting-room floor, but how can you possibly "review" a film without your own tastes intruding on your judgment? Without a sense of personal taste, you don't have a review, you have an encyclopedia entry. Jettisoning any semblance of "good" or "bad", however disingenuous those opinions may be, removes the flavor of the review.

Granted, "If you like this, you're a terrible person," seems to be what passes for reviews these days. Take, for example, the online petition circulating to shut down Rotten Tomatoes, the online movie-review aggregator, for "bias against DC movies", specifically the vastly-negative reviews generated for David Ayer's *Suicide Squad.* The perpetually-outraged internet mob alleges that Rotten Tomatoes has been bought-off by Disney and Marvel to slam movies set in the DC universe, that they only collect the negative reviews. Patently ridiculous, but that's the kind of paranoid world we live in now. Fans now control the studios. When *Suicide Squad* tested negatively, reshoots were ordered to "lighten" the film's tone. As a result, several scenes involving Jared Leto's Joker were jettisoned. This led to more outrage, and now I don't know what to believe. Except that, perhaps, "nobody is ever happy."

Every entry in the *Movie Outlaw* series was written from a standpoint of personal opinion. While I present the facts surrounding each film, how it was made, what pitfalls were encountered or avoided, how it was received, etc., I still choose to write about films I *want* to write about. I even qualify each entry as "you may not like this as much as I do." In the case of *Antichrist*, or other films I don't get/enjoy/tolerate, I try to find writers with contrary opinions. Because taste is personal. Taste is fluid. And I am not—nor should I ever be—an arbiter of taste. All I want to do is call attention to movies that I think deserve a second look. (Or in the case of *Antichrist*, no look at all.)

It. Is. All. Subjective.

When I choose a film, it's from a personal point of view. Not everyone is going to dig *Shock Treatment*—history bears me out on that one. Not everyone shares my passion for *Muppets Most Wanted*, as its box office returns reflected. Sometimes, when writing about a particular film, my experience having seen it is sometimes just as influential on my opinion as the film itself. We *all* have those movies—something that touched us at an early age, or made us rethink a long-held belief. Whatever. That's what movies *do*. As critics and reviewers, it's our duty to make sense of what we've seen. To try to do that completely objectively is just folly. Entertainment is never meant to be objective. That's what documentaries are for, and even those fall short of the goal. (Do you think *Religulous* or *Bowling for Columbine* don't have personal agendas? What about *Supersize Me*? What about *Triumph of the Will*?) Movies can be narratively impartial, but the critic can never be. It's the fateful nature of the job.

What the argument seemed to boil down to, at least from my perspective, is what usually lies at the bottom of all disagreements: fear. In this case, it's the very real, very valid fear, that while movies are important, critics are not. And I couldn't agree more. Who are we, as critics, to tell anyone what is "good" or "bad"? At heart, paychecks or no aside, we're simply consumers sitting in the dark hoping to enjoy something visually, aurally, and emotionally. Then we relay that reaction to the world, usually with far too many words, flourishes, and emphasis. No matter how high the pedestal is that we've climbed upon and claimed as our own, our proclamations to the gods are still, and only, opinions. Opinions are not facts. They are not universal truths. If I say *Yellowbeard* is worth your time, I'm not necessarily right and everybody knows it. It's simply a suggestion that you give it a chance. I'm only ever suggesting that you give these movies a chance. Maybe they'll change your life. Maybe they'll waste your time. I don't know. I'm not you. But *somebody* had to be first to eat whatever the hell that was that fell out of that chicken. Somebody else had to prove that it might be better if you take it out of the shell.

To that end, there are a couple of movies in this volume that are personal favorites of mine, and the fact that they may be a bit more mainstream than usual is a cross I'm prepared to bear. Sometimes I'll go for the obscure, other times I just want to write about certain movies. That's why I chose *Miller's Crossing* and *Videodrome* over some of the more-obscure titles in the respective filmmakers' resumes. It's also the reason I spend a lot of time on *Muppets Most Wanted*, despite the Disney connection. Sometimes, ya just gotta do what makes you happy.

That being said, in 2015, I returned to teaching, this time at my alma mater, Pittsburgh Filmmakers. Now I have a whole new perspective on what's "obscure". In my current circle of 40-plus-year-olds, *Buckaroo Banzai* and *Big Trouble in Little China* are not considered obscure. *A Chinese Ghost Story* is about as middle-of-the-road as you can get as far as my movie-buff friends are concerned. And yet, to the new generation of folks coming up quickly behind us, these are "old" movies, unusual titles. My jaw has stopped dropping when "kids" (i.e., anyone younger than me) tell me they haven't seen a certain "must see" movie. The absence of *Brick* in their education is no longer a cause for shock. I've stopped clutching my chest when people tell me they've never seen "the original Indiana Jones movies". I simply mock them for their inadequacy and then assign the titles. Like telling really old knock-knock jokes to toddlers, every vaudevillian finds a new audience every decade.

The movies I cover are and always will be things I don't want to be forgotten. I'm happiest when I can bring something new to someone with as deep a love of film as I have, especially if they're even bigger film scholars than I'll ever be. There's no greater thrill than to introduce something new to a peer. When someone comes up to me and tells me they'd never even *heard* of such-and-such before, my heart swells. (And because I'm old, and heart-swelling is a definite concern, I immediately sit down to recover.) It's almost as great a thrill as when I stumble across something heretofore undiscovered myself.

And that's the function of *Movie Outlaw*: my entertainment, then your introduction. Sometimes fighting ensues. That's the third great thrill. Telling each other that your taste is terrible and that your opinions are bananas.

Despite the recent outrage over *Ghostbusters,* a reboot that can stand on the Silver platform (to use Olympic terminology) despite all the criticisms of "pandering" and "my childhood is ruined", no one ever went to war disagreeing about a movie. The internet may be cold and heartless, filled with people ossified by untenable rage... I forgot where I was going with that. Anyway, stouter hearts prevail, here's fifty more movies to enjoy or not.

And the next time you see a trailer for something that looks abysmal, calculated, cynical, or just plain unnecessary, remember: you've already seen worse.

INTRODUCTION

By Scooter McCrae

Memories are like guns—they both have triggers, but you never know who or what is going to pull them.

The book you are now holding in your hands is a 300-plus page, fully automated weapon locked and loaded to spray fifty-something movies at you willy-nilly until you succumb to falling in love with author Mike Watt's belief that the highest and the lowest end of the cinematic art form share more similarities than differences. And I totally agree with him about that, as my own personal movie collection ranges from Andrei Tarkovsky and Stanley Kubrick to Jess Franco and Jean Rollin and everyone and everything in between.

You kids today have it lucky. I'm old enough to remember those thrilling years of using the telephone and mail to obtain rare archeological finds that consisted of fourth generation VHS tape transfers that rarely looked only slightly clearer than an ultrasound image of an embryo. Heck, if they had an English language dub track or subtitles, even better, but that was rarely the case and I've probably absorbed a couple of extra languages by osmosis from watching movies and trying to figure out what was going on based on not much more than a brief synopsis about it from a cult movies book.

Services like Video Search of Miami were not only charging $20.00 a tape for movies (brilliantly skirting copyright laws by charging for the transfer of the movie from one format to another, but not for the movie itself), but also purposely degrading the quality so nobody else would be able to make a useful copy off the one you were sold. And yes, I know this is true because I called up Tom W.[1] one time and asked him about it since I worked at a professional video transfer house back in the day and wondered what the heck was going on over there. VHS was never the champagne video format, but with some love and care in the transfer process it could look a lot better than the cheap bathtub gin for the eyes that was being proffered by most video dealers.

(There were some exceptions, of course, provided by a few companies that lovingly maintained high quality dubbing and even created their own readable subtitles for these releases, but that's a foreword for another book….)

Pardon me for letting my inner tech geek take a turn at the typewriter for a bit, but back in the 1990's one of the big innovations for film fans with a taste for esoteric delights that spanned the globe was unleashed upon an unsuspecting public. Panasonic introduced the game-changing AG-W1 video deck that allowed you to play a VHS tape from anywhere in the world and digitally transcode it so it would playback on whatever TV you happened to be watching it on. This was truly incredible, as back then you would generally have to have entirely separate systems in your home if you wanted to watch tapes from anywhere else in the world, which got expensive quickly and took up a lot of space as your NTSC deck would need an NTSC TV, and your PAL deck would need a PAL TV, and your SECAM….

Anyway, you get the point.

Sure, there were professional machines that also did this and even monitors that were multi-system so with the flick of a switch you could watch any format on it, but all these combined devices were prohibitively expensive for the average consumer. But the AG-W1 cost

---

[1] *Editorial Insert*: "I went to my attorney and told him my idea… to make copies of these impossible to find foreign films and sell them to movie fans. He found a 'loop-hole' in the Berne Act which allows people to make copies of a movie if that movie hasn't been registered with the Library of Congress. In the beginning, Video Search of Miami was a "request company." Somebody would write and tell me what they were looking for and I'd try to find it. That was ridiculous, of course. So I started publishing lists and we sent those lists to subscribers of Euro Trash Cinema. Eventually Mike Weldon [of *Pyschotronic*] got involved and we had even more names of potential customers." –O'Terror, Scarlett. 2010. "Interview: Thomas Weissner – Editor Asian Cult". Horror News.net. September 20. http://horrornews.net/13423/interview-thomas-weissner-editor-asian-cult/

only $2,000.00. Which, when you consider that a professional multi-system transcoder alone was in the $5,000.00 price range, was a relative bargain for those adventurous viewers who had the spare income at their disposal.

Machines like these made work easier for places like Video Search of Miami, and also created new opportunities for small mom and pop businesses to convert tapes for customers at a reasonable price. And much as I would have loved to own one myself, I never had that kind of extra scratch to invest—although, in the end, I wouldn't be surprised if I spent more than the cost of the machine in the process of obtaining converted tapes for my ever expanding collection over the course of many years.

Most of those Franco and Rollin movies (amongst many others) that I acquired have been released on DVD and even Blu-Ray since then. Admittedly, maybe not all of them, but give it time and eventually Franco's nearly 200 film output will eventually be more fully represented in the hi-def digital world we now live in…!

Okay, so we now return to the foreword for *Son of the Return of Movie Outlaw*.

Mike has the ability to find and share interesting films lurking just beneath the cineaste radar which are not, in fact, that traditionally obscure. Almost all of the movies in his books are not mysterious Slovenian cinema that was released 40 years ago into only five theaters for less than a week during a leap year. Many of them used to be regularly shown on TV stations looking to find stuff to transmit between the all-important commercials back before cable gave us theme specific channels for every possible genre from sports to weather to comedy and whatever other fetish has a hunger to be sated. Back when every station was its own tiny universe that supplied a little bit of everything to viewers over the course of the broadcast day.

Heck, there are even some movies released by major studios that Mike has rediscovered and held up for people to reevaluate. In our current technological age, it feels as if no film is lost anymore, and often there are great movies just within easy reach that are unknown for no other reason then the fact that there are just so many damn movies to choose from that a viewer needs to occasionally be reminded about the obvious or that even major studios have arcane delights waiting to be recovered from the depths of time gone by.

That being said, I'm also certainly glad to see that I'm not the only person who likes *Watchmen* and *Shock Treatment* (probably even more than Mike, based on his criticisms), so having a book like this tucked under my arm makes it feel like having an old friend close at hand to remind me that I'm not alone in my deepest, darkest cinematic loves.

—Scooter McCrae

Scooter McCrae is an essential part of '90s-'00s independent cinema, thanks to his films **Shatter Dead, Sixteen Tongues,** *and his latest, the award-winning* **Saint Frankenstein.** *Readers are invited to check it out at https://vimeo.com/ondemand/saintfrankenstein*

ABOUT THE CONTRIBUTORS:

DR. RHONDA BAUGHMAN, a Canton, OH native, is a long-time writer, reader, actress, and overall geek / film buff. When she's not pulling rank in corporate America, she's often discussing things no one understands but they're too polite to mention it. Find her on Facebook and Twitter.

MIKE HAUSHALTER, a lifelong film fan, Mike formed an anime club, "Moonlight Ramblers", in 1991, and he remains president for life. When that group disbanded in 1997, he and pal Matt Gilligan started up a review and interview 'zine called Secret Scroll Digest that ran until 2005. He has worked as firearms wrangler and craft services on several Happy Cloud Pictures productions, giving him insight into life behind the camera that many film reviewers lack. His greatest film disappointment is the time his grandma promised to take him to *Star Wars*, but they saw *Close Encounters of the Third Kind* instead.

ALLY MELLING holds a Master's in Film Studies from the University at Buffalo and instructed undergraduate film classes during a doctoral assistantship at Bowling Green State University. Dividing her residence between Ohio and Florida, Melling is currently senior editor for a nonprofit cyber education organization based out of Western Pennsylvania. She is also layout coordinator, as well as a contributing writer, for the horror and exploitation cinema publication Ultra Violent magazine. Her areas of academic focus in film analysis include body horror, Russian Formalist theory, and sensory-based cinema experience.

TERRY THOME is a lifelong film student (his words) and film scholar (their words). He's written for and contributed to several Fanzines, liner notes, and special features sections of DVD and Blu-Rays, and film reference books. He was the founder of *f.p.s. Films*, through which he held a series of repertory theatrical screenings of such films as *Hard Boiled, A Chinese Ghost Story, Project A Part II*, and *Doctor Butcher, M.D.*

BILL WATT retired in 2012 after 30+ in career counseling and adult education. He has certifications from Pitt University's School of Social Work and Duquesne University's Division of Continuing Education. He designed and conducted independent seminars on a variety of subjects including "Humor in the Workplace" and "Why Sherlock Holmes?" He has written for "Sirens of the Cinema" and is currently working on a humorous book of family history. He loves books and movies, not necessarily in that order on any given day.

ABOUT THE AUTHOR:

MIKE WATT is a general layabout, working towards the rank of rear admiral layabout. From a mostly-supine position, he has penned this book, the two previous, one previous to that for another publisher, two novels, a collection of short stories, a couple of plays, two-dozen or so screenplays, a handful of notices, six angry letters, and several Facebook posts that border on gibberish.

ACCIÓN MUTANTE (1993)

Slant Magazine: From where do you think people get this idea of perfection, of materialistic elegance and supermodel beauty?

Álex de la Iglesia: I don't know. It's not just an American way of life, you know. It comes from before. People need this perfection, to imagine happiness in perfection, and imagine other lives for themselves. These other lives here take place in the shopping center, because it's like a temple. A place where you can find perfection because there are no human beings inside. You go to a shopping mall, and you can say, "I love everything. I love the TV plasma, I love this stupid Sony thing, everything." Then you buy the TV, you put it in your house, and then it's not so good. Why? Because now, it's human. Same with women. You think about having sex with women, then you have sex with one, and it's no good. Why? It's not a dream anymore, it's a real thing.[1]

I once heard an Álex de la Iglesia film described as "a really sick joke told at a funeral. It's neither the time nor the place for it, but damned if it wasn't funny."[2] Best-known in America for the nihilistic black comedy *Dance with the Devil* (aka *Perdita Durango*, 1997)[3], de la Iglesia revels in sick humor. Taking well-worn horror tropes and blending them with absurd, politically incorrect comedy, he has a flair for grossing you out and making you laugh in spite of yourself at the same time. If it is possible to weep in despair while simultaneously vomiting

---

[2] I'm delightful.

[3] Starring the human-voice equivalent of the Emergency Broadcast System, a.k.a. Rosie Perez, Barry Gifford's novel *59° and Raining: The Story of Perdita Durango*. The title character also appears in David Lynch's *Wild at Heart*, played in that film by Isabella Rossellini.

and guffawing, that's the emotion de la Iglesia manages to capture with his movies. Like the best subversive artists, de la Iglesia is an unwell person. "I like to play with genres and construct my own movies...What I am trying to do is inject poison into these genres. In a happy comedy I like to introduce poison and make the movie freaky and weird, with a tasteless sense of humor."[2]

In his feature directorial debut, de la Iglesia imagines a future where the genetically imperfect "mutants" wage a war of terrorism against the beautiful people. Mutant Action ("Acción Mutante" in the native tongue) consists of the physically- and mentally-handicapped, including the slightly-smarter-than-the-others conjoined twins Juan (Juan Viadas[4]) and Álex (Álex Angulo[5]). By assassinating body builders, blowing up sperm banks, machine-gunning aerobics classes on live TV, and generally stomping up and down on the kinds of people other people find "attractive", the "Mutant Action" group sees themselves as leaders against a superficial world. "We don't want to smell good or lose weight!" Unfortunately, the leading members of the organization aren't terribly bright and don't trust one another. So, in that way, they're exactly like every other terrorist group.

Their leader, Ramon Yarritu (Antonio Resines[6]), fresh from prison for illegal firearms, crafts a devious plan to infiltrate the high-profile wedding of Patricia Orujo (Frédérique Feder[7]), heiress to the fortune of billionaire wheat magnate Lord Orujo (Fernando Guillén[8]), intending to kidnap her for ransom. Sadly, the bride slices into the cake, and therefore into Chepa (Ion Gabella[9]) hiding inside. Injured and alarmed, out pops the gunman who opens fire on the wedding guests. Those not killed initially are killed subsequently.

Mutant Action flees with Patricia, stapling her lips shut and escaping in their terribly unsafe space ship disguised as a fish delivery vehicle (their ground vehicle is an obscene ice cream truck), head for the barren mining planet Axturiax to collect the ransom. Sadly, Ramon double-crosses the others and kills off the majority of them along the way. (It's actually surprising how quickly the film dispatches characters we were just starting to get to know.) In the midst of the fray, the ship crashes on the planet, leaving Ramon and Patricia the only survivors. Or so they think. Though Ramon personally killed Juan, Álex survived the crash. He takes off after Ramon and Patricia, dragging the lifeless but connected Juan along with him.

The sole inhabitants of Axturiax are the abandoned and sex-starved male miners enraged and engorged at the sight of Patricia. Captured by the miners, Ramon manages to fight off the attempted rapists. As a result, Patricia develops a nasty case of Stockholm syndrome towards her hulking anti-hero. Ramon, for his part, begins to regret the entire escapade, feeling cursed and quite misused by the Universe. It seems that nothing will ever go right for him again.

Meanwhile, Lord Orujo uses the ransom exchange as a political opportunity, with the drop covered on live TV. Unbeknownst to Ramon, Lord Orujo plans to kill everyone on the planet with a portable nuclear device. And, honestly, that would probably be the best possible outcome for all involved.

Born in Bilbao, Spain, in 1965, Álex de la Iglesia studied philosophy at the University of Deusto, but wound up working in comic books. He served as the production designer for Pablo Berger's short post-apocalyptic film *Mamá*, and Enrique Urbizu's 1991 thriller *Todo por la pasta* (*Anything for money*). Teaming up with José Guerricaechevarria, they made the disturbing serial killer film short, *Mirindas Asesinas* (1991), which attracted the attention of Spain's most

---

[4] Appearing as Generalismo Francisco Franco (still dead) in de la Iglesia's *Balada Triste de Trompeta* (aka *The Last Circus*, 2010).

[5] Angulo is marvelous in de la Iglesia's 2nd feature, *El día de la Bestia* (*The Day of the Beast*, 1995), as well as in a sympathetic turn in Guillermo del Toro's *Pan's Labyrinth* (2006). Angulo passed away in 2014.

[6] *Cell 211* (dir. Daniel Monzón, 2009)

[7] *Three Colors: Red* (Trois couleurs : *Rouge*, dir. Krzysztof Kieślowski, 1994)

[8] A member of the Pedro Almodovar family, including *Law of Desire* (*La ley del deseo*, 1987).

[9] Open Your Eyes (1997)

successful director, Pedro Almodóvar, one of the country's few filmmakers to receive acclaim in the United States for *Women on the Verge of a Nervous Breakdown* (1987), and the erotic Antonio Banderas-Victoria Abril comedy, *Tie Me Up! Tie Me Down!* (1990) Almodóvar agreed to produce de la Iglesia's first feature.

Thanks to Almodóvar's name on the credits, *Acción Mutante* enjoyed brief cult success in the States, with fans of sick humor attracted to the film's wild make-up effects and irresponsible narrative. Playing the already-well-played-with tropes of the post-apocalyptic action comedy—ala *Radioactive Dreams* (1985), *Class of Nuke 'em High* (1986), every Italian knock off of *Mad Max* starring Fred Williamson[10], etc.—*Acción Mutante* is rife with characters who defy sympathy, but seem to evoke it anyway. Sure, Ramon is an unapologetic heel who murdered all of his hapless friends in order to keep a hefty ransom for himself, but he only did so because his friends were irreconcilably stupid and mindlessly violent. Even though all of the misfortune he suffers was brought on by his own actions, it's difficult not to feel sorry for him by the end when all he wants to do is give up and go home.

The pretty people victimized by Mutant Action are, to be perfectly honest, also awful people, shallow, insecure, smug, but do they deserve to die horribly in hails of gunfire? (Or left headless, naked, and floating in a pool of blood on a heart-shaped bed?) That's not up to me to decide. But I didn't shed too many tears when it happened. Álex is a vile, pernicious killer, ruthless and balding, but our hearts go out to him when he loses his brother, closer than most non-conjoined brothers tend to be. Juan was his best friend and boon companion, whether Álex wanted him to be or not. Topping the tragedy of death with the burden of carcass-schlepping is just karmic cruelty. And after listening to Patricia drone on during her wedding, seeing her lips stapled shut becomes an admittedly shameful blessing. After all, they're all trapped in an unsympathetic reality, the ugly people just as ugly as the beautiful people.

"The first half of the film drags somewhat—the scenes on the spaceship with Antonio Resines knocking off his crew are strained. The party scene has its moment but the outré costumes—oversized Madonna-styled pointed brassieres and the like—seem to strain too

L-R: The Interim leaders of Mutant Action: Quimicefa (Saturnino García),
Álex (Álex Angulo) and Juan (Juan Viadas), and Manitas (Karra Elejalde).

---

[10] The ex-football player and all-around awesome guy made a number of post-apocalyptic films in one spate, including *The New Barbarians* (1982), *1990: The Bronx Warriors* (1982), *Warrior of the Lost World* (1983)…

Hapless bride-kidnapee Patricia Orujo (Frédérique Feder)

much for that Almodóvar zaniness," wrote Richard Scheib. "However, once on the planet, the film picks up considerably with its series of bizarre incongruities—the Siamese twin dragging his stuffed dead brother around with him, at one point he left hanging via a noose around the other twin's neck; the family of bald hillbillies who have never seen a woman and their ten year old son who ties Antonio Resines up and sits gouging the wound and pouring salt into it when Resines gets out of hand; the climax in the bar where every element of the film comes together, including a TV crew covering the hostage swap who keep interrupting the coverage with commercials, including an hilarious ad for LSD flavoured cornflakes. There is not a great deal to *Acción Mutante*—the future background is sketchy, the story slight—but the wacky humour helps carry it. The film has its own title rap song which, during the opening credits, recites the names of the cast and crew."[3]

In case it hasn't been made clear, the future depicted in *Acción Mutante* isn't the slick, clean one from *Tomorrowland* (2015), nor is it the neon-drenched, crowded one from *Blade Runner* (1982). Nor, to belabor the point, is it the gritty desert world of *Mad Max* (though Axturiax does reflect that landscape fairly well). Rather, the Mutants take Action in a greasy environment, every surface covered with a gritty film, as if the entire world had been fished out of a stopped-up sink. Every member of the group looks like something unpleasant discovered accidentally behind a public toilet. "Hitchcock is like my mother and Polanski is like my brother. They're part of my family. Their movies are in my head, and so when I try to do something different, I can't,"[4] de la Iglesia offers by way of explanation. "I love Jack Kirby, Daniel Clowes, Poe and Lovecraft, Noam Chomsky, and Billy Wilder. All at once, in an eclectic manner. The transcendent and the comic, the ridiculous and the epic. Dreyer and *Hellzapoppin'*."[5]

"The producer of this Spanish splatterama, Pedro Almodóvar, has always strived to mix comedy and perversity. In director Álex de la Iglesia he's found a colleague who's up to the same tricks in the genre of blood-caked science fiction. And this futuristic, post-apocalyptic black comedy is ripe with high style and lowbrow laughs. Our heroes are a likable pack of bumbling cripples and freaks, who comprise the terrorist group Acción Mutante. Tired of being 4th class citizens, they drive around the burnt-out remains of civilization in an ice cream truck (accompanied by *Mission: Impossible* music) and lead murderous raids on rich, beautiful aristocrats—striking terror into the hearts of trendy and hip elitists. [...] The acting is appropriately broad, with Feder a stand-out, looking lovely even when covered in dried blood. And it's obvious that the filmmakers had a relatively luxurious budget to work with, evoking the dinginess of *Blade Runner* crossed with the demented humor of a top-level Troma pic! [...] This pic is packed with colorful chaos, razored satire on the media and high society, and cool special effects (from the same crew who worked on *Delicatessen*[11]). Perhaps a little too much is

---

[11] Headed by Jean-Baptiste Bonetto.

packed in, because first-timer Iglesia switches gears so often that the larger picture is often lost. Still, he never lets up, with his manic energy and maniacal sense of humor driving the film to its comic massacre finale."[6]

Following the cult success of *Acción Mutante* and his Satanic Apocalypse follow-up, *El día de la Bestia* (*The Day of the Beast*, 1995), de la Iglesia was given a larger budget and a shot at breaking into Hollywood. Unfortunately, *Perdita Durango* was not a raging success. "*Perdita Durango* is a curious oddity in de la Iglesia's oeuvre. It is his most overt attempt to crack the North American market (where he has only a small but dedicated following) with his first English-speaking film and a cast of recognizable actors like Rosie Perez, James Gandolfini and Javier Bardem. This alienated his Spanish fans who probably felt he had sold out, while his penchant for graphic sex and violence scared off potential distributors and mainstream audiences in North America, sending the movie direct to video. This reaction is unfortunate because *Perdita Durango* is de la Iglesia's most successful effort: a perfect mix of the ridiculous and the epic, with the right blend of genres (crime, horror, comedy, road trip) and a wonderfully eclectic cast that features his regular favourites (Santiago Segura) and colourful character actors (Screamin' Jay Hawkins)."

After the failure of *Perdita Durango*, de la Iglesia turned his attention away from English-only-speaking Hollywood and concentrated on delighting and disturbing Spanish audiences. His only other attempt to woo the unwashed American masses was with the joint British/Spanish produced *The Oxford Murders* (2008) starring John Hurt and Elijah Wood. (He also contributed to the Mexican-American anthology feature, *Words with Gods* in 2014.)

Álex de la Iglesia summed up his attitude towards Hollywood while discussing his award-winning 2000 film, *La Comunidad*. "In Hollywood cinema the main character always has to be good so you can identify with them. What I really like about *La Comunidad* is that the heroine is greedy too. That's what the whole movie is about—none of us are completely good. Unfortunately I have a very negative point of view about human behaviour. […] What I'd really like to do, but I haven't managed yet, is to take one of these rollercoaster blockbuster movies, keep all the action, but take out all the stupid American characters and replace them with bizarre people instead. You know, I always feel envious when I see American movies. It's like being a child watching someone playing with expensive toys. I want to say: 'Let me play with them!'"[7]

As usual, *Acción Mutante* is extremely difficult to find on DVD in this vast American wasteland. Those with region-free players can find a reasonably-priced DVD on Amazon, or can shell out a whopping $38 for a VHS. There are also associated T-Shirts and tie-in goodies to be found on Amazon.co.uk (including a tie-in book for the mere price of £411!—just $540.18 at current exchange rate).

NOTES

[1] Croce, Fernando F. 2005. "Interview: Álex de la Iglesia." Slant Magazine. August 29.
   http://www.slantmagazine.com/features/article/every-heaven-has-a-hell-an-interview-with-alex-de-la-iglesia

[2] LaFrance. J.D. "The Ridiculous and The Epic: The Cinema Of Álex De La Iglesia." Erasing Clouds.com.
   http://www.erasingclouds.com/1112delaiglesia.html

[3] Sheib, Richard. 1993. "Review." Moria. http://moria.co.nz/sciencefiction/accion-mutante-1993.htm

[4] Russell, Jamie. 2003. "La Communidad." BBC.co. July 2.
   http://www.bbc.co.uk/films/2003/07/02/alex_de_la_iglesia_la_communidad_interview.shtml

[5] LaFrance. J.D. Erasing Clouds.com.

[6] Puchalski, Steven. 1994. "Review." Shock Cinema. Archived: http://www.shockcinemamagazine.com/accion.html

[7] Russell, Jamie. 2003. "La Communidad." BBC.co. July 2.
   http://www.bbc.co.uk/films/2003/07/02/alex_de_la_iglesia_la_communidad_interview.shtml

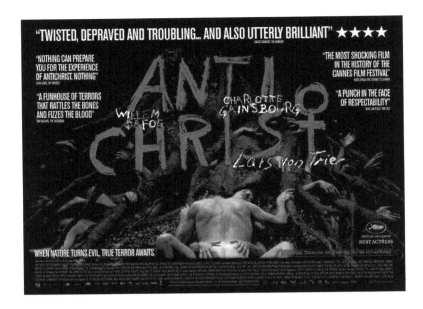

ANTICHRIST (2009)

Every now and then, a movie comes along that I'm told I *have* to see. Horror fans in particular are constantly on the lookout for the new "most disturbing and upsetting" thing, and the one they encountered in autumn, 2009, is Lars Von Trier's *Antichrist*. So insane and violent that many theaters "refused to show it", I was informed, and that "rampant censorship was afoot to keep this movie out of American theaters." Often, I respond that I'm the wrong audience for a Von Trier movie. The only project of his I've ever come close to enjoying was the original *The Kingdom* miniseries. There's a distance to his work that I don't appreciate and his Dogme 95 philosophy[12] always irritated me to a degree. *Dogville* (2003) and *Manderlay* (2005)

---

[12] First presented by Von Trier and Thomas Vinterberg at the Le cinéma vers son deuxième siècle symposium, in Paris, March 1995 as a "practical way forward" and to keep filmmaking "pure" by relieving the picture of all "artificial" elements. Von Trier's rules, referred to as the "Vow of Chastity," which filmmakers must adhere to and submit a form online stating they "truly believe that the film ... has obeyed all Dogme95 rules", are as follows:

1. Filming must be done on location. Props and sets must not be brought in. If a particular prop is necessary for the story, a location must be chosen where this prop is to be found.
2. The sound must never be produced apart from the images or vice versa. Music must not be used unless it occurs within the scene being filmed, i.e., diegetic.
3. The camera must be a hand-held camera. Any movement or immobility attainable in the hand is permitted. The film must not take place where the camera is standing; filming must take place where the action takes place.
4. The film must be in colour. Special lighting is not acceptable (if there is too little light for exposure the scene must be cut or a single lamp be attached to the camera).
5. Optical work and filters are forbidden.
6. The film must not contain superficial action (murders, weapons, etc. must not occur.)
7. Temporal and geographical alienation are forbidden (that is to say that the film takes place here and now).
8. Genre movies are not acceptable.
9. The film format must be Academy 35 mm.
10. The director must not be credited.
11. And the unofficial 11. None of the above shall actually apply to Von Trier.
12. (Read more at Suite101: A Short History of Dogme 95: Lars von Trier and Thomas Vinterberg's Cinematic Challenge http://www.suite101.com/content/a-short-history-of-dogme-95-a102049)

seemed like pretentious filmed plays and the minimalism failed to capture my imagination because I simply loathed all the characters he spread across his empty sets. This is all, of course, my personal taste. With all of his fans and supporters, Von Trier doesn't weep at my absence from his altar.[13]

Yet, in spite of my arguments against what I felt would be another Von Trier film lost on me, I had to admit that I found the idea of a Danish horror movie starring Willem Dafoe[14] intriguing and I work hard to avoid pre-disliking something. I got my hands on a copy and gave it a shot. The opening sequence, shot in positively heartbreaking black and white, with the gentle falling snow contrasted with the passionate lovemaking between the central couple, the agony of the early tragedy, I thought maybe this would be the one Von Trier movie that grabs me. I was even able to overlook the over-the-top use of Handel on the soundtrack.

Almost immediately afterward, for me, the center failed to hold and things fell apart.

As recounted *ad nauseum* in other reviews, *Antichrist* focuses on a married couple, irritatingly identified as "He" and "She"—Dafoe and Charlotte Gainsbourg[15]—who are wracked with guilt and grief over the loss of their infant son, Nic. Nic toppled out of an open window, falling in agonizing slow motion to his death (making it the most beautiful infanticide captured on film since Andy Warhol's *Bad* (1977)[16]), while He and She were having sex. It's easy to see where the torment would come from in this situation. She finds it difficult to cope and winds up in a hospital. He decides that the best thing for both of them is for him to help her through her depression and despair through psychology. He takes her to a secluded cabin surrounded by land that she inexplicably feared before Nic's death and forces her to face her fears in order to overcome them. That this seems like cruel manipulation on his part does not go unnoticed by the audience and you suspect that he's only doing this to punish her.

But then She feels that She *should* be punished. Not because She was indulging herself during Nic's accident but because, while doing research for an academic study on witchcraft and "gynocide", She came to believe that women are inherently evil. All women, herself included. In the midst of all this, bizarre portents come unto the couple—a stillborn fawn hanging from the backside of its mother doe, a self-disemboweling fox that announces "chaos reigns"—and in between long stretches of psychobabble and 500-frame-per-second slow motion sequences that defy you to detect movement at all, there is violent sex, emotional and

---

[13] The above nonsense is why I appreciated it when Troma's Lloyd Kaufman introduced the "Dogpile 95" Manifesto at Cannes in 2002. ""Long before Dogme 95 was born, Troma was making movies with poor lighting, amateur acting and crappy sound. However, we just have not been able to rise to the level of boredom that the Dogme 95 films have attained." Some of the Dogpile rules are:

* Shooting MUST be done on location with no soundstages. However, if your Mom's basement is a $500,000 soundstage, then by all means shoot there. Props and sets must not cost over $5 to make or produce, unless stolen or obtained through selling your body, or if you have a rich producer then spend his money. The point is, don't be stupid like Troma and spend your own money.

* The sound must never be produced apart from the images or vice versa. But if you thought that there should have been ambient sound that wasn't there at the time, you can put it in, or if your brother's band has a cool song, put it in. We won't tell...

* Use natural light whenever possible (Shooting illegally at night on private property is a good way to gain natural light through police flashlights and spotlight.), but if natural light seems too artificial, then by all means use some lights...

* Optical work and filters are forbidden. But what the fuck? If you can afford them, use 'em! Use your imagination! As the late Billy Wilder said "There mustn't be rules like #4."

* The film mustn't contain superficial action. So there better be murders, weapons, hard-bodied lesbians, boobies, and more boobies.

For more, skip the Dogme link and head to: http://www.dogpile95.com/content/home

[14] The Last Temptation of Christ (1988), Spider-Man (2002)

[15] *21 Grams* (2003), Todd Haynes' *I'm Not Here* (2007)

[16] Directed by Jed Johnson, in which an infant is hurled from a window—cut to what we hope is a watermelon exploding on the street.

physical torture and, finally, a sequence that angered me beyond words.

Not being a total schmuck, I was able to grasp that all of *Antichrist* was allegorical, set in dreamtime, and meant to be some sort of indecipherable visual poetry. I was able to grasp that because I—and many, many others before me—have been assaulted by this sort of self-indulgent artistry since film school. Kenneth Anger[17] may not have done it best, but at least he had a sense of humor about it. Bizarrely, Von Trier tries to obfuscate his message by burying it in the obvious, then masking it in the hallucinary. Midway through, I stopped trying to interpret what I was seeing and merely wondered how much longer I'd be asked to put up with this.

As each of the film's "chapters" ticked by, and the movie grew more and more pretentious, my patience was finally worn to a frayed shoelace with the "horrific" set pieces during She's ultimate emotional and psychological breakdown. In order to express my aggravation, I'll have to describe what was so maddening: Once She finally faces her grief and guilt and terror, she flies into a rage over a perceived fear that He is going to leave her alone in her loathsome environment. So she attacks him, rapes him, castrates him with a log, manipulates him to ejaculate blood, then drills a hole in his leg in order to attach a heavy grindstone to his femur. It doesn't take a student of either Jung or Freud or Phyllis Schlafly to interpret the rage in that sequence. Nor do you need any psychological insight to guess what's going on a few scenes later.

After a half-hearted hide-and-seek game taken from the climax of every horror movie, He and She finally, sort of, reconcile. In that they have sex again and he seems to forgive her for hobbling him with an instrument of labor. Midway through, she takes a pair of scissors and, in graphic close up, slices off her own clitoris. That's when I realized why so many people had been insisting that I check this out. More than that, I witnessed what I believe to be the very genesis of the film.

Most movies can be traced back to the inspiration. Sometimes you need to research the movie and the filmmaker and sometimes you can actually tell what specific image, idea or even line of dialogue, brought the movie to the front of the creator's brain. There it was in hideous close-up: this one image of female self-mutilation was the sole reason Von Trier made the movie. It's meant to be shocking and disturbing—as is the literal castration of He, rather than all the previous metaphor—and revolting and "Oh my God—I can't believe they showed that!" That angered me to no end.

The point to *Antichrist*: "dude, they show this woman slicing off her clitoris!" The sex, with its hardcore body doubles, and the torture that both the characters and actors are put through, are completely secondary to this shot. This, I have no doubt, was the sum total inspiration for this movie and the framing story is nothing but preamble to this singular hideous moment. It can be argued—hell, I'll even argue the fact—that the shot works thematically. If so much of her self-loathing is built around her femininity, why shouldn't she want to remove this defining aspect of herself, just as She similarly attacks He? But then to what end? Because by that point, He has every reason to believe her: women are inherently evil and it's up to this shattered, broken, ridiculously ego-centric man to put the world right. Which makes that final image of the faceless women symbols of what he's up against—the sum total of her thesis: gynocide.

As I've mentioned *ad infinitum*, if you spend the bulk of your life watching movies, particularly with a bent towards horror, you get to see a lot of "disturbing" things. There are visual endurance tests like *Cannibal Holocaust* (1980), and emotional nightmares like *In a Glass Cage* (1987). There are pure gross-outs like *Pink Flamingos* (1972) or *Men Behind the Sun* (1988), movies designed to see just how much you can take. So "shocking" wasn't the word for my response to this clitorectomy. I was purely and simply annoyed.

Before sitting down to watch *Antichrist*—again recommended by folks who I respect, but

---

[17] Legendary experimental filmmaker known for *Rabbit's Moon* (1950), *Scorpio Rising* (1963), among others.

with vastly different tastes than mine and who generally like endurance test movies simply to see what it takes to get through their desensitized psyches—I did a little research, read about how *Antichrist* was considered to be a misogynistic film, that the director was undoubtedly afraid of women (and certainly he has no trouble abusing or even martyring his female characters and too-often the actresses playing them), but I usually take these gut-reactions with not just a grain, but an entire salt-lick. Film critics are like anyone else—if they dislike something, it's the creator's fault, rather than "simply not to their taste". If Von Trier is a misogynist, and maybe he is, that doesn't necessarily make the narrative misogynistic.

Except in this particular case where the central female character—the only female character—believes wholeheartedly that women are born evil and deserve domination and torture. Okay, fine. An outrageous central conceit but valid as anything else you can hang a narrative on. That this idea is backed up with a closing image of He, after his liberation from the horrid She—a monster He more or less created, if you want to be honest—approached by of hundreds of women, their faces digitally blurred to featureless masks, similar to one at Nic's funeral where the spectators are supposed to be faceless in the wake of the parents' grief. Obviously this is supposed to mean... something. Are all these women the spirits of the oppressed? Are they meant to be female demons? Are they how He sees all women? None of that seems to be the point. It's all about the clitorectomy.

If you want to watch two extremely talented actors put themselves through an emotional wringer, there is no better recent example than this movie. This is full-contact *Who's Afraid of Virginia Woolf*. If you want to look at gorgeous cinematography interrupted by tedium, this is as highly recommended as the best of Bergman. But make no mistake reading this review: I was not offended by *Antichrist*; I felt insulted by it. Because I, and audience members like me, were forced to wade through so much tedious and self-abusing psychology, and even more tedious loveless lovemaking, to get to one single shot.

One critic I read mentioned that at one screening Von Trier was told that no mother could ever be as cold as She, who may have allowed Nic to fall out of narcissistic disinterest. He responded, "You've never met my mother." So there, perhaps, is his subconscious reason *Antichrist* was made. In the midst of a severe depression, Von Trier finally confronted his own hatred of his mother, so She and the rest of his female canon are representative of his yearning matricide.

If *Antichrist* is little more than a single shot meant to represent that personal hatred then, yes, many of us feel that our time was wasted with a long, irritating screed. By the time the credits rolled I realized that *Antichrist* was, at least to me, the very definition of pretentious: it wants to pretend that it's about something when, really, it's not about anything at all. Except, perhaps, the creator's own misery. Since we all have our own misery, why would we want subject ourselves to someone else's?

Willem Dafoe
& Charlotte Gainsbourg
in a film by Lars von Trier

Antichrist

ANTI-CHRIST "PRO" ARGUMENT

By Ally Melling

As an admitted cinema masochist and longtime fan of Lars von Trier (the two not being entirely mutually exclusive), I had a decent notion of what to expect walking into a downtown Pittsburgh showing of *Antichrist* upon its release in 2009.

Like all the other dedicated or morbidly curious, I had read the reviews scandalizing the graphic onscreen violence and sexual content. However, unlike many, I looked forward to it, or more specifically, to seeing what function von Trier would assign it. Previous von Trier films had solidified me as a lover of the Danish director's ruthlessness, the way he unapologetically assaults spectators with uncomfortable images and uneasy themes they never wanted to see but from which they cannot look away, like the bound viewers in Plato's cave. Unlike Plato's imprisoned, however, multiple audiences were free to reject von Trier's punishment upon the film's release. In my showing alone, at least five people got up and leave at various points in the film, a tell-tale sign usually reassuring I am watching work right up my alley. I knew what they chose to see—a few scenes of unsimulated sex, genital mutilation, and all-too-realistic gore—and no doubt they had read the buzzword reviews branding the film as unapologetically self-indulgent and misogynist.

What I argue—what people chose to overlook in their condemnation of *Antichrist*—is the reality of an extraordinary piece of highly stylized cinema, one comprising breathtaking cinematography, visionary imagery, and masterful performances from its leads. Furthermore, I maintain that if viewed through a critical feminist lens, *Antichrist* is quite the opposite of misogynist; the film communicates a rebellion against patriarchy and its socially imposed feminine roles, a message I fully endorse. Please do not misunderstand—I do not believe *Antichrist* to be von Trier's best work (*Dogville*, anyone?), nor do I hail it as groundbreaking per se. I am also perfectly able to separate my love of von Trier's films from my personal disapproval of his real-world antics (yes, it is possible to do that, you Kevin Smith fans). However, I maintain that *Antichrist*'s artistic praises and thematic merit have been far too unsung and underappreciated.

As a tale of a grieving couple—He (Willem Dafoe) and She (Charlotte Gainsbourg)—coping with the accidental death of their young son, Nic, *Antichrist* may appear a rehashed (*Don't Look Now* did the same), run-of-the-mill drama at first glance; however, the film takes a truly dark turn when She's grief and seemingly irrational fears spiral downward into violent madness. While it is nearly impossible to think of *Antichrist* as a horror movie in the common sense, horror film tropes surface subtly but seamlessly in a tapestry of unconventionality. As a therapist who commandeers his wife's recovery, He believes taking She to the place She fears most—their isolated, woodland cabin, "Eden"—will enable his wife to overcome her excessive mourning. Once transported to Eden, the viewer is given the initial perception that some sort of sentient presence watches over the couple and may even embody their very surroundings. Finally, in a *Shining*-esque turn of events, She succumbs to a mental break with gruesome consequences, as both He and the spectator discover She has been losing control for longer than led to believe.

Admittedly, *Antichrist* may seem misogynist taken at face value. The spoken notion that "nature is Satan's church" and women, being more natural, are inherently evil couple with She's actions to become a prevalent theme. Added to this is He's epiphany that She has adopted rather than rejected history's patriarchal brutality against women (e.g., the witch trials, the Inquisition). A philosophical theme of female evil is supported in the way She's growing madness is seemingly aided by the natural elements of Eden, from the thundering acorns to flesh-eating lichens to the "Three Beggars" (a fictional constellation turned tangible trio of woodland animals). Entertaining this theme, the spectator feels a sense of dread as flashbacks reveal that She been inflicting harm upon the couple's son for quite some time. Compounding the eventual outbreak of violence against her husband, She is finally revealed, again through flashback, to have chosen her orgasm over saving their son from falling to his death as the couple made love.

In the end, the spectator is left disturbed, unsure, and grasping for interpretation, desperately replaying the film in search of clues to concrete distinguish plot action from illusion and symbolism. These are the kinds of films that feed my soul. As a woman, is She inherently evil, explaining why She let her own son die, or is she just traumatized psychologically? If so, why the immense grief, pain, and despair? Are the natural elements of Eden truly evil, aiding and abetting She's actions? Or is She just insane, and He simply comes to share in her hallucinations through physical and mental distress? Of course, the beauty of films such as *Antichrist* is that there are no right or wrong answers; there are only interpretations to be made from von Trier's meticulously placed clues. As an egalitarian film student with a dash of feminist, I argue that von Trier's clues actually disprove the notion of *Antichrist*'s supposed misogyny, providing a unique but disturbing commentary on strong women's struggle to thrive in a society founded on male constructs. Furthermore, I believe the subtly of this message, particularly in terms of other von Trier films, only highlights the film's masterfully communicated complexity.

Editor Rob White was one of many to look past *Antichrist*'s misogynist label, calling the action "an opt-out from serious engagement, a critical short cut which reduces the film to the schematics of unconscious desire that von Trier so artfully dismantles in order to reach out to more visceral, counter-scientific causalities" (*Antichrist: A Discussion*). Dispelling the straightforward insanity of She's actions and beliefs, one can definitely view She's anxiety as feminist, especially in the scope of von Trier's entire "depression trilogy." My own first impression upon watching *Antichrist* was that She is a character steeped in the natural who is simply uncomfortable with abandoning her identity in favor of another. As a result, her child dies. Because of her inability and failure to fulfill that socially imposed role, She views herself as evil. It is an inability only in word; it encompasses the struggle between She's acceptance and rejection of the guilt of being a woman who, despite social constructs, did not want to sacrifice her identity to motherhood. She may also feel a shameful relief in her newfound childlessness. So great are She's ensuing moments of shame that she finally punishes herself by removing a source of female empowerment grounded in women's increasing appropriation of their own pleasure and sexuality (the clitorectomy scene). After all, sexuality is natural, and women who display desire are often viewed socially in terms of evil.

Odd as it may sound, I was not alone in thinking this. Examining She's role through a de Beauvoirian lens, professor Lori Marso draws attention to She's inability (unwillingness) to sacrifice. Marso draws a parallel between She as an oddity and the way women who are unable to take on the mother role in our patriarchal society are commonly viewed as selfish, strange, or even unwomanly. "Female characters whose love does not take the expected (demanded) form of self-abnegation and self-sacrifice, particularly when they are mothers, are generally depicted in film as freaks of nature" (Marso). Marso also states that She is "free from the forms of self-victimizing and self-destructive love" and poses the question of whether women in a patriarchal society can love at all when free of self-victimizing love.

While it is unnecessary to consider the subsequent two films in von Trier's "Depression Trilogy"—the aptly gloomy *Melancholia* (2011) and the sexual odyssey *Nymphomaniac*, released in two volumes in 2013 and 2014—to fully appreciate She's rebellion in *Antichrist*, doing so benefits the viewer's comprehension of von Trier's grand scheme of portraying strong, complex women. If She is an abnormal mother—an oddity in a patriarchal society—*Melancholia*'s Justine is an abnormal bride (unable to be content on her wedding day), and *Nymphomaniac*'s Joe is an abnormal wife (unwilling to be monogamous or motherly)—all three female leads failing at the three main social roles women are expected to selflessly and contently fill.

Added to this is the notion that the male characters of the Depression Trilogy always seem more than just a little oblivious. Von Trier bluntly confirms this observation: "The male protagonists in my films are basically all idiots who don't understand shit. Whereas the women are much more human, and much more real. It's the women I identify with in all my films."[1] (Gross). In that vein, *Melancholia*'s John and *Nymphomaniac*'s Seligman are pitifully out of touch with the realities the films' female protagonists clearly acknowledge. *Antichrist*'s He is no different. Self-assured, He rejects peer diagnoses of his wife's "atypical" grief and places himself in charge of her rehabilitation. She seems to recognize his folly from the start and only go through the motions to satisfy him, eventually commenting, "You're so damn arrogant." It is only when He realizes the gravity of She's anxiety that an interesting feminist role reversal ensues: He becomes the film's "survivor girl" in a horror gender swap I fully support.

It is worth noting that all three female leads of the Depression Trilogy initially realize their inabilities with a despair that manifests physically. "Their bodily suffering and pathological symptoms (depression, melancholia, nymphomania, anxiety, fear) are linked to an inability or unwillingness to conform to society's bourgeois and patriarchal expectations."[2] However, von Trier always includes a turning point when each heroine at least somewhat embraces her socially construed faults. *Melancholia*'s Justine eventually overcomes her debilitating depression to accept the inevitability of doom with utter calmness, and *Nymphomaniac*'s Joe leaves her family to re-embrace her desires and excel in a new profession. Regardless of whether it is driven by insanity, the turning point for She occurs in overcoming the fear of embracing her ideals of the nature of Eden and womanhood. In doing this, She appropriates the natural powers that once terrified her. It is the first instance wherein the spectator watches She begin to reject the shame of motherly inability and embrace her own natural identity.

The crowning achievement of *Antichrist* is how von Trier and Academy Award-winning cinematographer Anthony Dod Mantle (*Slumdog Millionaire*) collaborate to visually com-municate the couple's journey, particularly the ambiguous elements of Eden and She's transition from grief to pain to despair (the three central chapters of the film). This refusal to avert the camera's eye from female suffering is likely one reason why many construe the film as misogynist, but again, I believe the opposite is true. By unwaveringly, graphically, and elegantly depicting She's struggle in all its physical and mental discord, von Trier and Mantle accomplish the seemingly impossible: they confront the spectator with a tactile beauty in what is typically considered repugnant.

Shot with a high-speed camera around 800 frames per second, the film's high-frame-rate shots are a lovely and indispensable. *Antichrist's* black-and-white Prologue showing the couple making love while Nic approaches his doom is one of the most gorgeous displays of slow motion in film thus far, fully exemplifying cinematic chiaroscuro in all its dramatic contrast. The use of slow motion later resurfaces to communicate the ominous and fantastical elements of Eden. In an ethereally exquisite display of motion, She's imaginings of crossing into a nighttime Eden begin a motif drenched in the sinister overtones of the natural world. This motif reemerges through several additional slow motion images that entwine both He and the spectator in the impossible, grim elements of She's Eden. As Marso summarizes, "His images also prompt viewers to reconsider the lines between what is real and what is fantastical, and to question the limits, methods, and possibilities of communication—between humans, between humans and animals, even between humans and acorns, or humans and trees, given that SHE can 'feel the tree's strange personality.'" For example, He spots a doe (one of the Three Beggars) in the woods, a stillborn fawn protruding from its body (yes, nature is violent, and the young commonly die), and He later encounters a gore-covered fox (another of the Beggars) that tears at its own entrails and warns smug He that "Chaos reigns." In another dream-like sequence, He stands in a shower of acorns, completely inundated by the evil of the film's earthly universe. The seasoned spectator clearly recognizes these surreal nuances and additional point-of-view shots implying menace in nature as a clear homage to Andrei Tarkovsky's *Stalker* (von Trier dedicates *Antichrist* to Tarkovsky in the film's credits).

While it is true that slow motion has become widely overused in modern cinema, very rarely has the repugnant or sinister been portrayed more artistically or glamorously. Mantle echoes this sentiment in interviews regarding his methodology for filming *Antichrist*: "I'm pretty sure it was Lars's intention to make that contrast between the roving physicality of the rest of the film and the amazing stillness you get when you use a high speed. What you're seeing is slowed down so much that for the first time in the cinema I had the sense of watching a film in the way that I look at a painting."[3] This is an understatement—von Trier and Mantle paint an artwork that is highly stylized, able to render the most harmless, stunning aspects of the wilderness as both charming and eerily vile.

Mantle's slow motion shots are just one *Antichrist's* of technical highlights. Somewhat shaky handheld shots seamlessly freeze in their tracks, steadying and zooming to signify transitions into the surreal in a jarring, imaginative way, while other shots communicate the symptoms and mindset of She's suffering in sublimely physical ways. For example, one sequence shows corporeal manifestations of She's compounding grief in a series of blurry, fast-moving, close-up shots of different affected parts of the body. Watching this depiction, the spectator can physically feel the palpitations of anxiety, and indeed he/she has no other choice: Von Trier's camera is not one to turn away from the unpleasant. The director presents an equal opportunity critique of female suffering under patriarchy, whether it be the motions of grief stemming from shame or the physical disfigurations of self-punishment. Marso notes this in her analysis: "He unapologetically focuses his camera on women's intense experiences of pain, grief, anger, cruelty, melancholy, violence, desperation, pleasure, humor and ecstasy."

If Mantle's cinematography comprises the language of *Antichrist's* depiction of female suffering, Gainsbourg and Dafoe are indispensable as the gender-opposed speakers engaged in its brutal discourse. Gainsbourg, who received the Best Actress prize at Cannes for her performance, openly expresses the masked pain of loss (or, in this case, the shame of motherly failure) that sufferers typically conceal, bringing a genuine desperation and an uncompromising physicality to the part. She also successfully pulls off the transition from prisoner of grief (or self-doubt) to predator exacting revenge. It is a mesmerizing shift that initially seems abrupt but, upon further examination, reveals itself in Gainsbourg's meticulous pacing, carriage, and subtlety ("But this may not last—ever thought of that?"). Unafraid to appear unattractive, Gainsbourg fearlessly owns a role far more complex than those featured in a majority of horror-based films, so much so that it is impossible to imagine anyone else in the part. Opposite She, Dafoe is superb at conveying ego regarding the gravity of his wife's struggles, while also simultaneously inhabiting the identity of a grieving father who masks his own mourning and affection in almost cold, laughable professionalism. It can be risky to rely

SON OF THE RETURN OF MOVIE OUTLAW

on only two actors to carry an entire film, but this pair succeeds and excels, especially under von Trier's careful guidance.

Antichrist is obviously not for everyone. Regardless of whether it is enjoyed, I believe it should at least be acknowledged by anyone serious about cinema, diversity in the horror genre, filmmaking, film as art, feminist analysis, or film analysis in general. Very rarely does one find a film so well-acted, well-shot, and well-directed as to traverse the confines of the horror genre in the spectator's expectant mind. Mantle's imaginative and varied camerawork skillfully mediates von Trier's brutal vision and translates it to true visual art, setting the morose tale apart with lush, haunting, uncompromising imagery. The film is also subtly subversive, especially when placed in the context of the two subsequent films of the trilogy. In a time when cinema is overrun by portrayals of women who overcome odds to thrive in their expected social roles, it is refreshing to find not one but three interconnected films portraying strong female rebellion—the oddities who are unwilling/unable to sacrifice under the pressures of patriarchy. Although that is my preferred lens for viewing *Antichrist*, von Trier's calculated craftsmanship as an auteur allows for countless other readings and correlating details I have no space to mention here. Like David Lynch or Alejandro Jodorowsky, von Trier presents *Antichrist* with purposeful ambiguity, blurring the diegetic lines between the "real" and the merely symbolic.

As someone who delights in films that engage their spectators in critical thought, I absolutely rejoice when their directors take risks, excel technically, and display obvious vision to near perfection (see Nicolas Winding Refn's *The Neon Demon* as a more recent example). If you feel the same, *Antichrist* is a cinematic Eden not to be missed.

NOTES

[1] Gross, Larry. "The Six Commandments of the Church of the Antichrist." Film Comment 45.5 (2009): 38-46. JSTOR. Web. 30 June 2016.

[2] Marso, Lori J. "Must We Burn Lars von Trier?: Simone de Beauvoir's Body Politics in Antichrist." Theory & Event 18.2 (2015). Project MUSE. Web. 30 June 2016.

[3] Johnston, Trevor. "'Antichrist' cinematographer Anthony Dod Mantle: interview." Time Out London. Time Out England Ltd., n.d. Web. 30 June 2016. http://www.timeout.com/london/film/antichrist-cinematographer-anthony-dod-mantle-interview-1

Antichrist. Dir. Lars von Trier. Perf. Charlotte Gainsbourg, Willem Dafoe. Zentropa Entertainments, 2009. Blu-ray.

"'Antichrist': A Discussion." Film Quarterly. The Regents of the University of California, n.d. Web. 30 June 2016. http://www.filmquarterly.org/2009/12/antichrist-a-discussion/

ARMED AND DANGEROUS (1986)

Life's tough out there for an honest man. Seems like all the odds are stacked against you, that the bad guys get ahead by stepping on the backs of the good guys. Forget about finishing last; nice guys are often lucky if they get to finish at all.

Or so it seems for Frank Dooley (John Candy) and Norman Kane (Eugene Levy). Big-hearted honest cop Dooley has one bad day, needing to be rescued from a tree after trying to rescue a cat, he is later framed by crooked L.A. cops for stealing a television set. Humiliated, he's kicked off the force. Norman's fresh out of law school and his first case is defending Manson-esque white supremacist murderer Lupik (Glenn Withrow[18]) who threatens to kill him in front of the entire courtroom. Pleading for leniency for both himself and Lupik, Kane is promised by the judge that he will make sure Lupik will serve a sentence "so long he won't remember Kane's name", so long as Norm promises to find another line of work.

The pair meet cute at the Guard Dog Security Agency, a private group run by "Captain" Clarence O'Connell (Kenneth McMillan[19]) and his daughter, Maggie (Meg Ryan[20]). Some of the perks that come with joining the company include owning a gun and a weekly union contribution of $15, paid directly to upstanding union bosses Clyde Klepper (Jonathan Banks[21]) and Tony Lazarus (Brion James[22]). This latter handsome pair work for union president Michael Carlino (Robert Loggia), who Kane manages to antagonize within minutes

---

[18] Part of Francis Ford Coppola's S.E. Hinton craze of '83: *The Outsiders* (1983), *Rumble Fish* (1983)

[19] Baron Harkonnen in David Lynch's *Dune* (1984).

[20] Wide-eyed clone of Melanie Griffith.

[21] *Better Call Saul*'s Mike Ehrmantraut.

[22] "Lemme tell you about my mother…" *Blade Runner* (1982)

of their first union meeting by asking legitimate legal questions about liability.

On their first job guarding a warehouse, Dooley and Kane discover a pair of masked men raiding the loading dock. A shootout ensues and the bad guys get away, resulting in the pair getting their pay docked and their faces repeatedly sprayed by angry O'Connell spittle. When they complain further, they are reassigned to a toxic waste dump, where they encounter the shattered remains of a pair of guards previously robbed at a warehouse job. Determined to get to the bottom of all this corruption and shame, Dooley and Kane solidify their partnership and restore their good names to…whatever reputation they had before they became security guards. Disguises are donned; cars are crashed; much, much damage is done.

Following the huge success of *SCTV*, the entire veteran cast attempted to transition to movies. Some of them, like Martin Short, Rick Moranis, and Catharine O'Hara, were quite successful. For Joe Flaherty and Andrea Martin, not so much. Candy and Levy, favorites on the show, found some difficulty in the movies. The affable Candy is better-remembered for his supporting roles in *Planes, Trains and Automobiles* (1987), *Stripes* (1981), and *Splash* (1984). Among his few starring roles, he's appreciated most for John Hughes' inexplicably popular *Uncle Buck* (1989) (sadly less-so for his nearly perfect performance in the underrated *Only the Lonely* (1991). For his share, Levy bounced around in thankless supporting roles in bigger ensembles also like *Splash*, before finding a comfortable niche as the sweet-natured "Jim's Dad", the saving grace of the *American Pie* films. In between installments of the bafflingly-popular series, Levy returned to his improve days working on Christopher Guests' endlessly amusing satires, *Waiting for Guffman* (1997), *Best in Show* (2000), *A Mighty Wind* (2003), and the criminally underrated *For Your Consideration* (2006) (co-starring alongside O'Hara, Harry Shearer, Michael McKean, and a host of others). This was all after a remarkably unfunny failure (also co-starring Flaherty), *Goin' Berserk* (1983).

Armed and Dangerous, on the outset a *Police Academy* rip-off, was written by their *SCTV* buddy Harold Ramis, along with Brian Grazer, James Keach, and Peter Torokvei. Directed by Mark L. Lester, seemingly parodying his excessive successes with action movies like *Class of 1984* (1982) and *Commando* (1985), *Armed and Dangerous* is primarily a comedy with some action set-pieces, culminating with an extended and hilarious apocalypse provided by none-other than Steve Railsback as "The Cowboy", a gleefully-deranged trucker delighted to have his vehicle commandeered by Dooley[23] and provided the excuse to wreak absolute mayhem across Los Angeles.

"[The project had] been around for five or six years and there's probably been about fifteen versions of the script," explained Candy […]. "It had Belushi and Aykroyd at one point, then Harold Ramis [who co-wrote the script] and Dan, then Dan and I, with John Carpenter

L-R: Meg Ryan, Eugene Levy, John Candy, Steve Railsback.
Screencap copyright Columbia Pictures. All Rights Reserved.

slated to direct. When they dropped out, I was left with a contract and no movie. So Gene [Eugene Levy] came in, took my role and I took Dan's spot. […] I'm always hearing about these great scripts, but then they say, 'Oh, it needs a rewrite.' And then before you know it, there's another rewrite, and then it needs a little polish, and by the time it's done, it's almost unrecognizable."

---

[23] In one of the movie's best reveals, Dooley preps for the final show-down by dressing in his full motorcycle cop regalia (as seen on the poster) only to have his bike conk out on him a few minutes later.

Candy grinned. "I mean, can you just imagine the poor guys who came up with the original idea when they go to the movie with their family and they say, 'Hey, wait a minute. I didn't write that! Who's that character?' And of course if the movie bombs, then everyone dumps on those guys!"[1]

To give another example of Candy's character, let's turn to journalist Jimmy Callaway, who wrote in *Splitsider* that Candy was ready to walk away from the project except for one thing: "[E]ven if *Armed and Dangerous* is an awful movie, Candy wanted to do this movie exactly because he wanted Levy in it. Knelman talks often about how Levy was struggling since the demise of *SCTV*, and Candy, as his best friend, was willing to sacrifice his career on this movie in order to give Levy a higher profile here in the States. This, more than anything, is what makes John Candy who he is. His best friend is having a hard time making a go of it, so Candy flexes the Hollywood muscles he'd been developing and gets *Armed and Dangerous* off the ground. So even if the movie tanked and is regarded as a hunk of garbage, that was the way it had to be."[2] While at this point it's questionable how much "muscle" Candy had in Hollywood, the interpretation of the 'why' fits in with how Candy was as a person. Following *SCTV's* departure from the airwaves, Candy was anticipated to be a major star, a huge comedic force for the industry. But he wound up in one misfire after another—*Volunteers, Summer Rental, Brewster's Millions*—all in 1985 alone! According to those who knew him, it took a toll. "We all loved John," Steve Railsback told me at the 2016 Chiller Theater Convention in New York. "He threw himself into his work, made sure he knew everybody's name. We had a great time together those couple of days locked in that truck cab. But he loved to eat, he smoked maybe a half-dozen cigars per day. Everyone told him to cut back but he just wouldn't… Sweet man. Never met a person who disliked him."[24]

The movie hits as often as it misses. One memorable sequence, outrageous at the time, has Dooley and Kane hiding from the bad guys in an adult bookstore in Hollywood. To escape, they "borrow" outfits from a skinny leatherboy in assless chaps and an enormous Divine-esque drag queen. Levy and Candy play up the homosexual stereotypes for laughs, but without malice. The sequence

Levy and Candy: Undercover. Screencap copyright Columbia Pictures.

seems dated now—with the majority of the comedy relying on a shot of Levy from behind and in those assless chaps—but it's not nearly as uncomfortable as it could have been (the hateful homophobia of *Freebie and the Bean* (1974) springs immediately to mind when it comes to *Cruisin'* parodies). The joke is Candy in drag (a joke repeated in the nearly unwatchable *Nothing But Trouble* (1991)), and if that's all that it takes to put you guffawing on the floor, then you're the easy mark *Armed and Dangerous* was hoping to attract.

"*Armed and Dangerous* was a project that had died a quiet death, and then was resurrected by Brian Grazer, the producer," Ramis told The A.V. Club's Joshua Klein. "And Brian said, 'If I can find a director, can I make the movie?' And I said okay. So then he finds a director—and I mean, literally, he just found a guy—and it was not good. I tried to take my name off it. I took my name off in one place. I was both executive producer and screenwriter, and I can't remember which name came off.[3] But I gave up one credit."[4]

However, in the same interview, Ramis also said, "I can't imagine a successful comedy

---

[24] Personal conversation with the author, April, 2016. Quoted with permission.

movie without a successful comedy performance at the heart of it. […] For me, it starts with the writing. I always think that the writer is doing the vast majority of the director's work, in a sense. If you're a writer who is also going to direct, you're doing all your preparation: You're already visualizing everything, you're imagining how the lines are going to be read, you see the blocking in your head, and you know the rhythm and the pacing. Then it's a question of communicating it. It's a great luxury for me to be able to write on the films that I direct, and kind of a nice thing to be able to write enough to get credit, which is difficult for a director. When you're a big enough part of the process that the Writers Guild gives you a lot of credit, that's a good thing. It tells me that I've had a significant impact on the film as a writer. But selling that to the actors…"[5] So does the primary blame for *Armed and Dangerous* really fall on Lester's shoulders? Because Candy and Levy are, as I've said, terrific.

At the time, Candy defended Lester. "To be honest, the film went through a lot of directors and no one was really that interested. But Mark had a lot of good ideas and I think he did an admirable job."[6]

"Although Candy has kind words for the film makers he's worked with on his recent pictures, he maintains that he's 'frustrated' by his lack of control over his film projects," wrote Patrick Goldstein for the L.A. Times in 1989. "'The big difference is that with *SCTV*, we had complete control over what we were doing,' [Candy] explained in his new office here. 'We may have felt that the show was often on in a really late time slot, but at least we had the responsibility for all of our work, from the sketches down to the scenery. The problem with film is that you can't see it through to the end. You can't get your hands on the material. A lot of times, the project you saw at the beginning has completely changed by the time you see it on screen.'"[7]

When you get down to it, *Armed and Dangerous* is frequently amusing, rather than out-and-out funny. When Candy and Levy play off of each other, nothing else matters. Certainly not the almost-incidental plot. While it's fun to play "spot the character actor", watching Banks, James, and Tiny Lister[8] in early roles, wondering why Meg Ryan looks so dazed in every scene (the woman never blinks once in the entire film, it's like Lester smacked her in the forehead with a hammer prior to each take), recoiling from the effortlessly sleazy performance given by Loggia, there isn't a lot of meat to the film. Then again, there isn't much to any of the *Police Academy* movies, either. For my money, the movie is commendable for avoiding the mean-spiritedness that is often found in theatrical farces. Railsback's affectionate nickname for Candy is "Slim", and that's about the extent of the fat jokes.

At the time of its release—and neverending run on HBO—*Armed and Dangerous* was meant to be nothing more than a harmless diversion, an amusing interruption to the daily rut. It wasn't groundbreaking then, nor is it now. But it still deserves to be rediscovered by those too young to remember *SCTV*, when these talented men and women definitely shined. There are little moments of brilliance throughout *Armed and Dangerous* and it's worth sitting through it to see them.

NOTES

[1] Goldstein, Patrick. 1986. "John Candy's Ready To Take Control: My agent is always telling me--'it's not called show art, it's show business.' And I have to learn that . . ." L.A. Times. August 28. http://articles.latimes.com/1986-08-28/entertainment/ca-13992_1_show-business

[2] Callaway, Jimmy. 2012. "I'm Your Uncle Buck: The Low-Key Career Path of John Candy." Splitsider.com. October 1. http://splitsider.com/2012/10/im-your-uncle-buck-the-low-key-career-path-of-john-candy/

[3] In the final film, Ramis receives only a screenwriter credit.

[4] Klein, Joshua. 1999. "Harold Ramis." The A.V. Club. March 3. http://www.avclub.com/article/harold-ramis-13583

[5] Ibid.

[6] Goldstein, Patrick. 1986. L.A. Times.

[7] Ibid.

[8] Thomas Lister Jr.; June 24, 1958, best-known by me as President Lindberg in Luc Besson's *The Fifth Element* (1997).

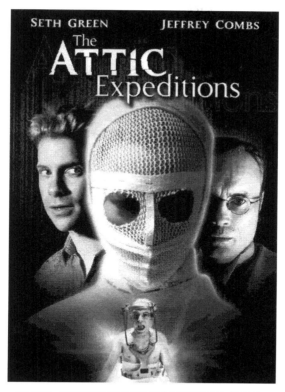

THE ATTIC EXPEDITIONS (2001)

There's a welcome trend that pops up for a while before vanishing again: movies that trust the audience, that don't automatically assume that the viewer is an idiot. We've seen the inverse far too often—the best example for me just happens to be on as I write this: Luke Wilson literally explaining, to the camera, how the main characters in *Soul Survivors* (2001) are in Limbo following an accident. Though the film adequately sets up this fact, the producers felt the need to "dumbsplain" via the empty vessel of Wilson. It was infuriating then and its impact hasn't lessened, even when bracketed by commercials. "Dumbsplaining" makes us appreciate movies that unfold without dialogue—such as the openings of *There Will Be Blood* (2007), *Up* (2009) or even the (ultimately irritating for other reasons) *10 Cloverfield Lane* (2016). In the case of *The Attic Expeditions*, the viewer practically has to do as much work as the screenwriter to decipher the twisting plot. While not as intricate as contemporary *Donnie Darko*, *The Attic Expeditions* has enough bends in its narrative road to keep the viewer on his toes.

We meet Trevor Blackburn (Andras Jones[25]) in an idyllic scene, sitting beneath a tree with his girlfriend, Faith, sharing a lazy spring day. Suddenly, Trevor is strapped to a table, about to undergo brain surgery and having no idea why. Four years later, Trevor awakens from his

---

[25] See chapter on *Sorority Babes*. Kasten describes Jones as "sort of an upcoming Johnny Depp type for a while there, and left Hollywood in a frustrated angry mess and moved to Seattle to pursue his career as a musician, which is what he'd been doing for several years. He flies back to do movie parts and stuff." (Interview, Ugo.com—see citation next page). Which remains true today. However, this from Jones: "I haven't taken a break at all. I've been doing Radio8ball. Doing The Radio8ball Show, which is a show I do at Theatre Off Jackson. I've done it in L.A. I've done it on the radio. We're filming it for webcasts, and ultimately, pitching it as a TV show. Being an actor and choosing to live in the Northwest definitely is taking me out of the L.A. casting game, but the acting game is once you've caught the bug, you're always training. You're always getting ready for when the call might come." - MacGuffin Film Podcast - Andras Jones Interview at Crypticon 2010. Archived at: www.transcribemyaudio.xyz/.../macguffin_film_podcast_-_andras_jones_interview_ at_crypticon_2010

coma and finds himself under the care of Dr. Ek (Jeffrey Combs[26]—I'm sorry, I'll never be ill enough to accept "Jeffrey Combs Healthcare"). Ek places Trevor in a group home dubbed "The House of Love" run by the mysterious Dr. Thalama (Wendy Robie[27]), filled with a chorus-line of wacky out-patients who are systematically—and mysteriously—murdered over the next few nights, while Trevor is plagued by nightmares where he is called to a trunk in the house's attic. And something is locked inside that trunk. What would Freud say about that? And this all happens before we discover that the entire group home is a closely-monitored experiment that the patients may or may not be actors, and the sole voice of reason is coming from a rival physician played by Ted Raimi![28]

It's David Lynch by way of Joe Dante, and it doesn't always work. Rogan Russell Marshall's (90% effective) script seems too disjointed at times, and the viewer is left with the feeling that there are things being deliberately left-out. The ending is a clear indication that Marshall may not have known where he was going, and wasn't sure where he was when he arrived. Still, at least there aren't any characters staring into the camera and telling you exactly what you've just seen, in case you were too dumb to figure it out yourself. It goes for a circular "the end is the beginning" tie-up, which both works and doesn't—which may indicate that it works all too well.

"The deal was that Rogan wrote the first draft, and he and I fucked around with other subsequent drafting," director Jeremy Kasten told journalist Daniel Epstein. "Because he was in Mississippi, we were writing a lot of it over the phone. So sometimes, we would just cover broad concepts, and the he'd go back and do it, and sometimes I'd take a pass at dialogue. A lot of the character names and stuff like that, we came up with together in the re-writes, but really, I have to say because so many of the germs, the cool ideas came from him, it really is his script, his sickness. [...] It took forever just to get it shot. We were raising money and shooting and raising money on and off. We shot for eighteen days in 1997 with like less than what people spend on a year college education. For the first eighteen days, we shot at the House of Love, and then we ran out of money before we even shot Jeffrey or any exteriors or anything, just stuff at the house. We hadn't shot the attic yet, so we raised money, and a year later, went and shot a couple more scenes and then raised money, and we just kept doing that until the movie was the movie. And a lot of people said along the way, 'Why don't you just try and make a movie out of what you have? It's so weird anyway, can't you just try and make it make sense?' But it seemed like it was going to need all the pieces, and actually, we ended up overshooting."[1]

The real joy of *The Attic Expeditions* is the cast. It's just too much fun to see Combs and Raimi sharing scenes together, and *Buffy the Vampire Slayer*'s Seth Green steals every scene he's in. (As a quick aside, the part was originally offered to *Adventures in Babysitting*'s Keith Coogan. "Yeah, Keith was a buddy of my roommate who was a grip on the movie. And we went to Keith because we were so excited that there was a movie star who was willing to be in the movie. Keith and I met and I was really, really excited about him playing Douglas, but he had to drop out, because we weren't paying him, and he got a paying gig," said Kasten. "And Keith is a great guy and I would have loved to have worked with him, but as it turned out Seth was a godsend for us both, because he was truly made for that role, I don't know that anybody ever could have said those words as well as Seth could have. With his amazing Jeff Goldblum impersonation going on in that role. And also, obviously, right about the same time, *Austin Powers* just came out right before we started shooting, so his resurgence into Hollywood was just happening. He got *Buffy the Vampire Slayer* shortly thereafter, and then it all fell into place. I think, in a lot of ways, it made it possible for us to get that movie done. Because even though we still had to finance it in bits and pieces a little bit at a time, and no studio or anything ever

---

[26] The great Herbert West from *Re-Animator* (1986)

[27] Nadine Hurley from *Twin Peaks*.

[28] Did you love him more on *Seaquest* or *Xena*?

stepped up and paid for us to finish the movie. [...] Seth spent most of the time on the set of the movie kind of punch drunk, because we were just so exhausted. They were such long days, and like I said, we were all just living together at that house, so it was more like summer camp, and he had this pirate character that he did, so the whole time on the set, [in a pirate voice] 'Arr, me matey, time to do my close-up'.")

Kasten expounded on Green in an interview with Nate Yapp. "I'd seen a lot of people at the time [Green] came and auditioned, and nobody seemed to know that the character is being both incredibly likable and dynamic, and also frightening and unnerving. Seth really came to the role with that. That being said, we did rehearse and we played quite a bit in finding the characters, because I had set out to do, and whether I succeeded is forever up for grabs with the fans, but we set out to make a movie where the actors were playing mediocre actors who were actually in this world that Dr. Ek created to drive Trevor out of his mind. So it's a delicate balance to find the moments where they'd slip a little bit and reveal the person they actually were and that would throw you off. Additionally, Seth is playing an actor who's playing a mental patient who, halfway through the movie, becomes possessed by the dead fiancé of the protagonist, so there's a whole other dimension for him to explore. We did a whole bunch of acting exercise with Beth Bates, who plays Faith in the movie, and Seth, where they would sort of walk around and say things and mirror each other to find some kind of middle ground where they had similar behaviors when they need to be there."[2]

Fellow indie actor Jones seems too down-key for particular scenes, but he grounds the goings-on in reality, showing the events through Trevor's fractured memory works well to build the mystery—did he or did he not sacrifice Faith for greater Faustian knowledge or is that something Ek implanted? Ek's verbal morality-jousting with Raimi's Dr. Coffee often sends the film spiraling into a different direction, conflicting with the uncertainty of Trevor's point of view, making the mystery too explicitly a conspiracy. But since we're never given a true definition of reality—medical trickery? Supernatural interfering?—it's hard to gain your footing. By the time all hell breaks loose in the final act, the viewer still has no clue what's going on. But for many lovers of bizarre movies, the impossible knowledge of "reality" is the frosting.

It may be surprising to learn that Kasten originally intended the film to be part of the hit-or-miss *Witchcraft*[29] series. "[Marshall] was an old friend of mine, and it was originally written to be [*Witchcraft IV: The Virgin Heart* (1992)] [...] I was a production assistant on *Witchcraft 4*, which is an absolute turd of a movie. Back in the video boom of the 1980s, they were just churning anything out, and you'll make a million bucks. I was working on it, and they didn't have a script yet, and I called up my friend Rogan, who is living in Mississippi. And I said, 'Hey man, rent the first three *Witchcraft* movies, and if you can write the fourth one in the next week, you're going to sell it.' He wrote it in five days and sent it to me, and I read it, and thought there is no fuckin' way I'm going to give them this movie. I'm going to make it, and I sat on it, and let the guy who produced those movies read it when they were done, because the other guy finished his script, like, two weeks later. And he said, 'I like it, the sex is great, just get rid of the attic and it's perfect.' So, obviously we just sat on it forever. And it took a long time to make."[3]

As reported by Michelle Erica Green, "Combs had been slated to do *The Attic Expeditions* a couple of years ago, but the filmmakers ran out of money after shooting most of the film and had to postpone. 'I was the final week—all of my scenes. So it went away, but to their credit, those guys tenaciously battled to keep it alive and get more money, and were able to put it all together. It's an interesting little movie, and the director and writer, Jeremy [Kasten], has a lot of enthusiasm.' [...] Nevertheless, it was a difficult shoot. 'I play a doctor who runs a private sanitarium where a lot of research is done, and it's primarily set up so I can get information from just one patient. I send him off to a halfway house with a lot of other people who 'need

---

[29] Originally produced by Jerry Feifer and Yoram Barzilai, spawing *sixteen* entries.

therapy' when in fact they're all actors under my employ. He's the only one who needs the help. Everyone else is playing mind games with him and messing with him until he gives over what I want him to give over.'"[4]

For the filmmakers and producers, *The Attic Expeditions* was less a *labor* of love than it was a vendetta. Kasten, Jones, Marshall, and many of the six producers (Melissa Balin, David Bouffard, Daniel Gold, Dan Griffiths, Jessica Kopp, Allen R. Larson) moved into the home serving as the House of Love set, sleeping on, as they call it, "Hot Sets", rolling out of bed and going immediately to work, for three months. An agreement with the house's owner allowed them to shoot for free in exchange for renovations to rooms previously fire-damaged in 1922. The pay was low, the days were long—the normal challenges for an independent production. With numerous fits and starts in the production, it was years before the film finally made its way onto video shelves, just in time for the video boom's turn to bust. Although Blockbuster acted as the distributor, little effort was put forth in promotion. There was a little assistance from new "indie-friendly" rules established by the Screen Actors' Guild, but nothing that really screamed "support".

As Kasten told Classic Horror.com "It was brand new when we shot the movie—we started shooting in 1997. So, it's almost ten years old. But they had made it very difficult for independent films and genre films specifically to get made, because, for example, if you're making an art film, it seemed like, for whatever reasons, people were having an easier time working with the Screen Actors' Guild to go off and make a little art film and sort of pretend they were gonna make a short and then extend it into a feature, and everybody would go, 'Oh my goodness, what happened here? Oh, how adorable. We've made a movie.' But with genre movies, nobody's signing on going, 'I'm just doing this because my heart is in the right place.' I mean, some of us are, but for the most part that's not the commonly held belief about genre movies and horror movies more specifically. And the LEA was a huge benefit to us, because we were able to say to the actors, 'Look, we can't make this movie for more than $200,000, so you know that all the money is going in the right places, and that our heart is in the right place, but we just don't have more money than that. So people came to our table knowing exactly where we were coming from and interested in being part of that with no sort of false hope that this is going to be a cushy movie in any way.'"[5]

And, of course, the critics did their best to kick the little movie into its proper place. "About as appealing as a tour of someone else's basement in the dark, *The Attic Expeditions* is an overly ambitious slice of Grand Guignol that is none too grand in conception or execution," wrote Ken Eisner for *Variety*. "First-time helmer Jeremy Kasten has edited cheapo genre pics, and he shows some visual flair, but overall tone is just higher than that of the fabled *Coven*,[30] as filtered through the allegedly satirical elements of *But I'm a Cheerleader*.[31]" Numbingly convoluted story centers on Trevor (expressionless Andras Jones), a shaven-headed mental patient apparently in stir for murdering his silicone-enriched [girlfriend] during a satanic ritual. But perhaps his tortured memories are merely the electrically implanted suggestions of the evil Dr. Ek (Jeffrey Combs), running an elaborate operation inside a halfway house where Seth Green, acting in another, better movie, runs rampant. Women are unfailingly presented as duplicitous predators."[6]

Even sympathetic reviewers were hard-pressed to wrap their heads around the continually shifting narrative. "What may or may not have happened is that an evil magician decided to reform his ways and hid the all-powerful book of black magic. At least two other groups of people are trying to get it back. First, a psychologist is trying to get the amnesiac magician to remember the location of the book by creating a fully controlled environment for

---

[30] *Coven* is the infamous 1997 black and white short film directed by Mark Borchardt, its making documented in *American Movie* (1999).

[31] Directed by Jamie Babbit, 1999.

him, ala *The Truman Show*[32]. (But who does the doctor himself work for? It is not clear.) Second, the magician's dead girlfriend is still wandering the earth, assuming different forms, engaged in her own plan to get the information," wrote Johnny Webb, trying to be helpful. "Or maybe not. Maybe time simply exists in some kind of endless loop. Maybe there is no reality at all. Maybe everything exists in some kind of recurring dream. The film suggests a myriad of possibilities and doesn't really commit to a single answer. In determining whether you'll like this movie, it is important to note that it is never completely clear what is going on, and the ending does not provide "closure". At any time, a character may be imaginary, or may be real, or may be the dead girlfriend assuming another form, or may be an actor hired to play a role in the controlled environment, or may be magick—because magick is real in the film's universe. […] Because the film is confusing and does not care to explain all the details[33] at the end, or even to try to make everything fit logically, many people simply don't like it. Most people prefer their films to have some grounding in reality rather than to exist in unguided free-fall. I don't insist on tying everything together, but I do like a clearer explanation than the one offered by this film. In spite of that personal preference, I thought it was fun. I believe that with a little more budget and a few minor script changes, this could have been an entertaining mainstream mindfuck movie, ala *Fight Club* or *The Game*, but without those changes it is often just kind of an incoherent and amateurish mess, albeit an entertaining mess in many ways."[7]

"*The Attic Expeditions* sounds [like] echoes of some (better) weird movies: *Jacob's Ladder* (in the way that the script offers different possible explanations for the protagonist's hallucinations, and jerks the viewer back and forth between those theories) and *Donnie Darko* (in that it seems the director intended to tell a fantastical story that "made sense" on a literal level, but lost control of the story when he took it one paradox too far). An interesting, confusing, out-of-control picture, it's as fascinating for its misses as for its hits. It falls just short of a general recommendation, but it is recommended to anyone interested in psychological, mindbending horror seasoned with heaping doses of confusion and who isn't a stickler for great acting."[8]

In keeping *The Attic Expeditions* under the radar, it was rendered obscure upon its date of release. Even when it made its way to DVD, horror fans were slow to respond to it. Bigger reviewers, and fans of "bigger" movies, paid no attention at all, reflecting the attention it got when pitched to "bigger" studios. "People are idiots, and there is such a lack of understanding of genre and of the fans, and it's a weird movie. I mean, admittedly, this is not a slasher film. This isn't even *Blair Witch*. It's a strange film, nobody involved with the movie comes from money and nobody went to law school. So we were just struggling just like we did at the beginning all the way through to the end practically."[9]

The end result seems to be, "If you enjoy this sort of thing, this is exactly the sort of thing you'd like." If closure isn't as important to you as the journey, you can do—and already have done—worse. It's a mystifying movie to be sure, but you can't deny that the filmmakers'

---

[32] Directed by Peter Weir, 1998.

[33] For Kasten's part, he has a definite take on the script: "I tend to believe Trevor Blackburn murdered his fiancee and then went crazy and has completely slipped off into a comatose state in his own mind. He's built the mythology of the ceremony and the magic and everything else in his head to justify his actions, and that he was probably just a very sick man to begin with. A very wealthy, but very sick man." As he told Nate Yapp, "I think that it became increasingly difficult for me to make Attic Expeditions a film where I didn't believe in a reality. I set out to do that, and I really fought to keep myself somewhat "tabula rasa" in that way, because I wanted to try to support the three possible explanations of reality in the film. Fortunately, while you're making the movie, there's so many questions, and it becomes your job to answers those questions. At times, I could sense the frustration from the cast and crew when they would ask what is really real. So I eventually came around to saying, "I don't know what's really real for you, meaning the audience, but what I believe is real is—" And as such, I think that there's one stronger voice as to the reality of the film than the other two possibilities that we tried to build in. We worked a lot in post-production and in putting the movie together to support the various levels of reality throughout the movie, and to make sure that at any given time, you could argue for any one of them." Yapp, Classic-Horror.com. 2004.

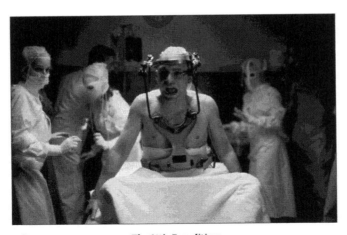

The Attic Expeditions
Trevor Blackburn (Andras Jones) awakens during brain surgery
©2001 Tae Tae Fly Productions

hard work is just dripping from the screen. Take, for just one example, Kasten's lengthy and painstaking single-shots, following characters in the midst of monologues as they drift through the various rooms in the House of Love. As any filmmaker knows, one-shots are difficult and extremely time-consuming, whether you're Orson Wells choreographing the opening of *Touch of Evil* (1958) or Jim Sharman's cost-cutting on *Shock Treatment* (1981)[34]. "I think that on any film, having experience in other departments other than directing is always an asset. Specifically in post-production and editing, it enables you to know really what you need and when you have it. The common belief for how a scene needs to be shot and covered is that you need your master wide shot, your medium shots, your close-ups, and then you have a scene. And in a lot of ways, that's the smartest thing to do, to cover a scene to be safe. But, as we both know, horror movies are their own kind of beast in a way, because you're not always going to stage the scene the way your audience is used to seeing and feeling the rhythm of editing or the progression of shots. Additionally, you most likely have some more complicated set-ups—some moving camera, or effects gags and that sort of thing—that cut into your day. So, planning out what you want to achieve an effect, and at the same time knowing that you can go into the editing room and up-cut it, and change the tempo of what you shot on the set is really important and very helpful," Kasten told Nate Yapp. "It also made me want to rehearse with the actors and that's something I hope to always have the opportunity to do in a movie. That way, you know that in the film that I know when I have what I need and the pieces I need in order to rehearse the scene at the tempo I would like to see it played in a movie. For example, the gameroom scene in *Attic Expeditions*, with Seth Green, it's three and a half minutes of him just making a monologue and he's just walking around and around in this giant room, and the monologue itself becomes more of a mindfuck and more and more complicated and he's moving faster and faster. We rehearsed it to a metronome. I knew that I was going to be having him move through the room to a waltz, so I had a metronome set to a 3:4 time, and then I would slowly turn the metronome up, and as we rehearsed, he would feel the rhythm of the waltz. So, I didn't get stuck with something that was a drag in the editing room, which is often the way dialogue works, is that you're pulling it up and pulling it up and making it more dynamic. Instead, I ended up with something that played exactly three and a half minutes that was exactly the rhythm."[10]

A lot of unfair criticism has been leveled at the admittedly low-key Jones and his down-to-earth approach to Trevor, who tries to handle his confusion and constant manipulation with more good humor than most would be able to muster. Kasten, however, liked Jones from the start. "Interestingly, Andras moved out of town and still does live in Olympia, WA. The casting director had suggested him and I watched some of his work and I thought he was very good, but I was concerned that he lived out of town and the difficulties of making such a low budget movie with somebody where you have to put them up and feed them and take care of

---

[34] See entry in this very book.

them and all of those things. Andras read the script and got my e-mail address from the casting director and started writing me these beautiful, very well thought out, lengthy e-mails about what he thought the movie was about, and how he saw the influences of Robert Anton Wilson and HP Lovecraft and Crowley and all this stuff that's going on in the movie that I think not only would elude most actors, but most people. And I was so impressed by that, we started a correspondence, so by the time he flew to LA to audition, we knew each other and we knew that we had a common vision for the role of Trevor. He got the part on the spot. I'd seen maybe a hundred people for that role and I just couldn't find somebody who could pull it off, who what I was looking for, so I went with Andras," Kasten told Yapp. "And I will say, I think that he had, in a lot of ways, the most difficult role in the movie. While we were making the movie, I would constantly liken what he was doing to being Dorothy in *The Wizard of* Oz— everybody else around her gets to play these fun, incredibly exciting, interesting characters, and Judy Garland is sort of forced to be Judy Garland and sweet and the true core of the film, but not really a dynamic character in the movie. Trevor in *Attic Expeditions* is much the same, in addition to which he's playing "tabula rasa." He's been wiped clean of his personality for the majority of the film, which is, for an actor, is an incredibly hard thing to ask them to play. You're saying, 'You have a glimmer of the person you once were, but for the most part, you don't even know who you are,' and that's tough."[11]

Let's give Jones the last word here: "I honestly have to say that [...] "*The Attic Expeditions* is my best work and, more than that, is the smartest, funniest, weirdest, and most subversive film by far that I have been in. There is an awesome cast including, Seth Green, Jeffrey Combs, Ted Raimi, Wendy Robie, and Alice Cooper[12], who are all really excellent, but the best part is that the director (Jeremy Kasten) and the writer (Rogan Marshall) really made a film to amuse themselves and their cleverest friends and I think that is what makes it so good to have been involved in."[13]

NOTES

[1] Epstein, Dan. 2008. "Interview with Jeremy Kasten." UGO.com. Archived: https://web.archive.org/web/20081202011440/http://ugo.com/channels/filmtv/features/atticexpeditions/

[2] Yapp, Nate. 2004. "Jeremy Kasten Interview." Classic-Horror.com. October 15. http://classic-horror.com/newsreel/jeremy_kasten_interview

[3] Epstein, Dan. 2008. Ugo.com.

[4] Green, Michelle Erica. "Jeffrey Combs Gets Reanimated: Weyoun Returns as a Hirogen." The Little Review.com. http://www.littlereview.com/getcritical/trektalk/combs.htm

[5] Yapp, Nate. 2004. Classic-Horror.com. October 15.

[6] Eisner, Ken. Review: 'The Attic Expeditions'. 2001. Variety. http://variety.com/2001/film/reviews/the-attic-expeditions-1200469418/

[7] Webb, Johnny, and Tuna. "Review." 2002. Movie House Commentary. http://www.scoopy.com/atticexpeditions.htm

[8] Smalley, G. 2011. "List Candidate: The Attic Expeditions (2001)". 366 Weird Movies.com. May 9. http://366weirdmovies.com/list-candidate-the-attic-expeditions-2001/

[9] Epstein, Ugo.com.

[10] Yapp, Nate. 2004. Classic-Horror.com. October 15.

[11] Ibid.

[12] In an amusingly disturbing cameo at the front of the film as an escaped patient trying to reason with his captors.

[13] Brown, Tony. "The Andras Jones Interview." Old Hockstatter Plaace. hockstatter.com/interviews/ajinterview.shtml

BAD BIOLOGY (2007)

Here's a riddle for you: What do you get a girl with seven clitorises? (The answer may surprise you!) As it turns out: "A man with a murderous, steroid-addicted penis."

I didn't say it was a particularly funny riddle. But it is a puzzler that witnesses madness.

Born with mutated genitalia, Jennifer (Charlee Danielson[35]) lives a life of overstimulation. Riddled with clitori, she stalks nightclubs in search of a man who can satisfy her and still live to tell the tale. Sex with her is hazardous, you see, due to her penchant for, during the overwhelming sensation, latching on to her paramour's ears and driving the back of his skull into the floorboards. Complicating matters further, her post-coital manslaughter is always followed by a premature pregnancy and immediate birth of a mewling mutant baby that quickly dies from lack of maternal interest.

Across town, junkie Batz (Anthony Sneed[36]) works to perfect a kind of steampunk masturbation machine to keep his drug-addicted monster cock from whipping around his head in blue ball fury. Can these two mixed-up kids, these mutated sexual predators, come together and find true happiness with one another? If you answered "No," then congratulations, you know a Frank Henenlotter film when you hear one.

The switch in points of view is actually disturbingly, and intentionally, abrupt. "Originally, we were going to intercut between learning who the Jennifer character is and who the Batz character is," Henenlotter explains. "As we were doing that, R.A. and I just felt that's exactly what every other film would do. That's not interesting. That's predictable. We show her story

---

[35] To date, *Bad Biology*, is Danielson's only feature-film credit, but her IMDb bio, written by "Chaz Kangas", has a character arc, so bravo!

[36] Producer on Henenlotter's *Chasing Banksy* (2013) and the director of the quite entertaining *Trump vs. Bernie 2016 Debate Tour* (Video short).

first and then bring in Batz. Yeah, we just spent twenty minutes introducing a character that's now pushed into the background. We know, folks, we know. Because we had narration for the Jennifer character, we thought we should do the same thing with Batz, but early on we realized no, he doesn't understand what's wrong with him. Take it out, take it out. There are a lot of things in the construction of the film that if you were teaching screenwriting, you'd say don't do it that way. That's precisely why I think the film worked. We tried to go in an opposite direction. I love *Bad Biology*. It's probably my favorite of my films."[37]

After *Basket Case 3: The Progeny* saw release in 1992, Frank Henenlotter took an extended leave of absence from the filmmaking world, concentrating on locating and restoring exploitation titles from the '50s and '60s, lost children of film history for Something Weird Video. Without Henenlotter's tireless intervention, titles like the Spanish sexploitation flic, *The Curious Dr. Humpp* (*La venganza del sexo*, 1969) would have been lost to oblivion. That may seem like sarcasm but it is in no way meant to be. As I've stated before, if "Art" can be defined as "anything made, with intent, by man", then all art is worthy of preservation, subjective "quality" be damned. And while we all can find something in the SWV catalog to be thankful for, Henenlotter's absence from the filmmaking scene was noticed.

Jennifer (Charlee Danielson) on a typical Saturday Night.
Courtesy of Bad Biology LLC. All Rights Reserved.

"I avoided a career [in Hollywood]," Frank told Andrew J Rausch. "I would have never fit in, in Hollywood. I just would not have fit in. I'm just not interested in those kinds of movies. I would have to clean up my act so much. I would have to compromise so much. There's no Hollywood studio that would have said yes to the scripts I did. Simple as that. Why go there and pretend to be something else? Yeah, for the money, but eh, I don't know I just want to make movies. [...] I stopped seeing Hollywood movies years ago. It's the same movie over and over and over again. That's not what the genre is. They already have come to me about it. The only way I'm going to do it is if they pay me so much money that I have to go along with it. But that hasn't happened yet. I wouldn't mind selling out. Honest to God, I'd be happy to sell out. I mean, I have a price tag like everybody else does. I wouldn't participate in the remake but, you know, I have a price tag. I've recently had people flirt with a remake of *Basket Case*, but I haven't inked the deal. I'm not anxious for a remake. I think that's the ultimate sell-out. I also think it isn't an easy film for them to remake because it doesn't fit into the slasher category. They probably have to make Belial legs, you know? And then he carries a

---

[37] Rausch, Andrew J. *Gods of Grindhouse*. BearManor Media. 2013. p. 57-58

Batz (Anthony Sneed) and his Magnificent Masturbation Machine.
Courtesy of Bad Biology LLC. All Rights Reserved.

machete and wears a mask."[1]

Sadly, the economic state of the world played a cruel part in Frank's extended hiatus. His first attempt at a comeback, an aborted effort titled *Sick in the Head*, his first attempt at collaboration with rapper "R.A. the Rugged Man"[38], was met with investor remorse and producer interference.

"After three years of the producers not being able to raise money, they took my script and cut out twenty-three pages and all the special effects. And I said, 'Well, what's left?' And they said, 'Well, why don't you make this story more like *Saw*?' Henenlotter told *Film Threat's* Matthew Sorrento. "I owned the script, so I took it back and said, 'Goodbye.' [...] If they wanted a *Saw* ripoff, they should have told me they wanted a *Saw* ripoff. Don't take a good piece of work, gut it, and try to pretend it's something else. [T]he deal was over right then. I didn't like where it was going, so for three years I was putting up with a lot of bullshit. And I kept saying to myself, 'Yeah, but the script is good, the script is good—I can still make it work if the script is good.' Then the script was bad—good-bye. There's no point anymore. What's the point of making movies you don't want to make?"[2]

Fortunately, their second attempt, which included an infusion of capital from R.A., resulted in the mind-boggling *Bad Biology*, the most glorious celebration of bad taste this side of John Waters. "He wanted to make a film, and came to me asking what we could do. And I said we should do something extreme, and I had a couple of visual ideas. I told him to let me think about it. And I had [Jennifer's] opening line already: I originally had it as "I was born with six clits." [The odd biological disposition of Henenlotter's main character leads her to serial fucking and repeated, rapid child-births as she searches for the divine lay.] [R.A.] said if we say "six," it will sound satanic, and we don't want that [for our holy focus.] He said, "Why don't we say 'seven' so it could be biblical?" So that's how we work. We had a list of shots that were like bullet points. I knew we wanted to do this, this, and this. And then I sat down and said, this is all what I want to achieve, now how to we get there. By the way, from day one we knew

---

[38] Born "Richard Andrew Thorburn" sometime *other* than 1974, as he insists. Which seems strange, but who am I to judge? "Well, he called me up one night out of the blue when he was signed with Jive Records. He was a 19-year-old rapper with a new contract, and asked if I would do a rap video. Now I didn't know the first fucking thing about hip-hop, but I just said, 'Sure.' We did a video, and Jive didn't know what to make of it. But we had a good time. Most of the videos of his that you find on YouTube are ones that I've done, despite my name not being on them." Sorrento, Matthew. 2008. "The "Basket Case" Returns(?): Interview With Frank Henenlotter". Film Threat.com. June 4. www.filmthreat.com/interviews/1199/

how it would end. [When we started] we knew the opening line, we knew the last shot, and other stuff in the beginning. So as we were writing it, it was like handball—it's better to play handball with someone else. When you write, you write pages, you rewrite pages, you rewrite the rewrites, and while you are doing that, you are on the phone late at night [discussing it]. We're doing the same thing with a new [script] now. I can't say that one idea is mine and one idea is [Thorburn's], because I wouldn't have had any of these ideas if we hadn't already worked together on other [unproduced scripts]."[3]

"Who knows where we came up with it all?" Henenlotter told *Ultra-Violent Magazine* editor Art Ettinger. "I remember saying that the opening shot should have her saying, 'I was born with six clits.' R.A. said, 'It's got to be seven, because six will sound satanic, and the world was created in seven days,' He was absolutely right. When he said that, I started thinking, why don't we put a religious angle on this and have her think she's doing god's work? Let's play with this. Also, right off the bat, I wanted to show a shot of a hypodermic needle going into a guy's dick. R.A. said,

Tina Krause (in vagina mask) with director Frank Henenlotter (the guy who put her in there). Courtesy of Bad Biology LLC. All Rights Reserved.

'What do you want to do that for?' I said, 'For the same reason you just made that face. It will creep everybody out. That's a shot no guy wants to see. That's why I want it in there.' When I approached Gabe about it, I sketched the last shot. I drew the legs, the blood on the floor, the trajectory of the penis baby, and where it should go on the screen. Gabe was laughing hysterically, and he was immediately on board. He was hooked. He asked what it was about, but I didn't know yet. We had a handful of images, and all we knew was that the last shot's going to be this penis baby. Let's figure out everything in between."[4]

All of the surprise of *Bad Biology* comes in the first act, with the deranged genitals leading the rest of their hapless conjoined bodies in murderous misadventure before meeting cute in the middle. From there on, the audience merely plays the patient game, waiting for the gutmunching carnage to ensue. And ensue it do! Especially once Batz's crazed member decides to divest itself of its troublesome host and its pesky moral platitudes. "[The script] was interesting because I had backstories for two characters," Henenlotter told *Film Threat*. "But I didn't want to repeat backstory. So I had my character Jennifer tell her backstory in voiceover, which was sometimes unrelated to the picture. And then I had the other main character, in a drug-induced hallucination, confess his. You had to know where these characters came from. In the case of *Bad Biology*, if we showed it, like in *Basket Case*, it wouldn't have been interesting. It was more interesting to hear their psychological explanation of who they are."[5]

For fans of grindhouse cinema, *Bad Biology* easily and eagerly recaptures the gritty sleaze of the first *Basket Case*. The film's low budget, contrasted with the clean HD image, adds to the movie's voyeuristic feel brought about by Jennifer's confessional narrative. Frequently breaking the fourth wall, Jennifer treats the viewer like a reality show camera, relating her plight of casual sex and murder to us with the ease of Facebook food-blogging. She's pretty matter-of-fact about it all: it sucks to have seven clitorises, and because of that sometimes people get hurt. When you climax. And seize their ears and bash their heads into the floor.

Frank Henenlotter and F/X maestro, Gabe Bartalos.
Courtesy of Bad Biology LLC. All Rights Reserved.

Batz has more of a cautionary tale: if you're self-conscious about the size of your penis to the point that you'll directly inject it with steroids, perhaps a healthy sex-life shouldn't be your primary concern. The minute the hypodermic comes out, "healthy" goes right out the window.

But as an actor in a Henenlotter movie, you're asked to do some unconventional things.

"Charlee [Johnson] was going out with R.A. at the time," said Henenlotter. "She read the first 30 pages of the script and she asked us if we would let her do. She loved the character and I was thrilled when I heard she wanted to do it. But even then, I tried to spook her a bit and scare her off. And she didn't get scared, thankfully, because she really was just what I wanted. She was absolutely perfect. She's got this fragile beauty, she's like the girl next door. She's not the kind of person you'd expect to star in this film and go as crazy as she does. An absolute delight to work with. […] Anthony I think heard about the film on Craigslist. He came to an audition and at the time he looked a little too…well I'm so overweight so I can say it. He looked a little plump. He was a little too healthy. And I said he didn't look like the kind of 'junkie' we needed for the character. So, he said 'Fine, I'll lose 30 pounds.' And this was 30 days until we started shooting. I figured "Yeah, right." And I never thought of him again, but sure enough he showed up 30 days later and lost 30 pounds for the part. I was so thrown by that commitment. I thought if you're really going to drop 30 pounds for this film, then I've got to take you seriously and I did. And he was great."[6]

Compared to Henenlotter's previous films, *Bad Biology* is closer in spirit to the drug analogy, *Brain Damage*[39], than it is to its more playfully psychotic *Basket Case* brethren. There's also a biting meanness that plagues the film throughout, which contrasts with Henenlotter's usual playful approach to sleaze and depravity. It's tempting to blame this tone on R.A.'s influence. The white rapper makes an appearance as himself midway through the film, shooting a music video in his NY brownstone backed up by topless models wearing grotesque full-face vagina masks. The sequence seems largely out of place, with R.A. creeping out the models almost as much as peeping tom Batz, discovered lurking upstairs by none other than Tina Krause[40] (also playing herself). While Henenlotter's staging points out how dehumanizing the vagina masks are, as voiced by Krause, R.A. doesn't seem to be too terribly put out by this attitude. Which begs the question, is the misogyny in this scene inherent, or has this reviewer become too sensitive in this overly-P.C. era? Truthfully, it's probably the latter explanation, because *Bad Biology* seeks nothing less than the total obliteration of political correctitiude. The inside-vaginal POV of Jennifer's multiple, squirming clitori is the best example of this punk rock attitude. Still, it's difficult to disagree with Kim Newman's assessment of the film:

"Henenlotter made *Frankenhooker* (1990), about a female monster stitched together from

---

[39] Another amazing film: a parasite voiced by John Zacherle (named Aylmer) delivers an addictive drug into the brain of its host, making it kill.

[40] *Animal Room* (1995); *Witchouse 3: Demon Fire* (2001)

blown-apart crack whores, and spun his first film into a trilogy with *Basket Case 2* (1990) and *Basket Case 3: Progeny* (1992). Then, he took a long sabbatical before returning with *Bad Biology* (2008), a love story featuring a girl with multiple clitorises who experiences unparalleled orgasms but gives birth within hours of sex to mewling mutants and a guy whose penis is a self-aware, python-like drug addict. He retains his unparalleled ability to come up with astonishing mutant ideas, but still has problems incorporating his freak characters into actual storylines and tends to trot out a series of murders in lieu of a plot."[7]

This is particularly true of the film's third act, in which Batz's deranged member goes slithering through the city murdering a number of shrieking scream queens (including Rachael Robbins among the zoom-down-the-throat cameos). It's fun to see the familiar faces during the black-comedy killing spree presented from killer penis POV[41], but the sequence quickly becomes repetitive, leaving the viewer impatient for the resolution of Jennifer's and Batz's storylines.

Yet, as *Variety*'s Rob Nelson points out, all of the above is what makes a Henenlotter fan special for his fans. It's also what gets him in constant trouble with the well-intentioned hysterics as the MPAA. "A well-earned NC-17 would hardly hurt commercial prospects given Henenlotter's fans, for whom crudely transgressive schlock is precisely the point. Midnight fest play will spawn horror-porn mag and blog raves—followed, after short refractory period, by uncut DVD. […] Played as stiltedly by Charlee Danielson as Henenlotter's so-bad-it's-rad oeuvre demands, the post-post-feminist heroine proudly forgoes prophylactics, the better to deliver her 'freak babies' within hours of conception. Sharp 35mm lensing includes a peek inside the femme's fave orifice, as well as aptly purplish p.o.v. shots from the hero's third eye. Spotty humor somehow serves the prevailing mood of gentle repugnance, while the pic's almost poignant preference of '80s-style prosthetics over CGI allows the male protag's prodigious tool to register as a rare work of rubber art."[8]

"I think excessive gore is often hilarious," says Henenlotter. "It's not realistic, it's not violence, it's just blood squirting all over the place. That was always my argument with the ratings board. How can you be taking all this seriously? You're [The British Board of Film Classification] going to give *Basket Case* an X rating because an unconvincing puppet is throwing blood around? Are you guys nuts? What are you protecting kids from? […] When we premièred *Bad Biology* [2008] in London I had dinner the night before with a bunch of people and one was a member of the BBFC. I said to him, 'I'd love to know your opinion after the film, unofficially of course.' I said, 'How much trouble are we in?' And he said, 'Oh Frank, you're not in any trouble at all, this is hilarious and harmless.' Then he said, 'But if this was 20 years ago we would have had you arrested.' And that's kind of chilling, you know?" But still a long way from the censorial excesses of the 80s and the Puritanism of even earlier days. "They just put out a restored version of *Dracula* with footage that was banned way back then," he tells me. "The big surprise was a shot where [Christopher] Lee is smiling and caressing a girl and then opens his mouth to reveal his fangs, and that was censored? You look at it now and think, how can that ever be transgressive let alone censorable? That mix of sex and horror always upsets everybody, which is why I like playing with it a lot."[9]

Fans embraced the outré madness of *Bad Biology* with open arms. It also marked the re-emergence of a horror icon who'd gained a reputation as a recluse. After years of focusing solely on the *Something Weird Video* catalog, Henenlotter was somewhat surprised to realize that a goodly number of people had been dying to meet him. "I had assumed, having not made a film in sixteen years, that no one would connect the dots between the guy who made *Bad Biology* and the guy who made *Basket Case*. We ended up going to London for the British premiere at FrightFest, and I was stunned when right in the lobby of the theater, all of these kids were

---

[41] Putting one in mind of Clive Cohen's brilliantly mind-boggling sleaze comedy/thriller/puppet extravaganza, *Exterminator City* (for which I shot a short sequence with my wife/partner Amy Lynn Best), which takes place in a distant future populated solely by killer robot puppets and naked women.

This is exactly what you think it is.
Courtesy of Bad Biology LLC. All Rights Reserved.

coming up to me with video boxes. I was actually thrown for a loop because I missed the obvious. I had been thinking of my films only in terms of theatrical. I didn't reckon with the impact home video had made on them. I mean, I know that seems so obvious, but I missed it. I just didn't see it, so I was very humbled by it. Then, maybe two months later, there was a DVD signing at Dark Delicacies in Los Angeles, and again, there was a mob there. The people were taking the stuff very seriously. They had memorabilia from my films that I never even saw before. So I realized, okay, I kind of had turned my back on the fans because I didn't know I had any, really. So I thought, let me make it up to them, and then I did a couple of conventions. More importantly, I went on Facebook, so I can talk to my fans. That was my way of trying to make up for all of my years of being invisible."[10]

Following *Bad Biology*'s release to home video, Henenlotter's directorial output has been focused on documentaries, including an excellent overview of the career of the infamous inventor of "splatter" and *Blood Feast* director, *Herschell Gordon Lewis: The Godfather of Gore* (2010); an analysis of nudie/roughie/sex 'n violence output of the '50s and '60s *That's Sexploitation!* (2013), and the most recent look at the world's most-famous street artist in *Chasing Banksy* (2015). For more info on any of the above, please visit Frank's official site, www.hotelbroslin.com.

Oh, and try and keep it in your pants.

NOTES

[1] Rausch, Andrew J. Gods of Grindhouse. BearManor Media. 2013. p. 57-58

[2] Sorrento, Matthew. 2008. "The "Basket Case" Returns(?): Interview With Frank Henenlotter". Film Threat.com. June 4. www.filmthreat.com/interviews/1199/

[3] Ibid.

[4] Ettinger, Art. 2015. "Interview with Frank Henenlotter". Published by Scott Gabby. P. 61

[5] Sorrento, 2008.

[6] Rob G. 2010. "Exclusive Interview: Frank Henenlotter!" February 8. http://www.shocktillyoudrop.com/news/14024-exclusive-interview-frank-henenlotter/

[7] Kim Newman. Nightmare Movies. Bloomsbury Publishing. 1988. P. 184

[8] Nelson, Rob. 2008. "Review: 'Bad Biology'". Variety. June 11. http://variety.com/2008/film/reviews/bad-biology-1200509124/

[9] Bett, Alan. 2013. "Exploitation: An Interview with Frank Henenlotter". The Skinny. May 10. http://www.theskinny.co.uk/film/interviews/exploitation-an-interview-with-frank-henenlotter

[10] Ettinger, 2015.

THE BALLAD OF CABLE HOGUE (1970)

"Sam Peckinpah was a genius for four hours a day," James Coburn once said of the embittered director. "The rest of that time he was drunk. He called himself 'a working alcoholic,' but he was much more than that. I think the alcohol sort of quelled all the influences that were going on around him so he could really focus on what he was doing with the film. He would shoot with three cameras and just...do it."[1]

Bloody Sam liked to keep people guessing.

By the time *The Wild Bunch* (1969) exploded across screens, signaling that a new type of Western, violent and demystified, had moved into the culture, Peckinpah—for whom the word "irascible" was invented—refused to be pigeon-holed. While *The Wild Bunch* repaired a lot of damage done to his reputation due to his uncontrollable alcoholism and often abusive nature on set, and critics were enthusiastic about the brutal, cynical anti-hero western, there was a lot of speculation over what he would do next. Remember, *The Wild Bunch* came on the heels of a disastrous shoot with Charlton Heston on *Major Dundee*[42] and a controversial and very public

---

[42] "The nod comes from Columbia in 1964. The deal: Charlton Heston, a $3 million budget, a three-hour flick, and a script about a Civil War major who runs down a renegade Apache in Mexico. Two days before the shooting starts, Jerry Bresler, the producer, tells Peckinpah one million's been cut from the budget, 15 days from the shooting schedule, and an hour from the running time. Peckinpah's down in Mexico with a cast of hundreds. Drives his crew around the bend. Some fights break out. According to Paul Seydor's book *Peckinpah: The Western Films*, Heston charges Peckinpah on his horse and tries to run him through with his saber. Fifteen crew members are fired. Nobody's getting any sleep. Peckinpah wears the same pair of jeans through the whole production. Starts to run over schedule. At some point falls in love. Hits $600,000 over revised budget. The guys in the Italian silk suits arrive, threaten to seize the footage. Heston offers to return his salary if Peckinpah is allowed to finish. The studio takes Heston's money, and Peckinpah finishes what he can. Flies to California and makes his first cut. Says it runs 'beautifully' at two hours and 41 minutes. Bresler chops off 55 minutes. Leaves out what the story's about. Adds a marching song by Mitch Miller's Sing Along Gang. When Peckinpah sees the release print of *Major Dundee* he gets sick." Carroll, E. Jean. 1982. "Last of the Desperadoes: Dueling with Sam Peckinpah."

dismissal from *The Cincinnati Kid*[43]. Peckinpah was considered a dangerous risk, not only because of his approach towards violence and subversion, but because of his reckless behavior towards cast, crew, executives, family, and random animals. After the apocalyptic ending of *The Wild Bunch*, audiences were primed for the next Peckinpah outing to be a literal bloodbath, possibly spilling from the screen and into the theater seats below.

Though completed before the release of *The Wild Bunch*, *Cable Hogue* was an ace up Peckinpah's sleeve. Sam being Sam, he refused to deliver the expected. Or even the desired.

The Ballad of Cable Hogue tells the story of its titular hero, played by Jason Robards[44], who "Found Water Where It Wasn't."[45] A prospector betrayed by his partners Bowen and Taggart (Strother Martin and L.Q. Jones, more or less repeating their roles as the sleazy bounty hunters from *The Wild Bunch*, but in surprisingly less-cartoony turns here), is left wandering in the desert without water or hope. About to perish, Hogue collapses beside a mud puddle. Digging with his hands, he discovers an underground spring. Never one to waste an opportunity, Hogue digs a well and opts to charge travelers for a drink of the only water between two stops on a stagecoach route. His first customer, the shady Reverend Joshua (David Warner[46]), also becomes his business partner, urging Hogue to register his claim on the property in town. After successfully obtaining a bank loan for his new venture, Hogue celebrates with a hot bath and roll with local soiled dove, Hildy (Stella Stevens[47]).

As time marches ever onward, "Cable Springs" thrives and Hogue's fortunes grow. His partnership with Joshua comes to an end when the reverend is run out of town for preying on "vulnerable" women. Evolving moral outrage drives Hildy out of town as well, and she takes up with Hogue at his flourishing camp. While the changing world amuses Hogue, it never vexes him. Watching a motorcar speed past the Springs without stopping, Hogue muses, "Well, that's the next guy's problem." Though the invention itself will prove to be Hogue's undoing, he goes to his grave with a smile, surrounded by the people who've grown to love him.

"There wasn't a star in the sky he hadn't nicknamed. There wasn't a man he was afraid of," eulogizes Joshua. "He never went to church but the whole desert was his cathedral . . . He built his empire but he was man enough to give it up when the time came."

The Ballad of Cable Hogue is *The Wild Bunch* with smoother edges. The central themes of the disappearing west and the displacement of the men who prospered in wilder times are still present, but this isn't a movie about ruthlessness, regret, or even alienation. *Cable Hogue* is about finding your way in the world when fortune seemingly turns a blind eye towards you. It hails resourcefulness and opportunity, and Hogue approaches it all with almost detached bemusement. He goes after what he wants, but he doesn't trample anyone to achieve it. Few gunshots are fired during the course of the film, little blood is shed. *Cable Hogue* is thoughtful and philosophical. So it should come as no surprise that it was roundly ignored.

"Peckinpah had bought the rights to *The Ballad of Cable Hogue* back in 1967 while he was still scrambling for TV assignments to make ends meet. John Crawford and Edmund Penney had written the haunting, allegorical screenplay about a stubborn desert rat who discovers a water hole along a stagecoach route at the dawn of the twentieth century. [...] When Ken

---

Rocky Mountain Magazine, March. Archived industrycentral.net/director_interviews/SAPE01.HTM

[43] "1964, December. four days after Peckinpah starts work on *The Cincinnati Kid*, [producer] Martin Ransohoff fires him. Says he's vulgarizing the picture." Carroll, E. Jean. 1982. "Last of the Desperadoes: Dueling with Sam Peckinpah." Rocky Mountain Magazine, March. Archived industrycentral.net/director_interviews/SAPE01.HTM

[44] Something Wicked This Way Comes (1983, dir. Jack Clayton).

[45] The framing of the woefully panned-and-scanned version that dominated TV for years cut off part of the sign bearing this motto, leaving it to read, "He found water where it was."

[46] *Time Bandits* (1983, d. Terry Gilliam)

[47] *The Nutty Professor* (1963, d. Jerry Lewis)

Hyman gave the project the green light in August 1968, Gordon Dawson and Sam did a minor rewrite, adding comical scenes, tightening up some sequences, and polishing the dialogue of others. The film would be a tribute to Sam's great-uncle, Moses Church, his grandfather, Charlie Peckinpah, and all the other wild and woolly entrepreneurs who carved their own empires out of the great untamed land in the nineteenth century, then faded into obscurity when "progress" eventually passed them by. Peckinpah's team—Dawson, who would function (without credit) as associate producer, cinematographer Lucien Ballard, art director Leroy Coleman, and prop man Bobby Visciglia—cranked pre-production into high gear in December 1968. The picture was to be shot in thirty-six days in the Valley of Fire, just east of Las Vegas, and in Arizona on a slender budget of $880,000."[2]

Cable (Jason Robards) and Hildy (Stella Stevens) meet cute in the first of many bathing scenes. German Lobby Card. Photo copyright Warner Brothers. All Rights Reserved.

What makes *The Ballad of Cable Hogue* stand out in Peckinpah's filmography is precisely its humanity and genteel nature. Hogue isn't a tough guy like The Bunch's Pike or Dutch, but he's no shrinking violet either. The main reason Taggart feels comfortable with betraying him is because when given the chance to gun his ex-partners down, Hogue hesitates, unwilling to make that killing shot. Taggart's underestimating of Hogue proves to be the man's downfall. Expecting a rough and tumble cowboy, Hildy is surprised by Hogue's tenderness and humor. Seeking an accomplice for his vices, Joshua is bemused by Hogue's incorruptible nature. Indeed, when it's suggested that Hogue raise the price for his water, he argues that there's no reason to take advantage of those in need. Hogue isn't the poster boy for Darwinism here; he simply wants to get by and is content to let others do the same.

Cable Hogue is one of the gentlest of westerns, to the point that the narrative often stops so that Hogue and Hildy can sing to each other (the earworm "Butterfly Mornings" dominates the second act and is so sickly sweet a song, you can watch Robards develop diabetes as he sings), and also bathe each other. While Peckinpah was never big on symbolism, water is the primary metaphor here: renewal through baptism (frequent bathing after a long drought); live-giving sustenance; an affordable commodity; and a pure Capitalist endeavor arguing that the self-made man is what made America great.

But the downfall of the West due to the interference of modern technology—a frequent theme throughout most of Sam's work—might have also been an unconscious metaphor for Sam's career. Alcoholism aside, Peckinpah's biggest demons sat behind studio desks and made critical decisions about how to shape art into something they perceived as more popular. Not that Sam ever made things easy on himself. There was no challenge thrown in his path that he couldn't make worse. "You never talked with Sam about things like motivation. I asked him one time, when we were doing *Major Dundee*. I said 'Sam, what is it that makes my character

Polish poster for Cable Hogue. The Internet is neat.

tick?' And he thought about it for a minute and finally said 'Drier. Dry. He doesn't give a shit.' And that's who that character was! And that's how I played him...It was really sad what happened to that picture. The studio took it away from him and re-cut it. We had a great knife fight in that picture [*Major Dundee*], between Mario Adorf[48] and myself. And it was a vicious fucking knife fight. While we were shooting it, people were yelling for us to stop! That's how real it looked. It was a terrific piece of action, and it was cut from the film...the night it premiered at the Paramount Theater, Sam saw the studio's cut and was just devastated. His hands were shaking. He had half a pint of whiskey and dropped it. It smashed on the floor. And my wife at the time said 'Sam, it's okay, it's only a movie.' "[3]

While Peckinpah's reputation preceded him then and follows him now, as Rick Moody pointed out in *The Guardian*, his violent spectacles seem almost tame to modern eyes— also telling for the argument that modernism ran over Sam in the end as well. "'Now, most funeral orations, Lord, lie about a man,'—so says David Warner, in his memorable turn as Joshua, the fraudulent preacher in Sam Peckinpah's *The Ballad of Cable Hogue*, from 1970. The same can be said of most film criticism—that it dissimulates or exaggerates about the film, about the director, about the movement, about the art. So let's aspire in this revisionist essay on Peckinpah to tell the truth. Although it's worth noting that when you believe what characters say in a Peckinpah film, you play right into the director's malevolent hands. Nevertheless, the first point that must be made, here in the 21st century, is that Peckinpah's films are not terribly violent. That's how he made his reputation: as 'Bloody Sam', the man who never met a bucket of theatrical blood he wasn't willing to splash around, and who always made certain you knew when the blood was about to flow, by means of slow motion. Still, by today's standards, the better part of the Peckinpah canon is not terribly violent—not when judged against today's rivers of gore. There are, in Peckinpah, no fountaining bodies, no bits of brain tissue splattered about. Anything released in the last twenty years is quite a bit more repellent. Seen any of those *Saw* movies?"[4]

Which is arguable, I suppose. Certainly students of mine have watched *The Wild Bunch* and wondered what all the fuss was about. It's difficult to see movies in the context of their times (*Birth of a Nation* anyone?). But then Moody doubles down on a point that I feel misses the integral point of *Cable Hogue*:

"In *The Ballad of Cable Hogue*, the Jason Robards vehicle that Peckinpah made in 1970, just after *The Wild Bunch*, the comic and light-hearted moments that also marked the first reel of *Ride the High Country* are back, even expanded. Though the filming apparently suffered many problems, not least of which was the director's frequent intoxication, the results are good-natured, even heartwarming. Robards' performance, in which he often appears alone, inveighing against God, or fate, or luck, is marked by an almost Beckettian slapstick existentialism. His scenes with David Warner, too, are funny, sly, and immediately accessible to cinemagoers who also admire Ionesco or Pirandello. While I am sure Peckinpah believed he

---

[48] A veteran German actor perhaps best-known for his role as the (possible) father of the ghoulish little boy in *The Tin Drum* (1979, directed by Volker Schlöndorff).

was remaking the western along more realistic lines—John Wayne and John Ford needed to be dispatched, after all—this is not the film that achieves that end. The western, in *Cable Hogue*, is comic, is populated by stock outlaws and tipplers. Its only generic innovation is its nihilism about the possibility of good. The preacher is a liar and pervert, the bank owner delights in the collapse of the revivalist's tent, the whore is the only girl in town, who does, of course, despite her short temper, have the heart of gold. Where's the realism in this?"

The realism is in the characters of the film. Of course the most reviled woman in town has a heart of gold, but the "good" citizens can't see that in her, or they would have to acknowledge her as a human being and not, to devolve the citizens further, the "harlot" that causes the crops to shrivel and the livestock to die. Hildy is the object of their ire so that they can go through the rest of their day believing themselves to be her moral superiors and overlook their own faults. Warner's Reverend Joshua is admittedly a weak man who also hides behind his projected morality. Only Hogue stands apart from the so-called "stock" characters. His love of Hildy is unconditional. He doesn't care what she does, but who she is. And she sees the same in him. Joshua sees this as well—Cable accepts people as they are. If they're scumbags in his eyes, it's because he recognizes their hypocrisy. It's probably the most no-nonsense cinematic equivalent to an alter-ego Sam ever put on the screen.

Though the film has an overlaid sweetness and an unhurried pace (save for some of the chase scenes undercranked for comedic exploitation), the shoot was a typical Peckinpah farce. "But when shooting began in January 1969, the simple low budget picture turned into a financial quagmire. The Valley of Fire became the Valley of Thunderstorms. Heavy rains and technical and logistical problems caused the production to fall ten days behind schedule in its first month of shooting. Peckinpah took his frustrations out on the crew. He fired thirty-six people from the production, an average of one a day. The dismissals grew so frequent that a car was kept on location for the express purpose of carting the fallen from the set, and a shuttle service transported casualties to the Las Vegas airport and fresh fodder out to the valley. Sam terminated camera mechanics, assistant directors, caterers, drivers, an animal handler, a set dresser, a projectionist, a gaffer, grips, a makeup man, and production manager Dink Templeton."[5]

Sam liked to just "get on with it". In the opening scene, Cable shoots a lizard for dinner. Sam being Sam, he opted to just blow up a poor, living animal. Several members of the cast and crew—including Sam's own daughter. Sharon, who'd witness her father's casual murder of all sorts of animals (rabbits, puppies, horses)—protested the merciless, unnecessary destruction.

"The screenplay for *Cable Hogue* dictated that as Hogue scratched out an existence from the barren desert he would kill lizards and rattlesnakes, rabbits and birds for stew meat. Sam insisted that live animals be used, and that some of them be killed on camera.

"When [Sharon's boyfriend and still photographer] Gary Weis learned that Sam intended to squib a live lizard for one shot and blow it up in slow motion to simulate the reptile's being shot by a rifle, he mounted a "Save the Lizard!" campaign. "I started leaving these phantom notes around, on Sam's car, on the bulletin board at the hotel where all the production notices were posted," says Weis. "They'd say things like, 'To kill a lizard on Thursday is bad luck for a hundred years—Akira Kurosawa.' I always signed the names of Sam's idols on them."

"Weis' efforts were in vain. Sam blew the lizard up anyway. Sharon was horrified. Looking at all those rabbits trapped in their tiny wire cages, knowing they would be slaughtered for a scene in a movie, was unbearable. [...] [It] was the way she, her sisters and brother, everybody and everything came second to his whims that infuriated Sharon, and she told him so. Sam shot back at her, "Who do you think is paying for your education?" and ridiculed her as naive. But it was bluster—Sharon's verbal darts were drawing blood.

"She and Gary really got to him," says Gill Dennis, an AFI intern on the production who ended up codirecting the documentary. "They were making him feel so guilty. Every time Bobby Visciglia took a rabbit off to kill it for a shot, Gary would film it and zoom in with the camera, you know?" The final confrontation came when Sam summoned Sharon and Gary to his hotel room one night. He launched into a tirade against his eldest daughter, accusing her of disloyalty. Did she have any idea how stressful it was to direct a movie? Under such high pressure he needed all the emotional support he could get, but instead she had betrayed him.

"Sharon's anger matched his own. She told him she didn't believe in what he was doing. 'Do you think making a dumb movie is going to be worth hurting so many people? All the people you've fired, all the people you've humiliated and degraded, do you ever think about that?'"[6] The confrontation with his daughter literally left him in tears—the real shock to those involved.

Because of the success of *The Wild Bunch* (despite releasing a shorter version edited without Peckinpah's consent, leading him to sue the studio), Warner Brothers more or less gave Peckinpah free reign on *Cable Hogue*, leaving him pretty much alone during the shoot, even when it ran 19-days over schedule almost $3 million dollars over budget. What was unforgivable was its poor performance at the box office. Once word got around that Bloody Sam's latest was barely bloody at all, interest waned, then vanished.

After a rough cut was screened for the studio heads, their apathy for the film bubbled to the surface. The regime at the studio had changed during production, and the current suits had no vested interest in *Hogue*. They recommended a happier ending—suggesting Cable and Hildy run off to New Orleans, eliminating the film's theme entirely.

"They gave Peckinpah a free hand to finish the film his own way, not out of respect for his artistic talent, but out of apathy. The picture was simply not worth the hassle of another battle with Peckinpah. Feldman was hoping the previews would save them. If audiences liked the picture, certainly the Warners brass would have to change its attitude. With its running time now hovering at about two hours, *Cable Hogue* previewed at theaters in Long Beach and New York at the end of January and beginning of February. Seventy percent of the reaction cards rated it from good to excellent. But this was not enough to change Warners' attitude about the picture. *The Ballad of Cable Hogue* was dumped into second-rate theaters across the country with barely a ripple of publicity—one billboard on Sunset Boulevard, an ad in the trades, only quarterpage ads in newspapers, and no radio or TV advertising at all. 'Warner Bros. didn't release it,' says Stella Stevens, 'they flushed it.'

"Though some critics found its allegorical style heavy-handed and pretentious, the film won many raves that were every bit as good as those for *The Wild Bunch*. But the reviews were not enough to save *Cable Hogue*. After a couple of weeks in second-run theaters it sank to the bottom half of double bills on the drive-in and grind-house circuit, then disappeared altogether. By 1973 it had grossed a grand total of $2,445,863."[7]

The disposal of the film was a heartbreaking blow to its director. Where once Sam was being bandied as the sure-bet director of *Deliverance*, he found himself on the outs with Warner Brothers and was forced to film *Straw Dogs* in England after American financing fell through. For years, when speaking at colleges and other engagements, he would suggest a screening of *Hogue*. It was, after all, his favorite film.

After *Straw Dogs'* critical failure, Peckinpah's alcoholism finally consumed him. With an already-terrible reputation, he found it harder and harder to get work in Hollywood. His disease forced limitations on him both as an artist and a craftsman. His sporadic output through the '70s and '80s include the muddled and unpleasant *Bring Me the Head of Alfredo Garcia*, and the nearly incoherent *The Osterman Weekend*. His final output before his death was directing the music videos for Julian Lennon's "Valotte" and "Too Late for Goodbyes". "Valotte" is a special favorite among Lennon fans: Lennon sitting alone in a studio, just him and the piano, while framed from the hovering point of view of an unseen overhead observer.

"Julian Lennon, his features and his voice so unsettlingly reminiscent of his late father's, sits alone at the piano in a recording studio, as the camera seems to hover, as if from hereafter itself, at the uppermost corner of the ceiling above the performance," writes Moody. "There's nothing flashy or cheap about the video (in an era when cheap was the order of the day), and everything about it feels understated, even graceful. But whose heavenly ken is depicted therein? From the top of that ghostly staircase? John Lennon's point of view, lamenting a son he insufficiently came to know? Peckinpah's, who knew his time was short and that his vision, as realised, was incomplete? Maybe Valotte was a sort of funeral oratory, too—one, as in

David Warner's speech from *Cable Hogue*, in which the orator was unable to lie."[8]

Even today, *Cable Hogue* gets little love. It's never been released to Blu-Ray. A stand-alone DVD offered by Warner Brothers is out of print, the remaining copies woefully expensive. Currently, the only place you can obtain it is by purchasing the *Sam Peckinpah's Legendary Westerns Collection* box set (which also offers *Pat Garrett* and *Ride the High Country*, so it's probably worth the money). While respect for it has increased over the years, it's still dismissed as "lesser" Peckinpah. How it can be thought of when compared to his latter output is baffling. As a standalone film, *The Ballad of Cable Hogue* is light-hearted and life-affirming. When placed in the context of Peckinpah's filmography, it's a remarkable piece of work from a man who usually saw only the ugly in men and the futility of life. *Hogue* was possibly the death rattle of Peckinpah's humanity. For that alone, it is important.

NOTES

[1] Simon, Alex. 1999. "James Coburn: Cool Daddy." Venice Magazine. February. Archived The Hollywood Interview. http://thehollywoodinterview.blogspot.com/2008/02/james-coburn-hollywood-interview.html

[2] Weddle, David. 1994. " 'If They Move…Kill 'em.' The Life and Times of Sam Peckinpah." Grove Press. P 383

[3] Simon, Alex. 1999. Venice Magazine.

[4] Moody, Rick. 2009. "Inside the head of Sam Peckinpah." The Guardian. January 9. http://www.guardian.co.uk/film/2009/jan/09/sam-peckinpah-retrospective

[5] Weddle, 1994. P. 383

[6] Weddle, 1994. P. 383-384

[7] Weddle, 1994. P. 387

[8] Moody, Rick. 2009. The Guardian.

BLOODBATH AT THE HOUSE OF DEATH (1983)

In 1975, on a Thursday, give or take a day, eighteen people were murdered to death at Headstone Manor via various means of dispatchment at the hands of red-hooded monks (hangings, multiple shotgun blasts, slashings, the shish-kebab skewering of four people in a bed like a shish kebab, a hatchet through the head, all either reminiscent of, or homage to, *Friday the 13th*). This pre-credit sequence is constructed like a straight horror picture with a slim amount of comedy, and this illustrates what is problematic about the film. Such gory elements are peppered throughout the narrative and they sit uneasily alongside the simple-minded daft gags tailored for and by comedian Kenny Everett and his fellow cast members (many of who had appeared at some stage on his television series). This is the film's funniest sequence.

Immediately following, we meet several pairs of scientists, two law-enforcement officers who may or may not be but probably are gay and a randy dating couple, all of whom head over to said Manor in "The Present" (as the titles tell us; aka 1983) to measure radiation and see if there was anything unusual about the day when those eighteen people were killed, mutilated and otherwise treated badly.

Meanwhile, Vincent Price heads up that cadre of red-hooded monks as a 700-year-old Warlock (or something) and this group only live to serve their master, Satan, who is also an alien, who is personified as Headstone Manor, the sentient and muchly evil house that must be vacant in order to achieve maximum evilness.

I think.

This *Airplane*-style horror comedy wants oh-so desperately to be *Return to Horror High* (1987). It tries so very hard. They even got Vincent Price to play a character referred to (in the credits only) as "The Sinister Man". There are buckets of blood and gags every few seconds.

Amazingly, to we who have been conditioned by *Family Guy*[49] and The Wayans

---

[49] Seth MacFarlane's *Simpsons* rip-off for stoners. You know perfectly well what I'm talking about.

Vincent Price as "The Sinister Man".
Photo copyright Goldfarb Distribution Nucleus Films Ltd (DVD). All Rights Reserved.

Brothers[50] to expect jokes to be stomped thoroughly into the ground, lit afire and yelled at, the jokes are quick and clean—they get in and get out and move on. Overall, it's generally funny, but it just goes on too long. About midway through, the story becomes hopelessly incomprehensible as Price and the monks burst into flames and are replaced by doppelgangers of our main characters who are quickly and gruesomely murdered and replaced again. Sometimes. And sometimes they're not. The nefarious plot is revealed five minutes prior to the end credit roll and it had left me behind at least half an hour before.

"Ultimately, *Bloodbath* is a frustrating misfire, but not without merit. It would be impossible for any screenplay penned by the legendary British comedian Barry Cryer not to have at least a few worthwhile gags. The scene in the local pub in which there is confusion about the exact number of deaths at the manor—which climaxes in a group sing-along—is an example of the silly yet charming humor that the filmmakers were capable of. Co-written by director Ray Cameron, the script works best when relying on its willing and talented performers whose collective comic timing is flawless. Everett seems restricted by a feature-length narrative and being confined to playing only one character, but he equates himself well in the lead role, while his occasional psychotic lapses into a deranged surgeon with kitsch German accent allow him to display some of his trademark zaniness. The remarkable Pamela Stephenson had demonstrated in the skit BBC series *Not the Nine O'clock News* that she is a talented comedienne and her presence in the film is most welcome. According to the supplementary material on the DVD, Stephenson was responsible for adding the peculiar lisp to her character's speech and this slight but important addition to her performance is an indication of her strong comedic instincts".[1]

Bloodbath at the House of Death was created to showcase the not inconsiderable talents of British comic Kenny Everett. His writing partners on *The Kenny Everett Show*, Barry Cryer and Ray Cameron, wrote the script with Cameron directing (his only feature film), and Everett stars as the primary scientist who harbors the horrible secret of once being German. The humor is very British throughout, in that it is more droll than hilarious. Their infrequent attempts at course American humor (involving profanity, naturally) usually falls flatter than the quick word-play or even slapstick. The funniest death scene in the film goes to the *Carrie* parody involving decapitation-by-can-opener. And if you still aren't sold, it's known among horror fans as "the movie where Vincent Price swears". And he swears an awful lot. Oddly, that actually is funny.

---

[50] *Scary Movie* (2000), *White Chicks* (2004)—dumbing down America since 1995.

By this time in his life Price was taking roles in order to stay working, to pay the bills and stay in the public eye. But that doesn't mean he was happy about every choice he made. According to his daughter, Victoria, "In a publicity interview at the time Vincent, rather testily but with some justification, complained, 'I'm bored talking about horror. I'm too old. Do you ask Al Pacino how he likes doing gangster roles? I'm bored talking about it.'"[2]

Ironically, 1983 also saw his acceptance of a job for a small honorarium: his narrative rap for Michael Jackson's Platinum record's title song *Thriller* (1982). Though he was often critical of the financial naiveté of his fellows, Price was angry at himself, as well as Jackson, for the contract he signed, which included no provisions for royalties. When he approached the superstar's legal division regarding the use of his voice on the massive best-seller's tie-in video, he was simply pointed towards the finest of print that eliminated any hope of residuals. As "thanks", Jackson sent Price a framed photo of the singer, plus the gold and platinum albums. After Jackson settled a child molestation case out of court, Price told Reggie Williams, his personal secretary at the time, "All I can say is that Michael Jackson fucked me—and I didn't get paid for it!" Yet, the album led to a resurgence of interest in the actor, with Disney seeking him out to play the villainous Rattigan in *The Great Mouse Detective*. Which is more than *Bloodbath at the House of Death* ever did.[3]

One of the things that screwed the film to obscurity involves a disastrous political appearance by Everett. "British political history is littered with celebrity endorsements that have backfired. It is not hard to imagine the delight of Young Conservatives in 1983, on booking Kenny Everett--then one of the biggest names on British TV—to appear at a youth rally. The idea, presumably, was to add a bit of youthful sparkle, anarchy even, to an event whose other principal draws were old stagers Bob Monkhouse and Jimmy Tarbuck. What they got, for their efforts, was endlessly replayed TV footage of a man with giant foam hands yelling "let's bomb Russia!", to loud Tory cheers, as Prime Minister Margaret Thatcher looked on. [...] Everett later said he regretted the incident and that he had taken the foam hands to the rally because the Tories "asked me first". But, for the party, the damage had been done."[4]

"Back in 1983, *Bloodbath at the House of Death* was quite a well-known title, mostly for the wrong reasons. The production coincided with the aftermath of Everett's infamous "Let's bomb Russia! ... Let's kick Michael Foot's stick away!" outburst at the Young Conservatives' annual conference, so the film's title was regularly invoked in the press. Although his conference appearance did little damage to Everett's popularity with his fans, the media turned on him. The knives were out and well sharpened by the time *Bloodbath* came out, and its vitriolic critical reception still taints the film's reputation," wrote Phelim O'Neill in The Guardian. "Today, it's virtually absent from film literature in print and on the internet. Even sites dedicated to Kenny Everett, Vincent Price or British films either omit it or give it a cursory mention, but how could they do otherwise when they've been denied the opportunity to see it? It's almost as if it had never been made. While some people might wish that were the case, it seems unusually unfair that a comparatively recent film boasting such familiar names as Price and Everett (as well as a slew of British comedy fixtures including Sheila Steafel, John Fortune, Barry Cryer and Pamela Stephenson) could just vanish. [...] Laurence Myers, who was called in to produce *Bloodbath* when its financing threatened to collapse, has a theory—and one that would most reasonably account for the film's disappearance. 'It's a fairly terrible film,' he says. 'I recall showing it to [censor] James Ferman who thought it was fine and funny enough, but thought we were showing him the reels in the wrong order. We weren't—the film just doesn't make sense.' "[5]

For the longest time, *Bloodbath at the House of Death* was only available on VHS from Media Home Entertainment, copies of which can still be found on Amazon. (There seems to have also been a tie-in novelization by Martin Noble.) Allegedly, there was a British DVD, from which the version I "obtained"[6] was struck, and it's head and shoulders above the VHS, of course. Particularly during the opening scenes when you can plainly see that the house was shot in unsuccessful day-for-night. On VHS, these shots are simply blurry blobs with windows.

No one saw an existing market for a sporadically funny horror farce known best as "the movie where Vincent Price swears." Yet, Nucleus Film's Marc Norris managed to track down

the film's original negative in order to finally release it to a tolerable DVD. "*Bloodbath* had accrued around £25,000 in overdue charges, and for a film with such limited marketability that price tag could have scuppered the whole endeavour. Fortunately Morris was able to haggle the amount down to a much more manageable figure when the lab realised that whatever he was offering would be the only money they'd ever see from the movie. Morris's offer was better than nothing, even if it was only marginally so. As a result, a near-pristine negative has been saved from destruction and the DVD of *Bloodbath* has a picture quality to rival its competitors on the shelves."[7]

One of the strongest arguments for film preservation is that celluloid negatives are degrading, but doing so at a faster rate than DVD or streaming interest emerges. Tens of thousands of movies are in danger of disappearing forever, much like the thousands of pre-WWII movies that have disintegrated already. My feeling is that everything is worth preserving, from two-reel silent comedies to, well, Kenny Everett's disastrous masterpiece. Every movie ever made deserves the chance to be someone's favorite. If *Bloodbath at the House of Death* can be rescued at the same time as Welles' *Chimes at Midnight* (1966), what possible argument could possibly stand against this?

NOTES

[1] O'Neill. 2008. "Bloodbath at the House of Death" 10K Bullets. October 8th, 2008.
http://10kbullets.com/reviews/b/bloodbath-at-the-house-of-death/

[2] Price, Victoria. 1999. *Vincent Price, A Daughter's Biography*. St. Martin's Press, 1999. P. 412.

[3] Ibid.

[4] Wheeler, Brian. 2004. "Ugly business for show people?" BBC news. May 26.
http://news.bbc.co.uk/2/hi/uk_news/politics/3746865.stm

[5] O'Neill, Phelim. 2008. "The films that were buried alive." The Guardian. August 22.
http://www.theguardian.com/film/2008/aug/22/comedy

[6] Neither the author nor the publishers condone the act of piracy even though it seems to be the only way to get certain titles thanks to the devil-worshipping media conglomerates. We say this with love.

[7] O'Neill, 2008.

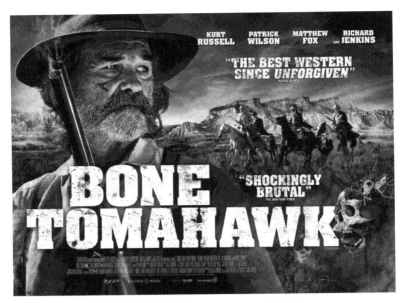

BONE TOMAHAWK (2014)

By Bill Watt

Reviews of westerns on Amazon often begin: "I don't like westerns, but"…and then a litany of what they liked about (fill in the blank). This usually means they know nothing about westerns so I pay them no mind.

Many, many, many years ago, I made an impossible pledge to myself that I would see every western made. That meant 'A' westerns, 'B' westerns, Poverty Row westerns, TV series, comedies, parodies, cartoons, if it had a horse and a horizon, I watched it. That means I've watched *Stagecoach* and *The Terror of Tiny Town* (the first and, as far as I know, the only all midget western), *Shane* and *Shame, Shame on the Bixby Boys*, *Abilene Town* to *Zachariah*, I watched them all. Then came the Spaghetti Western, and God help me, I even watched quite a few of those. I've seen German produced westerns, Japanese westerns, French and Australian westerns. I read and have read western novels, western history, western comic books and I listen to old radio westerns. I've written western articles and lectured on them. I know a little something about westerns. So, if I tell you that *Bone Tomahawk* is the best western of 2015, you can bet your saddle on it. And remember, 2015 was the year of *The Revenant* and Quentin Tarantino's, *The Hateful 8*. *The Revenant* is probably the closest we're ever going to come to what the West was like in the early 19th century, even with some historical inaccuracies. I don't know what the hell *The Hateful 8* was; it sure wasn't a western, no more than *Django Unchained*. Tarantino seems to think they are, but I refer you to the opening statement. And no, I won't debate the issue. I know there are many who will disagree with me on this, but watching it was three hours I'm never getting back and discussing it will rob me of more hours I can't spare. On to *Bone Tomahawk*.

"If you move in a hasty manner, I'll put a bullet in you."

It's 1890 or thereabouts and two drifters, Buddy and Purvis, (played by the frequently wonderful Sid Haig[51] and the usually annoying David Arquette[52]). Their occupation seems to be killing travelers. When they accidentally cross a burial ground sacred to a tribe of cannibal cave dwellers, Buddy is killed and Purvis narrowly escapes. Eleven days later Purvis arrives in

---

[51] See chapter on The Devil's Rejects.

[52] *Scream* series.

the small town of Bright Hope and his suspicious behavior while burying something comes to the attention of The Back-Up Deputy, Chicory, (Richard Jenkins[53]). Chicory informs The Law, Sheriff Franklin Hunt (Kurt Russell) of his suspicions and Hunt confronts Purvis in the local saloon—the outrageously named "The Learned Goat." When he is questioned Purvis tries to run and moves in a hasty manner and Sheriff Hunt shoots him in the leg. Well, after all, he was warned. Hunt has Purvis moved to the jail and sends John Brooder (Matthew Fox), An Armed Gentleman to fetch the doctor. Since one doctor is drunk, Brooder goes to the home of The Cowboy, Arthur O'Dwyer (Patrick Wilson[54]), to ask O'Dwyer's wife, Samantha (Lili Simmons[55]) to go to the jail to dress Purvis' leg. She is The Town Doctor. Sometime during the night Samantha, Purvis and the other deputy, Nick are kidnapped, a stable boy is murdered and horses are stolen. The only clue is an arrow found in the jail. Hunt consults with an Indian scholar (Zahn

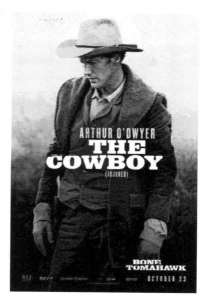

McLarnon, from *Longmire*), who informs him that it looks like they've been taken by cave dwelling troglodytes who live in "The Valley of Starving Men." Hunt, Chicory, Brooder and O'Dwyer form the posse that will go to the rescue.

"Pain is how your body talks to you. You'd do well to listen to it," Hunt tells O'Dwyer, who is recovering from a broken leg. But in the best western tradition, he will not consider staying home and let someone else rescue his wife. Pain in all its forms is a palpable character in *Bone Tomahawk*. It defines the characters as surely as a fingerprint. Physical pain, personal loss, weariness, ageing, even the pain of bad jokes are all present. It's unavoidable; it can't be ignored. A case could be made that westerns are always about pain and suffering; the maiming of Jimmy Stewart in *The Man from Laramie* (1955) comes to mind as a powerful example. As much as pain, responsibility is also a function of the western. Hunt goes because he's the law, O'Dwyer because of his wife, Chicory reminds Hunt that he's the back-up deputy and his age shouldn't be a factor and Brooder, well he has a history with these people and he has actual experience fighting Indians. These are the kinds of characters who used to populate western movies. The movie heroes we grew up with felt the pull of community, responsibility and loyalty.

The journey consumes the greater portion of the movie and that has earned some negative criticism. Director S. Craig Zahler clearly likes classical westerns and knows that good ones are less about wall to wall action and more about delineating character. Good stories of any kind require something from the audience besides presence in the seat. Too many modern

---

[53] *The Cabin in the Woods* (2012)

[54] "Nite Owl" in *Watchmen* (2009)

[55] *True Detective* (2014, HBO Series, created by Nic Pizzolatto).

filmmakers have convinced audiences that action must occur every six minutes; in addition, dialogue doesn't translate easily for the foreign markets, which is the primary reason for big splashy special effects loaded spectacles. It's amazing that a movie like *Bone Tomahawk* can even be made today. The degree of talent and the commitment to the project speaks volumes considering this was the smallest payday any of them had had in years.

The ending is the most talked about piece of the story, the confrontation with the sub-human cannibal troglodytes. There's nothing new about the melding of horror with westerns; novels, comic books and a few movies have used the elements with varying degrees of success. The final 30-40 minutes of *Bone Tomahawk* are truly horrific, but the troglodytes are not supernatural and for me it's the least interesting part. I got the feeling while I was watching that a small band of Comanches could have wiped out the whole bunch. That being said, it is exciting and suspenseful as well as nauseating.

I've read quite a few reviews of *Bone Tomahawk* since its release, but almost none of them have addressed it from an historical perspective. Since it is a work of fiction it's not bound by historical accuracy; the average viewer of westerns have always been tolerant of inaccuracies in the interest of a good story. For myself, I mostly ask that the characters not be encountering Apaches on the Northern Plains or shooting a Colt

Peacemaker twenty-seven times without re-loading. My family would most likely disagree, as I'm always pointing out historical gaffes, but I mostly view movies in the aggregate. S. Craig Zahler has taken pains to get a lot of it right. The costuming, the sets, the saddles, the guns (thanks to the go to guy for western authenticity, Peter Sherayko[56]) and the speech are appropriate to the times. Zahler loves words. I've read his first western novel, *A Congregation of Jackals,* which has a ponderous preponderance of pointed prose. He falls in love with certain words and phrases and uses them endlessly. In his novel nobody looks at anyone else; they gaze. Legs and arms are often appendages; people don't read, they peruse. Much of his writing takes patience. An example of this in *Tomahawk* is the repeated use of "The German" for the elegant telescope owned by Brooder. The language in the movie has a nineteenth century formality, an easy formality that sounds right and is excellently delivered by the cast.

There's always a temptation to reveal too much about the story, that's what Wikipedia is for. Still, I want to talk about several aspects of the movie that particularly impressed me. The dialogue is especially important and even though it sounds somewhat archaic to the modern ear it is an excellent approximation of the mannered speech of the late 19th century. It is by turns, revealing, humorous, pointed and poignant. A few examples:

O'Dwyer: "John... Make any flirtatious remarks in my wife's presence, there will be a reckoning."

---

[56] Western scholar and "Texas Jack Vermillion in *Tombstone* (1993)

Chicory: "It is the official opinion of the back-up deputy…"

Brooder: "If you want to question my morals…do it later."

Hunt: "We'll make sure all of this has meaning."

"Say goodbye to my wife. I'll say hello to yours."

The dialogue never feels forced; we believe these men spoke this way naturally. It takes effort on the part of the writer to produce dialogue of this caliber, even more is required to make it appear effortless. Another element that has become rare in movies is religion and/or its practice in a positive way. Too often, when religious people are portrayed at all, they're seen as fanatics or worse. Classical westerns respected the notion of faith; so too does Zahler in O'Dwyer's Catholicism. There are several scenes where O'Dwyer crosses himself and prays for blessings on their enterprise. O'Dwyer's faith sustains him and allows him to endure gut wrenching pain and the other travails of the journey. The concept of God was important to these folks, however we may feel about it today. There's a quirky appropriateness about the names of people and places in this movie: the sheriff as nominal head of the search party is named Hunt; the gunman with the shared past with the cowboy's wife is Brooder; the back-up deputy's name is Chicory, a hardy plant often used as a substitute, or backup, for coffee and is widely used medicinally; O'Dwyer, the Gaelic word for "black," a reference to the cowboy's mood. The name, Purvis, is almost self-explanatory.

I could go on about the remarkable performances of Kurt Russell (how did he get to be a senior citizen so soon!), Patrick Wilson (best performance with a broken leg), Matthew Fox (not "*Lost*" here), and Richard Jenkins (the back-up deputy everyone should have). They're all men to "ride the river with." And if you don't get that reference you need to watch some more westerns. No, you don't need me for that. A lot has been said about the length of the movie (132 minutes), I think I would edit certain scenes in the cave—you'll know what I mean—other than that I think the running time is fine. Horror elements aside, *Bone Tomahawk* is a fine western on its own and rewards repeated viewings. It is readily available on DVD and Blu-Ray. Make sure you watch the deleted scenes as well.

A final thought: Westerns have been declared dead so many times it's a cliché. They can't be killed, they're the heart's blood of movies. It's been estimated that 90% of all movies ever made are westerns. Whether set in the past, the present or even in the future, westerns survive. Ask an actor if he'd like to do a western and his eyes light up. Who doesn't want to do one? Who doesn't want to watch one? Search the internet for a few minutes and you'll find pages, blogs, essays and endless lists of favorite westerns. No genre is more durable, entertaining and just plain fun to watch. The late Glendon Swarthout put it this way: "For this is the marrowbone of every American adventure story; some men with guns, going somewhere, to do something dangerous." John Wayne weighed in with: "No one should come to the movies unless he believes in heroes." I think Loren D. Estleman put it best when he

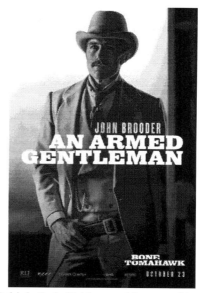

said: "If you don't like westerns, you don't like movies." I think Craig Zahler would agree with these sentiments.

Happy Trails.

BORSALINO (1970)

My introduction to French cinema, long before my "International History of Film" class inflicted *Breathless* (*À bout de souffle* (1960)) upon us, was a little gangster movie I happened to catch on late night TV starring a smooth-skinned clothes mannequin alongside a much more interesting fellow with Bogart's face. The mannequin, in his sharp suit and narrow eyes peering out from beneath a fedora, was the world-famous sex symbol Alain Delon. I didn't know that at the time. Besides, I was more fascinated by the guy with character, whose lumpy visage betrayed an effortless charm and sense of humor. That man, I would later learn, was launched to stardom by Godard's aforementioned slog. *His* name was Jean-Paul Belmondo, and soon after the credits rolled on *Borsalino* (1970), he was one of my new heroes.

Set in 1930 Marseilles, *Borsalino* opens with low-level gangster Roch Siffredi (Delon) leaving prison after a stint for robbery. At the top of his post-prison agenda is to seek out his former girlfriend, Lola (Catherine Rouvel[57]). But first, Roch stops by the dancehall run by the former colleague who put the finger on him, casually setting the bar and curtains on fire.

Now, during Roch's incarceration, Lola took up with the not-in-prison criminal François Capella (Belmondo), and Roch finds them together in Capella's pool hall. After the two men order Lola around for a while—Roch demands she get her coat and leave while François tells her to sit back down—the two men realize their impasse and settle the matter with some knock-down fisticuffs. By the end of this constrained Gallic donnybrook[58], both men are

---

[57] *The Marseille Contract* (1974, dir. Robert Parrish)

[58] "Shooting begins in mid-September 1969. One of the first scenes is Siffredi-Capella meeting which ended in a fight. [Director] Jacques Deray must work with the stunt Yvan Chiffre, which was imposed by Alain Delon (the two men are friends since the unfinished *Marco Polo* in 1962). He does not appreciate at all the right pass and informed Chiffre, from their first meeting, insisting that he is the only master on board. At the preparatory meeting of the scene, the director says that he wants a fight in the style of *The Quiet Man* by John Ford. [Chiffre responds] 'Immediately, I would point out that this is not possible: the morphology of the two players is not the

battered and exhausted. They manage to introduce each other and shake hands mere seconds before they collapse to the floor.

Through their mutual love for and abuse of Lola, Capella and Siffredi decide to join forces, figuring they can do more damage together. After unsuccessfully fixing horseraces and boxing matches, they are contacted by Rinaldi (Michel Bouquet[59]), a lawyer for Marseilles' greatest crime bosses, Marello (Arnoldo Foà[60]) and Poli (André Bollet[61]). Longing for a change in regime, Rinaldi convinces the pair to take on the big bosses and take over their operations. Starting by sabotaging Marello's control of the fish market business by surreptitiously dropping rotting fish into Marello-owned baskets and inciting a riot among the customers. Quickly, Poli recognizes the chaos as the work of the new boys and puts out a contract on them. They respond by murdering him first.

Finally, things are going the duo's way and they begin their climb towards the top of the criminal food chain when Rinaldi is killed by a button man known as The Dancer. After a brief war, Roch and François now oversee all criminal activity in Marseilles. With danger looming around every corner, François decides that he wants out. Then the movie has only a few more minutes to go, and if you've seen a gangster movie of any country, you can guess what will happen by the end.

In 1970, *Borsalino* was one of the most expensive French movies ever produced, with the bulk of the financing coming from Paramount Pictures, who were eager to capitalize on Delon's rising status as an international star, thanks to head-turning roles in *Purple Noon* (1960), *The Leopard* (1963, starring Burt Lancaster), Jean-Paul Melville's *Le Samourai* (1967), and the critically well-received, but box office failure, *Once a Thief* (1965), in which he co-starred with Ann-Margaret and Jack Palance. One of the top draws in French cinema, Delon's only major competition was unconventionally-handsome Belmondo, the darling of the French New Wave, thanks to his star-making turn in the aforementioned Godard worldwide success, *Breathless*.

Though the pair had worked twice before in *Be beautiful and shut up* (1958, dir. Marc Allégret) and René Clément's 1966 *Is Paris Burning?*, the two superstars had never been paired together in equal roles. For several years, Delon sought a project in which he and Belmondo could co-star, and finally found the perfect property in the form of the book, *Bandits in Marseille* by Eugene Saccomano. The actor was particularly fascinated by a chapter on a notorious crime pair Paul Carbone and Francois Spirito, who ruled the prostitution and opium markets in 1930s Marseilles, rising from simple pimps and racketeers to Nazi collaborators. Belmondo, surprisingly the more image-conscious of the two, at first turned down the role of Capella. But Delon was undeterred.

"We wanted to make a gangster film," said writer Jean-Paul Carrière, "but to a certain French tradition, that of Jacques Becker. That is to say, a certain intimacy and a sense of humor in a violent history. The first problem was to find the tone and the charm of the film. The second scenario was to issue a two-hour movie with no plot and no drama built node. We wanted to do a column, we wanted to make a river that has at the limit, no beginning, no end, and which carries the secondary characters, stories that intersect, intersecting."[1]

Originally titled *Carbone and Spirito*, the production was announced to the public in March of 1969, days after Belmondo received the finished script and accepted, on the condition that his name appear first in the opening credits and that the pair have an equal amount of close-ups and dialogue. Almost immediately, Delon's production company received threats in the

---

same in *The Quiet Man*, there is. [Victor McLaglen] and John Wayne, which are both 195m. Alain Delon and Jean-Paul Belmondo has a rather elongated morphology, which implies a totally different fight style. (...) In the presentation of my arguments, Jacques Deray was angry red.'" Lombard, Philip. 2009. "Borsalino (1970)". The Devil Dead.com. September 21. Translated by Google Translate (with further editing by *Movie Outlaw*). http://www.devildead.com/histoiresdetournages/index.php.

[59] *The Bride Wore Black* (d. François Truffaut, 1968).

[60] "Inspector A", *The Trial* (d. Orson Welles, 1962)

[61] *The Return of the Tall Blond Man* (*Le retour du grand blond*, dir. Yves Robert, 1974)

press from Carbone's surviving brother, Paul.

Because the script originally incorporated elements of the pair's collaboration during the Occupation of France, [Director] Jacques Deray received threatening phone calls, and even the town of Marseilles felt the need to distance themselves from the project. Delon, who never hid his ties to the French underworld[62], flew to Corsica to meet with the Carbones to work out a compromise. "'Upon his return,' remembers Jacques Deray, 'everything starts on new foundations that compromise only the spirit of the film's working title. *Carbone and Spirito* will be amended [as well as] the name of the characters. The story ends in 1939—some critics will blame us. *The Heroes of Marseille, 1930*, new title, are now called Roch Siffredi, name borrowed from our well-known manager featured in Marseille, and François Capella."[2] Delon employed four writers, Jean-Paul Carrière, Jean Cau, Jacques Deray, and Claude Sautete, to fictionalize the exploits of Carbone and Spirito and remove the traitorous Nazi bullshit, and craft the story into, basically, a buddy-crook adventure.

Never satisfied with the title, Delon fancied something that could be universal and evocative, like *Casablanca* or *Vera Cruz*. Ultimately, he settled on the world-famous hat makers, Borsalino, who manufactured the omnipresent headgear synonymous with gangsters, the fedora. The Borsalino Hat Company also contributed to the film's financing.

"'Borsalino' stands for hat. Not just any hat, the most fashionable and best quality hat. Ever since 1857, when two brothers named Giuseppe and Lazzaro first created this iconic Italian hat in Via Schiavina in Alessandria, the Borsalino has fascinated stylish men and women. [...] With its elegant shape, quality materials and refined versatility, the Borsalino has been successful not only in international markets, but also on the big screen. [...] Stars and celebrities such as Humphrey Bogart, Gary Cooper, Antony Quinn and Alain Delon, as well as Robert De Niro, Al Pacino, Robert Redford, Warren Beatty, Federico Fellini, Paul Newman, Alberto Sordi, Vittorio Gassman and even Johnny Depp, Leonardo Di Caprio, Denzel Washington, Justin Timberlake, Kate Moss, Nicole Kidman, Naomi Campbell, and John Malkovich have all chosen to be immortalized wearing Borsalino hats. [...] In the book *Cinema wears a hat. Borsalino and other Stories* by Gianni Canova (2011), Roberto Gallo, the president of the Borsalino Foundation, says "I think the hat is full of contents, primarily the ability to change the human being, not only outside. A hat changes a person, it makes one a character or nonentity, exalts or depresses, pulls down or gives strength, protects or abandons, reveals or hides. Because it is not a mask or an armor, it changes a person and makes one look different in the front of the mirror and in front of others, it

---

[62] "Delon, who in a varied career has also promoted boxing matches and peddled airplanes, ran away from home at least once and was expelled from several schools before enlisting in the French navy at the age of 17 and serving in the last stages of France's war in Indochina. On his return he got to know some highly dubious French gangland characters, many of whom have since met untimely and violent deaths: men with nicknames like Z, Bimbo, Petit René, Tany, Le Boxeur and Le Coréen.

"The cinema probably prevented him from going bad, but he loves to cultivate his relations with France's finest gangsters," [Bertrand Violet, author of the unauthorized biography *Les Mystères Delon*] concludes. "That is his way of proving he was a man of character. If there was ever a prison for him, it was one he built himself." The actor himself was rather more succinct in a magazine interview yesterday. "All my life, I've played at being Alain Delon," he said. "For the rest, I couldn't give a damn." Henley, John. 2000. "Nervous publisher sneaks biography of Delon into shops." The Guardian. September 30. www.theguardian.com/world/2000/sep/30/filmnews.books

arouses emotions and makes you think. Just like the movies."[3]

Deray and Delon both insisted on absolute realism, with Deray saying, "'Marseille is the third character in the film.' He immersed himself in newspapers and archives of the time and gets even with Jacques-Henri Martigue, which provides him with his photos taken in the thirties. 'At that time, there was still no car museum, and I was able to recover a lot of the time cars. I also completely transformed several streets of Marseille! We had removed nails, antennas, traffic lights ... I brought the old steam trains in stations ...' The decorator, François Lamo, then built a model 50-meter high bridge of the ferry, which crossed the port of Marseille in 1944."[4]

By most accounts, filming went smoothly, with little friction between the cast. A notorious prankster, Belmondo spent most of his time between scenes trying to get the cast and crew to crack up. At one point during filming, Delon and Belmondo bet a policeman a thousand francs to jump fully clothed into a fountain. The cop won the bet. "'With John-Paul, we were in perpetual laughter,' recalls Catherine Rouvel. 'Someone had to come and ask us to stop filming because we an inconvenience!' What about the two stars, which the press is watching, [was there] any disagreement? 'There was no real conflict,' says Jacques Deray. 'We can not say that there was an overflowing friendship between them, but they did their job. It was in front of them a director who liked the players [enough] to give equal importance to

Top: Jean-Paul Belmondo as Capella. Bottom: Alain Delon as Roch.
So as to give neither actor an advantage, both of these photos are the same exact size.
Copyright Adel Productions / Marianne Productions / Mars Film. All Rights Reserved.

both and not play with respect to the other.' The makeup artist Charly Koubesserian, [...] adds: 'Left to break legends, I testify that everything went well during this shoot. There was of course a competition between the two stars, a friendly competition and clashes [here and there]—because there were few—were only the usual clashes between two stars."

On screen the pair have decent chemistry together, with Belmondo's humor overshadowing Delon's brooding, but the film suffers slightly from an uneven tone, lurching from comedy to violence without warning. Many of the action sequences are poorly staged as well, particularly the opening fight scene—while the actors are selling every punch, Deray's camera always seems to be in the wrong place, betraying the choreography by showing punches missing by a mile. The set design and costuming are often the real stars of a scene, with the actors simply moving through the spaces rather than living in them.

"The interiors, whether seedy or sumptuous (especially a gambling casino in the Chinese style) display the paraphernalia of their period as meticulously—and in their very completeness, somehow as inauthentically—as any museum reconstruction. The exteriors are if anything even more complete—to the degree that some rather elaborate scenes seem to be held beyond all dramatic need so you can see that the next car around the corner, the next walker on the block, will be, down to the last particular, genuinely of the period," wrote Roger Greenspun in his NY Times review. "Jacques Deray's direction seems not so much to lead, as to accede to the demands of the scene designer and the costumer. There are, indeed, six costume credits. But where he has his way, he is equally indulgent—photographing the sunlight through what looks like layers of scrim, introducing gratuitous motor trips simply as you may admire the cars, staging fist fights and beatings that manage to be both dull and unusually brutal at the same time."[5]

The detractions did little to sway filmgoers, however, as it broke box office records throughout Europe, though it fared poorly in the U.S., much to Delon's and Paramount's disappointment.

To add insult to injury, due to contractual obligations with Paramount, the film's opening credits read "An Alain Delon Production", coming before Belmondo's title card. As a result,

Belmondo sued Delon and the company for breach of contract. "We are still what you in America call 'pals' or 'buddies'," said Delon at the time. "But we are not friends. There is a difference. He was my guest in the film but still he complained. I like him as an actor but as a person, he's a bit different. I think his reaction was a stupid reaction... almost like a female reaction. But I don't want to talk about him anymore." Despite the suit and more than a decade of avoiding each other, Delon and Belmondo did work again, more amicably, in the 1998 feature *Une chance sur deux* (directed by Patrice Leconte, co-starring Vanessa Paradis[6]).

Helping to fuel the *Borsalino*'s European success was the on-going, and so-called, "Markovic Affair", when Delon's ex-bodyguard, Stevan Markovic, was found dead in a garbage dump outside of Paris in 1968. The ensuing investigation uncovered a potential blackmail scandal against then-French president Georges Pompidou,

Pompidou's wife, Delon's longtime and shady friend, François Marcantoni, and Delon himself.

"The investigation uncovered a tangled tale of drug-dealing, blackmail and compromising pornographic photos that implicated numerous celebrities and politicians, sparking rumours that ultimately touched the wife of the future president, Georges Pompidou. Delon, who knew Pompidou well and was a very close friend of the Corsican gangster who was initially charged with the murder, François Marcantoni, was questioned intensively by the police, but the crime was never solved."[7]

While the controversy continued to rage into the early '70s, European filmgoers flocked to see a film starring a potential real-life gangster. While Delon was never charged with any wrongdoing, his mystique as a suave and dangerous man of few words prevailed in the public eye. To capitalize on *Borsalino*'s success, Delon produced and starred in the 1974 sequel, *Borsalino & Co.*, also directed by Deray. Much more violent and absent much of the cheeky humor of

the original, due in part to the lack of Belmondo, *Borsalino & Co.*'s through-line concerns Roch's revenge on the people who murdered Capella, resulting in way more bloodshed than the first.

As is the case with many of our discussed films, neither film is easy to find. *Borsalino & Co.*, the only one of the two offering English subtitles, can be had for a small fortune through Amazon. *Borsalino's* import DVD is similarly pricey, but at least it comes dubbed into Italian and Castilian, with Spanish subtitles for those illiterate in a multitude of languages. Since Delon is still alive[8], a letter-writing campaign is encouraged. Nothing is more fun than harassing an old French guy over movies he'd made decades ago and over which he likely has little control. But wouldn't it just be neat to do so?

NOTES

[1] Lombard, Philip. 2009. "Borsalino (1970)". The Devil Dead.com. September 21. Translated by Google Translate (with further editing by *Movie Outlaw*). http://www.devildead.com/histoiresdetournages/index.php.

[2] Ibid

[3] Belcastro, Angela. 2012. "Borsalino | Vintage Italian Hat". Ganzomag.com. Jul 22. http://www.ganzomag.com/borsalino-hat-vintage.html

[4] Lombard, The Devil Dead.com. 2009.

[5] Greenspun, Roger. 1970. "Review". New York Times. August 14. www.nytimes.com/movie/review?res=9E00E2D61638E336A05757C1A96E9C946190D6CF

[6] French singer, actress, and no-longer-with-Johnny Depp.

[7] Henley, John. 2000. "Nervous publisher sneaks biography of Delon into shops." The Guardian. September 30. http://www.theguardian.com/world/2000/sep/30/filmnews.books

[8] As of May 30, 2016.

LE BOSSU (1997)

(a.k.a. ON GUARD)

Lagardère (Daniel Auteuil[63]), a lowly sword-for-hire, develops an unlikely friendship with Phillippe the Duc de Nevers (Vincent Pérez[64]), who has to his name oodles of money, a devious and dastardly cousin, Comte du Gonzague (Fabrice Luchini[65]), a brand new baby courtesy of duchess Blanche du Caylus (Claire Nebout[66]), and a deadly and very specific fencing move called "la botte de Nevers" (which involves the fight-ending technique of thrusting one's sword between the eyes of an assailant). If Phillippe marries Blanche, then their baby will become the heir to all that is Nevers' and Gonzague will find himself with only a generous pension. Before Phillippe and Blanche can consummate their marriage, Gonzague and his deadly assassins, the red-wearing Peyrolles, sneak into the castle and murder the entire wedding party. Phillippe is stabbed in the back by a masked Gonzague but Lagardère arrives just in time to "brand" the assassin—stabbing him through the hand and vowing vengeance: *"Si tu ne viens pas à Lagardère, Lagardère ira à toi!"* ("If you don't come to Lagardère, Lagardère will come to you!")

Fleeing with the infant, Lagardère fakes their death with the help of a traveling troupe of Italian actors and remains with them for the next sixteen years. Meanwhile, the baby, Aurore, has grown into a beautiful young woman (Marie Gillain[67]) who develops unusual feelings towards the man she believes to be her father. He has taught her all the skills she needs to survive: juggling, laundry, and the "Nevers Attack". Unable to avoid Paris forever, the troupe

---

[63] Best-known as "Ugolin" in *Jean de Florette* and *Manon des Sources* (dir. Claude Berri, 1987).

[64] "Christien" in *Cyrano de Bergerac* (directed by Jean-Paul Rappeneau, 1990), but also, sadly, *The Crow: City of Angels* (1996, Dir. Tim Pope).

[65] "Julius Caesar" in *Asterix and Obelix: God Save Britannia* (aka *Astérix & Obélix: Au service de Sa Majesté*; directed by Laurent Tirard, 2012)

[66] "Pierre Beaumarch" in *Beaumarchais* (French: *Beaumarchais l'insolent*, directed by Édouard Molinaro, 1996)

[67] Perhaps best-known as "Anne" in *Hell* (*L'enfer*, directed by Danis Tanović, 2005) notable for being the last script written by Krzysztof Kieślowski (with Krzysztof Piesiewicz), part of a proposed trilogy, prior to his death in 1996.

performs in the heart of the city. When Aurore uses the highly recognizable Nevers Attack to fend off a would-be rapist, Gonzague realizes that Lagardère is still alive and the jig, as the French do not say, is up.

Lagardère is driven into hiding once again—this time disguised as a hunchback accountant to Gonzague himself! Gonzague is hoping to amass another small fortune in American Louisiana, selling land along the Mississippi. Lagardère conspires to bring about a happy ending for everyone (save, of course, Gonzague).

While no more or less complicated than Dumas' *The Three Musketeers*[68] or Victor Hugo's *Notre-Dame de Paris* (a.k.a. *The Hunchback of Notre Dame*[69]), *On Guard* was adapted from the 1858 novel, *Le Bossu* by Paul Féval, père. Published fourteen years after Dumas' *The Three Musketeers*, *Le Bossu* helped firmly establish the swordplay action subgenre ("roman de cape et d'épée"). In fact, so popular was the novel that Lagardère's vow, '*Si tu ne viens pas à Lagardère, Lagardère ira à toi!*' became a proverb in French language. An immensely popular author at the time Féval received as much acclaim for his work as Dumas, but grew increasingly dissatisfied with his adventure story output and made multiple attempts at social satire and religious tracts. Audiences weren't interested. They wanted his sword-and-cape adventures. They wanted his detective novels—in fact, his 1862 novel, *Jean Diable*, is considered to be the first "modern" crime novel, involving a Scotland Yard inspector on the trail of a seemingly unstoppable criminal who goes by the name "John Devil". So influential was *Jean Diable* that Féval founded a literary magazine under the same title in the same year. In 1862, Féval founded the magazine Jean Diable, named after his eponymous novel. One of the magazine's editors was Émile Gaboriau, whose own police detective character, Monsieur Lecoq, famously inspired Sir Arthur Conan Doyle's own Sherlock Holmes. How's that for "Six Degrees of Nineteenth Century Literature"?

Arguably, *Le Bossu* was one of Féval's most successful novels and was adapted to film numerous times over the years, most notably the 1959 version directed by André Hunebelle, starring Jean Marais and the popular comedian André Bourvil (who was best-known under his last name mononym), as Lagardère's valet, Passepoil[70]. The film was a blockbuster and led to Hunebelle reteaming his leads in the rousing *Captain Blood (1960)*.

"Si tu ne viens pas à Lagardère, Lagardère ira à toi!" Lagardère (Daniel Auteuil) and the "Nevers Attack". Photo courtesy Philippe de Broca.

---

[68] Filmed in 1997, directed by and starring Kiefer Sutherland who starred in *Truth or Consequences, N.M.* with Kevin…Pollak. (Anyone can play *Six Degrees of Kevin Bacon*).

[69] Adapted in 1996 by Disney (directed by Stephen Herek) which starred Demi Moore who co-starred in *A Few Good Men* (Rob Reiner) with… Kevin Pollak .

[70] A character given a bit of a short shrift in the '97 film, played by Didier Pain.

Philippe de Broca directs Daniel Auteuil and Marie Gillain (as Aurore de Nevers). Photo courtesy Philippe de Broca.

Le Bossu was directed by Philippe de Broca[1], a man who cut his proverbial teeth as an assistant to some of the greatest voices of the *nouvelle vague*, working with Claude Chabrol on *Le Beau Serge*, and François Truffaut on *The 400 Blows* (*Les 400 Coups*). Chabrol even produced de Broca's first film, the 1960 comedy *Les jeux de l'amour* (*The Love Game*). De Broca's influence over modern French cinema can't be understated. "In the entry on Philippe de Broca in The New Biographical Dictionary of Film, the critic David Thomson writes that 'when the cinema of charm is assessed, de Broca must always be remembered'," wrote A.O. Scott in the *New York Times*, who wasn't overly-enthralled with the director's new adaptation. "Though [*On Guard*] breaks no ground—hardly surprising, given that its source, an 1857 novel by Paul Féval called *Le Bossu* (*The Hunchback*), has been adapted for the screen five times before—Mr. de Broca's film is full of durable cinematic pleasures: a little sex, a lot of sword fighting and a plot that combines heady passion with complicated political intrigue."[2]

Given a plain title by American suits who were well aware that audiences couldn't care less that the phrase is actually *en garde*, which means "engage", *On Guard* is a rousing, exciting and very clever movie[71]. The film belongs entirely to Auteuil who can be both brave, foolish, clever, sad, and comical all at the same time. For swashbuckling fans, here's your new favorite movie, for hardly ten minutes goes by without a duel, and by the end you'll be able to perform the "Nevers Attack" on your own, stabbing foreheads to your heart's delight!

For modern reviewers, the idea of a new and sincere swashbuckling film, for which the American comparisons seems to stop at the Errol Flynn era, strikes as somewhat ridiculous. "You don't make a movie like *On Guard* without real love for your material and without real conviction in it. The tendency now is to assume that a glaze of irony is needed before audiences will buy something this old-fashioned. But parody was always a part of swashbucklers, and de Broca's sure grip on the tone of this tale allows us to believe in it emotionally even as we are amused by the far-fetched adventure-story conventions," wrote Charles Taylor for *Salon*. Yet, he continues, "It's a completely satisfying picture (and I can't remember the last time I was in a screening room where the assembled critics broke into applause when a movie ended). What I'm saying is that de Broca honors our collective moviegoing past in a way that Hollywood appears to have forgotten how to do. *On Guard* is a piece of ornate costume jewelry proffered with love. And like any gift given with love, it may assume more of a place in your affections than the most precious gem."[3]

For modern audiences, the subplot of Lagardère and Aurore falling in love might make one a bit uncomfortable, seeing as how, while he isn't her biological father, he did play the part for her entire life. The semi-incestual considerations aren't really addressed as Lagardère is more concerned with the fact that by restoring Aurore to her noble position, he'll remain as "a nobody", with no title, no status and no money. Aurore, as a naïve teenager, sees only hopeless

---

[71] *The Crow: City of Angels* (1996, Tim Pope), which co-starred Thomas Jane, who was in *The Punisher* (Jonathan Hensleigh) with John Travolta, who was in *Pulp Fiction* with Bruce Willis *and* Rosanna Arquette, both of whom are in *The Whole Ten Yards* (2000, Jonathan Lynn) with…Kevin Pollak.

romance in poverty with this dashing man she's known her whole life.

"The problem may be that swashbuckling adventure stories tend to be considered juvenile entertainment. Though the film is not especially graphic—it is far less bloody than most PG-13 action blockbusters—it addresses sexuality and violence with a brisk candor that may ruffle American sensibilities," wrote Scott. "'Do you dabble in sodomy?' the duke asks Lagardère as they climb into bed together one chilly night—a question nobody would have asked Errol Flynn or Douglas Fairbanks, at least not onscreen. Later, Nevers's daughter, Aurore, reared by Lagardère with a traveling Italian theater troupe, grows up into the meltingly beautiful (and briefly naked) Marie Gillain, and promptly falls in love with the man she had always thought of as her father. And he with her. Converting "a father's love into a lover's love" presents no problems that a bit of clever counter-conspiracy can't clear up."[4] If you can get past the above and just chalk it up to "it's the times they lived in", you'll have no trouble with *On Guard* as it never fails to be charming and thrilling and touching.

In France, *Le Bossu* was well-received—in no small part due to Auteuil's status as one of the most popular actors in that country—and was nominated for multiple awards, a BAFTA Nomination for Best Film, and eight César Award Nominations for Best Film, Best Actor, Best Actress, Best Supporting Actor, Best Cinematography, Best Editing, Best Music, and Best Production Design in 1998, winning for Best Costume Design. Naturally, the movie was given only a limited release in the U.S., Koch-Lorber assuming once again that "subtitles equal death" at the box office. It is available commercially on DVD with a handsome transfer and gorgeous audio—the score is almost a character in and of itself, accompanying Lagardère through all his adventures.

The Lady and the Hunchback. Photo courtesy Philippe de Broca.

NOTES

[1] http://www.philippedebroca.com/

[2] Scott, A.O. 2002. "A Swashbuckler Gets Even." NY Times. October 18.
http://www.nytimes.com/2002/10/18/movies/18GUAR.html

[3] Taylor, Charles. 2002. "On Guard: This far-fetched and far-flung adventure romp might be old-fashioned, but it's also one of the best swashbucklers in movie history." Salon. October 18.
http://www.salon.com/2002/10/18/on_guard/

[4] Ibid

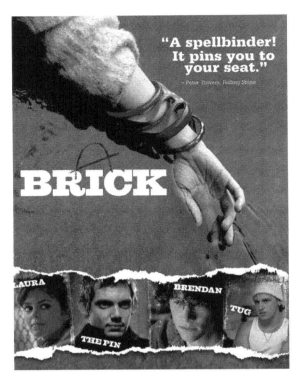

"A spellbinder!
It pins you to
your seat."
– Peter Travers, *Rolling Stone*

BRICK

LAURA · THE PIN · BRENDAN · TUG

BRICK (2005)

Brendan Frye (Joseph Gordon-Levitt) spends his days isolated from his peers, and only partially voluntarily. A year ago, he betrayed a friend to the authorities. He lost his girlfriend, Emily (Emilie de Ravin[72]), to a new and dangerous crowd. Once on top of the world, Brendan is now a loner, angry at existence itself. One day he gets a note from Emily, instructing him to go to a nearby pay phone. She calls, terrified, repentant, in danger. Her tearful call is fractured; Brendan can only make out a handful of words, among them "brick" and "pin". She terminates the call before telling him where she is. Just as she does, a black car drives by, someone inside flicks a distinctive cigarette out of the window. The next morning, he finds Emily lying dead at the mouth of a drainage tunnel. Determined to find her killer, Brendan reconstructs the Emily's final days, following the clues into an underworld of drugs, bad dames, and worse criminals.

The above description is *Noir 101*. It's *Out of the Past* (1947) updated for a new millennia. Except that instead of dark, rain-slick streets, the world of *Brick* is overcast day. Brendan's base of operations, far from a dingy office slashed with venetian blind shadows, is the parking lot behind his high school. The authority at odds with him is the "Vice"—as in "Principal". And far from the hardened gumshoe you'd expect, Brendan hides his face behind long shaggy hair and glasses, he walks with his hands shoved deep into the pockets of his gray windbreaker. Sneakers make no "click clack" noise on the concrete. The criminals he's up against aren't the cigar-chomping hoods cut from Al Capone cloth; they're kids in wife-beater t-shirts, or tall, skinny drop-outs in capes and canes and other youthful affectations. Brendan's femme fatale leading him down this rabbit hole isn't a slinky dame with a troubled past, she's simply Laura, a girl who may be well-to-do, but she's taking the same classes (presumably) as he is.

"When I was in high school, I had a bit of a superiority complex. And you know, read *Catcher in the Rye* when I was fourteen, and got a big kick out of calling everybody phonies. And

---

[72] *Lost*'s "Claire Littleton."

I think Brendan has a lot of that in him," Gordon-Levitt told Peter Canavese. "He thinks—he looks around at the world and sees it as a corrupt, petty, no-good affair. And then when he loses his one love—his one thing in the world that he does connect to—Emily—when he loses her to that, it really, really sends him to the back of the school and to just hunch over and harden up. And then when she turns up dead, my God, it's all he can do to keep from falling apart. The only thing he can do to keep from just breaking down is to set this goal for himself and pursue it ceaselessly. That's what he does—even though it doesn't make any sense, and he's hurting himself and he's hurting other people by doing it, that's all he can do. And I think it speaks a lot—I think it says a lot about that kind of superior attitude. And that's where you end up if you keep that sort of "Oh, I'm smarter than everyone" attitude. You end up alone. And you probably end up hurting yourself—and are more than likely to end up hurting other people too."[1]

"Who was Em' eating lunch with?" Brendan asks his ear-to-the-ground-guy, Brain. This is one of *Brick's* many distinctive post-pubescent noir slang phrases. Just as in the post-war '40s detective stories, it's important in the world of *Brick* to know what the cliques are and who comprises them. Emily's move from the outcast class into the better-off rich kids and their world of drugs and fast cash is as much a change of social status as it is economic. Either way, Brendan is left behind, even after—or especially because—he once attempted to "save" her by informing on his own former friends, placing him in "The Vice's" pocket. These days, because of his actions, Brendan is the school's biggest outcast, moving freely through the groups because he is an island unto himself. When approaching Dode (the always-terrific Noah Segan[73]), a burn-out in leather jacket and acne cover, Brendan warns off the stoner droogs, "I've got all five senses and I slept last night, which puts me six ahead of you!" When goading a popular (if ineloquent) jock into disclosing information, Brendan proves he can throw a punch as well as take one. This comes in handy when pursuing the source of all Emily's problems, Tugger (Noah Fleiss[74]), right-hand-man to the drug lord, "The Pin". Brendan never backs down and always gets back up, even when it becomes increasingly clear that Emily was the instrument of her own demise. Especially when he learns what the word "brick" refers to and why certain parties would be willing to kill to retrieve it.

"[Director Rian] Johnson threads the needle a hundred different ways, but before getting into all the little things he gets right, here's how the concept pays off: The common denominator between crime fiction and high school is a mood of heightened emotion obscured by a thin veneer of cool. There's never a time in a person's life where they feel things more intensely than in high school, nor is there a time when they labor as hard to keep those feelings under wraps," wrote Scott Tobias for The A.V. Club. "By evoking the stylized, rat-a-tat dialogue of vintage Dashiell Hammett detective novels—with words like 'yeggs' (guys), 'heel' (walk away), 'jake' (drugs), 'shamus' (detective), et al.—Johnson finds a new way to suggest teenagers' capacity for couching their real problems in language. He also raises the stakes: Crime fiction deals with matters of life and death, and if that isn't literally true of adolescence, it certainly feels that way to those on the inside. So by introducing a dead body into the equation, Johnson provides an incident that justifies that level of intensity."[2]

Brick was the incredibly impressive film debut of Rian Johnson, a southern California filmmaker who came out of the same "school" as Lucky McKee, whose own landmark film, *May*, put him on the indie darling map. (Johnson was an editor on *May* and even pays homage to the film's main character, played by Angela Bettis[75], in *Brick's elaborate* costume party scene.) Largely inspired by The Coen Brothers' *Miller's Crossing*[76] (with no small amount of debt owed

---

[73] *All About Evil* (dir. Joshua Grannell, 2010)—See *Fervid Filmmaking*.

[74] *Storytelling* (directed by Todd Solondz, 2001)

[75] A member of the Lucky McKee film family, Bettis directed McKee in *Roman* 92009), and returned to being directed by him in *The Woman* (2011).

[76] See Chapter in this very book!

to *Things to Do in Denver When You're Dead* (1995), which also played with the gangster-slang of Damon Runyon to its great effect), Johnson deftly melded the darkness of the detective story with the inherent nihilism of the high school drama, creating a distinctive world for Brendan and his fellows. As in *Miller's Crossing* and the Dashiell Hammett stories that inspired it, there are no authority figures in *Brick* beyond "The Vice" (played by *Shaft's* Richard Roundtree); there are only the loosely-defined "classes"—which is a little ironic considering that there are no classes attended in the film. School is a setting, not an institution; the film doesn't concern itself with the tedium of the eight-hour school day, but the extra-curricular activities orbiting the schedule.

"The world of [Hammett's books struck me as so amazingly vibrant, scary, funny, intriguing, you name it... so I decided I wanted to take a crack at an American detective movie," Johnson told Tim Ryan. "The decision to set it in high school was, initially at least, just to give it a different set of visual cues, so you couldn't just take a glimpse at guys in hats and shadowy alleyways and switch your brain into 'I know what this is' autopilot mode. I wanted people to experience the genre in an unexpected way. After I started working on it, though, it became much more than that for me, and in many ways became about the emotional experience of being a teenager."[3]

"[T]he thing about *Brick* is even though the dialogue and a lot of the camera-work and costumes and everything are kind of over-the-top or beyond reality, the emotions never are. The emotions are all very genuine," said Gordon-Levitt. "And the whole point of doing as much practice as I did to get the words as down as I did was so that when we actually doing the scenes when it actually came time to do them, I didn't have to think about doing the words at all. I could just feel what I needed to be feeling. And Brendan is not feeling good. Pretty much there aren't almost any moments in the movie where he's not either in pain or just barely keeping pain at bay."[4]

"Someone once asked Hammett, who worked as a detective himself, if Sam Spade was based on anyone he knew," said Johnson to The Telegraph's Daisy Garnett. "He said no: Spade was based on what every detective he knew wished he was. That's more the essence of it. Brendan isn't me or a version of me, but I am using the heightened world of detective fiction to communicate very impressionistic memories of high school, the feeling you got looking at the unobtainable girl who ruled the school or the library early in the morning when the geeks are huddled around the desk lamps."[5]

The unique structure of the script is a huge part of *Brick*'s success, but isn't the whole story. There isn't a false performance in the film, but it is anchored by its star, Joseph Gordon-Levitt, a critical darling thanks to his long-running role in *Third Rock from the Sun*, but not yet a bona fide star. When *Brick* hit theaters, the stars had aligned. Gordon-Levitt's turn as a young male prostitute in *Mysterious Skin* (2004) garnered him acclaim and helped push *Brick* into the forefront of critical attention. He's the lynch-pin around which the plot revolves, but he's equally matched by Fleiss, former child-actor Lucas Haas[77], and especially Nora Zehetner as the mysterious Laura. Remarkably, the performances ring true and compliment the heavily-stylized story. At no point are the characters "acting" like adults, or ever feel artificially older than their years. Brendan holds himself as a weary traveler, yet at the same time he's very aware of his outcast status, that those who interact with him want to use him for their own ends or simply desire him to go away. Everyone is navigating post-pubescence and this mystery is the embodiment of the angst and anguish that colors every high schooler's day. For once, the central problem really *is* one of life and death, far removed from the melodrama of *The Breakfast Club* or *Pretty in Pink* (where everything just seems to be apocalyptic turmoil).

Credit also has to be given to San Clemente, CA, where the film is set. Johnson's own alma mater, San Clemente High School, provided the film with its primary location, a sprawling concrete bunker standing solid against a cloudless grey sky. The streets in *Brick* are

---

[77] *Witness* (directed by Peter Weir, 1985)

virtually deserted; in this film, more than three people equal a crowd, as if every person not involved in the mystery have cleared out of the way to avoid being caught up in the coming apocalypse. The emptiness mirrors Brendan's soul. As Johnson says on the DVD commentary: "Teen movies often have an unspoken underlying premise in which high school is seen as less serious than the adult world. But when your head is immersed in that microcosm, it's the most serious time of your life."

An admitted introvert himself, Johnson had difficulty getting *Brick* made during his first few years out of film school. He gives complete credit to his friend and producer, Ram Bergman, for keeping the project afloat, and encouraging everyone involved to "pass the hat" among friends and family to raise the meager $500,000 budget. With the exception of the Pin's paneled rec-room, all the sets were found already standing—a phone booth that plays a key role in the plot was real, "borrowed" by the prop masters and carried from one location to the next. Like the best of the no-budget filmmakers, everything had to be begged for, borrowed, stolen, or stretched to accommodate the limitations of the budget. That the 35mm film got finished at all is an amazing accomplishment.

"'Film school is great for meeting people, but really the only way you learn how to make films are by watching them and making them,' [Johnson] said. 'I got what I know largely from watching and re-watching the usual suspects: Scorsese, Fellini, Kubrick, Kurosawa, Hitchcock, Lynch, Spielberg, and so on,' he said. 'You see something like the editing in *Goodfellas*, the way he pops into those quick tracking shots, and the next time you're making a short with your friends you try a crude version of it. Trial and error.'" Miles David Moore reported for Scene4.com. "During those years, he supported himself however he could, but the period as he described it was far from unpleasant. 'I got lucky and had some really nice day jobs,' [Johnson] said. 'I did some random assistant editing work, worked at a preschool for deaf children for a few years, then produced promos for the Disney Channel.' He had no industry mentors to speak of, but his USC friends formed a mutual support group. 'When my friend Lucky McKee got his film *May* made, we all worked on it,' Johnson said. 'That was a real galvanizing shot in the arm—just seeing that it could happen, it was possible for one of us to jump that seemingly uncrossable gap and make a feature.'"[6]

Well-received at The Sundance Film Festival in 2005, awarded the Sundance Film Festival's Special Jury Prize for Originality of Vision, *Brick* launched Johnson's and Bergman's careers. After a slightly disappointing sophomore effort with *The Brothers Bloom* (starring then it-guy Adrian Brody), Johnson and Bergman made *Looper* with Gordon-Levitt transformed via remarkable prosthetics into a young Bruce Willis, the two actors playing the same character in a time-traveling crime thriller. *Looper* was a box office success and critical darling, leading Johnson directly to leading the production of the upcoming *Star Wars Episode VIII*. (And if that isn't success, who knows what is?)

Though *Brick* was well-received in 2005, not everyone dug the unique mixture. The New York Times usually pedantic Steven Horden, for instance, missed the point entirely when he wrote: "*Brick* is even less dramatically convincing than Alan Parker's 1976 gangster spoof, *Bugsy Malone*, which cast children as hoods and featured the 13-year-old Jodie Foster vamping it up like Rita Hayworth in *Gilda*. (*Brick* has nothing half as spicy.) Even a guilty pleasure like *Cruel Intentions*, which took *Dangerous Liaisons* to high school, landed some uncomfortable emotional punches because it was acted rather than pantomimed. The underachieving cast of *Brick* merely goes through the motions. The women are especially pallid. Isn't a deep whiskey-and-cigarette-ravaged voice a prerequisite for playing a noir siren? Or has the Hilary-Britney-Mary-Kate-and-Ashley chirp stamped out precociously womanly voices like the 19-year-old Lauren Bacall's in *To Have and Have Not*? Maybe *Brick* is a comedy. There is something cute, if not outright ludicrous, in the spectacle of dewy young actors striking the poses of hard-boiled demi-mondaines and desperadoes and failing utterly to make them come alive. The movie seems to have its tongue stuck in its cheek during a final showdown in a suburban basement, during which the impervious mother of a teenage drug lord is upstairs baking cookies. But funny it's not."

(Contrast that with Damon Wise's take on the film for Empire Online: "True, it gets

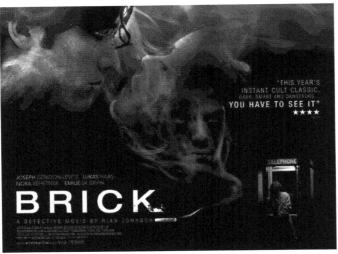

convoluted at times—though it's not quite as murky as Howard Hawks' 1946 adaptation of Chandler's *The Big Sleep*, which even the novelist himself couldn't fathom. [7] Johnson follows his own story with a fast-paced logic that sometimes leaves question marks dangling, but all those points add a little more to ponder and savour once the bigger conundrum is finally cracked. It will certainly split people into those who buy the conceit and those that don't, those who see daffy, sub-*Bugsy Malone* (1976) drivel where others gobble up its *Usual Suspects* goose-chase and debate its *Donnie Darko*-like demands for interpretation. But *Brick* wasn't made for everybody. It's a film that nobody should agree on. Like Brendan himself, we should just be proud to differ.")[8]

While *Brick* remains a cult favorite, it has faded from public consciousness in the ensuing years. Fortunately, it's very easy to find on DVD, usually in bargain bins. While this is sad for Focus Features, it bodes well for anyone on a budget who wishes to check it out. Especially valuable is Johnson's slightly schizophrenic audio commentary, where members of the cast and crew are "invited" to contribute periodically during the film's running time (which gives the track a confused nature, the guests seeming rushed by Johnson's structured audio plan here). Johnson's infallible memory makes the track essential listening for indie filmmakers and is a mini film class in and of itself.

NOTES

[1] Canavese, Peter. 2006. "Joseph Gordon-Levitt—Brick—02/10/06" Groucho Reviews.com. February 10. http://www.grouchoreviews.com/interviews/152

[2] Tobias, Scott. 2009. "Brick." AV Club. May 21. http://www.avclub.com/article/embrickem-28276

[3] Ryan, Tim. 2006. "Interview with *Brick* Director Rian Johnson." Rotten Tomatoes. April 20. https://editorial.rottentomatoes.com/article/interview-with-brick-director-rian-johnson/

[4] Canavese, 2006.

[5] Garnett, Daisy. 2006. "Drugsy Malone." The Telegraph. April. 30. http://www.telegraph.co.uk/culture/3652004/Drugsy-Malone.html

[6] Moore, Miles David. 2007. "The Most Serious Time of Your Life: Interview With Filmmaker Rian Johnson." Scene4.com. January. http://www.scene4.com/archivesqv6/jan-2007/html/milesmoore0107.html

[7] Not 100% true. While adapting *The Big Sleep* in 1946, screenwriters William Faulkner and Leigh Brackett couldn't figure out who killed the character of chauffeur Owen Taylor, or if he'd committed suicide for his part in the central scandal. As reported in *The Raymond Chandler Letters*, Chandler told his friend Jamie Hamilton: "They sent me a wire ... asking me, and dammit I didn't know either." Hiney, T. and MacShane, F. *The Raymond Chandler Papers*, Letter to Jamie Hamilton, 21 March 1949, page 105, Atlantic Monthly Press, 2000.

[8] Wise, Damon. 2006. "Review". Empire Online. April 28. http://www.empireonline.com/movies/brick/review/

BUG (2006)

Agnes White (Ashley Judd[78]) is a middle-aged woman living in fear of the outside world. Having made her home in a rundown Oklahoma motel, she hides from the daylight and the people who move around comfortably within it. Her phone rings almost constantly; she's convinced that it's her ex-con ex-husband looking for her, but there's never anyone on the other end of the line. At night, she waitresses at a lesbian bar and then parties until dawn with her best friend, R.C. (Lynn Collins[79]).

One night, R.C. notices a tall, attractive man standing by the bar's juke box, having wandered in but minding his own business. She thinks he might be just the thing to get Agnes "back on the horse", so to speak, and invites him back to Agnes' room to party. When Peter (Michael Shannon[80]) arrives at her motel, he tries to comfort them both: "I'm not an ax murderer," he tells them. An emergency on the part of R.C.'s girlfriend leaves Agnes and Peter alone. He confides that he's a former soldier and is "in between" permanent residences. She offers to let him spend the night on the couch. He chooses the floor.

The next morning, Agnes awakes to the smell of coffee on the stove and the sound of the shower running. She smiles to herself and thanks him out loud. But from the bathroom emerges Goss (Harry Connick Jr.[81]), her ex-husband, fresh from prison and looking for a place to stay, hoping they can pick up where they left off. She orders him out. He knocks her down and takes money from her purse. That's when Peter returns, witnessing the aftermath, but

---

[78] The non-singing Judd sister.

[79] "Kayla Silverfox" from *X-Men Origins: Wolverine* (directed by Gavin Hood, 2009)

[80] Sure, he's General Zod in the controversial *Man of Steel* (directed by Zack Snyder, 2013), but especially wonderful in *Midnight Special* (directed by Jeff Nichols, 2016).

[81] Non-Judd singer.

doesn't confront the angry, possessive Goss as he storms out. Stunned, humiliated, Agnes puts her walls back up, but slowly Peter manages to break through them. She tells him that she and Goss once had a son together. In a grocery store, she took her eyes off the boy for just a minute and he just disappeared. The police were no help and she's half-convinced that Goss took their son out of spite, something the con has always denied.

Neither Agnes nor Peter had ever confessed their secrets to anyone else. Desperate for human contact, the pair fall into bed.

Recovering from their emotional and physical intimacy, they lay in bed when something bites Peter. He insists it's a tiny aphid, but Agnes can't see it. Within minutes, he's convinced her that the room is crawling with them. "Infested." He's alarmed, but isn't surprised—he wasn't discharged from the military, he tells her, he escaped from a program of medical testing and his former captors are out there looking for him. The Army, he tells her, put bugs in his blood. There's an egg sac embedded beneath one of his teeth—he removes the offending tooth with a pair of pliers.

Agnes replaces her own terrors with Peter's. They hang dozens of fly strips from the ceiling. One day while she's out getting supplies with R.C., Peter uncovers a toy microscope amidst her boy's toys, things she'd kept for years. He uses the toy to study his blood, seeing millions of creatures crawling in the plasma. Fearing for her friend, R.C. tries to drag Agnes away from Peter, but Agnes clings to her new lover and cuts R.C. from her life. Meanwhile, the phone continues to ring and helicopters circle the motel, their rotors shaking the room, causing the lights to flicker, the walls to tremble. To keep out governmental spying signals, they cover the walls with plastic sheeting and tin foil and they black out the windows. The only illumination inside is purple, the unnatural shade produced by the dozen bug zappers hung from the ceiling.

Their isolation is interrupted by the arrival of Goss and Dr. Sweet (Brian F. O'Byrne[82]), a man claiming to be a military psychiatrist who wants to take Peter back with him, return him to his treatment. Peter, Sweet tells her, is dangerously delusional, believing himself to be the subject of grotesque experiments. Agnes doesn't believe him. Peter suddenly emerges from hiding and brutally—*brutally*—murders Dr. Sweet. That's when Agnes realizes that there is no escape—not from the bugs, not from intruders of any sort, and not from the pain that has plagued them both for so many years. They have to destroy the bugs, to keep the infestation from spreading to the world. They have to purify themselves with fire.

Throughout 2005, the internet was abuzz with the news that legendary director William Friedkin was returning to the horror genre. The man who'd changed the face of horror with *The Exorcist* (1973) was going to terrify us once again. All we knew was that the film was called *Bug*, and its big star was Ashley Judd. As it turned out, *Bug* was nothing like we'd all anticipated. First of all, it was an adaptation of a play by a writer named Tracy Letts, the titular insects were not of the giant variety, and the horror, while very real, was psychological. Gorehounds took to the message boards in typical outrage, declaring that they'd been cheated, misled. The startling image of a nearly-naked, blood-covered Michael Shannon would turn out to be as far from *American Psycho* as you could get. *Bug* was nothing but a "talky", "boring" "snooze-fest". This was after its successful premiere at Cannes and despite opening at #4 at the Box Office against *Pirates of the Caribbean: At World's End* and *Spider-Man 3*. Though it had a wide release, *Bug* quickly disappeared as more summer blockbusters pushed it off the screens.

I missed *Bug* at the theater but caught up with it on DVD. With the film's opening moments, I was enthralled. Up until that point, I'd never been particularly impressed with the non-singing Judd, and actively hated her "big" movie, *Kiss the Girls* (1997). But in *Bug*, she was unglamorous; her Agnes was so damaged you could physically feel her pain. Then there was Shannon, the truly unknown element. As he's proven since, Michael Shannon is hypnotizing. I'm not sure if it's his deep voice, authoritative even when uncertain, or those wide, unblinking

---

[82] "Bobby" in Sidney Lumet's final feature, *Before the Devil Knows You're Dead* (2007).

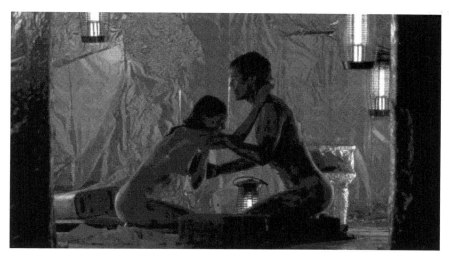

Agnes and Peter bug out. (…I don't feel good about that joke.)
Photo copyright Lionsgate. All Rights Reserved.

eyes filled with sensitive danger. His physicality, too, is an important part of his mystique. In *Bug*, Peter is physically intimidating, but by and large avoids confrontation. (Contrast that to Shannon's role as a prohibition agent on the HBO series, *Boardwalk Empire*, where he looks like the Frankenstein Monster at a desk job.) When he's onscreen, you literally cannot look at anyone else.

"By and large, all of the fans of *Bug* I have encountered for the play and the film have been pretty straight up, just normal people," Shannon told *Slant*'s Kurt Osenlund. "I think people who were truly paranoid couldn't watch it, or maybe would be afraid to see it. Or maybe it wouldn't live up to their own hallucinations. I don't know. I made a conscious choice once I did the movie—I had performed *Bug* over 200 times on stage; I did it in London, I did it in Chicago, and I did it here in New York. And there was actually a production going on in L.A. and they called me, and I said no, I said I was all Petered Evans'd out. It was a tough role, because when I was doing the play version, we would do it eight times a week, sometimes twice a day. I love that character to death, but man, it was intense."[1]

When Shannon and Judd are together in *Bug*—and it's a two-person film for the majority of the running time—their chemistry is undeniable and the tension they create, with their madnesses converging, is breathtaking. Literally: there are scenes in *Bug* that, no matter how many times I view the film, I forget to breathe. This is particularly true of the apocalyptic ending.

"I was really comfortable with the script and I wasn't bright enough to me intimidated or scared that people might compare me to whomever did it on stage. That's the excitement and the challenge like wow, how do I get myself from where I sit right now with what I know and how I feel, to what the character knows and feels on the page in a three dimensional and dynamic performance," Judd told Blackfilm.com's Nicole Schmuelian. "The process for me is simply about surrendering and being really willing. I would sit around before I went to Louisiana to do the film and joke around with my sister. I would give her a funny off-hand summary of the film, which of course is so bizarre and she would say, 'how are you going to do it?' I would say, 'I have no idea.' I was confident at the same time that I could do it because it is a magical process. Again all it takes for me is that surrender and the willingness and then everything comes together."[2]

In the same conversation, Friedkin expounded, "The [actors in *Bug*] own the characters; once you get ready for the cameras the writer doesn't own them anymore the director doesn't own them. They own them. The first quality I look for in an actor is intelligence. Now I am sitting next to arguably one of the most beautiful women in the world but that is why she is in this movie, it didn't need a beautiful women. It is very difficult to take that beauty away from her because it is deep it is inside. But what she had was knowledge of how to portray this person and find those qualities in herself. It is what Michael had; he is not beautiful, she is. Intelligence is all, in other words they understand what they are doing. Then there is not intellectualization of it, it simply okay I get it, let's go. I would try to do everything in one or two takes which they weren't crazy about because actors love to do, they'd do it all day. If I had said to them 'let's do this one scene all day', they'd love it. What I found is when I get in the cutting room of something it is usually the first or second take that has the spontaneity. That is what I am interested in, is spontaneity much more so than perfection. Unless it is Shakespeare or something where the words have to be exact. If they look like they are in character to me it's a take. Then the script girl might say to me, 'Well they didn't get these words right,' and I would thank her and say, 'Yes, but it looked real to me.' There is no improvisation in this, Tracy Letts wrote everything that is there and if you messed with it by improvising you would screw it up. Yet they could come to it fresh."[3]

Friedkin and Letts add another layer to the tragedy of two irreparable people, however, and that's the subjective nature of Peter's madness. During his commentary, even Friedkin is at a loss to say what is real and what is conjured from the couple's paranoia. He can't even say for certain whether the helicopter shots are indicative of imagined threats or genuine surveillance. The director himself isn't clear as to whether or not Dr. Sweet is a real person. He enters with a wide-eyed, frantic Goss, but the jealous ex-husband swiftly disappears from the scene and is never glimpsed again. As the climactic conflagration engulfs the room, melting the bug zappers, the scattered toys do not melt; the tin foil remains unconsumed. We're never given any evidence of Peter's blood creatures save from Agnes' POV as she looks into the microscope—and what she sees multiplies by the millions. So shattered by her grief and loss and loneliness, Agnes is not only willing to believe Peter's slightest fears, but is eager to share them. It's a connection to another person, toxic though it may be, that she hasn't felt in far, far too long.

Bug was the first collaboration between Friedkin and Letts, the second, of course, being the stomach-churningly tense *Killer Joe* (2011)[83]. While the latter could have been improved by Shannon's presence (he created the role of "Chris" on stage, a character played by Emile Hirsch in the film), Shannon originated the role of Peter in Letts' stage version of *Bug* (in Chicago's A Red Orchid Theatre), and his comfort with the role is obvious. He doesn't make a single misstep and his Peter remains captivating from the moment of his inauspicious entrance in the film, even with his slight build the man fills the frame. Friedkin's adaptation never feels like a "filmed play"; the claustrophobia inside the motel room removes any artifice. After the first act, where the action jumps from a grocery store to the bar to the parking lot, we're shut inside that room with Agnes and Peter. That *Bug* was filmed inside a real motel room and not a built set adds to the realism, not to mention our own desperation to escape before things get really bad.

"Tracy Letts is the best playwright in America today, without a doubt. His last play [*August: Osage County*] won the Pulitzer Prize. People now recognize him. He wrote for himself. He felt no obligation to an audience, or to the actors or the director what it is about. And now people understand totally. They get it that it is on the oppression of the strong against the weak, the oppression of organized religion. [...] Most of the films I am most a fan of that I have made over the years deal with people in claustrophobic situations, like Harold Pinter's *The Birthday Party*, it is the favourite film of mine and it all takes place basically in one room. About one third of *The Exorcist* takes place in one room. The Tracy Letts films that I have done are really brilliantly written and they are about themes that I'm drawn to which are paranoia and obsession. And they played out in tight spaces, not in open country, the Wild West or even in the Streets. If you look at *The French Connection*, even how it is shot all over New York, it is

---

[83] See Movie Outlaw Rides Again.

basically a claustrophobic film, these guys are locked in their own world."⁴

At the story's heart, and this is the testament not only to Letts' writing, but the performances of the two leads, are two shattered people that we really *like*. We want to see the pair get better, to overcome their grief and loss and heal before our eyes. That the opposite happens, in the worst possible way, makes the ultimate tragedy crushing. Just as we have no escape from that room, neither do Agnes or Peter. Whether their immolation is real or imagined is irrelevant. By the end, they are consumed, whether by fire or by each other's pain. It's a movie that doesn't just oppose the existence "Hollywood Happy Ending", it belies it all. Unlike the bugs in Peter's blood, the possibility for any happiness between the two of them is undeniably imaginary. "There's evil in all of us. Our lives are a constant struggle of our better angels. For our better angels to defeat the evil that's in all of us. Most of my films are about the thin line between good and evil, between the policeman and the criminal, for instance."⁵

Over the past decade or so, Friedkin, who used to be a staple of high concept moviemaking, became less interested in film and turned to directing opera. It's a little telling that his most recent films have both been Letts adaptations, with his last film to date, *Killer Joe*. "[W]hen I started making films and when I hit a stride in the early 70s I was very much part of the zeitgeist—what the people were interested in is what I was interested in. To some extent that isn't the case anymore. I would not want to make *Spider-Man* for any reason, or any amount of money—which is not to be taken as a criticism of it, it's just about sensibility and taste. It's not my taste. I don't like hip hop music. I've listened to it, but I prefer to listen to Shostakovich or Rachmaninoff or Dave Brubeck or Frank Sinatra. But that's just my taste. […] The only difference between directing an opera and directing a film or doing a play is there's no camera on the stage. That's the only difference. Everything else is the same. You are still trying to, on the stage, put people in different relationships to each other. You use lighting instead of a close-up camera to highlight people and put others in relief. The good actors want the same thing as the great singers want, which is a psychological underpinning for their characters and a staging that works. But I don't look at *Bug* and say, 'Oh this is a play I'm going to adapt.' I look at the script itself; I look at the basic raw material. If this was a novel about these people it would be just as powerful, and just as powerful on the screen, I feel, because he's written some really terrific and unusual roles."⁶

Bug, thank God, is readily available on DVD. I do have to point one disappointing aspect of the presentation: surprisingly, for as erudite Friedkin is in interviews, his commentary is perhaps one of the worst ever recorded. For the bulk of the film's running time, all the director does is narrate what you're seeing on screen. "And here in this trailer is Agnes. Obviously alone. And here's Peter at the juke box. R.C. is going to tell Agnes that she should talk to him." It's a tragic missed opportunity for a director of some of the most dramatically intense movies to impart advice or divulge some filmmaking secrets. That being said, the movie remains unique and transfixing.

NOTES

¹ Osenlund, Kurt. 2013. "Interview: Michael Shannon." Slant Magazine. May 1.
  http://www.slantmagazine.com/features/article/interview-michael-shannon

² Schmuelian, Nicole. 2006. "An Interview with Ashley Judd, Michael Shannon and Director William Friedkin."
  Blackfilm.com. May. http://www.blackfilm.com/20070518/features/buginterview.shtml

³ Ibid.

⁴ Gomarasca, Manlio, 2011. "Interview With William Friedkin On Killer Joe And His Previous Films" Cinema Scope
  #49. November 11. Archived at Arte.tv. http://www.arte.tv/sites/olivierpere/2012/09/04/interview-with-
  william-friedkin-on-killer-joe-and-his-previous-films/

⁵ Faraci, Devin. 2007. "Exclusive Interview: William Friedkin (Bug)". CHUD.com. May 22.
  http://www.chud.com/10373/exclusive-interview-william-friedkin-bug/

⁶ Ibid.

A CHINESE GHOST STORY (1987)

By Terry Thome

Ning Choi-San (played by Cantopop singer Leslie Cheung) is a taxman that travels throughout rural China collecting the taxes from various businesses in the Tang Dynasty. When a rainstorm renders his Ledger illegible, he's forced to stay in the only free accommodations available in the area, Lo Ran Temple. Ning Choi-San is warned to stay away by the townsfolk who tell him the Temple is haunted but, in desperation, he ignores the warnings.

Arriving at the temple, he accidentally runs into two battling swordsmen who seem to be fighting over who is superior. Ning Choi-San clumsily diffuses the situation and the swordsmen run off in different directions. Later on by a campfire, one of the Swordsman, Hah Hau (Lam Wai), hears the sound of a woman singing. He comes upon a girl bathing in a stream. She seduces him and he is drained of his Yang energy by an unknown force. The girl, named Nip Siu-Sing (Joey Wang), seems to be a siren, luring men to their deaths with her song.

The remaining Swordsman, Yin Chik-Ha (A truly memorable performance by Wu Ma) advises Ning Choi-San to leave the Temple, otherwise a fate worse than death may await him. Ning Choi-San shrugs off his warnings and takes up refuge within one of the temple's living quarters to replace the washed out ink in his Ledger. Then he hears the siren's call…

A Chinese Ghost Story is one of those gateway to the East movies for adventurous filmgoers. Made in 1987, it was a hit all over Asia but failed to make much of a ruckus in the West, where it was only shown in Chinatown Theaters. When Jonathan Ross included scenes from it in his piece on Tsui Hark in the fall of 1988 on his *The Incredibly Strange Film Show* program, filmgoers in Europe began to pay attention. When that episode was aired in America two years later on *The Discovery Channel*, US film fans began clamoring for expensive bootlegs from black market sources. It quickly became a must-see item.

It's easy to see why people were excited by this film. It was one of those kitchen sink

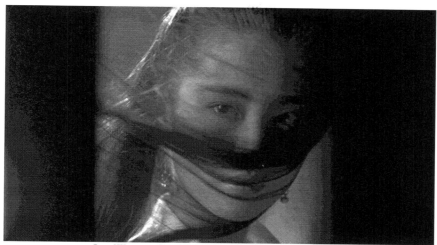

Joey Wang as Siu-Sing. Photo copyright Film Workshop.

"Hey-you-gotta-see-this!" movies, containing a break-neck mix of comedy, action, horror, romance and musical numbers all tightly rolled into a cohesive whole. That sort of thing was common in Hong Kong films of the period, but in the West it was an invigorating experience. The smooth, snaky, low to the ground camera prowls never fails to remind one of the POV demon "Samma-cam" in the first *Evil Dead* movie and the quick cut action sequences move more like a ballet than what was happening in US action films from the same year.

But for all the dizzying cinematography and rapid fire editing, *A Chinese Ghost Story* is, at heart, an old fashioned romance. While we, at first, are led to believe that Siu-Sing is an evil spirit luring men to their demise, we soon find that she is actually a slave to a 1,000 year old hermaphroditic Demon Tree Spirit (Lau Siu-ming), sporting an enormously long tongue, who uses Siu-Sing to drain the Yang energy from "evil" men so (S)He may remain youthful. Siu-Sing's family was too poor to bury her properly in a family lot, so she was buried under the Demon tree. Siu-Sing sees that Ning Choi-San is a good man and tries to make him leave the temple but, smitten, he refuses to leave without her. They begin to fall in love. However, as these stories all seem to go, Siu-Sing has been betrothed by the Tree Spirit to the Dark Lord of the Underworld, where she will live in eternal servitude to Him. Ning Choi-San decides to find a way to rescue Siu-Sing and free her so she can be reincarnated.

At first Swordsman Yin refuses to believe the young ghost. "Ghosts and Men shouldn't mix," he warns in one of the many, many subtitle variants available. But, while his resolve is strong, his heart is soft and he agrees to help the two young lovers. While they recover the Urn that holds Siu-Sing's ashes, they find they still must storm hell to rescue her.

And that, really is the crux of the film. It's not just a tale of star crossed lovers, it's the ultimate tale of star crossed loves. Ning Choi-San and Nip Siu-Sing can never, ever be together. The choice comes down to Ning. Does he love her enough to save her soul for reincarnation? I think you probably already know the answer, but getting there is all the fun. Tsui Hark, who produced the film under his Film Workshop production company and, by most accounts, directed it as well (Martial Arts director Ching Siu-Tung officially gets the director's credit) packs the film with bloodthirsty zombies (the bodies of the men robbed of their Yang energy), beautiful and deadly ghosts, battles that take place on horseback and high above in the trees and Hark makes it seem effortless and sensible.

Unfortunately, for English speaking audiences, it's been a bit of a rough haul. The best set of English subtitles are in the theatrical release from Rim Films Distribution (with a confusing "Presented By Dean Shek" credit at the start), but those wonderful subtitles have never seen a video release. The Chinese language has proven extremely difficult to translate over to English and most attempts for this film seem to be halfhearted, to say the least.

The great Ng Wu Ma as Swordsman Yin. Photo copyright Film Workshop.

There's an English dub (from the UK Hong Kong Legends DVD) that has found its way to an occasional American Television airing, and it's not bad, but this film is so very Chinese that hearing these characters speak English just feels like a cheat.

But, in the end, it's really about the visuals. It could be a silent movie and it would still thrill. And it was all done pre-CGI with some of the most imaginative effects ever committed to celluloid.

Since the worldwide success of *A Chinese Ghost Story*, there have been two official sequels (in 1990 & 1991, respectively), a 40 episode television adaptation from 2002 (*Eternity: A Chinese Ghost Story*), an animated feature ("A Tsui Hark Animation") from 1997, and a theatrical remake, released in 2011. They're all entertaining and are worth a viewing, but none of them have come close to the perfect balance of genres that is *A Chinese Ghost Story*.

Leslie Cheung and Joey Wang. Photo Copyright Film Workshop.

THE COOK, THE THIEF, HIS WIFE & HER LOVER (1989)

In 1989 I was sixteen and utterly obsessed with movies.[84] I had this burning desire to see everything. Fortunately for me, Pittsburgh at the time was rife with repertory movie houses with a constantly updating roster of new and classic and foreign films. My friend John Bulevich and I would travel all over the city hitting one theater after another, every day throughout the summer, seeing two, three, four, five movies per day, then return to his house or mine to watch two or three more. In this way we binged on the '70s dramas, black and white classics, the French New Wave, Hong Kong action—everything that shaped our own tastes in filmmaking. We were determined to see everything.

The first X-Rated movie I'd ever seen was the VHS re-issue of *Midnight Cowboy* (1969). I was astonished that the movie, amazing in its own right, had received that controversial rating, one I'd only associated with hardcore pornography or "underground" stuff like *Fritz the Cat* and *Pink Flamingos* (both 1972; neither of which I'd laid eyes on at the time). But *Cowboy* had been an easy one to lay hands on. Neither John nor I looked our youthful age, so video stores rarely questioned our choices. Movie theaters were another story. Though, again, we'd never been stopped, there was always that anxiety that we'd be "carded" at the box office and humiliated in the eyes of the other cinephiles. We'd both endured uncomfortable moments waiting to see *Lair of the White Worm* (1988) at the Forbes Theater (he because the attendant knew that he was fifteen, me because a crazy, shaved-head Valerie Solonis cult member hit me in the face with a dead chipmunk for daring to attend Ken Russell's "woman hating" latest), and we weren't eager for a repeat. But it couldn't be helped. Not when we'd read how "deliciously disturbing" *The Cook, The Thief, His Wife & Her Lover* was. A movie rife with sex, violence, and even cannibalism! Nothing would keep us away. Not the bus strike, not a lack of

---

[84] Unlike now, of course.

"appropriate" I.D., and certainly not the movie's strong NC-17 rating.

The film's rating and my underage status ensured I was going to witness something taboo. I was unfamiliar with filmmaker Peter Greenaway at this point. I had nothing to prepare me for what I was seeing. While the final shots were not violent to my eyes—not compared to the horrorshow last act of *Taxi Driver*, for instance, or the bloodbath of *The Wild Bunch*, which had played at the Playhouse just the previous week. But there was something decidedly *forbidden* about the film. Not just because of the emphasis I'd put on it during my excursion to see it, but because the film's photography and subject matter, particularly during those last few minutes, showed me a world I'd never experienced before.

As composer Michael Nyman's "Memorial" fills the speakers, the film introduces us to the first major character, the lavish Le Hollandais Restaurant, located in some unspecified part of London. It's very early morning, the sun has not yet risen, and the meat trucks have arrived. Moments later, the brutish Albert Spica (Michael Gambon[85]) arrives with his gang, seizing one of the restaurant's workers, demanding the money he owes. They strip him naked and smear him with dog excrement, humiliating him while beating him. Once the gangsters depart, the man's co-workers help him clean up, doing their best not to add to his debasement. Meanwhile, the head chef, Messeur Richard Boarst (Richard Bohringer[86]), prepares the meals of the day.

The camera drifts lovingly through the kitchens while Boarst's "kitchen boy", Pup (Paul Russell[87]), sings in a gorgeous soprano to the film's score. Soon, we're inside the restaurant's main halls, each cavernous room a different, overpowering color. (It would be years later that I would recognize these lateral dollies and vivid color schemes as signature Greenaway motifs, creating living paintings on screen.) Spica and his gang returns once again, this time with wife Georgina (an ethereal Helen Mirren[88]) very much in tow. It is revealed that Spica, a grotesque simian with delusions of gourmand, has taken over the restaurant, basically forcing Boarst and his crew into slavery, while steadily driving away the upper-class clientele with his unmeasurable boorishness and violent outbursts. He believes he appreciates the finer things, but the unmistakable stink of the gutter hangs about him.

Disgusted and bored with Albert, Georgina begins a surreptitious affair with the gentle Michael (Alan Howard[89]), whom she often witnessed sitting alone, sipping wine and reading from a new book each night. She's drawn to his gentility, his obvious intelligence. The danger adds to their passion as they make love in the restrooms and kitchens. Michael owns a bookstore; he's everything that Albert is not. Unfortunately, Albert is a cunning observer of human behavior. The affair does not stay a secret for very long. And once uncovered, the depths of Albert's depravity is unveiled. He has his gang torture Pup for information. His revenge on Michael is grotesque, but poetic, as Albert force-feeds the man pages from his beloved books. Eventually, his animalistic urges prove his downfall, and Georgina teams with Boarst, and everyone he's ever victimized, to exact their own vendetta.

That's the plot of *The Cook, The Thief, His Wife & Her Lover*, but it's barely a summary of what the film is *about*. Sitting in the balcony of The Pittsburgh Playhouse, Greenaway's masterpiece opened, for me, an unforeseen door into cinema. I was astonished by its power and, for one of the very first times in my life, I started to see the themes behind the story. I knew nothing about Greenaway at this point, but I quickly recognized his usage of color and music to counter-act the actions, as well as the lateral movement from one room set-piece to the next, revealing parallel action hidden from view. I recognized, somehow, the way he

---

[85] Long before he became *Harry Potter*'s Albus Dumbledore.

[86] "Patrice" in Angelina Jolie Pitt's *By the Sea* (2015).

[87] Who would later play "Ariel" in Greenaway's *Prospero's Books* (1991).

[88] John Boorman's *Excalibur* (1981) and everything else ever made since then.

[89] In one of the strangest credits, he provided the voice of "The Ring" in Jackson's *Lord of the Rings* trilogy.

fetishized the presentation of the food. I marveled at the way he had costumes[90] change in a single shot, to match the rooms' visual motifs, particularly one disturbingly violent shot where he drags Georgina through the restaurant, her dress and his cummerbund magically transformed by each room's décor. Suddenly, everything I thought I knew about art and film seemed insufficient. It was as much an awakening of the scholar in me as it was the daring victory of seeing the film in the first place. And for months afterward, *The Cook...* haunted me.

"Visceral". It was the first time I'd ever fully understood what that adjective meant when it came to film. You could smell the food Boarst presented; you could feel the silk of the tablecloths. When Georgina's and Michael's post-coital afterglow is interrupted by one of Albert's rages, they flee through the kitchens and Boarst prepares an escape for them: inside one of the meat trucks, left for a week unattended due to Spica's arbitrary anger, the meat inside spoiled, the full boar's heads rotting away. Michael and Georgina have no choice but to board, completely naked, and endure the stench and rot until their getaway is achieved. When the scene ended, you could still feel a foul sheen on your own skin. Visceral, indeed.

The violence inherent in the film is less shocking and more grotesque, due to its abject realism. When the blood does flow, the audience has already been bludgeoned by Albert along with the rest of the players. He's a vile creature, but one familiar to everyone. Albert Spica is beer-swilling truck driver who claims NASCAR is art. He's the overweight asshole who demands your local video store open an X-rated section. He is every ghoulish, pantomime human you've ever encountered at the grocery store or the violent political rally. He is violent pretention. He is the enemy of art and culture, even while extolling himself as the expert. He is Baron Harkonnen and he is too, too familiar. A disease that screams. And we can't wait to see him get his. Greenaway doesn't disappoint. (And Georgina's final words to him are the pinnacle of divine vulgarity.)

At the time of its release, Greenaway's film was decried in his home country for being an indictment of Margaret Thatcher and her anti-intellectualism. In the U.S., naturally, it was the sex and nudity that upset us. "What is his motivation here?" pondered Roger Ebert. "I submit it is anger—the same anger that has inspired large and sometimes violent British crowds to demonstrating against Margaret Thatcher's poll tax that whips the poor and coddles the rich. Some British critics are reading the movie this way: Cook = Civil servants, dutiful citizens. Thief = Thatcher's arrogance and support of the greedy. Wife = Britannia Lover = Ineffectual opposition by leftists and intellectuals. [...] This provides a neat formula, and allows us to read the movie as a political parable. (It is easily as savage as Swift's 'modest proposal' that if the Irish were starving and overcrowded, they could solve both problems by eating their babies.) But I am not sure Greenaway is simply making an Identikit protest movie, leaving us to put the labels on the proper donkeys. I think *The Cook, the Thief, His Wife, and Her Lover* is more of a meditation on modern times in general. It is about the greed of an entrepreneurial class that takes over perfectly efficient companies and steals their assets, that marches roughshod over timid laws in pursuit of its own aggrandizement, that rapes the environment, that enforces its tyranny on the timid majority—which distracts itself with romance and escapism to avoid facing up to the bully-boys."[1]

A British expatriate now living in Holland, Greenaway is a polarizing figure in contemporary cinema. Out of necessity, he evolved from a classically-trained painter into a relatively obscure and occasionally inaccessible filmmaker, then finally into a shameless and tireless self-promoter, primarily to combat the near-endless onslaught of criticism from aesthetes and fellow intellectuals. Many find his critiques of the lingering death of cinema to be tiresome and combative. For Greenaway, movies have been uttering one long death rattle since 1983. "Cinema has died and I even know exactly when it happened—on September 30, 1983, when the TV remote control appeared on the market. And now only a small number of people attend strange places known as the 'cinema', as compared with the watching of movies and

---

[90] Jean-Paul Gaultier designed the costumes; Giorgio Locatelli created the prop food.

videos at home. This is understandable—why should one sit in darkness? Man is not a nocturnal animal. Cinema has turned into wallpaper. Besides this, movies are based on literary narratives that have changed little since the 19th century," Peter Greenaway told the Russian publication, Kommersant, in 2014. "Cinema does not have its own Joyces or Borgeses. For over 8,000 years, our life has been dictated by men of letters, they wrote all the holy books, all the instructions—from diapers to aircraft carriers. Maybe it is high time to change the paradigm in the digital age. However, cinema surely has nothing to do with this."[2]

"At 67, Greenaway is no longer interested in cinema *per ce*—it's a half-dead medium wasted by taking its cues from books, 'telling bedtime stories for adults. *Harry Potter* and *Lord of the Rings* are illustrated books. Not cinema. I want to be a prime creator. As every self-regarding artist should do'."[3] He believes that cinema has ceased to evolve. In order to survive, it has to reflect what we think, not what we see. And it would be best if we could get rid of the frame altogether, the rectangle too constrictive for projected human thought. As he told *The Guardian*'s Catherine Shoard, if Rembrandt were alive today, he "would have been shooting on holograms. He would be post-post-James Cameron. [...] All really worthwhile artists, creators, use the technology of their time and anybody who doesn't becomes immediately a fossil."[4]

Greenaway feels that the artist—as well as the art—has an expiration date as well. In 2012 he famously declared that, thanks to Holland's practice of doctor-assisted euthanasia, he will kill himself when he turns 80. "I admit that death is not just about you, it's also about the people who love you. I have a child of 11 and a child of eight and they're not going to want Daddy to disappear. But I am seriously thinking about it and I could do it in Holland," he told Xan Brooks. "I can't think of anyone who has done anything remotely useful after the age of 80. One or two late prints by Picasso. One or two late paintings by Titian. Now you might say, 'Well, I've got this grandfather who's a beautiful old gentleman and rocks the cradle.' But really, is he not just taking up space? OK Grandad, happy 80th birthday. Here's your cake and here's the needle."[5]

I've written before that Greenaway is one of the few filmmakers that makes me feel that I'm too ignorant to properly appreciate his work. I'm not a scholar of Pre-WWI European art or their important movements. I know little about Chiaroscuro composition. But I do grasp his major themes: sex and death. "[W]hat else is there to talk about?" he asked Shoard. "[A]ll religion is about death and art's about life. Religion is there to say: hey, you don't have to worry—there's an afterlife. Culture represents the opposite of that—sex. A very stupid Freudian way of looking at it, but one is positive and one is negative. [...] I don't know much about you,' says Peter Greenaway, [...] 'but I do know two things. You were conceived, two people did fuck, and I'm very sorry but you're going to die. Everything else about you is negotiable.'"

He's been under criticism for years for his portrayals of sex and death in their rawest forms. He bristles when accused of creating pornography, but it's almost as if his umbrage is also carefully manufactured, with a tongue-in-cheek approach relishing that his art has the power to challenge and even offend.

"'Are you trying to make me out to be a pornographer?' he demands of Brooks. No, I tell him. Not necessarily, although I am interested in where he draws the line. Goltzius[91], after all, reasoned that the depiction of sex makes his art more saleable. I'm wondering if, in the process of staging a movie, Greenaway performs the same calculations. 'That's a very naive question,' he says waspishly. 'You've seen my previous films: they've always been pretty frank about notions of sexuality. You've seen it in *The Cook, the Thief*. You've seen it in *Drowning By Numbers*, *The Baby of Macon*[92]. So this subject is nothing new. Maybe inch by inch we push things forward a little bit, but I believe this is a credible and honourable use of a contemporary vocabulary. It's

---

[91] Hendrik Goltzius, a late 16th century Dutch printer known for his best-selling erotic prints and engravings, the subject of his film 2012 film *Goltzius and the Pelican Company*.

[92] Again, see *Fervid Filmmaking*.

Michael Gambon as the demonic Albert Spica.
Photo copyright Allarts / Elsevier-Vendex. All Rights Reserved.

a film about how sex and religion refuse to get into bed with each other. So throw away your Daily Mail hat because I don't believe it fits you anyway. You're fishing for some sensationalism and I don't think that's worthy of you."[6]

There's never been a Greenaway film that didn't both astound and exhaust me. His movies make you work as many of your senses as cinema is capable of engaging and his visuals often trigger the rest. As mentioned, you can smell the aroma of the kitchens in *The Cook, The Thief...* You can breathe in the omnipresent rot of death in *A Zed and Two Noughts*. The characters that populate *Drowning by Numbers* experience both pain and pleasure in such overt ways, your skin tingles in response. In *The Cook, The Thief...*, *The Baby of Macon*, even *The Pillow Book*, he engages your rage at injustice and ignorance. But, predominantly, it's the beauty of his images and sounds that overcome you. When it comes to Greenaway, I have to fall back on that old adage, "I don't know much about art, but I know what I like."

"*The Cook, the Thief, His Wife, and Her Lover* is not an easy film to sit through. It doesn't simply make a show of being uncompromising—it is uncompromised in every single shot from beginning to end. Why is it so extreme? Because it is a film made in rage, and rage cannot be modulated. Those who think it is only about gluttony, lust, barbarism and bad table manners will have to think again. It is a film that uses the most basic strengths and weaknesses of the human body as a way of giving physical form to the corruption of the human soul," wrote Ebert. "[…] It goes without saying that the timid souls of the MPAA's Code and Ratings Administration found this movie too hot to handle. They refused it an R rating. That left the distributor, Miramax, with two choices: Self-apply an X rating, or release it unrated. They have taken the second course (with an "adults only" warning in their ads), because an X-rated movie cannot play in most of the theaters in America—the contracts with the landlords won't allow it. We live in a country where there is no appropriate category for a serious film for adults. On the one hand, there's the R rating (which means a film can be seen by anyone in possession of a parent or adult guardian) and on the other there's the X, which has been discredited by its ironclad association with hard-core porno. Why not an A rating, for adults only? That would be the appropriate rating for a movie like this. But then, God forbid, the theaters might actually have to turn potential customers away! And so the MPAA enters its third decade of hypocrisy, and serious filmmakers like Greenaway, filmmakers with something urgent to say and an extreme way of saying it, suffer the MPAA's tacit censorship."[7]

In an extremely frustrating way, it would seem that American prudishness, added to its perceived rejection of anything non-American, has hindered *The Cook, The Thief's* legacy. It's difficult and expensive to obtain on DVD—a few years back I was forced to purchase not only a British Import DVD, but also a Region-Free player on which to watch it. Netflix, bless their hearts, do offer it via their streaming service. To date, there's no Blu-Ray offering, which is the true tragedy. For me, *The Cook, The Thief...*has never looked the same as it did when its vibrancy exploded across the little screen at the Pittsburgh Playhouse. The available prints are darker, muddier, grittier visually to match its tone, but muting the beauty contrasting with the abject ugliness of its story. It deserves better—all of his work deserves better. But I guess this is why he plans to leave us in 2022. Until then and after, I will continue to seek out his challenging work, and hope to be better for having seen it.

This screen cap looks so much better in color.
Photo copyright Allarts / Elsevier-Vendex. All Rights Reserved.

NOTES

[1] Ebert, Roger. 1999. "Review." Chicago Sun Times. January 1. http://www.rogerebert.com/reviews/the-cook-the-thief-his-wife-and-her-lover-1999

[2] Dyakonov, Valent'n. 2014. "Peter Greenaway: Cinema has died and I even know when it happened." Russia Beyond the Headlines/Kommersant. April 16. http://rbth.com/arts/2014/04/16/peter_greenaway_cinema_has_died_and_i_even_know_when_it_happened_35945.html

[3] Shoard, Catherine. 2010. "Peter Greenaway's pact with death." The Guardian. March 18. http://www.theguardian.com/film/2010/mar/18/peter-greenaway-nightwatching

[4] Ibid.

[5] Brooks, Xan. 2012. "Peter Greenaway: 'I plan to kill myself when I'm 80'." The Guardian. November 15. http://www.theguardian.com/film/2012/nov/15/peter-greenaway-plans-to-kill-himself

[6] Ibid

[7] Ebert, "Review." Chicago Sun Times. 1999.

**PETER O'TOOLE · MARIEL HEMINGWAY
VINCENT SPANO**

creator

PRODUCERS SALES ORGANIZATION
y KINGS ROAD PRODUCTIONS Presentan
Una Producción STEPHEN FRIEDMAN en un Film de IVAN PASSER "CREATOR"
VIRGINIA MADSEN · DAVID OGDEN STIERS   SYLVESTER LEVAY
CHARLES MULVEHILL   JEREMY LEVEN   JEREMY LEVEN
STEPHEN FRIEDMAN   IVAN PASSER

CREATOR (1985)

Another volume of *Movie Outlaw*, another underrated film starring Peter O'Toole. "[O]ne of these days we'll look into our microscope and find ourselves staring right into God's eyes, and the first one who blinks is going to lose his testicles."

In Carl Reiner's *The Man with Two Brains*, as Dr. Michael Hfuhruhurr attempts to transfer the brain from one subject into the body of his wife, he is confronted by Dr. Alfred Necessiter, who accuses him: "Dr. Hfuhruhurr, you're playing God!"

To which Dr. Hfuhruhurr replies, "*Somebody* has to!"

Directed by Ivan Passer, written by Jeremy Levin (adapting his novel), *Creator* tackles that eternal question posed by Dr. Necessiter: at one point does one's scientific curiosity supplant morality? If something *can* be done, *should* it? Actually, this is the question posed by every movies with the premise "scientific progress goes *boink*"[93].

O'Toole in this outing plays Dr. Harry Wolper, a brilliant eccentric who tools around a small California college town on a bicycle, seeking discreet assistants for his unorthodox experiment. Namely, Harry wants to bring back his dear departed wife, Lucy, via cloning. Lucy died during childbirth, 30 years previously, and her resurrection has been Harry's obsession the entire time. To achieve his goals, he tries to hire rudderless pre-med student Boris Lafkin (Vincent Spano[94]), offering a 12-credit course in "The Big Picture". When that fails to sway him, Harry tells him that he knows the name of the beautiful student he noticed Lafkin pursuing. And just like that, Boris is on Team Lucy. Though Boris is skeptical of not only Harry's experiments but also the idea of eternal love, he discovers that this girl, Barbara Spencer (Virginia Madsen[95]), may be his own Lucy.

To further his experiments, Harry and Boris "borrow" lab equipment from the

---

[93] My dearest apologies to Bill Waterson, Calvin, and Hobbes.

[94] If you haven't already, try and check out a lovely, underrated Italian film titled *Good Morning, Babylon* (directed by Paolo and Vittorio Taviani, 1987) about the making of D.W. Griffith's *Intolerance*.

[95] See *Movie Outlaw Rides Again* for a look at Madsen in *Electric Dreams* (1984).

university, right out from under the nose of the jealously underfunded Dr. Sid Kuhlenbeck (David Ogden Stiers[96]), who'd love nothing more than to see Harry forced into retirement—both to be rid of him and to take over his obscenely-bedecked laboratory. Meanwhile, young Meli (Mariel Hemingway[97]) has answered Harry's ad for an ovarian donor. Smitten with him almost immediately, the brash, no-nonsense girl from the streets moves in with Harry. He finds her both fascinating and useful, a possible home for Lucy's gestation.

As can be expected, things don't go smoothly. Sid and Harry are constantly at odds over scientific ethics; publically, Sid questions Harry's sanity. Meli grows frustrated with Harry's obsession, urging him to seize the present and forget the past. Worst of all, Barbara comes down with old movie disease and falls into a coma. A desperate Boris stays by her side, reading to her, talking to her, believing against all evidence that his presence will bring her back to life. In the end, he will beg for Sid's expertise, literally seizing the man's leg in supplication. All of this comes to a head as Harry's experiment reaches its pass/fail status.

Creator began an exorcism for novelist Levin. "The starting point was that my wife died of a cerebral hemorrhage when she was 23," the author told *Starlog* in 1985. "The original novel was done in diary form, set in the last year of Harry's life. Each day had an entry of about five pages so the finished book was something like 1600 pages long. What happened was that I continued to cut it down until the book was ready. [...] The book was purchased by Putnam in March 1978 and Lorimar bought the film rights almost immediately, and by that September I was working on the first draft of the script. It wasn't until the following spring that the book was published. By then, I was well into the film version, working closely with [then-]director Jonathan Demme [*Citizen's Band*] on all five drafts. [...] In the book, Boris Lafkin is a character in a book that Harry is writing. What happens during the story's course is that Boris is asserting his control over the story's direction, taking it away from Harry. Finally, Boris has his way until his girlfriend has a brain hemorrhage and then he must beg Harry to come back and write a happy ending. That's what I was working on when I did my five drafts for Lorimar."[1]

After Lorimar collapsed upon itself following the failure of the high-profile flops *Tank* and *Power* in 1984, *Creator* went on the back-burner until it was bought by King's Road Productions, an indie filmmaking company that produced *All of Me,* among others, for Universal. Levin reportedly wrote an epic *fourteen* additional drafts until finding approval with producer Stephen J. Friedman. Ivan Passer (*Cutter's Way*) was brought aboard to direct. "'When I began working on the script again, I thought too much was happening as originally structured,' Leven says, 'so I streamlined it by making Boris a student working directly with Harry. This gave me an opportunity to have them learn from each other without having to use the device of the novel. After that, everything fell into place. [...] Lucy, Harry's dead wife, plays in the tale. At first, she was seen through flashbacks and even inside the cells Harry successfully animates. "Every time he looked into the microscope, he would actually see Lucy,' Leven adds. 'We took that bit out in the end, but she's there in the flashbacks, establishing Harry's great love for her.'"[2]

Though it strives to ask the big questions regarding God's role in science, and vice versa—"[T]here is no *real* science fiction used in this film," Levin is quick to point out. "I really don't want people confusing *Creator* with *Star Wars* or *Brainstorm*. With the progress being made in biology and gene-splicing, we should be able to create humans in the not-too-distant future. I carefully researched how the process would be done and it's all reflected in the movie."[3]— *Creator* is very much a throwback to the *Love Story* period of the '70s and early '80s, both with Harry's May-December romance with Meli, and specifically Boris' never-say-die-damn-you! endless love for Barbara. The classic Big Love themes are peppered with the '80s growing affair with technology, presenting Harry's garage lab as a home-made network of beakers and

---

[96] He will always be Charles Emerson Winchester III from *M*A*S*H*.

[97] Best-known for her role in Woody Allen's *Manhattan* (1979).

chrome cylinders; Boris has a jerry-rigged robot made out of plywood and a tape-recorder, where his voice reminds him of his daily to-do list and gives him an electric shock if he oversleeps his alarm. It's all very "sciencey", reminding me of a line from *MST3K: The Movie*, "This is before science had any specific purpose."

The presumption is that miracles happen, whether by God or man standing hand-in-hand with technology. This same presumption brought us *Short Circuit* (1986) and *Weird Science* (1985), sharing space with all the classic '50s science-gone-wild fantasies, ala *They Saved Hitler's Brain*. The science on display in *Creator* is both metaphysical and quaint in light of modern technology. Today, if *Creator* were to be remade, Lucy would emerge as the sensual creature from *Splice* (2009), or a horror ala *Species* (1995). In *Creator*, Lucy is as desperate a *raison d'être* for Harry as Sid's grasp of biology and medicine is for Boris. Lucy and Barbara both represent the inability to let go, but Boris can no more give up hope than Harry. In the end, science both cures and delays. It's up to the human spirit to determine what is hopeless and what is possible. Both, however, seem to rely on miracles.

Creator's strength lies in the performances by O'Toole, Stiers, Spano, and Madsen. They're a fascinating quartet brought to life as three-dimensional beings by the actors. Spano's love for Madsen's Barbara is so visceral that we can't help but share in his pain as he humiliates himself before Sid to garner his expertise and heal the coma-laden young woman. Boris and Barbara are magical together, with an undisputable chemistry that everyone in the '80s tried to have with Madsen, but very few achieved. Typically, Madsen is on her own in these movies, her charisma carrying both sides of the love equation, though sometimes she manages to elevate her co-stars, as was the case with the distant Lenny Von Dohlen in *Electric Dreams*. Her portrayal of Barbara is as much a kindred spirit with *Dreams'* Madeline as O'Toole's Harry shares characteristics with most of his comedic roles. Spano, for his part, has never been better than here, as the idealistic, naïve Boris. There's a sincerity, too, that's refreshing, particularly considering how potentially manipulative the story could be.

Though she was speaking of *Sideways* (2004) during her interview with Alex Simon, Madsen's opinions about "modern audiences" is likely a timeless truth: "I think there's a lot of people out there who are hungry for something that's more real. We all know that reality TV isn't real, it's just the latest soap opera. With film, the powers that be have underestimated the audience way too many times, and they want something where the audience can feel again, and can feel characters and listen to beautiful dialogue. I think in many ways Hollywood continues to shoot itself in the foot. The audience is like 'We're onto you. We know you want us to cry now. We know we're supposed to applaud now.' I'm surprised there's not a neon sign in most movie theaters that says "applause," that's how dumb I think Hollywood feels audiences are. But audiences are not dumb. The young audience isn't dumb either. Kids will always want to see a titillating horror film. But they also want to see a good story as much as anyone, maybe even more. In general I think people have just been hungry for a moving experience. What's funny about *Sideways* is that, even though it revolves around two men, and men love it, it's also a chick film, and also a good date movie, and has also caught on with a younger audience because of the comedy. The comedy is smart in this movie, and that's why younger people dig it[.]"[4]

It's only Hemingway that threatens to sink *Creator*. There has never been a line that Mariel Hemingway couldn't flatline upon delivery, and her inadequate performance here underlines her entire career. O'Toole has proven time and again that his effortless charisma can elevate even the dourest of co-stars. *Beckett* (1964), *My Favorite Year* (1982), even in the wonderfully dreadful *Caligula* (1979) or *High Spirits* (1988), it's O'Toole's generosity that brings his fellows onto his own level. Nothing can be done with Hemingway. Her brashness comes off as bratty and her sensuality is non-existent. She's meant to be an unpretentious foil for Harry, as well as a sexual superior. As played by the bland Ms. H, Meli is none of those things. Her attempts to bring Harry into her modern day world just comes off as argumentative and even a little shitty. Perhaps it's the fault of Leven's script but Meli is just off-putting throughout. You actually start to root for Harry's Lucy experiment to be successful, as if the resurrected character could finally bring some life into the good doctor's situation. After a

L-R: Boris (Vincent Spano), Meli (Mariel Hemingway), and Harry (Peter O'Toole) in a not-at-all posed promo photo.
Copyright Universal Pictures. All Rights Reserved.

while, you almost wish Harry would stuff Meli into one of those flash-frozen cylinders, if only for a moment's peace from her grating voice.

(As an aside, I've often found O'Toole to be a confounding personage, particularly in the choices of his later-period roles. After reaching amazing heights in the '60s and '70s, he seemed to settle into a bit of complacency in the '80s. (It's a complaint I have with Malcolm McDowell as well.) One theory that abounded was that O'Toole's drinking limited the roles he was offered in this period, which seems a little disingenuous considering that he was a much greater hell-raiser during the height of his respect. "'Drinking problem?' he answers, tilting his glass and draining the last ounce of his Polish vodka." Reported Guy Flatley. "Why, no, not at all. Drinking is the easiest thing in the world. Oh, it's true—people like myself and Albert Finney and Richard Harris and Trevor Howard do drink. And since we do our drinking in public, we've been known to do a bit of jumping, shrieking and leaping. So what? We're bloody professionals and not one of us has ever been soused on the job. Do you have a drinking problem, or can I fix you another drink?'"[5]

While the film did reasonably well in theaters, and positively thrived on HBO, not everyone was as enchanted with it as I was. "It tries to do too many things. It gives us two love affairs, a professional rivalry, a goofy campus, a mad scientist's obsession and a deathbed soap opera. By the end of the film, there are so many problems to resolve that the characters are reduced to running from one to another," wrote our beloved Roger Ebert. "We could, I think, have probably done without the Hemingway character—who is fun, but an unnecessary complication. And maybe we could have done without some of the all-too-heartwarming bedside scenes. *Creator* is ambitious and tries to do a lot of things and does most of them well, but it's a close miss."[6]

In the end, *Creator* is both pleasant and comfortingly melodramatic, life-affirming even as the science of prolonging life is unspecific. Its ultimate message is something about the power of the human heart. Sometimes, this simplicity is all you need. Fortunately, this is one of those rare occasions where you won't have to look to hard to find it. *Creator* is currently available in a no-nonsense DVD and on Amazon Prime. Have at it. And a message to even the hardest-hearted of you: have tissues ready.

NOTES

[1] Greenberger, Robert. Jeremy Levin: Creating 'Creator'. Starlog #92. March, 1985. P. 40

[2] Greenberger, 1985. P. 41

[3] Greenberger, 1985. P. 42

[4] Simon, Alex. 2004. "Virginia Madsen Serves It Straight Up In Sideways." Venice Magazine. December. Archived at http://thehollywoodinterview.blogspot.com/2008/05/virginia-madsen-hollywood-interview.html

[5] Flatley, Guy. "The Rule of O'Toole." Movie Crazed.com. http://www.moviecrazed.com/outpast/otoole.htm

[6] Ebert, Roger. 1985. "Review." Chicago Sun Times. September 20. http://www.rogerebert.com/reviews/creator-1985

DEBBIE DOES DAMNATION (1999)

There's a common argument among artists and critics, particularly from indie filmmakers: the filmmaker often discounts criticism with "why don't you make your own movie and then you can comment on mine." It's both valid and dismissive. On the one hand, the filmmaker is defending flaws and limitations against unsympathetic "drive by" critics who, it is argued, could just as easily make a low budget film under the same conditions. From the critic's point of view, it's an insulting retort, saying that the "average" person has no right to a contrary position unless the critic has walked a mile in the same moccasins, thus diminishing the right of opinion. There's validity to each side. On the other hand, if you notice that a wall is crumbling, you do not have to be a licensed brick layer to make that observation. You don't have to be a gourmet cook to point out that your burger is underdone. On the other hand, telling a filmmaker that their efforts are worthless because their film doesn't look like a polished Hollywood offering isn't especially constructive either. Thus both parties will make their points loudly—OFTEN IN ALL CAPS!!—and will devalue their arguments themselves. Debate is rarely employed after the shouting begins.

I've been on both sides of the fight. Personally, I feel that it's always better to try and fail sincerely than to dismiss an idea outright for fear of criticism. Wearing the critic's hat, I feel it's valid to point out a flaw if it's especially egregious, particularly if your argument has a leg to stand on. I'll never disparage a filmmaker for trying something different. On the other hand, I'll beat up on James Cameron all day long because "Unobtanium" is lazy, cynical, and disrespectful of its audience, particularly when making the most expensive film in history. When you're spending a million dollars per minute to make a film, there's no excuse for laziness.

---

[98] Hand-drawn poster by Eric Brummer. Found on the Internet. Copyright Eric. All Rights Reserved. Don't sue me.

Jeanin Lake as Debbie and director Eric Brummer…maybe. I might be wrong. Probably am. Copyright Eric Brummer.

Being on both the art and commerce side of filmmaking, however, often results in a strange phenomenon of over-forgiveness. Once you know what grueling work it is to make a movie, it's easy to be sympathetic to even the least entertaining movies so long as you can allow yourself to recognize the work on screen. It's this sympathy that helps movies like *Manos: Hands of Fate* can get a restoration and Blu-ray release. The so-bad-it's-good syndrome thrives on audiences finding entertainment where those of lesser imagination find only narrative pain and suffering.

I have labored under this affliction for nearly as long as I can remember, at least since, at a young age, I discovered irony. Hence my affection for movies like *Fearless Frank, Shock Treatment,* and the no-budget *Twilight* parody, *Taintlight.* They're not "good" movies by any stretch, but they're not trash to be discarded. I actually employ the opposite opinion: everything is worth saving. Every movie is someone's favorite.

That's the reason I found great value in satirical pornography like *Cafe Flesh* or *Final Flesh.*[99]

It's the precise reason why I enjoyed Eric Brummer's faux-porn fantasy adventure, *Debbie Does Damnation.*

After making a modest splash on the underground film community with such inventive shorts as *Electric Flesh* (1997), and *Joanna Died And Went To Hell* (1995, a pseudo-precursor to *Debbie*), Brummer went on to a lucrative career in pornography. "Brummer played drums for a series of West Coast punk bands while growing up in the Los Angeles area, but ever since he received his first Super-8 camera for his thirteenth birthday, his true love has been filmmaking. He eventually started creating his own short films and collaborating with filmmakers as varied as Huck Butcko, Greg LeWalt, LeMonte Fritz, Peter Haskell, and Russ Forester," wrote Jeff McCoy for MICRO-FILM Magazine in 2000. "'I started the Hollywood Underground film nights in 1996,' says the [then] 35-year-old filmmaker, 'then Tyler Hubby and I started the Hollywood Sub-Cinema Conspiracy later the same year. We showcase underground films every month and people are catching on. But LA still has a lot [of ways] to go before there can really be an *underground* scene. […] I can't really define [what makes a film "underground"], but usually the film has to be some sort of crazy project that no one in their right mind would finance, but they make it anyway, going against the grain, with only the money they worked for, just to get their vision out. I've seen some pretty low-budget stuff that blew me away."[1]

The director of such productions as *Cock Crazy Quickies* 2-4, *DDD* is a return to his non-pornographic roots. Basically bringing a Norwegian Death Metal album cover to life, *DDD* tells the story of a young, nubile suicide (Jeanin Lake) who, on her way to Heaven, accidentally drops into Hell. She's recruited by a demonic talking skull named Traygor to retrieve the devil's horns before they can fall into the hands of one of two warlords feuding to replace the Prince of Darkness. The Warlords, Klegor and Tansitor are played respectively by Dukey Flyswatter and William Smith, but damned if I can tell which one is which. Part of this problem is that the $1,000 movie was shot silent on black and white Super-8mm film and then post-dubbed, so a lot of the dialogue, provided by Brummer, sounds like the mad ramblings of a drunken bench warmer.

---

[99] See chapter in this very book.

"If you ever tried to imagine what a fantasy horror movie with a $1000 budget made by a pornographer as a one-time hobby would look like, then here it is. And no, it's not pornography, but the nudity leaves nothing to the imagination," wrote Zev Toledano. "Naked girls find themselves transported somehow to a hellish world full of warriors, human-eating monsters, flying angels, a decapitated supreme-being and talking spider-skulls. Some are given quests to grab a sword and retrieve the lost devil's horns, but they get eaten at random by a Claymation monster, which is promptly ignored by everyone else. Interchangeable naked girls keep 'fighting' with various men in cheap horror make-up using home-made props in a confusing stream of scenes and locations. Will one of the heroines reach her goal or will she get so confused that she'll fall into some clothes by mistake and take a taxi home?"[2]

There's almost no plot to be found in *Debbie Does Damnation*. In its place are fully-nude actresses wielding plastic swords, paunchy men in costume armor, and a slew of entertaining clay monsters animated in styles ranging from "painstaking stop-motion" to "lump on a wire". Skulls with bulging eyes and thrashing tongues, flying demons, and snake creatures all cavort in a juvenile homage to Ray Harryhausen. *Debbie Does Damnation* is the end-result of every hyper-active adolescent left alone in his basement studio, provided they had easy access to willing nude models.

With a style reminiscent of both the highbrow worlds of German Expressionism and the lower-budget productions of Ted V. Mikels and Al Adamson, Brummer crafted a dark, dank Hell for Debbie's cavorting. Some of the settings may be clumsily crafted, almost like set pieces rejected from *Forbidden Zone*, the limited resources hardly hamper *Debbie*'s manic pace and tasteless proceedings. "*Debbie* is far from a perfect film, but it works remarkably well as long as one accepts it for what it is. Brummer manages to present his own unique vision of Hell, using nothing more than *mise-en-scène*. Costumes, props, and sets are combined with lighting and camera techniques to evoke a particular location or atmosphere, daring to convince us that his apartment is Hell. And why not? The film's grainy, black-and-white photography helps obscure the shabbiness of the sets, while providing the stark imagery appropriate for so grim a setting," writes McCoy. "Similarly, his frequent use of close-ups, blurred camera moves, and choppy editing contribute to the sense of being plunged into a chaotic netherworld. The brisk editing also propels the film from high point to high point with a minimum of extraneous connecting shots. (*This may be a moot point when it comes to the fabled 2-hour, XXX edition of DEBBIE, which presumably contains an extraneous barrage of "connecting shots" of a different sort.* —ed.[3]) It makes things a bit confusing at times, but it also adds to the episodic, arbitrary nature of the film. Necessity indeed proves to be the mother of invention."[4]

While I agree whole-heartedly with McCoy, my opinion is forged more from my inherent sympathy towards the indie filmmaker more than a great appreciation of the film. It's loads of fun, particularly if you enjoy Claymation gore, which I do, but it's hard to deny that the charm comes in fits and starts. The movie sings when the animated creatures are about, and drags while the unclad humans wander through the mumbly Popeye voice-overs.

Now, the usual caveat—*Debbie Does Damnation* is unavailable on DVD, at least "officially". Several of Brummer's non-pornographic shorts can be found online, with *Electric Flesh* on YouTube as of this writing. I obtained *Debbie* as part of a VHS trade back in college and I have no idea what the source material was. As far as I know, it was originally provided by Brummer itself. But if you're a dedicated *Movie Outlaw* reader, you're used to doing the legwork.

NOTES

[1] McCoy, Jeff. 2000. "Stairway to 'Damnation'". MICRO-FILM #3. Fall.

[2] Toledano, Zev. "Extreme Movies". The Last Exit.net. © 2000-2016
 http://thelastexit.net/cinema/main.html#Debbie%20Does%20Damnation

[3] "Ed" in this case is MICRO-FILM editor Jason Pankoke.

[4] McCoy, 2000.

THE DEVIL'S REJECTS (2005)

"Hardcore" and "disturbing" horror movies are made every day to satiate the ravenous appetite of the "extreme horror" fan. Every month or so, we get a *Green Inferno*, or a *Human Centipede*, or a *Serbian Film*. Particularly among the indie horror market you'll find movies plumbing the depths of depravity, from Ryan Nicholson's *Hanger, Live Feed,* or *Gutterballs*, to the misanthropy of TOETAG's *August Underground* trilogy. Fans of extreme horror live for the latest endurance test. How far can you push that envelope? How horrific can you make the torture and murder? Does *Cannibal Holocaust* still reign supreme for its agonizing impaling scene? Or is it the extended invisible demon rape scene in *The Redsin Tower* (2006)[100] that captured the title belt? As violent as Rob Zombie's *The Devil's Rejects* (2005) may be, with its rampant bloodshed and unwavering sadism, it barely registers as "extreme" for the *Murder-Set-Pieces* crowd. Though one thing is clear: *The Devil's Rejects* is a mean movie. Mean-spirited, mean-natured, cruel, and manipulative. It's probably the best movie that shock-rocker Zombie ever made, and yes, that's meant to be a compliment. It's every bit the promised road trip through Hell and it ends just as grimly as it begins.

Introduced in his freshman film, *House of 1,000 Corpses* (2003), the cannibalistic killer Firefly Family[101] is back to terrorize, only this outing seems like the true story that inspired *House*. Where the first film had a black humor to it that undercut some of the more gruesome set pieces, *Rejects* offers few respites from the depicted acts of awful.

Beginning more or less where *House* left off in 1978, Texas Sheriff John Quincey Wydell (an outstanding William Forsythe[102]), brother of the late lawman George Wydell (the also-late Tom Towles[103])—murdered by Otis Firefly (Bill Moseley[104]) in *House*—leads a posse to the ranch home of the *loco-familias* and orders their surrender. The Fireflys, however, don't know the meaning of the word. Both groups open fire, winnowing down the numbers on either side.

---

[100] See *Movie Outlaw Rides Again.*

[101] A clan of demented cannibals who've adopted their names from Grouch Marx characters. I felt so smart when I realized this during *House of 1,000 Corpses.* Then Zombie has Robert Trebor's (uncredited) Gene Shalit-esque character point this out to Wydell in this film, totally sucking the pompous wind out of my pretentious sails. Thanks ever so much, Rob.

[102] *Weeds* (1987); See *Movie Outlaw Rides Again* for a look at his frightening turn as John Wayne Gacy in *Dear Mr. Gacy.*

[103] Otis in *Henry: Portrait of a Serial Killer* (1986).

[104] Best-known as "Chop-Top" in *The Texas Chain Saw Massacre 2* (1986)

Only Otis and Baby (Sheri Moon Zombie[105], whose backside is as immune to covering as it was in the previous film) manage to escape the carnage. While the rest of the clan is gunned down, Mama (Leslie Easterbrook[106] replacing Karen Black[107]) is arrested. Meanwhile, Otis and Baby set out to reunite with her father, killer clown and fried chicken enthusiast, Captain Spaulding (an affably menacing Sid Haig[108]).

The trio light out for a safe haven with Spaulding's brother, Charlie Altamont (*Dawn of the Dead*'s Ken Foree) and his assistant Clevon (Michael Berryman[109]), but Sheriff Wydell is hot on their tail. A brief sideline at a rundown motel yields up more victims for the remaining family. Mentally and physically torturing members of the traveling band, Banjo and Sullivan (including Geoffrey Lewis[110], Lew Temple[111], comedian Brian Posehn, and Priscilla Barnes[112]), they leave their victims behind with their signature "The Devil's Rejects" written in blood on the wall, a calling card justifying the film's title.

Reaching Charlie's, the trio are unaware that the vengeful Wydell has sent ahead the "Unholy Two" (Danny Trejo[113] and wrestler Diamond Dallas Page), a pair of the filthiest bounty hunters this side of *The Wild Bunch*. Once in custody, the remaining Fireflys are returned to their family ranch where Wydell exacts ironic cruelty rivaling that of the killers'. He nails hands to chairs, staples morgue photos to their respective murderers' chests, shocks them with cattle prods, inflicting upon them the same horror they delivered unto others.

Via the intervention of the horribly scared Tiny (Matthew McGrory[114] in his final role), the Fireflys manage to escape Wydell's wrath, the ranch transformed into Satan's inferno. But their escape is short-lived as they encounter the rest of the posse out on a desert highway, speeding along through their final jaunt into arguable glory, set to Lynyrd Skynyrd's "Free Bird", now utterly co-opted for the younger generations.

Zombie insists that *House of 1,000 Corpses* was never meant to inspire a sequel. It just happened. "I always had a vague idea for a story in mind, because I knew that if the first film was successful, they would want to do another one. So I wanted to make sure they had a logical follow-up, and I didn't want to scramble to create an idea. So when I wrote the first film, I always had this little trailing idea of the brother of that sheriff [who was killed by the Firefly clan in *Corpses*][115] coming back to avenge his brother. And basically, you know, that was all I had for an idea. And then the whole thing sorta started formulating into a real idea the day after *House of 1000 Corpses* came out, because Lionsgate made back all their money the first day. They were all thrilled and wanted to make another movie," Zombie told Arrow in the Head.

---

[105] Born "Sheri Skerksis", also seen in Tobe Hooper's remake of *The Toolbox Murders* (2004), and does a very good job as the lead of Zombie's very near-miss, *The Lords of Salem* (2012), also starring *Shock Treatment*'s Patricia Quinn.

[106] The *Police Academy* series, but also the early Johnny Depp/Rob Morrow teen sex comedy, *Private Resort* (1985).

[107] There's some conflicting information regarding Black's absence here from the role she created in *House*. Some reports claim she wanted an untenable salary increase. Others say that she had a falling out with Zombie over the amount of violence in *Rejects*. Regardless, when her cancer entered the fatal stages in 2013, Rob and Sherri Moon rallied fans to help pay for her treatments. Black passed away on August 8, 2013.

[108] Sid has more credits to his name than the next two people combined. A staple of '70s exploitation movies, director Jack Hill often paired him Pam Grier in movies like *The Big Doll House* (1971) and *The Big Bird Cage* (1972).

[109] A marvelously erudite man usually cast as mindless killers in such films as *The Hills Have Eyes* (1977) and *Cut 'n Run* (1985).

[110] *High Plains Drifter* (1973), *The Way of the Gun* (2000). Lovely, lovely man who passed in 2015.

[111] Adrienne Shelly's 2007 *Waitress*.

[112] Bond Girl (*License to Kill*, 1987), best known as Terri Alden on *Three's Company*.

[113] America's most-acceptable Mexican, aka "Machete".

[114] Best-known as the Giant in Tim Burton's *Big Fish* (2003)

[115] Tom Toles' death scene in *House* is one of the film's few deadly-serious moments. In a long crane-out shot, the camera holds on Otis standing over the lawman, gun trained on his skull for much longer than anticipated. The wait for that final gunshot is excruciating and powerful.

"The first film turned out a little wackier and campier than I originally intended. But as we were shooting, that's the tone that it was turning out to be. Movies sometimes dictate their own course, so I just sort of went with it. And on *Devil's Rejects*, I really wanted to scale it back and try to make something a lot grittier and nastier when those moments dictated. I wanted the violence to be a lot more horrific and the characters to just seem more like real people, and not cartoon characters."[1]

Far removed from the visual eye-candy of *House*, edited with a music video sensibility, not to mention Zombie's own "gothabilly" aesthetic, *The Devil's Rejects* is grittier, with a filthy realism that coats the images with a film of its own. Shot on Super-16mm, Phil Parmett's photography rides the razor's edge of ultra-realism. There are moments in *Rejects* that feel like a particularly miserable travelogue, where your companions are the worst humanity has to offer. Gone are the Fireflys' fanciful costumes and war paint. No white-face priest this time around, Otis is emaciated, wearing long, filthy hair, scraggly beard. Spaulding doesn't spend much time in his clown make-up, preferring to be terrifying without relying on coulrophobia.

"It's almost like a really violent Western. The Firefly family is not in the house anymore. They're on the run. All I'll say is that in the beginning of the movie, the house gets raided by the cops and the family takes off on the road. It's a super-violent, demented crime thing. It's *Rocky Horror* meets *Goodfellas*. It's a *lot* more brutal than the first film," Zombie told *Fangoria* in 2005. "With sequels, people sometimes have the tendency to go campier as the characters become more familiar, like, say, Freddy Krueger, who starts off as a child killer and by the end, he's a lovable, wacky guy with the one-liners. Our intention is to go in the exact opposite direction. We're trying to dig deeper and do a more serious movie. [...] It's funny, they're *so* radically different, but in a way I believe everybody's going to like. To me, the first film was this semi-violent, kind of wacky horror movie. This new one is a really true-to-life, violent story. It's got the same tone as something like *Henry: Portrait of a Serial Killer*. There's nothing fun-loving or wacky about it. We've tried to turn Otis, Spaulding and Baby into very real characters and make all the situations realistic so that it's much more intense."[2]

With the possible exception of the ill-fated members of "Banjo and Sullivan", *The Devil's Rejects* is bereft of protagonists. There's nary a sympathetic character to be had, though each of the brutals reveal moments of sensitivity (mainly due to the nuances brought to the roles by the respective actors). These few fleeting moments provide the backbone of Zombie's genius structure. While by no means an exemplary script, with dialogue relying heavily on the word "fuck"[116], it's the film's structure that is remarkable. Casting the vile family in the traditional "protagonist" role—the criminals on the run from the law—and the grief-filled, vendetta-consumed Sheriff in the role of the villain, *The Devil's Rejects* inverts expectation. Through no fault of our own, we're almost forced to sympathize with the Fireflys, while finding ourselves reviling the lawman who understands that the only "justice" to be had for their crimes is in their own deaths. In a twisted way, Wydell's "justice" is, well, justified. These are wretched human beings, amoral killing machines who delight in torture. You get a sense that, prior to his brother's death, Wydell was a just peace officer, a law-abiding, upstanding man of the badge. The Fireflys created the instrument of their own demise. That can't be denied. Yet still, when the tables are turned, you can't help but question if their own pain and misery is deserved, even as our brains are screaming "Are you fucking kidding? YES!!"

---

[116] A friend of mine once remarked that, without the word "Yeah", all of Zombie's songs would be instrumentals. The same is true here with the unavoidable "F-Word".

By toying with our emotions and expectations, both conditioned by a hundred years of previous good-vs.-evil outings, Zombie betrays a little stroke of brilliance here. He didn't set out to make a horror film this time out, but a violent road movie, or something more akin to the hardboiled westerns of Anthony Mann, or the anti-hero films of the '70s, ala *Dirty Mary and Crazy Larry*, or *Prime Cut*. Every time you find yourself rooting for the killers, something trips in your morality center, desperately dragging you back to reality. No one here is worthy of empathy, but because of the way we watch movies, we find ourselves sympathizing regardless.

L-R: Baby (Sheri Moon Zombie), Captain Spaulding (Sid Haig), Otis B. Driftwood (Bill Moseley). Photo copyright Lionsgate. All Rights Reserved.

This dichotomy was magnified for Amy and me when we watched the movie opening weekend. After years of attending conventions, we'd built up a solid friendship with Moseley, Easterbrook, Forsythe, Temple, and Haig, not to mention McCrory, Dwayne Whitaker, and Steve Railsback, and especially the film's chief effects artist, Robert Kurtzman. We brought sympathy with us. Before the first half-hour's worth of commercials had ended, we were already on the side of the villainous family because they were played by friends, some of whom considered us "family" as well. When you have a personal connection to a film, it's difficult to separate the art from the artists. Which is about the best testament to the actors' skill I can give. When Bill, as Otis, delivers Tex Watson's famous line, "I am the Devil, and I am here to do the Devil's work," prior to eliminating a victim, part of me wanted to cheer, just as chills engulfed the rest of me.

House was initially produced under the auspices of Universal Studios, shooting on the studio backlot, constantly interrupted by the tram tours whose importance trumped the "little" spook-show horror film. Upon completion, the film was slapped with an NC-17 rating and Universal, experiencing severe backlash against film violence due to the Columbine murders, dropped the movie from its roster. Later, before the ink was dry at MGM, Zombie made a joke that the new studio lacked any sort of morals for agreeing to distribute *House*. That was all she wrote for MGM's involvement. Finally, he found a home for the little jokey drive-in flick at Lionsgate, albeit under the demand for cuts—a few for violence, the rest for running time. *House of 1,000 Corpses* made back its budget on opening weekend. This bought Zombie the luxury of being left alone on *The Devil's Rejects*. With the new autonomy, the director decided to stretch his muscles with an extreme tonal shift. Rather than make a horror film, Zombie opted for something closer to *Badlands* (1973) and *Bonnie and Clyde* (1967). The violence in *Rejects* obliterates both.

"Actually, I would say that this film is at least as influenced by '70s crime movies and action movies, anything from *Dirty Harry* to *Bonnie and Clyde*. And I think what sets that decade apart for me is that those movies were made in a time where the director was key. The director was the god on set with the vision. And I think as the '80s crept in, it became more about actors and gimmicks and studios, you know. I still think the '70s was the last great time where films were being made for the sake of the film and not for the sake of the money. Even though, of course, people were always trying to make money, it seemed like art was still important. And I think now that's what sets those films apart, no matter what type of film you're talking about."[3] Zombie elaborated in *Fangoria*. "We're playing it very down and real. It's much more violent than the first one, but it's never violence like, 'Wow, I love gore effects.' It's more like, 'Ugh!' It's very real and nasty. You can have *Friday the 13th* violence which is very cartoony, where you have 'split somebody's head with a machete'-type scenes and it's kind of funny. This is not like that at all. It's pretty gnarly. Movies like *Badlands* and *In Cold Blood* were the inspiration. The first film is very colorful. This one is very bleak-looking and stark. It's just a violent character piece."[4]

The Devil's Rejects really pushes its "R" rating, and it's one of the few times I felt the MPAA got things right. This is not a movie anyone under eighteen should see, less for its prurient elements—the nudity and bloody special effects—but for the overall grimness of tone. "I am a little bit fearful of the MPAA because compared to the last film this film is brutal," Zombie confessed to *Arrow in the Head*. "We went into it with a very humorless attitude. I mean, there are funny moments because the characters and actors are charismatic and I sort of took the approach that basically my villains are my heroes. That works sort of like Charles Manson does. I mean you don't like him but he is charismatic enough that you want to watch him and that is what these characters are like. The tone of the film is really dark and really brutal. Like there is a scene where Otis and Baby, when they first escape, take this sort of country western group husband and wife couples hostage in a motel, it's sort of like a home invasion and they sort of just torture them. […] It was brutal to film and it really was tough for the actors and that was never the experience before there was always that, 'Oh it's a horror movie isn't this spooky and this is fun.' This one really hits some tones. It was really bothering people," explains Zombie. "I just think that this is what this film was meant to be. It is a sequel in a sense to the last movie, but I don't want to be held to the rules of the last movie. There are things in the last movie that just don't play in this movie. They just don't make sense."[5]

There's very little humanity on display in *Rejects*. After a carjacking, Spaulding tells the driving mom's child, "I ever hear you hate clowns, I'm coming back to kill you!" During the excruciating scene in which Otis and Baby menace the musicians—literally and metaphorically raping Barnes—Baby's piercing cackle tears through any sense of hope that still remains. Wendy Banjo's (*Boston Public*'s Kate Norby) grisly demise is almost as comic as it is devastating, and if you allow yourself to laugh, you'll hate yourself later. Because there are so few moments not steeped in violence, the movie stands apart from its previous outing. As uneven as it is, *House of 1,000 Corpses* is rife with black comedy. *Rejects* is, to paraphrase Brother Theodore, "stand-up tragedy".

"*The Devil's Rejects*, a wild-ass road movie of down-home slaughter, recalls many other tales of homicidal sadists in the rocky American Southwest," wrote Owen Gleiberman. "The difference is that Zombie doesn't pretend to be on the side of the victims. He makes no bones about his identification with the sexy outlaw serial killers, a brother and sister played by the hippieish Bill Moseley and the Marilyn Chambers-like Sheri Moon Zombie (the director's wife), who commit many squalid and hideous acts, terrorizing their victims with knives, axes, and shotguns, all in the name of sociopathic cool. They're the movie's "rock stars" incarnate. Zombie's characters are, to put it mildly, undeveloped (he features two kinds of women: sexy young sluts and beat-up old whores), but there's no denying the leeringly grotesque egghead-devil charisma of Sid Haig, who returns from *House of 1000 Corpses* as Captain Spaulding, the clown so ugly you forgot to laugh."[6]

Few critics outside the horror community really embraced *The Devil's Rejects*, rejecting it (pardon the pun) for its brutality and nihilism. Where it found favor was in positive comparisons to Wes Craven's original *Last House on the Left* and Tobe Hooper's *The Hills Have Eyes*. "I think people respond well, because I think you have a feeling when you're watching those movies that everything's not going to be okay. And I think that was a result of all the guys like Wes Craven and Tobe Hooper, who were products of the Vietnam era, where clearly everything was not going to be okay all the time. It can be very upsetting to watch a movie where it soon becomes obvious that there are no rules and you don't know what's going to happen and it's not going to turn out nice. It's really unsettling. And I do feel that today, movies just don't have that feeling. They're much nicer. And I think that when it comes to certain types of movies, like horror movies, you don't want to go in feeling that you're being protected by the studio or the director. You want to feel like all bets are off, if you want that experience. And that's what I tried to do with this movie, that everything isn't going to turn out okay, it's not going to be nice. It doesn't matter what actor you see. They're not safe. [Laughs.] Anything can happen."[7]

What little amusement can be had in *The Devil's Rejects* comes largely from the unusual way Zombie employs the soundtrack. Aside from "Free Bird", he uses Southern Rock classics to counterpoint the action. Otis and Baby make their way across a river during the Allman Brothers' "Midnight Rider". Other incongruous set pieces feature Three Dog Night's "Shamballa" and Joe Walsh's "Rocky Mountain Way". Even for those raised on those songs, it's difficult to reconcile past nostalgia with the new violent context of those scenes. Thanks to *The Devil's Rejects*, whenever those songs pop up on the radio, my mind goes to much darker places now. No longer do I yearn for the open road; I now fear it.

I've often wondered if I would have enjoyed *The Devil's Rejects* if other actors had played the parts. It's a difficult thought experiment because Zombie wrote the characters for the actors. Another actor playing Captain Spaulding would be inconceivable. Sid Haig brings that awful man to life. As Mama, Leslie Easterbrook's crazed performance as Mama blows away Karen Black's more serene depiction in *House* and it's absolutely called for. Any time you think Easterbrook has gone completely over the top, particularly in her agonizing scene Forsythe torturing her for info on her escaped maniac children, she finds another, higher bar over which she leaps and clears. She froths and writhes to provoke Wydell, and he responds in the exact manner she hopes.

Clearly, I'm not the only horror fan with connections to the actors who felt the same way. At one Cinema Wasteland, I overheard a young man tell Haig he'd hoped the Fireflys survived at the end. "You missed the point," Haig told him. "If we'd lived, next stop woulda been your house!"

NOTES

[1] Tobias, Scott. 2005. "Rob Zombie Interview." The AV Club. August 2. http://www.avclub.com/article/rob-zombie-13946

[2] Carnell. 2005. "A Devil of a Time." Fangoria 255. P. 32

[3] Tobias, 2005.

[4] Carnell, 2005.

[5] JoBlo. 2004. "Set Visit: Interview with Devil's Rejects Director Rob Zombie". Arrow in the Head. July 15. http://www.joblo.com/movie-news/set-visit-interview-with-devils-rejects-director-rob-zombie

[6] Gleiberman, Owen. 2005. "Movies." EW.com. September 20. http://www.ew.com/article/2005/07/20/devils-rejects

[7] Tobias, Scott. 2005. The AV Club.

THE DIVIDING HOUR (1999)[117]

Four criminals, having pulled off a successful bank job, wreck their car on the way out of town and pick the absolute worst place to hole up until the heat is off. In a strange farm house, in the middle of nowhere, a young woman and her elderly father are sitting on a supernatural hot-spot. Things are about to get, well, bad.

The masterminds of this heist include brothers Josh (director Mike Prosser) and Zach (Brian Prosser), stoner Dean (Greg James), and the vicious wildcard of the group, Peter (Brad Goodman). Dragging themselves from the wrecked car, they limp along a deserted highway where they're picked up by a local man, Al (played by Jay Horenstein), who takes them to a remote farmhouse where they may be able to call for help.

The owners of the house are Dawn (Jillian Hodges) and her invalid father, Lewis (Max Yoakum), who sits catatonic, staring at the wall. Unfortunately for our Fine Young Criminals, the phone is down. Tired and hurt, the group opts to lay low at the house and make themselves at home. Soon, it becomes clear that something more is going on in this unassuming house, and that they won't be the house's only visitors.

In 1999, I was a budding journalist working for a free weekly, *GC Magazine* (my editor at the time was *American Nightmare* director Jon Keeyes, who gave me my first big break), an oversized newsprint publication distributed exclusively to Texas strip clubs. As the resident film and book reviewer, I was given free rein to write about whatever I wanted, interview whoever I wanted. In this nascent era of the Internet, I put out a call for screeners for independent films. Among the very first submissions I received, all on VHS, was Mike Prosser's *The Dividing Hour*, which had been generating very good buzz from others in the indie community. "H.P. Lovecraft's heist film!" wrote one messageboarder. "It's *Reservoir Dogs*

---

[117] Portions of this chapter were taken from "Mike Prosser and The Dividing Hour", *GC Magazine*, September, 2000, and "Jillian Hodges: Renaissance Woman." GC Magazine. October, 2000

(1992) meets *The Sentinel* (1977)," wrote another. (In point of fact, the Tarantino comparisons with any even-remotely crime-related film were already getting tedious during the run-up to Y2K, though Prosser himself admitted that the movie was meant to be an amalgam of *Reservoir Dogs* and *Carnival of Souls* (1962).)

What was striking about *The Dividing Hour*, from my point of view, was how it was structured like a "real" movie, rather than a series of disconnected scenes gradually revealing a plot, which was a prevalent problem with what the smugger pre-bloggers derisively called "Camcorder Coppolas". Sturgeon's Law—"ninety percent of everything is crap"—was constantly evoked, so when something exceptional revealed itself, it was cause for celebration.

From the nearly-wordless opening showing the criminals post-heist changing their appearances in a rest stop, on their way to Canada, as a viewer I was along for the ride, just to see where it was going. Prosser wastes no time establishing the interpersonal tensions while getting the quartet to the farmhouse. Once there, unease becomes the definite tone.

Whatever is happening beneath the surface inside that rustic house begins affecting the minds of the newcomers. Zach sees shadowy figures moving through the woods. Peter's sanity deteriorates rapidly as his aggression increases. Josh, aware that Dawn and Lewis are in danger from his partner's wrath, sets off down the road in search of another phone, only to make a horrifying discovery at the site of their crash. Meanwhile, it becomes increasingly clear that Lewis, who they suspected of being deaf and blind, is keeping watch over something none of the others can see or hear, but can increasingly sense. Violence is coming, from this world and another.

"[Co-screenwriter Dave Walker] had suggested we make a movie about a house that was the gate to hell, a tried and true topic of horror films. It soon took shape as a crooks-on-the-run flick. The gate to hell aspect shifted and changed focus; further rewrites incorporated allusions to Greek mythology just before going into production," Prosser told me in 2000. "Dave and I outlined the story carefully and wrote alternate scenes. I think it's a testament to any writing team's abilities when they forget who wrote what. I focused primarily on the plot points and the big climax while Dave's strong suit was writing some very colorful dialogue."

Mike Prosser, a Portland native who worked as a puppeteer at the Portland Petting Zoo (teaching kids about the importance of flossing—"Hey, I was in the 6th grade"), set his sights on making a feature-length horror film in high school and, after some fits and starts, finally completed this goal after college. "Obviously the biggest setback on any film project is the funding. We were lucky enough to raise enough to finance the project to be shot on Hi-8 video. Video allowed us to make mistakes and learn our hard lessons at a minimal cost to our investors. Other setbacks were various external forces."

The Dividing Hour was a relatively quick shoot for the crew, but, as he pointed out above, not without its challenges: "Our first day of shooting was the opening bank robbery, shot at a local video store which used to be an old First Interstate Bank. Despite our calls to the local police previous to the shoot, cops arrived, guns drawn thinking the guys running past off-screen camera equipment in ski masks minutes before were an actual threat to the community. When the owner of the store announced that the police were on the phone and had the building surrounded we thought it was a joke. We heard no sirens and saw no cop cars from our vantage point. Further investigation verified that it was indeed no prank call on the other end of the phone. I quickly collected the guns (real guns with their firing pins in place, unloaded mind-you, but the owner of the weapons was not on the premises), put them in a drawer, and proceeded to get frisked. Realizing that this was all a mistake, they uncuffed the owner of the store and we all had a good laugh. Thank God they never asked to see our 'prop guns' otherwise I may have been laughing behind bars. The other big issue was the day we shot the overturned car in the creek. We had had a mechanic remove the engine so we could get the Dodge Dart into the creek and manually turn it over. Now supposedly this was county property which we had received a verbal okay to shoot on. But, of course, when shooting began we were confronted by a man claiming to own the land.

Thankfully he had no problems with us shooting there, but he did mention he knew someone who had driven their truck into the creek and were reported to the EPA who then fined them for polluting the river. They just drove the car into the creek... we flipped one over in it, not to mention the remaining fuel that came out of the tank and floated down stream. Thank God the statute of limitations is up on that one. We proceeded to shoot. Later we heard sirens in the distance. We thought, 'Wouldn't it be funny if they were coming for us?'... they were. Someone way down stream spotted the car in our isolated location and called the fire department to help anyone in the wrecked car. Nice thought, but they should have checked it out themselves. Lesson learned, always notify the proper authorities and make-sure they get the message and return your call. A receptionist is not a reliable verifier of notification."

Unfortunately for Prosser, he also decided to co-star in the film as one of the crooks. In fact, Prosser's character is more or less the leader of the trio of misfits. And how did Prosser take to directing himself at the same time as the rest of the cast?

"Poorly," he says with a laugh. "After being up until all hours prepping the sets and organizing props and equipment with Jeff Yarnall and Greg James, I hardly knew my lines half the time. Thank God I wrote the dialogue, I could improvise a little. I had off screen help from David Walker and Jeff was another set of eyes for my performance. I could always go immediately to the tape and review it. Directing is a very delicate art, balancing motivation of cast and crew, being the voice of reason, and the source of the vision. Seeing as how we had a two-week preproduction, I was not as fully prepared for all of those areas as I would have liked. Needless to say I've learned my lesson about playing a lead in your feature directorial debut...don't do it. Concentrate on telling the story and guiding the performers. At least I could rely on me showing up every day."

"Sound was a big issue in this film," says Jillian Hodges. "The house where we shot the outdoor locations was located out in the middle of nowhere, literally—it's on a back road in the middle of farm country in Forest Grove, Oregon. It was perfect—isolated and quiet—or so we thought. As we started to shoot, the neighboring farmer turned on his plow and began to till his fields. Here we were trying to shoot scenes in which the bewildered boys find themselves cut off from civilization, and there's the sound of a great big plow in the background. Pleading with him didn't help—we actually waited, hanging around the set, until he was done- a couple of hours, if I recall. Finally, he was done and we could get started. However, we then discovered that if we turned on our generator close enough to stay plugged into the equipment for which it was generating electricity, it too made a sound that completely drowned out the actors' voices and everything else. Another hour or so for our handy D.P., Jeff Yarnall, to rig up some sort of system so that we could shoot undisturbed by the obnoxious hum. Then, we discovered that this back road happened to also be a scenic route, popular on weekend afternoons for touring. There was nothing we could do but hold up the shoot every time a car went by. Getting a whole scene was torturous—the scene in which Dawn is talking to Zach and he tells her about the bank robbery took maybe twenty takes to shoot—just to get through it without stopping! And we ended up dubbing it anyway!"

On the DVD commentary, the Prossers express mild regret that Hodges, as Dawn, was "too attractive" to be a believable doomed-farmer's daughter. There's an old saying about hindsight, after all. But Hodges's Dawn has a perfect innocent sweetness that makes us fear for her safety throughout the film, particularly once Peter develops an unsavory fixation on her (Goodman is legitimately frightening). A classmate of Prosser's at Southern Oregon University, Hodges was Prosser's first choice for the role. "When I graduated, I had no idea what I was going to do or where I was going to go—but I was ready to act!" she told me (also in 2000). "Mike had moved up to Portland, Oregon a little earlier and I got a call from him that summer, as I was trying to figure out what to do. He wanted me to take a look at this script and see if it was something I would be interested in doing. I was absolutely interested, but the logistics of the shoot were going to be difficult. It would mean I would have to commute up to Portland, a five hour trip, every weekend, which were the only times we could shoot, since everyone worked. But I was up for it and we got started by the end of the summer."

Stuck in the middle of proverbial nowhere, behind-the-scenes tensions grew as well over the course of the shoot. This is inevitable. Filmmaking is grueling and often unrewarding, at least from a monetary standpoint. Midway through the production, personalities began to

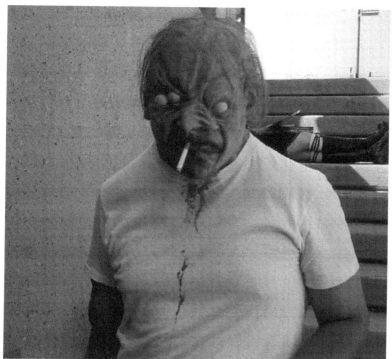

A Gimp About Town. (Greg James wearing the impressive mask.)
Photo Courtesy Mike Prosser

clash, equipment failed, the usual. From Hodges' point of view, however, it was just part of the job. "We had a lot of fun—the camaraderie was great. Everyone was dedicated to the project and really involved in what they were doing, not to mention willing and ready to help out everywhere. We had parties at the end of the day and, I think, really enjoyed each other and the process of filmmaking. However, it was also pretty trying at times—it was a first time experience filmmaking for most of the cast and crew and low budget movie making is always frustrating. You never have everything that you need—people are working on short fuses because they are up all night building sets and painting—everyone's doing three jobs... There were some temper flare ups and compromises. Overall, though, I'd say we learned a lot—we certainly came away from it with a better understanding of what it takes to make a movie."

And now that it is over and the hard work has finally yielded the finished product, what does Ms. Hodges feel about the world of low-budget horror movies? "It is a deep, dark well of turbulent, exciting and torrid emotion." I wait for her to continue. "No, seriously, there are a number of really talented, dedicated people out there who will do anything to express themselves in the medium of film. And that's what it takes in low budget filmmaking—you have to give it everything and be so dedicated and so persistent that you will finish it no matter what. There is nothing easy or simple or cheap about making a movie—if you're going to do it on a shoestring budget, you better really want to do it. This means that there is also a wonderful, rich world of low budget films—the people involved are usually highly creative, interesting and often surprisingly clever. It is a wonderful forum for budding filmmakers to get started—although it's more of a long shot—you have to produce something pretty spectacular and then have it seen at the right place and the right time-working your way up as a production assistant in Hollywood can be demoralizing and exhausting. I myself am a huge fan of low budget horror movies."

Most fans will find that one of the highlights of the film comes at the climax in the form of a good old fashioned stop-motion creature ala Ray Harryhausen. Combined with computer-generated animation, the sequence is quite effective and makes for a very creepy climax.

"The combination was pure necessity. I had worked on stop-motion projects at Will Vinton Studios (*The Adventures of Mark Twain*[118]) and knew my buddy Webster Colcord[119] could come through for us. The end sequence was originally supposed to contain CGI tentacles as well which never came to be... Guess it'll have to wait for the special edition... hehehe. The digital work that was done utilized Adobe Photoshop and After Effects to do composites of the blue screened animations and convert our two story location into a one story farmhouse. The morphing was done with Elastic Reality, a very user friendly consumer grade morphing program."

By the end, Prosser and company were relatively happy with the final product. "*The Dividing Hour* is maybe 60% of what I envisioned it to be. The more knowledgeable I become about the process the more disappointed I am that we weren't more experienced and shrewd about our creative process. We may trim the film slightly and clean up our archaic sound for the DVD which we hope to get authored soon... perhaps with a few new goodies. But it does stand as a testament to persistence and creativity for me personally. The reaction was better than we'd ever expected. When we shot the film we were saying, 'If this is the best piece of filmmaking we ever do, someone just shoot us now.' We knew our potential was greater than what we were able to achieve. Never in a million years did we think the response would be so overwhelmingly positive, or that we would get a two-page interview in *Fangoria*'s 20th Anniversary issue, or appear on *Roger Ebert & the Movies* as one of '22 All Time Great Cult Videos'. Just goes to prove how far you can get with a little self-promotion, hard work, and an original story."

Independent films always have a rough row to hoe. First the filmmakers have to stuff their creative instincts down and vomit up business personas to scrape as much budget as they can to get the dream started. Then its long days and nights of hard work and little sleep, usually malnutrition is involved. Sometimes there are hallucinations. Often, there is despair. Once it's finally finished, edited, scored, and—a onetime slightly easier feat than today—distributed, one has to contend with critics who hold your "little" film up to the same standards as omnipresent Hollywood fare. There's no winning.

"You'll have to forgive a fair amount in this film, which suffers from outdated video stock (it actually looks better in its initial VHS version than the "Newly Remastered" DVD) and muffled sound recording. The filmmakers also made a common indie film mistake in casting themselves and their relatives in the lead roles, resulting in protagonists that are unmemorable and lacking in charisma. Furthermore, *The Dividing Hour* is a product of its time in many respects, with wisecracking criminal protagonists right out of a Quentin Tarantino movie (though without the fine acting and brilliant dialogue of Tarantino's films); Tarantino buffs will also recognize the moniker 'The Gimp'[1] in the end credits," wrote Adam Groves in a typical review for the film. "Yet for all that the film was crafted with a great deal of skill. Director Mike Prosser has an eye for striking visual compositions that (nearly) offset his muddy imagery. The film is also admirably stately and expansive pacing-wise (eschewing the music video editing so prevalent during the 1990s), and its gradual shift from quirky crime drama to full-blown supernatural chiller smooth and unobtrusive. As for the last act monster effects, they're extremely primitive but startlingly effective nonetheless."[2]

Occasionally, you get a review that talks you off the ledge: "If you think that such terms as 'shot on video' or 'direct to VHS' automatically imply a substandard product, then this marvelously-executed feature from independent filmmaker Mike Prosser will change your mind. Masterfully shot on digital video, this dark morality tale proves that if talent and a deft knack for storytelling are involved, the limitations of the medium become incidental," read the review on *Pit of Horror* (no reviewer bylined, probably Rich Carlin). "It would be criminally

---

[118] See *Movie Outlaw Rides Again.*

[119] *Deadpool* (animation supervisor, 2015).

spoiling to reveal more in this review. Suffice to say that the revelations made late during the movie vastly remove the story from a mere "criminals on the run" premise and elevate the tale to embrace near-religious concepts. The climax of the film even features some rather impressive CGI effects, none of which are over-used; rather, the CGI is employed only when needed, and the result makes for some genuinely startling images. [...] At 89 minutes, *The Dividing Hour* is a slick, finely-written piece of independent filmmaking which repeatedly demonstrates that talent--not technology--is the salient focus of creating a good piece of work. Anyone interested in ordering a copy should follow this link. It's some of the best twenty-three bucks[3] you'll ever spend."[4]

When DVD became a viable format, Prosser re-edited *The Dividing Hour*, tightening the already-streamlined film and producing a cleaner, less VHS-y looking image for a 2003 re-release. From most standpoints, the film holds up perfectly well. If you're a fan of indie filmmaking, you already know what pitfalls you'll encounter in terms of uneven performances or technical flaws. Again: all part of the game. While the director found steady work as an actor, with appearances on *Grimm* and *Leverage*, he wouldn't direct another film until 2012's *Recovery*.

Obviously, I recommend *The Dividing Hour*. I think it's a fun time and the audio commentary is an interesting resource for other indie filmmakers yearning to commit slow suicide for the sake of art.

NOTES

[1] The film's nickname for the climactic monster, for those unaware that the word "Gimp" was not, in fact, invented by Mr. Tarantino. It was, like the rest of his ouvre, borrowed from something else. If this reads like snark, Mr. T. and I have a complicated relationship.

[2] Groves, Adam. 2007. "The Dividing Hour." Fright.com. http://www.fright.com/edge/DividingHour.htm

[3] $29.99 if you want to buy the original VHS from Amazon. $7.09 if you're cool with DVD.

[4] No author cited but probably Rich Carlin (or maybe Petch Lucas). "The Dividing Hour: Review". Pit of Horror. http://www.pitofhorror.com/features/special/divhour.html

DON'T BLINK (2012)

A common complaint you'll hear from horror fans of a certain age is the lack of "adult horror" in cinema. At least since the '80s, the horror movie has long been in the domain of teenagers, with "college student" the cut-off age of maturity, generally around 22- or 23-years-old. Just enough to keep the final girls nubile, the love interests rock-hard ab-wise, and the survival skills just this side of non-existent. It's the domicile of the slasher killer, the doomed road trip, the abandoned cabin/campsite/grain silo cookie-cutter gore adventure. In other words: "Kid horror".

Keeping with terms of the rare beast "adult horror" seems to indicate more worldly terror like *Don't Look Now* (1973), *The Changeling* (1980), *The Tenant* (1976), horror movies quickly redefined as "thrillers" so as to avoid the "H-word" stigma. Horror movies are for kids, it's implied. "Thrillers" are for adults. Less emphasis on the red stuff in the latter seems to be the yardstick measuring the maturity of the fright. Adult horror is generally concerned with loss and regret. "Kid horror" has to do with losing. Emotional horror as opposed to visceral. Is this valid? Sure. At least as valid as any other horror-based hypothesis.

So if you accept the premise that modern horror movies are preoccupied with physical debasement leading to the sick thrills of the "wet scenes", then "adult horror" therefore concerns itself more with the emotional or psychological trauma of the terrible events. Both types serve a purpose, but the former seems to be the default conceit. Too few modern horror movies still professing to be *horror* concern themselves with rational, logical, or emotional. With that in mind, those thirsting for more intellectual exercises in terror should welcome the low-key chiller, *Don't Blink*.

Discovered during a pull on the Netflix "Wheel O' Random" streaming service, this non-descript offering that I almost passed over because of the stars. Cast primarily with TV actors and former A-List—Brian Austin Green[120], Mena Suvari[121], Zack Ward[122], Joanne Kelly[123]—

---

[120] "David Silver" from *Beverly Hills 90210*.

[121] American Beauty (1999)

[122] Best- and forever-known as Scut Farkis from *A Christmas Story* (1983)

Don't Blink[124] seems at first glance designed to be ignored. The title is fairly nondescript and the description—"Ten people arrive at a secluded mountain resort to find it completely deserted. With no gas for the return trip, the visitors are forced to stay and investigate the mystery surrounding the abandoned lodge."—uninspired and uninvolving, you wouldn't be faulted for giving it a miss. But thanks to lazy Sunday doldrums, I gave *Don't Blink* a shot and was pleasantly surprised. More than that, the film's central terror is, from an existential (and very "midlife crisis" oriented) suitably terrifying.

Perhaps satirizing modern man's need for constant attention—via Tweet or FB post—*Don't Blink* involves some unexplained phenomenon that causes people to disappear when you're not looking at them. Divert your glance for even a second, and your best friend, the person you were just talking to, has completely vanished. Without a trace. Without a scream. They're just simply gone.

How do you fight that? What possible bit of logic can you deduce to combat something that makes you cease to be? When ostensible leader Jack suggests that perhaps a "crazy guy" is running around, Ward's response is utterly perfect: "I wish it was a crazy guy, Jack. I can fuck up a crazy guy."

But nonexistence? That's an extrovert's nightmare. It's even high on the list of nightmares for introverts. One by one, Jack's friends cease to be. And there's no explanation for it.

Don't Blink recounts the ultimate existential nightmare, a cosmic "unknowable" familiar to Lovecraft fans, but tapping into something heart-wrenchingly primal for those raised with constant technology. An online presence is both the first and last example of existence, of permanency. It might be the primary reason we're so obsessed, as a culture, with documenting the minutiae of our lives for the rest of the world to witness. To bear witness to. In the face of a democracy that hears no separate voice, confronted by corporations considered to be individuals when individuals are discounted, Facebook and Twitter are the ledges from which we scream "I exist!", and the only instances where we receive, not an echo, but an answer. *Don't Blink* is that terror that occurs when the answer doesn't arrive.

So what makes it "adult horror"? Aside from the presence of *adults*—i.e., those past their twenties, on furlough from day jobs and synergy meetings—*Don't Blink* defines its adulthood in how the characters react to the phenomenon. Unlike in slasher movies, where the groups splinter into victim factions, replete with violent arguments over who is in charge and whether they should all split up or stay together—the characters in *Don't Blink* don't turn on each other, but instead discuss the situation, volley remedies. Their cars won't start—they've run out of gas and even coasting down the hill gains them little ground. There's no blame bandied about, no fingers pointed. Just the realization of a desperate situation and the need to find a solution.

"Claire and Jack have a heartfelt conversation in near complete darkness about fear and their personal lives. It's a very intimate moment," said director Travis Oates. "The two actors, Brain and Joanne asked me if they could try something. They wanted to have their characters scared yet laughing at the situation—the ridiculousness of it all. My immediate reaction was 	hat laughing would destroy the mood. However, I let them try it, even though the day was running long. It turned out to be so human and touching. Sometimes, when you're a director, you need to have enough faith in yourself to try something that you think won't work."[1]

Like the hapless heroes in the cult favorite, *Cabin in the Woods*, the protagonists of *Don't Blink* are at the whim of circumstances utterly out of their control. There's no understanding the phenomenon threatening them. All they can do is lock eyes on one another and pray that morning will erase the danger.

"The film also benefits from strong direction. First timer Travis Oates (who also penned the screenplay, his first) is more well known as a voice actor, having worked on properties as

---

[123] "Secret Service agent Myka Bering" on TV's *Warehouse 13*.

[124] Nothing to do with Weeping Angels this go-around.

diverse as the recent Winnie-the-Pooh videos like Pooh's *Heffalump Halloween* and providing voices for the *Lego Movie* game adaptation. But don't let the kids' stuff material fool you—*Don't Blink* isn't afraid to be dark. In a smart move, however, it doesn't start out that way. *Don't Blink* plays like a strange romantic comedy in the first 10 or so minutes. The couples arrive, they joke, and only then do things start to get weird. And even once they're definitely weird, the film doesn't go the traditional horror route. There are no specters haunting the house, and nothing like gore when people disappear."[2]

"Well, I've been a professional writer for quite some time now. I've been writing for television and film for almost a decade. Most of what I do is polishes and dialog passes so it doesn't end up on IMDB, but I have also sold six films and seven TV pilots. I got tired of none of them being made, so when I sold ACME Comedy Theatre I made it a goal of mine to direct my own film. Zack Ward found funding for the project and the rest is history!"[125] Oates told Terry Wickham in 2015. "Zack Ward and I had been friends for a number of years, (I had directed him in a few comedy shows). He was looking to produce a film and he knew that I was looking to direct one. I offered to write a film for scale if I had the opportunity to direct. [...] The development side of things happened incredibly fast. We were funded, greenlit and starting production in less than three months. The production itself was only a month. Post took longer. It's funny, the first time I ever pitched a TV show the network bought it in the room. I thought, 'boy this is going to be easy.' I didn't sell another pilot for two years."[3]

There's a strange misstep in the last few minutes of the film, involving the arrival of government forces in the know (led by *Star Trek: Voyager*'s Robert Piccardo) that leads to a false sense of hope but it quickly undercut by the nature of the malevolence. That the rescuers, aware of the situation, would charge in and immediately succumb is an extra terror beat the script didn't need. Fortunately, it's easy to interpret this as the last mad dream of the film's final survivor who can see the ultimate demise rushing towards them.

What makes *Don't Blink* most effective for me seems to be the element that confounded a lot of other viewers, if the Netflix user-reviews are any indication, and that's the lack of closure. The phenomenon is never satisfactorily addressed—nor, as far as I'm concerned, should it be. Explanations remove terror. "I love horror films, but I'm very rarely scared by them," Oates told Mike Haberfelner. "Generally, I feel let down when I find out the "why" of what's going on. It the "not knowing" that scares me. When I saw *Blair Witch Project*, it was at a festival, and the buzz was that the film was actually found footage. They did a great job marketing it that way, in the very beginning (this was way before it came out in theaters). When I saw it, it scared the hell out of me, because in the back of my mind, a little part of me thought it might be real. You're never given a true explanation about what's happening in the film, and, as a result, the movie stuck with me."[4]

Unfortunately, decades of cinematic hand-holding has spoiled modern audiences.

"What's ultimately bothersome about the script is that, as things veer closer toward the supernatural, it becomes more and more likely that we're going to be left hanging at the end, without a hint of what the hell's going on," wrote "Porfle" for HK Film News. "I'm not asking for blueprints or diagrams or anything, but, heck, it's easy to gradually make a story as baffling and irrational as the writer wants it to be as long as he isn't planning on ever explaining anything anyway."[5]

On the other hand, Mike Haberfelner of *Search My Trash* had less problem with this element. "*Don't Blink* is an accomplished piece of indie horror that above all else gets the

---

[125] "I was as a producer from inception. I had worked for years to raise capital to make a movie with no success, just a bunch of lying D-bags wanting to waste time and pretend to be in "Hollywood" while having drinks with Scut Farkus. It was heart-breakingly annoying. Fortunately my producing partners, Carl Lucas and Alan Trevor introduced me to a real investor and we moved forward. The writer/director, Travis Oates, was already a close friend of mine who had sold many scripts to the studios so it was great opportunity to bring another talented friend into the fold." Haberfelner, Mike. 2014. "An Interview with Zack Ward, Star and Producer of Don't Blink." Search My Trash. September. http://www.searchmytrash.com/cgi-bin/articlecreditsb.pl?zackward%289-14%29

uncanny part of its story just right: There's something creepy and life-threatening happening which is unexplicable [*sic*] (and fortunately remains unexplained), and it's not something represented by any big special effects (or any special effects at all), but simply by the fact that a person goes missing for no good reason—which in its simplicity is all the more worrying. Now add to this an engaging story arc brought to life by an atmospheric directorial approach and carried by interesting characters embodied by a competent ensemble cast, and you've got yourself a pretty good and rather original piece of horror cinema."[6]

Which isn't to say that Oates was unaware of how the ambiguity would affect viewers. "Just as the audience of the film is sharply divided on the ending, so were the people making the film. Carl Lucas, one of the producers, was adamant about keeping the ending the way it was, others felt differently. I went back and forth. My own mother hates the ending, but my wife loves it. I do know, by the way, what is happening in the film, and there are clues to the "secret". In fact, someone contacted me on twitter and guessed exactly what was going on. He caught every clue. So it is there...but it helps if you know a thing or two about theoretical physics."[7]

With the acres and dozens and millions of movies that are floating around the ether around us, ready to be downloaded or On Demanded, the chances of landing on a good one at random is equivalent to all of those well-worn sayings involving needles and haystacks. So if you're at a loss some evening, spin the Netflix wheel and give *Don't Blink* a shot.

NOTES

[1] Wickham, Terry. 2015. "Travis Oates On Directing Don't Blink." Mantaray Pictures.com. FEBRUARY 10. http://wordpress.mantaraypictures.com/2015/02/10/travis-oates-on-directing-dont-blink/

[2] Sullivan, Gordon. 2014. "Don't Blink." DVD Verdict. October 31. http://www.dvdverdict.com/reviews/dontblink.php

[3] Wickham, Terry. 2015. Mantaray Pictures.com.

[4] Haberfelner, Mike. 2014. "An Interview with Travis Oates, Writer and Director of Don't Blink." Search My Trash. October. http://www.searchmytrash.com/cgi-bin/articlecreditsb.pl?travisoates%2810-14%29

[5] Porfle. 2014. "Don't Blink." HK Film News. September. http://hkfilmnews.blogspot.com/2014/09/dont-blink-dvd-review-by-porfle.html

[6] Haberfelner, Mike. 2014. "Review." Search My Trash.com. www.searchmytrash.com/movies/dontblink_282014_29.shtml

[7] Wickham, Terry. 2015. Mantaray Pictures.com.

DOOMSDAY (2008)

If you want to know the true measure of a filmmaker, see what he does when given an ungodly amount of money. If you're Peter Jackson, you make the amazing *Lord of the Rings* trilogy, (then burn out and churn out the bloated and unappealing *Hobbit* trilogy). If you're James Cameron, you defy all logic, make your "Thundersmurfs" movie which, proving definitively that there is no god, rakes in more cash than the gross national product of most countries. Somewhere in between slavish obsession to source and obsession with self lies Neil Marshall's *Doomsday*, a portmanteau of nearly every movie that ever touched the director's heart.

Building on general good will and healthy box office returns of his first two modestly-budgeted fantastic films, *Dog Soldiers* and *The Decent*, Marshall accepted £17 million pounds from Rogue Pictures to produce the ultimate 12-year-old boy movie, a tale set in the near future where a nasty, organ-dissolving virus has crippled Europe, forced the United Kingdom to wall off Scotland (building up the ancient Hadrian's Wall, built by the Romans in 122 A.D.) in quarantine, until, of course, a rag-tag band of soldiers has to venture into this no-man's land in order to obtain a possible cure once the virus resurrects itself in society. Leaving behind the cold world of technology and bitter politics, Major Eden Sinclair (Rhona Mitra[126]) finds her team up against tribal cannibals and medieval warriors, leaping from one impossible battle to another to reach the one man who can cure the world, the now-mad Doctor Kane (Malcolm McDowell). Ever capable, Sinclair leads her dwindling team across Scotland, pursued by howling tattooed punk maniacs, keeping both eyes—one organic, one bionic—on the pre-Roman stronghold in Glasgow where the cure awaits. Along the way, the viewer is treated to one amazing set piece after another, pitting HALO-level marines against armored knights on

---

[126] Previously seen in Stan Winston's *Skinwalkers* (2006). Before that, she inflamed Kevin Bacon's invisible loins in *Hollow Man* (2000)

horseback and mohawked scavengers in tricked-out funny cars. It's delightful nonsense born from mixing all of your action figures together.

"What happens in the context of the story is the British government quarantines Scotland and leaves everyone inside to die because there simply is no alternative," Marshall told Comic Con audiences. "They can't evacuate, they can't do anything about it. There's no cure and as a result of that the world isolates and cuts off Britain because they don't want to take the risk either. It's easy to do with Britain, it's an island so we just don't let anybody out … we tried to apply a real logic to it like, Britain wouldn't need an army anymore because not being able to fight overseas so the army becomes kind of the police force and it becomes this police state which is the only they could combat these levels of crime and unemployment and all this other kind of shit that's going to go down there. And uh, you know, it becomes a brutal and nasty place to live."[1]

As much sheer, unadulterated gonzo fun *Doomsday* is, where it falls flat is with its hero. While Marshall was quick to list his influences (before anyone beat him to it by ticking off familiar scenes on some sort of Action Geek Check List)—*Escape from New York, The Road Warrior, Excalibur, 28 Days Later*—he neglected to include a main character who could stand shoulder-to-shoulder with the likes of Max Rockatansky, Snake Plisskin, or even Merlin. As Sinclair, Rhona Mitra is fine. She kicks ass. She has her shit together. She can be described with casual profanity indicating her capacity for well-doing normally reserved for male counterpoints. But Sinclair isn't interesting. In place of character, she has a bionic eye that she can roll around and use it to surreptitiously record damning evidence for future means ending. On her team is a handful of interchangeably also-capable badasses who are occasionally killed as narrative demands. None of them are interesting either.

"My dad actually introduced me to [horror movies] when I was a boy," Marshall told *Fangoria*. "He allowed me to watch all the old Universal classics and *Doctor Who*—I was terrified, but loved it! […] I decided I wanted to make movies, and particularly direct, when I was about 12, walking out of *Raiders of the Lost Ark*. That was it—I had no idea how to do it, but I was determined."[2]

More interesting than anyone is Sol (Craig Conway[127]), son of the elusive Dr. Kane (cum-Col. Kurtz), the schizo leader of the marauders festooned with a magnificent yellow Mohawk and a killer recipe for barbecued mercenary. But apart from a marvelous song-and-dance celebration-slash-human chow-down set to Siouxsie and the Banshee's "Spellbound", Sol doesn't have too much to do. Neither does his mad dad and narrator, played with his unfortunately typical lack of interest by Malcolm McDowell[128], who spends most of his screen time muttering bitterly about how he and the rest of Scotland was left to die, but didn't just to spite those on the English side of the wall. But Kane isn't all that interesting either. So, in terms of character, we're down to the lunatic Sol and, possibly, Sinclair's CO Nelson, but Nelson is only compelling during his scant screen time because he's played by Bob Hoskins, and Bob Hoskins could invigorate the color beige without even trying.

"That's just my geography; it's what I know. Also, for this story to work, it has to be plausible. Since the Romans built this wall 2,000 years ago, I'm sure we could do the same thing now; it's not completely impossible. Geographically, it's logical; it works. So I thought that's the only place you could do it. You could do it between Canada and the U.S., but it seems to me that that border is way too big to make it happen. So this works for the story. And I like writing about that home turf, actually. But there's also the medieval aspect of it. Scotland has all these castles that are still standing today, and they will still be standing in thirty years' time. So there's the idea that even in the future this past will exist, so I could make the medieval world happen as well."[3]

---

[127] Previously seen in Marshall's *Dog Soldiers* (2002).

[128] "Neil Marshall is a tremendous talent. […] He's sort of an English Rob Zombie, if you like." Carroll, Larry. 2007. "Malcolm McDowell Delivers 'Doomsday' Details." MTV.com. August 27. http://www.mtv.com/news/2429077/malcolm-mcdowell-delivers-doomsday-details/

Don't make the mistake of thinking that the outraged infected in this outing are anything close to being zombies. The "zed-word" is never uttered or even implied. "It's almost become movie lore over the past ten years or whatever that virus equals zombies. Every film that's had a virus in it has produced zombies or mutants of some kind. Everything from *Dawn Of The Dead* to *28 Weeks Later* to *I Am Legend* or *Resident Evil*. It's all about the virus creates zombies. This film's not like that. It's more like *Outbreak*—it's about a virus that actually kills people. We wanted to keep that grounded in reality, because this is inspired by headlines about the SARS virus, avian flu and such-like, much more than anything that's going to turn you into a blood-sucking freak," Marshall told *Cinefantastique Online*. "I'm only interested in doing stories if I'm involved in the characters, because the characters take you through the story. With *Dog Soldiers*, I told the cast, "This is a soldier movie with werewolves; it's not a werewolf movie with soldiers." It was absolutely basic to me that these soldiers had to be realistic, three-dimensional, involving characters, and their story had to be something that we wanted to go with. The same with *The Descent*: The through-line was that it was Sara's story, about the loss of her family and eventually the loss of her mind. In *Doomsday*, the emotional core to the movie is Major Sinclair's story, which starts off in the present as a little girl and is resolved thirty years in the future. She finally finds her homecoming and redemption after this very long journey that she's had. That's the emotional core to the film, and everything else grows around that. So the characters are very important to me."[4]

Without anyone remotely tolerable to relate to, Marshall sacrifices *Doomsday* on the altar of spectacle. Fortunately, it's a decent altar on which to be sacrificed, as *Doomsday* starts at "11" and only manages to climb higher. Crowds of panicked families are machine-gunned by grim marines even as the hordes of infected breech the barriers. Scavenged automobiles sail high in the air, propelled by apocalyptic fireballs. Knights on horseback run down the technologically-advanced soldiers. Sinclair battles foes in gladiatorial games. Lip service is paid to the film's ethical conceit: at what cost should humanity be preserved? How many thousands should be sacrificed for the sake of millions? Blah-blah-blah-*kablooey!*

"It's like everything times 100. The scale is just on a different planet compared to the other ones. Those ones were like a cast of six people in a small dark hole or in a cottage and this is just a much bigger cast and the scale is … it's a huge journey across the country and it takes in several different worlds, I guess, different environments and uh, it's huge. We got castles, we got gang warfare, we've got futuristic London, destroyed Glasgow…" Marshall told Andrew Rivas. "The story idea sprang from an image that came into my mind … six years ago is when I came up with it, which was this vision of a bunch of futuristic soldiers in futuristic body armor and all this kind of stuff standing off against a knight in shining armor on horseback rearing up in front of them and I thought … what context could this image happen in a film and what story is there? So this concept of a virus breaking out in Scotland and if they rebuilt Hadrian's Wall, basically isolating and quarantining the whole country … Chernobyl was kind of a big inspiration where you know they kept people out of this hot zone area and I thought what if that happened to Scotland and there was this virus and they cut it off—literally blocking it off—and locked people in and left them to die. And then from that came, okay if you leave people to die and people survive … what happens to them in this country and in this castle so things like that … what if they became like a feudal society and they regressed. Everyone else is kind of carried on but they've regressed and became this different society and if you'd leave them for 25-30 years and then go back and discover what's there … that's exactly what we're doing in the story."[5]

In 2006, just prior to *Doomsday*'s announcement, Neil Marshall was adopted into a group of horror filmmakers dubbed "The Splat Pack" by Total Film Magazine's Alan Jones, "for their dedication to the genre, which they say has been hijacked by watered down PG-13 fare." Jones included among this group, "Alexandre Aja (*The Hills Have Eyes*), Darren Lynn Bousman (*Saw II* and *Saw III*), Neil Marshall (*The Descent*), and James Wan (*Saw*). There's also scribe Leigh Whannell, who came up with the idea for *Saw* with Wan and penned all three of those pics. Serving as something of mentors are subversive looking rocker-director Rob Zombie (*The Devil's Rejects*), Quentin Tarantino and Guillermo del Toro. 'We all have the same agenda: to bring back really violent, horrific movies,' says Roth, a New England native who has the looks of a leading man and is the son of a Freudian psychoanalyst who teaches at Harvard."[6] The term never officially caught on—certainly not as well as Packs "Rat" and "Brat". It also never fit Marshall particularly well, despite the amount of red splashed about in his films.

"The lone Brit in the Splat Pack, Neil Marshall's films dealt more with monsters than torture, but by virtue of being a new horror filmmaker in the early 2000s, he tends to get lumped in with the others. His debut movie, *Dog Soldiers*, was a lot of fun, but not quite gory enough to grab itself an 18 certificate. Not to worry, though—his 2005 follow up, *The Descent*, definitely was. If there's any justice in the world, and there probably isn't, *The Descent* will be recognised as a horror classic for the ages."[7]

That being said, *Doomsday* ups the ante for blood and gore, while still not technically being a "gore" film. "When I first saw the *Doomsday* script," [FX creator Paul Hyett] recalls, "I was wondering if Neil would want me to calm down, thinking it wouldn't really be bloody, but this is in fact much gorier than *The Descent*. It has been wonderful-this one has so much for me to do, from the infection makeups to loads of really good gags. We have decapitations, arm choppings, people squashed by tanks, spiked baseball bats in faces, heads exploding, gunshots..." And at $30 million, Hyett adds, "It's the highest budgeted gore movie ever." But don't make the mistake in thinking that this is another film riding *The Walking Dead* wave. "We were always clear that this isn't a zombie movie, so we don't want the infected to look like that. They're sick and weak, not wanting to grab people and eat their brains or rip them apart. [...] They're ill, and they die from the infection. [To achieve the unique look the team] pulled the eyes down, exposing the inside—you've never really seen eyes like this before."[8]

It's fortunate that *Doomsday* moves as well as it does, never slowing down to give the viewer a moment to catch his breath and reflect upon how goofy it all is. It was designed with popcorn sales in mind. When people proclaim that all they demand from a film is to be "entertained", *Doomsday* lacks only that callback to *Gladiator*: at no point does Sinclair ask the audience, "Are you not entertained?" Because it's difficult to not be, what with all the rad carnage and destruction. If ever a movie was made to constantly remind you "it's only a movie," it's *Doomsday*. Unlike dour post-apocalyptic fare like *Terminator: Salvation*, *Doomsday* never once takes itself seriously. Even during moments when it might benefit from some self-reflection.

Modern audiences have evolved a sense that sniffs out empty calories in entertainment, and sometimes that lack of discretion pays off, ala the indescribable success of the *Fast and Furious* franchise, or the aforementioned *Avatar* (though I think the latter might have employed some sort of post-hypnotic suggestion, which is the only rational explanation for the popularity of that wretched excess). *Doomsday* suffered no such luck. While it eventually made back its budget through home video, it opened and closed with little fanfare at the box office. *Mad Max* pastiche failed to attract attention the way that genuine *Mad Max: Fury Road* would do almost a decade later.

Doomsday's relative failure did affect Marshall's upward trajectory. While playing the "What if" game results in mere conjecture, it's telling that his follow-up feature, *Centurion*, was budgeted at only $12 million, and was dinged by critics for being a version of Walter Hill's *The Warriors* set during the Roman occupation of Gaul. This, too, did poorly at the box office and may have sent Marshall back to "the minors", aka television.

And yet Marshall has only exceled on the small screen, directing *Game of Thrones* (including the exciting and vicious "Blackwater Battle" episode in Season 2, as well as episodes of the pirate adventure *Black Sails*, DC's *Constantine*, and NBCs *Hannibal*.

But even with all of this success, none of his successive projects have contained the childlike glee of getting to use all his new toys, as displayed in *Doomsday*. The realities of art vs. commerce slapped Marshall down hard at the box office, and it seems as if he had to follow the edict that the time had come to put away childish things. For all its faults, *Doomsday* is an adventure unfolding on a rainy weekend afternoon, told by an overzealous, hyper-caffeinated dreamer. Sometimes, you need a couple of hours of unrestrained joy, even if, at the end, the toys have to go back into the box.

Lee-Anne Liebenberg[9] as Viper. Screencap copyright Rogue Pictures. All Rights Reserved.

NOTES

[1] Rivas, Andre. 2007. "COMIC CON: Talking 'Doomsday' with Neil Marshall." Coming Soon.net. August 2. http://www.comingsoon.net/movies/news/519207-comic_con_talking_doomsday_with_neil_marshall

[2] Blom, Paul. 2008. "Doomsday: The End is Nigh." Fangoria Magazine #271. March. Starlog Publications. P.49

[3] Biodrowski, Steve. 2008. "Interview: Neil Marshall Directs "Doomsday"." Cinefantastique Online. March 7. http://cinefantastiqueonline.com/2008/03/interview-neil-marshall-directs-doomsday/

[4] Ibid

[5] Rivas, Andre. 2007. Coming Soon.net.

[6] McClintock, Pamela. 2006. "Blood Brothers." Variety.com. December 24. http://variety.com/2006/film/news/blood-brothers-1117956275/

[7] Dobbs, Sarah. 2013. "Whatever happened to the Splat Pack?" Den of Geek. April 16. http://www.denofgeek.com/movies/25208/whatever-happened-to-the-splat-pack#ixzz4GOKt0Kf7

[8] Ibid. P.48, 50

[9] "South Africa's Sexiest Woman in the World," 2005, as per *FHM Magazine.*

DOWN AND DIRTY DUCK (1974)

Poor Willard Isenbaum. He's a lonely insurance salesman, literally and completely colorless in a world of free love indulgence. Chalk white from head to toe, Willard springs out of bed one morning declaring that "Today is the day!" He joyfully tells his landlady (and possibly only friend) that he plans to profess his love for his co-worker, Suzie, even though he's never spoken to her. Nevertheless, instilled with a confidence he's never felt before, Willard drives to work and presents Suzie with a cup of hot coffee—which he proceeds to spill all over them both. "Maybe today isn't the day," he sighs.

After heaping more humiliation upon him, Willard's female boss (who is fond of displaying her joy of "going commando") sends him to the tattoo parlor of "Painless Martha", an aged artist who has just filed a claim against her own death. She persists in the belief that she will be "killed by a wizard on Tuesday". Willard's insistence that she's still alive holds little sway over Martha—until she tells her the company won't pay out until she actually dies. After receiving such news, she immediately keels over from a heart attack. During this circular argument, Willard is stripped naked by Martha's giant duck, searching for the perfect place for Willard's new and exciting tattoo. According to her will, care for the duck will go to the person who kills here. I.E.: Willard.

So now our loveless, luckless, helpless, hapless non-hero Willard is stuck with a 6-foot talking duck who is determined to get the poor schlimazel laid. Unable to get a word in edgewise, Willard is dragged along on a series of surreal adventures, attacked by homosexual body builders, mistaken for a lesbian by a pair of other lesbians, assaulted by cops, thugs, pimps, and other and sundry rapscallions, before he finally discovers, to his delight and horror, that the Duck is female! And so, all's well that tail feathers. Or whatever.

For many, many years, all I heard about *Down and Dirty Duck* (or, rather, it's "Official Title", simply *Dirty Duck*) was how awful it was. Conceived as a quickie rip-off of Ralph

Bakshi's landmark *Fritz the Cat*—the first X-Rated animated feature—Roger Corman approached animator Charles Swenson[129] with the lowest-of-low budgets and the order to produce on the cheap. To that end, Swenson—who had previously produced Harry Nilsson's *The Point* and provided the Mothers of Invention with his quirky animation for *200 Motels*—teamed up with his brother Mothers Mark Volman and Howard Kaylan (as well as character actor Robert Ridgely[130]) to come up with an outrageous answer to Bakshi's horny Crumb-laden feature. Swenson and company took Corman's $110 grand and produced *Cheap!*—reportedly so it could be released as Roger Corman's *Cheap!* (The film got as far as test screenings under this title before Uncle Rog' caught on.)

    "In order to keep "*Cheap* cheap, Swenson did almost everything himself (except the voices and music)," wrote Jerry Beck in his book, *The Animated Movie Guide*. The production was completed in 1974 and reviewed in Variety at that time, but the film wasn't widely released until 1977. The resultant work, *Dirty Duck*, is raunchier than *Fritz the Cat*, and quite crude in other ways—particularly in character designs. The unappealing rushed, squiggly Jules Feiffer-esque characters often make you wonder how

Willard freaks out. Photo courtesy Charles Swenson. All Rights Reserved.

a film like this could have been produced."[1]

    Once it was rewarded with the coveted 'X' rating, Roger's New World Pictures basically abandoned it. Giving the feature little publicity, and the magical 'X' keeping it out of major New York theaters, combined with scathing reviews from critics, *Dirty Duck* quickly withered on the vine. Until it reached home video. And then it withered and died over the course of several years. Any time I came across a listing in a video book, the words "deplorable", "reprehensible", and "amateurish" sprang from the page, convincing me that the movie was a huge waste of my time.

    As detailed in Karl Cohen's book *Forbidden Animation*, "Variety called it a 'crudely constructed entry, obviously aimed for an adult trade easily satisfied... has little to recommend.' "[2]

    Charles Solomon in the L.A. Times called it a "sprawling undisciplined piece of sniggerring vulgarity that resembles nothing so much as animated bathroom graffiti." He also called it "degrading to women, blacks, Chicanos, gays, cops, lesbians, and anyone with an IQ of more than 45."[3]

    The New York Times called it a "zany, lively, uninhibited, sexual odyssey that manages to mix a bit of Walter Mitty and a touch of Woody Allen with some of the innocence of Walt

---

[129] Co-directed, with Fred Wolf, *The Mouse and His Child* (1977).

[130] "The Peculiar Purple Pie-Man of Porcupine Peak"! from the *Strawberry Shortcake* animated specials. He was also the voice of *Thundarr the Barbarian*.

Disney [and the] urban smarts of Ralph Bakshi."[4]

It was during the research for my chapter on *Twice Upon a Time* for *Fervid Filmmaking* that my mind finally made a critical connection: namely that Swenson co-wrote *Twice* with John Korty, Suella Kennedy, and Bill Couturié. When [animator Jimmy] Murakami started a production company of his own with partner Fred Wolf, Swenson joined them, in time becoming a partner in what would become Murakami/Wolf /Swenson. Here, Swenson worked on a

large variety of projects from commercials to theatrical re-leases. His work for tele-vision includes: Harry Nilsson's *The Point*, (ABC's first *Movie of the Week*), Peter Yarrow's *Puff the Magic Dragon* and *Strawberry Shortcake, The Blinkins* and *Carlton Your Doorman*." As well as the narratively elusive *Mouse and His Child*, and, later, worked on *Rugrats* and *Aah! Real Monsters!* Suddenly up was black, white was down, left remained where it was, and right ran away with the spoon. See, I *really* like *Twice Upon a Time*. I also have a deep fondness for *The Point*, and animation in general. So how terrible could it be? The answer, my friend, is blowing in the wind, because *Down and Dirty Duck* is actually funny, subversive, and completely unselfconscious. And rather than undercutting *Fritz, Dirty Duck* actually tips its ink-and-paint hat to Brother Ralph in a number of clever ways. The one that springs immediately to mind occurs early in the film, when Willard leaps into his car and inserts his key into the dash: the key morphs into a penis, the key a vagina—just as Bakshi would do in the "Maybelline" sequence of *Heavy Traffic*.

One thing absent from *Dirty Duck* that is prevalent in Bakshi's films is Ralph's trademark misanthropy. Where Bakshi even today takes flack for perceived racism, sexism, homophobia, and glorification of rape and violence, Swenson takes a profound stand from the perspective of an older hippie, cynical in thought but still romanticizing the psychedelic flower power of the '60s. Despite running into characters with names like "Big Dike" and "Little Dike", "Big Fag" and "Little Fag", as well as a number of black characters leaning *wayyy* back as they keep on truckin', very little of the humor is "punching down". Even when the pair are forcibly shrimped by the body builders, our heroes are never angry or offended, merely simply bewildered. "Please stop sucking my fingers," Willard says. "Watch the feathers! Unhand my feathers!" yells Duck. It's outrageous, it's raunchy, but it doesn't come off as homophobic. Like the best satire, nothing is off-limits in *Dirty Duck*, but that doesn't mean anything is inferior, either. Willard's a nebbish with notions both romantic and sexual—while his boss dresses them both down (figuratively and literally), he imagines himself as a big black basketball player (though still chalk white), dribbling and shooting while his boss bloviates and even when he's assaulted and humiliated, he doesn't fantasize about murder or rape, just the desire to be stronger, smarter, more charming. Like everyone else. That the duck, his new constant source of embarrassment and abuse, becomes his ultimate sexual object and willing partner, is just poetic justice.

As far as the art being "amateurish", I suppose that depends on your point of view. Critics frequently compare the film to the art of Jules Feiffer, and fans of Bill Plympton or *Dr. Katz*'s "Squiggle Vision" will find plenty to admire here, particularly when Swenson imports some fantastic design work, with Willard schlepping through fields of photographed flowers,

119

or crowds of faces straight out of *Yellow Submarine*. Plus, fans of Zappa and the Mothers will be pleased by the film's adulation.

> **Willard:** Say, how did you come to be a duck?
> **Duck:** Well, I was a turtle for a while, but that wasn't going anywhere. Then my mother gave me the chance to be a duck, and I sort of flowed from there... [while the Duck is talking, a caricature of Frank Zappa rises like the sun over the horizon]
> **Willard:** Oh, Eddie, you have GOT to be kidding.

For the Zappa-deficient, I'll demure to Zappa expert, The Reverend Patrick Neve:

"There are a few Zappa references peppered throughout the movie. For one, the duck is

roughly the same character that Jeff Simmons morphed into in *200 Motels*. At one point the main character and the duck are lost in the desert, and the duck is explaining how he came to be a duck. He says he used to be a TURTLE, but that wasn't too happening, so he got some advice from his MOTHER and he just sort of FLO'd from there. If by any chance these references are too subtle for the more chemically aided members of the audience, at this point a cartoon version of Frank Zappa's grimacing visage is looming over the entire scene, having just risen like the sun over the horizon. Later, *200 Motels* is specifically namedropped. It's almost as if this movie is a sequel to *200 Motels*, sans Zappa involvement."[5]

For further clarification, co-writers and co-stars Mark Volman and Howard Kaylan were once members of '60s group The Turtles. After the band's breakup, a legal snafu prevented the pair from using either "The Turtles" or even their own names when performing. To solve this problem, they became "Phlorescent Leech and Eddie", aka "Flo & Eddie", and they joined The Mothers of Invention in 1970. However, after a series of unfortunate events, Frank Zappa was injured during a concert in London in 1971, when an audience member pushed the musician off the stage and onto the concrete floor of the orchestra pit, resulting in a large number of serious injuries, leaving Zappa wheelchair bound for months. During his recovery, the Mothers put their careers on hold and Volman and Kaylan were left unemployed. To avoid starvation, they recorded a number of albums under the "Flo & Eddie" moniker, which included songs for this very film. (Including the hilariously appropriate "Cheap", *Dirty Duck*'s opening credits song.)

"*Dirty Duck* is one of the most overlooked animated features of the 1970s, a glorious experimental mess of a film, which, from today's vantage point, looks incredibly creative and daring, and something current Hollywood studios would never attempt," wrote Jerry Beck for Cartoon Brew.[6]

However, what's controversy without a little more controversy? After its release, New World and Swenson were charged with plagiarism from an underground artist named Bobby London. In 1971, London created a comic strip titled "Dirty Duck", which was picked up first by *National Lampoon*, then later Playboy, where it continues to run today. Though *Down and Dirty Duck* has nothing to do with London's character, the charges continue to haunt the film.

"Hi, I caught your reference to my comic strip although you never mentioned me," wrote London to the *Dirty Duck* section of the Zappa fan site, "Information is Not Knowledge". "The movie was a knockoff of my work which, in turn, has made people think my work is a knockoff of *Fritz the Cat*, which it isn't. I created the strip in 1971 and it was picked up by National Lampoon in '72, then Playboy in '77 where it still runs and I find it odd that

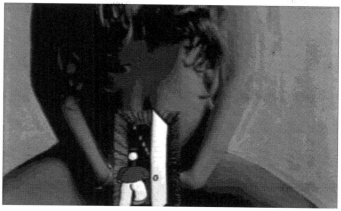

you've never seen it. Crumb's lawyers, btw, refused to help me stop these guys."[7]

"There is no reason the duck should be a duck other than to give the film a catchy title," Beck also wrote. "Swenson managed to make an interesting picture despite his budget, cleverly animating over still photos and clip art. He captures the feeling of underground comics of the time, and predates edgy homegrown animation efforts such as *Beavis and Butt-Head* and the first *South Park* film."[8]

Since its escape in '77, *Down and Dirty Duck* has fallen into obscurity, if not downright unknownity. It never received an official DVD release, and those "unofficial", or "bootleg", versions out there are taken from the original VHS dump. Swenson rarely mentions it in recent interviews—preferring to talk about his new career as a fine artist—and time hasn't been especially kind to it. But what's our *Movie Outlaw* motto? "You've already seen worse."

"The uncensored film proved that there is not necessarily a large audience for an animated work that shows a lot of sex and demonstrates free speech by starring a nice-looking, foul-mouthed fowl. Swenson says, "It didn't have a big following...but it is still in video stores." He says he was never informed of any censorship problems with the work, but he was not in close contact with New World once he was paid for his work. [...] When Swenson showed it at an ASIFA-San Francisco event in the early 1980s, he got bored about halfway through the tape and asked if anybody needed to see it to the end."[9]

NOTES

[1] Beck, Jerry. *The Animated Movie Guide*. "An A Cappella book." p. 66

[2] Cohen, Karl F (1997). *Forbidden Animation: Censored Cartoons and Blacklisted Animators in America*. North Carolina: McFarland & Company, Inc. pp. 90

[3] Ibid.

[4] Ibid.

[5] "Dirty Duck." Information is Not Knowledge. Maintained by Román García Albertos. 2015-11-18
http://globalia.net/donlope/fz/videography/Dirty_Duck.html

[6] Beck, Jerry. 2008. "Trailers From Hell: Dirty Duck." Cartoon Brew. September 3, 2008
http://www.cartoonbrew.com/feature-film/trailers-from-hell-dirty-duck-6827.html

[7] Information is Not Knowledge, Albertos, 2015.

[8] Cohen, *Forbidden Animation* p. 89

[9] Ibid.

FINAL FLESH (2009)

"Your discomfort is with humanity, not with us. Just calmly sit there and watch someone writhe."[1]—Vernon Chatman.

Something very strange occurred during the latter days of the VHS boom. With pornography still frowned upon and difficult to market in "straight" magazines, production companies started accepting amateur scripts from aficionados looking to see their fantasies brought to life. Okay, maybe it wasn't new or strange, but it became subversively popular. My brush with these sorts of "movies" came from a company called W.A.V.E.[131], which specialized in "murder fetishes". For a fee, folks could mail in their scripts, or even simple requests, to witness their favorite starlets drowning in quicksand, shot full of arrows, chloroformed, carried around unconscious, and sleeping while positioned in provocative poses. One of W.A.V.E.'s most popular performers was Tina Krause, a talented actor from the indie horror world who crossed over to the more-lucrative fetish flicks when money got tight. Over the course of a handful of films, Tina sank, got strangled, suffocated, and hunted for sport. Naturally, budgets would barely cover a trip to Whole Foods, but none of its hardcore fans seemed to mind in the slightest.

Then, or before, possibly during this period, the Triple-X producers dipped a toe into this game as well. Short scripts or ideas could be sent in and your favorite underground porn stars would act it out for your audience of one.

Enter Vernon Chatman.

Savvier readers may recognize him as the co-creator of the hilariously subversive *Wonder Showzen*—a parody of educational children's programming, particularly *Sesame Street*, in which puppets and humans would interact in the most horrifying way possible. He's also a producer

---

[131] www.wavemovies.com

on Louis CK's *Louie*, as well as a "consultant writer" and producer for *South Park* (and the voice of "Towlie"). His other credits include *Late Night with Conan O'Brien*, and the ill-fated 2001 Comedy Central show, *That's My Bush!* When it comes to fooling around, Chatman doesn't fool around.

Chatman decided to write a script specifically for small-house porn producers. Dividing the script into quarters and sending them off to the four winds, Swenson received the footage and edited into the feature *Final Flesh*. The result is 80 minutes of bemusement. And if you think you're confused by the end of the film, think how the poor actors felt. In at least one segment, you can picture a thought balloon over the head of one nudie cutie thinking, "Can I drop the dialogue and just fuck already?"

As the opening title card explains, in big, Gothic script:

"Deep in the greasiest creases of the internet, there are websites whereupon one can hire professional porn production companies to do the sick and custom bidding of your panting loins' dankest yearn, executed precisely and splayed on video for your greedily lapping eyes only. Staunchly withholding judgment and questions, they pledge to enact fantasies in earnest, and at a price.

Naturally, a person known as Vince Chaman (not to be confused with the person who is actually Vernon Chatman) submitted his Purest Truths © to these bewildered sexmaritans, in 4 scripts commissioning an 8 part prepocolyptic tritych in D minor, to test the inadvertent sensual limits of the Flesh Psyche©."

Each segment of *Final Flesh* begins with a small family—a "father", a "mother", and a "daughter", waking from a deep sleep to discover the apocalypse is upon them. After this epiphany, the trio ponders the meaning of their existence and remaining time on Earth. Their dialogue is beat poetry and non-sequitur set to surreal set pieces. And not a second of sex to be had.[132]

With the companies charging anywhere from $800 to $1,200, depending on the complexity of the script, Chatman insisted that the casts play the scenes straight. It was the "amateurish sincerity" that would bring the surrealism to life. "No one will believe it if I say a friend told me about a porn site, but it's true. A friend said, 'Hey, there's this porn site. They'll shoot any fetish you want. You should make a music video.' But I immediately thought that I wanted to hear them talk, I wanted to see them do, you know, things. Everything. So I just wrote a script wherein it seemed like everything was a fetish, but everything was just insane. There's no sex in it. The purpose was to have these porn-producer companies grapple with some shit. And hopefully it turns out funny, to grapple with scenes that I think are secretly comedy scenes, but they take sincerely as simple, noble porn," he told The AV Club's Josh Modell. "It's a cinematic exquisite corpse. The whole idea was a blind collaboration with people whose job it is, in a really generous and sincere way, to take the script incredibly seriously, because it has a real purpose. Porn has a purpose, and they're trying to serve its purpose. But then I'm just trying to make fun of shit. I tried to leave [casting] wholly up to them. I tried to make it a truly throw-it-in-their-court, let them do whatever they want, because I didn't want to influence anything. There were a couple of the companies that wanted me to choose the girls, and I stayed out of it. I said, 'Whoever's the best actress,' or actor in some cases. But there was one that I couldn't resist saying 'Please use her,' because of her hair. She was the most porn-starry one of them all. She was the one who shook the jar full of meat until it became milk. They were happy to do it. [...] I can't tell if they would just rather her sit and read the Koran on the toilet, or take two dicks in the ass. I don't know which is a better work day for them. [...] The whole point of this is to try to create inadvertent comedy on purpose and get people to interpret something as sincerely as possible. So I played up a little bit of

---

[132] Okay, there is one sequence involving a girl self-penetrating with a wooden spoon, but no one involved seems to be happy about it.

insanity and just told them that they had to stick exactly to the script."[2]

"There is simply no describing how... speechless this one will make you. And it's not just one retarded idea, it's a neverending stream of insanity and prank fetishes that could only have come from a heavily medicated mind. A woman washes herself in water from a jar labelled 'tears of neglected children' then reads from the Koran. Another woman holds a knife to her throat while claiming she is turning British. And so on. Imagine 70-minutes of the following type of scenes, each only lasting a few seconds before switching to the next absurdity and non-sequitur: A man, his wife and daughter (in panties) are sitting on the floor. The man says 'I was born and raised by lesbians. Wanna meet my daddy?' After which he pulls out a large dropper out of his pants. The daughter takes it, says: 'Hi grandpa. Get yourself some gramps.' Rubbing herself with the dropper and then: 'I'm going to kill your dinner with karate...hiyaa!' And this is a moderately insane example amongst over a hundred."[3]

While many critics have tried, it's pointless to try and critique the acting of the individual segments. Each trio soars and fails to different heights and depths. The first segment definitely has the most stereotypical "porny" performances, with the actors stumbling over their absurd lines with little emotion beyond elation upon reaching the end of each sentence. Everyone seems to be doing their best, with the final group seeming to approach things with a little more panache, as far as presentation goes. As several reviewers have pointed out, this last segment may have been produced by people who may have had indie film ambition at one point in their careers, performing the scene as a kind of beat poetry and attempting a more stylish presentation. "That was just ambition. That one was clearly people who were more interested in erotica and putting a doily on their porn. Those people were in California, in Los Angeles. It ran the gamut. The first one was in Minnesota. The second one was in Florida. The third one was in Florida. And the last one was people in porn valley. Basically, if you see this movie, you don't need to travel to those places. You've seen it. You've appreciated it. You've taken it into all your pores and cells, and just go wash and be done with it. Just live your life and die, already. [...] For me, the whole exercise is to try really hard not to care. You know what I mean? It is what it is. What you get back is what you get back. And it's also that there's real variety... I still have no idea what they're thinking, you know? Even if they're really in on it. But there's something when you're sure that they've chosen not to think, that is fun."[4]

However, Chatman is insistent that this was never meant to be exploitation of underprivileged porn actors. "[In some cases,] I felt they were exploiting me, for one, because I was so creeped-out by everything. But I don't know. I was just fascinated by the exploitation of it all. [...] I hope it doesn't come off entirely as making fun of people who don't know what they're doing. I just hope that the context is shifted, because I don't know who's gonna get it. The second group of actors, they look incredibly healthy and educated and together. I'm serious. Their house, or whatever house they used, is really nice. It's way better than my place. There's obviously some laughing at people. But hopefully, at least for me, you're watching people grapple with something, but you sympathize, you identify with the person trying to grapple. You know what I mean? So if you're a dick, this movie is mean, but if you're a decent person, fuck you, this is a good movie. [...] I was trying to make an accidentally terrible movie on purpose, but I fucked up and made a brilliant piece of cinema that will change the way we breathe and the atoms in the air."[5]

"Baby, I'm going to come so fast, the babies we make are already in this morning's obituaries."

As reviewer John Gholson pointed out, *Final Flesh* is an extension of the themes Chatman explored in *Wonder Showzen*, only instead of literal cloth-and-plastic puppets, this time around, the puppets are human, creating, "in his own words, "a seventy-two minute punchline" [...] Along the way, Chatman explores his darkest fears, many of them the same themes that propelled Wonder Showzen—the finality of death, the purpose of God, the crumbling of the American family, and Chatman's unusual, terrified respect for nature. It's next-to-impossible to take any of those concepts seriously here, through the wooden, mealy-mouthed mumbles of a naked porno chick who has no idea what it is she's even saying. I guess that reveals some of what makes Chatman tick, that by tempering his hopeless fears with accidental (oftentimes embarrassing) comedy, it's easier for us all to digest. It's harder to dwell on how we're all doomed to die the moment we're born, when a bimbo is pulling an entire raw steak out of her panties for no discernible reason. Chatman is a skilled surrealist, juxtaposing images and thoughts to create a comedy nightmare that manages to feel familiar, even through all of its absurdity. While *Final Flesh* may be a jaw-dropping trainwreck when it comes to filmmaking fundamentals (in one segment, you can hear the director call action before every shot), the concept makes it a must-see,

This frame grab is as representative of the film as anything else. Copyright Vernon Chatman. Don't sue me.

especially for open-minded viewers. It's a one-of-a-kind film that probably deserves to stay that way, because, for what it is, it's perfect."[6]

As far as experimental filmmaking goes, *Final Flesh* is both fun and fascinating for about an hour. Midway through the third sequence, the presentation starts to become both repetitious and a little tedious. Chatman's insistence that the movie is not meant to be at the expense of the actors, that claim begins to strain credulity, particularly when the technical difficulties become more blatant—shouts of "Action" and "Cut" become more prevalent, boom shadows and light stands have increasingly lengthy cameos. Yet, if Chatman had acted as the film's "director", the final product would have a much different tone, perhaps more mean spirited or even farcical—if that term can be applied derogatorily against a project that exists because of pure moxy on the part of people more attuned to more physical activity.

In terms of an ambitious experiment, *Final Flesh* succeeds, following in the neat footsteps of Rinse Dream when it comes to giving pornography and nudity an existential gravitas. The entertainment value, however, is delivered in diminishing returns. But even that may be part of Chatman's intention. After the initial schadenfreude wears off, the viewer is left feeling uncomfortable, if not a little bit sorry for those involved, particularly those completely out of their depth but forging ahead regardless. Maybe the self-hating introspection that comes over you before the end is the prize at the end of Chatman's Cracker Jack box.

Now if none of the above bothers you, by all means, seek out *Final Flesh*. It's worth checking out regardless, even if it does become an endurance test of sorts. That being said, good luck checking it out, as the only existing "official" DVD (from Drag City, the company that brought you Harmony Korine's *Trash Humpers*) is out of print and listed on Amazon for over $200. And while it is indeed great fun, cheaper fun can be had.

"All of the molecules in my body are screaming in agony. But there are three writhing in ecstasy. Here's one on my thumb bone."

NOTES

[1] Modell, Josh. 2009. "Vernon Chatman and John Lee of Xavier: Renegade Angel." The A.V. Club. February 12. http://www.avclub.com/article/vernon-chatman-and-john-lee-of-ixavier-renegade-an-23741

[2] Ibid.

[3] Toledano, Zev. "Final Flesh." The Worldwide Celluloid Massacre. thelastexit.net/cinema/main.html#Final%20Flesh

[4] Modell, Josh. 2010. "Vernon Chatman." The A.V. Club.

[5] Ibid.

[6] Gholson, John. 2010. "Review: Final Flesh." Moviefone.com. July 2. news.moviefone.com/2010/07/02/review-final-flesh/

GLORIA (1980)

"I'd do anything for you, Jeri, but I can't take [your children]. I hate kids. Especially yours."

Today John Cassavettes seems to be known as either one of two men: the Hollywood tough-guy actor of *The Dirty Dozen*, or the borderline-avant guard creator of such challenging studies of the human condition as *Mikey and Nicky* and *A Woman Under the Influence*. While his highly-scripted movies seem improvisational thanks to his unique directing style, making them darlings of "serious" film scholars, they were so far from being considered commercially viable by Hollywood that they were almost considered a different species of thing all together. Therefore, in order to raise the funds for these personal explorations, Cassavettes took work when it was offered and even then he wasn't always successful. Between 1977 and 1984, for example, Cassavettes attempted to finance a number of projects by accepting roles in such disparate films as Brian DePalma's *The Fury*, an adaptation of Brian Clark's euthanasia stage play *Who's Life Is It Anyway?*, and the inarguably trashy B-monster movie *The Incubus*.

In 1980, he wrote what he considered to be a simple pot-boiler for the sake of a direct studio sale. Originally intended for MGM's meal ticket Ricky Schroeder[133], mob-moll-on-the-run-with-child screenplay *Gloria* ultimately wound up at Columbia Pictures. Having written the title role for his wife, Gena Rowlands, Columbia slouched toward the opportunity but only under the condition that Cassavettes also direct. Overnight, the director's intended sell-off script became his responsibility. Even today, the resulting movie remains an odd duck in his filmography.

Jack Dawn (surprise appearance by Buck Henry[134]) is a mob accountant whose off-hand

<hr />

[133] Newt Dobbs in *Lonesome Dove* (1989).

[134] Co-Creator, with Mel Brooks, of *Get Smart!* Nominated for Academy Awards Best Adapted Screenplay for *The Graduate* (1968) and Best Director for *Heaven Can Wait* (1979). But don't hold that against him.

remark to one of his cronies leads to the discovery that he's been skimming from the outfit for years. With a price on their heads, the Dawn family is packing up to leave, hoping to be ahead of the button men coming for them—and if it weren't for the cleaner's unfamiliarity with the neighborhood, their grace period would have been even shorter—when their middle-aged neighbor, Gloria Swenson, runs out of coffee. Jeri Dawn begs her friend to take the kids with her and hide them, and the hard-nosed Gloria reluctantly agrees, leaving with six-year-old Phil (John Adames). Before he goes, Jack gives Phil a little book, referring to it as the Bible. "This is everything I know about everything in the world. It's your future. Always be a man. Be tough. Don't trust anybody." Phil barely arrives at Gloria's apartment before his parents' window explodes out and his father's voice vanishes from the phone.

Stunned—and probably more in need of caffeine than before—Gloria is suddenly responsible for a whole other life. "What do I do with you? What do I do? You're not my family. You're the neighbor's kid. You're probably too young to understand about making a living, but I have a job. I have my own life. My cat…"

With neighbors and cops filing the hallway, Gloria manages to bully her way out of the building with Phil. The kid's only way of dealing with the situation is to heed his father's words and "be a man". Overcompensating, he channels machismo by way of Harvey Keitel, alternately bossing Gloria around and clinging to her out of terror. "Look, I'm trying to tell you something," he tells her at a flophouse hotel room that night, "You're a good kid, Gloria. You ever been in love?" Later he gets stuck in a loop, trying to make sense of things. "I am the man! I am the man. You are not the man. You… you are a stupid person. A pig!"

"You're not the man," she tells him calmly, tired beyond words. "You don't listen. You don't know anything. You're driving me crazy."

It occurs to Gloria just how bad things have become when she realizes that she knows the murderers. Having once been the girlfriend to boss Tony Tenzini, she did time for this relationship. She can't go to the cops—the media has already painted her as Phil's abductor—and she can't go to the crooks. She doesn't even like this kid, but makes her decision when a car rolls up to them on the street. "We're not interested in you, Gloria. We just want the kid and his book." Gloria responds by shooting at them. The car flips and she escapes with Phil on a bus, knowing that she's in it completely now.

This all seems like standard thriller material, maybe better suited for Sharon Stone (who starred in the 1999 remake) than the unconventional Rowlands. But it's Rowlands who makes the journey worth taking. First and foremost, the utter absence of sentimentality raises this above the level of the average kid-com drama. Gloria remains conflicted throughout the film and on several occasions not only entertains the idea of leaving the kid to his own devices, but actually does so at one point. Her crisis of conscience isn't played for laughs either. She doesn't return to save him in a gruff-but-loveable way but in a genuine "what choice do I have?" fatalism. The men she's dealing with aren't big on the negotiations, so in many cases crisis resolution comes at the barrel of her gun.

While Gloria is not nurturing, Phil isn't all that lovable either. Masking his fear behind TV machismo, the little Puerto Rican kid acts like a stunted Freddy Prinze[135] and is frequently obnoxious in a way that only real kids can be. (Fortunately he never sinks to the depths of, say, *Shane*'s [136] Brandon deWilde, who was nominated for an Academy Award for his glass-shattering whine, lazy eye, and Mortimer Snerd overbite. Adames' performance, however, did

---

[135] The up-and-coming comedian and star of TV's *Chico and the Man*. Died in 1977 from a self-inflicted gunshot wound, either as a suicide attempt or a game of Russian roulette, depending on who you talk to. Managed to sire Freddy Prinze, Jr., who found love with *Buffy the Vampire Slayer*'s Sarah Michelle Gellar.

[136] Directed by George Stevens, 1953, starring a long-suffering Alan Ladd. "The final scene, in which the wounded Shane explained to the distraught Joey why he had to leave, was moving for the entire cast and crew except Brandon De Wilde. "Every time Ladd spoke his lines of farewell, De Wilde crossed his eyes and stuck out his tongue. Finally, Ladd called to the boy's father, 'Make that kid stop or I'll beat him over the head with a brick.' De Wilde behaved." https://en.wikipedia.org/wiki/Shane_(film)#cite_note-11

earn him a Worst Supporting Actor Razzie award, tying with Sir Laurence Olivier's whatever-he-was-doing in *The Jazz Singer*.) We believe his phony bravery and his laughably chauvinistic advances. Yeah, Gloria might pack a gun and talk tough, but she's still a girl and needs a man. Right? TV says so! "He don't know the score," he says of a hotel manager who denies them one of the ritzy room. "He sees a dame like you and a guy like me. He don't know." It precisely because he doesn't burst into wailing tears every few seconds—despite the fact that his whole family has been violently murdered—is what keeps us rooting for him. It's probably what keeps Gloria from chucking him into traffic as well.

Despite the winning formula, Columbia started to get cold feet as Gloria reached conclusion. Cassavettes was hardly a box office sure-thing like Friedkin or Scorsese and despite the gritty material, his camera spent more time on characters' faces than on the gun play or set pieces. Cassvettes feared, and for good reason, that the studio might ultimately shelve the film. Fortunately, a well-timed retrospective of his work at the Museum of Modern Art helped to change their mind. It also helped that its screening at the Venice Film Festival resulted in its tying with Louis Malle's *Atlantic City* for the Golden Lion award. "It was television fare as a screenplay but handled by the actors to make it better. It's an adult fairy-tale. And I never pretended it was anything else but fiction. I always thought I understood it. And I was bored because I knew the answer to that picture the minute we began. And that's why I could never be wildly enthusiastic about the picture—because it's so simple. Whereas *Husbands* is not simple, whereas *A Woman Under the Influence* is not simple, *Opening Night* is not simple. You have to think about those pictures." *Cassavetes on Cassavetes*, By John Cassavetes .

Ironically, the same critics who'd savaged his previous movies for being too esoteric now praised Gloria for its mainstream appeal, while his supporters accused him of pandering to a "Hollywood" audience. "For once, his characters aren't all over the map in nonstop dialogue, as they were in *Husbands*, the talkathon he made in 1970 with Peter Falk, Gazzara and himself," wrote Roger Ebert. "*Gloria* is tough, sweet and goofy. […] Well, it's a cute idea for a movie, and maybe that's why they've had this particular idea so often. You start with tough-talking, streetwise gangster types, you hook them up with a little kid, you put them in fear of their lives, and then you milk the situation for poignancy, pathos, excitement, comedy and anything else that turns up. It's the basic situation of *Little Miss Marker*, the Damon Runyon story that has been filmed three times."[1]

(Then there's this from Jonathan Rosenbaum, who reminds me that film criticism is often, by its very nature, an exercise in masturbation: "According to some local scribes, this all takes place in Never Never Land, unlike such alleged *True-Life Adventures as An Unmarried Woman, Manhattan*, and *Kramer vs. Kramer*. I'd argue, on the contrary, that it's merely a fantasy serving different class, race, and temperamental interests, which include separate definitions of what's real or important. Recalling Godard's equations of cinema and voyeurism. I often wonder if "taste" in film criticism is any more than a rationalization of unacknowledged erotic preferences. From this standpoint, *Gloria* gets me off in a way that middle-class chic never could.")[2]

NOTES

[1] Ebert, Roger. 1998. "Review". Roger Ebert.com. January 7. http://www.rogerebert.com/reviews/gloria-1998

[2] Rosenbaum, Jonathan. "Gloria." http://www.jonathanrosenbaum.com/?p=18496

THE GREAT RACE (1965)

February 12, 1908, 11:00 am, seventeen men in six cars took part in a race from New York to Paris, attempting to traverse the globe in 169 days. Facing unfinished infrastructure across three continents, with progress oftentimes measured in feet rather than miles, the six teams faced grueling conditions, hazardous weather, and the barely-tested technology offered by the relatively new internal combustion engine. The trip took them to San Francisco, then by ship to Alaska, after which they traveled to Vladivostok, Siberia, by steamer, in order to cross the Siberian Tundra into Europe. The American Team, headed by George Shuster, an employee of the Thomas Automobile Factor, and the only non-independent interest in the race, was first across the Paris finish line in the Thomas American Flyer, July 30, 1908, having covered approx. 16,700 km, becoming the definitive winner despite the arrival of the German Team having arrived four days earlier (they were penalized by the judges for having shipped their Protos vehicle by railway and bypassing Alaska). "Just doing his job", Shuster was nonetheless victorious in a race covered by traveling journalists, Skipper Williams and George MacAdam, writing for sponsors The New York Times and the Parisian paper, Le Matin.[137]

The Great Race is not necessarily the story of this competition.

At the turn of the 20th Century new mechanical marvels were unveiled on a thrice-daily basis. The motorcar, the aeroplane, the velocipede, the…uh, bumbershoot, and the great hickey-jig. Helming these magnificent vehicles were men with nerves of steel and heads of lead, yielding a brand new profession among the mechanically-inclined and the affable wealthy: the Daredevil! The Daredevils would put on displays of remarkable courage while promoting the latest wheel-mounted terror, engaging in races, stunt spectaculars, wing-walking, barn-storming, and…uh, well, getting injured a great deal. And in 1908, there were no greater daredevil rivals than the Amazing Leslie and the dastardly Professor Fate!

Yes, the Amazing Leslie (Tony Curtis), whose clothes are always clean and whose hair is always perfect! Watch him dangle from a hot air balloon even as Professor Fate (Jack Lemmon) attempts to skewer it in his bicycle-powered Fate Blimp! Watch them test out their rocket-powered rail-cars—as Leslie succeeds and Fate blows himself up. The crowds just love Leslie and revile Fate, failing at all turns to see the villain's obvious superiority. Confronting

---

[137] As detailed in the documentary *The Great Auto Race*. Produced by Michael Hamm/Kerrie Long, Frame 30 Productions Ltd. http://www.thegreatestautorace.com/

each other after yet another contest, Leslie challenges Fate to a race: New York to Paris, overland in specially-designed automobiles (or "auto-mo-beels" in Leslie's vernacular). To be sponsored by the greatest wallets in America! Fate accepts faster than you can say, "I accept!"

The world is agog in anticipation! Within weeks, seven teams have been selected to make the two-thirds-around-the-world journey. But thanks to Fate's slightly-less dastardly assistant, Max Meen (Peter Falk), four cars are sabotaged (as well as, accidentally, The Fate Mobile, "the Hannibal Twin-8"). The race is now closer than ever before it even starts, with Fate and Max, The Leslie Special (with co-pilot and loyal mechanic Hezekiah Sturdy (Keenan Wynn), and a Stanley Steamer helmed by lady journalist (!) and vocal suffragette Maggie DuBois (Natalie Wood). Who will win? Traditional good or bad, nasty evil? Never have the stakes been lower!

The course is set: the drivers will traverse the United States to the Bering Strait, then it's off through Asias Major and Minor, and finally on to the great continent of Europe. Trouble quickly looms in the small border town of Boracho, where outlaw Texas Jack (Larry Storch[138]) is jealously enraged by the attention shown to Leslie by songbird Lilly Olay (Dorothy Provine[139]). A massive saloon brawl ensues, with Jack repeatedly demanding "Everybody give me a little fighting room!"

Meanwhile, Maggie's car has broken down, forcing her to accept a lift from the Amazing Leslie and Hezekiah. Wanting an exclusive with Leslie, and irritated by Hezekiah's bitching about women drivers, she cuffs the mechanic inside a train and sends him back to New York.

Reaching the Bering Strait, the four competitors are forced to share warmth inside the Leslie Special (after an interfering polar bear finds its way into the Hannibal Twin-8). The next morning, Leslie and Fate are horrified to discover that they're adrift on an ice floe.

"Don't say anything," says Leslie to Fate. "I wouldn't want to alarm Miss DuBois."

"I won't say a word," replies Fate. "I'll just wait until the water reaches my upper lip, and then I'm going to mention it to *somebody*!"

In Russia, Hezekiah is waiting for Leslie, who is shocked—shocked, I say!—that Miss DuBois deceived him. He ejects her from the vehicle and she is immediately snatched by Fate, who now finds himself in the lead!

Unfortunately, the next stop on their journey is the troubled little country of Pottsdorf, where the foppish sop of a Crown Prince, Hapnick (also Lemmon) is an exact double of Fate's. Recognizing a scheme when they see it, the even-more-villainous-than-Fate Baron Rolfe von Stuppe (Ross Martin[140]) and General Kuhster (George Macready[141]) kidnap the Prince and force Fate to replace him. But with Max's help, Leslie thwarts the ruse, which leads to a lovely fencing match between Amazing and the Baron. After which, all parties engage in an epic pie fight.[142]

Following the thwarting, the race is down to the wire. Who will win? Leslie or Fate? The answer may surprise you!

Following huge box office successes with *Breakfast at Tiffany's* (1961), and the drama *Days of Wine and Roses* (1962 also starring Lemmon), Blake Edwards[143] directed *The Pink Panther*

---

[138] See *The Monitors* for more Storch goodness.

[139] Provine starred in Lou Costello's last screen appearance (and only solo effort sans Abbott), *The 30 Foot Bride of Candy Rock* (1959).

[140] Forever and always Artemus Gordon on TV's *Wild Wild West*, always effective at undercutting Robert Conrad's inherent smarminess.

[141] "General Paul Mireau", *Paths of Glory* (1957). That famous villainous scar on his cheek is real, incidentally, received when his car crashed on an icy road, throwing him through the windshield.

[142] So epic, as a matter of fact, the scene took three days to film, with a reported 300+ pies used in the sequence. Another report reports that filming was interrupted by a weekend off, and thus many of those crème pies "turned" in the interim. It's also further reported that Edwards was so exasperated by Wood—and vice versa—that he reportedly took great joy in hurling the first desert at his leading actress, nearly knocking her over (as seen on screen).

[143] Born William Blake Crump (1922).

(1963) and its follow-up *A Shot in the Dark* (1964), introducing British madman Peter Sellers to the United States. Soon after, Sellers-fatigue set in and Edwards searched for something new to take his mind off of his Goon-induced PTSD. Over at United Artists, Stanley Kramer was producing and directing an all-star cast in a nation-spanning scavenger hunt comedy titled *It's a Mad, Mad, Mad, Mad World.* Looking for something to rival that, Edwards and screenwriter Alfred A. Ross discovered the Great Auto Race of 1908 and thought it would make for a great live-action cartoon for Warner Brothers. Conceived as a tribute to the silent slapstick comedies of the early Hollywood days, particular in homage to Laurel and Hardy, Edwards and Ross crafted a daffy, sprawling comedy rife with characters who have little parallel in real life. [144] While the race course was exploited for maximum comedy.

Jack Lemmon as Professor Fate and
Tony Curtis as The Amazing Leslie.
Photo copyright Warner Brothers. All Rights Reserved.

"Edwards has been called many things: a 'manipulative sock-bam director' (Manny Farber); 'the last of the traditional sexists' (Stuart Byron); 'post-Hitler, post-Freud, post-sick-joke, with all the sticky sentimentality of electronic music' (an acute assessment by Andrew Sarris in 1968). He has always had his passionate supporters, yet it's not hard to see why his critical and commercial fortunes have been so erratic [...] Edwards is a master of slapstick, a genre that, despite the prestige of the great silent clowns, still rarely gets the respect it deserves; his formal brilliance is also bound up with his use of the Scope frame, meaning that up till the advent of 'letterboxed' DVDs it was impossible for modern home video consumers to get a full sense of his achievement. There's no denying either that his blend of Hollywood gloss and New Age 'sophistication' has its dated aspects—shading at times into old-fogeyism, as with Dudley Moore's gibes at the Beatles in *10* (1979)," wrote Jake Wilson for Bright Lights Film.com. "Factor in Edwards' taste for racial stereotypes, and the clean-scrubbed niceness of his frequent star Julie Andrews, and he begins, indeed, to look like a figure from a bygone age. In fact, he began his directing career at the moment when the system we now call 'classical Hollywood' was nearing collapse; he is one of a handful of auteurs —with Bob Fosse, Sam Peckinpah, Robert Aldrich—who not only survived the wreck but made it the formal and thematic basis for their subsequent work. In the sense film scholars use the term today, Edwards is not a 'classical' director—even if *Wild Rovers* was consciously modelled on Greek tragedy, and equally ancient precedents exist for the picaresque forms of *The Great Race* (1965) or *Skin Deep* (1989). Rather, inconsistency and excess are his trademarks: he burns through genres, smashing them together or pushing them to self-annihilating extremes. This approach is seen at its peak in *The Great Race,* which begins as a nostalgic tribute to the slapstick of Mack

---

[144] Though not based on him, Leslie's wardrobe was likely inspired by that of real life participant in the Greatest Auto Race, G. Bourcier de St. Chaffray, a French aristocrat and white-suited dandy. In order to win the Greatest Auto Race, he reportedly bought up all of the petrol Vladivostock. He still came in third. Maggie DuBois was inspired by the women's suffrage movement and, to their likely chagrin had they been alive, journalists Skipper Williams and George MacAdam. While Fate is likely a relative of Snidley Whiplash.

Sennett before evolving into a parodic dictionary of cinematic forms, taking in the western, the swashbuckler, science fiction—the gadgets of the villainous Professor Fate (Jack Lemmon) are 'steampunk' before the term was coined—and a screwball-style battle of the sexes."[1]

As much as I personally love *The Great Race*, a favorite in the Watt household during my formative years, its structure is unfortunately a progression of diminishing returns. The first act, with Leslie and Fate battling each other in dubious feats of daring-do, and the establishing scenes leading up to the race, is the strongest part of the film. Once the race is underway, the pacing frequently bogs down, until is virtually slams on the brakes (pun intended) upon reaching Pottsdorf. The *Prisoner of Zenda* parody wears thin after a few minutes and continues to drag on long after it should have been resolved. Save for the magnificent sword fight between Curtis and Martin (and the brief scenes of Fate attempting to imitate the hapless Hapnick—in particular a throwaway line where Fate is joined in bed by a dozen puppies, he lifts one, looks into its eyes and tells it, "I hate you.") the Pottsdorf sequence could have been whittled down, or even out, as an unnecessary C-plot. It just delays continuous interaction between Lemmon and the scene-stealing Falk. For far too long in Pottsdorf, we are denied Fate's trademark prelude to disaster: "Push the button, Max!"

What's particularly damning during Pottsdorf is the pie-fight. Though a staple of silent and two-reeler comedies, it feels like a rehash of the saloon brawl, minus Larry Storch. While it stood as the "greatest on-screen pie fight" (at least until the tragically excised sequence from *Dr. Strangelove*), for modern audiences, that's a superlative equal to "the world's greatest water polo bout". Swell idea, but who is it *for*? (Maybe it's just me.)

What makes *The Great Race* so great has less to do with the script and more to do with the delightful actors and the deft little surreal touches Edwards throws in as business. From the animated little gleam in Leslie's teeth when he smiles to the ice flow sequence where Max snaps off a bit of Fate's frozen mustache, the interactions make the stock characters endearing, grounding them as the plot gets more and more strained. Edwards and company are aiming for the cheap seats with the gags and keep them coming (at least until we reach Pottsdorf).

Natalie Wood survives the
"World's Greatest Pie Fight".
Photo copyright Warner Brothers.

It's not that Pottsdorf scuttles *The Great Race*—far from it. But it is indicative of the uneven nature of Edwards' entire filmography. *A Shot in the Dark* is superior to the original *The Pink Panther* because it focuses on Clouseau and not David Niven's Phantom, for example, or the other subplots that the latter wears as an albatross. In later years, say *Darlin' Lili* on, Edwards seemed incapable of sustaining consistency. Personally, I feel that *S.O.B.* is the best of his later career, with a possible runner up from *Victor/Victoria*, but I think *10* has always been overrated, and things like *Skin Deep, Micki + Maude, Blind Date, Sunset* and in particular *A Fine Mess* are all unmitigated disasters. Especially egregious as Edwards was clean and sober at this point in his career, with the full support of (inexplicable) wife Julie Andrews for decades.

As many reviewers over the years have pointed out, Edwards seems to have a problematic relationship with women. While the majority of his films have strong female characters, they are inevitably disseminated into two defining traits: object of desire, long-suffering spouse. In point of fact, those competing traits serve as the plot of many of his films, *10* and *Micki + Maude* in particular. *Blind Date* even jettisons the wife, leaving Kim Bassinger's character existing only as the prize in the capture-the-flag contest between Bruce Willis and John Larroquette.

As Wilson pointed out in his Bright Lights Film article: "Wood, it's worth noting, had a miserable time during the *Great Race* shoot, and her arch performance communicates an uneasy suspicion that her sexuality is being exploited, burlesqued, or both. Andrews, Edwards' wife for forty years and his regular leading lady from *Darling Lili* (1969) onward, serves as a more satisfactory quasi-maternal love object, though her string of films with her husband must stand as one of cinema's more perverse examples of an artist-muse relationship. Plainly, Edwards sought to free his wife from the governessy persona established in *Mary Poppins* (Robert Stevenson, 1964), and *The Sound of Music* (Robert Wise, 1965)—but the aim is pursued with an aggression that remains disconcerting no matter how far she's understood to be in on the joke. If there's something adolescent in Holly's beatnik act as in Maggie's claims of 'emancipation', the characters Andrews plays for Edwards are undeniably adults; yet just for this reason, she serves for him as the ultimate 'straight woman', who needs to be knocked off her pedestal and mussed around a bit. So in the Hollywood satire *S.O.B.* (1981) she's a movie star persuaded to tarnish her squeaky-clean image by flashing her 'boobies' onscreen; in *Victor/Victoria*, she's a struggling cabaret singer who finds success as a mock drag queen, 'a woman pretending to be a man pretending to be a woman'; and in *The Man Who Loved Women* she's an authority figure who 'cures' her anxiety-ridden patient only when he inadvertently gets a peek up her skirt and recognises her as a 'female' no different from the rest."[2] While this is often chalked up to an internal "battle of the sexes", the running theme, repeated time after time in his work, becomes problematic.

Still, the movie's charm is inarguable. Fate is the gentlest of villains, an eternally-frustrated wanna-be genius who can't fathom Leslie's success. His jealousy drives the film and Lemmon owns it. This is Fate's film, not Leslie's, though Curtis never once allows Leslie to be too dull or "perfect". The chemistry of the four leads is also remarkable. The romance between Leslie and Maggie never feels strained, though it does feel obligatory, as they keep up their antagonistic bickering until the very predictable end. (As independent as Maggie is, convention dictates that she fall in love at the end. The fear of the unmarried woman.) What Fate doesn't realize is that Leslie is Bugs Bunny and he's merely Daffy Duck, doomed to failure by his own hubris. Which is just hysterical.

"I have tremendous memories of *The Great Race*, which to this day is one of my favorite films of Jack Lemmon," Lemmon's son Chris told Alex Simon in 2009. "I was about ten or eleven when that film was made, so going to that wonderland was just amazing. I remember riding around in the Fatemobile with Pop. I have memories of Tony Curtis giving me fencing lessons when he was in the famous scene with his shirt off with Ross Martin. So I was there fencing with The Great Leslie. Blake Edwards made golf carts that looked just like all the cars they drove in the race, and he insisted that everyone race to lunch every day from whatever location they were on in the golf carts. So I remember racing in Pop's Fatemobile golf cart against Blake, whose golf cart was, of course, the Pink Panther. That was one of the classic moments of my life because Pop, as you may remember from the book, was a horrible driver. [...] He literally did back a Jag XKE over the back of a parking structure. He took Bill Bixby's old MG-TC and wrapped it around a tree up in the Hollywood Hills. [...] Basically the final line of the book was, he may have been a lousy driver, but boy was he a great actor."[3]

And when asked by Adrian Wooten what of his performances he was most proud of, Curtis responded: "It's easy for me to say *Sweet Smell of Success*, *The Boston Strangler*, *The Defiant Ones*, because the whole attitude is very limited. You're not asked to fill up the screen with idiosyncrasies, you're kept like that. Compared with comedies, where you're open to do anything you want. You can find any kind of trick to do, any kind of action you wanted. So the physical action in a scene would dictate what that scene is and what should be played. As for my favourite performance, I'd say *The Great Race*. I love that movie. That's one of the best fencing sequences ever done in movies. That's one thing I'd try to do in all my movies: I'd find something to do in it where I would match other actors in other movies. That sabre sequence, I tried to match another actor [Ross Martin]—with the sabre, bare-chested. I got a buddy in a bank, he said to me, 'Didn't you ever wear a shirt in your movies?'"[4]

The Great Race has lived particularly well on cable TV and VHS. A now out-of-print bare bones DVD used to be the best source, but our heroes at Warner Brothers Archive have made a lovely Blu-Ray available, complete with a 16-minute promotional documentary produced at the time of release. The whole package makes for a nice time-capsule of Hollywood prestige pictures as well as a little glimpse into the madness of the nineteen-oughts.

Photo copyright Warner Brothers. All Rights Reserved.

NOTES

[1] Wilson, Jake. 2011. "Crazy Dreams: The World Of Blake Edwards." Bright Lights Film.com. January 31. http://brightlightsfilm.com/crazy-dreams-the-world-of-blake-edwards/

[2] Ibid.

[3] Simon, Alex. 2009. "Chris Lemmon Sheds Light On Jack Lemmon: The Man Behind The Magic." The Hollywood Interview Blogspot. June. http://thehollywoodinterview.blogspot.com/2009/06/chris-lemmon-hollywood-interview.html

[4] Wooten, Adrian. 2008. "Tony Curtis." The Guardian. April 23. https://www.theguardian.com/film/2008/apr/23/guardianinterviewsatbfisouthbank

The amorous life
and misadventures
of a virginal young
pinball player...

his Chicks...his Chums
and a host of
assorted weirdos
in all colors.

a STEVE KRANTZ production · produced by STEVE KRANTZ · written and directed by RALPH BAKSHI · an AMERICAN INTERNATIONAL release · color by DeLuxe®

HEAVY TRAFFIC (1973)

Michael Corleone (no relation) is a young budding cartoonist who spends much of his time in a Brooklyn pinball hall, spinning the chrome ball and daydreaming about his life. As the ball careens from flippers to bumpers, lights and sounds filling his vision, we enter his mind. Michael's world is now animated, the people in bright colors against a muted, almost diseased live-action backdrop. Reflecting the ugliness of the trash-strewn city, the people in Michael's life are grotesque caricatures of human beings.

We are introduced first to his parents—Angelo ("Angie") is a put-upon, working-class Italian slob married to Ida, an equally-miserable shrew of a Jewess who keeps an axe hidden somewhere down the front of her threadbare housedress. They fight constantly, violently, spilling marital blood whenever they meet. To Michael, this is all normal.

Unemployed, Michael spends much of his time in a bar trying to woo Carol, the black bartender. To win her affections, he draws cartoons of the bar's patrons, particularly the legless but muscular bouncer, Shorty, who gets around on a wheeled platform, riding the conveyance like a skateboard and hurting people he doesn't like—or who hassle Carol. For her part, Carol believes she's better than all of this, and she's probably right, but like the rest of her acquaintances, she doesn't do much to improve her situation until forced to.

Another regular barfly is an albino transvestite named "Snowflake", who gets off on rough sex, which she acquires by "surprising" paramours with her unexpected male genitalia. After being beaten savagely by one such john, it's Carol who takes the fall for not controlling the situation and is fired by her unctuous boss. Shorty offers to take her in, but she tells the man that she and Michael have a "thing" going and goes home with the young cartoonist.

This imaginary "thing" becomes real and begins a series of comedically-tragic, tragically-comedic situations. First, Angelo's racism bubbles immediately to the surface upon meeting Carol and he throws his son out of his home, "shamed" by his offspring's penchant towards miscegenation (though, of course, not in those words). His attempts to get his virgin son "deflowered" by Rosa, an overweight, alcoholic part-time prostitute are thwarted by Michael resisting the rape, as well as Ida violently interfering once again.

Following this, Michael and Carol move in together and try to save enough money to go to California. He gets her a job as a taxi dancer by claiming she's the "fourth Andrews sister" ("they kept her in the back") and pitches a comic book idea to a dying executive. Since the idea involves God being shot to death, the executive doesn't live through the pitch. (Who hasn't been there?) Meanwhile, a single flash of her panties gives another old man a heart attack, so Carol is fired from her new job. As for Angie, so distraught over his son's betrayal, he seeks permission from the Godfather to put out a hit on Michael. The Godfather refuses—bad idea to mix business with personal. Undeterred, Angie takes the streets to find someone who will rub out his son.

Desperate for money, Michael and Carol turn to crime. Carol lures a rich businessman back to her apartment where Michael beats him to death with a lead pipe. This final transaction earns his demise—Shorty wheels around a corner and fires a bullet into Michael's head. The

camera follows the bullet in ghastly slow motion as it tears the young man's head apart while the nightmare of his life flashes in a cycle of grotesqueries and psychedelic madness.

Back in the real world, the pinball machine tilts and the "real" Michael trashes it. As he storms out of the arcade, he runs into the "real" Carol on the street. After

Lobby card featuring Carol and Michael. All images courtesy Ralph Bakshi.

some friction, the pair's unmistakable chemistry clicks and they walk off together through a much nicer part of New York.

"Bakshi was born on October 29, 1938; his father was a Russian immigrant who worked in a sheet-metal factory, his mother worked in the garment district. He has one older sister. Brownsville was not exactly fertile soil for a budding artist, and in Bakshi's case, the urge to draw was late in coming. In his adolescence, he remembers, 'it was the usual bullshit—guys, gangs, basketball, broads. I was playing the part, with my blackjack and things, and whatever the guys were doing, I was doing. I went to Thomas Jefferson High School, and one day, I was walking around, really depressed, I don't know why. I got a lot of girls, my hair's combed back in a d.a[145]. ... The academic thing was okay; I was able to skin by without doing much work, so that was cool. I was walking on the second floor and there were some drawings up, by kids in the senior class, that had all gotten blue medals and green medals and red medals. I just looked at them and I said, man, I can do better than that. Mind you, I had never drawn in my life. Sometimes my ego is unreal." It was the principal of Thomas Jefferson that stepped in and saved Bakshi from a life of mundane crime. "I went to his office the next day, and he tells me I'm nothing, I'll never be anything, I'm a typical hoodlum, etc. He told me there was nothing I could do, and I said, bullshit, I can draw. He said, 'If you can draw, you don't belong in this school, and we'd like to get rid of you anyhow. There's a school uptown called the School of Industrial Art that takes guys like you.' The School of Industrial Art started in the eighth grade; it was a vocational school, but it was highly specialized training. So, if you were a really good

---

[145] "Duck's ass."

artist, you could leave junior high school to go there. The last chance to get in was coming up; you had to take a test. I got very excited—something really hit my head. I almost started to tremble. I couldn't explain it. I went up the next day to the principal with my cards saying I was allowed to take this test. There were about thirty kids in this auditorium, all latecomers like me for various reasons. There was this model up there, and the test was that you had to draw the model in different poses. Out of the thirty kids, they took ten, and I was one of the ten.""[1]

Ralph Bakshi first met animation producer Steve Krantz on the ill-fated Canadian television program, *Rocket Robin Hood*, produced by Trillium Productions, a division of Al Guest's company, The Guest Group. Unbeknownst to Bakshi, hired to replace Krantz-fired supervising animator Shamus Culane, Krantz and Guest were in the middle of a bitter lawsuit that almost landed Bakshi in jail over "misappropriated" animation and art sheets. This should have been Ralph's first red flag against working with Krantz and his Krantz Films, but hindsight will always be, as they say, like staring backwards out of your ass.

With Krantz Films, Bakshi directed the notorious *Fritz the Cat*, the world's first X-Rated animated feature film, based on the popular comic book drawn by the irascible Robert Crumb. Crumb's hatred of the final product—and of Bakshi—became the stuff of legends, but the film broke box office records. With *Fritz* bringing in big bucks, Bakshi was free to write his own ticket. Unsatisfied with the world of funny animals, he wanted to tell a real story, with "humans fucking". To that end he revisited *Heavy Traffic*, a film previously rejected by Krantz as being too shocking for investors. Now that *Fritz* had folks championing his vision, Ralph set out to make his most personal film, if not particularly autobiographical as some critics have read into the narrative.

A native of Brooklyn neighborhoods, the Jewish Bakshi grew up among the predominantly black urban poor and his upbringing became as much a part of him as his love of art. But Bakshi's view of the world was hyper-real, with the New York of the '50s and '60s very much that of Burroughs, Bukowski, and particularly Hubert Selby, Jr.: a nightmarish landscape of poverty, drugs, prostitution, mobsters, gangsters, and grotesqueries of all ethnicities. With a pitch-black sense of humor, Bakshi's penchant was to make all that was ugly even worse in his depictions. Starting with *Traffic*, critics leveled accusations against him of racism against blacks, Jews, and Italians, glorification of violence, homophobia, and unforgivable sexism. To Ralph's mind, he was simply painting what he saw. It was all hideous to the point of absurdity. Nothing was beneath contempt and, therefore, beneath mockery.

While not as biting or savage as his follow-up, *Coonskin*[146], *Heavy Traffic* was a shock even to those who'd accepted the unconventional *Fritz the Cat*, which put an undeniable spike in the heart of the Disney-influenced public idea of "animation". *Fritz* was an awakening slap that got mainstream attention and put a spotlight on the burgeoning counterculture. *Heavy Traffic* was a bottle broken across the faces of even the most open-minded.

Scatological, inappropriate, violent—"uncomfortable" isn't a strong enough word for the emotions evoked by Bakshi's first "original" feature (i.e., not based on an existing property, like *Fritz*). "Terrifucking"? "Absurdifying"? (The first time I viewed it, probably at a much too-young of an age, the friend I was with explained that he'd felt like his "soul had been kicked in the balls".) Nothing is taboo or off-limits for Ralph and it's only the rubbery ink-and-paint bodies of the characters that allow us to see their shreds of humanity. Angie, the arguable villain of the film, is a shattered man who can't even remember what his dreams used to be. His racism is really the culmination of a lifetime of disappointments and his rage and shame in his son has little—if nothing—to do with Carol's skin color. It's just the final sociological slap to a castrated working-class man who can't bear to face his peers any longer. Carol's independence, which attracts Michael instantly, repels Angelo just as quickly. The "uppity nigger" one-upping him is the final straw as his ego hits rock bottom but still keeps digging.

Ida, perhaps once beautiful before shackled to this proto-Homer Simpson, lives for her

---

[146] See *Fervid Filmmaking* for more info.

son and for her husband's death. Happiness isn't even a concept that fits in her worldview. There's only "another goddamned fucking day" to live through.

On the other hand, while Michael is accepting of all races, he's also blinded by his youthful naiveté, allowing for flexible situational ethics and the immortality that comes with being in your early 20s. Maybe one day he *could* become a successful cartoonist, but not unless he plays by at least *some* of the rules. And even so, there's no guarantee that a sudden, horrible death isn't just around the corner. Something we all try not to think about.

"Ralph Bakshi's second animated feature (precipitated by a split with producer Steve Krantz, which would only be fully realized after the film's release) is, like *Fritz the Cat*, a tale of sex and drugs," wrote Jerry Beck (a little reductively). "The film presents a gritty, often chaotic view of a New York populated by Mafiosi, prostitutes, transvestites, and feckless young thugs (running themes in Bakshi's films; the Godfather here is essentially a warm-up for the even more grotesque creature in Bakshi's next movie, *Coonskin*). Characters stream in and out of Michael's life, with his squabbling Italian gangster mother and shrewish Jewish mother as focal points. A sequence involving an eccentric pigeon-chasing black man, Crazy Moe (voiced by playwright Charles Gordone, also used in *Coonskin*) is surprisingly philosophical, beneath the vulgarity. As with Fritz, Bakshi used a mixture of New York [animation] veterans (Martin Taras and Nicholas Tafuri), Hollywood veterans (Lloyd Vaughan, Irv Spence), and relative up-and-comers (including Milt Gray and Mark Kausler, the latter animating a rough-hewn

Ida reacts appropriately when Angie suggest Rosa deflower Michael. Image courtesy Ralph Bakshi.

adaptation of the song "Maybelline"). As with most of Bakshi's other films, the subject matter and approach to storytelling can be difficult for viewers to accept. Sequences such as a pitch for a comic book in which God is shot to death, leaving an aging publisher in shock, were and are undoubtedly a change from what one expects in animation, and with a certain intellectual point beyond the titillation and revulsion."[2]

To facilitate Bakshi's vision for the film, Krantz sought out a financier sympathetic towards artists and their temperaments. Failing that, he contacted the ingenious b-movie maven, Samuel Z. Arkoff. For his part, Arkoff was completely open to the idea, not only from an artistic standpoint, but also after viewing *Fritz*'s box office take, and gave Bakshi full reign.

For Ralph, the idea of melding animation with live-action was elating. "'I was ecstatic,' Ralph remembers. 'I got to pull a bunch of tricks that I couldn't do on *Fritz*. Instead of tracing photographs, we used actual photographs for the backgrounds, actual pieces of live-action, and real humans instead of animals fucking. It's exactly what I wanted to make—and because of the success of *Fritz*, I had some respect. Sam Arkoff said, 'It's Ralph's film!'"

While the imagined adventure Michael embarks may seem incongruous by the end—or worse, prophetic—Bakshi's use of the pinball machine as a metaphor for life's arbitrary whims was the unifying element. "The two flippers at the bottom of the board are the only controlled element—that's *your* influence over the universe. Once the ball is whacked, it goes careening through a gaggle of obstacles—bells, gates, chutes—sometimes dodging but mostly colliding. Left. Up. Sideways. To the right. Diagonal. Then flushed into the gutter. To Ralph, that's fate—once you wake up in the morning and walk out the door, anything can happen. Anything. Sometimes you get the high score, other times you have to feed in another quarter. 'You never really know what direction you're gonna get pulled or pushed in,' he says."[3]

To push boundaries, Ralph insisted that the fantastic be presented with a realistic undertone, which meant photographic backgrounds—the prostitutes cat-calling Michael on the street are real streetwalkers trying to attract the attention of the weird dudes with the hand-held cameras trolling the boulevard—omnipresent piles of trash, incomprehensible street scholars, and ad-libbed material. For the elastic, violent characters to exist in this world, their voices needed to be authentic.

With Arkoff's blessing, Ralph also allowed innovation among his animators. Styles meshed and conflicted within the same shots. "Another of Ralph's innovations can be seen in such free-bodied moment like the Mark Kausler-animated "Maybelline" sequence. As the Chuck Berry tune begins, the film shifts from a full-color shot of Michael to a nearly black-and-white montage—a window to Michael's active imagination. It chugs at only a few frames per second; pencil lines are still visible under the marker drawings. It's rough, but totally intentional "Ralph is very unusual in this business," explains Barry Jackson, who started painting backgrounds for Ralph on *The Lord of the Rings* (1978). "He sees what the artist does as both 'art' and part of the production. Look at the 'Maybelline' sequence. Who else does that?' [...] As far as Ralph is concerned, there are no rules. No formula. No punches are pulled. The scenes of domestic violence between Angie and Ida prove just that—Ida shoves Angie into the oven, Ida attacks him with an axe that she keeps tucked away in her garter, and Angie pummels her clear off the balcony onto a clothesline. Yeah, it's brutal, but Ralph was just 'drawing what most people would like to do when they're out of their head with rage.' In parts, it parallels Ralph's hazardous relationship with Krantz. They were stuck in a corrosive marriage."[4]

Midway through production, Bakshi and Krantz found themselves at odds over *Fritz's* success. While Krantz insisted that the box office numbers were inflated, that there was no income due to the red-tape and creative accounting from Paramount, he had no trouble flaunting new expensive cars, clothes, and mansions in front of his lesser-paid employees. With Bakshi owed an untold amount of money, his disillusionment with Krantz grew and he began seeking new venues in which to create, before Traffic was even finished. After overhearing a conversation between Bakshi and producer Albert Ruddy, regarding an idea Ralph had for an "Uncle Remus" update then-called *Harlem Nights*, an enraged Krantz locked Bakshi out of his studio and tried to replace him. According to Bakshi, Krantz was convinced that *he* was the genius behind his animations, just as he believed that it was Walt Disney who provided the creativity and held the whip. Reportedly, the first person he called to replace Ralph and complete *Traffic* was Warner Brothers' superstar Chuck Jones. Quickly, Arkoff intervened and threatened to pull financing unless Bakshi was re-instated.

Ultimately, despite intense negotiations by both Bakshi and Krantz, the MPAA slapped an X-Rating onto the "dangerous" cartoon, limiting its exhibition options. Ultimately, it didn't matter. Among critics, *Heavy Traffic* was considered one of the best films of 1973, sharing that title with *American Graffiti, Mean Streets,* and *Last Tango in Paris.*

"In the glass top of a pinball machine the figures start to materialize, like emanations from the mind of a player obsessed with a game that can only end in "TILT." They strut, creep, hobble out into the squalid streets—these characters whose passing miseries become the substance of Heavy Traffic, Ralph Bakshi's animated movie, a cruel, funny, heartbreaking love note to a city kept alive by its freaks, and always, always dying," wrote Roger Greenspun for the NY Times. "Bakshi's subject is really the city, New York City, the sum of his many characters' lives, and yet desolate, depopulated. Generally it looks as if news of some impending disaster had reached everybody in time to leave New York deserted—except for the creatures in the movie, who live together in the shadow of a doom they don't understand but somehow express. At one point Michael goes to the movies, and he sits utterly alone in a cavernous Broadway theater while on the screen, in actual film clips, Harlow stars with Gable in *Red Dust.* It's like always being haunted by the ghost of yourself, a familiar, unshakable terror."[5]

Predictably, accusations of racism were leveled upon release. Though nowhere near the heights of hysteria reached by The Reverend Al Sharpton's condemnation of *Coonskin, Heavy Traffic* received its own share of indignation, and not without reason. Most critics contend that Bakshi is an equal-opportunity offender, his caricatures always get him into trouble. In the case of *Traffic*, the one character that continues to make people squeamish today is that of Carol.

Like Will Eisner's Spirit sidekick, Ebony White, Carol is a product of her time, when women in general and black women specifically began to empower themselves. Carol is sassy, removed from the big-lipped minstrel designs of some of the other denizens-of-color, but no less problematic for modern-day white guilt America. "She's a living embodiment of the soul-sistah archetype: brash, sassy, vulgar, unabashedly sexual. She has the spit-fire tongue and voluptuous figure of a classic Blaxploitation heroine. (Also a set of permanently high-beaming titties.) Stereotype or not, Carole is a total fox, the Venus de Milo of ass-cleavage. She has a mouth on her, and a brain in her head; it's easy to see why Michael falls for her. Okay, yeah, I'm in love with a cartoon. What of it, jive-ass honkey muhfucka?"[6]

"One standout segment illustrating some of Michael's story ideas relates a post-apocalyptic fable about Mother Pile, a garbage heap literally fucked into sentience by a sex-starved survivor type," wrote Roger Wilkins in his review of Shout Factory's bare bones Blu-Ray release. "The legend continues with Wanda the Last, the sole remaining human female, who gets scooped up by the *prima noctis* prerogative of the Big Guy Upstairs. (Their relationship gives the term "second coming" a whole new spin). If only Bakshi's later foray into fantasy, the woe-begotten *Wizards*, possessed even an ounce of this sequence's black humor and unabashed irreverence. Elsewhere, Bakshi's battering-ram subtle use of racial caricature—never more trenchant than in the bitter beleaguered battles between Michael's Italian father and Jewish mother—paves the way for the relatively more nuanced handling of this brand of material in *Coonskin*."[7]

Despite its poisonous X-Rating, *Heavy Traffic* did well at the box office, attracting as much acclaim as derision and, this time, without having to suffer an outraged, impossible-to-please underground cartoonist's attacks. In many ways, it furthered Bakshi's credentials among the undergrounds, attracting (albeit short-lived) friendships with folks like Vaughn Bode and Gilbert Shelton, giving the still-not-yet-called-that "counterculture" some much-needed positive press. *Traffic*'s achievement meant that Bakshi became the first—and to date, only—director to have back-to-back X-rated animated successes.

Again, however, to modern eyes, Bakshi's work comes saddled with decades of controversy that overshadows the groundbreaking work in animation, social satire, and racial attititudes. His work, *Coonskin* and *Traffic* in particular, often seem to be prefaced by back-peddling and pre-emptive apologies from white-guilt-ridden reviewers of which I count myself among. We're as much a product of our times as Ralph was. Sometimes it's difficult for the two to meet.

An R-rated version was released in a Region 1 VHS and DVD by MGM Home Entertainment on 1999. On July 16, 2013, Shout Factory and MGM released an uncut *Heavy Traffic* on Blu-ray for its 40th anniversary.

NOTES

[1] Barrier, Michael. "FUNNYWORLD REVISITED: The Filming of Fritz the Cat, Part One". Reprinted from Funnyworld No. 14, Spring 1972. Archived: michaelbarrier.com/Funnyworld/FritzPartOne/FritzTwo.htm

[2] Beck, Jerry. "The Animated Movie Guide." Chicago Review Press; 1st edition (October 28, 2005). P. 87

[3] McDonnell, Chris (2008). "*Heavy Traffic*".*Unfiltered: The Complete Ralph Bakshi*. Universe Publishing. pp. 89

[4] Ibid

[5] Greenspun, Roger. 1973. "Heavy Traffic." New York Times. August 9.
http://www.nytimes.com/movie/review?res=EE05E7DF173EE76BBC4153DFBE668388669EDE

[6] McIntyre, Ken. "Heavy Traffic". Movies About Girls.com. Monday, March 7, 2011.
http://www.moviesaboutgirls.com/2011/03/heavy-traffic-1973.html

[7] Wilkins, Budd. 2013. "Heavy Traffic Blu-Ray review." Slant Magazine. JULY 18, 2013.
http://www.slantmagazine.com/dvd/review/heavy-traffic

Photo courtesy Ralph and Liz Bakshi

RALPH BAKSHI INTERVIEW

In 2008, I pestered Ralph Bakshi into a phone interview, ostensibly for *Film Threat*, but also for a book I'd been planning (for a publisher which shall remain nameless), focusing on "Movie Outlaws". Other marks...er, *subjects* included director William Richert and stunt woman Jasi Cotton Lanier. This is the first time this interview has appeared in print anywhere. This interview appears here verbatim, with the only editing done for clarity. This is Ralph in his own words, off-the-cuff and conversational. We bounce around a bit, though truthfully, I didn't have to say very much.

Heavy Traffic grew out of the success of Fritz the Cat (1972), but you were fought quite a bit by producer Steve Krantz. Following Traffic, you were fought by producers on Coonskin (1975) and Hey Good Lookin' (1975)[147]. *You fought every step of the way to get your films seen.*

I'm not going to take a heroic stance. It was very hard on me and the family and it's always a surprise when it happens. There were so many difficulties along the way but I was just trying to make the film that I wanted to do. The thing that kept me going wasn't any sort of hatred of these people, I just wanted to make as much of the film in my way as I possibly could. And I really didn't think there would be another film. Everything I couldn't do on *Fritz* I tried to do on *Traffic*. I never thought there would be another film after *Fritz* and I never thought there would be another film after traffic. Because in those days animation was not a medium that people respected or loved other than Disney. Because when Disney released the film people went but they stopped going in the '70s. So animation really wasn't a big deal financially. The studios didn't care about it. Studios executives didn't care about it. And

---

[147] Unreleased until 1982.

everybody I ever worked with thought I was out of my mind and couldn't care less what I was doing. That had the two repercussions: A) that allows me to do things that they had no idea that I was doing, and B) they had no idea how to release the film or they hated the films, they were disgusted by the films so they never got behind the films. So it worked both for me and against me. Very difficult.

I know you started out in the business wanting to be a strip cartoonist but wound up in animation what made you choose that medium and decide to fight for films in animation?

That's a very good question. First of all I'm 71. I grew up on comic strips that were a major medium. This is before computers, of course. Before any easy access to the movies other than the movie theater. Which cost you money to get in. The kind of stuff we have for kids and adults today, from the computers, the DVDs, wasn't available except for comic strips, which was a national entertainment. You know, it took all the stuff from movies and DVDs and blogs and stuff—that was the comics. People used to line up at the newsstand to catch the new addition of what happened to *Dick Tracy* or *Little Orphan Annie*. Today comic strips are virtually dead. During the Golden age of comic strips you have a great cartoonist like Windsor McKay, and *Krazy Kat* and *Terry and the Pirates* of course *Prince Valliant* and *Barney Google*. What I'm saying is comic strips were sensational. I wanted to be a comic strip artist. That was the game. I love comics as a kid. That's what's got me interested I devoured them. I'd eat them for breakfast if I put cream on them, you know? So after high school I got a job in the animations Studio to earn a living. That was a Terrytoons. Sweeping floors, things like that. I don't mean that as a joke. I went in polished cels before they went the cameras, so the animation was clean, dust free, and that was a tough job because you can't get dust off of plastic no matter how hard you try. (Laughs) It was a torture task. Basically if you could hang on doing this you go on to the next step. And then I went on painting cels.

I wanted a job to earn a living. That was very important in the '50s. In other words college wasn't an issue because you couldn't afford to go to college. We were immigrants' sons; there wasn't that kind of money to send us all the college. We don't want to do the work and buy our own cars anyhow.

The one thing about comic strips was that basically you did everything yourself. You wrote it you drew the characters, you designed it. It was a one-man production. Animation wasn't. Animation was a bunch of people collaborating. And that didn't interest me too much. On the other hand as I got more and more involved in animation—I kept moving through Terrytoons, through the company and the jobs so fast, you know, my enthusiasm for the art form over cartooning—love all the animators I love the work and I love that we weren't Disney. I love that we were funky instead of slick. And all of those early things I loved about Terry tunes I ended up hating. Because Disney was king and I hated that—it bored the shit out of me. Disney wasn't—he had nothing. His quality level was sensational, you know what I mean? But the quality overtook with they were making, in other words. It had to be slick and brilliantly animated, but they weren't saying anything. And to cover up on their not saying anything they went all the way over on technique, which is pretty much what they're doing today in a way, with Pixar and stuff. I'm not putting them down, they're great movies, and people love them, but they're not saying anything in the tradition of *Traffic* or *Coonskin* or something. Again with the technique, what they're doing is amazing. Technically.

So I loved Terrytoons because it allowed me to be myself, and honest, and it taught me a lot about—somewhere along the lines I got the impression—what I'm saying to you now, it was a slow learning process. As I talk to you now, at 71, took me years to learn. But I finally learned that what you say is more important than how it's animated. I wasn't animation freak, you know all the guys in the industry gave the animators the idea that if they didn't have Disney's money they couldn't do anything good. But that was an excuse. A total rationalization. I'm serious. My studio, Terrytoons, asked for thirty feet of animation per week[148] from every animator. That was the budget. Thirty feet a week. Disney's budget was two feet a week. You see all the guys were complaining, "How can we do any good work at thirty when Disney's guys are great and they do two?" And I eventually understood that if you had to do anything, [the attitude was] fuck the animation. In other words, do it reasonably well, or do it bad or do it the best you could, but having the idea is important. And that's what I based my whole life on after that. In animation, when I found that I found *the Grail*. In other words, I got very excited. As a young man, I was offered $800,000 total budget to do *Fritz the Cat*. Now at that time, Disney was making animated features for $14 to $15 million, okay? And someone offered me $800,000. If I was normal, I would have turned it down. I said, 'I can do this for $800,000.' Anyone else would've turned it down. But I said 'that's easy', and I did it. And I did it because I didn't place the animation at the level of Disney. I said well listen guys, let's have some fun let's animate Terrytoon style. Let's do thirty feet a week, you know, but let's do *this*. [laughs[149]] Instead of that, you know? And the screaming in the yelling and the fighting began. That's another story

And I'm like that today. Budgets aren't everything. So I grew to love animation, and I got good at it, and comic strips were fading from my mind. I was getting more and more excited about the potential of animation. Especially when I got *Fritz the Cat* out. You know what I loved at Terrytoons? I created *The Mighty Heroes[150]*. Everyone seemed to like it. It seemed to me that animation was easier for me. I never got that good at comic strips. What's funny about comic strips—it was King Features [Syndicate], it was newspaper comic strips, and it was a lie. I only got good at my craft when I didn't have to lie, I could tell the truth about how I felt. All the comic strips were basically bullshit. They were vanilla ice cream. And I realized after a while that you weren't allowed to say anything of any importance. Until [Jules] Feiffer[151] came along, I respected him as an artist because he started to say something. But I was already deep in animation by that time.

Even after Fritz, you struggled with having freedom. Is it safe to say what they wanted was another Fritz, rather than Traffic?

Traffic was my own. What these guys need—these Hollywood guys, the guys that buy and sell the films—is a property. A book, an article. I don't know why. Something original hasn't made it. As far as *Fritz The Cat* goes, which I liked very much, is that it sold 25,000 books at the time. It was a massive best seller. But outside of the underground guys, Crumb wasn't the massive artist that he is today. *Fritz* was just a powerhouse. They printed it big. Big, nice color cover. Black and white inside. It was cheap, so they could do that. I had this book. I flashed the book at the meetings, saying 'these animals are cute'. I really played down the obscenity angles. They went for *Fritz*. They wouldn't have gone for *Traffic*. Krantz wanted me to do *Fritz 2*, after the huge success of *Fritz*. I thought, well, they're gonna do *Fritz 2*[152]. I was going to do *Heavy Traffic* or I was gonna quit.

See, these guys in the industry, they didn't know what I was doing, or what I'd do next. They just cared that they had Ralph Bakshi in the room after *Fritz*. After *Fritz*, I was the boy wonder. And they didn't care what I was going to do. Until they didn't know what to do with it. After a while, I couldn't get stuff past them, but there was a period where I took advantage

---

[148] At peak quality, that would be 480 individual drawings. Even if corners were cut, and you shot every drawing for two frames, that's still 240 separate drawings every week.

[149] Bakshi has a very high-pitched laugh. It's delightful and infectious.

[150] CBS animated series, 1966– 1967.

[151] Jules Feiffer went from working as a "ghost" for Will Eisner's *The Spirit* (while Eisner was off fighting in WWII) to becoming one of the most celebrated political and satirical print cartoonists of all time.

[152] And, after an angry split from Bakshi, Krantz did indeed produce *The Nine Lives of Fritz the Cat (1974, directed by Robert Taylor)*. It isn't nearly as awful as history has painted it, but the design and the animation are all sub-par when compared to Bakshi's *Fritz the Cat*.

He's X rated and animated!

of their stupidity. Their arrogance. I knew what I was doing. When I pitched *Coonskin*, I made it sound much funnier than it was. I didn't discuss the issues. The pitch was very important in those days, particularly when I knew which guys never read screenplays. [laughs] After the pitch, I could write the screenplay I wanted, they'd never read it. Ruddy was running around 'such a funny movie! I'd never heard such a—*The Godfather* in animation! ha ha ha!' That's what sold him. He'd just done *The Godfather*, so putting the Godfather in animation was the funniest thing he'd ever heard. The fact that his sons—"Ha ha! His sons are queers!" Put it together, it's like devastating! That's what a director can do when no one's looking.

Is Heavy Traffic your version of Hubert Selby, Jr.'s Last Exit to Brooklyn? I know you wanted to direct that as a life-action film at one point, and an animated version was discussed.

Selby became a very good friend of mine. We did a couple of screenplays together and I very much wanted to do a live action movie of *Last Exit to Brooklyn*. This was after *Traffic*. He hung around the studio a lot. He thought *Coonskin* was the greatest movie ever made. But Selby taught me a lot. So did Burroughs. Richard Price[153] was a huge Selby fan too. Price wanted me to introduce him to Selby. But *Heavy Traffic* is definitely my *Last Exit to Brooklyn*. Because what Selby taught me was that it was okay to be totally honest.

The main difference seems to be that while Traffic has hope, Last Exit doesn't.

That's very astute. That's… yeah. The difference is—first of all, I loved all the people in *Heavy Traffic*. Even though I may make fun of them and put them down. But I'm very much in love with the city. They have faults and they're shallow and they're stupid. But running through *Traffic* is a love of New York and a love of the characters. And that's what drove me forward. There's a lot of hope. There's also a lot of Jewishness in *Traffic*. A love of the old buildings. I didn't feel a sense of despair that nothing would never work out. I never doubted Michael would have made it because the whole thing is a fantasy. He's definitely in love with Carol and he met her at the end again. She may have been a hooker or whatever. He loved her. She was black—remember that, at that time. Of course it was very anti-religion, all the things that made people crazy. Mixed marriages, or, with Catholics, you can't get divorced. If you have a bad marriage you should be able to get divorced. There's just a little more hope in *Traffic*.

Selby didn't really love the people [in *Last Exit to Brooklyn*]. He may have hated them. Look what he did to that girl. 100 guys fucking gang raped her in that lot.[154] He didn't really care for those people. I'm not putting him down. He just thought they were useless. I didn't think anyone in Traffic was useless.

Both Heavy Traffic and Coonskin are analyses of racism, and both got you into a lot of trouble that prevails to this day.

---

[153] Novelist, best-known for *The Wanderers* (1974), *Clockers* (1992).

[154] *Last Exit to Brooklyn* comprises six separate vignettes. Bakshi is referring to the climax of "Tralala", the story of a young, idealistic part-time prostitute in the titular short story.

Traffic was my life, autobiographical. Those were the people I grew up with. *Coonskin* was a black movie. It wasn't my life. It was me trying to understand how black people lived. So I read all the black literature I could. I had black experiences. But unless you're black, you don't understand. I was a step back, making a picture about black people, and their problems in white America and the people that put them down. And being white, I knew the white attitude of racism against black people and how it's used against them. The cop was no lie; the godfather was no lie. I knew these people and how they despised black people. Now, wrapped around all of that, as a kid I loved the Uncle Remus tales. I loved Br'er Rabbit and Br'er Fox and I loved the language of how it was written. I loved the lyrics, when I could figure out what they were saying. Took me sometimes two or three times to read a page. With that dialect. But I loved it. So I was also doing a sort of a folk tale, using black folk tales and black pop art and black humor and music and talk about that. One of my favorite lines, when a black man attempts to move into an apartment in Brownsville, as soon as he stepped inside everyone left. I mean the whole fucking block! They'd try to get into a better neighborhood and they'd try and they'd try, and eventually some landlord in some building would let them in. And then you'd hear the dialogue: [kvetching] "You let one in, you get two! And you're gonna get three! And I'm moving outta here!" Those were things I knew.

And of course I grew up with certain racist attitudes and I had to check myself on. So in this film, I was really wrestling with my own demons, which I worked out in the end. It wasn't as personal as *Traffic*, it was more intellectual than *Traffic*. More Mark Twain. More funky.

Brother Bear, Brother Fox, and Brother Rabbit, the stars of Coonskin. Photo courtesy Ralph Bakshi.

Every rapper in the world loves *Coonskin. Coonskin's* been screened over the last ten years to standing ovations. Blacks loved the film. They never disliked the film. Ask any black person who's seen it and they'll tell you. Here's the story of *Coonskin*—you're not gonna like it, but here's the story.

During the '70s every studio had—blacks had been trying to break into the studios. And at one point, every studio had to hire a black person to fill a quota, like what they call "affirmative action" now. Now, the original name for *Coonskin* was *Street Fight*. I'd also called it *Harlem Nights*. The working title. *Coonskin* was never on my mind. Albert Ruddy, the producer, changed it to *Coonskin No More* and he asked me if that was okay and I said 'sure'. I made a mistake. I wanted to keep working and I wanted to keep Ruddy happy. It didn't really matter to me. I wasn't thinking about a title at that point.

The picture was finished and we're headed for the Museum of Modern Art, who screened it and said it was the most amazing thing they'd ever seen. They also screened *Traffic*. And *Fritz*. I was like a regular there. [laughs] But before that, this young black executive, nice guy, comes into Al's office and tells us in the meeting that we have to have that we have to change the title. They tested it and it's offensive to black people. Al Ruddy stood up from his desk and told him to go fuck himself. "I don't need anyone telling me what to do!" Etcetera, etcetera. The guy looked at Al and me and just left. And I knew we were in trouble. I looked at Al and I couldn't believe what he'd did.

The next day, we had the screening at the Museum of Modern Art. I flew in for it. Sharpton was there with all these black guys in the back, angry as hell, but they hadn't even seen it. They were just convinced it was racist. Now I always thought that this guy called Sharpton and said 'take care of it'. To this day I believe that. And that's when we had the Museum screening. Now the black guys who were standing in the back with Sharpton, carrying sticks the whole time, Sharpton started walking up the aisle and told the guys to follow and they wouldn't come! They liked the movie. Sharpton was almost in the middle between the back and the front and I'd come up the front, to get to the lectern, answer questions. And I told Sharpton that he was a fucking sell out, that he's a middle-class little shit guy. That his friends liked the film and that he's full of shit! I used those words. The guys in the back said, 'Look, Al, you can go up and kill the guy, or let's go home.'

Now, I'm giving you the short version. There was screaming and yelling. But they left. I left—visibly shaken. I knew we were in trouble. In those days everything [wound up with] demonstrations. The next day, Al Ruddy gets a call from Paramount, the Corps have all the elevators blocked in the Paramount building in New York and none of the executives could come down.

To my "great luck", the guy who bought the film, Frank Yablans[155], who was a tough Jewish guy who stood behind the film and got it released, got fired from Paramount. Not because of the film. He got fired and this other guy, Barry Diller[156], came in. And Barry Diller said 'What's *Coonskin*? Who's Ralph Bakshi? Let's get rid of this mess." Called Ruddy— "What's *Coonskin*?" He didn't want any part of it. He just took over last week! That could be checked out. He didn't release the film! The guys who take over from the guys who get fired never want to touch what they started. The guy who bought *Wizards* got fired before they could release it and Alan Ladd, Jr., bought it. I've had some great luck and I've had some horrible luck when it came to making money to support the studio. We never had enough money it was always touch-and-go.

Al gave it to Bryanston[157], which was a very strange operation. He met those guys while he was making *The Godfather*. I'm not going to say any more. And they released it for a couple of days or so, and that was that. A couple of theaters got smoke-bombed. And then white people, who don't know black people from a hole in the head, especially in those days, didn't want any part of it. Because the minute they heard the word "racist", it automatically was. In those days everything was racist! [laughs] Guys will pat me on the back and tell me I did such a great job. I could show you letters from right wing organizations who wanted me to speak! About how my American rights were being squandered! I'm like a man without a country.

There was an article in a magazine, *Blax Poetic*, who said it was the greatest black movie of all time. But that didn't mean anything because it cost me my studio. It cost me my reputation for a long time. And it cost me a sort of status, that black people would stand up behind me. It reminds me of how the Muslims should stand up, against the way their religion treats women,

---

[155] Producer of *The Godfather* (1972) and *Chinatown* (1974).

[156] For what it's worth, during his tenure at Fox, Diller did greenlight *The Simpsons,* so he does have a legacy.

[157] Bryanston Distributing Company was at the time run by Anthony "Big Tony" Peraino, who was prosecuted by the federal government on an obscenity charge stemming from the production and distribution of the film *Deep Throat.* Their other notable release at the time was Tobe Hooper's *The Texas Chain Saw Massacre*, both rumored to have been financed with mob money.

it's no good. They should really stand up but you don't see that either. Plus, after that, my lawyers and agents thought that I was a racist [now]. They had no idea what I'd done. Very disappointing. My family was threatened. All kinds of things came down. Today that's all gone, but it was very difficult living through it.

No one saw the film.

See, my family in the '40s, 1946, they were immigrants and they were told that if you move into a black ghetto, there were no grocery stores there. There was maybe one general store every five blocks or something. Because white people wouldn't go in there. And you could make a decent living supporting the neighborhood with a general store. Everyone needs to eat—milk, bread, whatever. That sort of thing. So they took their savings and we moved to a black neighborhood and opened a store. They weren't racist, my parents. We serviced the neighborhood and all my friends were black. The crazy thing was that I had to walk 50 blocks to school every day because the schools were segregated. Across the street and a half a block down was the school all my friends went to. But me and my sister, walked the 50 blocks to our school in the white neighborhood. There and back every day. I tried to get into the black school and they wouldn't have me! It caused a furor. My mother took me in one day—"I don't want him walking across the city at night. It's dangerous. We live half a block away!" They wouldn't have it. The black teachers—terrified of this crazy white woman wanting her white son to sit down with everyone else. Think of it!

My father got deathly ill, so we had to go back to New York. But then, my mother wrote everything down in this big book, what people owed, same as when we lived in Brownsville with the Jewish grocery stores. You couldn't pay, you could owe. And everyone loved us. We lived above the store. The Black people loved them. We loved them. Never had any problems with anyone. Never. I learned a lot. Because all my girlfriends were black too.

We used to go to the movies to see black cowboys, black detectives. All these black movies [so-called "Poverty Row productions"]. I'd go back to New York and tell people about all these black movies and nobody knew what the hell I was talking about! They had their own films, made movies for their own theaters. For black theaters. I went into a barber shop once with my mother. Get my hair cut. Guy says—I'll never forget this: "Lady, we don't do white hair." [laughs] That's where *Coonskin* started.

Was Wizards your examination of Judaism?

Yeah. Well… *Wizards* was my fear of the future. Atomic bombs and terrorists. My fear of religion and racism coming back, which you're getting [now] with Muslim [conflict]. It was what Israel meant to me as a Jewish person. And it's about racism and digging up the past to use it again. Which is exactly what's going on now. I'm not down on Muslims—I'm down on racism and terrorism. All the things that were said about Jews, and how they're being treated. And how Israel is being isolated even though everything they do involves the entire planet. It's very similar to Nazi propaganda. That's what *Wizards* was about wrapped around the fantasy elements. I learned from Coonskin to understand temptation to… *Wizards* allowed me to hide stuff. Again, very personal films.

And *Wizards* was made at a hard time. *Coonskin* and *Hey Good Lookin'* made back-to-back but not released. Which was very hard. Didn't think I'd survive it. In the '80s I had a nervous breakdown—probably. I was so fuckin' tired that when the phone rang in the studio I started to shake. I just couldn't take another phone call. No matter what it was, you know. What I'm saying is I was pretty beat up.

You could say that I was heroic, but I'm not. I got the shit kicked out of me. I really did. Got back-stabbed by every studio executive. Movies weren't released. Negatives were given away. It was pretty horrific. Now everybody's buying my films, *Coonskin*'s coming out on DVD. All the films are going on DVD. Originally, *Hey Good Lookin'* was animation over live-action, but after *Coonskin*, they were looking for a reason not to release it. So they told me the live action doesn't work with the animation. So they tore it apart and had me redo it. After eight years, ten years. That was just an excuse. The producer called me and asked if I had the original negative so we could release it, but I don't think [the producer] is still alive. I think I came through the phone and strangled him. [laughs] I told him what I think of him, what he did to my family.

Does the original version of Hey Good Lookin', *with the animation/live-action composite, still exist?*

Warners still has [original *Hey Good Lookin'*] in their vaults. I have whatever was the composite. I had a work print and a mixed track. I never got to the composite. Warners has a rough composite. My wife says, because she likes me, that it was an incredibly great film. It had a black gang and a white gang in it. I had written it right after *Coonskin*, so I was still looking at racism, going down the same block. Just trying to show how these skinny white guys hated black guys. My wife says that it's one of my best films, the way it was. So that hurt. I fought for what I wanted but you pay a certain price. If I hadn't paid that price, I'd be very rich today. I'm not complaining. But it cost me a lot of … the human mind, if the adrenaline kicks in too many times, it's not healthy. I have the same thing that soldiers get coming home from the war. I'm dead serious. I can't take too much pressure and I overreact at the drop of a hat.

Ever since I left Hollywood I was that way.

So that's the story of those films. I thought I'd lost, I thought I'd failed. But all these generations of college kids, and the emails, and the people who continue to find these films is overwhelming to me. I went to this college convention—these, they're eighteen, they're nineteen, they're twenty, all coming over to tell me they'd discovered these films and were absolutely in love with them. And my older generation guys still love them. Now all these movies are on DVD, still being sought after, so I do feel like I succeeded in some degree.

AN EXPRESSION IN ANIMATION FOR THE ADULT IMAGINATION

Ralph Bakshi, creator of "Fritz the Cat," "Heavy Traffic" and "Wizards," brings you the outrageous '50s the way they really were.

I left the business entirely. When I left, I left. I just couldn't do it anymore. I got the shit beat out of me. My family couldn't take it anymore. So it came to a point where I had to choose—they didn't ask me to choose. No one asked me to choose. I had to choose between seven-days-a-week aggravation, not being able to pay the bills to run the business, or the house, or the … which was very difficult. Either leave animation and save my family, or stay and lose them. So I left my animation. I'd done these films.

Does that mean you've given up animation for good?

My favorite film of all time is *La Strada*. When I saw that movie in 1955, still in High School, I was mesmerized. It taught me everything I needed to know. Talk about Selby, you talk about *La Strada*. About what could happen on film. Fellini fell apart after *La Strada* and *Nights of Cabiria*. Everything after was ridiculous. Pretty, but my god! Those two movies from Fellini. I work—I animate, I don't talk about it, I just do it. I'm working on a movie now and it's devastating, but I'm doing it. I do a lot of drawing and painting, which I like. Keeps me kind of sane and gives me something to do. I love drawing so much. But I would like to finish another film, yeah. If somebody came to me with some low budget money, I would probably do it [work with a team out of the house].

You had mentioned in other interviews that entire animated features could now be made by a handful of people—or even one person—sitting at a computer. Is that something exciting to you?

Hell, yes... We discussed earlier, all the excuses the animators make to themselves. They can't do it at that price. Or the studio stopped hiring. Which was actually a thing for a while. They might be getting back into shape, but there was a point where everything was Pixar and Disney laid off all their [traditional] animators. These guys were crying out of a job. I told them honestly—everything I did on *Traffic* with 400 people can be done in one room on the computer! Everything! All those special effects I used to stress about, with the opticals and the shadows, the live-action matting, which was all very difficult in my day, very expensive, you can do on the computer now! Everyone! So guys, what are you crying about? Go to work.

Want to hear a funny story? Young guy comes up to me at the Comic convention, has his wife with him. He said 'I took your advice'. He'd taped my talk. She's now working [full time] while he and his buddies are working on a film! And she's furious with me. She hates my guts! He quit his job because of me. And I'm laughing my head off and I said to her, 'Look, if he's any good, you have a good chance of becoming very rich.' I think she felt a little better after I said that. They could make millions of dollars off this film if he's right. 'Cause he'll own it.

I grew up in a time when directors and their vision was really respected. A lot of good films were made. Producers and studios have total control again. Studios had all the control when I grew up and then some time it moved to where the directors had more of a say. You know, like Marty Scorsese made *Mean Streets*, that kind of thing. A lot of great films were made. Directors had more control. Now it's gone back to the producers and the studios and you don't open your mouth up. The kind of films that have been made today and the money being made is astronomical. Directors are not being bandied about the way they used to. You hear about them, but they never talk out of line. Most of them have sold out and do the studio changes. I would never accept studio notes on any of my films. I'd tell them, "look, you may be right, but then that would be your film. This is *my* film. Doesn't mean that I think you're stupid, or that you're not right, it just doesn't work for me. I can't do it." All the directors take the notes now. You don't go up against... The kind of budget it takes to make a movie, I guess the studios have to have control. $180 million! You know what it costs today to make films? So it's very hard to give the control back to the idiots—the directors and the actors—if you're spending that kind of money. So I don't see it being possible.

I'm saying with the computer and the internet and the streaming movies, I think going direct-to-DVD is the way to go. I'm saying if you drop your bullshit aspirations to be a hundred-billionaire, with your big house with three pools—you gotta understand that everyone in Hollywood is in it for the money. I don't care what your initial reason was to make films. In film school, everyone wants to be a great director and writer, once you get to Hollywood and you see the kind of money being thrown around, all bets are off. That's what they want. But if you give that up, that glory train, and go direct to the DVD, get it on YouTube, god knows what you can do! I'm all for finding a way out of Hollywood. There's a guy I know in Brooklyn, printed his own book about growing up in Brooklyn, he goes on the subway and has to sell 16 books a day [to make a living]. He's sold 35,000 books! I think it's a glorious time!

At the time of this interview, Bakshi had been working sporadically on a brand new project titled *The Last Days of Coney Island*. On February 1, 2013, he launched a Kickstarter campaign to complete the film and it was officially premiered on Vimeo on Ralph Bakshi's 77th birthday on October 29, 2015. Check it out, as well as ample behind-the-scenes video, at http://vimeo.com/lastdaysofconeyisland

HELL IS FOR HEROES (1962)

The Siegfried Line. That was the English name for heavily-guarded stretch of murder running for 390 miles along the borders between France, the Netherlands, and Switzerland. The Germans dubbed it "Westwall", and it was dotted with pillboxes, anti-tank traps known as "dragon's teeth", heavy guns, mines, and mortars. In the fall of 1944, less than 100 American G.I.s held that line for 48 hours awaiting reinforcements. This is the story of the 2nd Line of the 95th Infantry Division, in particular the six men who defended that line.

Squad leader Sergeant Larkin (Harry Guardino) and his men are taking a well-deserved rest behind the lines at Montigny, Meurthe-et-Moselle, France. They've been on the front line for weeks and rumor has it they're heading home. Exhaustion and boredom are displaced by tentative hope. Busying themselves as they wait, scrounger Corby (Bobby Darin) collects looted flatware and offers fountain pens for $7.50 each--$8.00 with ink; Corporal Henshaw (James Coburn) works on a jeep, fixing it until he can figure out what's wrong; Kolinsky (Mike Kellin) writes a letter home; Cumberly (Bill Mullikin) reveals his secret to his unflappable ease: focus on something worse that's happened to you and the present won't seem so bad. Meanwhile, their unofficial camp mascot, Homer Janeczek (Nick Adams), a polish "D.P." ("displaced person"), once again pesters Sgt. Larkin for a uniform so he, too, can "kill Krauts".

Into this camp comes the anti-social Pvt. Reese (Steve McQueen). He carries with him his haunted past along with an M3 submachine "grease gun". Platoon Sgt. Pike (Fess Parker) knew Reese in North Africa. The loner was an excellent soldier but cracked up at his last camp, stealing a jeep and almost running over an officer. It would seem that he can't handle cease fires. A court martial busted him down and got him transferred to the 2nd Line. Camp Captain Loomis (Joseph Hoover[158]) worries that the prospect of the war ending might make Reese even more unstable. Pike

---

[158] "Charlie Hasbrouck" the reporter who printed the legend in *The Man Who Shot Liberty Valance* (1962).

delivers the news to the men that instead of stateside, they're all returning to the front lines, to provide support for the 1st Line, hunkered down at the Siegfried Line. The morning after their arrival, they discover that the 1st was moved out overnight, leaving the undermanned 2nd alone against an unknown number of enemy combatants lurking out there in the woods and hills, a lone pillbox looming over them like a siege tower.

The key to their survival is hiding their thin numbers from the Germans. This means making the noise the Germans would expect from a heavy platoon—patrols, tank maneuvers, chatter. Corby discovers a German microphone hidden beside the camp phone. Like any threatened animal, the 2nd Line has to appear "big."

"Homer" (Nick Adams) and Pvt. Reese (McQueen).
Lobbycard Copyright Paramount Pictures. All Rights Reserved.

The ideas start flowing once PVC Driscoll (Bob Newhart) accidentally rolls up with a requisition of typewriters for another company. Henshaw takes his jeep and modifies the engine to roar and backfire like a tank, then drives it around to make it sound like there are more rolling in. Driscoll has only served the army in a secretarial capacity—"All I've ever done is type!"—and almost blows Reese's head off while fumbling with his rifle's safety. To keep him out of the way, Larkin gives Driscoll the duty of ad libbing into the German mike and lie about the camp's numbers. "Sir...sir, the biggest problem I'm having is with entertainment. We've shown *Road to Morocco* seven times already. The men... well, sir, they know all the lines. No, sir, please, don't send any more men here. I have five men in each foxhole. There's still a war over in Japan, sir. You might send them over there."

When Larkin is killed, command falls to Henshaw, who decides, with Reese, to try and take out the pillbox with explosives. This, however, requires the pair to crawl through a minefield, feeling ahead of them for the three tell-tale wires and mark the spots for the man behind. When this mission fails, Reese finds himself in line for another court martial under Loomis, which will mean the end of his career and freedom. Before that, however, they'll have to join the 1st Line and push forward to take the hill.

Hell is for Heroes was conceived by screenwriter Robert Pirosh. Pirosh was a war hero in his own right, having seen action during the Rhineland and Ardennes campaigns, fought during the Battle of the Bulge and won the Bronze Star. His film career focused on paying tribute to the American infantry, winning an Academy Award for his screenplays for *Battleground* (1949), nominated a second time in 1951 for writing *Go for Broke*, which he also directed. Both films focus on WWII infantry divisions. His original conception for *Hell* was to show a lighter side of vicious, hideous war. According to Bob Newhart, Henshaw originally had a pet duck. Part of his deal for *Hell* was that, like *Go for Broke*, he would direct and Bobby Darin would be the youthful lead. Things changed radically when Steve McQueen was hired. The screenplay was restructured to focus more on Reese, much to the consternation of just about everybody. A predictable head-butting with McQueen caused Pirosh to step down from the directing role, ceding to tough guy filmmaker Don Siegel. Later during filming, Pirosh stepped away from the film entirely.

As directed by Don Siegel, from the new script by Pirosh and Richard Carr, *Hell is for Heroes* is a (predominantly) no-nonsense tale of front line dog faces facing the end of the long war in Europe. Once the 2nd Line arrives at the Line, we're treated to one harrowing sequence after another—the minefield crawl, a forest excursion to hang rock-filled ammo boxes from trees to give the illusion of constant GI patrol, not to mention the final (and I don't say this loosely) hair-raising final push towards the German pillbox. *Hell is for Heroes* isn't shy about its violence, either. One soldier's death is a prolonged scream of "My God!" Another sequence stars Henshaw and his flamethrower, and the horrific results it produces.

While Hollywood churned out dozens of WWII adventures following the war's completion, *Hell is for Heroes* stands out as an unusual entry, not only for its taciturn anti-hero McQueen, but also for its baffling inclusion of Newhart, billed as "Introducing Bob Newhart, The Button-Down Mind", capitalizing on the comedian's breakthrough comedy albums (in fact, *The Button Down Mind of Bob Newhart* was at No. 1 on the charts at the time of his casting). This results in the shoe-horned sequence with Newhart performing what is essentially a protracted version of one of his "telephone" routines.[159] The sequence is funny and sticks around just long enough to give the film some much-needed levity, so it doesn't necessarily seem out of place. However, following the sequence, the mike line is cut and Driscoll has nothing further to do, more or less replaced by the return of Nick Adams' Homer. According to Newhart, again, the telephone bits were originally scripted, but it was up to him to provide the dialogue.

This incongruity didn't go unnoticed by Newhart, incidentally, particularly when his album success started bringing in new and exciting offers, his fee for nightclub work having quadrupled. For days Newhart would approach director Siegel and beg to be killed off.

"On a daily basis, I would pester Don Siegel with suggestions for my previous demise. I was aiming for just the right amount of verisimilitude.

"'Now, Don, in this particular scene, I see that a tank is coming over the hill,' I said one day. 'Maybe—and I'm just offering this up because it could be funny—but maybe I could roll under the tank and get killed.'

"Siegel's reply: 'Bob, you're on the movie until the end.'"[1]

Far from being the only dissatisfied participant, Newhart was in good, if irritable, company. Shooting in California during the height of a long, hot summer, the players were drenched in sweat by the end of each take. McQueen, notoriously difficult to get along with anyway, was angry that his manager agreed to the role without securing a certain price. Darrin, the other egomaniac on board, overheard Siegel say that McQueen was his own worst enemy, and reportedly said, "Not while I'm alive!" Adams, a legendary—if you'll pardon the expression—"star fucker" who hitched his star to

---

[159] My personal favorite of Newhart's is the "Driving Instructor" sketch, where a replacement instructor meets his student for the first time: "Erm, you're Mrs. Webb, is that right?... Oh, I see you've had one lesson already, who was the instructor on that Mrs. Webb?...Mr. Adams... I'm sorry, here it is. Mr. Adams. Just let me read ahead and kind of familiarize myself with the case...Erm, how fast were you going when Mr. Adams jumped from the car?...Sev..., Seventy-five. And, and where was that...? In your driveway... How far had Mr. Adams gotten in the lesson?...Backing out...I see, you were backing out at seventy-five and that's, that's when he jumped.... Did he cover starting the car...? And the other way of stopping...? What's the other way of stopping...? Throwing it in reverse... that's, that would do it, you're right, that would do it..."

Natalie Wood, James Dean, Sal Mineo, and even Elvis Presley, reportedly fought for a larger slice of character pie, which may explain the re-emergence of Homer in the film's final act.[160] Add to all of this an edict from the studios that the production stay within its meager budget and deal the best it can with faulty props and cheap stock footage, *Hell is for Heroes* became more of a mantra than a title.

In the gossip circles, word got around that McQueen and Darin got into a brawl, with "punches thrown". "One well-known actor, who asked to remain anonymous, said at once about the rumor, 'This one could very well be true. I've worked with both Darin and McQueen and, in my humble estimation, they're the hardest guys in the business to work with. They have egos a mile long, they want things done their own way, and they are complicated fellows who can't help bringing problems to any job. I'd say they were bound to clash," reported the *TV Radio Mirror Magazine* in 1961. "Bobby is like McQueen in many ways. He relentlessly pursues his star. He made up his mind to make his career in show business when he was eighteen. 'I set out to become a star at twenty-one and the greatest star of all by twenty-five,' he modestly allows. It is one of the statements that tend to act like dust in the eyes of his fellow performers. But, in his own way, Bobby is a dedicated showman. He is a conscious perfectionist and demands the same of all who work with him. 'He doesn't mind stepping on toes, all in the name of improving a scene or an action,' one technician ruefully points out. This stepping-on-toes naturally resulted in a wave of rumors about a blow-up with Nick Adams, and then the big explosion with McQueen.[161] But, aside from characters and reputations of the principals involved, the heat and the demands of their roles, there seems to be no solid evidence of a feud, fist fights, or anything but the usual tantrums that are an inevitable adjunct to a difficult show. 'Fights? We were too busy dodging rattlesnakes,' snorts Nick. 'We killed seventeen rattlers while we were sweltering in that heat. Naturally, we were not exactly relaxed and cozy.'"[2]

"The unit publicist was fingered for the leaks and was summarily dismissed," wrote Newhart. "Unfortunately, they had the wrong man. It turned out that Nick Adams was trading with the gossipmongers: some dirt from the set in exchange for a splashy item on his next movie. But upon hearing the unit publicist had been fired, Adams felt terribly guilty. I'll never forget the image of Adams chasing the guy's plane down the runway, yelling out: "I'm sorry! I'm sorry!"[3]

"I think something was happening in the ownership. I always suspected that Y. Frank Freeman's son was the person who urged his dad to buy his company [Paramount Pictures]. I got the feeling that the movie side of the business kind of went on—Mr. Freeman approved things, obviously, but by the time I got there, he was not a young man. I think they were just kind of running it as a business, which is sort of unusual. With *Hell is for Heroes*, all of a sudden there was an edict that there would be one or two more days, and that's it. So we didn't finish the script. My scenes that made sense for me to be in the movie were never shot. All of my gut-impact material was

---

[160] One of the more tragically pathetic stories from Hollywood's mid-'60s era, Adams had grown up poor and dreamed of stardom his entire life. Both his looks and talent were middling—okay, but nothing sensational—and to combat this, he rode coattails for a living, following those he saw to be "in power" to the biggest parties and galas. It's rumored he fostered sexual relationships with Dean and Mineo. As offers started to dry up—he went from co-starring in *Rebel without a Cause* in '55 to *Invasion of Astro-Monster* in '65. With his career in a spin, he grew more depressed. On February 7, 1968, he was discovered dead in his home in Beverly Hills, from an apparent overdose of sedatives. There was some speculation—later dismissed—that Adams was murdered because of a Hollywood tell-all book he'd planned to write, outing the homosexual stars of the screen. (Himself included.) In Gavin Lambert's bio of Wood, *Natalie Wood: A Life* (2004), her public relationship with Adams, including an "almost Vegas marriage" was one of the Warner Brothers studio arrangements, in order to hide Adams sexuality from teen audiences.

[161] "Steve always thought of himself as a re-actor, not an actor. I think he got that from John Wayne (laughs). What can I tell you about Steve? (His first wife) Neile used to call him a "male nymphomaniac." (laughs) He had an incredibly dynamic personality. He was like a kid. He said to me one time "Why can't they make a movie about just one guy--me!" (laughs) He even had a script idea about a guy who crashes in the desert, and trying to survive. While we were shooting *Hell is for Heroes*, we were shooting up in Redding, where it was so hot, I mean 110 in the shade. And the studio gave him this convertible. And we'd be driving along the road, and all of the sudden he'd shoot off the road and go tearing through the woods, as fast as he could until he ran into something! So he wore this car out in about a week and a half, and they sent a guy out who said "What the hell happened to this car?!" Steve said "I dunno. It just stopped running." (laughs)— Simon, Alex. 1999. JAMES COBURN: COOL DADDY. Venice Magazine. February. Archived The Hollywood Interview. http://thehollywoodinterview.blogspot.com/2008/02/james-coburn-hollywood-interview.html

at the end of the picture, with incoming troops relieving our group. There was a nice tie-up," Fess Parker told Michael Barrier. "Don Siegel seemed to me to have the old Hollywood mantra down: stick with the money [that is, give the most attention to the highest-paid stars]. He was competent, but as far as his giving me any sort of directions or instructions or help as a director, none. And that's usually the case. There are some people who do try to lead or suggest or something, but most of the time, if the scene works, the good people let you bring what you bring. And if it's obviously wrong, they'll tell you."[4]

Ultimately, the movie's original low budget of $900,000 had grown under Siegel to over a million dollars more. Paramount brass sent down the order that once the final order of film stock ran out, production was over. This goes a long way to explain the abrupt ending—the last desperate push towards the pillbox and the completion of the mission. Then the stark titles: "The End."

For such an unusual little movie, it's more or less fallen into the wayside of movie history. Fortunately it's readily available on both DVD and Netflix.

Mike Kellin as Pvt. Stan Kolinsky, Bobby Darin as Pvt. Dave Corby, Bob Newhart as Pfc. James E. Driscoll.
Lobbycard Copyright Paramount Pictures. All Rights Reserved.

NOTES

[1] Newart, Bob. 2006. "I Shouldn't Even Be Doing This: And Other Things That Strike Me As Funny." Hyperion Books. P. 148-149.

[2] No author cited. "Hell Breaks Loose on Location", TV Radio Mirror Magazine. December 1961. Archived http://www.bobbydarin.net/heroesarticle.html

[3] Newart, Bob. 2006. P. 147-148.

[4] Barrier, Michael. 2004. "Fess Parker: An Interview". Michael Barrier.com December 20. by Michael Barrier. http://www.michaelbarrier.com/Interviews/Parker/interview_fess_parker.htm

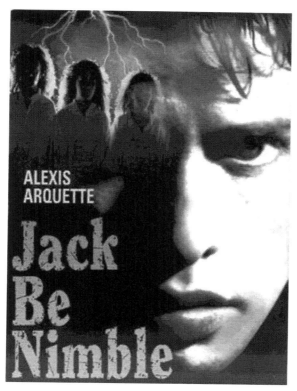

JACK BE NIMBLE (1993)

Young children Jack (Alexis Arquette[162]) and Dora (Sarah Smuts-Kennedy[163]) Sharp are surrendered to an orphanage by their mother and survived by staying close together. However tragedy strikes again as they're separated by the system: Dora is adopted by the nice and kind Birches, Jack is adopted by the strange and cruel Gough family. As the siblings grow, their memories of each other begin to fade, but their psychic connection grows. Their lives parallel in grotesque ways, as the horrors Jack suffers translate to dreams and vision for Dora. Suffering extreme abuse at the hands of the Goughs, Jack's sweet nature twists and deadens. After a severe beating with a length of barbed wire, Jack makes a decision. In metal shop, he builds a strange machine with twirling parts and flashing lights driven by a single candle. Using this dynamic-hypnotism machine, Jack commands his parents to commit bloody suicide.

Free for the first time in his young adult life, he sets out to reunite with Dora in the hopes that they may both track down their birth mother. Dora is hesitant to leave her comfortable life with the older Teddy (Bruno Lawrence[164]) behind, but feels Jack's pain and hopes this quest will brighten the darkness in his heart. Unbeknownst to the pair, Jack's four evil step-sisters are hot on their trail, with their own goal to revenge their parents and put an end to Jack the usurper. Between Jack's murderous impulses and the three-Gough-Girl juggernaut, all of New Zealand is in danger.

"*Jack Be Nimble* was the feature-length debut of New Zealander Garth Maxwell[165]. Maxwell was a promising young talent who debuted with the Cannes Award-winning gay love short *Beyond Gravity*

---

[162] Bride of Chucky (1998)

[163] This Is Not a Love Story (2002)

[164] Actor and musician perhaps best-known for *The Quiet Earth* (1985).

[165] A vet of New Zealand TV, Maxwell is best-known in this country for directing multiple episodes of *Hercules* and *Xena*.

(1989) and went onto the modestly acclaimed polysexual love story *When Love Comes* (1998)," wrote Richard Scheib. "*Jack Be Nimble* gained modest genre acclaim when it came out but leaves much to be desired. As a film, it is so incomprehensible in its random plotting, frequent shifts of tone and jumbled melting pots of incongruous genre elements as to be downright weird. [...] A scene where Bruno Lawrence introduces Sarah Smuts-Kennedy to marigolds under the pillow as a handy source of psychic amplification verges on the laughable. Maxwell compensates somewhat with an occasionally ambitious visual style in the early scenes—a toy clown placed on young Jack's cot with its lips sewn up, the disheveled Gough daughters moving in unison like some ominous chorus of Greek harpies—but eventually he and the film get lost amid the plot incomprehensibilities."[1]

Shot in six weeks in and around Auckland, New Zealand "for a budget of $1.5 million New Zealand (about $750.000 U.S.)"[2] *Jack Be Nimble* premiered at Cannes in 1993. Not so much a "lost" film as it is neglected, Garth Maxwell's *Jack Be Nimble* is an off-putting and disturbing little story about childhood scars carrying pain like a psychic river. The "abused orphan" is a well-worn trope of dark fantasy, a staple of nearly every fairy tale, and the desperate wish of every unhappy child—the idea that somewhere out there in the world is the real mother and/or father who will beg forgiveness and finally make everything better. Even the wonky hypno-machine seems an element of juvenile wish-fulfillment. "'I made one of those, or at least I tried to make one, when I was in my teens.' chuckles Maxwell of the device. 'I used to construct these things with flashing lights and little electric motors which spun pieces around and things sparked and connected. It wasn't specifically for hypnosis. But it made a great noise and had an incredible dramatic effect when I dragged it into the living room and forced my family to look at it with all the lights off.'"[3]

While our sympathies lie with the brutalized Jack, Dora is the audience's first-person entry into the story, and it's her moral outlook that even allows us to forgive the young man for his murderous rages. At the same time, we question if she is "moral" because she was raised with kindness, which would mean that Jack's upbringing makes him "immoral". Maxwell presents this "nature vs. nurture" discussion in hues of nightmarish darkness. Because so much of *Jack Be Nimble* is the internal chaos made external, it's difficult to get a logical foothold on the proceedings.

"A friend of mine told me that he had been whipped with barbed wire as a child," recalls the director. "He mentioned this fairly casually, and it's not the sort of thing you hear and forget. So I wanted to place that into a more accessible story, one that would allow me to experiment cinematically with images, pace and characterization. Also, I wanted to do something that had an impact and expressed some of my anger about the way people are programmed when they grow up-how they are damaged by parents and how they can transcend that and get over it. I know that sounds fairly serious. But to do those sort of things I thought it would be easier to work in a more fertile realm, which is how we got the 'Hansel and Gretel' analogy and the look of the film. We attempted to look away from realism as much as possible into a kind of horrific dark-forest kind of feel."[4]

Just as Scheib indicates above, *Jack Be Nimble* is a narrative mess. A lot of the elements do seem to be incorporated from other stories. Jack's hypno-machine, for example, is utilized once, then is smashed to bits a few scenes later, never to be addressed again. The Gough sisters and their malevolent pursuit of Jack seem to be more a force of nature than characterization—especially as they move in grim unison, a trio assembled into a single being. And their revenge on Jack is both horrifying and appropriate.

As Mark Salisbury wrote in *Fangoria*: "Maxwell is quick to point out that this element is in no way autobiographical. 'I've got one sister and she's absolutely gorgeous. The four in the film are like the manifestation of hideous anonymity. They had these two hellish parents and became the extension of the mother especially, and just move about and wreak havoc. I wanted a really memorable image and also, because there is only one scene where they have anything to say. I wanted them to have a powerful visual impact.' "[5]

Yet, *Jack Be Nimble*'s structure may be less chaos and more dream logic. The entire movie seems to be one extended nightmare, with lapses in logic that still seem organic, even if they're difficult to parse with the "real world". If, perhaps, one were to consider the entire film taking place in Jack's fevered subconscious, the whole is easier to digest. (Of course, this could be a theory driven by a need to justify the messy script, because there's nothing in *Jack Be Nimble* to indicate amateurishness or misstep. There is similar rationalization, for instance, to blame the sluggish pace of *The Magnificent Ambersons* on thoughtless editors and studio execs. How could Orson Welles ever be blamed for that film's clumsiness? We defend the things that bring us happiness, especially when they are, by nature, imperfect.) Maxwell describes the film as a "Hansel and Gretel"-type of allegory, so my interpretation may be close.

"I knew that it was all about atmosphere, and suspense. I wanted a number of set pieces, which had a clearly signaled structure, which could proceed in a measured way, heading towards some unspeakable outcome. Those are the sequences which audiences loved, coupled with the appropriate music. I credit Chris Neal's atonal, surging strings with really supporting the film, becoming a big part of its identity and success. Other genre elements, like human hair—and Sarah had this massive black volume of hair which we used in many ways visually, hair was a real theme, like the farmer's daughters hacking their hair off before they do bloody battle at the climax. Grant Major [Production Designer] introduced me to the Symbolists, and Arnold Bocklin, and we studied his paintings for a sense of brooding landscape, like *Island of the Dead* with those cypresses, which are a very NZ feature too. We wanted it to feel elemental, blood, water, wire, twisted macrocarpas, the sun seen flickering through poplar trees as you drive, but we wanted the film to feel like it wasn't set quite in the present—sometime between the Victorian era, and say the fifties. Wardrobe choices went that way as did choices of cars and props. Keeping the dowdy fairytale aspect tangible."[6]

As far as the performances are concerned, Smuts-Kennedy is very good as the sympathetic Dora, and the Gough sisters are perfectly menacing in their monolithic way, but *Jack Be Nimble* belongs to Alexis Arquette as nimble Jack. Best-known today as the transsexual sibling of David, Patricia, and Roxanna—having transitioned to female 2006[166]—Arquette is perfect in her portrayal of the hopelessly broken protagonist. While it's tempting to project that the actor's troubled gender identity informed his performance, the fact is, it's just a marvelous portrayal of someone beaten down and marginalized exacting the only revenge he can think of. This is a rare "straight" role for Arquette, who is probably best-known for his tragic role as the doomed transvestite "Georgette" in *Last Exit to Brooklyn* (1989) (where he breathes wonderful life into Selby, Jr.'s character from the story "The Queen is Dead"). "I wanted the film to have its best shot, I wanted to work with a really good actor and I wasn't certain I could find that person in New Zealand [.] It required someone who could make the damaged character of Jack compelling. We need to have sympathy and compassion for him even though he is basically a murderer, a very disturbed psychopathic kid. I had seen Alexis in *Last Exit to Brooklyn* and realized he was prepared to take on the kind of roles that weren't necessarily flattering and gave him the opportunity to display his range."[7]

For Arquette, it seemed to be a unique chance to grow as an actor. Prior to (and even following), Arquette was usually cast as a loser or a drug addict. In *Threesome* (1994), his character was basically told to stay in the closet if you wanted to be successful. "I'm the openly gay one. What that film says is, "If you want to be gay and you want to be respected, stay in the closet. Don't let your love be known, don't let your desires be known to anyone. Don't let anyone know you love Stephen Baldwin. But if you're going to be openly gay, you're going to have to be a mincing, obnoxious queen." That's how I was directed, and I fought him all the way. And the director himself is gay. I don't know if he wants to admit that, but I will, freely, and it's weird that a gay person would carry on the stereotypes," Arquette told *Index Magazine* in 1999. "My agents—I want to fire them right now, I want to fire them this moment, because all they ever do is send me up for gay roles or drag queen roles. And it's like, okay, that's fine, they know I can do that. But before they knew that A) I was gay, and B) that I had done drag stage work, I was getting the normal auditions. People only know what they know and they only believe what they see. They're very limited, most people in this town. It's amazing how uncreative so many people in the film business are. They're people who should be CPAs. All of them should just go away. So often I'm labeled the 'outsider' or the 'bad boy' because I speak my mind. You know, I'll walk in and say, 'Who wrote this shit?' I do speak my mind. Luckily, I came out when I was very young so I don't have to worry about that burden anymore or

---

[166] As documented in the 2007 film *Alexis Arquette: She's My Brother.*

have fear of that. And coming out was just the sort of thing like—I have sex with men. That's it. Can we get past that? Like right now, I have been seeing, for about two years, a woman. And people don't understand that it's my own personal life. People see me out with her at a premiere, they think, 'Oh, you're trying to pretend like you're straight now?' They don't get it. They'll never get it. It's frustrating because you can never get past it, you're always this person who's thought of as one thing and not as an actor, which is upsetting to me because I feel that I've proven myself as being able to do the work, but you can never get past the label."[8]

Despite Arquette's presence, and despite Maxwell's sexual identity, the director insists that *Jack Be Nimble* is not meant to be perceived as a "gay horror film." "'Jack *Be Nimble* is not overtly a gay film,' the director says. 'But one of the reasons I feel quite personally attached to the film is the depiction of alienation. Gay people growing up have a kind of daily pressure just to exist. And some degree of constant self-assurance is required to feel good about yourself so that you can get through the day. That was really what I was looking at with Jack; he's really alone, he's the most lonely boy in the world,' Maxwell continues. 'He can't find his sister. He's struggling to have a sense of value rather than just being hired labor on this farm.' […] The point was a) to make an entertainment and b) to say something about the consequences of violence and alienation and the kind of psychological position that that puts you in. Possibly that explains why the film moves around so much; I was trying all these different things. Maybe I was being overly ambitious, but since you only get one chance to make a first feature, you might as well go for it.'"[9]

For American horror fans, there could be a cultural disconnect as well, with the preference being for more straight-forward fare. There's a reason that exorcism movies, for example, moved quickly from the spiritual to the visceral over the years. People tend to remember the projectile vomiting over the catechismal crisis. "Adding to the fairy tale-like atmosphere are the almost-caricatured characters of Jack's evil family—from brutish father to uptight and cruel mother to the silent yet menacing four sisters. I also liked the use of chiaroscuro throughout the film. Deep, dark shadows dominated the first part of the film, only to be juxtaposed with lighter, brighter colors later in the film. Most of the film carried with it a bleak atmosphere, though, and utilized the contrast of light and dark to show just how black the darkness really was," wrote Sarah Jahier. "Story-wise, the plot wasn't that developed, and it felt like writer Garth Maxwell (who also directed) was a bit all over the place with the psychic/telekinetic/hypnotic powers of the lead characters. Nonetheless, the result was intense interactions between the two siblings. Actors Alexis Arquette and Sarah Smuts-Kennedy, who played Jack and Dora respectively, had a great chemistry and really gave the roles their all. I was surprised at how intense and serious Arquette could act, considering I only remember him from *The Wedding Singer* and *Bride of Chucky*. And Smuts-Kennedy (poor girl, doesn't she have a separate stage name?) was equally good as Dora, even in the intensely awkward sex scenes she had to do with the creepy older guy."[10]

NY Times' Stephen Holden felt that the film took a severe left-turn after the introduction of the hypno-machine. "[T]he film loses some of its ferocity as it takes more metaphysical paths. Jack and Dora finally do reunite and seek out their original parents. Although the bond between brother and sister is deep, it is troubled by Jack's unquenchable rage against the world. He is insanely possessive of his sister, who has begun an uncertain love affair with a loner named Teddy (Bruno Lawrence), who has telepathic abilities similar to hers. What makes *Jack Be Nimble* a superior genre film is that it never loses its focus on childhood trauma and obsession and their tragic repercussions. In the film's opening scenes, where the children watch their mother go crazy, we see the events mostly through their frightened, uncomprehending eyes. Curtains blowing in the wind and a children's song on the phonograph assume an ominously scary resonance that haunts them for years. It is only much later that the pieces of what actually occurred are put together, for both the viewer and the characters. In the scenes of Jack's humiliation, the images of mud, pigs and the family's glowering, hateful faces conjure the most frightening fairy-tale figures of childhood fantasy. In the end, the movie shakily aspires toward a transcendent resolution. The voices in Dora's head and her ability to transmit and receive mental calls from others, it suggests, are not just freakish abilities but latent gifts possessed by many. *Jack Be Nimble* becomes a cautionary fable of parental irresponsibility and its dire consequences."[11]

"I remember when the film came out, and I remember not bothering to see it. More fool me. But I came to view it recently as part of my role introducing films for TVNZ Heartland [...] Difficult to classify in the best possible way, I'm gonna call it a gothic horror drama. Informed by the works of Brian De Palma, Dario Argento and David Lynch, its own uniquely haunting flavour shines through above all else," wrote Dominic Corry for the New Zealand Herald, when *Jack Be Nimble* was rediscovered in 2014. "Horror movie guru Kim Newman, quite possibly my all-time favourite film critic, gave it four stars in Empire magazine, describing the 'deeply weird melodrama' as a cross between

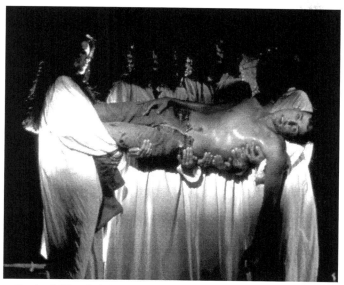

Quadruple Pietà: Jack (Arquette) and his beastly sisters (Kristen Seth, Amber Woolston, Tracey Brown, Wendy Adams)
Screengrab copyright Essential Productions. All Rights Reserved.

Stephen King and John Irving. There's a lot of weird, nasty stuff going on in Jack Be Nimble, and I was entranced by all of it. The boldness of the vision is undeniable. It's difficult to make the argument for a greater focus on genre in New Zealand cinema without sounding like either a heartless number cruncher or a shallow fanboy, but *Jack Be Nimble* embraces genre in a way that never compromises its artistic ambitions. Like Vincent Ward's The Navigator, it beautifully combines a resolutely personal vision with bold genre elements. The result is a film as immediately captivating as it is resonant. It's one of the strangest New Zealand films ever made, and dark in a way few get to be. It deserves way more of a cult reputation than it currently enjoys, and feels ripe for rediscovery."[12]

In recent years, New Zealand has become a Mecca for film production, thanks in part to the Sam Raimi-produced *Hercules* and *Xena* television shows, and in much larger part to native son Peter Jackson, who put the little island on the map first with his ultra-gory *Dead*Alive* (aka *Brain Dead*), then with the critically-acclaimed *Heavenly Creatures*, and finally the culmination of nerd-prayer, the *Lord of the Rings* and *Hobbit* series. Eclipsed by those mega-productions are the numerous other films produced slightly-to-the-right-of-Down-Under filmed and released beneath the cosplay radar.

"How many major studio released horror films of recent years have challenged both the staid horror junkie and mass audience in terms of intensity, viscerality or originality? One would have to go back to 1980 (*The Shining*) or 1979 (*Alien*). The ground breaking horror films of the last ten years have come from the independents [...]. It may seem strange to think of horror films in these terms, but the dichotomy between majors and Indies often suggests the venerable 'art' versus 'industry' issue. The level of creative interference seems to rise equal to the level of financial assurance. The higher the investment, the higher the compromises. Compromises which usually revolve around questions of tone (more upbeat, less intense), subject matter (less risky) and style (less arty). In fact, several recent indie horror films which have garnered critical and fan acceptance straddle the line between commercial and art film: *Henry: Portrait of a Serial Killer*, *Dust Devil* (Richard Stanley, 1992), *Nekromantik*, *Der Todesking* (*The Death King*, Jorg Buttgereit, 1990), *In a Glass Cage* (Augustín Villaronga, 1988), *Jack Be Nimble* (Garth Maxwell,1992), *Dellamorte, Dellamore*, *Nadja* (Michael Almereyda, 1995), and *The Addiction* (Abel Ferrera, 1995). These films share formal and thematic qualities that have more in common with art cinema than popular cinema: stylized *mise-en-scene*, ambiguous narratives, symbolic imagery, complex morality. Although Dario Argento cannot be considered an independent in his native country, this trend toward an art cinema aesthetic has been greatly influenced by his excessive, uncompromising style (elaborate set-pieces, flamboyant camera movements that go beyond narrative purpose, stylized *mise-en-scene*)," mused Donato Totaro in his 1997 article, *The Quick and the Good*. "A final indie film which merits attention is [the abovementioned] *Jack Be Nimble*, the New Zealand feature film debut of writer-director Garth Maxwell. At under one million dollars, the film should be an inspiration to other low-budget filmmakers and proves that horror can be a venue for serious subtext and social criticism. The film weaves themes of child abuse and alienation into a symbol-laden, visually stylish, psychic horror film. It begins audaciously with a speechless four minute sequence, which shows a young boy (Jack) and girl (Dora) abandoned by their mother and subsequently adopted by separate families. The film cleverly crosscuts between the two families to contrast the varying treatment the children receive (abuse/indifference). A close-up of an ornamental pig on Dora's birthday cake cuts to a real pig on a farm miles away, which Jack is forced to watch slayed. An overhead shot looking down through the hanging pig's ears to the blood-filled bucket dissolves to an overhead shot of the red icing on Dora's cake. The film never matches this great opening sequence, but it is an ambitious, assured debut feature.[13]

"My dream would be for a NZ film industry that was capable of that level of sophistication. Not just peddling hobbits. *Blue Jasmine* I loved. Nicholas Winding Refn's *Only God Forgives* is astonishing, incredible. […] I try to see the new Kiwi films at the main Film Festival, which is such a great resource for us all. Sometimes things that people think I'll love just don't work for me. I suppose I want more, more craft, more colour, more sensation, more oddness! But with an adult sensibility. Dish it up, I can take it!" Maxwell told Corry. "To me [*Jack*] is a success, even though financially that didn't seem the case—it was pirated from early on in the UK, USA, all the main territories. I think we managed something fierce and original. The energy of the writing was not smoothed out by teams of script editors as happens now, and the actors took it to the level it needed to be working at. It retained its wicked, funny edge—it feels appropriately over the top but still moves you."[14]

NOTES

[1] Scheib, Richard. "Jack Be Nimble." Moria.co.nz. http://moria.co.nz/horror/jackbenimble.htm

[2] Salisbury, Mark. "Jack Be Nimble - Jack Be Sick" Fangoria #135, 1994. P. 51

[3] Ibid

[4] Ibid

[5] Salisbury, Fangoria #135. P. 52

[6] Corry, Dominic. 2014. "Kiwi cinema at its twisted best." New Zealand Herald. May 22.
    http://www.nzherald.co.nz/entertainment/news/article.cfm?c_id=1501119&objectid=11259561

[7] Salisbury, Fangoria #135. P. 52

[8] Lee, Chris. 1999. "Alexis Arquette, 1999." Index Magazine.
    http://www.indexmagazine.com/interviews/alexis_arquette.shtml

[9] Salisbury, Fangoria #135. P. 53

[10] Jahier, Sarah E. 2009. "Jack Be Nimble." Fatally Yours Reviews. July 16.
    http://fatallyyoursreviews.blogspot.com/2009/07/jack-be-nimble-1993.html

[11] Holden, Stephen. 1994. "Review/Film; Gothic Horror With a Point to Make." New York Times. June 10.
    http://www.nytimes.com/movie/review?res=9C0CE7DB133AF933A25755C0A962958260

[12] Corry, Dominic. New Zealand Herald.

[13] Totaro, Donato. 1997. "The Quick and the Good." Offscreen Magazine. Volume 1, Issue 2 / July.
    http://offscreen.com/view/horror_cinema

[14] Corry, Dominic. New Zealand Herald.

L.A. STORY (1991)

"I have a favorite quote about L.A. by Shakespeare: 'This other Eden, demi-paradise, this precious stone, set in the silver sea of this earth, this ground, this... Los Angeles.' Anyway, this is what happened to me, and I swear, it's all true."

"Wacky Weatherman" Harris K. Telemacher (Steve Martin)[167] lives the quintessential L.A. life. Rather than quiet desperation, Harris's attitude is one of simple complacency. He's relatively successful, has an appropriately glam girlfriend, and has embraced the California lifestyle. He may not enjoy kissing people hello, but he does it, because, dammit, that's what you do in L.A. It's also perfectly natural to drive exactly three houses down the block to visit a friend because, hey, "Walk? Nobody walks in L.A.!" We first meet him in a perfectly-coiffed park, riding a stationary bike in the stationary bike path, musing about the perfect oasis that is the center of universe for all who thrive there.[168]

Something is missing in Harris' life, however, and it's a hole he doesn't know how to fill. Sure, it's fun to roller skate through art museums while your best lesbian friend records you, but does that really make for a fulfilling existence? But, on the other hand, what is there to complain about? "Let us just say I was deeply unhappy, but I didn't know it because I was so

---

[167] "Tele" from the Greek, meaning "movement over a long distance." "Macher", from the Yiddish, meaning a "doer". ("He's such a *macher* 'cause he works his *tuchus* off."—Weird Al.)

[168] "The entire film has a very dreamy quality to it, which I really liked. This is enhanced by a slightly over exposed look and the use of trance music by artists like Enya. Steve Martin gives us a look at LA as both a house of crazies and as a sort of transcendent paradise, where people rise every perfect morning to take "Slo Mo" showers. It walks a very interesting line between the real and the unbelievable that I found very charming and funny." Roddey, Judge Dean. 1999. "Review". DVD Verdict. October 27. http://www.dvdverdict.com/reviews/lastory.php

happy all the time."

Then, at an outdoor luncheon with his closest acquaintances, the answer to Harris' question sits down at the table: Sara (Victoria Tennant[169], Martin's then-wife), a young English journalist on her first visit to California. She's fresh, unusual, and to Harris, exotic—from her introduction ("Yes, I'm shattered [from the long flight from London], but it's nothing that some sleep and a good fuck wouldn't cure, as my sister used to say.") to her failure to grasp proper American driving etiquette ("Right side! Right side!"), to her delightful schedule of calling her mother every morning in order to accompany her on the tuba.

> **Sara:** "What would be the proper time of morning for sustained booming noises?"
> **Harris:** "Oh, sustained booming noises. Around nine, nine-fifteen."

Once Sarah arrives, the magic that Harris yearned for is suddenly all around him. His Virgil through this new journey of love comes from the most unexpected of places: a large highway traffic sign. For no discernable reason, Harris's car malfunctions, coming to a stop before the signpost, which immediately requests a hug. It gives him two messages for the future:

First, "The weather will change your life…twice."

Second, "You will know what to do when you unscramble how daddy is doing."

This encounter launches a series of events that could be construed as fate, as destiny, or a midlife crisis. Over the following few days, Harris loses his job after pre-recording the weather ("This weekend will be sunny and 72 degrees. Just like always."), failing to predict a moderate storm that sinks his producer's boat. A simple quest to pick up a pair of pants results in an infatuation with a much younger woman named Sandy (Sarah Jessica Parker, in perhaps *the* role of her career). (Or, because this is L.A., "SanDeE*"). A free spirit and fan of high colonics—"They really clean out your head!"—"Someone should tell him he's doing it wrong."—SanDeE* never walks anywhere—she bounces, she spins, she glides, even standing still she's never motionless, as if traveling via her own private summer breeze. (Or, as Hal Hinson writes in his sadly cynical review, "who suffers, it seems, from something like spandex poisoning."[1]) She is the living embodiment of L.A.'s joy.

Then he discovers that his girlfriend, Trudi (Marilu Henner) has been cheating on him with his agent. At first, he sees this as a pathway to dating Sara—storming out of Trudi's apartment, his woeful stomping transforms into a very happy dance—but Sara may or may not be trying to mend her relationship with her charming ex-husband. Free of responsibility, but also direction, Harris searches in vain for new employment, and decides to see how things go with SanDeE*. In a series of "only in the movies or possibly Los Angeles" events, both couples wind up at the same beach resort getaway and that's where things get messiest.

Trapped by pride and social norms, Sara and Harris fail to reconcile. On the night Sara is to return to London, Harris tells her, "All I know is, on the day your plane was to leave, if I had the power, I would turn the winds around, I would roll in the fog, I would bring in storms, I would change the polarity of the earth so compasses couldn't work, so your plane couldn't take off." And, impossibly, something just like that happens.

For many, many years, Steve Martin was a hilarious human being. He was passionate about comedy, would rehearse to the point of obsession. Though his career started on clumsy footing—*Sgt. Pepper's Lonely Hearts Club Band* (1978), or for a better example, *The Jerk* (1979), which I've always found grating, but know many people who think it's the funniest movie ever. Personally, I prefer the dour Americanized Dennis Potter film, *Pennies from Heaven* (1981).

"I think in those early films," he said, "I was still finding my way, still trying to figure out what kind of films to make, and I believed that the kind of films I should make, with the exception of *Pennies from Heaven*, should be extensions of what I was doing onstage. The same

---

[169] By way of trivia, Sir. Lawrence Olivier was Tennant's godfather.

kind of character, more or less. And then, right around *All of Me*, I dropped that and saw that movies were very different from just doing some crazy jokes. I think in the early films, there are moments that are pretty funny, but the stories are always sort of weak. I wish they'd worked a little better. But I think there's something in each one of them that's a little daring. I really can't evaluate them that well, because it's me."[2]

Now, far be it for me to criticize a man's search for inner strength, the yearning to grow as an artist and story teller. Why, that would be like aliens coming down to Earth to tell Woody Allen that they preferred his "earlier, funnier movies." And that's just absurd, right?[170] "I feel like I have a niche, but I'm not going to put any qualitative value on it. What I've done or am still doing is slightly off-base. There isn't anybody really doing it. Don't ask me why. I always feel like I do things, finish them, and move on to something else. Like stand-up comedy, then my early films which were kind of silly, dopey comedies, and then they started changing, getting into more legitimate stories. I feel that *L.A. Story* is the end of some kind of cycle for me. I don't know what I'll do next."[3]

With exceptions, his post-Millennium career has focused on more serious dramatic stories for both screen and stage. He turned his short story, *Shopgirl* into a contemplative story about age-gap relationships; in *Novocaine,* he starred as an unhappy dentist caught up in intrigue and murder. He's positively sinister in Mamet's *The Spanish Prisoner.* In between these more serious turns, he starred in the lackluster *Grand Canyon,* and the abysmal *Bringing Down the House* and *Housesitter.* In fact, the last truly funny movie he made was the Frank Oz-directed *Bowfinger.* But all of that aside, *L.A. Story,* for me anyway, is his perfect movie. At the same time outlandish and low key, *L.A. Story* introduced me to magic realism in a way that Gabriel Garcia Marquez never could. Blending a simple tale of finding love into the idiosyncratic nature of Los Angeles mixed with Shakespearean allusions, *L.A. Story* accomplishes more in 90 minutes than the whole of *Winter's Tale* (2014) ever managed.

For the romantics—or folks who've gone off their depression meds—*L.A. Story* has numerous beautiful, tear-jerking moments, all set to various lovely Enya songs. One sequence has Harris and Sara sneaking away from a tedious dinner party to wander their host's garden, becoming children in adult clothing while stone lions bow to their innocent love. The film's climax, borrowing liberally from Shakespeare's *The Tempest*, can chisel through the most be-stoned of hearts.

Washington Post reviewer Desson Howe wrote that *Story* is "One part La-La-land gagfest and two parts valentine (to Martin's real-life spouse Victoria Tennant)," which perfectly explains the natural chemistry the two have on screen.[171] While Howe is somewhat appalled by the "impossible situation" Tennant is forced into. "But then there's that romantic stuff. Tennant (who appeared in Martin's much-better *All of Me* (1984)) is a respectable performer, but Martin has scripted her into an impossibly precious, eccentric corner. She's witty, sweet and direct. She's nice enough to let her still-smitten ex (Richard E. Grant) down gently. She even plays the tuba. What a woman, we are required to conclude."[4] I'm sorry, but this is romantically egregious. To quote Hunter S. Thompson, "Buy the ticket, take the ride." If you find that the romance is too saccharine, maybe you should visit a cardiologist to make sure your heart isn't Grinch-sized. Just as the city is romanticized, so is Sara (and to an extent, so is SanDeE*, the precursor to the Manic Pixie Dream Girl). The film is a fantasy, so why should the romantic angle be any less fantastic?

---

[170] Please tell me you've seen *Stardust Memories.*

[171] "That would be awful if it was. I don't want to spend seventeen million dollars of someone else's money on an homage to my wife. I'll do that at home with a box of candy. You could take another actress and put her in there and tell the same story. The movie was an allegory about romance—how it feels. It happened to star my wife. I wanted to movieize that state. [...] This is about the first blush of romance. As opposed *to L.A. Story II,* which, if there were one—don't worry, there won't be—would be The Married Years. After romance is love: trust and knowing the person. You love for different reasons." Sheff, David. 1993. "Steve Martin". Playboy. January. Archived at: http://davidsheff.com/article/steve-martin/

"That's difference between the British and Americans. We stay friends with our exes. You kill them."
Richard E. Grant, Victoria Tennant, Steve Martin, Sarah Jessica Parker.
Image Copyright Tri-Star Pictures. All Rights Reserved.

And at the same time, the movie is delightfully screwy. In an attempt to impress SanDeE*, Harris tries in vain to get a reservation at L.A.'s hot new trendy restaurant, L'Idiot (so swanky, it has staff dedicated to offering floss (a *flossier*?). After giving his occupation, his after-tax income, and justifying selling a condo—"Yes, in this soft market!"—he is granted an in-person interview with the unctuous maître d' (Patrick Stewart) and the surly chef. "You think with a financial report like this you can have the duck?" As Harris guesses, this is all part of "The New Cruelty". Yet later and without effort, Roland manages to get them all a table for lunch, showing up Harris in front of Sara without malicious forethought. Roland, actually, is not a bad guy; he's just as smitten with Sara as our hero. "That's the difference between English and Americans," he tells Harris. "We maintain friendships with our exes. Americans kill them." *L.A. Story* is also a movie without villains. "Another thing is that [Martin's] humor is never cruel," [Victoria] Tennant said. "He's never mean or sarcastic. There's always a sweetness in his work." [5]

British director Mick Jackson, introduced to Martin by Tennant, brings Martin's lovely script to life in a very straightforward manner, allowing the magic to occur organically without showy camerawork or editing, making the kind of movie that would have starred Cary Grant and Audrey Hepburn were it made thirty years earlier. Jackson and Martin also fill the movie to the brim with cameos, including Rick Moranis as a funny gravedigger; Chevy Chase in a mercifully brief walk-on as another rich victim of "The New Cruelty"; Woody Harrelson as Harris' sucker-sucking producer; Paula Abdul and Iman also appear. And, always welcome, Kevin Pollak!

Let's not discount the role played by an inanimate object (and no, I don't mean Chevy Chase). The towering highway sign is not only a literal *deus ex machina*, but it's also a clever creature on its own. Martin transforms the L.A. phenomenon ("I've only seen them on and working once in fifteen years," he told Ebert.) into an electronic oracle of Delphi, imparting the age-old riddle to be solved in order to find happiness. From its "Hug Me" introduction to the revelation that it was, in a past life, a set of bagpipes and continues to look for its voice again, the Sign—as in, "Dear God, give me a sign!"—is as important to Harris' life as the weather proves to be.

But, as it says in the film's tag, "What I really want to do is direct."

The strangest cameo, however, was left on the cutting room floor. Despite numerous appearances in the movie's trailers, John Lithgow as superagent Harry Zell, the jet setting, cell-phone lugging, skipping powerhouse ("Skipping is the perfect balance between walking and running," Zell advises.), Zell is mentioned twice in the finished film, in hushed and reverent tones. In the deleted scenes, Harris turns to Zell for guidance on getting his career back on track, obeying each ridiculous lesson but with far less confidence. But both Jackson and Martin determined that the Zell subplot got in the way of the central love story. Losing Zell does work to the film's benefit, though, and fortunately the anniversary preserves the scenes, albeit with unfinished special effects (particularly Zell's magnificent introduction landing in the middle of the strip on his personal jet pack. This is a man to be listened to!).

The city, of course, is also a main character, transformed into a fairy tale kingdom rife with activity that would only be absurd to those who aren't from there. Gone is the smog and the overcrowding; present are the upscale shops and pastel people. Lest you think that the magic is coming specifically for Harris, there are quick shots of other people staring up at the traffic signs, presumably receiving their own spiritual messages.

As Roger Ebert wrote in his review, "There are scenes that in other hands might have seemed obvious (for example, the daily routine of shooting at other drivers while racing down the freeway), but somehow there is a fanciful edge in the way they do it, a way they define all of their material with a certain whimsical tone. [...] The film is astonishing in the amount of material it contains. Martin has said he worked on the screenplay, on and off, for seven years, and you can sense that as the film unfolds. It isn't thin or superficial; there is an abundance of observation and invention here, and perhaps because the filmmakers know they have so much good material, there's never the feeling that anything is being punched up, or made to carry more than its share. I was reminded of the films of Jacques Tati, in which, calmly, serenely, an endless series of comic invention unfolds."[6]

As he told Ebert in 1991, "'I started writing it about seven years ago,' Martin said, 'before I even started writing *Roxanne*, and then I put it in a drawer, because it's the kind of thing that's very scary to think of ever being made into a movie. You're risking a lot. I'd think, no, I can't do this, then I'd get encouraged again, and I'd pick it up and do it. [...] '[B]ecause a lot of the ideas for the movie occurred to me in little bits.[172] I'd make a note and put it away. In this movie, every scene has to have an angle because the story itself is a sort of regular love story. So there's always something going on behind the action. I always had to think of a place, or an idea, or an attitude, or something that lifts the scene up a little. [...] "Like, for example, the gravedigger scene with Rick Moranis, which has fun with *Hamlet*. All the scene really achieves, on the story level, is to make the man and the woman interested in each other. But having Rick as the gravedigger gets this other thing happening, too, at the same time, rather than just having the characters standing on the sidewalk. Or like the scene outside the automated teller machine. You're killing two birds with one stone. You're showing a little bit of the relationship between myself and the young girl, SanDeE*, and yet you're also getting this gag going on at the same time.'

"*L.A. Story* is such an original and particular movie, I said, that it must have been almost impossible to pitch in a meeting with studio executives. Is this kind of project tough to sell, or to get financed? 'A little tougher, yeah. I have a feeling a lot of studios wanted to make it, but they didn't want to pay for it. They wanted it to be very cheap. As it turns out, the movie was very cheap by today's standards, but it couldn't be that cheap, it needed some class to it. I think it's a risky film. At least, it was seen as risky when we were pitching it. I don't know if it seems

---

[172] "Did you start right out with the notion of a communicating billboard? "No, that only came within the last year and a half or two." And yet that was really the organizing principal, wasn't it? "Yeah. It shows you how drastically things can change. The original draft had me leaving L.A. and ending up in Turkey, because I wanted something that was just the opposite of L.A. Turkey didn't make it into the final draft. I never got out of L.A.'" Ebert, Roger. 1991. "No Longer Crazy, Just Wildly Talented, It's Steve Martin." Roger Ebert.com. February 3. http://www.rogerebert.com/interviews/no-longer-crazy-just-wildly-talented-its-steve-martin

so risky now, when you can see what we had in mind. It's like *Roxanne* was a very risky film, at least in my head, before we started rolling, but then when it opened people said well, it's OK, I had a good time, I enjoyed it, it's OK to tell my friends to go."[7]

Released in February of '91, *L.A. Story* managed to knock the box office favorite *Home Alone* out of its 11-week number one spot, met with acclaim from critics and moviegoers alike, giving the struggling TriStar Pictures a desperately-needed win. But in recent years the movie has fallen into a sad obscurity. You can't throw a rock at any of Comcast's eight bazillion channels without hitting *Father of the Bride* or *Parenthood*, but *L.A. Story* rarely makes an appearance.

However, the real tragedy to me is that after this wild, romantic love story, Tennant and Martin divorced just three years later, in 1994.[8] "I can't describe it specifically, but it is more about an attitude. We're a couple forever. I came from the philosophy that it lasts as long as it lasts. As soon as you accept the vision that it is going to work forever, it can," Martin told *Playboy* in '91. "I once went to a psychiatrist who said that your emotions follow your intentions. If your intent is to last forever, your emotions go that way. Once I saw that, I could see that it can last forever. As our marriage goes on, I like her more and more and admire her more and more. Romance is about a feeling and marriage is about so much more: the intellectual, the compassionate, the friendship. It has to do with a way of life, too, a circle of friends. Part of the deal is that you strive to be together as much as possible. We've been together for eight years and we recently took a vacation in which we spent seven weeks essentially in one room. And it was great. It was, like, better than ever. [Laughs] I'd better be careful. People say, "We have this perfect marriage" and two weeks later they're divorced. [...] Not us."[9]

But in the universe of *L.A. Story*, I like to think that Harris and Sara lived happily to a ripe old age, stone lions bowing as they pass.

NOTES

[1] Hinson, Hal. 1991. 'L.A. Story'. Washington Post. Feb 8. http://www.washingtonpost.com/wp-srv/style/longterm/movies/videos/lastorypg13hinson_a0a9d3.htm

[2] Ebert, Roger. 1991. "No Longer Crazy, Just Wildly Talented, It's Steve Martin." Roger Ebert.com. February 3. http://www.rogerebert.com/interviews/no-longer-crazy-just-wildly-talented-its-steve-martin

[3] Grobel, Lawrence. 1991. "Steve Martin: But Seriously Folks." Movieline.com. The Vault. February 1. http://movieline.com/1991/02/01/steve-martin-but-seriously-folks/

[4] Howe, Desson. 1991. "'L.A. Story' (PG-13)" Washington Post. February 8. http://www.washingtonpost.com/wp-srv/style/longterm/movies/videos/lastorypg13howe_a0b2db.htm

[5] Ebert, Roger. 1991. "No Longer Crazy". Roger Ebert.com. February 3.

[6] Ebert, Roger. 1991. "Review." Chicago Sun Times. Feb. 8. http://www.rogerebert.com/reviews/la-story-1991

[7] Ibid

[8] " While filming a miniseries, [Tennant had] fallen for a hunky Australian TV star and returned only to tell Steve she was leaving. The divorce was not friendly. When questioned, Tennant claimed that she found Steve to be 'emotionally unavailable', and this distance has caused him many problems. Some performers switch off when not on stage, and even Steve's friends say that he switches off more than most. He's polite to people, but uninvolved. Tommy Smothers of the Smothers Brothers even said that 'To spend time with him is like being alone'. And, though he's bright, curious and hilarious with his closest friends, he finds it impossible to be that way on dates. It may have been nature, or nurture, as his family were far from close that way. He recalls many a silent dinner-time in his childhood." Wills, Dominic. "Steve Martin—Biography." TalkTalk.co.uk. http://www.talktalk.co.uk/entertainment/film/biography/artist/steve-martin/biography/118

[9] Heartbreaking. Sheff, David. 1993. "Steve Martin". Playboy. January. Archived at: http://davidsheff.com/article/steve-martin/

THE LEGEND OF SIMON CONJURER (2013)
(a.k.a. DEADLY LESSONS)

Simon Conjurer (pronounced, sporadically, as Con-JUHR-er) is a gentle, long-haired intellectual college professor who takes time out of his curriculum to help people with their fears and problems. When we first meet him, he is teaching a group of 10-year-olds not to be afraid of airplanes by hypnotizing them, having them pretend that they are floating through the air on their own. And then the children rise from their seats and do just that. In awe of his power, a nurse begs Simon to help her son Roberto, a suicidal teenager who refuses to answer to any name but "Rebel".

To convince Rebel to join Conjurer's night class, the professor—off camera—shackles the teen and basically kidnaps him, the whole time telling him he's free to go. With nowhere else to go, Rebel agrees to attend the class so long as he can drive Conjurer's obscene Humvee, which he promptly crashes. Again, off-screen.

There are nine other members of Conjurer's latest session. Going around the room, Simon identifies them by name and ailment, deconstructing each person into their chief malady. "Tears" is a manic-depressive borderline schizophrenic; Platehead is a compulsive gambler; Lulu is the teenaged anorexic; "Toons" suffers from confused sexuality; Scorpio has an uncontrollable temper. Elements of their backstories will be introduced as needed.

Simon's nemesis is the "Pulitzer Prize Winning" psychologist, Dr. Crazx (pronounced "Cray-zacks"), a corpulent megalomaniac[173] whose books are endorsed by Saddam Hussein. He's obsessed with two things, apparently: chocolate bars and the destruction of Simon Conjurer. To bring about Simon's end, Crazx kidnaps one of the young girls from the opening flying class and hurls her off a rooftop, effectively framing Conjurer for murder—or, more appropriately, child endangerment or manslaughter (depending on how far you want to go) by blaming Conjurer's "fantasies" implanted in the girl, making her believe she could fly at will. Maybe. Anyway, the cops are now after Simon and his class follows him into the city to gather evidence that will clear him of wrongdoing.

Before they leave, Simon shows off impressive strength—defending himself from one of Scorpio's rages, he hurls the man across the room—and passes out leather-bound books that somehow knows the future, as well as private details about each member of the group. The book is titled "Prophet without a God", and it may have been written by Conjurer, or it may have been written by Crazx in the future, or it may have written itself.

---

[173] Voight in appropriately disgusting make-up created by Ryan Nicholson.

The group breaks into Crazx's ridiculously-lavish apartment, replete with a boa constrictor in a giant tank, multiple well-endowed statues, and an overall décor of "minimalist gothic". Throughout their scavenger hunt, each member experiences an epiphany that explains their one-dimensional obsessions—Toons realizes he's confused because as a kid, he walked in on a minister fucking a teacher; Tears was raped at knifepoint; Rebel misses his absentee—or possibly dead—father. Scorpio's epiphany happens off-screen…maybe. The group leaps into a truck to escape Crazx and discover, later, after the truck pulls over, that the drivers are terrorists and the truck is loaded with explosives. Sometime during the dissolve between riding and not-riding, Scorpio subdued the drivers and found satisfaction in lashing out violently against "bad guys", instead of "random passersby". At each magical realization, Rebel keeps the count: "Two down, eight to go," and etcetera.

Any time the group finds themselves in trouble, or in a lull in action, they consult their books for insight. One passage details an encounter Simon had with Crazx on a rooftop which resulted in the villainous psychiatrist pulling a cutlass on the hippie magician, forcing him to walk the length of a mechanical stone gantry, leading to his plummeting "death" (the book doesn't mention if he splats; since he's still there in front of them, it's unclear if this is a fictional passage, something that happened in the past, something yet to come, a bad episode of *Lost*…). Another sequence has Simon joining his lover, Dean Elkwood (Danielle Kremeniuk), in a lengthy shower sequence—she's naked, he's in a three-piece suit, and they're both standing in an indoor stone grotto beneath a waterfall. If this is just a passage in the book, how is Toons able to spy on them? Or, as it is brought up earlier, is the book communicating to them all telepathically, enabling them to all experience the same hallucination? Oh, and we did mention that Simon is being pursued for murder, right?

In 2006, I was working for *Film Threat* when I got a call out of the blue from Jamie Greco, a performer and publicist I knew from Troma. Jamie asked me if I was available to interview Academy Award Winning actor Jon Voight. I said "Sure." He said, "Great, I'll connect you."

My interview with Voight took place pretty much that very minute, while the actor drove via limo to the New York premiere of his latest film, *The Legend of Simon Conjurer*, in which he appeared under heavy prosthetics, playing the villain. At this point in his career, Voight had pretty much taken a back seat to his daughter, Angelina Jolie, who was constantly in the news at the time thanks to her bizarre past relationship with Billy Bob Thornton, a new pregnancy, her highly-publicized marriage to Brad Pitt, etc. Meanwhile, Voight was appearing in big budget films like *Pearl Harbor* and (at the time) the upcoming *Transformers*, as well as the critically-acclaimed *Holes*, *Ali*. But, as no one would let anyone forget, Voight was also the villain in the indescribable *Karate Dog* (2004). The basic consensus was that once you made the money that the Voight-Jolie-Pitt family had, you could do whatever the hell you wanted and fuck the critics. For those of us in the low-end of the critical spectrum, this was a highly-respectable stance.

And he made this *Simon Conjurer* thing sound amazing. "Yeah, it's a murder mystery but it's full of other things," Voight told Jordan Garren & Brian Morton at Rogue Cinema (making me realize just how unspecial I was at the time, thinking Voight had chosen me to interview him). "Let me read from a flyer that we put out, and it's kind of interesting. [Reading from the flyer] 'This movie will provoke the metaphysical mind and may be a way to tap into one's own healing process' and that's the most interesting line of the whole flyer. What could it possibly be? What it is, is a very whimsical form, a fable form that contains a lot of information. It's a very complex piece, and it has a happy ending too, it has a very positive, hopeful ending after many twists and turns. It's really something, it's completely original, you'll never see anything like it, and it's really an amazing piece full of things that you'll want to see."[1] We couldn't wait to check it out. Except that, after the New York premiere, *The Legend of Simon Conjurer* vanished from the face of the Earth.

A quick Google search of *The Legend of Simon Conjurer* yields dozens of pages offering torrents, downloads, VODs, but little in the way of information. In fact, the most common search term relating to the film is "Is 'Simon Conjurer' a hoax?" Many speculated that the film was so bad that the director removed his name from credits, leaving only a "?" in its place. On screen, the credits are presented in children's drawings on the walls of the elementary school, with "Written and Directed by" written on a blackboard, the name erased at the head of the edit. The truth is, the director and star, Stuart Paul, never intended to use his name in the first place. In fact, it was Voight who convinced him to at least adopt the pseudonym, "Q. Mark" for promotional materials. While you might think at first blush that this is a cynical or pretentious act on the part of Paul, apparently his insistence on anonymity was genuine. Paul, as it turns out, is the strangest member of an already-strange entertainment family.

"Well, I'll tell you who he is. His name is Stuart Paul, he's an interesting guy, listen, this fella is the most interesting man I've ever met and he's the person I most admire and I must tell you, I know a lot of great people. This guy is the top of the list and he's the person I go to. I feel very privileged to have him in my life that I can go to him and ask him about different things. Whenever I have a question, which is every day, about lots of things, about the world situation, about different problems people are having, questions that I have about my own life, stuff like that, I always ask Stewie and he always gives me an interesting answer, something I couldn't have expected and usually it puts me on track, he's like a compass for me. And he's also my best buddy, which means we have a lot of fun, we laugh a lot and all of this. Anyway, he's been writing screenplays and he's had an interesting life, a very challenging last ten years of his life, and he wrote this screenplay after all this time of wrestling with real challenges and I was interested to read if, of course, and I was quite taken with it, I thought it was terrific and then there was a role in it, that was an amazing kind of role, which I thought maybe I could play, I said, Stewie I can play this role, so also it might help him get the picture made, of course, and all of that. But I'm always amazed to be part of his thoughts and his stories and his intentions, which are quite ambitious. Anyway, that's how I got into this and now I'm trying to do my best to make sure that people know it's out there. Here's a simple story for you two guys, the simple line of the film, is that there's ten dysfunctional people who are following a kind of magical teacher and their paths cross with a kind of a murder plot which they have to solve. My character is kind of a dangerous, Pulitzer Prize winning psychiatrist/novelist who is extremely negative and all his negativity has made him very popular and I'm a bit of a villain of the picture."

Paul is the brother of director/producer Steven Paul, who made his debut with the film *Falling in Love Again* (1980—which was also the ostensible film debut of Michelle Pfeiffer). The film also apparently launched the careers of the rest of the family. Mother Dorothy Koster Paul became a casting agent and manager; sister Bonnie Paul co-starred in the film (with Stuart); somewhere along the line, Steven Paul became Voight's manager (along with Gene Wilder, Michael Cimino, and the late Bob Clark). While Steven Paul has become a controversial name in Hollywood—serving as the producer of the "whitewashed" *Ghost in the Shell*, the ill-advised *Ghost Rider: Spirit of Vengeance*, and our personal favorite, *Never Too Young to Die*—Stuart Paul seems to come and go. He last surfaced in 2013 with the short film, *Settlers of Catan*, inspired by the classic video game and starring Whedonites Fran Kranz and Amy Acker. Ironically (or not so), that's when brother Steven's company Crystal Sky decided to finally release *Simon Conjurer* to DVD under the dreadfully-bland title, *Deadly Lessons*, with Stuart Paul's name still conspicuously absent from all promotion, save for the omnipresent "Q. Mark".

"We still had to have something once Stewie said he wasn't using his name, so we had some fun. We thought it would be a nice way to let people get excited. It actually ended up distracting from the fact that this film is not only original and humorous, but also very serious. It provokes a lot of serious questions. The poster says something like: 'Will provoke the metaphysical mind and may tap into one's own healing process,' so it suggests something not only unusual for filmfare, but just a pretty far-out idea of what the medium can be-a new genre almost. It says, let's do something else with film, with story and let's see if we can get to another level of audience interaction."[2]

As Stuart Paul told The Nerdist, "Usually the things I work on are from crazy whacked-out universes that populate my head, but every once in a while the universe slaps something right in front of you. It happens. You don't need to put a lot of bells and whistles on it."[3]

Now, prior to Voight's promotional push, *Simon Conjurer* was already the subject of controversy, even if nobody knew it. Flying beneath the radar even in production, the film then-called *Sunrise* was the object of a medium-profile industry strike that led to Voight withdrawing from the Screen Actor's Guild's membership and resetting his status to "Financial Core", giving up union's insurance coverage and other benefits. On January 25, 2005, *Daily Variety*[4] ran the following letter from Voight:

> Jon Voight
> January 25, 2005
>
> Dear Fellow Actors,
>
> Please know that I am deeply moved by your recent nomination for SAG's "Outstanding Performance by a Male Actor in a Television Movie," and I want to express my sincere gratitude for that honor. Since then, you may have heard that the SAG board has excluded me from the awards ceremony on February 5, 2005.
>
> The published explanation given for my exclusion is not accurate, and I feel I owe a truthful explanation so that what happened to me, should never happen to another actor.
>
> The truth is that during the Summer of 2003, I was approached by a dear friend who had a lifetime vision of directing a piece he had written. He explained to me he had very little money and he would need to feel complete freedom, if there was any possibility to bring his vision to fruition.
>
> When I read the script, I was so moved! It was original, it was spiritual, and I felt it would be important, and an answer to many of our personal sufferings. It wasn't too long before other people felt the same as I did, and supplied just minimal funds so my friend could begin work on his project.
>
> I knew by law I could participate in the project without violating the Guild's rule against non-union work by electing "financial core" status. I called the Guild to request that status. My request was met with fear and panic from the SAG officer in charge of "financial core." "Jon, you must not do this," she said. "You will open the door to all our actors running for financial core." I thought to myself, "What's so bad about that?
>
> There could be multiple reasons, financial and otherwise, why many creative people might want to do a non-union movie under the protection of 'financial core.' 'Core' membership is an entitlement of any union member, protected by federal law." I needed a few days to think about this.
>
> Before I had arrived at a solution, all hell broke loose! Suddenly, there was what can only be described as a brutal attack on the small production, not only by SAG, but other unions as well. They came down hard. It was vicious and ugly. I thought I was living a part in the film, 'On the Waterfront'.
>
> Our Guild exacerbated the assault with the false announcement to the press that I was the film's producer. My peers, who were rushed off to join the angry mob on picket lines, had no idea that I was not the producer, and that I had not worked one day as an actor on the film, but the false information they were led to believe was immediately released to the press.
>
> The unions' scare tactics worked. The crew was frightened to continue, and a small filmmaker's creative endeavor was shut down after 2 1/2 weeks of work, leaving great financial losses.
>
> The ugliness did not end. The attacks on me and the production continued on with the vicious taunts and lies spread over the internet. It went on for months, leaving in its wake extreme stress and mental anguish

for all involved. If this could happen to me, a veteran actor of 40 years and an Academy Award Winner, I shuddered to think what would be in store for other actors. I wouldn't want this to happen to anyone ever again.

Because of all the cruel bullying and unfair play, I then decided to apply for "financial core" to see if I could help salvage in any way this original pure vision. I understood that I would give up my right to vote in union matters, but I would be able work legally in non-SAG films, as well as SAG films. As a "financial core" member, I willingly pay the same dues as all other SAG members, which support the efforts of the guild to negotiate and administer our contracts, efforts I concur with. I contribute and participate in the various benefit funds on the same basis as a full member. Given the structure of the contracts, my support of the Guild exceeds that of most members.

I would hope to think that the anguish and stress that was put upon me would have been enough, but it was not. The SAG board chose to bring me once again what they think is shame, and apparently to warn other actors off joining financial core, by announcing to the press that I was not invited to the ceremony to which my fellow actors nominated me for a union film. All this is because of my willingness to uphold the right to our personal pursuit of freedom and liberty. I am neither sorry nor ashamed for my decision to join the "financial core." My sorrow comes only for a union that can be a great force, that can accomplish much good, and protect, promote, and nourish the actor in his individual pursuits, but does not yet understand that there will be some that will be happy to follow the union in all its rules and regulations, but there may be some that will differ and follow a destiny of their own choosing, and that is their right, and that is our country's Constitution.

I congratulate all my fellow nominees, and wish everyone the best.

With great sincerity,
Jon Voight (Signature)

Production moved to Kelowna British Columbia. Nearly everyone involved moved on. The movie faded to oblivion. But thanks to the Internet, *Simon Conjurer* stayed alive, mostly in a years-long argument on the IMDb thread "Is this a real movie??"[5] Posters argued the legitimacy of the film's very existence, most arguing that the production was an elaborate internet hoax (though failing to explain what point such a hoax would serve), starring "Jon Voight impersonator" Mark Hagel. Others attacked filmmaker and make-up artist Ryan Nicholson, claiming he lied about his own involvement with the film, even accusing him of doctoring behind-the-scenes make-up photos. The anger towards the unreleased film was matched only by the negative reaction to finally seeing the finished film itself.

Simon Conjurer's disappearance was a nagging point of personal consternation for me, as I did a fair bit of promotion for it on *Film Threat* at the time. Over the years, I'd resigned myself to never laying eyes on the movie that gave me the opportunity to talk to Jon Voight. (Or did I interview Mark Hagel instead?)

A chance Facebook conversation with Nicholson revealed that *Simon Conjurer* was indeed quietly released to DVD in 2013. And…well, it's a movie that was finished.

It's difficult to describe my reaction to what was finally called *Deadly Lessons*. It's definitely a unique film. It certainly defied my expectations. It could not be mistaken for anything else. After the whimsical opening sequence with flying children (also featuring some surprisingly-shoddy digital wire-removal), the disjointed narrative left me feeling disoriented, but wondering if that was the point, or if several linking scenes had been left either unfilmed or were excised from the already ponderous 137-minute running time. Conjurer's initial encounter with Rebel is missing, the two appearing side-by-side for the first time with Rebel handcuffed in the front seat of the ridiculous Hummer. This despite the fact that Rebel is the film's narrator. The truck chase that results in Scorpio's aggression awakening is also conspicuously missing, as is any sense of logic regarding Crazx's and Conjurer's past. Their rooftop fantasy begins with a theological discussion about their search for God and the absence of discovery. It ends with an unperturbed Conjurer plummeting through the air, lazily waving his arms as he falls.

While the largely-unknown actors are game for anything, their characters are little more than sketches—"the alcoholic", "the overeater", "the anorexic" (played by Paul's niece and Voight's goddaughter, Skyler Shaye)—and their dialogue ranges from preachy to filler. My initial reaction to the group was summed up on the aforementioned IMDb boards by a disgruntled viewer: "Ok, ok, ok this is what happened... They were doing a workshop and typically dumb exercises, and the director/teacher/coach calls up his good friend John Voight to come by and do a master class. So, they're doing their stuff before the master: the "Mirror" exercise, the "What if..." exercise, the "Waiting for Godot" exercise, the "Psycho Drama" exercise, various heavy breathing exercises, plus a few primal stage screams—and being the generous, reinforcing kind of guy he is, Voight says, "Hey, you kids are great! Why don't we find a location and turn this into a movie?" You know, the way Judy and Mickey say, "Hey Kids, let's find a barn and put on a show!" What we have here, Folks, is real, but is it a movie or just an elaborate showcase of "budding talent," for which we are, as usual, the paying beta testers?"[6]

While Voight is completely over-the-top, eyes a'popping, mouth smeared with chocolate, gasping and groaning, at the edge of cardiac arrest in every scene, Paul as Simon is an admittedly calming presence, a long-haired professor reminiscent of every Liev Schreiber performance. The magic he professes to find in everyday life, manifested as disappearing doves and flying children, seems to be a metaphysical building-block for not only Conjurer's personality, but it is likely an extension of Paul's personality as well. Voight pointed out to me that Simon is closely based on Paul, so it's no surprise that his performance is the most relaxed and honest of the film. By contrast, Germaine De Leon's Rebel is one twitch after another, rolling his shoulders and talking out of the corner of his mouth like Freddy Prinze playing a lesbian mechanic. Rebel also disappears around the film's two-thirds mark, the other characters commenting on his absence, only to reappear in a clumsy coda as he rejoins his no-longer-dead father and nurse mother. The other characters merely exist to fulfill the needs of Paul's metaphysical storyline, though each one tries to give their character a stand-out moment, primarily through their contractually-promised monologue (each character gets one).

It would not surprise me to learn that *The Legend of Simon Conjurer / Deadly Lessons* is the dramatization of Paul's religious/psychological beliefs. One commenter alleges that Paul was "kicked out" of the Church of Scientology, implying that the artist was too strange even for the Children of Hubbard. "It's a very good question, how much of this is based on this guy, Stuart, because Simon Conjurer, the magical teacher in the piece is very much like Stuart," said Voight. "But the movie is told in a fantasy way with much magic, but there's just as much magic in Stewie as far as I'm concerned, he's really an amazing fellow. If people go to see this film and want to ask questions about him I certainly would be available to answer them, even though I don't think you'd be able to drag Stewie in front of anybody to talk. He'd never talk about himself, he's like a Salinger type of guy, but, on the other hand, anybody who ever meets him is always delighted to find that he's full of fun and he's such a warm and embracing guy and takes care of people and cares for people, you know, he's just a wonderful guy to be with. He just keeps himself away from the crowd and out of the spotlight."[7]

The unavoidable problem is that Paul's philosophy seems incomplete. Is Simon a Christ figure? Is Crazx the God character manipulating the lives of all the others? Is Crazx's psychology damaging (ala Scientology) versus Simon's magical realism? Self-realization is all the addict needs to overcome his or her individual disease? Some understanding and personal forgiveness the keys to physiological recovery? If that is the message, it's muddled beneath the sloppy editing and clumsy execution.

But you can't accuse Paul's final product of being amateurish. The cinematography—a tug of war between two photographers, Howard Atherton and Douglas Milsome—is lush and beautiful, giving the indescribable events a rich environment in which to cavort. Michel Legrand's bombastic score seems to have wandered in from another movie, but it strengthens the idea that the narrative is a boundless fantasy transplanted from the by-gone Golden Age of Hollywood. It's probably the most sincere, inept, gorgeous, and confounding car wreck you'll ever see.

"It's a totally new piece and that reason by itself to see it, but there's lots in it. People are saying that people aren't making movies about anything and I say *that The Legend of Simon Conjurer* is completely the answer to that, it's really about a lot of things. And it's done in a playful way, so you know that nobody's gonna get hurt, so go check it out!"[8]

NOTES

[1] Jordan Garren & Brian Morton. "An Interview with Jon Voight." Rogue Cinema.com. 2006
   http://www.roguecinema.com/an-interview-with-jon-voight-by-jordan-garren-brian-morton.html

[2] No author cited. "Man of Many Faces." 2006. NY Press. June 14. (Updated Feb 17, 2015).
   http://www.nypress.com/man-of-many-faces/

[3] Ratcliffe, Amy. "Director Stuart C. Paul Discusses His Short The Lord Of Catan." 2014. Nerdist.com. August 14.
   http://nerdist.com/director-stuart-c-paul-discusses-his-short-the-lord-of-catan/

[4] Archived at Box Office Mojo: http://www.boxofficemojo.com/misc/?id=1672

[5] http://www.imdb.com/title/tt0758763/board/nest/40948236?ref_=tt_bd_1

[6] http://www.imdb.com/title/tt0758763/board/thread/45273062. Fri Apr 28 2006 11:06:50

[7] Jordan and Morton. Rogue Cinema.com. 2006

[8] Ibid.

JON VOIGHT: CHARACTER OF EVIL[174]

New Yorkers have all the luck. This coming Friday, June 2nd, Jon Voight will be at the Village East Theatre for the premiere of his latest movie, the odd and exhilarating *The Legend of Simon Conjurer*. He's holding a Q&A and an autograph session "for as many people as the theatre can hold" (so says the film's official site: www.thelegendofsimonconjurer.com).[175]

Hell, the first 25 people through the door get in free!

Some people reading this won't be that thrilled with the news. They belong to a sad subsection of our culture who only know Voight as the father of Angelina Jolie (if they're aware of him at all). The rest of us, those who love film and its rich history and all the talented artists involved, know him as *Midnight Cowboy*'s Joe Buck and *Deliverance*'s Ed Gentry, as well as the myriad of other memorable characters he's played during his 40-plus-year career. With *Simon Conjurer*, Voight adds the latest persona to his canon, the brilliant and evil novelist/psychiatrist, Dr. Axel Crazx (pronounced "CRAY-zax", in case the spelling didn't give it away).

Looking very much like Orson Welles in *Touch of Evil*, buried under make-up and a fat suit, wolfing down chocolate bars in psychotic frenzy, Voight's Crazx has a beef with the title character, a healer who organizes group-therapy for a variety of addicts. He feels that Conjurer is a blight on society, an abomination… this from the guy whose novel "Nothing Matters Except Death" is advocated by Saddam Hussein! The word "antagonist" springs immediately to mind. "Yes, there's no other way to describe him," Voight tells me as he drives across Manhattan to his next engagement. "He's hiding a dark side, an evil side. He's a psychologist and an award-winning novelist—a very popular fellow. He's popular because he's so negative. Look up on the internet all the novels he's written—I recommend this because they're very funny! 'Life is Not Worth Living'. [laughs] 'I've learned a lot from [Dr. Crazx] and look where

---

[174] Originally published on Film Threat.com, 2006.

[175] A sadly-defunct website, it can be accessed through the Web Archive where you can read the almost-certainly manufactured pull-quotes from fictional news sources:
http://web.archive.org/web/20061231113031/http://www.thelegendofsimonconjurer.com/

it's brought me!' Saddam Hussein. They really are hysterical."

Apparently, there is no correct way to describe this new film. Written and directed by "?" according to the poster and "Q. Mark" according to the Internet Movie Data Base, even the movie's star seems hard-pressed to summarize the story. "It's interesting... I just came back from talking to some students at Kingsborough Brooklyn College. Really neat to speak to the people there, the faculty and the kids. They asked how to describe the movie and I said 'Well, it's such an unusual movie; it's difficult to put it into one category.' The person said, 'it's part mystery, it's part fantasy, it's part psychological, part spiritual'—and I said 'You're right! It's all of the above. And there's also some humor in it. It's very unusual, very interesting piece.' So in describing it, I'd say that it may be best termed as a fable because it's a very complex story, brings up many complex ideas and provokes many, many thoughts, but it does it in a very simple form. Which is what a fable does. The names—Dr. Crazx, Simon Conjurer—all have some playfulness to them."

(At this point, Voight's car passes through a tunnel and I lose contact with him. A few minutes later, my phone rings. "How's the interview so far?" the actor asks with a laugh.)

"When someone does something totally original in this day and age it's to be cherished, you know? And this piece is completely original and quite amazing. And there are some serious considerations there. It's an intriguing, other kind of experience. We're asking a different kind of thing from the audience. They're going to come in to an adventure they've never been on before, and they're going to be asked to ask questions and to explore something. There are many open-ending aspects to it, but there is a conclusion and a hopeful conclusion as well. So it's a quite intriguing piece. When I got the screenplay I said, 'Boy, this is a very extraordinary piece of work. It's brilliant in its structure.' I really think it's quite special."

And the actor insists that Crazx existed nearly in whole on the page when he received the script. "Pretty much, I delivered what Dr. Crazx is—I didn't fool around with it. The speeches are very complex. You couldn't improvise Dr. Crazx very much. He's a lead character and he speaks in an extraordinary way. Here's a piece of his dialogue in the midst of a river of dialogue: 'Simon Conjurer is no less than a monster in disguise. A horrid incubation. Let us not wait for him to reach his full maturity.' Very clever, you know? And like I said, this is at the end of a river of invective about this man's character and activities. He goes on and on. It's very ornate language."

The labyrinthine dialogue was only one of the challenges Voight faced on "Conjurer". Next comes the make-up that rendered him almost unrecognizable. If it weren't for his trademark piercing blue eyes, one would be hard-pressed to pick him out of the cast of virtual unknowns that round out the rest of the cast. "It takes a while to get it on," he says of the facial appliances. "And [the way we designed it] as an all-encompassing piece, it covers almost my entire face. I have some make up on my face as well—and then there's the fat suit. As I was putting on the make-up I got closer and closer to the character. By the time it was all on, I felt like the fellow. I kind of played around with it. It made me feel quite funny, actually and strange. It was fun. You don't always find the whole character until you put the makeup on and give it a shot. Of course, I'm doing a lot of other work outside of it, but the make-up helps you come to life."

At first glance, the "Written and Directed by ?" may strike the callous film scholar as a clumsy marketing ploy, the last act of a desperate publicist. Indeed, the website even plays this aspect up with an article about the pursuit of the mysterious creator, who bears more than a passing resemblance to the lead character. Because this journalist is dedicated to the truth, he was able to discover the truth behind the auteur's identity, but also knowing how to play the game, I ask if we're going to keep this a secret for the purposes of this article. Voight laughs. "No, no, I'll tell you who he is. His name is Stuart Paul and he's the lead in the film as well," he says, confirming my information and officially establishing me as "not an idiot".

Best known for the odd indie *Emanon* from 1987, Paul dropped off the proverbial entertainment map after being credited for the story for *The Double 0 Kid*. But as it turns out, he actually has been fairly active, to one extent or another, if only just writing. He's just completely under the radar. His recent emergence, such as it is, was only to bring to life a story that he abjectly believed in—one that captured Voight immediately. And Voight applauds Paul's decision to keep quiet about his role in *Conjurer*.

"The reason he didn't want his name on any of the credits and the reason that started was that he doesn't like the vanity in Hollywood," he explains. "He said 'I won't put my name anywhere on it!' Then it became a kind of thing because it was hard to follow through on anything. You call up the IMDb they have to have the name [to list the movie]. And I said, 'Well, here's what you do: we'll call you 'Q. Mark'. For question mark. It's a funny thing but there's a serious root to it. But he's going to stick with this. He'll never put his name on any of his pieces anymore. Life experience hones people into different things. This is a very mature Stu we're dealing with. Very unusual guy. Good guy. I wanna see all his movies now. I want to see what he's going to come up with next. He's got a lot of scripts that he's written lately and I want to see them all done. It'd be exciting to me as a film-goer to see his work and see his ideas come to be."

Far from being a mystery in Voight's life, the director and his star have actually had a long friendship prior to the cameras rolling on *Conjurer*. "He's a friend of mine and a person for whom I have a great admiration for as a kind of moral force in our lives. He has very strong understandings. He's one of those people who will tell me honestly what he feels about everything. He never lets me get away with anything and always tells me exactly what he feels. He's the type of guy who keeps my feet on the ground and very humbly. A very, very rare type of pal. It was very interesting [to finally work together]. We're very close, you know. We don't always agree—as any two people don't always agree. But he's the director and he's the boss and my very best friend. We had a lot of fun and it was exciting to work with him. Watching him make his decisions was quite interesting."

Returning to the IMDb, a quick glance at Voight's page reveals over sixty distinct roles in film and television. He got his start in a small role on *Naked City*, which led not only to additional television, but also to his first feature, the obscure and goofy superhero comedy *Fearless Frank* (1967)[176]. *Frank* has its similarities to his breakout performance in *Midnight Cowboy*, which would come just two years later in 1969. In *Fearless Frank*, he plays a wide-eyed country boy arriving in the big city for the first time, only to be murdered by gangsters and resurrected by a mad scientist. In *Cowboy*, it's the same story, only with sickly street people and male hustlers, rather than mad scientists and gangsters. When I point out these similarities, Voight laughs. "That's funny, isn't it? It *is* funny that the silly character, *Fearless Frank*, would be prophetic and that I'd go on to play that guy in earnest later. I was just doing a silly thing and then all of a sudden we go and do it seriously. Wow. Any man who knows *Fearless Frank* is a dangerous man!"

Those similarities aside, you won't find too many other parallels between the rest of the characters he's played. Granted, he's played heroes and villains and statesmen and presidents, usually men of stature, but he isn't an actor that can be accused of repeating himself that often. And I ask if this plays a conscious part in his decision-making. "I suppose in some ways it is. I don't want to repeat myself. I don't think there's anything wrong with doing something similar to one you've already done. But each character seems to be unique and I want to find that particular person. It could be a quirk that is unnecessary. I set out to play the character and I start with a clean table and work to find things to draw upon. I never know why people think I'm good for this or that [character], but because I am a character actor, people don't know what I *can't* do. They say, 'Listen, I can't figure out this role, maybe Jon has an answer', and they throw the script my way. It usually has to do with a certain kind of presence required for the role. A strength or something—they think that I have a commanding aspect. I'll play someone with a force of stature or a force of negativity—whatever it is. A coach or a president. Or the wise bad guy in *Heat*. A stature they're looking for me to fulfill. I'm very thankful that I'm working as often as I am and that people are excited to work with me. It's a

---

[176] See *Fervid Filmmaking* for more. Seriously, it's just a fascinating piece of writing.

great feeling. I think I've covered pretty much the gamut, but every time I'm offered a role, it's completely new territory to me. For some reason, I don't see things in categories, I guess."

Which is pretty amazing, I say, given the trash that so often comes out of Hollywood. Voight gets quiet on me for a second, then continues. "Well, I don't know about that," he says. "Look, I'm just an actor, a working actor, and there are a lot of wonderful actors working today. And especially, I must say, looking at the nominees this past year. Phillip Seymour Hoffman and Heath Ledger, Joaquin Phoenix and Terence Young, who I'm very impressed with. All these guys are going to have very long careers and they're all character actors. They're really strong character actors and they're all the real deal. That's a great bunch of guys who have paid their dues and are now stars. People can get movies made when they get one of those stars and I think that's a wonderful thing. These guys are artists. They're real and they're exciting. I remarked watching, 'look at this year! It's a great year for character actors.' Real artists! You think of the leading men, but you don't always think of the character actors. And there are a lot of them. And when they also have that leading man aspect to them, the charisma, they become a true force. And we have a bunch of them coming up and I'm so happy."

The traffic noises outside of the car begin to increase. I turn up the volume on my phone and ask him if there are any other movies coming up as exciting as *Simon Conjurer*. "Not *as* exciting," he says playfully. "I've just done a thing called *Pride and Glory*, which is a gritty story about a cop family in New York. I play the head of the family, a chief of detectives with two sons and a son-in-law, who are played by Colin Farrell, Edward Norton and Noah Emmerich. Then there's… then I have a movie coming out in the fall called *September Dawn*. It's a very extraordinary powerful piece. A Romeo and Juliet story set against a massacre—a historic event that happened in 1857. It's quite interesting. I've done some very interesting pieces now. I'm going to do a thing called *Transformers*, I'm getting ready to step into that one. It's a family movie."

And, of course, any movie geek worth their salt knows all about this upcoming blockbuster. Some of us can't wait. Others are just bewildered by the very concept. *Deliverance*, *Midnight Cowboy*, *Coming Home*, *The Champ*, and now *Transformers*? Something doesn't compute, even with the campy TV movie *Karate Dog* (2004) on his resume. So I ask: 'What attracted you to a project like *Transformers*?"

"Well, it was offered to me, and I'd worked with Michael Bay before [on *Pearl Harbor*]. And I like family movies—like *Holes*, other things. I like to stay in touch with younger audiences. I think it's going to be an extraordinary piece. The imagination that will take to build these *Transformers* and stuff like that. It's going to be a visual feast. And my challenge is to make the other story interesting. The human aspect of things. It's quite a challenge, actually. I'm going to be working with some great actors. John Turturro is going to be in it. Shia LeBouf is going to be in it. And I know that Michael is relying on me to bring a force to the character and an authenticity. That's what I'm thinking about now. How do I do that, given the power of this piece, and my character? I'm looking forward to it."

I take another quick glance at the official site for *Conjurer* and have only slightly more information about the mystery than I had before. Paul's character stares out at me beneath a shock of curly hair. Voight's grotesque Crazx looks even crazier than he had been during my first visit to the site. It doesn't really look like anything else, and I firmly believe in Voight's assessment that it will be a unique and challenging film. So how have the audiences taken to it? "No idea," he answers. "I haven't seen it with too many audiences yet. It's going to be fun. I'm going to go to the screening on Friday night and then address the audience afterwards. And I can't wait!"

LOVERS AND OTHER STRANGERS (1970)

Richie Vecchio: Don't you understand, Joan and I are just not happy together.
Frank Vecchio: You hear that, Beatrice? They're not happy together.
Bea: I heard, Frank.
Frank Vecchio: So who's happy?
Bea: Who's happy?
Frank Vecchio: What, do you see me running around dancing in the streets?
Bea: Do you see your father running around dancing in the streets?
Frank Vecchio: What are you, better than me? You think your mother and I are happy?
Richie Vecchio: You mean you and mom aren't happy?
Frank Vecchio: [together with Bea] No!
Richie Vecchio: Then why did you stay together?
Frank Vecchio: [pause] We're content.
Bea: We're content.
Frank Vecchio: These kids today, all they're looking for is happiness.
Bea: Don't look for happiness, Richie. It will only make you miserable.

Growing up, my parents often asked me how school was with the time-honored query, "What's the story, Ritchie?"

When family gossip would arise, while wondering why one couple hadn't yet divorced or otherwise enacted a murder-suicide pact, my parents would look at each other and say, "And *they're* still together."

If a friend was invited over, my father would say, "Now we have so-and-so's happiness to worry about."

It was years before I finally saw *Lovers and Other Strangers* and finally discovered the source of all these family sayings.

Based on their play, Renée Taylor and Joseph Bologna, along with David Zelag

Goodman, adapted their four blackout vignettes into an interwoven story about love and all of its dysfunctions, leading up to Mike (Michael Brandon[177]) and Susan's (Bonnie Bedelia[178]) wedding. As the film starts, Mike is getting cold feet. He can't go through with it. He wants to grab every ass he sees—"And that's not normal, Susan!" During the credits, Mike presents her with reason after reason, some of them perfectly reasonable, as to why marriage is a sham, a scam, old fashioned, ridiculous. It's 1970, for Christ's sake! And they've been living together for a year and a half. How hypocritical can you get?

Meanwhile, Mike's brother, Richie (Joseph Hindy[179]), and his wife Joan (Diane Keaton), and are considering divorce, which makes no earthly sense to their Italian-American parents, Frank (Richard Castellano) and Bea (Bea Arthur). Using food and threats to make their point, the Vecchios are unwaveringly against divorce. It just isn't done. Telling an anecdote about one of their friends: "Vinny chased her down the block and grabbed her by the hair. And Carmel spit right in Vinny's face. Then he started choking her by the throat over the open window. And the super had to come up and pick Vinny off Carmel. And *they're* still together."

On the WASP side of things, Susan's father Hal (Gig Young[180]) and Bernice (Cloris Leachman) are having their own problems. Hal has been seeing Bernice's sister, Kathy (Anne Jackson[181]) behind everyone's back. The upcoming wedding has Kathy in a constant state of hysteria and has been trying to pry a commitment out of Hal for months now. He can't do it. He has to think of Bernice's happiness too. Which leaves Kathy sobbing for most of the film.

Then there's Susan's sister, Wilma (Anne Meara), and her fizzling marriage to Johnny (Harry Guardino). She wants to bring passion back into their coupling. This makes Johnny feel henpecked and threatened, particularly of Wilma's newfound "obsession" with feminism. She doesn't know who the boss is anymore! "Let's not start that up again," says Wilma.

Finally, Mike and Susan decide to spread some chaos by fixing up his friend Jerry (Bob Dishy[182]) with her friend and bridesmaid Brenda (Marian Hailey[183]). Jerry gets all of his moves from *Playboy*'s advice column, while Brenda has read every female empowerment book available, as well as several that she may have made up. (It's hard to tell.) She wants to go to bed with Jerry, but her dignity is at stake, and her standing as a woman, and her responsibility to the female sex, but should she deny her own desires at the cost of upholding her ideals? Somewhere along the line, Jerry's desire to get laid is subverted by his need for an end to the conversation.

---

[177] "Senator Brandt" in *Captain America: The First Avenger* (2011), and by way of coincidence, voice of the "Street Cat" in *Heavy Traffic*. (See Chapter)

[178] Another co-incidence, she almost ran me over while leaving the set of *The Prince of Pennsylvania* (1988), which was filmed in my home town. I didn't get Keanu Reeves autograph because I didn't expect him to work again. Hope that didn't hurt his feelings…

[179] *Where Are the Children?* (1986)

[180] Academy Award winner for *They Shoot Horses, Don't They?* (1969)

[181] "Dr. Nolan" in *The Bell Jar* (1979)

[182] "Jack Jerome" in *Brighton Beach Memoirs* (1986)

[183] *The Seduction of Joe Tynan* (1979)

Though very obviously a '70s film, *Lovers and Other Strangers* still feels fresh today thanks to the human race's obstinance against change. As long as there is and will be sexual couplings and impending marriages, there will always be infidelity, confusion, stalwart parents with specious reasoning, and a gap in understanding. (Despite Hal's insistence to Mike that he gets it, he really gets it. "There's no gap," he smiles and reassures. For that's what Hal does: he smiles and he reassures. He just doesn't solve problems. Out of respect for everyone else's feelings, of course.)

While there isn't a phony performance in the bunch, not every character will endear themselves to every viewer. (From my point of view, Jerry would be better off hiring a prostitute than suffering through another of Brenda's gear-switching inner-turned-outer monologues.) The movie is ostensibly about Mike and Susan, their family members get much more attention from the script and direction. Honestly, that's okay, because the real stars of the film are Bea Arthur and *The Godfather*'s Clemenza, Richard Castellano. There is no conversation between the two that isn't comedy gold, from dialogue to their expert timing. Having created the role of Frank onstage, Castellano's reprisal in the film gives him the opportunity to own the part completely. Even modern reviews of the play sing Castellano's praises, so you can't help but feel sorry for present and future actors playing Frank Vecchio.

The other standout pair are Wilma and Johnny, though Guardino has to work twice as hard in his scenes because he's up against the marvelous Anne Meara.[184] As Wilma, Meara plays frustrated and pleasant at the same time. She wants affection and passion, not an argument on traditional sexual bedroom roles. Johnny is nothing but male insecurity.

"Nag?" she says in response to his dismissal. "I have done everything but nag. I have suggested, implied, rubbed against you while passing, worn provocative nightgowns, perfumed my underwear. I have tried every subtle way to reach you except showing stag films."

"Wilma, I get the feeling you're trying to make my virility look impotent."

"When did the feeling first hit you?"

"The day I married you. I was dynamite with other women."

"Well, sure. They were lucky just to be there with the holder of the world's championship three second record in intercourse."

"Out of all the women in the world, I had to marry an equal-time orgasm fanatic! You read a couple of *Ladies Home Journals* and all you know now is, *me too*!"

When she attempts to argue that there is no "boss" in their relationship, that they're equals, he challenges her to a wrestling match to prove her wrong.

Lovers and Other Strangers was written at a time when the Equal Rights for Women Act was in hot contention across the country. For the first time in… shit, it seems like *ever*, women were publically calling for an end to the male patriarchy, picketing and marching for equal pay in the workforce and equal time in the bed room. The end of the Sexual Revolution came as a complete surprise to the male population when they discovered the female section had a thing or two to say about "free love" and "free will". Considering the ERA is *still* a controversial conversation says something about our Cro-Magnon society. To realize that the ERA has still not passed says even more.

Lovers and Other Strangers marked the directorial debut of Cy Howard, a TV writer whose credits included *The Smothers Brothers Comedy Hour*, and he handles the material in the best way possible: he cast the right actors, then got the hell out of the way. There's nothing fancy about his direction and that's absolutely what the script called for. These people may seem larger-than-life, but underneath the bluster, they're all just actual size, trying to make sense of the world around them when all of their preconceived notions are suddenly challenged.

As Bea repeats to Frank while neither are listening, "You live and you learn. What are you gonna do?"

---

[184] Husband Jerry Stiller makes a cameo near the end as a guy pushing a "talented" little girl to sing at an appropriate time (which never comes). How Stiller and Meara managed to produce such an irritatingly unfunny offspring as Ben Stiller is a genetic mystery never to be answered in our lifetime.

MERRY CHRISTMAS, MR. LAWRENCE (1983)

(a.k.a.: SENJŌ NO MERĪ KURISUMASU)

When David Bowie died unexpectedly of liver cancer in January, 2016, the world went into mourning. The internet plastered tributes to every page—thousands of images of Bowie as "Aladdin Sane" and the infamous lightning bolt bisecting his face; the Thin White Duke captivating audiences; and, of course, the cult of Jareth the Goblin King mined the world for new pictures of the cod-piece-bearing white-haired inspiration of '80s' kids puberty. The one role that seemed to be overlooked, however, was perhaps his greatest: that of Maj. Jack 'Strafer' Celliers, the uncompromising and haunted soldier from the Tom Conti-starring *Merry Christmas, Mr. Lawrence*.

The 1983 WWII drama, a co-production between British Japanese studios was directed by the legendary Nagisa Ōshima[185], produced by Jeremy Thomas, with a screenplay by Ōshima with Paul Mayersberg, adapting the experiences of Sir Laurens van der Post's during his time as a Japanese POW, depicted in his collections *The Seed and the Sower* (1963) and *The Night of the New Moon* (1970).[186] The film concerns itself with the complicated relationships between the

---

[185] Director, In the Realm of the Senses (1976)

[186] "The film is heavily based on author/activist Laurens Van der Post's novel The Seed and the Sower, an erstwhile memoir of his days as a POW under Japanese heels in Southeast Asia. Van Der Post had visited Japan years before the war, and spoke the language, quickly gaining the respect of his captors and thus a window into their cultural practices. Van der Post developed some understanding of the Japanese mindset, while remembering that they were aggressors in this cataclysmic conflict. In that sense, he was never an apologist for the Japanese cause, nor did he seek to aid and abet the enemy, as the Arabist T.E. Lawrence did, blowing up rail tracks in an effort to halt his nation's imperialism. Rather, Van der Post's cinematic stand-in, Lieutenant Colonel John Lawrence, is a cautious pragmatist realizes he is a prisoner, albeit one enjoying a position of some privilege based on his linguistic skills and his status as an officer, so important to the rigidly hierarchical Japanese." Butcher, Terrence. 2010. "Exoticism and Eroticism in 'Merry Christmas Mr. Lawrence'." Pop Matters.com. October 21. http://www.popmatters.com/review/132431-merry-christmas-mr.-lawrence/

British POWs and their Japanese captors, in particular a strange and strained series of encounters between the New Zealand-born Celliers and the camp's "martinet" camp commander, Captain Yonoi (Ryuichi Sakamoto[187]). But the over-arching theme of the movie is the clash of cultures, neither of which truly understand the other, and the extreme difficulties that arise when one group baffles the other.

Mr. Lawrence begins with the titular character, British liaison Col. John Lawrence (Tom Conti[188]), summoned to defend a Dutch soldier from execution by the camp enforcer, Sergeant Hara ("Beat" Takeshi Kitano[189] in his film debut). The soldier and a Japanese guard were caught in a sexual encounter, but the Dutch soldier insists that that the guard had been raping him over a series of weeks. The guard claims that his generous attentions were misinterpreted by the soldier. Regardless, homosexuality is against camp policy and the complex Japanese Bushido code. Lawrence successfully manages to spare the soldier's life, but Hara calls for the guard to commit seppuku to atone. The ceremony is interrupted by Yonoi, who decrees that the ritual suicide will be carried out at a future time, leaving the guard partially disemboweled for the time being.

While Lawrence is the Hara's go-to man, due in a large part to Lawrence's having lived in Japan and understanding the language, he is not a voice of authority. Unfortunately, neither is Group Capt. Hicksley (Jack Thompson[190]), the POW's official spokes officer, who constantly butts heads with the Japanese over the Geneva Convention rules. While Lawrence and Hara have a grudging respect for each other—with Lawrence almost affectionate towards the cynical and hard-nosed soldier—Hara still insists on rules being followed to the letter, though he may bend those rules at his own whim. It's this unpredictable humanity that Lawrence works to exploit for the good of the prisoners.

Into this tense situation comes Maj. Celliers (David Bowie), a proud and decent man who immediately flaunts the camp's rules, smuggling food into the barracks, for instance, following a camp-wide punishment fast imposed by Yonoi, to cure their spiritual laziness. For Yonoi's part, upon meeting Celliers he felt an instant connection with the stalwart soldier, sensing a hidden shame within the blond man that he himself struggled with. (Celliers never recovered from his shame of betraying his younger brother in boarding school, allowing the weaker sibling to be hazed and essentially tortured by upper classmen; Yonoi's shame stems from the fact that he was posted to Manchuria at the time his Army comrades, the "Shining Young Officers" of Japan, staged a coup d'état in Tokyo, the "February 26, 1936 Incident", and were executed after the coup's failure. Yonoi's regret at missing the opportunity to share with his comrades' "sacrifice" never left him and he has dedicated his career to erasing that shame.) While Celliers' realizes the true nature of Yonoi's fixation—a homoerotic attraction that neither can safely acknowledge—Yonoi's Bushido code forbids the relationship. And it's here that the internal struggle centers.

Matters are complicated when a wireless is found in Celliers' and Lawrence's barracks. Yonoi orders both men imprisoned in a make-shift sweat box, starved and beaten. With a wall separating them, Lawrence and Celliers share bits of their past to pass the time and subvert their torturers. Surprisingly, Hara orders them before him. Drunk and inexplicably jovial, he allows the pair to return to their barracks, yelling "Merry Christmas, Mr. Lawrence!" Though this act was not on Yonoi's authority, the commander does not punish Hara further and actually seems relieved that the young Celliers has regained his freedom without having to compromise his own orders.

Soon, however, Yonoi's conflicted feelings towards and frustrations with Celliers has him questioning his own reasoning. Desperate to reassert his authority, Yonoi orders every man in

---

[187] Better-known as a musician and composer of *The Last Emperor* (1987).

[188] See *Movie Outlaw Rides Again* for chapter on *Gospel According to Vic* (1986)

[189] *Sonatine* (1993)

[190] Most recently seen in Baz Luhrman's *The Great Gatsby* (2013) as Nick Carroway's doctor.

the camp—including the sick and immobile—to stand at attention while he disciplines Hicksley. Celliers steps forward and, rather than accept Yonoi's challenge to combat, nor allowing himself to stand by while Hicksley is executed, does the unthinkable: he kisses Yonoi on both cheeks. Stunned and instantly humiliated, Yonoi collapses.

Maj. Celliers (David Bowie) and Capt. Yonoi (Ryuichi Sakamoto). Photo Copyright Oshima Productions. All Rights Reserved.

Some short time later, Celliers receives his punishment: buried up to his neck in the dirt and exposed to the elements. There will be no escape for the officer. Yet just before he succumbs, Yonoi visits him one last time, to cut a lock of Cellier's golden hair.

Years later, the war has ended and Lawrence is afforded the chance to visit Hara, now himself a POW of the Allies, about to be executed for his war crimes. "What did I do that was worse than anyone else?" Hara wonders.

"You are the victim of men who think they are right," Lawrence says. "Just as one day you and Captain Yonoi believed absolutely that you were right. And the truth is of course that nobody is right."

They then laughs as they share the memory of that fateful Christmas where Hara's generous nature got the best of him. The two men enjoy the reminiscence, and then Lawrence leaves Hara to his fate. As the door closes behind him, he hears Hara repeat that blessing from years ago, "Merry Christmas, Mr. Lawrence!"

Merry Christmas, Mr. Lawrence is a film that benefits from repeated viewings, possibly requiring even back-to-back sittings-through. A cursory glance may reveal very little but a lot of talk between career soldiers with little to do but converse and pontificate. "They're a nation of anxious people, and they could do nothing individually, so they went mad *en masse*," says Lawrence. It's definitely a colonial point of view, but the statement gives weight to the character of Hara. While the other Japanese guards seem to live in fear of Yonoi, the older, more experienced Hara is really the one who runs the camp—something he's all too aware of, resulting in acting without the commander's authority. He jails and releases the Western prisoners at both will and whim, and for these actions, which he feels were justified by circumstance and his own judgement, leads him frustrated in the end, when he is on the other side of the bars. Yonoi's actions are motivated by his sense of shame—mirroring Celliers' own sense that he was derelict in his duty towards his brother, but unwilling to show "weakness" by way of favoritism should he protect the younger sibling. Like Hara, Lawrence feels he "knows" his enemy, tries to find common ground, but neither are willing to accept that the other is just as confounded by cultural differences. Ultimately, neither the British, nor the Japanese, can definitely understand what the other is thinking or really why they feel that way, even when you take into consideration that the conflicts are born of similarities!

Draping these inherent cultural gaps in the background of war both amplifies and obfuscates the miscommunication. It's not just the language barrier that keeps the pair apart but the defiance of "the other". The central conflict between Yonoi and Celliers is driven by feelings of personal failure that can never be erased. Both are duty-bound, both are defined by almost universal ideals of masculinity; they turn their inner conflicts outward, turning their inner struggle into external battles of will.

"There are numerous interpretations for Yonoi's intense fixation with Celliers, but homoerotic desire seems to be at the core. The film's Wikipedia entry suggest that Yonoi is not necessarily gay, but instead sense a kindred spirit in Celliers, as both men are struggling internally with a shameful episode in their pasts. That may be true, but Yonoi's interest carries an intensity equivalent perhaps to contemporary Japan's hunger for Western pop culture, and I couldn't help thinking of the blond-tressed white women who flock to Japan to cadge generous tips serving inebriated businessmen at hostess bars. Sakamoto himself is a curious physical presence, all hooded eyes, severe cheekbones, and pouty lips, giving him the appearance of a petulant schoolboy, but for his conspicuous makeup, which, as told in the extras package, wasn't uncommon for Japanese soldiers of that era to daub on; they wanted to appear immaculate at all times, particularly around the 'barbarian' Westerners they were guarding. Yonoi's mush-mouthed English is dramatically appropriate here, as it conveys his emotional deterioration against the increasingly manipulative Celliers, fighting to maintain his haughty composure as his love-struck inner child—a female one?—takes control," said Thomas Butcher. "This isn't new territory for Ôshima, as anyone who has seen his 1999 *Gohatto* will know. In that picture, set in feudal Japan, a soft-featured, impossibly pretty young man, with a notably fey demeanor, joins a group of samurai warriors, and chaos quickly ensues. Indeed, erotic obsession, and the arrival of an interloper who causes a sexual disturbance, a twist in the sobriety of an insular clique, are familiar themes in his oeuvre. As such, he might be an excellent choice to helm a story—coming very soon, I expect—about the first openly gay soldier serving in the U.S. Armed Forces. Sadly, Ôshima's health has been ravaged by a series of strokes, and future projects are unlikely."[1]

Lawrence and Hara understand each other from a personal, if not cultural, basis, but both are still culturally biased. Despite his education and experience, Lawrence still views the Japanese from an educated, white man's perspective. Hara views the English from a Japanese point of view. Without meeting in the middle, "true" understanding can never really be reached. The only consensus is, while the ostensible enemies are confounding, the war is still the ultimate display of irrationality, and both cultures are caught in the middle. While Hara and Lawrence are comfortable with the cultural disparities—at least during their private moments—neither Celliers nor Yonoi can give an inch: their manhood will not allow quarter. The curse of the upper-crust upbringing: compromise means losing moral high ground. It isn't until Celliers embraces his shame and forces Yonoi to embrace his own, that the conflict is broken. That Celliers is punished for this crime really doesn't make much of a difference for him. In his mind, being buried up to the chin in sand and left to die in the sun is a martyrdom he can accept. Yonoi's trophy—a lock of Celliers' hair taken surreptitiously—is the only acknowledgement of "love" he can allow himself to make. Executing Celliers was the proper thing to do from a military standpoint, but it isn't something he'll ever forgive himself for—something that is implied by Hara in the end, but not said explicitly, because Hara has no words for what the other man felt.

"Here's a movie that is even stranger than it was intended to be. *Merry Christmas, Mr. Lawrence* is about a clash between two cultures (British and Japanese) and two styles of military service (patriotic and pragmatic). That would be enough for any movie, and there are scenes when it is enough, and the movie works pretty well," wrote Roger Ebert in 1983. "This is interesting material, especially since Ôshima plunges a little more deeply into the psychology of his characters than your average prisoner-of-war movie is likely to. There are hints of a homosexual attraction between Celliers and Yonoi, eventually leading to one of the movie's most awkward moments—a parting in which the British soldier actually seems to be saying that both sides were right in the war and both sides were wrong. It's awkward, not because of the subject matter, but because of the contrasting acting styles. Here are two men trying to communicate in a touchy area and they behave as if they're from different planets. The overstatement in the Japanese acting ruins the scene. It's strange: Japanese acting styles never bother me in all Japanese movies (especially not when they're modulated, as in the contemporary films of Kurosawa). It's only when you have actors who are clearly on different wavelengths that the Japanese histrionics become distracting. What this movie needed was a diplomatic acting coach."[2]

Because *Mr. Lawrence* is such an odd-duck of a film, courtesy of renowned artists, both now and then, at the top of their game, albeit in a much quieter way than their fans are used to, different reviewers focus on different things. For some, it is another entry in Ôshima's heart-wrenching oeuvre: "Ôshima indulges the tear-jerking tropes of prison-camp movies but avoids their moralizing, as Japanese and British are shown to be both brutal and human. In fact, Ôshima's primary insights are that it's not just brutal to be human, it is human to be brutal, and that the expression of the erotic often emerges, through the constraints of what Cassavettes would call "society," as violence. In a 1983 interview (included in the exemplary extras of Criterion's DVD release) he states, "That thing we call eroticism results from human beings wanting to somehow connect with each other [...] eroticism is proof that we are alive." In *Merry Christmas, Mr. Lawrence*, Ôshima furthers his critique of nationality, of borders, as restrictive of this connection. All to the accompaniment of a layered, and incredibly '80s, synth score."[3]

"'Stop using the term 'New Wave' once and for all! Evaluate each film on its own merits!' protested a critic-turned-auteur from Kyoto named Nagisa Ôshima in an angry 1960 denunciation of both Shochiku—the studio that funded his daring anti-Stalinist milestone, *Night and Fog* in Japan, before pulling it quickly from theaters—and the lazy critics who excused what Ôshima deemed censorship with the argument that Japanese New Wave films were simply in decline," wrote Aaron Hillis for *The Village Voice*. "Ever the feather-rustling outsider, even among his like-minded peers, the now 76-year-old Ôshima is the radical mind and guts of an iconoclastic filmmaking generation (once removed from the postwar humanists: Kurosawa, Kobayashi, Ichikawa) whose questioning, prodding, and deconstruction of its society's codified corruption and hypocrisy ran parallel to La Nouvelle Vague. (The knee-jerk comparison of Ôshima to Godard makes sense, since both figureheads' films spill over with politics, sex, youth, discourse, and experimental rigor, though Ôshima may be the more dedicated to his lefty, anti-authoritarian cine-activism.)"[4]

Today, Takeshi Kitano is a superstar in Japan, that country's "answer to Clint Eastwood, Lee Marvin, Don Siegel and Jean-Pierre Melville all wrapped in one," wrote Alex Simon. A hard-nosed action actor and director, the working-class-born Takeshi started out as a comedian, a member of a stand-up comedy duo (known in Japanese as a *manzai*) with his friend Nirō Kaneko (also called Kiyoshi Kaneko). They took on the stage names Beat Takeshi and Beat Kiyoshi and became known as "The Two Beats", their comedic style "punching down" at the poor, women, "the ugly and the stupid". After the duo dissolved, Takeshi gained greater fame on Japanese television. Coming from a working-class neighborhood run by Yakuza, the comedian fell in with gangsters again during his stint in comedy theater.[191] Some of these men helped him gain a foothold in the cinema, which led to his being cast in *Merry Christmas, Mr. Lawrence*, his first opportunity to play something other than comedy.

"*Merry Christmas Mr. Lawrence* was done when I was sort of at the peak of my popularity as a comedian, and was suddenly becoming very well known throughout Japan as a comedian. But, I knew that this was not going to last long, being a stand-up comic. I knew I had to do something different, and that is when Mr. Ôshima offered me the role in *Merry Christmas Mr. Lawrence*. Without knowing what acting really was or what filmmaking was all about, I said 'Okay, that would be great.' I thought I might surprise people, playing this kind of part. After

---

[191] "Well, they have this theater where most of the comedy performers gather. It opens at 10 in the morning and stays open 'til 9 in the evening, so these were my working times. My principal place for my performance was theater, rather than clubs, like here in the States. Although there are clubs there where you can make a lot of money, but principally it was the theater. What happens if you perform in nightclubs, or cabarets, these are the places where the Yakuza guys hang out. If they like your performance, they'll invite you to have a drink, then tell us legendary stories of the big bosses, and that's how I came to acquire that knowledge, some really interesting stories." Simon, Alex. 2008 "'Beat' Takeshi: The Hollywood Flashback Interview." The Hollywood Interview. July 26. http://thehollywoodinterview.blogspot.com/2008/11/beat-takeshi-hollywood-interview.html

seeing the film, I thought my performance was not bad at all, actually, so I was looking forward to see the reaction of the audience. One day I snuck into a theater to see their reaction, and was quite surprised to find that the first scene where I appear, the whole audience suddenly burst into laughter, as if I had suddenly appeared on stage doing a routine! I was devastated by their reaction, because this character was supposed to be very intimidating and mysterious, not somebody to be laughed at! (laughs) But here they were, still perceiving me as this funny, crazy comedian. After that, I only accepted parts playing serious, dark, evil characters. It took ten years of my playing those types of roles before I was perceived as being a serious actor."[5]

While *Mr. Lawrence* boasts four exceptional performances (Thompson providing a fifth), most modern audiences are no-doubt attracted to the film because of the rare appearance of Bowie in a film bereft of genre tropes. There are no songs for him to fall back on, no capitalization of his otherworldly manner stuffed into the persona of an alien or a Goblin King. As Celliers, he's the most down-to-Earth he's ever fallen. "He also sprinkles the role with personal touches. As he's waiting for execution, he pulls some tricks out of the old mime closet, miming a shave and a last meal and cigarette (itself a moment of rebellion to his captors). There are also several moments of singing in the film and Bowie, obviously the capable singer, sings out of tune so well that it doesn't even seem forced. All of these touches add up so that while you never forget that you're watching David Bowie (because really, how can you?), he inhabits the role of Celliers and brings him to life. In many moments he conveys several emotions bubbling under the surface with just a simple expression," wrote Rajan Khanna. Bowie himself said of the experience that he had never played "anything so unstylized before" and that the process was rewarding for him. Ôshima, by all accounts doesn't rely heavily on rehearsals and rarely shoots more than two takes, so the working environment seems to have been highly collaborative which no doubt helped bring out the best in Bowie's performance."[6]

Just as Nicholas Roeg was inspired by Bowie's "Diamond Dogs" tour to cast him in *The Man Who Fell To Earth,* reportedly, Ôshima cast Bowie after seeing the singer in a stage performance as John Merrick in *The Elephant Man,* and was taken by the man's ethereal presence.

"Bowie's screen performances are always doubled: He's always David Bowie at the same time as he inhabits a character. He can't help this, of course. He's David freaking Bowie and he's never going to blend. But that doubling effect also describes his mode of queer performance, in which his gender, sexuality or, indeed, species is never taken for granted. In *The Hunger* (1983), he makes a convincing 200-year old vampire. Of course, Tony Scott's film is a lesbian cult classic for its sex scene between Catherine Deneuve and Susan Sarandon. But even though Bowie's character has been unceremoniously boxed in the attic by that point, the eroticism of the Bowie-Deneuve-Sarandon triangle imbues both the film and its production history with a potent cocktail of iconic stardom and bisexual potential," wrote Rosalind Galt for Salon. "Nagisa Ôshima's film is complex and resonant, a rare assemblage of talents from Ryuichi Sakamoto to Takeshi Kitano and Tom Conti. But what seduced me utterly was the perfect meshing of Ôshima and Bowie's perverse coolness. The scene in which Bowie, playing New Zealand prisoner of war Major Jack Celliers, kisses Sakamoto's Japanese Captain Yonoi is surely burned into the memories of many a young pervert, and the film is not only homoerotic. The high-stakes power dynamic in this forbidden attraction crackles throughout, and Bowie manages to look at once rebellious and louche while shackled by the wrists and more so when finally buried in the ground and bound with rope around his chest. There's a lot else going on in the film but I hope it's no disservice to Ôshima to say that as a young viewer, I experienced *Merry Christmas, Mr. Lawrence* as at once a sexual and a cinematic revelation."[7]

Sakamoto never intended to pursue a career as an actor, though coincidentally his first film as an actor marked his first time as a composer as well. Though well-known throughout Japan for his music, following Bowie's death, Western journalists rushed to Sakamoto—who was back in entertainment news thanks to his score (with Alva Noto) for Alejandro G. Iñárritu's "Let's kill Leonardo DiCaprio for an Oscar!" *The Revenant*—to get his take on the Thin White Duke. "I never pursued an acting career, it's not my intention, but it's a fact that I acted in a film for the very first time with David Bowie, who was amazing. And it was my very first film music. So two very new things came to be at the same time. Working with David Bowie, I was with him for a month, every day, on a very small island in the South Pacific Ocean. For a month! [laughs] It was an amazing experience. He was very nice guy. Very straight-forward," he told Fact-mag's Miles Bowe. "I still cannot believe [Bowie is dead].

Celliers and Mr. Lawrence.
Photo copyright Oshima Productions. All Rights Reserved.

Even now I can't believe, especially because the new album came out two days ago. This morning I carefully listened back to each track of the new album. His vocals sound not like a cancer patient—because I know that. I was diagnosed with cancer two years ago, so I know what it is. It doesn't sound right."[8]

Strangely enough, playing the film's titular character, you'd think Tom Coni—whose own father had been a political prisoner during WWII, one of more than 4,000 men of Italian descent imprisoned on the Isle of Man by the British government "amid general suspicion of their loyalties"—would have gotten a little more press than his supporting actors. After scouring numerous reviews and interviews, Janet Maslin gave him the most attention in her '83 review: "Mr. Conti has some fine moments here, too, but his is the more passive and less mysterious role. He is also saddled with some of the film's more simplistic dialogue, and some of its more obscure responses. *Merry Christmas Mr. Lawrence,* is closer to a curiosity than to a triumph, though its conception is certainly ambitious. Mr. Ôshima has staged the film in a spacious tropical setting and filled it with a great number of extras. Even so, Mr. Bowie always stands out from the crowd."[9] Most contemporary interviews seem far more interested in his take on Bowie than on his own performance. It's not surprising, but it isn't necessarily respectful either of the great, and largely unsung, actor. But it seems like something he's gotten used to. (He's still around and working, by the way, and can be seen briefly in *The Dark Knight Rises* (2012).)

Perhaps one of the most difficult films in this book to get a handle on, the remarkably good news is that it was rescued from obscurity by those saintly titans at Criterion Collection. Their DVD offers a gorgeous transfer of the print and, as Butcher points out, extras numbering more than double the running time of the film: "Including interviews, five featurettes are clustered here, the longest being a 55-minute documentary bio of Van der Post, who was both an anti-apartheid Afrikaner and a godfather to one of Queen Elizabeth's grandchildren, eventually becoming a Commander of The British Empire. Who would have guessed that Robert Redford (!) was considered for Lawrence, that the original screenplay ran nearly 200 pages, or that Ôshima rarely shot more than a single take? We also get a deluxe 28-page booklet of print interviews and the *de riguer* theatrical trailer, apparently a necessary curio for obsessed fans. Whew!"[10]

Sergeant Gengo Hara (Takaski Kitano) and Mr. Lawrence (Tom Conti).
Photo copyright Oshima Productions. All Rights Reserved.

NOTES

[1] Butcher, Terrence. 2010. "Exoticism and Eroticism in 'Merry Christmas Mr. Lawrence'." Pop Matters.com. October 21. http://www.popmatters.com/review/132431-merry-christmas-mr.-lawrence/

[2] Ebert, Roger. 1983. "Review." Chicago Sun-Times. September 16. http://www.rogerebert.com/reviews/merry-christmas-mr-lawrence-1983

[3] Krute, Clinton. "Merry Christmas, Mr. Lawrence." Bomb Magazine. http://bombmagazine.org/article/4724/merry-christmas-mr-lawrence

[4] Hillis, Aaron. 2008. "Best of the New York Film Fest's Nagisa Ôshima Tribute." The Village Voice. October 1. http://www.villagevoice.com/film/best-of-the-new-york-film-fests-nagisa-Ôshima-tribute-6388781

[5] Simon, Alex. 2008 "'Beat' Takeshi: The Hollywood Flashback Interview." The Hollywood Interview. July 26. http://thehollywoodinterview.blogspot.com/2008/11/beat-takeshi-hollywood-interview.html

[6] Khanna, Rajan. 2012. "A Hidden Acting Triumph: Merry Christmas, Mr. Lawrence." Tor.com. January 11. http://www.tor.com/2012/01/11/merry-christmas-mr-lawrence/

[7] Galt, Rosalind. 2016. "David Bowie's magic dance." Salon.com. January 13. http://www.salon.com/2016/01/13/david_bowies_magic_dance_his_explosive_cinematic_sexuality_from_the_goblin_king_to_merry_christmas_mr_lawrence/

[8] Bowe, Miles. 2016. "Ryuichi Sakamoto reflects on his unique time with David Bowie." Factmag.com. January 13. http://www.factmag.com/2016/01/13/ryuichi-sakamoto-david-bowie/

[9] Maslin, Janet. 1983. "David Bowie In 'Merry Christmas'." New York Times. August 26. http://www.nytimes.com/movie/review?res=9C00E2DA143BF935A1575BC0A965948260

[10] Butcher, Terrence. 2010. Pop Matters.com.

MILLER'S CROSSING (1990)

What we have here is a fairy tale about gangsters.

Sometime in the early '30s, in some unspecified city, two gangs are in charge of "runnin' things". (Which ain't gravy.) On the one side, you have Johnny Casper (Jon Polito[192]) and the Italian mob, running numbers, fixing races, you know: business. On the other side, you've got Leo O'Bannon (Albert Finney), pretty much the owner of the town, running out of the Shenandoah Club. One day, Johnny turns up with a wart on his fanny, sez he's been placing bets on the horses, but any bet that goes through Bernie Birnbaum puts Johnny on the wrong end of the fix—worse, on the short money! It's getting so an honest businessman can't rely on a fix. So, in short, he wants Leo to do the right thing, and let him kill Bernie Birnbaum (John Turturro).

"Sorry, Casper. You're looking for a license to kill Hebrews, and I'm not selling any."

Bad play, thinks Leo's right hand, Tom Reagan (Gabriel Byrne). And Tom tells him so. See, there's a complication. A big complication. Seems Leo's gal is Verna Birnbaum (Marcia Gay Harden), Bernie's sister. And she's also stepping out on Leo behind his back—with Tom! So Tom knows exactly what kind of person Verna is. Putting Bernie down deep might smooth some future problems with Caspar. Leo doesn't want to hear that.

The next morning, Rug Daniels, one of Leo's grifters, turns up dead in an alley. Leo had him tailing Verna, so the short money is on Verna getting spooked, popping Rug in the shadows. A little boy and his scruffy dog are the ones to find Rug; the boy steals Rug's namesake toupee. "They took his hair, Tom," Leo ponders out loud. "Jesus, that's strange."

"Maybe it was injuns," Tom replies.

Now Johnny's no yegg. He knows Tom has Leo's ear. So he tries to buy some good

---

[192] "Det. Steve Crosetti", *Homicide: Life on the Street* (1993-1994, NBC created by Created by Paul Attanasio)

favor, offers to square Tom with his bookie, Lazar, to whom he's in for a mint or two. Tom's not too stellar with the ponies. One numbers guy sez to Tom, "Horses got knees?"

"I dunno," sez Tom. "Fetlocks."

"Well, if I was a horse, I'd be down on my fetlocks praying you don't bet on me."

The last bet Tom placed, on Thunderclap, the horse barely made it out of the gate.

But Tom doesn't want Johnny's ugly money. He doesn't turn against Leo. So Johnny has his goons, Frankie and Tic-Tac, try to beat some sense into the consigliere. It won't be the first time.

So, now Leo has Chief O'Doole (Thoma Toner[193]) and the Mayor (Richard Woods[194]) hitting all of Caspar's joints. Then one night, Johnny sends some boys to ventilate Leo. But the old man is still an artist with a Thompson, and he sends two of them dancing to their graves. Even takes out the getaway car. Seeing no end to this, Tom finally pleads with Leo to think things through. When Leo insists on protecting Bernie, Tom confesses that he's the one stepping out with Verna. After taking many right crosses to the jaw, Tom and Leo are quits.

But Johnny isn't so quick to accept applications. "You been to college? We only take yeggs what's been to college. Ain't that right boys?...I'm joking, of course." To prove his new loyalty to the Caspar gang, Tom has to give up Bernie. The hitch he doesn't see is that he has to drive out with them, to Miller's Crossing in the woods, and do Bernie himself.

Out there in those woods, Bernie is beside himself, and Tom's not looking too good either. "This is wrong, Tommy! You don't whack people!" He gets down on his knees, begs, pleads through his tears. "Look in your heart, Tommy! Look in your heart!"

As Verna said, Tommy does have a heart after all. "Even though it's small, and feeble, and you can't remember the last time you used it." He fires into the air and tells Bernie to vanish.

Johnny's right hand, the menacing Eddie Dane (J. E. Freeman[195]), doesn't buy it. Neither Tic-Tac (Al Mancini[196]) nor Frankie (Mike Starr[197]) watched the hit. All Tic-Tac said was, "You gotta put one in his brain. The first one puts him down, the second goes in the brain. Then he's dead. Then we go home."

See, Eddie Dane has a vested interest in all this too. It's not that he's not loyal to Johnny, Christ knows, but Bernie's been stepping around too, with Eddie's "boy", Mink (Steve Buscemi), and now Mink hasn't been around. Something stinks.

It's all gonna come to a head. A man can only be pushed so far before he starts pushing back. But Tom's smart. That's his weapon. He sees all the angles. Especially when Bernie returns, rearing his ugly head, letting Tommy know that he knows, "Me turning up, I thought, might not be so good for you. But then I think, that might not be so bad for me. You get me my money or I start eating in restaurants."

"We should just get outa here," Verna tells Tom.

"What about Bernie?"

"He can come with us."

"You, me, and Bernie? Where we gonna go, Verna? Niagara Falls?"

Everyone thinks they've got Tom pegged. But as he's quick to point out, "Nobody knows anybody. Not that well."

Miller's Crossing was the third feature film written and directed by the Coen Brothers, known separately as "Joel" and "Ethan", whose stars were only starting to shine after the critical successes of *Blood Simple* (1984) and *Raising Arizona* (1987). After working as script-doctors and editors on an almost depressing number of low budget horror films—including

---

[193] *Doubt* (2008)

[194] *In & Out* (1997)

[195] Wild at Heart (1990)

[196] "Capt. Harry Nugent" on *Colditz* (BBC 1972-1974, Created by Brian Degas, Gerard Glaister)

[197] "Frenchie" in *Goodfellas* (1990)

Sam Raimi's landmark *The Evil Dead* (1980) their stars were finally rising.

"I'd started working as an assistant editor on low budget, sort of, splatter movies," recalls Joel. "Then Ethan and I started writing...a lot of these guys came in and wanted scripts written, these producers who were looking for very low budget things. [...] They mostly had "Dead" in the title. The best one was *The Evil Dead*, Sam Raimi's first movie, and that's how we got to know Sam, who's an old friend of ours. The rest were all those sort of early 80's *Friday the 13th* knockoffs: *Fear No Evil, Nightmare*...you know, they were all..."

"Scantily-clad girls running from guys with big knives," [Ethan interjects].

"Right. *Evil Dead* was the only really distinguished one I worked on."

[Said Ethan,] "Having written these things, especially for Sam, and going through the process of watching people raise the money for their own movies, starting with very limited, or no experience, as we had, in production...we figured, if they can do it, why not us?[1]

A decade later, they're working on a period drama, a gangster piece titled after a nickname they'd given their main character, Tom Reagan: *The Bighead*. Sort of a reworking of Dashiell Hammett's *The Glass Key*. For those unversed in Hammett (or Chandler), *Miller's Crossing* is a network of double-crosses and playing against the middle. All Tom wants to do is keep the peace, but there are too many pawns running around the board vying for king. Queering all the deals just to keep a girlfriend's crooked brother alive seems like a real bad play. "Think about what giving up Bernie gets us, and what crossing Johnny Caspar loses us."

"Christ, Tom, you know I don't like to think," sez Leo.

"Yeah, maybe you should think about starting."

"When I read that script, I was just like anybody I think who read it, just really impressed by how visual and literate and how complex those relationships in the story actually were. When you unravel what that movie is about, it's even more audacious that someone could base a storyline on that single conversation between Steve Buscemi's character and mine at the bottom of the staircase. All the twists and turns, the betrayals..." Byrne told Alex Simon in 2007. "There's laugh out loud moments in that movie, whereas on paper, it didn't necessarily read that way. When Albert Finney turns around says 'They took his hair, Tommy. They took his hair!' (laughs) And of course, we'd just seen the kid run off with the guy's rug in the earlier scene. I asked the Coens what their inspiration was to write the film, and I forget whether it was Joel or Ethan who said to me: "You always see gangsters in the street, but you never see them in a forest." I just thought that was so brilliant. Plus, there's so much amazing imagery: the hat floating by the camera through the forest, which is one of the most original images in film history. [...] [T]here's *The Third Man*, there's also *The Glass Key* in there, the original *Scarface* with Paul Muni. I remember looking at those old gangster films and thinking 'What can I steal out of here that won't be too obvious? And I think it's in *Scarface* where Paul Muni lights the match off the policeman's badge. It's just a throwaway bit, but in order to set up that shot in *Miller's Crossing*, it was this really complicated process, where we had to fix the cop's badge with sulfur and all kinds of props for that bit to work. And it was this wonderful, Coen-esque cop character: 'I'm just speculatin' about a hypothesis, Tom!' (laughs) It looked like a throwaway moment, but it really helped establish Tom's disrespect for the law, and everything, really.[2]

Filmed in New Orleans by a more-disciplined Barry Sonnenfeld (more disciplined than he will be on, say, *The Addams Family*, at least), *Miller's Crossing* is a buffet of crime delight. There isn't a boring character to be seen, and every single one of them seems to have a life outside of their scenes—including Frances McDormand as the Mayor's sassy secretary; including director Sam Raimi as a dim-witted, hair-triggered cop. All the pieces fit smoothly together, but it takes a while before the picture comes clear. While Hammett fans will be quick to follow along, many of the twists provided come from character development, rather than forced necessity dictated by the plot. The inevitable ending this time around isn't necessary inevitable. It's come by honestly, but it doesn't come down unnaturally to "them or us"; other escape routes are available to all parties, and it isn't destiny pushing them towards a showdown, but stubbornness, in the cases of some, naiveté and misplaced trust in others. In the case of Tom Reagan, his final confrontation with the pursuing demons ends with him just being fed up with trying to get people to listen to reason. When he finally manages to tie up the ends, he picks up the phone and places another bet. As he says several times during the course of the film, "Nobody knows anybody. Not that well." And if we, the audience, think we can tell what anybody is thinking, we're just as deluded.

With 20th Century Fox providing the financing, the Brothers had written a plum role for their *Arizona* star, Trey Wilson. The once Nathan Arizona would next play Leo O'Bannon. Except that two days before shooting, Wilson died of a massive brain hemorrhage. Nothing against Albert Finney, who signed on as a replacement and is fucking brilliant, but you can't help but wonder "what if?"

"Yeah, we shot that in and around New Orleans, and I think if they'd had an election for Mayor that year, Albert [Finney] would've won it, hands-down," said Byrne. "He led the St. Patrick's Day parade and was up and down Bourbon Street every night. The last thing you'd think of Albert after talking with him was that he was an actor, which is the greatest compliment I can give him. You'd talk with Albert about race horses, football, politics, what was going on down the road. I never heard him talk about acting, and I'm not someone who likes talking about acting, either, or talking about the business. We had many great conversations. I remember after we shot that scene in the park, we were two hours from New Orleans, and myself and Albert came back together in the van. We didn't have separate cars in that film, everyone just went in the van together. It was great. Coming back, I just sat with Albert for two hours and he told me all about where he was born, and where he was brought up, what working in England was like in the 1950s and '60s…he told me how he turned down the lead in *Lawrence of Arabia*. I said 'Did you regret it?' He said "No Gabe, I didn't regret it, because the next year I won the Oscar for *Tom Jones*." (laughs)"[3]

"The old man's still an artist with the Thompson." Albert Finney as "Leo."
Screengrab copyright 20th Century Fox. All Rights Reserved.

(By way of trivia, Finney had such a great time on set that he stuck around well past his last day. If you look closely during the scene where Tom bursts into the woman's room—"Close your eyes, ladies, I'm coming in!"—Finney can be seen in drag as an outraged older lady.)

One of the film's major set pieces involves an attempt on Leo's life. Two gunmen enter Leo's home, kill the other occupants—one while smoking a cigarette which ignites the newspaper he was reading, the smoke drifting up through the floorboards alerting Leo to their presence—and mount the stairs. As Leo takes them out one by one—machine-gunning one with a Tommy Gun, the bullets sending the man into what the Coens refer to as the "Thompson Jitterbug", where he twitches with each impact, his finger convulsing on the trigger of his own weapon, stitching bullets through the walls, floors, and even his own toes—while the most Irish of all songs, "Danny Boy", plays on his Victrola.

"Well, it's actually a little too obvious, yes!" said composer Carter Burwell. "The Coens knew something had to be playing on Finney's record player when the assassins arrive and they stuck in 'Danny Boy' assuming we'd ultimately find something else because it was just too obvious. And wouldn't it be nice if we found another Irish piece that people weren't as familiar with? But they cut the scene to 'Danny Boy' and after trying lots of different traditional pieces there, nothing was really quite as good. Ethan looked up the singer of our version of "Danny Boy", Frank Patterson, and asked if he would be interested in performing the song to our scene. Frank was very interested; he said 'This film will introduce the song to a whole new audience!' He didn't seem at all off-put by the actual content of the scene, some guy getting his head blown off! He was very excited by it. [...] Larry Wilcox did the arrangement and we recorded it in this extremely old-fashioned approach. Frank would watch the film with us, and Joel and Ethan would say, 'Now if you could hit the word 'bend' here and hold it until the car explodes...' He memorized the visual cues, sang while watching the film, the conductor followed Frank, and the orchestra followed the conductor. I think Frank got it in two takes. It was kind of amazing."[4]

Burrell's score drives the film in a way most modern scores fail, bringing out the flavor of the scenes in a beautiful way without being obtrusive. In many ways, the score is an additional, invisible character. "From the time we read the script together, before they even shot it, we all agreed it would be nice to use a big orchestra. We didn't know what a really big orchestra was, but something that sounds like one—bigger than a banjo! So while they were shooting I was learning about orchestration and how the whole thing works. It was really fun. I had an excess of time, three months, to write the score, which is a lot more than I usually get. And also, uniquely, they had money left over after the shoot—they'd actually come in under budget on the movie—so we could afford a large orchestra and could do everything we wanted to do. So it was a great experience. I love whenever this business gives you an opportunity to do something new."[5]

Unlike the novels that inspired them, there's no mystery driving the plot of *Miller's Crossing*, except for why the characters behave the way they do, usually against their best interests. ("You always know why you do things?" Tom asks Verna...of course, later, he insists that "you do thinks for a *reason*."). Instead, it's the interactions of the characters, all of them outwardly familiar tropes but unique, breathing individuals beneath the facades. In this film, the people are the mystique.

"At the beginning of *Miller's Crossing*, we had two setups: the first was of a drinking glass with ice cubes, then a close-up of Polito. We did not intend to show right away who was holding the glass. You see someone walk off with the glass, you hear the tinkling of the ice cubes, but the character is not visible in the shot. Then you see Polito, you listen to his monologue, and the ice cubes are always part of the scene, but they escape view. Then you see Albert Finney, but you still do not know who is holding the glass, and finally, you get to Gabriel Byrne in the background. All that was set up and laid out in the storyboards. We intended to create an aura of mystery around the character who was going to become the hero in the film. Polito is important in this scene because he's the one who provides the background information as he begins to tell the story. We held back Gabriel's entrance into the conversation. He is the last one to talk, five minutes after the beginning of the film."[6]

It also marked the beginning of the "Coen Brothers Stock Company," introducing audiences to actors like Polito, Turturro, and Buscemi, who would join Frances McDormand and go on to play more prominent roles in future Coen pictures. "There's a little bit of a mix always going on. Even from *Blood Simple* on, we would write specific parts for a specific actor, someone whose work we knew or who we knew personally and were friends with. So there's always been a mix of parts for specific actors and parts where we're not sure who's going to play them. In *Blood Simple*, for example with Emmet Walsh's part, we wrote that for him. We knew his work. Holly [Hunter]'s part in *Raising Arizona*, was written for her, but Holly was an old friend of ours."[7]

They also introduced the world to Marcia Gay Harden (who would go on to win an Academy Award in 2000 for her role as "Lee Krasner" in Ed Harris' *Pollock*). "In 1989, Harden was appearing as a character called *Lucy the Fat Pig* in a New York University production. 'Basically, I followed the male lead around, making snorting noises,' she says.[198] Donna Isaacson, a casting director, was in the audience. 'Now here,' Isaacson recalls thinking, "is someone with nerve. She just went with it. There was no holding back." Isaacson set up the meeting with the Coen brothers that eventually led to the unknown Harden beating Julia Roberts, Demi Moore and Jennifer Jason Leigh for the female lead in *Miller's Crossing*. At the time, Harden was studying acting as a graduate student, even though she had already done so at the University of Texas, had done years of summer stock and was rapidly approaching 30. 'I was old to be in grad school,' Harden says. 'But I wanted to have resonance. I felt like I could get a reaction from an audience, but it didn't feel like anything I did came from deep inside of me'," reported Margy Rochlin in The Guardian.[8]

"So I graduated, I'd been brought in to see the great Milos Forman for *Valmont*, and it got down to being very close between me and Annette Bening, and that was a big to-do in the casting world, because Annette had credits and I didn't. So naturally the person who doesn't have credits, people are asking, "Well, who's that? Who's that upstart just coming out of school?" [Laughs.] So I didn't get that part, but I did get attention, and that was valuable. Then Donna invited me to meet the Coens, and I was doing a play, *Les Liaisons Dangereuses*, down in Norfolk, Virginia, so I was going back and forth by train to meet with the Coens, and—although it's unusual for this time—you used to get the script a good two weeks in advance to read before going on auditions, so you had time to prepare. So I was able to check out old movies like *The Public Enemy* or Dashiell Hammett's *The Glass Key*, things like that, to really get the feeling of that world they were creating. And it's easier when you're a single kid right out of school than when you're a mom with three kids and craziness in your life to actually do that work, to do all of that work that goes into enhancing an audition. I auditioned for them three times, and against all odds they cast me. It is typical for them to give newcomers a chance, however. They've done it for Frannie McDormand, they did it for Holly Hunter, they did it for me, and they've really helped a lot of other New York actors toward roles of prominence and longevity. So I'll always be grateful to the Coens and to Donna Isaacson, because they sort of gave me my start."[9]

"[H]er feature-film debut as a two-timing floozy in the Coen brothers' Prohibition-era gangster drama *Miller's Crossing* was so silkily confident and original, she seemed destined to land on top of the Hollywood A-list. Instead, she went on to a television movie called *Kojak: None So Blind*, did a lot of babysitting and found out how hard it is for people to separate buzz from reality. 'Everyone thinks offers are always pouring in,' she says. "Offers have never poured in. Never. I was auditioning a lot, but I didn't get the jobs. I had to pay off my school loans, you know?""[10]

---

[198] "I had gone back to grad school, so I was studying at NYU Tisch School Of The Arts, and I was in the master's program there, which is really a program of shredding affectation, shredding ego… not literally, but the outer surfaces, the things that you think make you you, so you can acquire neutrality. And once you acquire neutrality, you can begin character work, filling it with the core of you, which is what will make your character different from any other character. So [casting director] Donna Isaacson had come to see a play I was in where I was playing an invented character, *Lucy The Fat Pig*, in a Shakespeare gender reversal of *A Comedy Of Errors*. All the guys were girls; the girls were guys. And I was Lucy The Fat Pig, who had no lines. So my chagrin at being cast in my senior year of the master's program in a character that had no lines led me to creating this series of different kinds of grunts and snorts for Lucy that were, in essence, lines. They were her responses. And it was absolute bawdy physical humor that we were able to explore in that play. Beanbag breasts would fall out, a skirt would "accidentally" be ripped off and the underwear would show. It was all on purpose, but we made it look as if it wasn't, and the audience was just screaming with laughter. Anyway, Donna had come to see this, and why it made an impression on her for *Miller's Crossing*, this dark film noir, I simply have no idea. [Laughs.] But she saw whatever she saw." Harris, Will. 2012. "Marcia Gay Harden on her favorite character and working with Clint Eastwood." NonStopPop. October 11. http://www.avclub.com/article/marcia-gay-harden-on-her-favorite-character-and-wo-86533

"After a film noir and a madcap comedy, the Coen brothers were again, according to Ethan, making 'a conscious effort not to repeat ourselves' when they undertook the writing of *Miller's Crossing*. They started from a genre they wanted to do, the gangster film, and an image: 'Big guys in overcoats in the woods—the incongruity of urban gangsters in a forest setting.'" Read the official Production Notes. 'We weren't thinking so much of gangster pictures,' adds Joel, 'just novels.' And while their first film had been inspired by the plot-driven pulp fiction of James M. Cain, for this one they turned to Dashiell Hammett: 'He took the genre,' Joel explains, 'and used it to tell a story that was interesting about people and other things besides just the plot. In Hammett, the plot is like a big jigsaw puzzle that can be seen in the background. It may make some internal sense, but the momentum of the characters is more important.' "[11]

When it came time to cast *Miller's Crossing*, John Turturro was already known to the Coens due to his friendship with Frances McDormand. As a matter of fact, they'd had the actor in mind for *Barton Fink* when they hit their famous writer's block on that picture, prompting them to focus on something completely different. That's when "Bernie Birnbaum" appeared on the page. "They'd seen me do a lot of plays, and so they said they were going to write a part for me. Then they wrote two parts for me in a row![199] [Laughs.] Those are big things. When someone writes something for you, you really want to return the favor. So I put a lot of work into it, and tried to give them a little surprise back. Actually I'm going to be directing these three one-act plays on Broadway soon, and Ethan is one of the writers. Woody Allen is one and Elaine May is one and Ethan is one. So I'm working with him again. This is, I guess, the sixth time we've worked together," Turturro told The A.V. Club. "The Coens are like a mom-and-pop operation. They write it, they edit it, they do the whole thing. They're involved in everything. It's very low stress, working with them. There's almost no stress. If I could make a movie with them every couple of years I would, just because of the pleasure of it."

Arguably, Bernie's big moment in the film is when he's "taken for a ride" by Tom, Frankie, and TicTac, dragged out to Miller's Crossing to die. Terrified, Bernie lays his soul bare before a queasy Tom. "Tommy, this isn't right!" he sobs. "You don't whack people! Look in your heart, Tom! I'm begging! I can't die out here. Not like a dumb animal! Look in your heart!" It's a nakedly emotional moment: Bernie without his slick patter or confidence. This is a man who knows that this is the end and the only "angle" he has to play is honesty, groveling before his executioner, begging for him to see reason.

"I don't remember how many takes [that scene took]. I just know it was 13 degrees, that's all. It was really cold. You know, it was a long time ago. It was a hard scene. Sometimes you think about movies, and you say, "Well, I want to try to do something that's not exactly in a movie." If you've ever been in a very dangerous situation, you know that people will do all kinds of things to keep themselves alive. It was very well-written, but you want to imagine what it's really like to be in that kind of situation. It depends on what you're willing to do, and in real life you would do a lot of different things. I tried to capture a little bit of that. I had a couple close encounters throughout my life before that, and you store that stuff in the back of your mind. It's how you do it, but it's what they choose and how they put it together too. But that was my goal when I did that, was to do something that was almost a little difficult to watch, because people aren't trying to be heroic at those moments."[12]

While much has been written about the leads, the film's primary antagonist, the one who provides the bulk of the immediate conflict, Johnny Caspar, aka "Giovanni Casparo", played

---

[199] "They said at the end [of production on *Miller's Crossing*—the guy, [executive producer] Ben Barenholtz, said there was this other movie. The way he talked, it sounded like 'Bart And Fink'. I thought it was 'Bart *And* Fink'. I was like, Bart And Fink? I don't know about that." And I didn't completely get it when I first read it. Their scripts you have to read a bunch of times. And now I guess people can read them easier—some of their scripts—because they know their sensibility. But their sensibility can be quite different, depending on the movie that they're linked to." O'Neal, Sean. 2011. "Random Roles: John Turturro". The A.V. Club. June 28. http://www.avclub.com/article/john-turturro-58178@seanoneal

by veteran character actor Jon Polito, usually gets a short shrift. Subsequently appearing in the majority of the Coen's films, Johnny Caspar is arguably Polito's meatiest role of his career. "I do consider myself a character actor because everything I've played has been one hell of a character," Polito told Adam Pockross. "I think a character actor, more than a leading man, is someone off to the side. They're either the baddie, or they are the best friend. A mother role is a character actor part. It's the stuff that fills in the plot from the center of the movie, which is usually your leading man or leading woman. […] It's a funny thing about character actors. You hear stories about when there was demands for better salaries and stuff for actors. What happened to us was when these stars went up into the $20 million range, they cut the salaries of the character people way down. And yet people think character men are rich, but in fact in the end, some years were as low as $50,000 and less, and some years they were maybe as high as $120,000. But not more than that. They're really middle class, and most of the time lower middle class. That's what an actor is, except in the fact that they have panache and charm."[13]

Unlike Turturro, Johnny Caspar hadn't been written with any particular actor in mind. Polito, however, had that character in his sights from the audition. "I knew they were looking for the part and were close to casting. ... I was asked initially to read for another part by the casting person. I don't think the Coens knew this. I was asked to read for the Dane. But I had read the script and the only part I ever wanted to play was Johnny Caspar. So I said, 'No. I will not read for anything but Johnny Caspar.' […] So anyway, I would not read for the Dane, and I went off and did a play, *Other People's Money*, and I did an arc on *Miami Vice*. And they came back to me after about a month and a half ... and said, 'We still haven't cast the part, we would like to see Polito for this part.' And I only read the first scene, and the Coens stopped and said, 'Wait outside.' And then they asked me to come back in, and then without even prepping, they wanted me to read the whole role, the whole scene, the whole performance. So I read, I sat in that casting room and read every scene. […] I think that generally my career changed with *Miller's Crossing*, and therefore there was a gangstery thing that went with a mustache. So I would say the character Johnny Caspar. And *Miller's Crossing* led to a whole bunch of recognition. But then again, I was on *Seinfeld* in the "Reverse Peephole" episode where I had a comb over and talked with a bad accent. I played his landlord. And of course, *Seinfeld* at the time was major and that lasted for about five years. Now I'm only recognized for surviving this long."[14]

"A striking feature of *Miller's Crossing* is it's incongruous, by the standards of a gangster flick, deployment of beautifully serene, autumnal outdoor settings in the eponymous location outside of town which the film's structure continually brings it back to. Views looking up to the forest canopy gliding peacefully by underline the contrast with the grimy urban environment of violence, sleaze and corruption which harbors and even normalises most of the action. Importantly the settings determine how differently the conflicts will be resolved: in the forest it's by recourse to the spirit, as the merciful sparing of one life exemplifies, in contrast to the rule of lead justice repeatedly seen in the harsh, garish city settings. Echoing the naturalness of Tom and Leo's friendship, only in the wild can humanity peak through."[15]

The prominent image of *Miller's Crossing* is a black fedora landing on the forest floor, resting before the camera before the wind picks it up with the leaves, swirling it away through the tree. Later, Tom tells Verna about a dream he has about the wind blowing his hat off.

"And you chased it and chased it until you finally caught it. Only it wasn't a hat any more. It had changed into something beautiful," she responds.

He scoffs at her. "No. It stayed a hat. And I didn't chase it. Nothing more foolish than a man chasing his hat."

Because of the way we've been taught to "read" films, that lonesome image of a hat without a wearer seems like a heavy metaphor, a symbol perhaps for Tom's relationship with Leo. Certainly, the shot is repeated at the end, only with Leo now, walking through the woods while Tom watches him go. It evokes the final shot of *The Third Man* and seems to evoke the opening. That Tom does not pursue, his face remaining unreadable as he watches the object of his machinations abandon him. Is Leo Tom's "hat" in this case? That Tom does not chase after him seems to give weight to his summation of his dream. Then you realize that you're dealing with the Coens, who love misdirection and misplaced symbolic meaning. Perhaps in this case, a hat is just a hat, Leo is just Tom's former friend and boss, and he's too tired to chase after a man who likely didn't deserve all the protection his consigliere provided.

"In this visual strategy the film evokes an unusual association with the America-phile film noir of France's Jean-Pierre Melville, particularly his *Le Circle Rouge* (*The Red Circle*, 1970), whose similarly wintry scenes of masculine showdown in the muted space of quiet woods evokes a strong resonance," wrote Westcombe. "If that seems a long bow to stretch, consider the bridge between *Miller's Crossing* and Melville's brilliant black and white gangster thriller *Le Doulos* (1963), which ends with the gangster protagonist's final fate underlined wistfully by the shot of his fedora coming to rest, alone in the frame, in the dirt of the forest floor, in anticipation of the (likely) homage with which the Coens open their title sequence here, a fedora being blown off its bed of fallen leaves in the forest of their imaginary America."[16]

"'The hat really becomes a big symbol in the film,' notes unit manager Ron Neter. 'Every time Tom gets knocked down, the hat falls off, and people are always handing it back to him.' Five identical hats were made for Byrne to wear during the filming, but another "generic" one was used for the opening shot of the credits: a hat blowing away from the camera across a field, which was filmed at high speed using a special lightweight hat that could be controlled with a fishing line. This shot, the last to be filmed, 'was one of the first images we wrote,' according to Ethan. 'The idea of the hat blowing away in the woods, without really knowing how it was supposed to fit in.' Unlike the other early image of thugs in the woods, this one was left unexplained and floating free of any plot connection, except for a dream Tom describes at one point to Verna."[17]

Lest this entire chapter revolve around headgear, here's Christopher Orr's take: "The Coens are characteristically mum on its meaning, but the general contours seem clear enough. It is Tom's cloak and his armor. It keeps his motives and intentions hidden ("under his hat") and it protects his brain, his "smarts," his "thinking" from the weaknesses of his "heart." (The words "smart," "think," and "heart," appear in pretty much every scene with Tom, the first two always in direct opposition to the third.) Without his hat, Tom is vulnerable—not merely physically (though he certainly is that: Nearly every removal is the prelude to a beating, and just before the Dane intends to kill him he contemptuously flings the hat away), but emotionally, too. Why does he impulsively—and uncharacteristically—give in to his desire to sleep with Verna, his boss's girlfriend? Because she has already taken his hat away from him at a card game. The second time that he sleeps with her, he dreams of his hat blowing away, perhaps never to be recovered. And what does he do at the conclusion of the film, after he's lost not merely Verna, but Leo as well? He lowers his hat over his eyes. He's going to need it now more than ever."[18]

For no reason, here's a screengrab of Sam Raimi as "Snickering Gunman."
Copyright 20ᵗʰ Century Fox. All Rights Reserved.

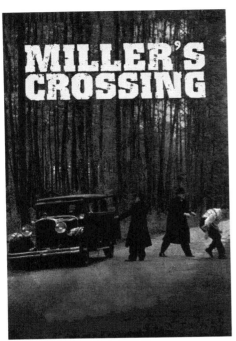

Astonishingly, *Miller's Crossing* was an incredible bomb, overshadowed that summer by Martin Scorsese's *Goodfellas*, which more or less devoured every smaller movie in its path. Released a year ahead or behind, *Miller's Crossing* may have been a hit. At any rate, it found its audience on VHS and DVD. While the *Crossing* cult doesn't come close to dishing out the worship received by *The Big Lebowski*, its numbered admirers are nothing to sneeze at.

"What else would you expect from a Princeton philosophy grad teamed with his equally pulp-loving cineaste brother than an exploration of the 'mind/body' split, articulated through 1930s Hollywood gangster imagery? Whatever brutalities or sordid corruption they engaged in, it was "always for a reason", Gabriel Byrne's Tom Reagan, the increasingly isolated and independent underworld protagonist keeps reminding his more instinctive (read: violent) and less reflective confederates throughout *Miller's Crossing*. What it earns him is an increasingly gratuitous series of beatings, from which he emerges with little more damage than a bloody lip, his philosophies intact," wrote Roger Westcombe for Crimeculture.com. "Nevertheless there's a chill at the heart of *Miller's Crossing* that rebuffs affection, unlike their best films, *Barton Fink* (1991) and *Fargo* (1996). Perhaps this is a by-product of the screenplay's two-stage creation, as they were forced to abandon it halfway through, finding themselves hopelessly stalled and incapable of resolving the plot complexities. (Presumably its uncredited basis, Dashiell Hammett's *The Glass Key* was no help.) Only after switching to convey a writer with writer's block in Barton Fink were they able to return and unkink their own. By that second half the Cartesian duality in *Miller's Crossing* has itself 'taken a powder' (the deployment of '30s slang in *Miller's Crossing* is superb throughout) in favor of an increasingly Byzantine spider's web, itself a genre stereotype."[19]

As usual, the NY Times' Vincent Canby missed the point of the film, longing for something the Coens neither promised nor delivered. "The film's production notes say *Miller's Crossing* had its origins in a single image, that of men in black overcoats in the middle of a forest. It's an evocative image that is used with effect twice in the movie. Not as good is the elaborate but haphazard and jokey film that the Coens have concocted to surround the image. Their screenplay more often brings to mind *Dick Tracy*, but without that film's wit, class and Stephen Sondheim songs, than the pre-World War II Warner Brothers gangster movies to which the Coens are apparently referring."[20]

Even the critic I generally agree with and admire, Lord Mr. Roger Ebert, seemed at a loss to see *Miller's Crossing* for anything other than its surface presentation. "But I think about the room [Leo's office from the opening sequence]. What a wonderful room. All steeped in dark shadows, with expensive antique oak furniture and leather chairs and brass fittings and vast spaces of flooring between the yellow pools of light. I would like to work in this room. A man could get something done in this room. And yet the room is a key to why *Miller's Crossing* is not quite as successful as it should be—why it seems like a movie that is constantly aware of itself, instead of a movie that gets on with business. I do not really think that Leo would have such an office. I believe it is the kind of office that would be created by a good interior designer with contacts in England, and supplied to a rich lawyer. I am not sure a rackets boss in a big American city in 1929 would occupy such a space, even though it does set him off as a sinister presence among the shadows. [...] I am also not sure that the other characters in this movie would inhabit quite the same clothing, accents, haircuts and dwellings as we see them in. This doesn't look like a gangster movie, it looks like a commercial intended to look like a gangster movie. Everything is too designed. That goes for the plot and the dialogue, too. The dialogue is well-written, but it is indeed written. We admire the prose rather than the message. People make threats, and we think about how elegantly the threats are worded."

The argument can—and has—been made that the Coens are more interested in presentation than content, particularly with their earlier films. It wasn't until *Fargo* (1996) that critics began to herald the brothers as visionaries, aka "Serious Filmmakers". That *Miller's Crossing* is only beginning to be appreciated now comes as little surprise. *The Wizard of Oz* was a bomb when it was released in 1939 and wouldn't be embraced by the public until a decade later. Maybe the trite phrase "the best art takes time", which I just coined, applies all-too-well in this case. But for its detractors, all I can say is: "Jesus, Tom."

NOTES

[1] Simon, Alex. 1998. "Brothers' Keepers." Venice Magazine. April. Archived at The Hollywood Interview By Alex Simon and Terry Keefe. http://thehollywoodinterview.blogspot.com/2008/02/coen-brothers-hollywood-interview.html

[2] Simon, Alex. 2007. "Gabriel Byrne: The Hollywood Flashback Interview". The Hollywood Interview. July 5. http://thehollywoodinterview.blogspot.com/2015/07/gabriel-byrne-hollywood-flashback.html

[3] Ibid

[4] Morgan, David. "Knowing the Score." Archived on Carter Burwell.com http://www.carterburwell.com/projects/Millers_Crossing.shtml

[5] Ibid.

[6] Anderson, J. Todd. "Miller's Crossing Is Touching And Studiously Crafted Love Letter To American Film Noirs And The Seventh Art In General." Cinephilia and Beyond. http://www.cinephiliabeyond.org/the-coen-brothers-millers-crossing/ - Quote taken from Palmer, R. Barton. "Joel and Ethan Cohen." University of Illinois Press. 2004. p.182-183

[7] Simon, Alex. 1998. Venice Magazine.

[8] Rochlin, Margy. 2001. "Marcia Gay who?" The Guardian. March 29. https://www.theguardian.com/film/2001/mar/30/culture.features2

[9] Harris, Will. 2012. "Marcia Gay Harden on her favorite character and working with Clint Eastwood." NonStopPop. October 11. http://www.avclub.com/article/marcia-gay-harden-on-her-favorite-character-and-wo-86533

[10] Rochlin, Margy. 2001. "Marcia Gay who?" The Guardian. March 29. https://www.theguardian.com/film/2001/mar/30/culture.features2

[11] *Miller's Crossing* Production Notes. "Miller's Crossing Homepage." Archived https://web.archive.org/web/20091022145629/http://geocities.com/~mikemckiernan/mcprodnotes.html

[12] O'Neal, Sean. 2011. "Random Roles: John Turturro". The A.V. Club. June 28. http://www.avclub.com/article/john-turturro-58178@seanoneal

[13] Pockross, Adam. 2014. "Jon Polito: That Guy From That Thing (Who You Definitely Know)." Yahoo Movies. March 28. https://www.yahoo.com/movies/bp/jon-polito-guy-thing-definitely-know-225543635.html

[14] Ibid

[15] Westcombe, Roger. "Miller's Crossing." Big House Film Reviews. http://www.crimeculture.com/Contents/FilmReviews/MillersCrossing.htm

[16] Ibid.

[17] *Miller's Crossing* Production Notes. "Miller's Crossing Homepage." Archived https://web.archive.org/web/20091022145629/http://geocities.com/~mikemckiernan/mcprodnotes.html

[18] Orr, Christopher. 2014. "30 Years of Coens: Miller's Crossing". The Atlantic. September 30. http://www.theatlantic.com/entertainment/archive/2014/09/30-years-of-coens-millers-crossing/379895/

[19] Westcombe, Roger. "Miller's Crossing." Big House Film Reviews.

[20] Canby, Vincent. 1990 "Review/Film Festival; In 'Miller's Crossing,' Silly Gangsters And a Tough Moll". New York Times. September 21.

THE MONITORS (1969)

"We are here to serve humanity.
Here to reaffirm gentility.
Light the way from fear to sanity.
Carefully promote tranquility.
Grant us neither gift nor gratitude…"

"The Monitors are your friends. The Monitors bring peace. Peace brings happiness. Be kind. The Monitors are kind. Helping others helps you. Happiness comes from helping others."

Welcome to the future, where the world has been taken over by The Monitors, a race of humanoids of unknown origin, identified by their overcoats and black derby hats. The Monitors wanted to bring peace to the Earth, but the inhabitants were resistant to the idea. "We're forced to control the world," says their leader, Jeterax (Shepperd Strudwick). "We wanted to be partners."

In the Monitor-monitored world, war, aggression, civil disobedience, regular disobedience, everything "bad" has been outlawed, and the Monitors patrol the streets with spray cans of knock-out gas in order to keep the peace peaceful.

"If you don't like air pollution, war, body odor, hard pizza rolls, exercise, hairy musicians, sexy blonds, tooth decay, smiling heroes, population explosion… you'll love The Monitors"

Xavier Cugat sez "The Monitors are a stone groove, man. They never lose their cool."

Worldwide peace doesn't sit well with certain members of society. For one thing, there's the shadowy organization S.C.R.A.G. (Secret Counter Retalitorial Group, nonprofit), run by

Col. Stutz (Larry Storch) under the command of General Blackwisher (Keenan Wynn)[200]. For another, there's pilot Harry Jordan (Guy Stockwell), who is just generally dissatisfied with the world. "Yeah, the Monitors are great. I still hate them."

Against his wishes, and before he knows it, Harry gets dragged into a tug-of-war between S.C.R.A.G. and the Monitors by actress and Monitor agent Barbara Cole (Susan Oliver). Desperate for his attention, Barbara accidentally gets Harry fired from the film they're working on (he's given his walking papers by Peter Boyle). When he's lured out of his apartment by a message from Stutz (dressed as a Monitor-friendly street preacher), a riot breaks out among Stutz's supporters. In the ensuing melee, the Monitors arrive with their spray cans. They spritz Harry's comedian brother, Max (Avery Schreiber), and in retaliation, Harry sprays the Monitor. This is a crime of the highest order and Harry is sentenced to immediate Indefinite Detention.

Fleeing from the bowler-wearing peaceniks, Harry, Barbara, and Max are picked up by Stutz and they lead The Monitors on a grand chase during which Stutz's armored Buick rams a Monitor roadblock, sending one of their cars over a cliff. Harry leaps out to rescue the car's driver and is arrested by the others. Meanwhile, Stutz conscripts Max and Barbara into S.C.R.A.G.

Stutz: "You're not going anywhere, you both know too much."

Barbara: "Well you told us!"

Meeting with Jetterax at The Montors' base of operations—a re-education spa nicknamed "The Peace Room"—Harry voices his complaints. "We used to vote and choose who installed parking meters or who decided when to make left turns."

Jetterax: "And did you? Vote?"

Harry (angry, then conceding): "…Sometimes."

While Harry joins with the disaffected Monitor agent, Mona (Sherry Jackson), Stutz's ambition starts to get the better of him. The organization is in possession of an "Inversion Bomb", which S.C.R.A.G. intends to use against the Monitors. Stutz intends to sell the device to the Monitors for a reward. During all of this, the savvy Monitors are growing increasingly frustrated with their subjects' resistance to happiness.

Based on Keith Laumer's 1966 novel, Myron J. Gold's screenplay mines the thin story for heightened satire, thanks to the four yerars that transpired between publication and production. In 1966, Laumer's America was only beginning to descend into chaos. Following the assassination of President John F. Kennedy, Americans were growing increasingly paranoid, resulting in the rise of both the hippies and the "America-first" jingoists. As Johnson escalated involvement in the Vietnam War, the idea of "peace" at home or abroad was devolving into a fanciful idea. By 1969, "idealism" had multiple definitions, depending on which side of the college campus you were standing on. Still, Hollywood relied on the idea of the lone heroes acting against malevolent outside forces. The flip given by *The Monitors* is that the alleged bad guys controlling the world are pacifists, their antagonists are home-grown ex-military nutcases, and the heroes are ostensible entertainers mildly irritated by what they see as a lack of choice in a supposed utopia. The message of *The Monitors* is that humans will never be satisfied, especially if they get everything they want. Harry doesn't want peace, but he doesn't want to see anyone killed, either. During his stand-off with Jetterax, he holds the implosion bomb in his arms and insists that he's a coward. "I don't want anyone to die. I just want you to go home to wherever the hell it is you come from!"[201]

With choice eliminated along with aggression and pollution, humanity should be satisfied. But it's obvious that society longs for conflict. Without disorder, what is man's purpose? Since the Monitors' arrival, for instance, The President of the United States (Ed Begley) sits alone

---

[200] Known as "The Pacifist General" whose slogan was "Better fed and Red than dead." Stutz is outraged: "A lie! A vicious Red smear aimed at overthrowing a fine American who's just as keen for killing as the rest of us!"

[201] Rewatching the film, I wondered if Edgar Wright had seen *The Monitors* prior to writing the satirical climax of *The World's End*, in which benevolent aliens leave the planet exactly the way they found it, taking their technological advances with them, leaving a stubborn humanity to start over, but still feeling like "we" won.

and lonely in the Oval Office, his desk covered in cobwebs, waiting for … "I don't know for sure. But it's my duty to be here when it happens." He yearns for "the good ol', bad ol' days."

"We don't rule, Mr. Jordan," says Jeterax. "We only serve. But clearly it's too early in your history for us. I only hope it's not too late in your history."

"*The Monitors* was a collaboration between Second City and Bell & Howell, the film equipment manufacturing company who financed the movie in an attempt to establish Chicago as a major center for film production," wrote Examiner.com's JM Dobies. When it tanked at the box office, that idea went out the window, but the film remains a fascinating, if flawed, oddity. It's a decidedly different take on the usual alien invasion flick, all about these seemingly benevolent extraterrestrials dressed in black suits and bowler hats, who come to Earth to save humanity by eliminating sex, violence, and politics…well, two out of three ain't bad."[1]

With a sparse 85 minute running time, *The Monitors* is long on ideas but short on plot and character. Given the talent that came out of Second City over the past half-century, it's also surprisingly short on laughs. Granted, the jokes aim more for drollery than guffaws, but why have, for example, the very funny Avery Schreiber aboard if you're not going to give him anything to do? (Though he does perform "The Swamp Draining Song" in its "original tongue, which I created," he says as Max. And it's a fun 30 seconds of nonsense noises.) Stockwell makes for a fine hero, resembling Russ Tamblyn. Oliver's Barbara's purpose is to browbeat Harry into loving her. Wynn has a few funny moments, but the bulk of the comedy is laid on the shoulders of Storch, and Stutz becomes quickly unwelcome, his authoritarian mania wearing thin over the space of a few scenes.

Where *The Monitors* largely fails is in the story department, and it feels like a long SCTV sketch stretched too far. Linking the sequences of plot are testimonials given on The Monitors' behalf delivered by a host of cameos including the entire Arkin family (Alan as an English-challenged garbage man celebrating the Monitors' delivery of a "better class of garbage"; son Adam praising the fact that since the Monitors' arrived, he hasn't been bullied or beaten up), Xavier Cugat, Jackie Vernon, Stubby Kaye, and even Chicago Senator Everett Dirksen[202]. Battling on the score is the electronica "Monitors Theme" giving way to the rah-rah of the "Monitors Cheer" on one side, and Fred Kaz'[203] score, including "Run", sung by Odetta Holmes, and the treacley "Voice of the Flower" sung by Sandy Holt, the latter doing its best to firmly date the film.

Chicago's futuristic city structure provides an excellent backdrop for the not-quite-now satire, giving a nice alien feel to the modern world. "The Monitors is very much of movie of its time," wrote Lee Bey. "But there's a reason to check out the film: the jaw-dropping, wide-angle photography that depicts Chicago—which I don't believe is actually named—and its modernist architecture as an otherworldly place. The modern Meigs Field terminal makes a couple of appearances. Even the Thornton Quarry gets into the act as the setting for a chase and a car explosion. The film's director of photography, Vilmos Zsigmond (billed here as "William) would go on to shoot classics such as *The Deer Hunter, Close Encounters of the Third Kind* and the more-recent Woody Allen flick *You'll Meet a Tall Dark Stranger* [.]. His colors are lush and crisp in this new print that just popped out of nowhere on Netflix."[2]

This emerging Vilmos Zsigmond style—a few years before *Close Encounters of the Third Kind* (1977), a few years after *The Incredibly Strange Creatures Who Stopped Living and Became Mixed-Up Zombies* (1964)—is as eclectic as his career, helping the relatively low-budgeted film achieve a "worldwide" look. In many instances, his photography syncs with Roy Henry's Art Direction to give us the feeling that we're watching an Italian comedy, like *The 10th Victim* (1965) or Fellini's *8 ½* (1963). Patrick Kennedy's editing, too, gives a heightened reality, particularly when we get flashes of Harry's thought processes. While discussing his career as a pilot, we're given

---

[202] Senator Dirkson was still in office when this film was made, and died just prior to its release. During his career he recorded four albums of music, primarily patriotic songs, including the Grammy-winning "Gallant Men."

[203] Jazz pianist Fred Kaz served as "Second City's" musical director for "Second City" for three-plus decades.

shots of a jet plummeting towards earth[204]; while speaking with Barbara and Mona, we get three-frame shots of tigers and parts of a woman's naked body. The subliminal images are very much of the decade in which the film was made, but these instances are almost the sum total of information given about Harry's character. And in this case, it's very effective.

Kennedy also utilizes stock footage in montage to show the past events that inspired the Monitors to invade (as well as elements of wishful thinking on the part of the disaffected President). This didn't work especially well for Howard Thompson, who wrote in his NY Times review in '69: "But the movie is neither as funny nor as stinging as it was intended to be. We are asked to consider a Monitor-controlled existence as the just deserts of a blighted nation. To underscore this there is a head-on documentary montage depicting Establishment folly, ranging from a rocket-launching (apparently at Cape Kennedy) to the temple scene in Griffith's *Intolerance*. But it's not easy to bleed for humanity one minute and chuckle at the specimens frolicking through the picture the next. The endless wisecracks seem none too wise or witty, or, for that matter, new. Even a thickly accented monologue by Alan Arkin, as a sanitation worker, seems curiously antiseptic."[3]

(It doesn't seem to play too well with modern audiences either, as Scott Ashlin wrote: "When it comes to '60s satire, I sometimes suspect that you kind of had to be there. I wasn't, and Lord knows I never seem to get the joke. (Well, okay—so I got *Dr. Strangelove, or How I Learned to Stop Worrying and Love the Bomb*, but that really is about it.) *The Monitors*, based on a story by Keith Laumer[,] is among the purest examples of the breed, coming across almost as what might have happened if the "Laugh In" crew had produced a satirical sci-fi movie—which is to say that most of it left me utterly unamused, and more than a little pissed off. [...] The take-offs on late-60's TV commercials mostly work, but they're just about the only thing in the movie that does. [...] The worst part, though, is that *The Monitors* is not content simply to be a screwy farce, an enterprise at which it might possibly have succeeded. No, this movie wants to make us think! We should be thinking! about how it seems all too plausible for human beings everywhere to rise up in defense of violence, venality, and hate in response to those evils being removed forcibly from the world by outsiders from another planet. We should be thinking about what it means that this movie's creators had to portray the S.C.R.A.G.ers as completely insane militarists in order to make them seem less sympathetic than the essentially good-hearted aliens. But all I was thinking! about was how much funnier the anti-war shtick was when Stanley Kubrick did it five years earlier, and how much more convincing Michael Rennie was as a purveyor of "peace— or else!" at the beginning of the preceding decade."[4])

"It's a movie that could have only been made in the '60s, the late '60s to be precise, the age of Aquarius, the Hallucination Generation, the crazy days of peace, love, and the Tet Offensive," wrote Dobies. " The movie may have failed during its brief theatrical run, but it gained new life thanks to numerous airings on the late, late, late show on local UHF stations in the '70s, '80s, and beyond (it was a highlight of my old UHF movie show *Surreal Cinema*, which lives on in reruns in Northeast Florida). Insomniacs, stoners, and fans of incredibly strange films ate it up and formed a small but fervent cult."[5]

While *The Monitors* is virtually unknown outside of film addict circles, it's another one of those productions that seem just as topical today as it did when it was made, which sort of undercuts Dobies statement above. Look at the world now—or, rather, at the time of this writing, July, 2016. As a country, the U.S. has been embroiled in a half-dozen wars for almost twenty years now. We're at the moment in the midst of an election run between the first-ever female Democratic nominee, and the possibly last Republican nominee. Political groups are again taking protests to the streets while both sides of the political spectrum promise prosperity, blow jobs, and puppies for all (provided "all" fall into the very specific "white male" category). A quick glance at Facebook would reveal hatred, anxiety, and frustration; people arguing just for the sake of arguing, with the arguments quickly dissolving into name

---

[204] Presumably somewhere over Macho Grande.

calling and enmity even if both sides, at heart, agree with the other. If The Monitors were to arrive tomorrow, eliminate war, strife, poverty, and misery, humans worldwide would fall into a funk, believing that their rights were somehow infringed upon, that "happiness" was mandated and mandatory. We'd want those bowler-wearing illegals off of our planet post-haste.

"We've looked into your minds," a sad Jeterax says to Harry, "but I don't think we have, and shall never, fathom your hearts."

They're here to serve humanity…
Screengrab copyright Commonwealth United Entertainment

NOTES

[1] Dobies, JM. 2010. "Second City Sci-fi: The Monitors (1969)". Examiner.com. February 1.
www.examiner.com/article/second-city-sci-fi-the-monitors-1969

[2] Bey, Lee. 2011. "Recently re-released obscure late '60s sci-fi comedy showcases Chicago architecture." WBEZ.org.
March 23. http://www.wbez.org/blog/lee-bey/2011-03-22/recently-re-released-obscure-late-60s-sci-fi-comedy-showcases-chicago-archit

[3] Thompson, Howard. 1969. "The Monitors (1969)". New York Times. October 9.
http://www.nytimes.com/movie/review?res=9B05E1DD1F3BE73ABC4153DFB6678382679EDE

[4] Ashlin, Scott. "The Monitors." 1000 Misspent Hours.com. http://www.1000misspenthours.com/reviews/reviewsh-m/monitors.htm

[5] Dobies, JM. 2010. "Second City Sci-fi: The Monitors (1969)". Examiner.com. February 1.
www.examiner.com/article/second-city-sci-fi-the-monitors-1969

MUPPETS MOST WANTED (2014)

It's difficult being a Muppet fanatic these days. Since Disney bought the rights to the characters in 2004, they haven't seemed to know what to do with the furry troupe. For many years, my opinion was that Disney pursued the Henson family for the purchase of The Muppets solely because they didn't already own them. The past decade hasn't really proved me wrong. After doing very little with the franchise aside from producing what I consider hands-down to be the worst Muppet special ever created, NBC's 2008 *A Muppets Christmas: Letters to Santa,* Disney sat on the franchise. They cancelled the license held by the Palisades Toys, who'd been producing exquisite action figures of the characters, but failed to replace them with any commensurate merchandise. Hell, we're *still* waiting for them to release DVDs for Seasons 4 and 5 of the original *Muppet Show* because, it can be safely surmised, Disney doesn't feel like dealing with the hassle of the music rights that truncated the first season DVD collection (even though they now own 90% of all human entertainment since the dawn of time).

Let me clarify something, because I'm going to return to this complaint about a dozen times in this chapter: *Letters to Santa* is not bad because of the Muppets in it. The Muppet sequences are handled nicely and the whole special is directed with aplomb by the beautiful, beautiful man, Kirk Thatcher. But the script—four different writers for one 45 minute special!—relies far too heavily on the human stars. This is what sank the inventive *Muppets Wizard of Oz*.[205] Disney had no faith in The Muppets carrying their own stories, giving the characters a back seat to whatever nonsense the humans had going on. It's almost racist.

Like most Muppet fanatics who worshipped Jim Henson nigh unto a god up to and far after his death in 1990, when we learned of the Disney purchase, finally happening after two

---

[205] With egregious co-star David Allen Grier actually referring to them as "the most famous *puppet* troupe in the world". "Puppet troupe"? Then how do people interact with them? If you can't suspend the disbelief that the Muppets are real, how can you accept audiences to accept the rest?

decades of negotiations and false starts (including a brief sale to the German company EMTV that went absolutely nowhere and bankrupted said company), we were elated. After all, who does merchandising and marketing better than Disney? For the hardcore Muppet acolyte, we expected to see all of the shows and movies remastered in great, wonderful, chocolate-covered special editions, to watch swaddled in Muppet pajamas, blankets, silk underwear, sheet sets, decorative hats, and artisanal singing cheeses.

We got a couple of crummy inaction figures and a few China-made and quite hideous plush toys that may or may not have been bootlegs before Disney absorbed the various sweatshops in charge of manufacturing. We got truncated repackages of the specials. The first DVD reissues came full-frame. Suddenly, it felt like the House of Mouse was punishing fans for being fans in the first place. There was no expansion of Muppet attractions at the parks—hell, even their new t-shirts were stylized cartoons, rather than photographic images of the characters! Apart from a few inspired web-only shorts and the continual abusive-husband promise of a new TV show, nothing transpired.

So…to quote nobody involved in Jim's original vision: "what the holy goddamned *fuck*, Disney?"

In 2011, The Muppets and their fans met a very unexpected savior in the form of sporadically-funny Jason Segel. As it turned out, the biggest comedic proponent of full-frontal male nudity was also a huge Muppet geek—both of which he proved in *Forgetting Sarah Marshall*, in which Siegel's character creates an all-puppet stage version of *Dracula*, and sobs while trying to cheer himself by playing *The Muppet Show* theme on the piano. A few months later, it was announced that Segel and his writing partner, Nicholas Stoller, would be bringing The Muppets back to the big screen. Finally, in the wake of *The Muppet Movie* (1979), *The Great Muppet Caper* (1981), *The Muppets Take Manhattan* (1984), *A Muppet Christmas Carol* (1992), *Muppet Treasure Island* (1996), and *Muppets from Space* (1999), we would finally get the follow-up we'd all been waiting a decade to see. The awesome, love-inspiring title: *The Muppets*.

Okay, so the title was less-than-thrilling, but at least our beloved characters would be back where they belonged. And it was…fine. Like the majority of the TV specials, *The Muppets* (2011) focused on the trials and tribulations of the main human characters—Segel and Amy Adams, both perfectly pleasant—and a new, rather dull little Muppet character named Walter (Peter Linz). Walter and Siegel's Gary are brothers, though Walter always felt that there was something different about him. When Walter discovers old episodes of *The Muppet Show* he does what the rest of us did: he became instantly obsessed. So the rest of the film concerned itself with the "getting the band back together" plotline that so often centers in "reboots". Even more familiar, the throughline was that the Muppet Theatre, disused for twenty years, was about to be bought and demolished by an Evil Oil Baron named "Tex Richman" (played by Chris Cooper[206]—who *raps*!).

How many times had we been given that plot? How many times do the Muppets have to put on a show in order to save their theater? Hell, *A Very Merry Muppet Christmas* (2002) had the same exact storyline, only instead of the evil oil baron they had to face an evil Joan Cusak.

Still, that all seemed like nitpicking because it meant the Muppets were back. The lively score was by *Flight of the Conchords'* Bret McKenzie and his centerpiece song (sung by Segel and Walter), "Man or Muppet" took home the Academy Award for Best Song that year, and the studio took in $165 million at the box office. Even if the new movie felt just a little lacking—hearing the Muppets being told that they're irrelevant by every major human character got pretty depressing pretty quickly—the prospects for more was just too exciting. A sequel was announced pretty much before the end credits rolled.

"They really want it," said Stoller. "It's very…it was very encouraging and exciting. I've never been part of a franchise before. They want to do it. They want it as soon as possible, which is good. I'm not sure exactly when they want to release it. I think it was something like

---

[206] *American Beauty* (1999), and *Lone Star* (1996)—see *Movie Outlaw Rides Again.*

L-R (Foreground) Dominic Badguy (Ricky Gervais), Gonzo the Great (Dave Goelz), Fozzie Bear (Eric Jacobson), Kermit the Frog (Steve Whitmire), Miss Piggy (also Eric Jacobson, so probably somebody else here, since Fozzie is speaking). Background: Behemoth, Beaker, Scooter (David Rudman), Bunson Honeydew, Animal (Matt Vogel), Zoot, Sweetums, Rizzo the Rat, Pepe the King Prawn (Bill Barretta), Dr. Teeth.[207] (Somewhere in there must be Louise Gold, Peter Linz and/or Mike Quinn.) A/P Photo by Jay Maidment. 2013 Disney Enterprises, Inc. All Rights Reserved.

next summer, but I don't know if that's…I don't think that that's realistic in terms of getting it all together in time. But to want to do it so quickly is great. It certainly makes us want to write it quickly."[1]

As is usual in Hollywood following any success, the urge was to repeat whatever worked in the first place. But as is usual with The Muppets, what worked once doesn't always work again, because with all the old jokes and vaudeville songs, The Muppets embraced freshness, or, at the very least, recycling done in a new way. "[B]y the time you're in a room sitting down together, you're pretty sure what you're going to do. The initial ideas about what the films going to be about as a whole is a much more general- producers, studio, everyone's in the room just throwing ideas around, so at that stage there's all sorts of crazy ideas, who knows. I mean, Piggy and Kermit get married and Piggy's family turn up and there's some sort of problem, or Kermit's stag weekend, who knows? [laughs] There's lots of different ideas you can do like that. So there's lots of different roads you go down initially, and then you bring it back, and then you end up with the purity of the simplest idea often works best. Like- what if there's an evil Kermit? And what if there's a world tour and he gets replaced and no one noticed? Just these funny comedy premises, and it just means you can build a central narrative

---

[207] Of the many additional Muppet Performers who may or may not be performing above:

Additional UK Muppet Performers: Don Austen, William Banyard, Daisy Beattie, Sue Beattie, Lynn Robertson Bruce, Dave Chapman, Marcus Clarke, Richard Coombs, Sue Dacre, Phil Eason, Iestyn Evans, Damian Farrell, Andy Heath, Paul Jomain, Mark Mander, Alison Megowan, Helena Smee, Katherine Smee, Andrew Spooner, Olly Taylor, Chris Thatcher, Robert Tygner, Fiona Wilson, Sheila Clark, Matthew Crowfoot, Geoffrey Felix, Rachel Leonard, Tony Lymboura, Stan Middleton, Colin Purves, Neil Sterenberg, Mandy Travis.

LA Muppet Performers: David Barclay, Tim Blaney, Julianne Buescher, Tyler Bunch, Kevin Carlson, Nathan Danforth, Alice Dinnean, Tanya Haden, Patrick Johnson, Sean Johnson, Brian Jones, Bruce Lanoil, James Murray, Michael Oosterom, Brett O'Quinn, Michelan Sisti, David Skelly, Art Vega, Alex Villa, Chase Woolner. Thanks much to http://muppet.wikia.com/wiki/Muppets_Most_Wanted#cite_note-EW-1-30-13-5

engine to drive the story forward, which is really one of the most important things about the movie. So that, to me, once we had those pieces in place everything else kind of fell into place actually."[2]

Where *The Muppets* retold the "getting the band back together" story (literally and figuratively), *The Muppets* sequel would necessarily have to be more action-oriented. (Right?) It was quickly announced that the new film would concern itself with international jewel thieves. Which sounded…familiar. "[…] I think it's similar to the first one in that the first one certainly had dramatic connections to the first Muppet movie, but it was a whole new thing, hopefully. This is the same thing. We love *The Great Muppet Caper* and we love *Muppets Take Manhattan* and whatnot. So this has some elements of that, but it's different because it's in the tone of what James and I like to do."[3]

As an example of the marketing machine behind the film, several of the Muppet characters were used in "exclusive' interviews in print, video, and on the web. "I can actually tell you quite a lot because I have a press release in front of me, which makes it very easy!" "Kermit the Frog" told Entertainment Weekly. "The idea of this film is that our gang is on this global tour, and we're selling out these grand theaters all over Europe—in Berlin, Madrid, London—but we sort of get into a little bit of trouble when we run across my doppelganger. He's the world's number one criminal, Constantine, and he happens to look an awful lot like me. I won't tell you any more than that, but let's just say mayhem ensues." When asked if he was playing both roles, Kermit responded: "No. We talked about putting me in makeup and having me play both roles, but we decided Constantine needed to be a guy who could do a Russian accent. And, you know, I'm a pretty accomplished actor and all, but besides the *Muppet Christmas Carol* and *Muppet Treasure Island* films, I've only really ever played myself. The great thing is, I have like 3,000 relatives back in the swamp, so it was quite easy to find a frog who could play Constantine."

As for their human co-stars: "Ricky Gervais is kind of like a Muppet, if you think about it. He fits right in. He's about our size. I actually think when this film ends it's going to be hard to get rid of him. He keeps following me back to my hotel in London, which is very strange, but we're thrilled to have him. Then, of course, we have Tina Fey—and it's hard to beat Tina. I know her because I was lucky enough to get asked to do a little spot on one of the last episodes of *30 Rock*. She's playing a feisty prison guard named Nadya, which should be fun. Then we have Ty Burrell, who's playing a French Interpol agent. But personally, I'm not going to be going to France for the French scenes. It's best if I don't go there. It's a frog thing."[4]

Returning to the jewel-heist trope, fans were initially concerned that the sequel would retread the ground already traveled by *The Great Muppet Caper*. Director James Bobin promised, like the first, that it would be familiar and unique at the same time. "Personally, I've always liked movies about big diamonds, like *Pink Panther* and *The Thomas Crown Affair*. I've always found those films really interesting, and they have a good energy about them, which I like. So, that was certainly an inspiration. Also, there was the idea from the last movie where we did bits from *The Muppet Show*, so I thought, "Why not do a world tour and keep putting *The Muppet Show* on, again and again and again?" So, we could combine *The Muppet Show* elements with this caper-style story. That's our film. And then, the doppelgänger is a classic old movie troupe. Obviously, Kermit is the most beloved frog in the world. So, we thought, what if there was a bad version of this guy? And the rest is history, as they say."[5] Filmed under the equally-uninspired title *The Muppets…Again* (a title that figured in two songs, again handled by [Bret] McKenzie), what we eventually got was something that the first reboot should have been: a zany, often-insane, charming, and less-sentimental caper film, *Muppets Most Wanted*.

Utilizing a classic set-up, Constantine (Matt Vogel) , "The World's Most Dangerous Frog", identical to Kermit in every way except for a thick Russian accent and a prominent mole on his face, replaces everyone's favorite "the Frog" and gets him sent to a Russian gulag. Meanwhile, Constantine and his "Number Two", Dominic Badguy ("It's pronounced "Bad-Gee". It's French."), played by Ricky Gervais, book the Muppets on a world tour in order to pull off a series of museum heists throughout Europe. Meanwhile, Kermit tries to make the best of things in Siberia, making tentative friends with the camp commander Nadya (Tina Fey) and his inmates, Prison King (McKenzie's *Conchords* partner Jermaine Clement), Big Daddy (Ray Liotta), and Danny Trejo (Danny Trejo…who else would play him?), and even… puts on a show using the prison talent.

Most miraculous is the tone struck in the script by Stoller (minus Segel[208] who wanted "to pursue more human-related projects,") and director James Bobin. Without the burden of having to re-introduce the characters to a new audience (or a seemingly forgetful older one), Stoller and Bobin were free to let the Muppets run wild, managing to recapture some of the old sardonic edge the troupe had when written by the late Jerry Juhl. McKenzie's songs this time around had less schmaltz and more of the bite from his best *Conchords* bits. Instead of the suicide-inducing "Pictures in My Head" song Kermit sings in *The Muppets*, full of regret and missing his friends who have all gone their separate ways, we get the wonderfully daffy "Interrogation Song" headed by one of the greatest match-ups in movie history: Sam the Eagle (as an Interpol agent with a "really big badge") and French inspector Jean Pierre Napoleon (played with gusto by Ty Burrell, doing his best Jacques Clousseau impression). Rather than an irritated Jack Black held hostage, we have a herd of cattle trampling Salma Hayek. *Plus* a waltz performed by Christof Waltz (and Sweetums)![209]

The tender moments this time around are more plot-driven than sentimentally-forced. While Kermit languishes in prison, the rest of the troupe are perfectly willing to accept the Constantine as their fearless leader—moronic accent and grumpy nature included—because he promises he can get them "anything they want". If Piggy wants to do a five-song tribute to Celine Dion, or if Gonzo wants to reenact the running of the bulls on stage, Constantine/Kermit's response: "Sure. Who cares?" (And the fact that the villainous amphibian, who practices his Kermit impression to less-than-stellar results—"The lov-vers, the dreamerz, and cheeeeeese….Nailed it."—gets severe stage fright on opening night is a wonderful humanizing moment.) Only Animal notices the differences, and later Walter and Fozzie, but Constantine manages to get them out of the way fairly quickly. "Walter, Fonzie and their dog have decided to leave the show forever," Constantine explains to little dubiousness. Well, Rowlf thinks something is up: "Walter too? We just did a whole movie about him joining."

Rather than keeping Gervais or Fey in the forefront, *Muppets Most Wanted* puts the title characters in the dead center. Finally, after so many years, the humans take a backseat to the Muppet madness, as it should be. The Muppets always worked best when the humans are brought into their world. They don't work as well when thrust into our reality because of the incongruity. Are they real animals? Are they puppets? If so, why doesn't anyone look down and talk to the puppeteers? After *Muppets from Space*, the cognitive dissonance of what the Muppets *were* bogged down nearly everyone who tried to reintroduce them. The magic of the Muppets is that they exist in a Muppet reality. You *go* to Sesame Street and you're invited to the Muppet Theater. One of the reasons the original Muppet movies seemed strange, even when Henson and Frank Oz were at the helm, was because the Muppets were trying to interact with our universe instead of the other way around. *Who Framed Roger Rabbit?* worked so well because

---

[208] "It's true [that I won't be in the sequel]," said Segel, "but it's totally amicable. My goal was to bring the Muppets back and I did that, leaving them in very good hands." […] Adding, "All I wanted to do was to set the stage for them to do whatever they wanted. I'm sure I'll return in some capacity here and there, but that was half a decade of my life. Five years of hard work. I'm ready for a little puppet break." Beard, Lanford. 2012. "Jason Segel not involved in 'Muppets' sequel." Entertainment Weekly. March 5. http://www.ew.com/article/2012/03/05/jason-segel-not-involved-muppets-sequel?cnn=yes

[209] Waltz was originally pegged to play Insp. Napoleon but had to drop out due to scheduling conflicts. His little moment with Sweetums has to be the best consolation prize in history. From Radish's Collider piece: "When Nick [Stoller] and I write the script, we're writing people's names in often. Obviously, certain people have to be that person. You can't do the Christoph Waltz joke with anybody else because it is about a waltz, so that's impossible. A lot of people approached me, just on the street, and asked if they could be in the movie. More often than not, I got them in. One of them was Lady Gaga." Gaga's line in the "We're Doing a Sequel" song: "More one-liner cameos!"

Promotional still featuring Constantine, The World's Most Dangerous Frog (played by Matt Vogel).
A/P Photo by Jay Maidment. 2013 Disney Enterprises, Inc. All Rights Reserved.

humans interacted with the toons and the rules were established early on. In the Muppet movies—all of them save *Muppets from Space*—thrust the Muppets into a reality they couldn't control. In *Muppets Most Wanted*, the human world may look like ours, but the Muppets are the masters of reality here. Putting a dangerous frog in prison makes sense in this universe, and therefore, nobody is tempted to look down at puppeteers when dogs and frogs and bears and chickens surround them. In *Muppets Most Wanted*, there are no men behind the curtain. Just Muppets.

"Though hardline detractors of the Muppets' half-Disney, half-*Flight of the Conchords*, minimally Henson 2011 reboot were largely in the minority, there are a few pointed moments in the ragtag gang's latest romp that seem explicitly aimed at assuaging their complaints. When Walter, the whistling dynamo but otherwise nondescript newbie Muppet protagonist from the earlier film, hightails it out of the felt frat's fold to rescue a wrongly imprisoned Kermit, one of the seasoned puppets muses how he could abandon them after 'all that time we spent with him.' Rizzo the Rat concurs: 'Yeah, some would say at the expense of other, more well-established Muppets,'" wrote Eric Henderson for Slant Magazine. "In fact, the balances are checked right from the get-go. As the crew launches into the musical number 'We're Doing a Sequel' as though it marks uncharted territory for them, Dr. Bunsen Honeydew stops everyone down to point out that their current enterprise actually marks their eighth feature-film venture[210]. The interjection is a tossed-off bit of preschool meta in a manner that's far truer to the classic Muppet spirit, and characteristic of why *Muppets Most Wanted*, for all its borrowed and recycled gags, is a far more satisfying tribute to Jim Henson's legacy than its predecessor. Instead of flexing their credentials, writer-director James Bobin, screenwriter Nicholas Stoller, and songwriter Bret McKenzie here yield to the strength of the franchise's ensemble. The problem with the previous film wasn't so much that it ignored Miss Piggy, Gonzo, and the rest. What left a sour aftertaste was the condescending sense that the filmmakers (working closely with star Jason Segal) were on a kind of rescue mission, as though the Muppets were some sort of charity case in need of an update for millennials. What they failed to realize was that the Muppets have always been, from the very first episode of their variety TV show, a knowingly dated vaudeville act. As canny as the reboot was about providing a taxonomy of Muppet fandom to reflect the feelings of the generation that's never known a world without them, its ambition plainly didn't walk the walk."[6]

---

[210] "I don't mean to be a stickler / but this marks the seventh sequel to our original motion picture."

As an amateur Muppet expert, it's my opinion that *Muppets Most Wanted* is actually the purest of the Muppet movies, second only to *The Muppet Movie* for me, and largely because of that film's presence in my DNA. Stoller and Bobin pulled off a little minor miracle with *Muppets Most Wanted*. Even the score worked better than the previous reboot, albeit without a standout Oscar-bait song like "Man or Muppet". (Though we do get to hear Danny Trejo sing, with the other inmates, "I Hope I Get It" from *A Chorus Line*.) "There's a bit of back and forth," said MacKenzie. "James and Nick would come up with the moment in the film that needs a song, and then they'd throw it to me. They often suggest lines that don't rhyme, and I just play around with it and try to combine the idea for the song, and also make it a song that works by itself, which is the challenge. I now have quite an extensive catalog of Muppet impressions. I can do Miss Piggy quite well. That's my weird career. So, I play a rough version, and then we get together and work out the bits. James often has an idea that's visual, and he needs to change a lyric to shoot the visual. And then, we record it with The Muppets. So, there's lots of back and forth. I had this idea to have this flashback that's a dreamy moment where Piggy is thinking about her future and sees her with Kermit, growing old. I thought it'd be fun to have a little pink frog and a little green pig, which was an idea that was around from the last film that I hadn't got in. James just manages to lift the song higher with the visual."[7]

"Movie tropes are tropes for a reason, because they've worked in the past, but often kids aren't aware of them and so they're enjoying it for the first time. I love that about it. It's really fun. Simple ideas work really well for children, and I have kids so I am aware of the idea that there are things that they just latch onto and that's the thing about the movie they really remember. So the mole, I'm not at all surprised that's the thing they remember. That's really fun."[8]

So, of course, nobody went to see it.

"Among the weekend's other new offerings, Disney's *Muppets Most Wanted* was a dud in its opening weekend, thanks in part to a saturated market for family titles. The sequel, facing competition from holdovers *Mr. Peabody & Sherman* and *The Lego Movie*, opened to $16.5 million in North America to come in No. 2, compared to a $41 million launch for *The Muppets* over the Thanksgiving holiday in 2011, including $29 million for the weekend. Nevertheless, Disney's financial exposure is limited, thanks to a reasonable $54 million budget," reported the Hollywood Reporter, reportedly. "And *Muppets Most Wanted* could make up ground overseas. It opened in its first eight markets over the weekend, grossing $1.5 million. [...] Disney distribution chief Dave Hollis said the opening was 'definitely disappointing,' considering that prerelease tracking suggested *Muppets Most Wanted* had every shot at opening north of $20 million. However, he said there was never a comparison between the first film and the sequel, since Thanksgiving is a concentrated time for family moviegoing. 'They are totally different propositions,' he said."[9]

Despite Disney's unprecedented marketing machine churning out Trailer Parodies, TV commercials tie-ins, and web-based content that should have translated into a $20 million dollar weekend, it fell short by $3 million and the studio decreed it to be a "disappointing" opening, despite ranking #2 behind *Divergent*. Over the next couple of weeks, Disney watched the numbers drop off and decided to yank it after a month. It had critical acclaim—" Even if the 21st century Muppet features don't quite reach the pinnacle established while Jim Henson was alive, "Muppets Most Wanted" is often as good as or even better than 2011's "The Muppets," which wonderfully relaunched the cinematic shenanigans of Kermit, Miss Piggy, Fozzie and all the felt-covered rest."[211]—great word of mouth, a dozen or so parody videos

---

[211] Duralde, Alonzo. 2014. 'Muppets Most Wanted' Review: Caper Sequel Proves Second Verse Can Be as Good as the First." The Wrap. March 12. http://www.thewrap.com/muppets-wanted-review-caper-sequel-proves-second-verse-can-good-first/-- Who also wrote: "Purists who nit-picked *The Muppets* for moments of hipness or smuttiness or something else that they claimed somehow besmirched the Henson legend will no doubt find some tiny throwaway moment objectionable, but overall *Muppets Most Wanted* remains sensational and celebrational, proving beyond a doubt that these beloved characters will continue to lead a plush life on the big screen for years to come."

"The Pig With the Froggy Tattoo" anyone?—and delighted Muppet fans across the world. So what the hell happened?

(It sure isn't the criticism levied by the Chicago Tribune. I'm not even sure which movie Michael Phillips saw that fateful pre-opening day: "In the previous, pretty good Muppet movie, Jason Segel and Amy Adams helped lighten the load and spark a connection between the human and nonhuman characters. Here, the atmosphere's soured; the beloved Muppets are treated as dismissible straight men, women and critters, for the venal real-world populace. [...] The air of defeatism hanging over the storyline in "Muppets Most Wanted" is meant, I think, to stoke our sympathies for the Muppets and to set up the London-set climax for a heartening load of pathos. Many Muppet fans will be happy to see the gang, including the Swedish Chef and the drummer Animal, once again. But the film's blobby, overextended and more bizarre than eccentric. The cameo laundry list this time includes Tony Bennett, Lady Gaga, Tom Hiddleston, Salma Hayek and Christoph Waltz."[10])

Then there's the on-going misperception that The Muppets are a kiddie-only franchise, something Henson spent his entire life combatting, only to be fought down by critics such as Christopher Lawrence: "For a kids' movie, *Most Wanted* is all wrong tonally, too. Constantine brandishes a gun and a bomb, and not one of those jokey bombs that just covers the victim in black streaks. It's a real, violently destructive bomb that threatens to leave the Muppets looking like a bargain bin at Hobby Lobby. And, clocking in at nearly two hours, *Most Wanted* is too long and tedious for its target audience. The little ones at the screening started getting restless long before the finale."[11]

"If you talk with industry insiders, they'll flat-out tell you that *Muppets Most Wanted* box office take was seriously undercut by a surprising strong *Mr. Peabody & Sherman*. Three weekends into its domestic release, this DreamWorks Animation production sold an estimated $11.7 million worth of tickets. Which meant that the family-friendly *Mr. Peabody* took an over-sized bite out of the audience that Disney had hoped would want to go see *Muppets Most Wanted* instead," wrote Jim Hill. "That said, there are also those at the studio who say that—as soon as Jason Segel made it clear that he didn't really want to be part of a follow-up to *The Muppets*—Disney should have had the smarts to go in another direction with this production. Given that Segel not only starred in the 2011 Walt Disney Pictures release, Jason also executive-produced *The Muppets* as well co-wrote that movie's screenplay with Nicholas Stoller ... Well, Segel's absence was obviously going to be felt. Especially since *Muppets Most Wanted* was being sold as a direct sequel to *The Muppets*."[12]

To this day, I have no answer for that question. I do know, however, that Disney decided, once again, to abandon the brand, but are unwilling to yield the reins to anyone else. A proposed Netflix series was kyboshed by Disney and ABC, resulting in a rushed and disappointing *Office* knock-off boringly titled *the muppets.*, and done in a documentary style, ala *The Office, Parks and Recreation*, etc., with the characters barely able to tolerate each other and Piggy and Kermit recovering from a terrible break-up. *Big Bang Theory* showrunner Bill Prady, a Muppet associate for years, and Bob Kushell took the blame for the show's cynical nature and midway through the season Kushell exited, with Kristen Newman brought in to retool the premise, bringing back both a sweetness and the lacking zaniness to the show. But it was too late. Audiences rejected the "too real" nature of *the muppets.*, and for good reason. Who the hell wants to watch a depressed Kermit the Frog? Who wants to see Piggy alienating friends she'd supposedly worked with for forty years? It was a cynical appeal to jaded Gen-Xers who rejected it *en masse*. Though Disney owns ABC and The Muppets, they opted to cancel the series after a single season.

Meanwhile, *Muppets Most Wanted* continues to be the rather unappreciated offspring despite getting all of the elements *exactly right*.

Theories abound, of course, which turn into conspiracy theories for the most frustrated Muppet fans. On numerous message boards, the question has been bandied about that the surviving Henson children, having moved on following the Disney sale and having no real stake in The Muppets as an entity, the absence of the "Henson" name might turn off the casual fan. Lisa Henson serves as the CEO of The Henson Company; Brian is the chairman and has moved on to producing and touring with the adult-oriented puppet improv show, *Puppet Up!* But they remain supportive of the characters' ongoing adventures: "I know that Lisa and Brian have seen the movie and loved it, which is always very important to me because of Jim's huge legacy to us," said Bobin. "With the first movie, when we're filming in Los Angeles, Brian came to set twice, and he and I talked about making Muppet movies. In fact, he and I are now the only people who've ever done two Muppet movies, so I share that with him. His opinion is obviously very important to me. On this one, it was harder because we were in London, so I didn't see him this time. But I know he's a fan of the movie, so I'm thrilled by that."[13]

As I said, I have no real answer as to why *The Muppets* have been failing lately. Their sporadic merchandise seems to sell well, and judging from the packed room at The Vulture's Muppet panel, filled to the brim with adults who teared up the instant Kermit and Fozzie appeared at the end of Steve Whitmire's and Eric Jacobson's arms (respectively), there's no diminished love for the characters. So the theory that I'm most actively working is that, for my generation, which grew up with the original *Muppet Show* and the Muppet movies, The Muppets may be too personal per person. Just as religion means different things to different people, every Muppet fan is protective of the characters in his or her own way. Which is why so many rejected the more cynical first-half of *the muppets* TV show, but embraced the zanier second (already doomed) half of the retooled season. Take Dana Stevens' Slate.com review: "And maybe this is just me, but I preferred the Kermit/Miss Piggy relationship in its latency phase, when the importunate Piggy only occasionally bothered the reluctant frog with baby talk and kissy noises. I don't need to hear pig/frog commitment squabbles or flash-forward to their future offspring, a green piglet and a pink frog (wouldn't it be a tadpole?) being wheeled in a pram. *Muppets Most Wanted* was co-written by director Bobin and Nicholas Stoller, who also wrote the last installment with its star Jason Segel: a nearly identical team for two very different movies. Could it be that Segel, with his sweet, boyish energy and enthusiasm for puppetry, is the missing element, the keeper of the Muppet flame who needs to step back in for the next movie to keep the spirit alive? In the absence of Jim Henson, he'll have to do."[14]

Yet, their "webisodes" have millions of views; old sketches on YouTube appear at the top of web searches. There's still great love and affection for The Muppets. Hell, this past weekend (August 7, as I write this), the Electric Mayhem appeared live at San Francisco's Outside Lands Music and Arts Festival, as part of a ticket that included Lionel Ritchie and Third Eye Blind.

I think what I'm looking for is someone who can recapture the spirit of Jerry Juhl. For those who may not know, Juhl was one of Henson's first writing partners and the head writer for The Muppets for over thirty years. He gave the Muppets their "second" voices—after those of their puppeteers, of course—set the bar for both the zaniness and the sweet sincerity that we've always, as a species, desperately needed[212]. The voice in Bobin and Stoller's script for *Muppets Most Wanted* came the closest to Juhl's since his death in 2005.

As Jim Hill mused in his article, there is and has been a "lost" Jerry Juhl Muppet script floating around Hollywood for decades. Titled "The Cheapest Muppet Movie Ever Made", it was first abandoned prior to production of *A Muppet Christmas Carol.* Then it was bandied about prior to *Muppets from Space.* In fact, Juhl had written a script titled "Muppets IN Space" which was also rejected, marking the end of Juhl's relationship with the troupe he helped establish.

"'The Cheapest Muppet Movie Ever Made" was:

---

[212] "'When people say about the Muppets, 'It's a gentle soul with a naughty sense of humor,' Jerry was just as responsible for that as my dad," said Brian Henson, Jim Henson's son, who serves with his sister Lisa as chairman and chief executive of the Jim Henson Company." Potts, Monica. "Jerry Juhl, 67, Award-Winning Head Writer for Muppet Shows, Is Dead." New York Times. October 9.
http://www.nytimes.com/2005/10/09/obituaries/jerry-juhl-67-awardwinning-head-writer-for-muppet-shows-is-dead.html

"[A] film that was supposedly so funny that—even in storyboard form—it reportedly caused Jim Henson and screenwriter Jerry Juhl to giggle uncontrollably: And what exactly was the storyline of this proposed Muppet movie? To give you the answer to that question, I'm going to have to turn to that national bestseller, Brian Jay Jones' *Jim Henson: The Biography* (Ballantine Books, September 2003). And to hear Jones tell this tale, the origins of "The Cheapest Muppet Movie Ever Made" can actually be traced back to a Henson associates staff meeting in early 1987. Where Oz had been grousing [...] to Jim and Juhl about the growing costs of (many of the future projects that they hoped to produce) at Henson Associates. If they were going to make another Muppet film, Oz said testily, they would have to "figure out a way to do a really low-budget kind of thing." That was all Juhl needed. Hunching over his Macintosh computer in his home office in California, he quickly pounded out a treatment for a film called *The Cheapest Muppet Movie Ever Made*.

"[...] Borrowing a page from Jim's own life during this point in the history of Henson Associates, as this film is getting underway, Kermit is far too busy to take on any additional behind-the-scenes responsibilities on the next Muppet movie. Gonzo—who has always dreamed of directing—then offers to take over production of this motion picture. Kermit reluctantly agrees but does seem pleased that all he'll have to do on this Muppet movie is appear in it. Rather than produce and then have to coax emotionally overwrought lady pigs out of their trailers.

"So Gonzo goes off and—because his contract says that he has now creative control over this entire project—completely rewrites the script for the next Muppet movie. The film that he now wants to shoot is called "Into the Jaws of the Demons of Death." Which—to hear Jerry Juhl describe the proposed storyline of the motion picture masterpiece that Gonzo wants to make—has this cheesy, terrible plot that made absolutely no sense whatsoever about something being stolen that led to a chase around the world.

"Let's Brian Jay Jones pick up "Cheapest" plotline from this point in the story. Gonzo now in his enthusiasm, Gonzo spends his entire budget on an impressive opening credits sequence, then has no money left for the rest of the film, As the movie proceeds, the film quality gets worse and worse, eventually eroding into black-and-white Super 8 film, then a slide show, and finally just storyboards -- until Gonzo sells out to corporate sponsors and finishes the movie in a beautiful, high-definition, widescreen format. Jim was delighted with the treatment, and put Juhl to work writing a full script, which he turned in as Jim was wrapping up *A Muppet Family Christmas* in Ontario. Jim, Juhl and Oz passed the script back and forth, and even Oz—always prickly about the treatment of the characters—thought it was a exciting project. "It's going to be the kind of movie the audience wants the Muppets to do," he told Jim. 'Just a little crazy and a whole lot of fun.'

"As it was written, "The Cheapest Muppet Movie Ever Made" actually wouldn't be cheap to make—Juhl's script called for erupting volcanoes and exploding islands, and for Meryl Streep to play Miss Piggy's stand-in—but the idea was funny and Jim thought he could manage things on a budget of $8 million."

But Jim's death in 1990 put "Cheapest" into Juhl's proverbial trunk. But then, many years later, circa 2004, following the Disney acquisition, then-Chairman of Walt Disney Studios Dick Cook dusted it off in an attempt to lure Frank Oz back to the world of Muppets. Hill continues: "Mind you, about this same time [late '80s], Frank Oz began cutting back on his involvement in Muppet-related projects. Mostly this was because Oz's career as a film director really began taking off in the late 1980s / early 1990s. Which meant that he then had less & less time to "...wiggle the dollies." (i.e., this was Jim & Frank's deliberately dismissive way of describing the work that they did with the Muppets. These two truly talented men felt that—if they avoided being precious about the puppets that they worked with—that would then make it that much easier for Henson & Oz to just concentrate on doing good work). [...] There have also been whispers that—on the heels of the July 1999 release of *Muppets from Space*—Frank wasn't entirely happy with the direction that the Jim Henson Company was taking with the characters. While Oz has never talked publicly about the matter, it is worth noting that Frank's last known performance as Miss Piggy was back on January 14, 2002. When he appeared alongside Steve Whitmire's Kermit the Frog as part of the 50th anniversary celebration of NBC's *Today*.

"With the hope that Frank might eventually find a way to drive the projected production costs of *The Cheapest Muppet Movie Ever Made* down, Cook asked Oz to meet with the studio's special effects department and continue to develop Juhl's screenplay. But about this same time in 2006, Jason Segel came a-knocking with his own pitch for a brand-new Muppet movie. One that aimed to revive this franchise by reaching back to the style & tone of the first three Muppet movies as well as the old *Muppet Show* TV series. In the end, given that what Segel was proposing was basically a reboot of the Muppets (which was really more in line with what The Walt Disney Company was looking for back then. Given that there was an entire generation of consumers out there who didn't know Kermit & Co. weren't emotionally connected with these characters) and given that Oz & Cook couldn't come to terms over *Cheapest* 's budget, Dick eventually opted to go with Jason's proposal. [...] After he departed Disney, Oz eventually went on to direct 2007's *Death at a Funeral*." [15]

Not-the-author with a genuine unidentified amphibious variety show host. Photo by Amy Lynn Best.

Even after Disney greenlit Segal's version of the "revival" film, as it was called to, before "reboot" took over, Cook continued to refer to *The Muppets* as *The Cheapest Muppet Movie Ever Made*, even as late as the D23 EXPO back in September of 2009, though it was clear that Segal's film had nothing to do with Juhl's.

As Kurt Vonnegut wrote: "And so it goes."

It isn't an easy balance to capture, sweetness and satire, as has been proven time and again. While the real world constantly changes, the Muppet world doesn't necessarily have to. There's no real reason to "update" the characters. Slipping drug references into dialogue among the Electric Mayhem musicians is sly and subversive and fits in with Jim Henson's established humor. A depressed Kermit wondering where his life went wrong, a Great Gonzo too afraid to launch himself out of a canon, a Fozzie Bear having relationship troubles with Riki Lindhome[213]—all elements of *the muppets* that we didn't need. The Great Gonzo staging an onstage "Racing of the

---

[213] Who I personally love, but who was mis-written for on *the muppets*.

Bulls", a Kermit stuck in a Russian gulag forced to put on a talent show, a Miss Piggy beating the crap out of a villainous froggleganger—we'll always have room for that.

Fortunately, Disney released *Muppets Most Wanted* on DVD and Blu-Ray with ample extras and goodies, including a pseudo "Director's Cut" known as "The Unnecessarily Extended Edition"[16]. So we'll always have that while we wait for The House of Mouse to finally do right by their multi-million dollar purchase.

NOTES

[1] Weintraub, Steve "Frosty". 2012. "Exclusive Muppets Sequel News: It's a Caper, Will Have New Muppets, Jason Segel Might Cameo, Possible Summer 2013 Release, More." Collider.com. April 13. http://collider.com/the-muppets-2-sequel-caper-nicholas-stoller-interview/

[2] Weintraub, Steve "Frosty". 2014. "Director James Bobin Talks Muppets Most Wanted, Finding the Story for the Sequel, Putting Together the Cast, Alice In Wonderland 2, and More." March 25. http://collider.com/james-bobin-muppets-most-wanted-alice-wonderland-2-interview/

[3] Weintraub, Steve "Frosty". 2012. Collider.com.

[4] Rottenberg, Josh. 2013. "A first look at the Muppets sequel, 'Muppets…Again!'—Exclusive." Inside Movies. Entertainment Weekly. January 30. Archived at: https://web.archive.org/web/20130131175709/http://insidemovies.ew.com/2013/01/30/muppets-sequel-exclusive/

[5] Radish, Christina. 2014. "Director James Bobin & Songwriter Bret McKenzie Talk Muppets Most Wanted, the Hensons' Reaction to the Film, the Pressure of Following an Oscar Win, and More." Collider.com. March 21. http://collider.com/james-bobin-bret-mckenzie-muppets-most-wanted-interview/

[6] Henderson, Eric. 2014. "Muppets Most Wanted". Slant Magazine. March 18. http://www.slantmagazine.com/film/review/muppets-most-wanted

[7] Radish, Christina. 2014. collider.com

[8] Weintraub, Steve "Frosty". 2014. collider.com

[9] McClintock, Pamela. 2014. "Box Office: 'Divergent' Breaks YA Curse With $56 Million Debut; 'Muppets 2' Bombs." Hollywood Reporter. March 23. http://www.hollywoodreporter.com/news/box-office-divergent-breaks-ya-690460

[10] Phillips, Michael. 2014. "REVIEW: 'Muppets Most Wanted" Chicago Tribune. http://www.chicagotribune.com/entertainment/movies/ct-muppets-most-wanted-20140320-column.html

[11] Lawrence, Christopher. 2014. "Miscalculations, tonal unevenness make 'Muppets Most Wanted' a dud." Review Journal. March 20. http://www.reviewjournal.com/columns-blogs/christopher-lawrence/miscalculations-tonal-unevenness-make-muppets-most-wanted-dud

[12] Hill, Jim. 2014. "Should Disney have made "The Cheapest Muppet Movie Ever Made" instead of "Muppets Most Wanted"?" Jim Hill Media. March 23. http://jimhillmedia.com/editor_in_chief1/b/jim_hill/archive/2014/03/23/should-disney-have-made-quot-the-cheapest-muppet-movie-ever-made-quot-instead-of-quot-muppets-most-wanted-quot.aspx

[13] Radish, Christina. 2014. Collider.com.

[14] Stevens, Dana. 2014. "The lovers, the dreamers, and Ray Liotta.?" Slate.com. March. http://www.slate.com/articles/arts/movies/2014/03/muppets_most_wanted_starring_kermit_the_frog_reviewed.html?wpisrc=hpsponsoredd2

[15] Hill, Jim. 2014. "Should Disney have made "The Cheapest Muppet Movie Ever Made" instead of "Muppets Most Wanted"?" Jim Hill Media. March 23. http://jimhillmedia.com/editor_in_chief1/b/jim_hill/archive/2014/03/23/should-disney-have-made-quot-the-cheapest-muppet-movie-ever-made-quot-instead-of-quot-muppets-most-wanted-quot.aspx

[16] For greater insight into the film, I recommend you visit The "Lost Commentary" page of ToughPigs.com: "Hennes, Joe. 2015. "Muppets Most Wanted: The Lost Commentary." "[W]hen *Muppets Most Wanted* came out on DVD and Blu-ray, we were incredibly saddened to learn that there weren't any commentaries or behind-the-scenes features to show off how the movie was made. We were left correcting people on Twitter who said that the movie used a lot of CGI and explaining why puppetry is still a complicated and technologically amazing art form. We felt it necessary to do our part and inform the masses! By "masses", we meant a room full of New Yorkers. At one of our Muppet Vault events, we invited Muppet performers Matt Vogel (Constantine, Floyd, Lew Zealand) and Eric Jacobson (Miss Piggy, Fozzie Bear, Animal) to join us for a live commentary. They wanted their stories to be told as much as we wanted to hear them." Tough Pigs.com March 23. http://www.toughpigs.com/mmw-commentary/

NEVER TOO YOUNG TO DIE (1986)

"Every now and then, a film comes along that throws together a group of actors that should never have even heard of each other, much less appeared in the same movie together. Witness *Never Too Young to Die*, a Steven Paul shlock-fest that throws together John Stamos (successful actor, failed singer), Gene Simmons (failed actor, successful singer), and Vanity (failed actress, failed singer). The only combination this film doesn't toss at us is "successful actor, successful singer", but that's probably because only one such individual has ever existed, and Jennifer Lopez was probably about twelve years old when this movie was made. Suffice to say, if *The Devil's Rain* was your idea of a "dream cast", then this film is right up your alley."[1]

There's no human way to adequately describe this movie. To use the old phrase, "It wasn't released; it *escaped*." Written by Steven Paul[214] and Anthony Foutz (based on a story by Paul and his brother Stuart), and more-or-less directed by Gil Bettman[215], *Never Too Young to Die* defies many laws of narrative, structure, story, and even physics, as it careens drunkenly through its overlong running time. It's so awful... so, so awful... that it's actually hypnotic. And though I despise the category "So Bad It's Good", there's no other box it could be forced into. There's not a rational moment to be had.

The wobbly Jell-O backbone of the story is that top super-secret agent Drew Stargrove (George Lazenby[216]) is murdered by elite uber-criminal, Velvet Von Ragnar (Gene Simmons[217]). Suddenly, Stargrove's gymnastics sensation and asshole fratboy son, Lance (John Stamos), is thrust into the spotlight after discovering his father's secret identity. Into his world

---

[214] Brother of *Simon Conjurer*'s Stuart Paul.

[215] *Crystal Heart* (1986) starring Tawny Kitaen.

[216] James Bond in *On Your Majesty's Secret Service* (1969). And then never again.

[217] Born "Chaim Witz" in August, 1949.

comes a ninth-tier Bond girl named Danja Deerling (Vanity[218]), sent to possibly keep Lance safe from Von Ragnar. Mostly, what she does is increase the volume on the post-pubescent stud muffin's sexual tension-o-meter, which he relieves at one point by angrily eating fruit. Lance sees Danja as the easy path towards revenge. Meanwhile, Ragnar's plan to poison California's water supply, by hacking into the Diablo Canyon power plant and dumping toxic waste into the reservoirs, is lacking only some sort of MacGuffin CD (which Ragnar refers to for some unknown reason as "RAM-K"), presumably containing oodles of cheat codes and walkthroughs. And who has this disk now that Papa Stargrove is kaput? Why, Lance, of course, and he enlists the help of his Asian genius-cum-whipping-boy roommate, Cliff (Peter Kwong[219]) to assist him in his quest to bed Danja. And save the day, of course. Can't forget that.

So far, this sounds like a clone of something Richard Grieco turned down to make *If Looks Could Kill*. But the above description leaves out several key details, like Ragnar is a cross-dressing diva (the VHS box refers to him as a "maniacal hermaphrodite") of Streisand-like proportions, whose army of followers have wandered over from an Italian post-apocalypse movie, decked out in leather and rainbow Mohawks. When not dressed as Frank N. Furter and breaking out into song, Ragnar disguises himself as a little weaselly ginger-beardo who hangs out with his I.T. guy (played by Robert Englund[220]). In between confrontations with Ragnar, Lance dodges homoerotic advances from class mates on the wrestling team, while storing away some truly homophobic remarks to use against the villain later.

I can only assume that *Never Too Young to Die* was created after a box of plot points and disparate characters was dropped down a flight of stairs. No two people seem to be in the same movie, to the point where conversations are little more than random sentences blurted out in turn. Look no further than during Lazenby's death scene, as he confronts the vicious Ragnar who just murdered the secret agent's partner:

> **Velvet Von Ragnar:** "A program disk was stolen from me, Stargrove. I believe you've got it.
> **Drew Stargrove:** Come on. This is stupid.
> **Velvet Von Ragnar:** You're right. It's *very* stupid. Assuming, of course, you want to see your son.
> **Drew Stargrove:** What kind of designer-drug are you on? How is Lance mixed up in all this?
> **Velvet Von Ragnar:** You know, oddly enough, I wasn't sure he *was*... until now.

---

[218] Famous for being Vanity.

[219] Hey, he was "Rain" in *Big Trouble in Little China* (1986)! And "Tommy Tong" in *The Golden Child*. 1986 was a good year for Kwong.

[220] Forever and always Freddy Krueger from the *Nightmare on Elm St.* series.

Drew Stargrove: Lance doesn't have a clue about my work!

Velvet Von Ragnar: Nor did his mother, but that didn't save her.

Drew Stargrove: You're threatening to *kill* Lance!

Velvet Von Ragnar: I'm not *threatening*, Stargrove. I'm *promising* to kill him, unless I get that disk.

Drew Stargrove: ...Ragnar, I've lost too much blood for your games.

Velvet Von Ragnar: Stargrove, you're about to lose a lot more.

[kills him with a shotgun]

The movie is delightfully terrible to the point that any intentional terribleness is secondary and beside the point. To enjoy *Never Too Young to Die*, several things are required from the viewer. First: chemical impairment. Second: some sort of party setting. Three: absence of expectations.

Foremost of these eliminated expectations is the hope for any possible heroics to come from young Lance. Stamos is naturally charismatic, that's the reason we haven't shot his Rebecca Romijn-losing ass into the sun, but yet Lance is an utter tool, obnoxious, privileged, sexist, and borderline abusive towards his nerdy acolyte, Cliff. For his part, Cliff is obviously in love with Lance—there's no other explanation as to why, as in an early sequence, he sits outside Lance's classroom to help him cheat on a chemistry exam via wrist watch communication. In one scene, after his car is totaled in a get-slightly-farther-away, he returns to his dorm to "borrow" Cliff's motorcycle, but Cliff insists on coming along—so Lance makes Cliff ride bitch *on his own ride!* When his inevitable love scene with Danja finally makes the scene, it seems like both actors are simulating sex at gunpoint. On the other hand, the loathsome-in-real-life Simmons is a delightfully campy sociopathic villain, and his chemistry with Englund's Riley is undeniable. You don't get more villain-y than the exchange they have regarding the toxicity of their intended poison:

Velvet Von Ragnar: Is the concentration lethal?

Riley: I'd say *worse!*

But that's barely scratching the surface. If all of the above can be dismissed, allow me to layer on some additional horror: Ragnar's favorite method of dispatch is via a sharpened nail on his middle finger, possibly dipped in some sort of poison though probably not; Ragnar's pet name for his acolytes is "My little turd balls!"; Lance has his own kick-ass theme-song-cum-earworm titled, "Stargrove!", which is just as catchy as Queen's *"Flash! (boom) A-aaaahh!" Flash Gordon* theme, but harder to remove from your cerebral cortex. The final climactic duel between Lance and Ragnar involve cutting grade-school insults along the lines of "You're gay!" The upper hand is gotten when Ragnar accidentally exposes a female breast-...and, during the ensuing wrestling match, Lance *bites it.* A move Lazenby's Bond never would have thought of, I'd wager.

Velvet Von Ragnar (Gene Simmons) and Riley (Robert Englund). Photo copyright Paul Entertainment All Rights Reserved.

Velvet Von Ragnar: "Don't you see the greatness in me? I'm female and male. Man and woman. I'm better than you are!"

Lance: "Yeah, but don't you understand something? You're only half of each. I'm a whole man. So, if you'll excuse me, I don't have a lot of time here. I gotta save the world."

"*Never Too Young to Die* is worth watching for the cast alone," offers Mitch from The Video Vacuum, before following up with more fighting words. "Stamos is actually pretty good in this flick. I don't know if he's exactly the 'New Breed of Hero' the video box makes him out to be, but he's a lot better than in that *Full House* crap. And Simmons is great too. There's one scene where he's on stage in a drag show and singing that's particularly out there. I don't know why he traded in acting for a reality show because the dude definitely had the chops to make a Grade-A movie villain. And then there's Vanity. I didn't pay close attention to her performance because I was too busy ogling her boobies. That's right folks, we get to see some Vani-ta-tas in this movie."[2]

I'm winding up my abuse of the story, acting, and performers, and I haven't even mentioned the hilariously-inept filmmaking. In the opening sequence alone, we get a variety of establishing shots of a power plant at night, then in daylight, then night again—all with straight cuts, so we know this is no time-lapse matter—which becomes just the opening salvo of the implausible. Props and bits of costumes come and go between angles. People teleport across rooms and back during even the most stationary of conversations. (This exemplary attention to continuity is rivaled only by the also-horrible but far-less fun *Children of the Living Dead*.)

And then, again, there's the song:

"Stargrove"
Music and lyrics by: Chip Taylor, Ralph Lane, Michael Kingsley, and Iren Koster (Yes, it took four people to write this song.)
(Stargrove!) Flying like you've never flown
(Stargrove!) Runnin' through a danger zone
(Stargrove!) Are you gonna stand alone?
Stargrove! Stargrove!

Not to mention the film's titular ditty:
"You're never too young
Never too young to die-iiieee.
And I don't know why…"

"*Never Too Young to Die* is precisely the kind of film that frequently fails to live up to its own promise. That cast, those roles, that plot—it all seems too good to be true. Yet, *Never Too Young to Die* doesn't disappoint. The movie consistently chooses excess and gloriously oversteps at each turn, reaching for action movie grandiosity and spilling over into outlandishness and absurdity. This naturally begs a host of tantalizingly pointless questions. How is poisoning the water supply a step towards world domination? Why is the disc with the water system codes not simply destroyed? Is Cliff the adult embodiment of Data from *The Goonies* (Richard Donner, 1985)? Why is Ragnar's Mohawked punk-powerhouse named, of all things, Pyramid? Why is Danja's seduction of Lance conducted like a blunt weapon? Why does Lance try to resist Danja through compulsive eating? How do two objects thrown from the same position travel in opposite directions when they collide?"[3]

Never Too Young to Die perfectly encapsulates the no-such-thing-as-too-much-cocaine film productions of the '80s, when cranking out product for home video was what kept so many companies alive. Maybe not everyone involved thought it was a great idea, but it's obvious that Simmons saw great potential in the role, since he forced KISS to cancel part of their '85 "Animalize Tour" so that The Demon could take part in the filming. Of everyone, he seems to be having the most fun, to the point where he may even be sucking the fun away from everyone else, leaving soulless husks behind. And Vanity.

No explanation necessary. Screengrab copyright Paul Entertainment.

"Simmons really throws himself into the role he was clearly born to play. Perhaps a bit too much. John Stamos should have done more movies like this. His only other role that's even a little bit similar is as the awesomely-named Grady Westerfall in *Born to Ride* (1991). There really should have been a Stargrove sequel—even a franchise, like Bond. They certainly say the name enough times, in true Brakus fashion. The whole thing was directed by Gil Bettman, who later directed *Night Vision* (1997). But this was indisputably his finest hour."[4]

I was first introduced to *Never Too Young to Die* by Low Budget Pictures show-runner Chris Seaver. The film's star came as no surprise since once-upon-a-time Seaver included a framed picture of Stamos as a non-sequitur cameo prop in all of his early movies (one of his fans justified this by dubbing the photo the "Stamos Configuration", separate from time and space and known for appearing at inopportune times (usually a character's death) and misplaced places). *Never Too Young to Die* had to have begun the filmmaker's obsession with the in-joke photo. As such, the movie never made it to DVD, and the existing VHS offering on Amazon will cost you upwards of $25. Fortunately for all, the Internet is a thing that may have been invented for the sole purpose of distributing this movie to the masses, since it can be watched *en toto* on YouTube.

This chapter is just a taste of the atrocity. For more info, by all means visit Dr. Winston Boogie's hilarious scene-by-scene takedown of the film over at Agony Barrel. "Unfortunately, we must endure one last round of painful comic repartee as they drive off into the distance. Danja tweaks Lance, asking if he got a good look at Ragnar's body. Lance tells her to knock it off, but she continues, saying, 'Really, I think the proper procedure would be to go back and —' before Lance cuts her off. The proper procedure would be to go back and do what? Was she suggesting Lance get some necrophiliac kicks with Ragnar's body, or what? We never find out, because the movie mercifully ends."[5]

NOTES

[1] Dr. Winston O'Boogie. 2002. "Never Too Young to Die. 1986". Agony Booth.com. May 1.
   http://www.agonybooth.com/recaps/Never_Too_Young_to_Die_1986.aspx

[2] Mitch. 2001. "It Came From The Thrift Store: Never Too Young To Die (1986)". The Video Vacuum. . Feb 19.
   http://thevideovacuum.livejournal.com/1017227.html

[3] https://makeminecriterion.wordpress.com/2013/08/14/never-too-young-to-die-gil-bettman-1986/

[4] Ty and Brett. "Review." Comeuppance Reviews. December, 2011.
   http://www.comeuppancereviews.com/2011/12/never-too-young-to-die-1986.html

[5] Dr. Winston O'Boogie. 2002. Agony Booth.com.

PERFORMANCE (1970)

"So remember who you say you are and keep your noses clean.
Boys will be boys and play with toys so be strong with your beast.
Oh Rosie dear, doncha think it's queer, so stop me if you please.
The baby is dead, my lady said, "You gentlemen, why you all work for me?"

"Often a movie will leave a viewer with a bitter aftertaste, but *Performance* makes you feel from frame one that someone is resting his dirtiest finger in the back of your throat," wrote Danny Peary in his highly-regarded book, *Cult Movies*. He continues, noting that John Waters' Odorama film *Polyester* and the "best-forgotten" Smell-O-Rama film, *Scent of Mystery*, *Performance* is likely the only picture in history which can be, and has been, discussed in terms of stench. Not surprisingly it was John Simon who, in his blistering attack on the picture, 'The Most Loathsome Film of All,' first called attention to the fact that the theaters in which *Performance* was initially shown constantly smelled from viewers' throwing up."[1]

Co-directed by Donald Cammell and soon-to-be cult auteur Nicholas Roeg, in many ways *Performance* heralded the end of the so-called "Summer of Love" for good. Originally conceived to be a "feel good romp" along the lines of The Beatles' *Hard Day's Night*, *Performance* spiraled into darkness rather quickly for all involved and resulted in a movie still considered controversial to this day.

London thug Chas works as an enforcer for feared underworld boss Harry Flowers. Specializing in intimidation, Chas extracts protection money from Harry's "clients" during the day. At night, he and his Droogs threaten barristers trying to indict Harry for criminal activities. To drive a particular point home, Chas and his gang show up at the lawyer's home, tie up, shave, and torture his driver, then pour corrosive acid all over the man's prized Bentley. Chas is Harry's favorite weapon—just point and fire.

Things go terribly wrong when Harry decides to bring one of Chas's old rivals into the fold. Joey Maddocks the bookmaker was an old gym buddy of Chas's and, though never explicitly explained, they may have been involved in a romantic interlude or two as well. Chas is desperate to work Joey over, bust up his business, and make sure the ponce never talks. Harry insists that the young gangster keep business and private affairs separate. However, after provoking Joey a little too hard, the bookie and his own gang show up at Chas's place and proceed to trash it and him. Joey and the boys beat Chas up, strip him and whip him with his own belt. But this is Vicious Chas, after all, who keeps a hidden guns and has no real qualms about using them. Murdering Joey brings the heat down on Harry—whose indictment is still on its way despite Chas's best efforts—and Harry, via Newton's Laws of Thermodynamic Revenge, passes that heat along to his protégé.

Needing to skip town, Chas gives himself a quick dye job with paint and turpentine and seeks out a safe house in which to hole up until his contacts can provide him with a new passport and identity. Through sheer coincidence, he overhears a musician talk about leaving behind a room rented to him by a man named Turner, a retired rock star, it turns out, with a decaying house in a crumbling part of London. Used to simply turning up and getting his own way, Chas scarcely bothers with an alibi, claiming to be an itinerant juggler, heralded through Europe. Turner's housemate, manager, and lover, Pherber, doesn't buy it, doesn't even want to take his money, but there's something about the obviously lying tough on her doorstep that she finds intriguing.

It takes some doing, but Pherber—with help from the waifish Lucy, whom she shares with Turner—manages to convince the one-time great musician that they could not only use the money, but that Chaz's presence might even lead to new inspiration. At first, Turner resists. He doesn't want another stranger in his moldering house, especially not one obviously lying about his past, obviously putting on an act for the freak artists. Gradually, Turner finds himself unable to resist Chaz's animalistic charms, his simmering violence. The two worlds collide violently, decadently, and terminally, becoming something very new in the end.

"In 1970 Donald Cammell sent a telegram to Warner Brothers urging them to release *Performance*, the film he had co-directed almost two years before. 'If *Performance* does not upset audiences,' he explained, 'then it is nothing.' […] He needn't have worried. In the end it upset almost everyone. One movie executive's wife would allegedly "vomit in disgust" at a test screening before the film was eventually made public. Early US reviews described it as "the most disgusting, the most completely worthless film I have seen" and "indescribably sleazy". Such audiences aside, dispute, ill fortune, infamy and death would enfold many of the principal people who made the movie," wrote Michael Holdern in The Guardian, 2005.

Though known mainly by genre fans for directing *Demon Seed*, Donald Cammell's career was sprawling and varied long before he stepped behind a camera. Born in Edinburgh, he was "brought up in a bohemian atmosphere, an environment he described as 'filled with magicians, metaphysicians, spiritualists and demons' including Aleister Crowley[221], the great inspiration behind Kenneth Anger's life and work. Cammell was a precociously gifted painter, winning a scholarship to the Royal Academy at age 16. He subsequently studied in Florence and made his living as a society portrait painter. While still in his late teens, The Times hailed one of his portraits as 'society portrait of the year.' He had a short-lived early marriage that produced a son. After its disintegration he moved to New York to live with model Deborah Dixon and concentrate on painting nudes, which helped him to satisfy his notable sexual appetite—he had the reputation of being irresistible to women—but not his creative desires. He moved to Paris and began writing screenplays; first a thriller called *The Touchables*, then a collaboration with Harry Joe Brown Jr. called *Duffy*. This caper movie was directed by Robert Parrish in 1968 (and featured James Fox), an artistic failure that frustrated Cammell to the point that he decided to direct. Through his friendship with Anita Pallenberg he came into the orbit of the Stones and

---

[221] Cammell was Aleister Crowley's godson. For those not in the know, Crowley was a bon vivant and self-styled "magician" who went by the "Magickal" name, "The Beast". He founded his own religion, Thelema, and identified himself as "the prophet entrusted with guiding humanity into the Æon of Horus in the early 20th century." https://en.wikipedia.org/wiki/Aleister_Crowley

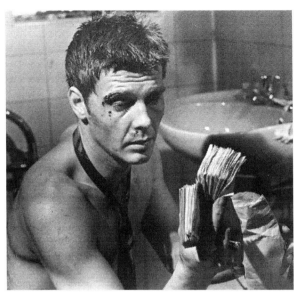

James Fox as "Chas".

moved to London.[2]

Now a Londoner, Cammell spent months developing projects to direct. Several times, he came close, but was hindered by a one-sided friendship with notoriously notorious Marlon Brando, who would often string Cammell along, it would seem, encouraging work on projects ostensibly to star, only to change his mind or otherwise back out, including a nascent version of *Performance*. "Having already seen discussions with Marlon Brando come to nothing over a gangster tale called *The Liars*, Cammell developed the screenplay into *The Performers*, which in turn became *Performance*. A social acquaintance of the Rolling Stones, Cammell was able to bring Mick Jagger into the equation, which served to reassure Warner Brothers—who agreed to underwrite the picture—that someone would go and see it, however it turned out. [...] Thirty-six years on it is difficult to imagine the sheer impact of involving the Rolling Stones in your movie in 1968. They were at the forefront of a youth culture that seemed a tangible threat, not only to the established order but order itself. Jagger's presence turned the making of *Performance* from a mere project into the event of the season. The Stones' reputation also presaged the project's aura as being somehow satanic."[3]

Filmed in 1968—a six-week schedule stretching into an interminable series of months—Cammell and Roeg holed up in that crumbling building with one of the biggest rock and roll superstars of all time, to make a movie that plays with the question of identity, and it's been said that no one emerged from that set untouched. Yearning for an acting career, Jagger threw himself into the role of Turner and embodied him, but only to the point that Turner is ultimately absorbed by Jagger. You never consider Turner to be anything other than a sad duplicate of the Rolling Stones' frontman. James Fox, on the other hand, a pretty boy playing tough for the first time, descended into London's underworld to prepare for the role. He returned as a genuine tough guy, bringing with him Johnny Shannon, an English actor with genuine mob ties, who joined the production first as an advisor, then finally as Harry Flowers, giving that role a surprising authenticity. "Willie, his nickname, was a great observer and was learning his craft," said Cammell. "He had already made some films and fell into this one with great gusto. He literally became a gangster in the name of research. He spent evenings in the company of London's most notorious thugs, to the extent that he actually frightened people. Now imagine this very macho, violent behaviour being shattered, once again, under Jagger's influence. It was perhaps a tragedy that Willie became so traumatized by Jagger's sexuality that he succumbed to it and ultimately quit acting altogether and went to India. It took him forever to snap out of it."[4]

Meanwhile, casting Pallenberg as Turner's lover Pherber created different, frightening challenges for Cammell and Roeg. A last-minute replacement for Mia Farrow and Tuesday Weld—both of which suffered injuries prior to shooting—Pallenberg was, at the time, dating Jagger's Stones partner, Keith Richards. "While you watch the film, remember that Keith Richards is waiting outside in his Bentley (writing "You Got The Silver") while Anita (his girlfriend) seduces Mick (his best friend) for real on the closed set. The way I heard the story, when Cammell called the scene, to the amazement of the crew, they kept going through orgasm. Keith refused to give Cammell the newly recorded *Let It Bleed* songs for the soundtrack because of all this.....he told friends he knew that if he was on the set and saw Mick, the Stones would have been history....but the band was his life so he just waited it all out," wrote Richard R. Carlton in his review. An apocryphal story has it that Cammell assembled all of the Jagger/Pallenberg scenes into a "blue reel" and submitted it for an award at an adult film festival.

"Anecdotes surrounding the production itself are legion. In a rare interview Nic Roeg recalls that his most extraordinary memory of filming was, having shot one of the movie's 'intimate scenes', arriving at the film lab (whose documentary department had mistakenly processed it and believed they had stumbled across pornography) 'to witness them destroying the film with a fire axe out on the pavement, and that brutality, used on something I thought was quite innocent, said something about the morality of the time.'"[5]

Richard Carlton continues, "This is one film where the legend does not obscure the brilliance of the plot, the direction of the scenes, and the players....the players with the famous goings on inside and outside the shoot. The cast was not only acting but actually doing the drugs and sex portrayed on the screen. The film pretty much destroyed everyone who worked on it except Mick and Keith and the Stones. Anita Pallenberg was incoherent for years afterwards, James Fox underwent a religious experience and ceased acting for a decade, one actor became a heroin dealer, another committed suicide, another committed murder and became a junkie before he died young. Stephen Davis (in his book "Old Gods Almost Dead") says that when the original Cammell and Roeg print was shown to the Warner executives, one's wife vomited and the whole audience left the screening room before the film ended. The true legend of the rock hard, satanic Rolling Stones was born when the band survived both *Performance* and the only live murder ever included in a movie during the Altamont Festival (shown in the film *Gimme Shelter*)."[6]

Warner Brothers was, as you would imagine, appalled by the film. Not only was it the exact opposite of what they were expecting, the visual language obscured the film's story, rendering it nearly incoherent even with a three-hour-plus running time.

A frequent complaint from the producers asserted that it took too long for Jagger to appear on screen; the gangster sections delayed the arrival to Bohemian Chelsea. Cuts were ordered. Along with Antony Gibbs, Brian Smedley-Aston, and an uncredited Frank Mazzola, were tasked with editing a viable product out of the film, resulting in multiple cuts and versions. In the U.S. *Performance* was eventually released in 1970 to the excitement of none, thanks to marginal publicity, with a nearly unwatchable 90 minute running time, Cockney accents clumsily dubbed over, and much of the film's mysticism removed.

"When they saw my rough cut, they were appalled that Jagger was not onscreen until maybe an hour into the film. So, in a vain attempt to keep it from being shelved permanently, I tried to rescue the work. I mean, I completely re-edited it three times, compressing it more and more. By then, Nick Roeg was completely absorbed in filming *Walkabout*, so he blissfully wasn't involved in any of this," Cammell told David Del Valle for *Video Watchdog*, stating that when Roeg saw what had been done in the editing room, "He [Roeg] wanted his name removed, because he felt that too many liberties had been taken with the continuity. You have to realize, it was a collaborative effort, yet it was my screenplay, my concept. I directed the actors and Nick did what Nick does best, which is the director of photography."[7]

"*Performance* was released during the summer of 1970, well over a year after its completion. It was shelved by Ken Hyman, the head of Warners, when he concluded that no amount of editing, relooping, rescheduling would cover up the fact that the picture ultimately made no sense. However, Ted Ashley, Hyman's successor at Warners, thought *Performance* salvageable—he assumed that any film with rock idol Mick Jagger in various states of undress would have some camp appeal. Ashley was wrong in guessing that the picture would be considered campy-the violence is too strong, the absurd humor too disguised, and Jagger too introverted. But coming at a time when young audiences were into heady, ambitious projects with blaring soundtracks and antisocial characters who turn on to dope and sex at the drop of a director's hat, and into anything Jagger did, *Performance* quickly gained a cult following. This cult has grown with the increased interest in the works of Nicolas Roeg."[8]

Indeed, it was Roeg who received the lion's share of the credit—when credit was grudgingly given at all—from the largely negative critical reviews. "I don't really want to discuss Nick, but I will say this: Nick went on to several features on the strength of *Performance*, and when you realize that the whole project was based on my friendship with Jagger, and the fact that Jagger trusted me, it does aggravate an already open wound. Enough said." Del Valle is quick to clarify in his *VW* article: "In the wake of *Performance*, Roeg directed a number of acclaimed motion pictures, while Cammell's appeared to stall. The common assumption that Roeg's success resulted in feelings of envy and sour grapes is unfounded: no ill feeling existed between the two directors. I emphasize this because, in the interview you are about to read, Cammell makes certain comments that might be mistaken for a kind of animosity that simply was not in his nature. If they were rivals, it was only as siblings would be. When he heard that *Video Watchdog* was planning to print the following statement about Cammell, Roeg said, 'I feel like a part of me has been taken away. He was like a brother.'"[9]

"Nicolas Roeg went to Australia to make *Walkabout* (1970), the first of a series of great films that would put him at the forefront of '70s directors. Although credited as co-director, Roeg's role on *Performance* was mainly a technical one. An experienced and respected director of photography, he looked after the camerawork while Cammell dealt with script, performance, characterisation and structure. Roeg was only present during the first stages of editing and had nothing to do with the final cut, which he initially disliked. After *Performance* Cammell's career would be a difficult one, resulting in the completion of only one film per decade. While Roeg's career flourished, it was widely assumed *Performance* was mainly his work while in fact it was Cammell's personal project from the outset and full of the themes and obsessions that would haunt all of his work—death, sex, transformation, the blurring of male and female, the power dynamics of often lethal mind games."[10]

"Brimming with explicit sex, brutal violence and drug use, the film was deemed too wild for release in its original form, so a re-edit was ordered. Cammell spent a year locked in a Hollywood studio fiddling with the film, reordering an already nontraditional story into a one-of-a-kind cinematic experience. Employing jump-cuts, elliptical storytelling and surreal imagery he instills a kinetic energy to the story propelling the viewer to abandon traditional ideas of movie watching and accepting the disjointed narrative as reality skewed by the haze of fading memory or drug use. It's baffling and bizarre, a movie that refuses to be pigeonholed. It isn't exactly a youth exploitation movie, or a crime drama or a drug movie, but in a way it is all of those and more. *Performance* is a challenging experience and one that hasn't lost one iota of its power in the decades since its initial release. 'I've seen a lot of films from that period again and they all seem to live in a time warp,' said Pallenberg. '*Performance* is completely timeless, it's extraordinary—you always discover something new and that's what makes a great film.'"[11]

It was submitted to the BBFC in August 1970 and the cuts list published here shows the Examiners picked up on the brutality of two particular scenes. They note potential for imitable behavior—"forcible shaving is something that could be imitated by young people"—and also look to reduce the association between sexual and violent images."[12]

With the squalor and sensationalism involved in the making, without having seen the film, one would expect *Performance* to be a drug-fueled orgy ala Kenneth Anger-meets-David Lynch. It's definitely strange, but the overall tone is off-putting, the rapid parallel editing deliberately disorienting. It's a movie at odds with itself as well as its audience, a squirming thing defying any attempt to grasp it.

Performance is actually two movies smashed together in a thematic particle accelerator. The first half is pure gangster drama, possibly one of the best British crime stories ever filmed, and you're instantly drawn into Chas' shady and dangerous world. Once he goes on the run and winds up in Turner's veritable Gormenghast, the movie becomes something very different. This 180-degree shift into psychedelia and "hippy drug nonsense" (as several of my students described it), *Performance* becomes something messy and intangible. For fans of Outsider Cinema, however, it's in the second half that *Performance* transforms into its own thing. While the film's visual cues are present throughout—using mirrors and multiple-exposures to

Pherber (Anita Pallenberg), Chas (James Fox), Turner (Mick Jagger)
Photo copyright Warner Brothers. All Rights Reserved.

question the idea of identity, how you see yourself versus how others perceive you, the abhorrent idea of gender fluidity in a hypermasculine world colliding with the Turner dimension sans boundaries—*Performace* begins in a world of straight cuts, hard angles, muted colors (except, of course, for blood red). Once entering Turner's world, the camera spins, gravity is defied, colors explode in multiple mosaic. If you struggled with the slang and thick accents at the head of the film, things won't go better for you in the second half, as philosophies are discussed and overlaid, obscure concepts about the nature of the performer to the performance, are tossed at the viewer like juggling pins, expecting the audience to keep everything aloft and in motion. *Performance* asks a lot of its audience, nearly defying you to keep up with it even as you're sure you're not getting all of the information you need.

Performance plays with Chas's latent homosexuality. His feud with Ritchie, for example, and his animosity towards the "lesser" hood, is strongly implied to have roots in a past affair, as Cammell intercuts the conversation with numerous photographs of Chaz and Ritchie shirtless, in boxing poses. The bodybuilder magazines found in Chaz's apartment are a homosexual dog-whistle, in a sense, harkening to the days when closeted men utilized the legitimacy of those publications as the only form of pornography they could publicly buy.

"*Performance* is about the trans-valuation of all values," Cammell told David Del Valle. "Perhaps the film is Nietzschean in the sense that I believe in living one's life that way. The film brings the Neanderthal gangster and the effete yellow book world of the rock star into one demonic fusion. The gangster is really more bisexual and in touch with his feminine side; once again, the fragmented self. It's really a provocative love story. The margin between love and hate is exceedingly narrow and I've made an effort to show that, where violence exists, it's as indicative of love as much as hatred."[13]

He argues with Pherber that, unlike Turner, he's "all man". Turner, she insists, is half man and half woman, making him a whole person. Shot of a mirror held close to Chas's face, the left side reflecting Pallenberg. She then holds the mirror in front of her face, reflecting him back. At one point she places the cameo mirror on the crown of Chas' head, mirroring the

227

bullet he will later put into Turner. She implies that Turner is stuck in the hotel, afraid to leave, or unable to leave. Mirrored ceilings add to the sense of distortion. Near the end, Chas rolls over in bed to kiss his bedmate—who, in at least one shot, *is* Turner—who turns out to be Lucy in Turner's robe. Misdirection or transubstantiation? I've read some theories that Lucy doesn't even exist as a person, but more a construct of Pherber's and Turner's ids and their desire for a superego. And who is Lorraine, the ten-year-old maid serving as a Greek Chorus for Chas, delivering exposition about the relationships of the adults? Is she Lucy's daughter, as is implied, or something that just comes with Turner's house and existence?

In the film's final moments, Harry's gang finally catches up to Chas and arrive at Turner's flat to bring him "home". By this point, Turner's obsession with Chas has become something almost metaphysical. When he tells Chas that he's coming too, Chas doesn't argue. He pulls his gun and hovers over Turner, with something other than murder on his mind. The camera assumes the path of the bullet, tunneling through Turner's brain, shattering an image of surrealist writer Jorge Borges at the terminal. Following the back of Chas's head, we follow the defeated gunsel to the car outside—but it's Turner we see through the window, even after we've discovered the dead, bloody rock star in a hall closet. Did Turner and Chas finally merge? Did Turner transcend his body and become Chas? The sudden appearance of credits offer no answers. Cammell's interpretation isn't much help either.

Del Valle: "At the end of the film, after Chas (Fox) shoots Turner (Jagger) in the head, it's Jagger that we see leaving the house with his old gangster cronies-presumably to be murdered by them. You meant to indicate that Chas had absorbed Turner's persona?"

Cammell: "In a sense, yes. I was thinking of Jorge Luis Borges and the Spanish bullfighter El Cordobes, who kisses the bull between the eyes before placing his sword therein. Jagger is very much that bullfighter. In terms of painting, if you look at the 'Memo from Turner' number, Jagger's character has already assumed the Harry Flowers persona (in terms of Chas' perception). So this further absorption seems natural. The 'Memo from Turner' sequence, by the way is probably the first rock video."[14]

"'Merger' is heard repeatedly in the dialogue, and Mick Brown points to Borges's theory that 'every man is two men,' realized at the end upon the fusion of Chas (the personification of violence) and Turner (pacifism). In the first half of the picture, gangsters (seen reading Borges on their coffee break!), businessmen and lawyers are so utterly lost in their oppressive performance that single-mindedness has left them homosexual. In the second half, Cammell examines what he called "the interchangeability of gender," via Chas's overbearing manliness, Pherber's domineering femininity, and Turner and Lucy's androgyny, narcissistic characters approaching the liberation of the female-man and the male-woman, a 'complete' individual," wrote Ray Young for *Flickhead*. Why this strange experiment? Why the merger of sex and race and personality? Cammell's formative years were lived with a father sensitive to the principles of Dante Rossetti and the Pre-Raphaelites. A movement against stale, formula-driven art, they mourned the death of one culture's passion and trumpeted the glory of another's birth. In this respect, Performance transcends every other youth and/or counterculture film of its period. Rapid fashion trends stunted "the Sixties," when automatic nostalgia dated movies within weeks of their release. They were products manufactured by calculating producers quick to capitalize on flighty, superficial tastes—indeed, Warners' own impetus for backing Performance. Cammell and Roeg's film may appear outwardly passé in its psychedelic drug use, music, hair and clothing styles, and Christopher Gibbs's Moroccan set design, but in truth its 'hippiedom' spans centuries, beyond the pre-Raphaelites, back to al-Hassan ibn-al-Sabbah and his declaration of moral freedom, "Nothing is true, everything is permitted."[15]

"The critics were not kind to *Performance*," wrote Perry. "Generally agreeing that without the presence of Jagger and James Fox it would have been unendurable. In 1970, we were curious to see if Jagger's dynamism would transfer to the screen; today, seeing *Performance* (as well as *Ned Kelly*, 1970), we better understand why he didn't click as a movie star. He is withdrawn, awkward, restricted so much that he sings his only song while behind a desk, and is forced to spit out through his swollen red lips such inanities as "I don't like music!" and "The only 'Performance' is one that achieves madness." Fox comes off better, especially in the beginning, when he exhibits a kind of Michael Caine blue-collar toughness, but later, Vicious Chas delights in turning the tables on the men who beat him up. When he reaches Turner's town house, he looks stranded among amateurs. It's one thing to have pros Dirk Bogarde and Sarah Miles emasculate Fox in *The Servant* (1963), but he is too strong to succumb to neophytes Jagger and Pallenberg. […] In fact, the two major themes of the film are very central to the films Roeg would solo direct, the magnificent, incomparably shot *Walkabout* (1970), *Don't Look Now* (1973), *The Man Who Fell to Earth* (1976), and *Bad Timing* (1980). The first theme is that in today's world the savage (Chas's world) and the gentle (Turner's world) exist side by side. From this theme we arrive at Roeg's second, more important, theme: man must be able to uncover and activate previously latent aspects of his personality (e. g. Chas's homosexuality), thereby discovering his true complete self, in order to adapt to a new environment. In *Performance* the only way for Chas and Turner, on the surface as opposite as Attila the Hun and Ravi Shankar, to emerge from their respective funks is by literally merging- there is no takeover of one person by the other-in mind and body. Such a merger is possible because, according to the men who made this film, everyone is part violent and part gentle; part male and part female; part "normal" and part "perverted"; part of each other. Such metaphysical concepts can be confusing, even unfilmable, and in the case of *Performance*, they are muddled beyond belief, and repair."[16]

That last assertion I don't entirely agree with. It's very true that *Performance* is a difficult movie, far from user-friendly and not 100% successful in delivering its kaleidoscope of themes. Repeated viewings always reveal new aspects of itself, the narrative unfolding like reverse origami, in a stream of consciousness that James Joyce would envy. While most would be drawn to *Performance* due to Jagger's presence, he fails to electrify except in one sequence, an ersatz music video to the song "Memo from Turner", in which Chas's two disparate worlds collide. Only while singing does Jagger come to life.[222] Fox is magnetic throughout and the real glue for the audience. As despicable as Chas constantly proves himself to be, without him, we'd have no gateway into Turner's moldy-cake world. The film forces us to see through the eyes of a psychopath, so there's no question that the glass we view is shattered and refracted.

Roger Ebert had a different take on Jagger's acting, however, giving the singer one of his few positive notices. "The surprise of the movie, and the reason to see it, is Mick Jagger's performance. It isn't simply good; it's a comment on his life and style. The ads emphasized his unisex appearance, and the role does so even more. When he slicks back his hair during a psychedelic fantasy, and seems to adopt the gangster's lifestyle, we're looking at acting insights of a very complex psychological order. Other than that, the movie is neither very good nor very bad. Interesting."[17]

"'I always thought *Performance* was a comedy,' says writer and codirector (with Nicolas Roeg) Donald Cammell. Perhaps a comedy of modern manners, psychedelic '60s style, but certainly not the kind of comedy that inspires knee-slapping. Marianne Faithfull[223] may have more put it more accurately when she said it "preserves a whole era under glass." It's the Swinging London that lit up the tabloid headlines in the late '60s. It's about the decadent lifestyles of rich rock stars who wore expensive clothes, trotted the globe and took mountains of drugs. It's about the violence of the notorious twin Kray Brothers, who ruled East London with an iron fist. It's about sexual experimentation and the relationship between sex and death. In short it's about the hedonistic stuff that made the '60s swing. It's the end of that era, a startling portrait of the Age of Aquarius in decay," wrote Richard Crouse. "'Donald Cammell was always aware of posterity as a director,' said Jagger. 'He always thought of film as this thing that freezes time. He was very aware of historical authenticity.' Mick Jagger, in his film debut, is perfectly cast as Turner. It may not have been much of a stretch for him to play a depraved

---

[222] The irony of one of Chas's first lines to Turner is not lost on modern viewers, "You're a comical little geezer. You'll look funny when you're fifty."

[223] Initially cast as Pherber but pulled out due to pregnancy.

rock star, but his take on Turner is fascinating. The story's bohemian character brought to life the media's perception of Jagger as a rock and roll Lucifer, an androgynous pleasure-seeker of the highest order who exuded pure, raw sexual energy. Although his dialogue occasionally falls into a druggy slur, he commands every scene he's in, bringing nuance to a character that could easily have been a caricature."[18]

The failure and shuttering of *Performance* by Warner Brothers (save for a limited VHS release in the '80s, the film remained unseen on home video until 2007) proved prescient for Cammell's career. Save for one modest hit, *Demon Seed*, the majority of his follow-up productions were mired in studio interference. Having his last film, *The Wild Side*, recut without his input drove him into a self-enforced exile.

Rather than regard *Performance* as a film that opened doors for future filmmakers, it is probably more instructive and accurate to see it as the culmination of a specific cultural moment. In terms of its aesthetics, its editing patterns and its recasting of pop culture as magickal ritual in a sexualised celebration of death, Cammell is quite explicit about the film's origins: Kenneth Anger was 'the major influence at the time I made *Performance*', much of which is 'directly attributable' to him. Anger was a friend of the Rolling Stones and Cammell at this time. Jagger provided music for Anger's *Invocation of my Demon Brother* (1969)—and was so unnerved by the experience that he allegedly wore a crucifix for months afterwards!—and Cammell played the Egyptian god Osiris in his *Lucifer Rising* (1973). It is not hard to see the Crowleyan Anger's vision of cinema as a magickal spell woven together of pop culture images imbued with esoteric significance at work in *Performance*," wrote Maximillian LeCain. "In fact, what is so special about *Performance* may well be that it is the furthest truly underground filmmaking has ever penetrated into the mainstream. Not just in terms of techniques pioneered by the avant-garde only to be snapped up for commercial purposes (of which *Performance* has many) but in the ideas and sensibilities that came together to create it. The world that gave birth to *Performance* was soon to dissolve. Rolling Stone Brian Jones, upon whom the character of Turner was substantially based, died; James Fox withdrew from acting and his social milieu to devote himself to Christian evangelism for a decade; the danger inherent in Jagger's image would mellow after the tragic events at the notorious Altamont concert in 1969. Donald Cammell went to Hollywood to edit *Performance*, a two-year struggle with studio heads who didn't know what to do with such a strange and outrageous film. He was to stay in Hollywood for the rest of his life. […]"[19]

"The death of Donald Cammell was as flamboyant and dramatic as anything he had ever filmed. Haunted by death and suicide for many years, he took his own life in 1996 at age sixty-two with a gunshot to the head. But he fired into the top of his head instead of the roof of his mouth with the result that he was alive and conscious for up to 45 minutes afterwards and, reportedly, was in a happy, almost euphoric state. The fact that he didn't die instantly was not accidental; in fact he allegedly requested that his wife and writing collaborator China Cammell hold up a mirror so he could watch himself die and asked her 'Do you see the picture of Borges?'," wrote Horden. "This was a reference to the climax of the only film that he is widely remembered for today, *Performance* (1968, released 1970), in which gangster Chas (James Fox) shoots reclusive rock star Turner (Mick Jagger). In a startling move, the camera plunges after the bullet into the hole in Turner's head only to end up confronting a photograph of Jorge Luis Borges, a writer much quoted in the dialogue and—like Burroughs and Genet—a literary influence on the film as a whole. Performance is a film about the merging of opposites, of male and female, of identities, of personae, of the apparently different worlds of gangsterism and extreme artistic decadence that are both revealed to function through the engine of the performative ritual of violence. Or, as the tagline had it: 'Vice. And Versa'."[20]

NOTES

[1] Peary, Danny. *Cult Movies.* New York: Dell, 1981. P. 356

[2] Le Cain, Maximilian, 2002. "Donald Cammell." Great Directors Issue 23. Archived at
   http://sensesofcinema.com/2002/great-directors/cammell/

[3] Holden, Michael. "Cast into darkness". The Guardian. 1 May 2004
   http://www.theguardian.com/film/2004/may/01/hayfilmfestival2005.guardianhayfestival

[4] Del Valle, David. "Interview with Donald Cammell." Video Watchdog Magazine. Archived
   http://www.drkrm.com/cammell2.html

[5] Holden, Michael. 2004.

[6] Carlton, Richard R. "The Film That Explains The Legend Of The Rolling Stones." Amazon review. October 25,
   2002. http://www.amazon.com/review/R3F5BI5Z0YAEGF/
   ref=cm_cr_dp_title?ie=UTF8&ASIN=B00IMRL2AA&nodeID=2625373011&store=movies-tv

[7] Del Valle, 1998

[8] Perry, 1987. P. 257

[9] Ibid.

[10] Le Cain, Maximilian, 2002.

[11] Crouse, Richard. "Son of the 100 Best Movies You've Never Seen." Published by ECW Press. 2008. PP 213

[12] BBFC http://www.bbfc.co.uk/case-studies/archive%E2%80%A6-rolling-stone%E2%80%99s-performance

[13] Del Valle, 1998.

[14] Ibid

[15] Young, Ray. "Cinema Obscura: Ruminations on Donald Cammell & Nicolas Roeg and Performance." Flickhead.
   http://home.comcast.net/~flickhead/Performance.html

[16] Perry, P. 257-258

[17] Ebert, Roger. "Performance". Chicago Sun Times. January 1, 1970
   http://www.rogerebert.com/reviews/performance-1970

[18] Crouse, 2008. PP 211-212

[19] Le Cain, Maximilian, 2002

[20] Holden, 2004

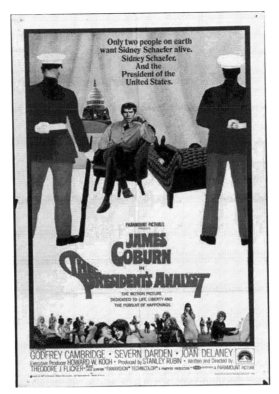

THE PRESIDENT'S ANALYST (1967)

"This film has not been made with the consent or cooperation of the Federal Board of Regulations (F.B.R.) or the Central Enquiries Agency (C.E.A.). Any resemblance to persons living or dead is purely coincidental, and so forth and so on."

"One day my secretary buzzed me with the message that two gentlemen were waiting to see me—from the Hoover Agency," recalls [producer] Robert Evans.

"Starched collars and all, they entered my office. No smiles, just gorilla handshakes and proper identification.

'I think you've got the wrong Bob Evans, gentlemen.'

'You're making a picture called *The President's Analyst.* Correct?'

'Correct.'

'We don't like the story.'

'Then don't see the picture.'

'Then don't make it.'

'Then get me a Paul Newman picture to take its place.' "

The FBI, Hoover in particular, didn't care for the way the FBI was portrayed. "Made fun of," they described. Evans, in typical Evans fashion, refused to back down.

"Within twenty-four hours, a half-crazed Marty Davis[224] was on the phone screaming.

'Are you crazy? You don't play games with Hoover. You don't play games with the FBI.'

'Fuck 'em. It's a free country, isn't it?

---

[224] "Martin S. Davis, the fiery executive who reshaped the unwieldy conglomerate Gulf and Western Industries into the entertainment and publishing giant Paramount Communications, died Monday in Manhattan. He was 72 and lived in Westport, Conn." Wyatt, Edward. 1999. "Martin Davis, 72; Created Modern Paramount." New York Times, October 6. http://www.nytimes.com/1999/10/06/business/martin-davis-72-created-modern-paramount.html

'No, it's not.'"

The concessions Evans made boiled down to changing the names of the agencies to the FBR and CEA. Again, Evans being Evans, he made sure everyone knew why the changes were made. And according to the producer, the FBI kept a tap on his phone for the next thirty years. "I hope what they've heard has made their faces as red as their necks."[225]

Dr. Sidney Schaefer (James Coburn) is a young, hip, and with it psychotherapist. Personally well-balanced emotionally, he's responsive to his patients' needs and open to their points of view. In fact, when his client Don Masters (Godfrey Cambridge) reveals that he's an assassin for the CEA, rather than react in horror[226] he responds with exuberance.

Dr. Sidney Schaefer: "Fascinating, Don... I suppose it's the conditioning of motion pictures, or television, or maybe it's just it's the times we live in, but... killing is serious business, yet this little card makes it somehow less shocking... acceptable in a way! You mean to say you can actually legally kill someone?"

Don Masters, CEA Agent: "Yeah, and it bothers me sometimes that I don't feel guilty about it. Don't you think that's psychotic behavior?"

Sidney: "No I don't! It explains your utter lack of hostility. You can vent your aggressive feelings by actually killing people! It's a sensational solution to the hostility problem."

Masters: "Doctor, are you trying to tell me it's all right to kill people?"

Sidney: "It's simply a moral question. Morality is a social invention, and in this case society has decided it's not only acceptable for certain people to kill other people... it's even commendable. Don! I've got to write a paper for the Institute on this!"

Masters: "I don't think the CEA would like that."

Of course, Masters' revelation is no revelation to the audience: we witnessed him nonchalantly murder a man right on a crowded city street, deftly stuffing him in to a rolling dry cleaning cart and barely missing a step. While Masters does have a few emotional problems to work out, his relationship with Sidney isn't a hundred percent therapeutic. Rather, he was sent to investigate the psychiatrist and determine if he'd be a good match for the President of the United States, a man who is the most "overworked, overtired, overburdened." Sidney jumps at the chance, barely taking the time to discuss it with his longtime girlfriend, Nan (Joan Delaney[227]).

Of course, the job isn't without its own stresses. For one thing, Sidney was chosen over the objections of Henry Lux (Walter Burke), the director of the Federal Bureau of Regulation (FBR—where all of the agents are under 5' 6"). Set up in a lovely apartment in Georgetown, Sidney will be at the President's beck and call, due to the man's extremely busy schedule, and must be available at any time of the day or night. To accommodate the President's needs, both Sidney's home and office are connected to the White House by a series of underground tunnels.

Exhaustion soon trumps exhilaration and Sidney realizes that he is completely unable to speak to a therapist of his own, saddled as he is with all of the U.S. state secrets the POTUS confides. In the interest of National Security, Sidney must bear the burden of his job in silence, but under constant observation, not just by the agents of the FBR and the CEA, but also the KGB and anyone else who happens to be in play. Once Sidney realizes that he's *the* inside man of Washington extreme paranoia sets in and soon he's seeing spies everywhere, including, possibly, *Nan*. And, of course, Nan is an undercover agent herself. "If I was a psychiatrist, which I am, I would say that I was turning into some sort of paranoid personality, which I am!"

Desperate to escape his situation alive, Sidney manages to sneak away from his overseers during a White House tour, posing as a PR agent eager to interview an "All American Family",

---

[225] Evans, Robert. 1994. "The Kid Stays in the Picture." Hyperion Press. P. 126-127

[226] As Alan Arkin does with John Cusak in *Gross Point Blank*.

[227] *Don't Drink the Water* (1969)

the Quantrills (Wynn, (William Daniels[228]), Jess (Joan Darling[229]), and their darling son Bing (Sheldon Collins[230]). The Quantrills are just the average, gun-toting, 2nd Amendment-loving Liberals (!)—"Now, son, I've told you never to confuse the house gun with the car gun."— who even help Sidney escape further assassination when they mistake foreign agents for average muggers and subdue them.

"Schaefer takes refuge with the Quantrills, a self-described 'typical American family' of militant, political 'liberals' armed to the teeth against right-wing "fascists" who 'ought to be gassed.' The father (marvelous William Daniels) boasts that they're for 'Negro' rights, yet Mom offhandedly calls going out for Chinese food 'eating Chink'; Arte Johnson's *Dragnet*-clone FBI agent reprimands their wire-tapping boy for using such bigoted argot," wrote Mark Borne at DVD Journal. "One minute Mom is asking Schaefer if he reads Gourmet magazine, the next she's delightedly kick-boxing international killers while dead-eye Dad blasts away with his .357 Magnum." [1] Bourne also described the film as "If Philip K. Dick had worked for *Mad Magazine*."

From there, Sidney goes deep undercover as a member of a hippie band headed by "Old Wrangler" (Barry McGuire[231]), thinking that his long wig and groovy glasses (and his talent for playing the gong) will keep him *sub rosa*. Unfortunately, the FBR and the Canadian Secret Service are on his tail and during one outrageous sequence a succession of foreign agents keep assassinating each other in order to be the first ones to assassinate Sidney! Eventually, KGB agent Kropotkin (the great Severn Darden[232]) and Masters arrive to protect him and bring him back to DC.

Unfortunately, there's the ultimate threat for Sidney to cope with: the TPC, aka "The Phone Company" (headed by *One Day at a Time*'s own "Schneider", Pat Harrington, Jr.). Far more insidious and omnipresent than any mere government agency, the TPC has developed the "Cerebrum Communicator", an electronic brain implant that will turn every living man, woman, and child, into a walking cell phone, capable of contacting any other at the speed of thought. Of course, to do this, the President will have to sign the necessary regulations, replace names with assigned numbers, etc. They need Sidney to blackmail the POTUS to achieve their ambitious goal and, thus, eliminate all the costly infrastructure and wires uglying up the world.

That slightly sick feeling in your stomach during the final act of *The President's Analyst* is the realization that so much of this satire has come true, and thanks to The Patriot Act, the TPC finally won. What was so outrageous in 1967 is an everyday reality: we are under constant surveillance by a network of government agencies who can't even adequately manage the Federal Post Office. Every stupid, short-sighted and belligerent official we meet during the course of the film is an everyday reality TV star now. Worst of all: we're all completely used to it. We traded our privacy and liberty to remain "safe", just as *The President's Analyst* predicted we would. Absurdity is the new normal.

With the exception of the outdated "Liberal" stereotype of the Quantrills and the extremely dated section involving the Old Wrangler and his hippies, *The President's Analyst* feels as fresh today as it did in '67, if not even more biting a satire than it was meant to be. While much of the political violence is played for laughs, the reality of average citizens press-ganged into serving the government then becoming disposable when their services are no longer required is just as frightening now as it was in that pre-Nixon era. (Edward Snowden, anyone?)

---

[228] *Magnum*'s Higgins and the voice of KITT.

[229] Groundbreaking female director of *First Love* (1977)

[230] "Arnold Bailey" on *The Andy Griffith Show* (1966-1968)

[231] Another word about Barry McGuire, best known for his song "Eve of Destruction". At the time of production, he lead the band Clear Light—evolved from "Brain Train—and were about to be signed by Elektra Records. Just after production, Cliff DeYoung signed on as their lead singer for the band's sole album release. Oh, and they were a last-minute replacement on *Analyst* after The Grateful Dead turned down the producers' offer.)

[232] *In God We Tru$t* (1980)

While Lux is an intentional parody of J. Edgar Hoover, ballooned to buffoonish farce, how much does the character resemble every single unctuous suit appearing regularly on Fox News or CNN today? And that we're all little more than phone-obsessed walking Wi-Fi towers is all the notice you need that the irony of the film has been murdered by modern reality. Still, that doesn't mean that *The President's Analyst* isn't immense fun. Though Sidney is less pro-active than what you'd expect from a Coburn character, he still oozes with the actor's unmistakable charm, even when he's coming apart at the seams.

Sidney (Coburn), Nan (Joan Delaney), Masters (Cambridge).
Photo Copyright Paramount Pictuers. All Rights Reserved.

Best-known today for co-creating *Barney Miller* with Danny Arnold, Theodore Flicker was primarily a TV writer and director who made his feature film debut writing and directing *The Troublemaker* (starring Buck Henry) in 1964. In the '60s, Flicker was a driving force in new forms of comedy, particularly a number of troupes he organized under "The Premise", which introduced new audiences to Henry, Darden, Joan Rivers, Mike Nichols, and Godfrey Cambridge.[233] One version in New York was titled "The Living Premise", groundbreaking as it featured an predominantly black cast with white supporting players, which, naturally, made the establishment very nervous. "Well, I would never say I discovered [Cambridge]. He was an actor, he worked here and there. At the Premise he got to show what he could really do and his career started to happen. Because I did the integrated Premise—the first integrated theater in New York—they opened a Black theater. The New York Times refused my first ad. I wanted an ad: The Premise—in Spades. They turned it down. So then it was The Premise—In Living Color. And they turned that down."[2]

Visiting the set of *Charade* (in which Coburn co-starred with Cary Grant and Audrey Hepburn), the writer first met Coburn and later pitched *The President's Analyst* on a whim. "[Ted Flicker had] come over to meet with his friend Peter Stone, who'd written the picture. So Ted was sitting in the background with his big black shades, watching us shoot. So Peter introduced us," Coburn recalled in *Venice Magazine*. "George Peppard and Elizabeth Ashley were having a Christmas party a few years later. Ted was there. He said 'I've just finished a script called *The President's Analyst.*' I said 'That's an intriguing title. Do you have a deal on it?' He said 'No.' So I took it home, read it, and wanted to do it. Ted said he wanted to direct it, so I said "Let me talk to Paramount." I had just done *Waterhole No. 3* (1967) over there. Robert Evans had just taken over, he loved it. Peter Bart read it, loved it. They said 'Can he direct?' I said, 'I dunno, let's find out.' So they put the whole deal together in five days! It was Evans' first film at Paramount. There are some great scenes in there. It was named one of the finest political films

---

[233] Prior to that, Flicker set up a Premise off-shoot in Washington D.C.'s upscale Shoreham Hotel. "Oh boy, that was a hoot. That was incredible. Originally I had the walls decorated with the flags of all those Balkan countries that no longer existed. Opening night we had all of Washington there including vice president Johnson. Somehow, Washington loved us. I think we played for six months. Only the communist representatives had the grace to walk out when we made fun of them. Hubert Humphrey sat next to Johnson and at the end of each scene he would explain to Johnson why it was funny. That was quite a night. It was quite a whole period." Nesteroff, Kliph. 2014. "An Interview with Theodore J. Flicker". Classic Showbiz.blogspot. December 3. http://classicshowbiz.blogspot.com/2014/12/an-interview-with-theodore-j-flicker.html

of the decade by the Sunday Times in London."[3]

Despite the script feeling well-worn today, what sets the film both apart from sixties satires and firmly within that era is actually Godfrey Cambridge's excellent performance. The comedian-turned-activist has a magnificent moment early on in the film discussing a painful memory with Sidney. "I was five," he says, as Don Masters. "And I knew there were colored people and white people. But then Mama took me to school, and it was almost all white kids. And nothing much happened on the first day. But on the second day, I was walking to school alone—my big brother, he was already in the third grade, and when you got a kid brother in kindergarten it can be kind of an embarrassment. So he ran on ahead to be with his buddies. Anyhow, there was a group of white kids on the street up ahead, and as I came up they started laughing and running and yelling, "Run! Run! Here comes the nigger! Run, run!" Here comes the nigger. And I looked around, and I didn't see any niggers. But if they wanted to play, so did I. So I started laughing and running and yelling, "Run, run! Here comes the nigger!" [whispers] Run, run. Here comes the nigger. Suddenly there was my big brother. And I ran up to him, and I started yelling, "Run, run, here comes the nigger!" And he hit me. Then he did something worse—he told me what a nigger was."

It's such a telling moment for Masters' character, and delivered so deftly by Cambridge that you can believe it's a real moment from the actor's past, that the man and the character merged in a way during the monologue. While the movie never again reaches the socio-political realism of that early moment, it can be easily extracted from the whole and held up to explain the racial environment of the '60s. Cambridge is both angry and heartbroken during the admission. Using today's backdrop of the "Black Lives Matter" movement, it's easy to see how little has changed—or, rather, how far we've slid backwards in 50 years.[234]

"Though predated by such efforts as John Frankenheimer's *The Manchurian Candidate*, the classic 1962 anti-McCarthy fable (also produced by Howard W. Koch), *The President's Analyst* is surprisingly barbed. One cannot say this sort of film would not be made today, only that it would be bowdlerized in the manner of an Austin Powers movie or have Will Ferrell in the lead and more gay jokes," wrote James Verniere. "Taking a cue from Hitchcock and *North by Northwest* scribe Ernest Lehman, writer-director Flicker uses such landmarks as the Whitney Museum, where Schaefer admires abstract sculpture; the Lincoln Memorial; the Washington Monument; and the Statue of Liberty as visual cues, giving his cartoonish political satire psychic and symbolic weight. [...] Produced by Koch (*Robin and the Seven Hoods* [1964], etc.) and Stanley Rubin (*Francis in the Navy* [1955]) and featuring excellent camera work by legendary William A. Fraker (*Rosemary's Baby* [1968], *Bullitt* [1968], etc.), *The President's Analyst* is an Austin Powers movie with teeth, and owes a huge debt to *Mad* magazine's trademark spoofs of hit movies. While considerably less scabrous and alienating than Luis Buñuel's indictments of modern Europe or Jean-Luc Godard's *Weekend* (1967), *The President's Analyst* has moments of genuinely offbeat power. Posing as one of Dr. Schaefer's patients in an early scene, Cambridge beautifully relates a haunting, even heartbreaking childhood anecdote involving racism, an anecdote that later turns out to be perhaps a fabrication. Also in the cast are Pat Harrington Jr., as a game-show-hostlike phone company spokesman, and future *Waltons* patriarch Will Geer, as Sidney's Mark Twain-like mentor. And watch for Dyanne Thorne, of *Ilsa, She Wolf of the SS* (1975) fame, as a cocktail waitress." [4]

---

[234] Cambridge left behind a lucrative stand-up career to campaign for Equal Rights in the U.S. At one point, he was one of the highest-paid comics working, black or white. "Mr. Hugh Hurd joined with Godfrey Cambridge and Maya Angelou in organizing one of the first benefits in New York for the Rev. Dr. Martin Luther King Jr., an occasion memorialized in Ms. Angelou's book "The Heart of a Woman." The benefit, held at the Village Gate in the late 1950's, raised $9,000 for Dr. King's civil rights movement. With Mr. Cambridge, Mr. Hurd founded and led a Committee for the Employment of Negro Performers in 1962. Their efforts prompted Representative Adam Clayton Powell Jr. of Harlem to hold hearings on racial discrimination in the entertainment industry." Saxon, Wolfgang. 1995. "Hugh Hurd, 70, Actor With Role In Early Civil Rights Movement." New York Times. July 20. http://www.nytimes.com/1995/07/20/obituaries/hugh-hurd-70-actor-with-role-in-early-civil-rights-movement.html

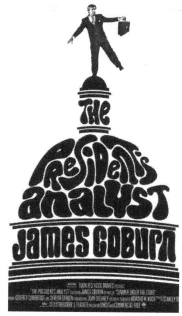

"The movie's style is of its moment—a veritable Nehru suit of zoomy, kicky montage interludes, ambient Pop Art, and Fun City locations. Indeed, shooting the sequence in which Coburn flees the fuzz past Café Wha? into Minetta Lane, the star was clobbered by a real cop. "Policeman's Ad Lib Steals Movies Scene," The New York Times reported—a notion that must have tickled Flicker, the mastermind behind the early-'60s improvisational cabaret known as the Premise. In essence, The President's Analyst is an extended Premise riff (psychoanalysis being a favorite butt), and the cast includes several Premise vets, notably Godfrey Cambridge as a CIA agent and Severn Darden as a Russian spy. That the latter is among the movie's more sympathetic characters reinforces the notion of the Cold War as Soviet-U.S. co-production, a setup for Flicker's final vision of America's soft totalitarianism, a Tinkertoy anticipation of The Matrix."[5]

Predictably, The President's Analyst was another box office failure that found its audience on home video years later. Thanks to music rights issues, two songs, including "Inner Manipulations" by McGuire, were absent from the VHS for years. And while the DVD restores those songs, there's a strange little scene missing in which Sidney and Nan meet in at an avante garde art house theater, parodying the rise of experimental film in the '60s. (A still from the film used to be featured on Roger Ebert's website, but the last time I visited the photo didn't load.)

NOTES

[1] Bourne, Mark. "The President's Analyst". Accessed January, 2016.
      http://www.dvdjournal.com/quickreviews/p/presidentsanalyst.q.shtml

[2] Ibid. Nesteroff, 2014.

[3] Simon, Alex. 1999. "James Coburn: Cool Daddy." Venice Magazine. February. Archived The Hollywood Interview.
      http://thehollywoodinterview.blogspot.com/2008/02/james-coburn-hollywood-interview.html

[4] Verniere, James. "The President's Analyst." P. 153-154 From "The B list : the National Society of Film Critics On The Low-Budget Beauties, Genre-Bending Mavericks, And Cult Classics We Love." edited by David Sterritt and John Anderson. 2008 Published by Da Capo Press.

[5] Hoberman, J. 2008. "The President's Analyst: A Paranoid Lark". The Village Voice. June 3
      http://www.villagevoice.com/2008-06-03/film/paranoid-lark/

SAVAGES (1972)

I have few regrets in life, but chief among them at the moment is that I didn't discover Merchant/Ivory's *Savages* during my pretentious film school years. After the first two years of being force-fed Brakhage, Anger, Antonioni, and Bertolucci, *Savages* would have been either an insufferable addition to our education, or a welcome relief via some (perceived) smart satire. That the movie could either be accepted as another esoteric art house film *or* a knowing parody of the same says more about this feature than any amount of criticism ever could.

During the late '90s, we of the aspiring artists who wiled away our part times working in video stores while pursuing our full-time careers being better than everyone else because we knew the inner workings of the studio system of the '70s. While the '90s were only beginning to shepherd in the "Era of the Indie"[1], *Clerks* and *Reservoir Dogs* still had to rub elbows with the established art house cinema, dominated by the team of Ismail Merchant and shockingly-American James Ivory, shoveling one costume drama after another onto small screens and Academy screeners. The biggest hitters of this early era were *Howard's End* and *Remains of the Day*, both starring Anthony Hopkins at his most stoic and least murder-y. *Howard's End* was especially egregious to we of the newly-anointed Church of Tarantino because its very title was a lie: that movie *never* ended. And as an usher at the prestigious Rex Theatre in Pittsburgh's South Side, I had to endure that stodgy, airless melodrama for five straight weeks. It made me boo repeated viewings of *Silence of the Lambs*.

But if I'd just known of *Savages* at this time…

I was vaguely aware of it. At my second job clerking in Classic Video, one of Pittsburgh's most eclectic mom 'n pops, we had almost random sections standing out among a sea of unsorted video boxes. The owner, Cathy Kelly, liked categories, therefore we had the city's only Opera section, for instance; nearby was one dedicated to BBC teledramas, boasting the only complete set of *I, Claudius*. And, to that end, we also had a Merchant/Ivory section, which I didn't even bother dusting during our slow summers. In '94, this section was remarkably thick with offerings, though the majority of them were the drawing room types written by Ruth Prawer Jhabvala, seemingly the lone champion of Indian colonialism at the end of the 20th Century. To give you an example of the type of our clientele, we couldn't keep *Room with a*

View in stock, nor *The Bostonians*. When *Howard's End* finally hit home video, fuggeddaboudit. In the center of this, rarely rented, was the 1972 *Savages*, with its cover art of people covered in grey mud converging on a stately New England mansion. Because I knew everything about film by the '90s, I was exceedingly disinterested in yet another long, dull exercise.

It wasn't until at least a decade later that I discovered the whimsical, carefree work

The Savages encounter civilization and vice-versa. Photo copyright Angelika Films. All Rights Reserved.

of *National Lampoon* and *Saturday Night Live* regular Michael O'Donoghue. A contemporary of Terry Southern, O'Donoghue's work, particularly for the legendary *Nat. Lamp* magazine and radio show, was scathing, often hilarious, but with a brutal edge. O'Donoghue, for instance, wrote a sketch for *Saturday Night Live* that never even made it to the censors. Titled "The Good Excuse", the sketch involved the interrogation of a Nazi Colonel. When asked "Why? What sort of obscene monster systematically murders millions of women and children?", the officer replied that the Party had a "really good reason". Once he whispered it to the soldiers, they had to nod and agree, "Gee, I ah…I guess I owe you an apology. […] When I saw that hundred-foot mound of human skulls outside your office, I just naturally jumped to the conclusion that you were some kind of demented fiend. What can I say—I'm sorry."[235] The summary doesn't do justice to either the sketch's savage humor or smart satire.

Cinema was undergoing a painful rebirth in the period between the late '60s and early '70s, with the new breed of later-called "Easy Riders" and "Raging Bulls" elbowing aside big Hollywood blockbusters. *Taxi Driver* shared marquee space with *The Towering Inferno*, newcomer De Niro up against Steve McQueen. During this time, surprisingly American director James Ivory and his production partner, Ismail Merchant, approached *Nat Lamp* writer George W.S. Trow and his friend, O'Donoghue, to expand on a simple idea they'd had involving a lost tribe of "Mud People" crawling out of the forest in pursuit of an errant croquet ball and discovering a sleepy, sprawling and abandoned estate. During the course of their investigations, the tribe drapes themselves in the discarded fineries and fripperies, metamorphosing into a polite, upper-class society spending a weekend getaway together. Tribal elders become captains of industry; the high priestess morphs into the home's dowager host; her consort becomes a sensitive poet and musician pining after a younger debutante. Imagine if the indigenous people from *The Emerald Jungle* decided to put on a performance of *The Great Gatsby*, shedding their wildness and embracing civilization, then discarding it once again, and that would be a succinct summary of *Savages*.

Far from dull, the film is captivating, often colorful, and frequently quite funny, to which I attribute O'Donoghue's smart sarcasm. After a lengthy credit sequence where the players are introduced ala a '30s comedy, *Savages* opens in black and white, aping travelogues from an even

---

[235] The point of the sketch, in case I didn't make it clear, was that there was, of course, *no* good excuse for the Holocaust. According to Dennis Perrin, who wrote a biography of O'Donoghue, "'The Good Excuse' is simple, aggressive, direct; it slashes the face of piety without losing its moral objective, namely, that the Holocaust and anti-Semitism are not and should not be beyond the satirist's reach. 'It's a hard thing to attack,' O'Donoghue later said, 'because everyone attacks it in the same pedestrian way.'" The sketch was killed outright by '80s SNL head Dick Ebersol who proudly proclaimed that there would be no Holocaust jokes on the air, missing the point entirely.

earlier era, complete with interstitial cards—"Tribal elders can often be distinguished by the colorful pebbles they've placed between their teeth. Though that isn't the case here."—and even a voice-over, inexplicably in German. Wearing over-sized pre-Colombian clay masks, the tribe is in the middle of a ritual sacrifice when they're interrupted by the aforementioned croquet ball. Since "spheres are unheard of" in the jungle, the Mud People follow its path.

Once they're inside the palatial estate, the film changes to a sepia tone, indicating a leap in time and development, an "Afternoon of Man" following "The Dawn". The Mud People find equivalence between their culture and the one they've just stumbled upon. Placing the ball at the feet of a bronze statue (possibly of Helena or Artemis, the huntress), the offering to the strange god seems to give the Priestess knowledge of this new world. Throughout the house, their masks begin to crumble.

The next shot is in dazzling full-color, pulling back from the red sequined leotard of Iliona (Ultra Violet, of Warhol fame), "a Decadent" we're told, straddling a swing like a trapeze, revealing an outdoor dinner party in full swing, the tribe fully civilized, yet still unable to express themselves any better than they were as savages. Where earlier they were grabbing each other on the path and humping away. Now they have to sneak away for their trysts. An abnormally-close pair, conjointly named "Hstr-Lsl", used to find "narcotic leaves" in the wild, have separated into separate beings, the transvestite Hester and the "Drag King" Leslie (Kathryn Widdoes). The brutal hunter is now Archie (Martin Kove), "A bully". The lame outcast is transformed into James (Sam Waterson), "The Limping Man". Their needs for food, clothing, and shelter obtained, the tribe evolves, or devolves, into clever urban modernites. But before too long, the jungle beckons them back, and they rediscover their savagery, wrecking what they've found and retreating into the trees. The audience is left behind to pontificate on the meanings of the film, the subtext of the interactions, the perceived racism of the thick-lipped insensitive caricatures of the Mud People during the opening. And I can't help but wonder if O'Donoghue laughed all the way through it, lampooning the "importance" of art.

After all, this is the guy who rose to prominence with an adventure comic strip in which the heroine, the frequently nude "Phoebe Zeit-Geist", dies during one of the opening sections and is passed around like cargo from one adventure to the next.

Had I only realized that the '70s was also a period where fun was being had at the expense of the establishment. Had I only had the foresight to understand that while the Scorseses and Coppolas were fighting for foothold in the shifting cinematic culture, there were other emerging artists thumbing their noses at the mainstream, and even the stuffy longhair culture of international art house cinema, I think I would have had more fun as a pretentious film student.

For what it's worth, O'Donoghue was less than thrilled with the final product. "On the editorial page of the *Lampoon*'s November issue, O'Donoghue "plugged" the film in mock ad-speak:

IF RAW SEX, TWIN-FISTED ACTION, and HIGH-VOLTAGE THRILLS are your cup of TNT, you won't want to miss *Savages*, A POWERHOUSE OF A MOVIE that BRISTLES WITH TENSION…Actually, *Savages* is about as exciting as a six-pack of Carnation Instant Breakfast, but we thought maybe they could pull a few of these phrases for reviews. In fact, here are a few more: FAIRLY EXPLODES ONTO THE SCREEEN, RIPS THE LID OFF HOLLYWOOD, MAKES *THE GODFATHER* LOOK LIKE BAMBI, MAKES *THE STEWARDESSES* LOOK LIKE *I REMEMBER MAMA*, AT LAST—A BLACK JAMES BOND, and I CAN'T REMEMBER WHEN I'VE ENJOYED A FILM MORE."[2]

NOTES

[1] Perrin, Dennis. "Mr. Mike: The Life and Work of Michael O'Donoghue". Avon Books. 1998. P. 387

[2] Ibid. P. 228

SCRAPBOOK (1999)

Indie filmmakers don't usually have much going for them beyond shock value. "Name" stars are rarely affordable; those that are usually carry the "cult" status. "Starring Gunnar Hansen" might set horror buffs atwitter, but Joe Average Movie Renter might not be so quick to jump. Big sets, lavish lighting set ups, even decent microphones are difficult to come by, even by today's tech-friendly standards. In the early- to mid-90s, the hey-day of independent horror, the best way to get your movie into video stores was to mire your film in gore and nudity. Any plot would do—hell, even any actors would do—so long as it had Don Dohler's ingredients: Blood, Boobs, and Beast. Pick two. As long as that criteria is adequately met, you could tell any story you wanted. The savviest of the micro-budget artists took advantage of this loose requirement and created something enduring. Such is the case of Eric Stanze's *Scrapbook*.

Prior to *Scrapbook*, Stanze was best-known for the surreal and ultra-violent tale of good vs. evil, *Ice from the Sun*, an almost overly-ambitious tale of humanity caught in a war between "all the angels of Heaven, and all the demons from Hell", with a group of unfortunates trapped in an in-between dimension where they are tortured Hieronymus Bosch-style (with a tiny bit of The Residents mixed in). It suffered from too much back-story—nearly fifteen minutes of exposition delivered over a repeat of six shots—but it made up for that with audacity and some truly uncomfortable special effects. Facing similar criticisms from print and online reviewers, Stanze decided to step back a bit with his new film and bring it back down to Earth. With scriptwriter and star Tommy Biondo, Stanze sculpted a close-to-home character-driven story about fame, murder, and survival.

Beginning a horrific prologue in which a kidnapped woman has a one-sided conversation with another, incoherent voice in the dark, only to discover that the other passenger is dying from a graphic wound. The frightened woman, Clara (Emily Haack), is to be the next victim of Leonard (Tommy Biondo).

Typical of Stanze's films, *Scrapbook* also has a lengthy and necessary back-story which immediately follows, showing Leonard as a young boy, seduced by his older sister. Her boyfriend, enraged by what he sees, drags Leonard from the room and rapes him. Something breaks inside of young Leonard. Something irreparable.

In the present, Leonard has abducted the boyish punk girl Clara to serve as the last chapter of his life-long work, a scrapbook added to by all of his past victims. Filled with pleas, photos, poetry, blood-work art, the titular scrapbook, almost a character unto itself, is a horrifying memento of pain, torture, and misery. With Clara finishing it for him, he can finally get it published and get the fame and recognition he always deserved. His victims' sacrifices will all be rewarded in the end.

When Clara fights back, Leonard strips her naked and beats her. At one point, as punishment for an escape attempt, he stuffs her into a plastic rain barrel, pours milk over her, then seals it over and lets it bake in the sun, letting the heat and stench overwhelm her. Removing her at the end of the day, he then rapes her and urinates on her. Through this, he tells her, she will learn that he's serious.

Clara finally realizes that the only way to survive is to give in to Leonard's wishes. With each entry she makes in his scrapbook, the better he rewards her. First with food, then with clothing. Then with something akin to kindness. Once she begins to grasp his points of vulnerability, a window of opportunity presents itself. And then opens.

Predating the so-called "torture porn" era of the post 9/11 zeitgeist, *Scrapbook* is an intense and difficult film to watch. Because of the extremely low budget, Stanze and Biondo keep the action confined to Leonard's filth-strewn trailer, walls covered with photos of dead and dismembered women, messages like "I Win!" scrawled in blood. The set is claustrophobic enough, but Leonard keeps Clara naked for the majority of the film, white skin vanishing beneath purple and yellow bruises as the story drags on. And you can't for a minute forget that what you're seeing, to a large extent, is real. The horror feels genuine, thanks entirely to the fearless performances by Tommy Biondo and Emily Haack.

The word "trust" is bandied about a lot in behind-the-scenes tales of filmmaking. For enduring the shoot and the occasionally unstaged violence, both Haack and Biondo deserve more kudos than actually exist in this world. This is Stanze's first so-called "Extreme" movies and the envelope has never felt so pushed. Skirting the boundaries of porn/not porn, a fellatio scene is unsimulated, as was the urination scene. Haack is allowed no modesty during the film's first act, so it's near impossible to separate your sympathy for Clara from your sympathy for the actress.

Biondo, too, gives one of the best depictions of severe schizophrenia in all of film history—not something I say lightly or frivolously. Leonard oozes unpredictable danger thanks to the subtle (and sometimes not-so-subtle) ticks Biondo infuses the killer with. An uncontrollable hand-movement here, a sharp change in emotion there, and Biondo is every mentally ill person I've ever met. It's a perfect performance—challenging and never once does Biondo go over-the-top. While it might be flip to say, his scenes with Haack had to have been just as difficult to perform for him as it was for her. Reviewers at the time focused on Haack's bravery and endurance; she was always quick to point out that Tommy was the one who had to brutalize *her*. He had to keep her in a perpetual state of anxiety; he had to force himself upon her. Remember, Leonard and Tommy Biondo are different creatures. It was Tommy's job to bring Leonard alive, to portray Leonard as the victimizer. "As an actor Biondo, contributes a genuinely terrifying vision of a sociopath. This man doesn't possess even the rudimentary mask of sanity that Michael Rooker's chilling *Henry* [*Portrait of a Serial Killer* (1986)] had. There's an utter emotionless vacancy that seems to go right to the core of the character. It is either a genuinely brilliant piece of acting, or Biondo was utterly out of his mind and had not a scrap of conscience."[1]

Granted, no one was in any physical danger during the filming—Stanze and his Wicked Pixel family are professional and supportive of each other, and all were protective of the two stars—the mental anguish took longer to recover from. A slap hurts for a few seconds; an insult can last forever. "Eric and Jeremy are very professional on set and know how to keep things serious and on task. They also know how to keep the atmosphere light when it's needed, and there were definitely times on the *Scrapbook* set when it was needed! The production was tough and we had a lot to do in a small amount of time. The pace was fast and the emotional strain we were going through started to take its toll on Tommy and me. But I trusted all people involved it really was a great experience because everyone works so well together," Haack told me for *Sirens of Cinema*. "As far as the sexual violence, nudity, and sexuality goes, I did not have a problem with doing it in this movie.

Tommy Biondo as "Leonard". Photo courtesy Eric Stanze. Copyright Wicked Pixel Cinema.

We felt it was necessary to not shy away from the graphic, horrific nature of rape and sexual humiliation. We have gotten a lot of flack about the explicit nature of our content. There are women that tell me I shouldn't promote violence and sexual violence towards women, but I don't see it as promotion. I see it as showing what can really happen, what does happen, without candy coating it. I think people are afraid of that. […] My experience on the set of *Scrapbook* exorcised many personal demons I had been dealing with. I was able to tap into my own personal feelings, reactions, and life experiences, so that helped me play Clara better. When we were on set, Eric would have us begin a scene and I found it easy to play off Tommy because, to me, he was so convincing and creepy. The only reactions I *could* have were fear, sadness, and confusion! […] I think I'm very close in personality with many of the characters I've played. I have been through hardships and tough times in my life that I can draw from, so in a way I am grateful for all the negative experiences I have had in my life. They help me reach those dark places I need to go when my character is being beaten or violated or is killing someone in cold blood. I've always been attracted to dark stories. I think fear, anger, sadness, loneliness, and despair are feelings we need to be more in contact with because they can consume us without us even knowing it."[2]

Very few movies of any budget have ever affected me the way *Scrapbook* infested my psyche. Having only just entered the B-Indie world in the late '90s, I was stunned to silence by *Scrapbook* in a way I had not been before, and it would be two years later before another indie horror, *August Underground*, would shatter my nerves again. I'm not being hyperbolic when I say that I almost didn't finish *Scrapbook*. The grit and the violence never felt like sleaze, though it remains one of the grimiest, fly-on-the-wall movies since William Lustig's *Maniac*. The whole time you're watching, you feel like you're peeping through a keyhole, watching something too intimate for comfort, yet powerless to stop it.

I'm not alone in this. "I have been watching horror films for almost a decade and a half and I can only name a few films that really left me feeling uneasy and uncomfortable. Scrapbook is another I can safely add to that list. I have watched several films with the topic of rape in the past but none touched a nerve like this film did. The portrayal of the rape was done in such a ferocious way that it almost feels real. From that point on in the film I was hooked because it was the first horror film that I have seen in my adult life that scared me."[3]

"Watching this film is challenge, and if you find yourself enjoying it then you should seek immediate psychiatric help, which is why I can't understand BBFC's cutting of it. Yes, *Scrapbook* dwells relentlessly and explicitly in sexual violence, but it's so disgusting that if you find it in the slightest bit arousing then, frankly, you've got serious problems already. I'm aware

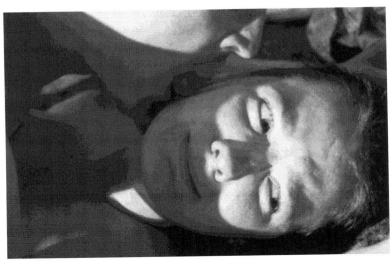

Biondo and Emily Haack (as "Clara"). Tommy Biondo as "Leonard".
Photo courtesy Eric Stanze. Copyright Wicked Pixel Cinema.

that none of this really reads like a recommendation. I'm calling this film things like disgusting, depraved, hard to watch and describing how repellent many of its sequences are. Well, who said movies have to be nice to be good? *Scrapbook* may often be hideous, but it is the film's intensity and atmosphere that I admire. It ends up being as potent an insight into the darkest impulses of people as has ever been filmed. It's also deeply distressing because it wants to make you feel like you are going through this torture with Clara. It succeeds in this because it feels unstintingly and upsettingly real, this film's boogeyman doesn't wear a white mask and lumber after babysitters, he's an average looking guy who'll kill anyone for no particular reason. Michael Myers isn't coming to get you. People like [Leonard] just might be, that's what's so disturbing about this film, it feels like it might have happened, yesterday, somewhere near you."[4]

Casual viewers may criticize the low production values, the occasional sound problems, inconsistent lighting—all the things that usually plague low budget, indie fare—but seasoned filmgoers understand that all comes with the territory. And if they're honest with themselves, even as they bitch, the casual viewer can't honestly deny *Scrapbook*'s power, or Stanze's finesse with delivering something both terrifying and honest. "One of my biggest complaints with low budget cinema is that it's difficult for independent films to convey a sense of realism on a restricted budget. It came as quite a shock to find that *Scrapbook* pulls off this feat despite its meager origins. I'm in two minds as to whether this is a good thing, as it stands this movie is one hell of a harrowing experience for the viewer and you get the impression it wasn't far off that for Emily Haack. [...] The movie itself could have so easily suffered from making its low budget obvious had it not been so well directed and edited. While the interior dialogues between Leonard and Clara have a 'hollow' sound to them (presumably from not being filmed on a proper soundstage), other scenes in the movie remove the obvious low-budget traits with a few crafty tricks. The exterior scenes, which could have been marred by wind noise, are overlaid with a grating electronic score which adds to the discomfort the viewer feels while witnessing how Leonard dishes out his punishments. Any prosthetic work is kept to a minimum, and any that is shown on screen is brief and works well."[5]

An on-going debate about the "need" for sex and violence in independent horror will likely never see an end. While it is true that indie filmmakers both feel the need to "push the envelope", so to speak, they also have the freedom to do so, unburdened by the necessity to submit the finished production to the MPAA for any kind of rating. So with the more extreme elements come the allegations of misogyny. Certainly Stanze and the Wicked Pixel crew have been on the receiving end of this criticism. "I do not see our movies as promoting or condoning violence towards women," says Haack. "As a woman who has experienced violence, why would I be involved in a project that I felt was promoting it? That is what I don't understand sometimes. Yes, we have violence in our movies, but we have it in there because it happens in real life and it is scary and sad and it conjures up emotions. And degrading to women? Have these people seen our movies? The women end up kicking ass and taking names! We get beat down but then we rise back up and get revenge. They are empowering, not degrading. But that's just my opinion. I feel that if you watch a movie that contains violence, degradation, etc., and you, subsequently, go out and inflict pain on someone else *because* of the movie then there was something wrong with you way before you ever watched that movie. Don't blame the media."[6]

"Leonard" turned out to be the role of Biondo's lifetime. "Tommy Biondo spent five years researching and writing *Scrapbook* which is, according to the opening credits, 'based on actual events'. The film was shot over just 13 days in 1999, but wasn't edited and finished until sometime later. Just as Eric Stanze had completed post production on the film and was about to send Biondo a copy, he received news that Tommy had been taken into hospital with head injuries from a film shoot he was on. Tommy Biondo died on August 6, 1999, at the young age of 26, having never seen the finished product which was finally edited and released in 2000."[7]

"Mr. Tommy Biondo, a man who had an incredibly impressive amount of independent film and video work under his belt at the young age of 26, passed away on Friday, August 6th, 1999. He died from injuries inflicted by an accident while on a shoot in Minnesota. Below is a nearly-complete filmography of Tommy's projects. Tommy worked on film/video productions as often as he could, helping out anyone who asked for his assistance. Due to this fact, there are many more projects that benefited from Tommy's talents that are not represented on this list. However, this string of titles is an amazing indication of Tommy's drive and energy in the world of independent filmmaking. We should all be inspired by his enthusiasm for the art as well as his generosity towards any other filmmakers who asked him to help out. Tommy submerged himself in his craft, learned as much as he could, worked as often as he could, and became the definition of the word "artist'," Stanze wrote on the Wicked Pixel website in 1999. "Tom started working with me when he was at the young age of 15. Over the many years we worked together, Tom impressed me more and more with each new project. Tom played a huge part in all the progress we'd made up to the time of his death. Of course, he played a huge part in our personal lives as well. He will be missed, admired, and dearly loved by all of us who had our lives enriched by Tommy Biondo.")

NOTES

[1] Inglis, Sam. 2011. "Scrapbook." Multimedia Mouth. January 26.
http://www.multimediamouth.com/2011/01/26/why-havent-you-seen-scrapbook/

[2] Watt, Mike. 2005. "Emily Haack". Sirens of Cinema #5.

[3] No reviewer listed. 2015. "Scrapbook (Review)." Horror Society. January 23.
http://www.horrorsociety.com/2015/01/23/scrapbook-review/

[4] Inglis, 2011.

[5] Benson, 2009.

[6] Watt, 2005

[7] Benson, Daniel. 2009. "Scrapbook." Horrortalk.com. February 15. http://www.horrortalk.com/reviews/movie-reviews/160-scrapbook.html

THE UNCOMFORTABLE NATURE OF VISION: AN INTERVIEW WITH ERIC STANZE[236]

You may not have heard of filmmaker Eric Stanze, and that's a shame. Stanze makes very interesting movies. They're not easy to watch, though, so be warned, should you happen across a copy of one of his movies. To date his most "popular" have proven themselves to be *Ice from the Sun* and *Scrapbook*, but these aren't your standard little grue fests. *Ice from the Sun* is an experimental horror movie that bombards you with images and filmic techniques, telling the oblique story of a game played by an insane sorcerer from another dimension, and a woman recruited by the servants of both Heaven and Hell to stop him. *Scrapbook* tells the story of a serial killer who kidnaps a young woman and proceeds to repeatedly torture and rape her for his own amusement, then make her write about her experiences in a journal kept by all of his victims. *Scrapbook* is one of the few low-budget independent horror films that can actually be classified as an important work.

By the end of these films, the viewer feels bludgeoned by the images and story that Stanze and his team at Wicked Pixel Cinema have crafted. They're not afraid to take chances, and their films can only be compared to the experimental artists of the '60s and '70s, folks like Kenneth Anger and (obliquely) Nick Zedd. And, perhaps, one other—Andy Copp, who wrote and directed another powerful and difficult film called *The Mutilation Man*, which was released last year onto a virtually indifferent audience.

A filmmaker's relationship with his audience is, of course, symbiotic. The audience relies on the artist for entertainment, the artist relies on his audience to provide his work an outlet. When a work fails to fall within the albeit oft-times flexible boundaries of genre definition (a definition, for example, that allows both *Scrapbook* and *Scream* to be classified as "horror"), sometimes an audience is hard to come by. Without an outlet, the filmmaker can and often does, struggle financially. Recently, Stanze has been producing films for Sub Rosa Studios, established by fellow filmmaker Ron Bonk (*The Vicious Sweet*), churning out violent fetish / extreme horror films for the mass market. In return for these movies, Stanze will find himself a

---

[236] Originally appeared on *Film Threat Online* in September, 1999.

bit more secure, financially, and free to make his more personal twisted and experimental tales.

"We're making the kinds of projects that Ron Bonk wants and staying on very short shooting schedules," says Stanze. "These are not projects that we want to spend three years producing. I wouldn't want to get into the specific numbers on it, but Ron and I are sharing the financial responsibilities of these projects pretty much fifty-fifty. And we're splitting the profits the same way. I look at it as I am taking what little money I have and investing it and letting it grow a little bit. And it lets me invest in something that I'm actually good at and in control of, rather than, say, stocks or something. This all gives me more production experience, and more importantly, it allows me to give a few other filmmakers out here in the Midwest a shot at directing their first movies. We have a handful of people here who are actually going to be doing the directing on these Sub Rosa Extreme movies while I supervise in an executive producer capacity, and this will be their sort of debut. My involvement is just to make sure that Ron is happy and that our investment remains healthy. So we're trying make sure that the person who ends up buying or watching the movie feels satisfied."

The partnership began as an idea of Bonk's, a way to expand the Sub Rosa film library and stock it with product specially developed by his company, allowing Sub Rosa to distribute brand new titles helmed by people he trusts, whose work he respects. As a filmmaker himself, Bonk has relatively high standards when it comes to what he will or will not distribute. Not every shot-on-video cheapie will meet with his approval. Every title in the Sub Rosa video catalog was hand-picked for distribution by him. While he often has to resort to selling certain "hard-core" titles to boost his revenue, that doesn't mean he wants every piece of shit that comes down the pike.

"I think for these Sub Rosa Extreme movies, the way it worked was Ron submitted to me a list of ten or fifteen titles and maybe two to three sentence descriptions that went along with each title. And it was up to me to pick the projects that I felt that I could handle within the amount of time we had to produce them. I took his descriptions and expanded each to a four-to-five page outline, and submitted those outlines back to him. And he would either approve them or say 'No, Eric, you missed the point completely'. But in each of those cases he said that he was happy with what we planned on doing. He of course had suggestions on where to tweak the storylines and how to make the stories into better movies. But he pretty much approved everything that I submitted to him and said 'Good, go make those movies'."

Audiences first became widely aware of Stanze through the release of *Ice from the Sun*, but die-hard b-movie fans remember his earlier efforts, particularly a movie called *The Scare Game*, which is more or less a prequel to *Ice*.

"We made *The Scare Game* the summer after I graduated from High School. I was only 18 years old—and that's why that movie is really bad. It had a lot of great ideas in it that we were very enthusiastic about, but after it was done, and picked up for home video—we look back at it now and see how poorly it had been done. We were just so young at the time. Completely inexperienced. I had zero training in high school in terms of film or video or lighting or anything like that. Absolutely no background except for some acting that I had done. How to make a movie was totally foreign to me, aside from some little camcorder movies I had shot with my friends for class projects. *The Scare Game* was originally conceived by DJ Vivona, who ended up playing the lead bad guy in the film. The two of us collaborated to flesh the idea out. We were two young kids with no experience and we made a really bad movie. What saved us, I think, is that we had set out to make a really surrealistic, bizarre horror movie. We weren't interested in making a traditional horror movie—like Sam Raimi's *Evil Dead*, or some run-of-the-mill slasher movie. And my theory is that we were so incompetent, and I did such a terrible job directing it, that it adds even more surrealism on top of what we intended. And that, I find, is what made it stand out at the time. It's certainly not a good movie, but it is one of the more bizarre things that you could possibly pick up off the video shelf."

For good or bad, Stanze and friends left their first footprint on the Earth with *The Scare Game*. Like all freshman efforts, it is, indeed, rough around the edges. But it truly isn't as bad as Stanze would like you to believe. "For years I thought, 'why am I even admitting that I made this movie? It is such a piece of shit!' But to this day, I hear from people who have seen *Ice from the Sun* and *Scrapbook* and some of my other movies, and I get comments where people say one of my recent, better movies is their favorite film, and other people say that they like *The Scare Game* the best. And I couldn't understand that for a long while. But I kind of stepped back from it, to see if I could look at it and see how badly we really fucked this up. I think people just latched onto *The Scare Game* because it showed them something they hadn't seen before, and there's a very wide visual palette to it, so you're at least looking at something different every five minutes. I guess, liking the concept of that movie, and feeling like we didn't do a very good job with it, was what motivated us to try it again, and do *Ice from the Sun* with a bigger budget. It actually is a sequel. If you watch the two of them back to back, *The Scare Game* actually ends where *Ice from the Sun* picks up, but we didn't advertise *Ice from the Sun* as the sequel because we didn't feel that *The Scare Game* was up to our standards, so we didn't want to call attention to it. But we wrote and created *Ice from the Sun* as a continuation of the story, the concept and the visuals. It was a chance to take all the additional experience I had as a director, a writer, and an editor, and apply that to a concept that we were still very enthusiastic about but just hadn't yet presented very well. Now we're still really into the idea and the story and we look at *Ice*—and I see things I could have done better, and I see things there that I wouldn't mind expanding on. We're looking to do a third movie in the series, continuing the story, continuing that sort of visual style. Partially because we feel that we can go to new places within the story, but mostly because I feel like I've grown as a director since I made *Ice from the Sun*."

Ice from the Sun is a study in stylized brutality. People are abducted from Earth and forced to play a sadistic game in another dimension. One man is forced to perform surgery on himself as his dead wife watches. Another woman is dragged naked behind a truck, only to have her torn and bleeding body covered with salt at the journey's end. Stanze plays with horrific imagery, and proves that it is still possible to shock even the most jaded of horror fans.

For all the praise it has received, there are criticisms leveled against *Ice*. One reviewer called it a "two-hour *Ministry* video", while others have cited an extended scene near the beginning where the entire plot is explained in detail via voice-over during a sequence comprised of three repeated shots. The sequence lasts for almost fifteen minutes.

"There are a lot of mistakes in the movie that make me cringe when I see them," Stanze concedes. "I feel they're things that I did wrong. [The backstory scene is] one of the bigger things that I think I should have done better. I should have known better. [But] It's hard to gauge how well you pulled something off. I've had scenes in all my movies where someone points out that the movie grinds to a halt during a sequence. I've had people say 'I was bored off my ass waiting for you to finish with all this dialogue'. At the same time, people who aren't really interested in the genre or who don't care about the visual style say 'You know that part where you stopped showing all the weirdness and just told the story, that was the better part of the movie.' So, no matter what you do, you can't please everybody. That backstory scene is one of the aspects of *Ice* that I'm not a hundred percent sold on, and one of the points that I wish I could have improved. I hope I find stuff like that in all my movies, where I can point to something and wish I could do it better. It forces me to try harder the next time."

While he will admit to enjoying E. Elias Merhige's pre-*Shadow of the Vampire* effort, *Begotten*, Stanze can't think of any experimental films that influenced *Ice from the Sun*. "I'd say [*Ice from the Sun's* style was] mostly instinctual. It was a combination of the story we wanted to do and the budget we were working with—that's what made up the look of it. We felt like this bizarre of a story would warrant a bizarre visual style. And we also felt that at this budget level, we were going to cut our own throats if we tried to do something that looks big budget. So instead of putting in swooping crane shots and extended dolly shots, we had to think, 'okay, we're shooting on Super-8, gritty, grainy, low-budget, let's just embrace that'. Let's go the other direction and utilize the low-ball aspect. We looked at a lot of techniques that were being used for music videos, and that style really influenced *Ice from the Sun* quite a bit. But then there were other points where we did look at classic surrealist films, decided what we liked, what we didn't like. We looked at stylistic techniques and whether they would apply or not to this particular story. We looked at a wide variety of sources. But ultimately it was the story and budget that dictated what we wound up with.

"I think I drew more from *Apocalypse Now*, as far as the story. I like that kind of movie, one that meanders. I like a movie to pursue a story from beginning to end, but I also appreciate a movie that isn't afraid to explore, which is something that *Apocalypse Now* does. I'm also into very unconventional techniques, even when used in a movie that isn't especially thrilling to me. Even if it's a technique that someone would probably tell me is the wrong way of doing something, there is a certain aspect about it that tells me that I should give it a try. And I like the idea of taking things that are taboo or offensive or confrontational or aggressive and using them as artistic elements. And not just for the sole purpose of pissing people off. Not that I care about pissing people off—I enjoy pissing people off. But I also like taking those non-mainstream elements that are shocking and aggressive and using them in an artistic manner."

After *Ice from the Sun*, which shot for eight months in several locations, his next production, *Scrapbook*, was more intimate. There are only three characters in the film, largely in one central location. The shooting lasted for thirteen days.

"Tommy Biondo conceived the idea for that," says Stanze. "Tommy was the production designer on *Ice*, and he's worked in some capacity behind the camera and as an actor in all of my films. He's always been very interested in serial killers, analyzing the psychotic deranged mind of a serial killer, that sort of thing. It's always been sort of a hobby of his—investigating that incredibly dark corner of humanity. Based on some of the research that he'd done, he felt that he could make a very dramatic movie. He brought the idea to me to see if I would be interested in helping him flesh out the script and possibly producing it. Jeremy Wallace, who produced *Scrapbook*, was very interested in making it because it was different from *Ice from the Sun*, and because it was very different from anything being made on our budget level. Which was important to Jeremy. He's like me [in that] he thinks that the best way to advance yourself as an artist is to always do something new. The fastest way to halt your upward career is to start emulating whatever the current fad is. Jeremy was big on doing *Scrapbook* simply because he'd never seen anything like it before, and he knew we could do it in a way that would be more in-your-face. We could be a lot more courageous than other filmmakers would be with the same type of story."

Scrapbook is a powerful, compelling movie, and one that is almost impossible to watch in one sitting. Biondo plays Leonard, a young man whose emotional and sexual abuse as a child shaped the very sick man that we see throughout the film. Kidnapping, raping and torturing young women is one of his main joys in life, but he also forces them to write about their experiences in a collective journal. Leonard sees this as his key to fame and fortune, which would, of course, cure him of his compulsions and allow him to be happy and innocent once again. His latest victim is a young woman named Clara, who suffers just as much as the others have suffered. But Clara figures out a way to turn Leonard's compulsions against him through his beloved scrapbook.

The movie takes the audience every step of the way through Clara's emotional and physical torment. As much of the dialogue was unscripted, to contrast, much of the action was not staged. Actress Emily Haack subjected herself to much of the rough play you see on film. With the exception of vaginal penetration, none of the sexual situations were faked—at one point Biondo urinates on a hysterical Haack. This was done for real, and with the consent of both actors. They would not allow themselves to hold anything back from the camera.

"It was a decision that we all made collectively that we weren't going to do it for simply drama or horror—if we were going to make a movie that focuses this much on rape and brutality, it was important that we do it in a way that makes a statement about it. For me, what I thought of, was when you see a woman who has been raped, and you see her on the news, or you see her coming out of the courtroom, she just has this deeply emotionally scarred look on her face. She looks crazed, and sick and absolutely distraught. Everyone else surrounding her, the crowd, her lawyer, the people in the courtroom, none of them even come close to having that look on their face. They all kind of look like 'yeah, it's normal, not a big deal'. And they all seem to look pretty calm about the fact that this woman has been violated. And I always found that to be pretty disturbing. How horrific must it be for a woman to go through that and have no way of effectively telling someone about her experience? You can't just tell someone about it and get it across how vast the emotional damage was. You can't do that. And not that we can get it across just by making a movie about it, but we decided that we would come as close as we possibly could. So that was why everything in *Scrapbook* was done to give an unsettling, ugly feel to the movie, to show that sort of attack in the worst possible light. If it made you sick watching it, then good, that's the reaction you're supposed to be getting. I don't think we glamorized that kind of attack, or that kind of violence, or that kind of invasion. To a certain tiny extent, however, it does glamorize it just by making a movie about it. So it was very important to us to pull together our artistic techniques and use them to make that movie as uncomfortable as possible. It hopefully takes the men who could never understand an emotional attack like that— and it gets them as close as they could possibly get to understanding. To feeling that kind of ugliness. It was a way of making a statement that we would all be comfortable with. It's not a movie I watch that often. I'm pretty freaked out by it too. But I wouldn't change it because I think we did it in the most appropriate way."

There is nothing in *Scrapbook* that isn't dead on, that doesn't feel real. And because of that, there is nothing in *Scrapbook* that is not claustrophobic, unsettling, uncomfortable or unnerving. There is ample nudity on the parts of both Haack and Biondo, and not a frame of this is devoted for titillating purposes. The audience, through Haack's character (and through Haack herself) feels just as exposed and brutalized as she. For Biondo's part, he gives the most realistic and terrifying portrayal of a serial killer ever committed to film or tape. This is not meant to be an over-statement, or meant to blow smoke about the actor. Anyone who has ever met anyone who was actually mentally disturbed will see that echoed in Biondo's Leonard. From facial tics to disjointed trains of thought, to sudden and horrible bursts of violence. Forget *The Cell* (2000), forget even Hannibal Lecter. No cinematic villain has ever come close to doing what Biondo achieves in *Scrapbook*.

"Tommy really did his homework. He knew that he wanted something absolutely horrific in that guy's past to make him turn out the way that he did. He also knew that someone capable of committing that kind of physical attack and doing that kind of emotional damage could also be very inviting and very normal looking. When we see him outside with the hillbilly, we see Leonard as very relaxed and we don't see that sinister side of him at all. Tom nailed that perfectly. Tom was also very into the idea of showing sex in the movie and making it as unappealing as possible. Instead of playing it coy and not showing anything, we decided to put it all out there. So that things you would normally find titillating, things you would normally find arousing—as you would with a lot of nudity and sexual content—we decided to present it in ways that would make it unsettling. We made it feel wrong. And that was something that Tom insisted on from the beginning, and it was something I completely agreed with. And it was also Tom's instincts to not just make it about these physical attacks, but the emotional abuse as well. Particularly someone like Leonard would want to wear his victim down emotionally so that they wouldn't be able to escape. It was at Tom's insistence that he do things verbally, say things to her that are humiliating to wear her down. It would keep her not only from escaping but also from thinking she could actually win if she did escape. A lot of thought went into it, especially for a movie that was 90% ad-libbed. There were these discussions about how these things would play out that led to how the actors did the scenes when the camera was rolling. All the thinking about it and discussing it did pay off."

As for Haack, her own performance is nothing short of harrowing and nothing short of remarkable. She goes above and beyond what is required of any other actress in a role like this. "By the time we hooked up with her, she had done some acting, but she was also well-rounded in that she had film and video production experience. She had edited quite a few projects. She really understood the process, but she had only played a few small or supporting roles in student projects. But she really understood the behind-the-scenes work and she used that as a jumping-off point as far as acting. She'd never played a leading role, and certainly she had never done anything that came even close to what she did in *Scrapbook*. I don't think she could have achieved this without drawing on some kind of personal source. It's a difficult part to just sort of walk through. And I don't think that she would have done this part at all if she hadn't felt that it would benefit her in some way and exorcise some demons. I had several meetings with her before casting her, to see what she thought about our take on the project, and to make sure she really understood what we wanted her to do. She was on the same page as everyone else from day one. We got really lucky with her in that she was a great actress, but also that she had an immediate connection with the material. She's out in L.A. right now, and she's been doing pretty decent, getting bit parts here and there on big TV shows. She got bit parts on *Malcolm in the Middle*, *Sex and the City*, she was in an Eminem music video, and she was on that *Sabrina The Teenage Witch*. I'm proud of her for going out there and actually pursuing this. I can't wait for her to get bigger parts, because she can definitely handle them. She's a very talented woman."

While the thirteen-day shoot did not always reflect the project's somber tone, it did take its toll on the crew from the beginning. "When we shot an attack scene, we tried to get as much of the action in a single take as possible. That allowed the actors to go into it with some momentum and do the scene from beginning to end. But without the benefit of cutting, it leaves the actors emotionally drained. It's difficult for the crew because at cut, the scene would end, we'd all have to step outside and get some air, because it was difficult for us to watch what was happening right there in front of us. We probably had a little more trouble with it, because we all really cared about Emily and it was distressing for us to see our friends, people that we genuinely care about, go through this. But the shoot also got very surreal when we started to kick into a self-preservation mode. The set was so thick with tension, so heavy with gloom, it almost became suffocating. All that constant abuse we were witnessing. We tried to desperately, between takes, push the gloom and doom away. So throughout the shoot we went back and forth, stunned at what we were doing from time to time, and there were these other points in the shoot where we were all laughing and joking and cutting up. The defense mechanisms kicked in that forced us to make some light of the situation and allow the stress to get away from us somehow. The laughing and cutting up from time to time allowed us to get back into the next scene a little easier. It was a weird shoot. Constantly a see-saw back and forth between the tension of the situation and striving to keep ourselves sane at the same time."

After wrapping, *Scrapbook*'s footage languished on Stanze's shelf for an entire year before he could find the time to edit it into a coherent film. On the day after he finished the final cut, Stanze and company received word that Tommy Biondo had died.

"He was on a shoot in Minnesota, and we were all back here in St. Louis. It was a freak thing. He fell and smacked his head on something. It wasn't something that you could look at and say 'oh, well that could kill somebody'. It certainly didn't seem like it would have been fatal. He literally tripped over something on the ground, smacked his head on the concrete, and that was it. I got a phone call that he was in the hospital, and twenty-four or forty-eight hours later he was pronounced brain dead. None of us could be there with him—it was very frustrating because he was so far away.

"It pisses us off that he spent all that time researching *Scrapbook* before we finally got around to making it—we spent several months in pre-production, then we shot it, and my schedule was so busy that I couldn't even get around to editing it for a year. So it sat there unedited for a year. He waited patiently; it was his baby. Every other day, I'd get an email from him, asking about the progress. He couldn't wait to see it. And one of the last emails I got from him, a few days before the accident, it said 'I'm looking forward to getting back to St. Louis, and I know that you're going to send me a couple of copies of *Scrapbook*, but I was wondering, when I get back, if you and I could get together and watch it. Just you and me. And talk about it over coffee or whatever?' I think he just wanted to talk about it with me, and see if I thought he'd done a good job, and where I thought he could have improved. He wanted that kind of feedback. And I emailed back 'yeah, I can't wait. It will be fun'. I had just finished packing up a copy of the movie to put in the mail to him when we got the phone call that he was in the hospital. He never even got the chance to see it. Which was an utter tragedy, since he spent all that time working on it. Six or seven years.

"It has not been the same since he left us. He was a huge creative force within the group. He was one of the more risky guys here. For Tom, if it meant quitting your job for four months to make a movie, he was perfectly okay with that. He worked on my movies, and he worked on a lot of other peoples' movies, and that was his whole life. He was the only person I've ever

known who was the definition of the word "artist". Everything else came after his desire to express himself, and after his desire to help everyone else express themselves artistically. The ideas that he brought to us—a lot of the darker and riskier stuff that we did, was at Tom's urging. I live in St. Louis, Missouri; it's a very conservative town. And every time I turn around, someone is telling me 'no'. 'No you can't do that. No, you're not doing that right. No, you shouldn't make movies like that.' And Tom's attitude was 'if this is what you want to make, let's quit talking about it and make it.' He was just an incredible person to collaborate with. We've only had one shoot since he died, actually. We shot the opening title video for our *Severed Head* compilation. That day of shooting felt really odd. It was a one day shoot. We tried not to dwell on the fact that it was our first shoot since Tom died, but we were all aware of it. We made it through the day, and we made it a productive day. Certainly, nobody broke down or couldn't handle it anymore. But it was a layer that was there in the backs of our minds the entire day: that we were shooting without Tom Biondo. We were all very close to him, and we were all friends. And anything that we do now, as we are much like a family, it will feel like we lost a sibling. It's been really difficult for us. We're still moving forward. It's not like it stopped us in our tracks. There were no logistical problems, but emotionally, it took us a while to get our bearings again. It will never be the same without him."

Our interview ends on a somber note. I ask Stanze if he has anything else he'd like to add.

"Yeah," he says, after a long pause. "I think maybe one thing: People give me a lot of credit for finishing the movies, and directing them and everything. They tend to focus on me. And I see a lot of guys with possibly unlimited potential starting to make their own movies, and failing miserably. Because it is incredibly difficult to accumulate the group of people that will support you and be devoted to you, and really help you through the very long and agonizing process that is making a movie. I don't know how I did it, but there is an incredible group of people working with me. This group is one of the big driving forces behind Wicked Pixel. I have Jeremy Wallace, and I have David Berliner, and these other people who are not only good friends of mine, but are also wonderful people to work with. And people give me a lot of credit for these movies, when in fact it is more of a group effort than anyone will ever know. I know that I am a very lucky person and I am very appreciative of the people around me. I know that none of this could ever have happened without their help and dedication. That's a big part of being a director... surrounding yourself with talented people."

Eric Stanze's movies are available through Sub Rosa Studios: www.b-movie.com. More information about Wicked Pixel Cinema can be found at: http://www.wickedpixel.com.

SHOCK TREATMENT (1981)

No discussion of "cult movies" can ever be had without at least a token mention of *The Rocky Horror Picture Show*. The so-called "Queen of the Cult Movies" has become a dominant presence in our country since its initial 1975 box office bomb and subsequent revival on the budding midnight circuit in 1977. Anyone with a passing familiarity with the cinematic phenomenon know the basics: newly-engaged young, whitebread upstanding kids blow a tire on a deserted road and seek help at a castle. Inside, they meet a variety of weirdoes and lunatics, not the least of which is the hypnotic, oversexed "Sweet Transvestite" and mad scientist, Frank N. Furter, who that very night plans to bring his new bodybuilding lover to life. Music and madness ensues.

Initially a box office bomb, *Rocky Horror* found new life on the new "Midnight Movie" circuit, mainly in New York City, playing alternately with *El Topo* (1970) and Jimmy Cliff's *The Harder They Come* (1972). Thoroughly embraced by artistic outcasts as well as the burgeoning LGBT community in the '80s, *Rocky Horror* has played in some theater across the country, every Saturday at midnight, for the past forty years. Audiences dress in costume and the majority of the theaters have their own, usually volunteer, "shadow cast" who perform the entire film in front of the screen, replicating the moves, costumes, and props. Annual conventions attract attendees from all over the world. The subversive, once-prurient offering has become a symbol of equality and harmony transcending gender boundaries. Any sense of persecution is generally left at the door while the misfits find their families in the darkened theater, hurling rice, toast, hot dogs and toilet paper at the screen at the appropriate time, warming the long-dead heart of William Castle.

"[…] O'Brien can claim to be a social revolutionary of some significance. Rocky Horror came just at a time when sexual stereotypes were being joyously exploded, and its success brought the party to even the prissiest backwaters. 'The period when *Rocky Horror* appeared, after the Free Love thing, was the point when the rigid ideas of sexual identity started to be attacked.' says Adam Matter, editor of the gay magazine, Attitude. 'You had glam-rock: David

Bowie, Queen and Marc Bolan pushing sexual boundaries. At the same time, Cabaret had introduced the notion of decadent, high-camp drama. For a lot of people, *Rocky Horror* was the perfect release. It was centered on a man who wasn't confined to a traditional sexual role: the whole point of Frank N. Furter is that he's sexually ambivalent and fantastically confident and glamorous at the same time. For a lot of people, that represented the destruction of the suburban sexual ideal."[1]

"'We always knew there would be a follow-up to *The Rocky Horror* Picture *Show*. There's always *a Son of ...* , a *Bride of ...* and a *Son* of ... *Rides Again,*' jokes actor/author/composer Richard O'Brien."[2]

While *Rocky Horror,* the brain-child of bored, out-of-work theatre actor Richard O'Brien, poked fun at uptight sexual mores among the English-speaking world, couching it in references to classic B-Movie science fiction and horror tropes, his satire got a little more savage in the follow-up. *Shock Treatment,* originally pitched as "The Brad and Janet Show"—after plans for a direct sequel, *Rocky Horror Shows His Heels,* were scuttled by 20th Century Fox suits who were desperate to capitalize on the newfound *Rocky* fame, they weren't *that* desperate to sink a pile of money into a sequel to a surprise re-emergence[237]—continued the adventures of the All-American couple as they navigate the pitfalls of married life.

"It seems that Jim Sharman, who has directed all of O'Brien's work on stage and screen to date, was responsible for the drastic changes in the initial draft, which read more like *Rocky Rises From The Grave* than the film it has become. Was the continuing saga of Brad and Janet some-

---

[237] As pitched to Fox, *Rocky Horror Shows His Heels* was to take place a short time after *RHPS*'s semi-tragic end. "Transsexual mad scientist Frank is revived from the dead by three of his gay cohorts. He is delighted to learn that the girl he seduced, Janet, is pregnant and about to give birth. He quickly turns a small town into a swarm of raging transsexuals. But then his body starts to decompose, the reviving formula ad mistered incorrectly, and Frank and his cronies are overwhelmed by the now irate townspeople. Janet and her baby are taken away from the melee by Frank's two former nemeses, Riff-Raff and Magenta." Read the production notes. (Archived at The Shock Treatment Network. http://www.theshocktreatmentnetwork.com/rhshh1.htm)

However, script readers found the proposed screenplay to be lacking. In 1979, Producer David Madden wrote: "Like the original Rocky Horror Show, this cannot be judged like a conventional script. Characterizations are grandiose and ludicrous in a Grand Guignol fashion, yet acted with the right style (as they were previously) the roles can be marvelously entertaining. There is hardly any dialogue, the script's structure consisting of bridging the numerous songs with brief expository conversations. The dialogue isn't as sharp as in the previous film, however, often tending to the obscure pun or the oblique reference. The settings, however, are suitably imaginative, with several possibilities for cinematic extravaganzas. The storyline is neither more nor less flimsy and incoherent than the previous version and runs a nearly identical narrative pattern. This one has numerous Rosemary's Baby references, and the gay jokes and attitudes are even more predominant.

The most important element of this sort of film is the score, since it's the music's quality that will determine both the youth word-of-mouth and the frequency of repeat viewings. The score, except for one song, is provided here on a cassette. Though the tape is woefully underproduced, banally arranged, and awkwardly vocalized, one can still find several good songs in O'Brien's Elvis Presley/David Bowie mode (notably "I'm Breaking Out," "Little Black Dress," "Looking For Trade," and "I Wanna Be An Ace") and only a couple of terrible ones ("I'm Gonna See My Baby" and "He Lived and Died for Rock 'n Roll"). But at this point the music seems markedly less consistent and energentic than that of the original show, lacking the irresistible, upbeat, dynamic tunes it needs (like "Sweet Transvestite," "Time Warp," "Toucha, Toucha, Touch, Touch Me"). Instead the composer has laden the score with lethargic ballads, particularly in the script's latter half; lyrics aside, the slow tempos and treatments are such that Como could sing many of these tunes.

If this project is to work, the composer must recollect that he's writing for a young rock audience; he misses here the drive and excitement that *Rocky Horror Show* possessed. If he weeded out the mediocre songs and wrote more lively ones as replacements, however, the score would definitely have the breadth of underground acclaim that the previous show had.

Essentially the question of whether to produce this film depends on one's satisfaction with the previous film's box office. With some rewriting of the screenplay and with substantial revision of the score and appropriate musical arrangements, this would certainly do at least as well as the previous film (provided that Tim Curry reprises his role). Moreover, perhaps it wouldn't take the sequel so long to gain the attention of the devoted youth cult. If this project were done, I'd suggest finding a new director (Randal Kleiser? John Landis?); the previous film was not nearly as visually exciting as the stage version, though it could have been. There is a modest but loyal audience for this film, and the first draft shows enough promise (though little polish as yet) to make the project worth pursuing." (Archived as well at The Shock Treatment Network: theshocktreatmentnetwork.com/rhshh4.htm)

thing he'd wanted to do since *Rocky*? 'Not really. It came to the stage where *Rocky* got into profit and I went to Michael White to see if he was interested in a sequel. (At that point, *Rocky* had made about 15 million dollars profit.) He agreed and I came up with a script which was very much *Rocky Rides Again*. Jim said that he wasn't really interested in going with that sort of concept and I didn't want to write a whole new script so we turned it around, chopped out a few characters like Frank, and made Brad the protagonist. Then over lunch we

L-R: Nation McKinley (Patricia Quinn), Harry Weiss (Mannin Redwood), Janet Majors (Jessica Harper), Bert Schnick (Barry Humphries), Emily Weiss (Darlene Johnson), Nurse Ansalong (Nell Campbell).
All Lobycards Copyright 20th Century Fox. All Rights Reserved.

decided that Janet should be the protagonist so I said 'That's all right. All we need to do is every time it says Brad we cross that out and put Janet and vice versa. It's very simple.' Two drafts later . . .'"[3]

Gone were the Sweet Transvestite and his sidekicks from the Planet Transsexual, as well as the semi-villainous (or at least, Nazi-sympathizing) Professor Everett Scott, and the "one from the vaults", Meatloaf's Eddie (though in fairness, he was killed and eaten in *RHPS*). Instead, O'Brien focused on the quintessential American town, Denton U.S.A., "The Home of Happiness". So clean-cut and pristine, Denton could only be properly presented to the world through the wholesomeness of television. Indeed, Denton may actually only exist on for the delight of a live audience.

Set inside a packed television studio, technicians hustle past the audience as it rushes in to occupy the limited number of seats, eager to watch their favorite shows live and in the flesh, all brought to you by fast food mogul, Farley Flavors (largely unseen, living behind the neon heart of the DTV studio sign overlooking the stage; otherwise he appears on a portable television). Following a rousing anthem to Denton, complete with smiling, gardening moms, and darling cheerleaders (including a black one!), Brad and Janet (Cliff DeYoung and Jessica Harper, replacing Barry Bostwick and Susan Sarandon[238]) are ushered to the stage to participate in "Marriage Maze", where the winners get to go home with their relationship intact. Losers are sent to the popular hospital soap opera "Dentonvale", for re-education by "official" medical professionals, Cosmo and Nation McKinley (O'Brien and *Rocky*'s Magenta, Patricia Quinn).

---

[238] Sarandon was riding high off an Academy Award nomination for *Atlantic City* and reportedly wanted too much money to return—"Susan Sarandon wanted half-a-million dollars," O'Brien told *Fangoria* in 1981. "That's a bit much, isn't it really? Especially if you are dealing with $5 million at that stage—she would have taken a chunk of about 10%." (Conroy, Mike. 1981. "Richard O'Brien and Shock Treatment". *Fangoria* Magazine #15. Vol. 3.); Bostwick was working on *You Can't Take It With You* for television; Tim Curry was approached to play Brad and Farley but was concerned that his American accent wouldn't be believable; Jonathan Adams, who played Dr. Scott in *RHPS*, was to reprise his role in *Shock Treatment*, returning again to his wheelchair as DTV's station manager, but changed his mind and was replaced by Humphries and the character Bert Schnick. Former Clear Light lead singer Cliff DeYoung, replacing Bostwick, was actually Jim Sharman's first choice to play Brad in *Rocky Horror*, but was working on the TV movie *Sunshine* (based on the memoir of Jacquelyn Helton) at the time and was unavailable.

"Marriage Maze" is hosted by the flamboyantly blind Viennese ghoul, Bert Schnick (Barry Humphries, in a rare appearance outside of his Dame Edna persona). The McKinleys are assisted by Nurse Ansalong (Little Nell Campbell) and "Rest Home Ricky" (Rik Mayall). They're all in the service of Farley Flavors (also DeYoung), who instantly recognizes Brad as his long-lost twin brother, raised in luxury while Flavors had to pull himself up by his bootstraps since the age of six. He will have his revenge, and Janet will be the face of his proposed franchise of mental institutions, hawking "Sanity for Today".

While the shows unfold accompanied by rousing musical accompaniment, the audience sits in rapt attention, applauding when appropriate, and even sleeping in their seats after DTV signs off for the night. Even Janet's parents have been absorbed into the Denton TV universe. If not for a brief glimpse of bright sunlight beyond the studio bay doors at the end, one would think that Denton—a town so steeped in '50s values, it would have made Ike proud, says Judge Wright (Charles Gray, another import from *RHPS*, possibly reprising his Narrator character)—didn't really exist at all. Eventually, schemes are uncovered, credentials are debunked,

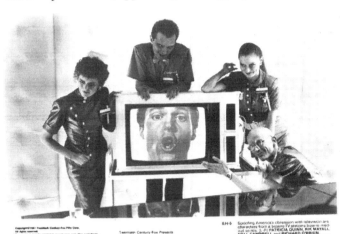

Twentieth Century-Fox Presents
SHOCK TREATMENT

SH-5   Spoofing America's obsession with television are characters (l-r) PATRICIA QUINN, RIK MAYALL, NELL CAMPBELL and RICHARD O'BRIEN as bizarre small-scale personalities in 6 bizarre TV stations. On the outs is CLIFF DE YOUNG as the stations' diabolical sponsor.

songs are sung, and O'Brien's skewering of Middle American "values" is complete.

In one sense, *Shock Treatment* shares the same opinion of "small town values" as David Lynch's *Blue Velvet*. Beneath the smiles and white skin, prejudice and fear lurk in all townsfolk (audience folk?). By setting the film entirely in a television show, *Shock Treatment* also prefigures the ubiquitous of reality TV, setting the stage for later productions like *The Truman Show* (1998). It also takes deserved pot-shots at the American penchant for personality cults and the desperation for starmaking approval. Janet Majors is groomed by the entire studio to be loved by "the people", to be the indisputable figurehead of Flavors' brand of sanity. Janet succumbs to the allure of fame in what might possibly the quickest Faustian bargain in history (and completely mirroring her role as "Phoenix" in *Phantom of the Paradise*).

"When you think how much of the world we view solely through the television screen it's surprising there haven't been more films dealing with the potential of mass manipulation via this medium. For all its attempts at objective documentation the TV eye remains unflinchingly subjective, as much a prey to the motives of programme makers as it is to the events portrayed. The world's most influential medium, it is also the most abused. Richard O'Brien is not the first, and certainly won't be the last person to commit his views on the influence of TV to film but *Shock Treatment* does make something of a unique statement in its depiction of the suburban town of Denton, USA, where the dividing line of reality between the screen and the viewer has completely disappeared."[4]

But like most strokes of brilliance, the single-setting was a decision made from necessity rather than forethought. While the original "Brad and Janet Show" script laid down all of the themes of closeted "perversion" that permeate *Shock Treatment*, the original idea was to follow the citizens of Denton inside their actual small town, with trips to the leather-loving banker's office, set pieces revolving around the town square, etc. Thanks to an unforeseen writer's strike, O'Brien, Brian Thompson, and director Jim Sharman (another *Rocky Horror* vet) had to rethink their Denton setting over a couple of days. "'It was because of the actors' strike in America,' explains O'Brien, who appears in the film as Cosmo McKinley, a zany TV shrink, and wrote the script and the songs. 'We were going to do location shots in the States—we were actually going to have an old house for the hospital and certain location shots, downtown Denton, etc. and with the SAG (Screen Actors' Guild) strike we couldn't turn a camera there. We had to find another way of doing it and once we'd come up with it I was frightened the strike was going to finish too soon and we'd have to go back to our original conception because I thought the new conception was much, much better. [...] It knocked a million dollars off the budget: we had a controlled environment which meant we could shoot at any time of the year if the weather was nasty and keep the whole thing very tight-knit and theatrical. It became more theatrical which is nice, because *Rocky* had a theatrical flavor about it and I think that element of it is quite important.'"[5]

As O'Brien told *Fangoria* in 1983: "A true sequel. Jim Sharman said 'I have no interest in doing that sort of movie. I have no interest in doing that: write a new story.' I said, 'I've no

Cosmo's seduction of Janet Majors. Photo copyright 20th Century Fox. All Rights Reserved.

interest in writing another story-what I will do is adapt this as a framework. I have done 10 songs already, we are going to have 15 songs-I have written 10 of the songs and I have no interest in throwing all that away; let's use it as a framework, as a basis." We went through five drafts. A university should study this--how you can adapt one story, it's most extraordinary. [...] We finally got the draft-it was still going to be realistic-naturalistic, realistic (houses, streets, real life site and location) and then the screen actors' strike. We had been promised $5 million at this stage, and then the SAG [Screen Actors' Guild] strike froze the money."[6]

O'Brien continued, "Jim was very good. He was going back to Australia in about a week's time. He had to go back to do the Adelaide Film Festival; Brian Thomson had gone already to do the Sydney Theatre Company and things in Australia. The whole thing was going down the tubes. How can you save the situation? Jim said it would be nice to try and save two years' work and do something with it-it's a good piece, there're some good songs, a good story now, strong. 'Do you want to do it on stage?' he asked. 'Well' I said, 'the West End is pretty sick at the moment; there's not a lot on except revivals and *Oklahoma* and *My Fair Lady* going back 20-30 years.' 'It would be quite exciting and I could film the stage show, take cameras into the theatre,' said Jim. I said, 'In that case, if we're going to do that, why don't we do it as a stage show but do it under controlled conditions in a controlled environment; do it on a sound stage somewhere and cast the audience just the same as we are casting the play.' And the whole thing suddenly started to shift and out of that we cut the budget by at least a quarter, we improved artistically tenfold I think. That was a hard thing to sell to the producers because they thought, 'They're just trying to save it'. I had to ring up the producers and say 'Listen, as far as I'm concerned, if the strike breaks tomorrow and you say 'go with the movie'—I hope it doesn't break tomorrow because this is much, much better than to go out and do it as a realistic thing, round streets and things.' So out of frustration and trouble came something rather wonderful, as always happens I think, and the less money you have the better off you are."[7]

Forced to relocate from the Dallas suburb of Denton—a lucky stroke of kismet—to a soundstage in Great Britain, the idea was floated to keep the setting encapsulated inside the DTV studio, making it the microcosm for the outside world. A resulting lower budget hampered things as well, but Sharman's solution, one from hunger, turned out to be one of the film's few strengths. With the cast and crew constrained indoors, Sharman untethers his camera and lets it drift in long single establishing shots introducing the surprisingly large cast of

257

characters and their environment.

One point of attack from those outside the cult—and even those within—is against the what is felt to be a comparatively weak score, even though, from both an orchestral and lyrical standpoint, *Shock Treatment*'s songs are more complex than those of the catchier, bombastic *Rocky Horror*. Several of *ST*'s songs were imported from earlier drafts of *Rocky Horror Shows His Heels* and shoe-horned into the *Shock Treatment* story. Other songs, like "Bitchin' in the Kitchen", were only slightly reconfigured. In *The Brad and Janet Show*, this song takes place in the Majors' home while Janet packs Brad's things for his trip to Dentonvale. In the film, the song is a double soliloquy, one of the more curious dramatic effects unique to musicals, where two people can have different interior monologues within the same tune.

The song "Lullaby", for example, is sung by the cast from their bedrooms as they prepare for sleep. The camera glides along outside, looking in at each room through windows. Ricky and Ansalong cuddle; Janet muses; Bert stares (but does not sing); Cosmo and Nation succumb to their allegedly incestuous desires, complete with riding crop and lingerie. As all lights go out, the camera spins back again, ending on a wide crane shot of a snoring audience, tucked in their seats for the night. The entire song was shot in one take, dollying from left to right and back. More astonishing: the scene was only shot once. "One and done and moving on," as nobody actually says.

For sheer photographic and choreographic brilliance, you need look no further than the song "Look What I Did to My Id", where all the greedy baddies adopt Flavors' white medical costumes and embrace their selling out in exchange for their dreams coming true. Sharman and cinematographer Mike Malloy limit the sequence to just three tracking shots, allowing the camera to basically join in on the elaborate dance. The same can be said for Malloy's inventive use of crane shots throughout, capturing the buzzing hive of DTV's stage, from the camera operators to Kirk the guy who runs the coffee cart.[239]

For the stand-out set pieces, the film's title song involves the majority of the cast trying to convince Brad to give in to his sickness and conform to mindless happiness. Janet's "seduction" scene comes in the form of "Little Black Dress", giddily performed by O'Brien as he presents Harper with her new, simple and chic, wardrobe. This leads directly to Janet's debut before the ravenous audience, singing "Me of Me", flinging her hat into the crowd as she embraces her fame. "'Jessica understood the irony of the film,' states O'Brien elaborating on his reasons for selecting Harper to portray Janet. 'It's a difficult thing for some American performers to be objective about television and the whole underside of pop stardom. But Jessica had no trouble at all with the irreverence of our script.'"[8]

The film's climactic song, "Duel Duet", is performed completely by DeYoung, playing both Brad and Farley as they confront each other over their filial differences, has only one instance of a body double during the entirety of the three-minute song. The rest of the song comprises back-and-forth cuts with DeYoung in both guises, effortlessly convincing the audience that we are seeing two men when really there is only ever one. It's DeYoung's sole moment to shine, the rest of the time he's either confined to a chair, a straight-jacket, or a rolling television, more of a talking prop than character.

---

[239] *Shock Treatment* is filled wall-to-wall with seemingly unnecessary characters given a strange amount of close-up time. Some of these folks include the Floor Manager, played by Ray Charleson (best-known as "Crow the Elf" in *Hawk the Slayer*); the aforementioned Kirk is played by Eugene Lipinski (*Arrow*'s Alexi Leonov); the wardrobe mistress is the late British dancer Imogen Claire ("Dorothy Trent" in *The Lair of the White Worm*); "fluff news" reporter Neely Pritt is played by former Mrs. Steven Soderberg, Betsy Brantley, who may be best-known for the trivia that she was the live-action double for Jessica Rabbit in *Who Framed Roger Rabbit?*; Neely's camera crew are played by original RHPS Transylvanians Perry Bedden (in his last film role) and Rufus Collins (also seen in Warhol's short *Kiss* (1963); Irwin Lapsey, president of Lapsey Autos, is played by Barry Dennen, best-known for his role as Pontius Pilate in the film version of *Jesus Christ, Superstar*, a role, strangely enough, once (very briefly) played by Richard O'Brien on the London Stage. For film buffs, *Rocky Horror* is just one long game of "Six Degrees of…" For *Rocky Horror* fans, everyone is one big family, and one of the few movies where the whole crew, from Cinematographer (*Empire Strikes Back*'s Peter Suschitzky), to the Casting Agency (Celestia Fox, U.K.), to editor (Graeme Clifford) are all name-checked by the audience.

"For Cliff DeYoung, his dual role in *Shock Treatment* is an actor's dream: he gets to play the hero, Brad *and* the villain Farley Flavors. 'I modeled Brad after David Eisenhower,' DeYoung reveals. 'Brad, with his clean-cut innocence and Mr. Squeak-Clean-America looks, is straight out of the 50's. But Farley is definitely not Mr. Clean. He's a snake-oil salesman with slicked-back hair who fine-tunes the fates of Brad and Janet to serve his own evil purposes. He's the great program director in the sky who makes everything happen.'"9

Despite the plot's requirements for Farley the villain, he's nothing close to a crazed Frank N. Further, neither in attitude nor energy. And the film suffers from that, even if Farley is precisely the villain *Shock Treatment* demanded. What most fans find tragic is that *Shock Treatment* delivers in inventive satire, but seems to have left most of the electric fun back home in the original film's Oakley Court.

With only the thin plot to keep it anchored, *Shock Treatment* is a rare movie whose text is overcome by its sarcastic subtext. Just as *Rocky Horror* played with the sexual repression rampant throughout Middle America—kept alive by its deep-set British roots—*Shock Treatment* is a furthering of O'Brien's fascination with the "American Dream": the idea that anyone can get ahead, become rich and famous, if they work hard or are, at least, white and in the right place at the right time. O'Brien's themes are mistrust of fame and the banality that comes with it. Once the DTV cameras are on, nobody is who they seem. The unctuous Ralph Hapshatt (Jeremy Newsome) loses his smile and his cool off stage, battling with ex-wife Betty.[240] Janet's parents, conservative by nature, are as quickly seduced by fame as their daughter, even lamenting, once Janet proves her mettle at the end and does the right thing by Brad, that "She let us down. She let us all down!" And turn their worship towards a newly-anointed Macy Struthers (Wendy Raebeck) as the face of mental health. Macy, the reason for Ralph and Betty's divorce, quickly abandons Ralph after Farley picks her from the crowd. Farley's

Humphries and O'Brien.
Photo copyright 20ᵗʰ Century Fox. All Rights Reserved.

quest for world domination involves running insane asylums in the same way as his chain of fast food restaurants, really does invoke the catch-phrase "Sanity for Today".

The satire existed throughout the multiple script drafts, but the cost-saving decision to keep it studio-bound is what made *Shock Treatment* prescient. In 1980-81, "reality TV" referred to shows like *Real People* and *That's Incredible!*, half-hour Stupid Pet Tricks for Human Beings, forerunners of *America's Funniest Home Videos* and *America's Got Talent*. The closest thing that resembled modern reality TV was the landmark 12-part PBS series *An American Family*, aired in 1973[241], or Michael Apted's septennial *Up* series (*Seven Up, Fourteen Up*, etc.). While slavish

---

[240] If you recall, the wedding of Ralph and Betty Hapshatt kickstarts *Rocky Horror*, introducing us to the "clean cut, All American" Brad and Janet. As Ralph, Jeremy Newsome is the only *Rocky* cast member to reprise his role.

[241] "Bill and Pat Loud and their five children, ranging from 14 to 20, allowed a crew into their Santa Barbara, Calif., home for seven months; from 300 hours of 16-millimeter film footage (this was long before digital camcorders), 12 hourlong episodes were produced. The premise was Warholian—applying a voyeuristic eye to unscripted moments—and so was the aftermath. Millions tuned in, and the Louds became a more or less new type of celebrity. As the openly gay eldest son, Lance, who had been a teenage pen pal of Warhol's, put it in *Time* magazine, the series fulfilled "the middle-class dream that you can become famous for being just who you are.' "[...] Mr. Gilbert and the Raymonds do agree on at least one thing: that *An American Family* has been unfairly credited with—or blamed—for starting reality television. The immersive, leisurely rhythms of the series are a stark contrast from the artificial situations (lab-rat housemates, gladiatorial contests) that dominate today's reality

259

fawning over the famous was nothing new then, the ravenous desire to join the club, humiliation in exchange for a fleeting fifteen minutes, was a relatively new phenomenon outside of *Let's Make a Deal!* In *Shock Treatment*, with instant fame came instant corruption. When that fame ended, cancellation followed, something worse than death itself. In *Shock Treatment*, the presumed "villains" win, but how could it be otherwise? O'Brien was commenting on American psychological culture; how do you defeat something nationally-ingrained?

"Observes producer John Goldstone: 'We are so influenced by the media—the way we dress, the way we talk, our behavior, values and dreams—that to a very real extent, the whole world has become one big TV show.' No one knows that better than Cliff DeYoung: "Years ago I was a regular on *The Secret Storm* and I invited my mother-in-law to visit the set because it was her favorite soap. She was very excited—until she actually got to the studio and watched us tape the show. Her reaction was far from what I anticipated. I asked her why she was so disappointed and she said, 'You ruined the show for me.' She was so hooked on the show, she thought it was real. But when she saw the actors getting ready, putting on their makeup, running lines, and the cameras rolling around, it totally destroyed the reality she had going in her head. Our film is going to bring that out,' De Young continues. 'Every part of life in *Shock Treatment* is in the context of a TV show.'"[242]

(Personally, I can't help but wonder if O'Brien is specifically having a go at *Rocky Horror* fandom as well. There's no doubt he's always been bemused by the cult, camping out in line every Saturday night, worshipping at the altar of Frank N. Furter week after week from the confines of the theater house. Draw your own conclusions with organized religion, of course. It certainly had the last laugh on President of the *Rocky Horror Fan Club*, Sal Piro. The first official "emcee" of the *Rocky Horror* midnight showings in New York, first at the Waverly Theater, then the 8th Street Theater, Piro organized *RHPS* events, managed fan mail, etc., and was essential to the growth of the phenomenon. In 1981, he was flown to London for a cameo in *Shock Treatment*. "When this movie was being filmed, Twentieth Century Fox wanted to promote it by making use of me and the fan club. I was hired to host a documentary entitled *The Rocky Horror Treatment*. This two-part film traced the development of the *Rocky Horror* cult in anticipation of the sequel, and the actual making of *Shock Treatment*. The biggest thrill for me was flying to London to shoot footage on the set of *Shock Treatment*. I interviewed the stars of the film and even made a cameo appearance. My "big" role was to stand talking on a telephone behind the staircase in the opening sequence. It was truly an 'if you blink, you miss me' role, or 'no, that wasn't a speck of dust in your eye, it was me.' But I didn't care. That week was the time of my life."[10] *The Rocky Horror Treatment* is a coveted rarity, airing once on syndicated TV, and then disappearing entirely following the film's box office disaster. It can be found on YouTube[243] in its entirety, but seems to be the *Star Wars Holiday Special* of the *Rocky Horror* crowd.)

"There exists the seeds of a decent idea here, but the broad social-comment subtext—the bland homogenization of a standardized, technologized, sterilized, and anesthetized middle-class America—has been done much better before (in *A Boy and His Dog* and Spielberg's *Close Encounters of the Third Kind*, to name just two). Between the tuneless music and forgettable lyrics, he completely uninvolving, uninteresting characters, and the no-win/no-lose/no-sense situations, the film has nothing to offer. If placed on trial, the Production Designer could probably plead he was just following orders, but the horrifyingly dull and blankly repetitive sets— meant to suggest that the town is the TV studio *is* the sanitarium—leave us feeling as caged-in as poor Brad in his padded cell. Sharman's dead, disconnected style of direction for *Shock Treatment* is intended to evoke the ennui and vacuity that haunts most of television. But

---

programs. With its grainy look and distanced camerawork, it resembles an art film more than any reality show."
Lim, Dennis. 2011. "Reality-TV Originals, in Drama's Lens." New York Times. April 15.
http://www.nytimes.com/2011/04/17/arts/television/hbos-cinema-verite-looks-at-american-family.html?_r=0

[242] Official *Shock Treatment* 1981 production notes.

[243] https://www.youtube.com/watch?v=Zk7sYfm2xpo

that is tantamount to making a gun control statement by shooting an N.R.A. member."[11]

As thematically different from *Rocky Horror* as one film can get, *Shock Treatment* arrived in front of studio suits in a baffling package. How would they possibly capitalize on the *RHPS* connection when the final product didn't bare even the smallest resemblance to the runaway now-classic? While Fox's marketing department had little idea what to do with *Rocky*, their best idea was to announce that *Shock Treatment* was "not a sequel...but an *equal!*" An unnecessary gauntlet hurled before a skeptical, growing audience, one that begged woefully unfair comparison. Despite the desperate shoe-horning, *Shock Treatment* could never have withstood the cult's scrutiny, and as far as the critics went, they weren't big fans of *Rocky Horror* in the first place, and had a field day attacking the new film's sluggish pace, over-abundance of unnecessary characters, and the many "uninspired" musical numbers.

"Deservedly dismissed upon release, this tiresome follow-up to *The Rocky Horror Picture Show* finds Brad and Janet (now played by the dreary Cliff DeYoung and Jessica Harper) the unwitting captives of a nightmarish reality TV show. A few decent Richard O'Brien-penned songs aside, *Shock Treatment* is one time warp you'll never want to do ever again," disparaged *Entertainment Weekly.*[12]

"Rather than maintain the level of crude, campy fun in the original, *Shock Treatment* deteriorates into lame, humorless nonsense that bores rather than amuses," despaired TV Guide.[13]

"*Shock Treatment*'s problems begin with this disjointed, vaguely metaphorical plot, but it suffers more from the many, many unmemorable songs, which slam the film to a standstill so the cast can cavort around, flashing their legs and smirking as though they're being much naughtier. *Rocky Horror* at least had the lure of forbidden sex and a pro-transgression stance; the squeaky-clean *Shock Treatment* instead pays some sloppy lip service to misbehavior without ever figuring out what that means. The film looks great, with vivid colors and sharp, snappy staging, but its 92 minutes drag by interminably. Tim Curry in fishnets might have helped, but a coherent storyline would have been far better," blergs The A.V. Club.[14]

None of these latter complaints are invalid. *Shock Treatment* is very much its own animal, not only in the *Rocky* world, but in the world of odd-ball musical comedies in general. In fact, the closest relative *Shock Treatment* has is with the Alan Arkin vehicle, *The Return of Captain Invincible* (1983), to which O'Brien also contributed songs and material. Like the swooping intro shots confined to the studio, *Shock Treatment* sets itself up with nowhere to go. The stakes aren't particularly high, Brad and Janet have no chemistry at their introduction, so it's hard to be too invested in saving their marriage if all we're doing is comparing them to Sarandon and Bostwick. The few absolute moments of joy are supplied by O'Brien, Quinn, and Nell Campbell during their brief scenes together, and by the irrepressible energy of Humphries' Bert Schnick, who seems devious and diabolical, but without purpose. "They should be sent to the Danube at dawn," he mutters near the end, referring to the Majors couple's newfound happiness. When he's questioned about this statement, Schnick replies, "Just...memories." Chilling if you think about it, but it doesn't really invite examination.

That *Shock Treatment* exists at all is a marvel warranting—and getting—endless debate. A sequel to a movie nobody originally went to see, completely devoid of every element that made people embrace the original in the first place. In a sense, this was the ballsiest move O'Brien and company could have pulled off: a sequel that could stand on its own. Even if it isn't a sequel. Really.

None of this, of course, matters to the hardcore *Rocky Horror* crowd. As I've pointed out before, a great number of movies that would have remained "lost" in the VHS dustbins are preserved by *Rocky* fanlove. The aforementioned *Return of Captain Invincible*, the Graham Chapman solo film *The Odd Job*, Martin Mull's *Serial*, even *Ferngully* all live on in one form or another thanks to their *RHPS* connections.[244] *Shock Treatment* sharing the bulk of its creative

---

[244] See *Fervid Filmmaking* for further info on *Captain Invincible*. *Movie Outlaw* for *The Odd Job*.

team with *Rocky Horror* cemented its place in movie history, even if it is considered a pale follow-up.

For the creator of the movies, however, O'Brien's attitude towards his creations over the years has vacillated between bemused and embittered. He'll be forever known as "The Creator of *Rocky Horror*", but little else. Maybe for his magnificent turn as "Mr. Hand" in Alex Proyas' masterpiece, *Dark City* (1998), or his cameo as Drew Barrymore's sleazy *Ever After* (1998—good year for O'Brien, eh?) paramour, the cleverly-named Pierre Le Pieu. "Mention *The Rocky Horror Picture Show* to O'Brien, and his aura of New Age calm starts to evaporate. The show brought O'Brien his wealth, but it also sealed him in a world of stocking, suspenders and giggle-strewn smut, preventing him, he believes, from achieving the success he deserves as an actor. 'I still get marginalised,' he says. 'There is a role out there for me which is going to blow everybody's socks off. But why they never offered me *Dr. Who* I'll never know. And why I've never been asked to play a Bond villain is a mystery. I'd be perfect for it. But you know,' he adds, heading back to the safety of crystals and karmic equilibrium, 'nothing eats at me.' It's hard to know whether to believe this. What you can believe, though, is that the whole *Rocky Horror* hoop-la has raked in close to £50 million pounds—and most of it bypassed O'Brien and poured straight into the coffers of 20th Century Fox."[15]

That being said, for years it Richard O'Brien teased that he'd been writing a direct sequel to *RHPS* titled "Revenge of the Old Queen" (a joke among fans being that the title should be "*Return* of the Old Queen", since "Old Queens don't get revenge."[245] "I'm up to the first song in the second act. I've written all the songs in the first act, as far as I know, and now I'm going to write all the songs in the second act. It seems a strange way to do it, but it seemed to me that I had to enjoy doing the work. Writing the sequel was so daunting, the whole concept of going down the same boulevard and not doing anything more than a soap opera carry-on, it had to have some kind of merit of its own including the same characters, and it was rather intimidating. I had the beginning of it from the original *Shock Treatment* screenplay that I'd written, which was very different from the *Shock Treatment* that ended up on the screen. Basically it's Janet having a baby and it's obviously Frank N Furter's baby. There'll be other people making claims to it, but it's not really about that. It's more a study of whether Frank's the right kind of person to become a parent. It's interesting getting the narrative sorted out; I've done a flow chart and it seems to work on a flow chart basis. [...] The thing that makes *Rocky* work in its own phenomenal way is that all that's been organic. I never tried to elicit that sort of response; it all happened naturally. It's interesting because when I used to go and watch B-movies and late-night schlock-horror as a teenager, we used to shout ruderies at the screen, but it was very yobbish, gauche, corny kind of stuff, and those were the very films that spawned Rocky. And then Rocky started to get this almost orchestrated response, and I thought that was a kind of growth in itself. Rather marvelous, really." As for the dubious return of the great Transvestite anti-hero: "Oh, he's resurrected. Dr. Scott is a scientist after all!"[16] Keep in mind, however, that this sort of rumor has been going on for at least a decade. The closest we're likely to get is the upcoming 2016 Fox TV-remake starring transsexual actress Laverne Cox (*Orange is the New Black*) as Frank, directed by Kenny Ortega. Fans have already drawn blood over this.)

But there's no stopping *Rocky* fans. While not shown as regularly as *RHPS*, *Shock Treatment* pops up at anniversary screenings, complete with its own shadow cast.[17] In 2015, Benji Sperring finally wore O'Brien down and received the rights to adapt the film for the King's Head stage in London, reverse-engineering the history of *Rocky Horror*. There hasn't been a Blu-ray edition yet, but it's popped up more than once on DVD, including as part of a double feature with its predecessor.

As far as *Shock Treatment* goes, as I've also frequently said, "Every movie is somebody's favorite." And, of course, "You've already seen worse."

---

[245] A play on the *Revenge of the Jedi* as opposed to **Return** *of the Jedi*.

NOTES

[1] No Author Cited. "A Horror Story." The Richard O'Brien Crusade. Archived at http://www.robcrusade.com/articles/seqind.html

[2] Mitchell, Blake and Jim Ferguson. "Shock Treatment: Not A Sequel But An Equal." Fantastic Films. January 1982, Vol. 4, No. 3. p. 57

[3] Norman, Neil. "Richard O'Brien." Face Magazine Interview. 1981. Archived The Richard O'Brien Crusade. http://www.robcrusade.com/articles/face.html

[4] Ibid

[5] Ibid

[6] Conroy, Mike. 1981. "Richard O'Brien and Shock Treatment". Fangoria Magazine #15. Vol. 3. P. 64

[7] Ibid

[8] Mitchell, Blake and Jim Ferguson. 1982. p. 58

[9] Ibid.

[10] Piro, Sal. "Shock Treatment Introduction." Archived at http://www.rockyhorror.com/shocktreatment/introduction.php

[11] Smithee, Allen. 1982. "Rocky Horror fans won't have to wait in line to see this turkey." *Cinefantastique*. Vol. 12, No. 1. February. P.51

[12] Clark, Jason. 2006. "Shock Treatment." Entertainment Weekly. August 29. http://www.ew.com/article/2006/08/29/shock-treatment-25th-anniversary-edition

[13] No author cited. 1981. "Shock Treatment." TV Guide. http://www.tvguide.com/movies/shock-treatment/review/117607/

[14] Robinson, Tasha. 2006. "Shock Treatment: 25th Anniversary Edition." The A.V. Club. October 18. http://www.avclub.com/review/shock-treatment-25th-anniversary-edition-8119

[15] No Author Cited. "A Horror Story." The Richard O'Brien Crusade. Archived at http://www.robcrusade.com/articles/seqind.html

[16] McCauley, Jim. 2000. "Richard O'Brien on the Rocky Horror Sequel." Daily Radar. Archived at the Richard O'Brien Crusade. http://www.robcrusade.com/articles/seq.html

[17] In the usual nature of full disclosure, from 1990 to 1995, I performed in the Pittsburgh shadowcast, "The Junior Chamber of Commerce Players", playing Frank or Brad nearly every Saturday night. In these pre-DVD days, *Rocky Horror* had just come out on VHS, allowing us to practice in our own living rooms. *Shock Treatment* wasn't released on video until 1992, but the film itself was rarely in circulation outside of *Rocky Horror* conventions. Eventually, the shadowcasts across the world began performing the "Equal" on special occasions. Which is why I understand just how goddamned difficult "Look What I Did To My Id" is to peform. (My role in *Shock Treatment*: Rest Home Ricky. My attempt to make it all about me came about in one of my first published pieces in Don Mike's *Faith Factory* newsletter, titled "The Ricky Horror Show", in which I boost Ricky to star status. Rik Mayall could not, at the time, be reached for comment. It's even harder to reach him now, since his death in 2014.)

THE SINFUL DWARF (1973)

(AKA DVÆRGEN)

By Mike Haushalter

A sadistic dwarf and his mother run a white slavery and heroin smuggling ring out of a decrepit boarding house. A pair of struggling newlyweds soon arrive at their doorstep seeking shelter and get more than they bargained for when the mother decides the young wife will make a good addition to their stable of sex slaves.

Way back when, there was a time when my friends and I seemingly had nothing but endless free time and nothing better to do with that time than watch movies. We ate up tons of movies in those joyful good old days and it came to pass that on an almost weekly basis we would endure a session we called "Man's Inhumanity to Man" night. On this night we would gather for many a shocking blood bath or grim friend test. We watched things such as *The Untold Story*, *Ebola Syndrome*, *Cannibal Holocaust*, the *Ilsa* films, *Make Them Die Slowly*, *Surf Nazis Must Die* and *Bloodsucking Freaks* to name a few of the films that would play out across our flickering televisions as we made off color jokes about horrors we witnessed. While *The Sinful Dwarf* was never viewed back in those less politically correct days it certainly could and would have—but back then we had never heard of the Sinful Dwarf. I only learned of it a few years back when it was "rediscovered" and heading to DVD. (Some further research in my favorite pre-internet film guides found that no mention of it was made in 1987's *Psychotronic Encyclopedia of Film* but that it was given a paragraph or so in Weldon's 1996 follow up, *The Psychotronic Video Guide To Film*, that likens the film to *The Gruesome Twosome* or a John Waters film without the humor.)

The Sinful Dwarf is a very dark, adults only fairy tale, not in a magical world of Disney fairy princess tale mind you, but an honest to goodness gritty evil fantasy parable of old meant to scare you straight and give you nightmare while doing so. Much like the original Grimm's tales, Classroom highway scare shorts or that after school special about angel dust. But unlike most of these cautionary chestnuts made with ill planned good intentions, the scary German filmmakers had nothing in mind but dollar signs and tormenting the English speaking rain coat crowd.

"A Fairy tale?" you may be asking, just bear with me for a moment and look at the film's characters and

Lola Lash as "Mum" and Torben Bille as "Olaf".
Photo Courtesy Severin Films.

urban blight spooky forest setting. Let's start off with the film's titular sinful dwarf, Olaf (Torben Bille[246]), a frog-voiced, twisted Rumpelstiltskin-like pedophile who is introduced in a scene where he lures a seemingly school aged girl to a fate worse than death with the help of a yapping dog toy. Then we have the film's nominal heroes; a recently married young English couple who seem to be on the lam like a grown up Hansel and Gretel. They are friend and family free and searching for shelter on the fringes of society. The wife, Mary (the beautiful Anne Sparrow who was rumored to have been married to Bille), is a naive airhead who's acting wavers between comatose and screaming. The husband, Peter (Tony Eades), is a blandly ineffective David Manners kind of hero who, like the Universal Horror heroes of the golden age, does very little to help his wife or himself survive their misadventures. We then have a drug dealer named Santa Claus who does indeed look the part and comes complete with a toy shop drug front. Finally, there is Lola Lash, Olaf's mom, who is Ursula, Maleficent and the evil step mother all rolled into one.

I'm going to pause here a moment and talk about Clara Keller, the actress playing Lola Lash, who seems to have much more invested in her part than the rest of the cast. While my search engine search of her didn't really bring up anything worth mentioning she certainly seems be adding a lot of emotion and nuances to her role, such as her anger and resentment in her musings of her character's salad days as a successful cabaret singer and her strange dealings with her visiting female friend. Is her casual almost-nudity part of an awakened lesbian seduction or has she just become such a sad alcoholic that personal dress and hygiene no longer matters?

I viewed *The Sinful Dwarf* multiple times while preparing for this review (and two times before) and each time I have watched it I have asked myself the same questions: What tragedy

---

[246] Of the Blu-Ray extras on Severin's excellent disc, "The Search for Torben" is the most fascinating. Torben Bille—playing Olaf as perhaps the most disturbing "evil little person" since Luis De Jesus' Ralphus in *Bloodsucking Freaks*. From his official bio on IMDb: "Torben Bille was born on October 31, 1945 in Koge, Denmark. Torben first became involved with show business when he joined a traveling troupe of artists as a child. Bille worked behind-the-scenes on a number of movies as either a property master or a stage manager. He achieved his greatest enduring cult cinema popularity with his unforgettably creepy and unnerving portrayal of the depraved and sadistic Olaf in the notoriously nasty exploitation sickie *The Sinful Dwarf*. Torben's other film roles were often strictly minor parts (he was the sole dwarf actor in Denmark in his day). Bille continued to work in the adult entertainment industry, most notably on Werner Hedman's enormously successful *Sign* series. He was rumored to be married to fetching blonde Anne Sparrow (his female co-star in *The Sinful Dwarf*), reportedly was the host of a children's TV show prior to working on more down'n'dirty adult-oriented fare, and even had quite the reputation as a ladies' man. Torben Bille died at age 47 on July 22, 1993."
http://www.imdb.com/name/nm0082350/bio?ref_=nm_ov_bio_sm

were our heroes running from? Why do they have no friendly faces to turn to? Also why does the film feature scenes of hard core pornograpy? Who thought these scenes would be titillating within the context of the film? Sure there is one almost romantic scene of lovemaking between our "happy" couple, but it is somewhat spoiled by the unknown prying eyes of an ogling Olaf. But the rest of the sex scenes involve doped up sex slaves being used against their will in a way that would shame even Ron Jeremy & Jamie Gillis. Nudity and even soft core sex is a staple to this sort of roughie antics but actual porn is unexpected considering the way it's shown and the fairly ugly even for seventies era adult performances.

This is a limited edition stuffed "Olaf" made by Severin Films specifically as a give-away promotion for *The Sinful Dwarf*. This is a thing that exists. And this is the appropriate reaction:

Anne Sparrow as "Mary". All photos courtesy Severin Films.

SKIN CRAWL (2005)

Just to warn you, this will be a fair analysis, but it won't be unbiased. It's impossible—I've known director Justin Wingenfeld for literally decades. We met during a theater audition in college. We worked on each other's student films. Hell, we worked on *Gladiator Eroticus* together! We went to each other's weddings. He's one of my best friends to this day. So no, no matter what I do, this will not be an unbiased chapter. *Skin Crawl* is uneven but it's solid, it's unique, and it has a very dark vision behind it.

Sometime in the 1700s, a group of angry white moralists break into the shack shared by three women they suspect of witchcraft. Taking the youngest with them, they take turns raping and beating her to death. The joke is on them, however. The three ladies *are* witches, and they cast a spell ensuring that no one will ever hurt one of their bloodline and escape unscathed.

Fast forward to the modern day of 2002. Margaret (Debbie Rochon[247]), unaware of her lineage to the sisters, is trapped in a miserable marriage with philandering milquetoast Howard (Kevin G. Shinnick[248]). Margaret intends to divorce him. As she's wealthy and will take everything, Howard panics. Fortunately, he's having an intense affair with Sadie (the excellent Julian Wells[249]), who has her own designs on Margaret's fortune. Through sexual trickery, she convinces Howard to have Margaret killed. On her way home from work, Margaret is abducted by two seriously horrific men. While Howard and Sadie play kinky schoolgirl games, Margaret is gruesomely stabbed to death and left in the woods to rot. Those familiar with horror tropes understand that this is not the end of Margaret's tale.

But without warning, the film reverses itself, traveling back through footage and time in

---

[247] *American Nightmare* (2001)

[248] *The Death of Poe* (2006)

[249] *Bite Me!* (2004)

order to present Howard's point of view. For him, Margaret is cold and castrating, caring more for gentle insects and spiders than she does for him. Sadie, however, is young and exciting and sexually insatiable. She gets him to reveal all the fantasies he has that Margaret will not indulge. Zoning in on his desire for anal sex, Sadie promises him that special favor if he agrees to get Margaret out of the way. And she happens to know someone who knows a couple of guys (John P. Fedele[250], Rodney Gray[251]) who will do it out of the goodness of their hearts, plus a big split of the insurance payout. The night of the murder, Howard and Sadie act out their various fantasies. Howard's guilt is immediately subverted by his lust. Sadie gets off as she imagines the carnage inflicted on her rival and how she's about to win the brass ring.

Then, again, we reverse through time and see the same events from Sadie's perspective (along with that of the two hired thugs). She's been playing Howard like a cello (or whatever instrument is the saddest and most pathetic...I'm thinking flutophone). Her earlier phone conversation with Howard, where he agrees to the murder, is replayed, but this time with a twist: she's already in bed with another man—the "guy who knows a guy". We see the past through her eyes—including the sodomy scene that we first saw her raving and enjoying, but from this new angle, her face betrays the discomfort and her intense dislike of Howard. She just needs to get this over with and move on.

And though the police turn up to interrogate Howard on his wife's disappearance, they immediately conclude that any woman in her right mind would leave this loser immediately. So he's off the hook, legally-speaking. Then Sadie arrives to pick up her payday, telling Howard that they're not right for each other, after all, "You're the one who agreed to have his wife killed so that you could fuck your girlfriend in the ass!" But this is a short-lived victory for her. For Howard, it's the final prelude before his comeuppance. And for the thugs, legitimately disturbed by the murder they committed, things won't end well for them either. For something shambled out of the woods, preceded by a small swarm of roaches and millipedes, looking for revenge for centuries of abuse and torment. The curse has finally awakened.

I was lucky enough to be one of the first to read an early draft of Justin's script and thought it was a great, sleazy cross between Italian exploitation and *Tales from the Crypt*. Justin had crafted a neat supernatural revenge story inspired by his love of the old Warren comics, ala *Creepy*, *Eerie*, and *Vampirella*. What wound up on screen was very different from what was on the page. In the script, the events unfolded chronologically, linearly. In the edit, Justin gives full credit to editor and stop-motion virtuoso Brett Piper for the non-linear time skipping. While some may find the technique tedious, complaining about "footage we've already seen", they missed the point. It's a small story of infidelity and murder shown from the various points of view of the players involved. It's as much *Rashomon* as it is *House at the Edge of the Park*. It's as much this unique structure as it is the excellent performances, and grimily realistic look of it all, that makes *Skin Crawl* a cut above the average microbudget horror.

"Welcome to the world of 'good news/bad news' horror film criticism," wrote Bill Gibron for DVDTalk. "On the analytic menu today—the under-baked revenge flick *Skin Crawl*. Lining up the likable elements of this outsider effort, we find a willing cast (complemented by current schlock scream queen Debbie Rochon) eager to deliver in the dread department. Similarly, first time writer/director Justin Wingenfeld wants to utilize a *Pulp Fiction* / *Rashomon* style for his narrative, twisting and turning the basic plot points into something surprising...and sinister. And finally, for you lovers of gore and gratuity, actress Julian Wells is in a near constant state of nudity, exposing her chest with routine regularity, while the finale features a decent amount of Italian terror inspired grue. It's actually a pretty impressive collection of pluses, each one an example of a movie trying to make a motion picture mountain out of a standard macabre molehill. But wait—that's only one side of the story. What about the negatives, you ask? Are the flaws facing this film fatal, or merely minor pitfalls along the road to a decent indie effort? Sadly,

---

[250] Ani*mal Room* (1995)—See *Fervid Filmmaking* for more info.

[251] Co-star of Paul Scrabo's incredible *Dr. Horror's Erotic House of Idiots* (in which Amy and I also cameo...fyi.)

the cons really cold cock this movie, delivering deathblows over and over again to something that is trying, stoically, to remain engaging and upright. Indeed, in the end, the problems completely scuttle the scares, resulting in a fright film without horror, a tepid tale of supernatural vigilantism that just falls apart."[1]

Another major criticism I've read—and heard during screenings—that the amount of sex and nudity is almost absurd. "Does this woman do anything but have sex?" Well, as Justin explains on the DVD commentary, "This is Sadie's job. Some people go to an office, she fucks people to get her own way."

"[Justin] wanted everything very small and authentic," Wells told me in 2006. "He didn't want me to be a cartoon villain and he wanted the plot and dialogue to convey the evil, rather than my performance. Rather than me twirling my mustache. [...] I was really blown away by the script and how talented he is. He's really a quiet force at E.I. and he should be much more on the front lines. And he's just a pleasure. Just calm and gentle...he's just a sweetheart. [...] Justin has no temper at all. They [Justin and Piper] both stay very calm and collected. And they both elevate the level of professionalism in cinema of E.I. that they're all accustomed to. They bring it up a couple of notches. They were very generous in terms of giving us creative license."[2]

At DVD Verdict, David Johnson liked it a little better than Gibron. "Skin Crawl is marketed as a horror film, but it would be more accurately described as a juiced-up, occasionally bloody Lifetime movie-of-the-week. Or, to lend it a tad more hardcore street cred, think of *Skin Crawl* as a super-sized episode of *Tales from the Crypt*. The first sequence, where we meet the witches and see them harassed by some colonial-era soldiers and so on and so forth, made it look like the rest of the film was going to play out as yet another half-baked horror movie. Actually, the horror elements are shuffled off until the final 10 minutes as the majority of the film is devoted to the shenanigans of horny, greedy people. And believe it or not, the story is pretty clever. [...] The script isn't genius, but for the shoestring this film was made on, and thus the homegrown direct-to-video movies category it will no doubt find itself pigeon-holed into, writer/director Justin Wingenfeld threw together a fairly interesting storyline, which is supplemented well by some novel filming styles. Wingenfeld will tell a portion of the story, then jump back and repeat that segment, but peeling back some of the layers of his narrative and revealing plot elements and characters that totally change the direction of the plot. It sounds like a gimmick, but Wingenefield [*sic*] manages to make it work here. The story itself isn't rich, and really ends up being boilerplate CSI mystery-of-the-week grist, but the success here is in the method, and that's executed quite well."[3]

As far as it being exploitative, *Skin Crawl* presents Sadie not only as a sexual being, but one that's self-empowered and utterly realistic. For example, there are no "L-Shaped Sheets" in this film. While Sadie lounges post-coital, or just hanging out at home, she doesn't cover herself. Why would she? She's in a familiar, safe setting. She's more comfortable nude (which Wells sells effortlessly). When she's on the phone naked, she'd have no reason to cover either—who can see her, and who cares if someone does see? Instead of feeling gratuitous, the nudity is casual, perfunctory, and something nearly all humans do in private or with lovers. (Howard is not exempt from this rule either, as Shinnick is just as naked as Sadie during their scenes together. "If the woman is going to be nude for sex, the man should be too.") As for the sex: "Ever watch a movie where two people are having sex and you can see they're still wearing their underwear. How is that even physically possible? Do they just wear crotchless underwear all day in case they get lucky?" It's a movie contrivance for which Justin has no patience. "Seriously, this is desensitizing nudity Paul Verhoeven would be proud of."[4]

The script also works hard to imbue all of its characters with dimensions that elevate them from their familiar tropes. While we feel sympathy for the loveless marriage between Margaret and Howard, neither are blameless in the state of things. The brutality of Margaret's murder actually weighs quite heavily on the thugs, Franco and D'Amato (obvious homages to the Italian maestros; the chief witch hunter played by Michael J. Thomas in the prologue is named "Nalder" after the bizarre actor and his character in the gory *Mark of the Devil* (1970)). As Franco, the usually comedic Fedele is just a common thug who hurts people for money, but he's never killed before and it haunts him. As D'Amato, Rodney Gray speaks scarcely a dozen words

Julian Wells as "Sadie". Bugs as themselves.
Photo courtesy POPCinema. All Rights Reserved.

in the film, but his unblinking menace betrays severe and utterly disturbing mental illness. Viewing Sadie's actions from different points of view also rounds out her character, transforming her casual greed and manipulation into utter amorality. Even Ruby Larocca, a producer on the film and familiar on-camera face in the indie horror world, stepped in at the last minute to play Franco's wife, interacts with the brutish man but displays no fear of him. Indeed, the minute he leaves to kidnap Margaret, she slips off her shorts and beckons to a third cohort (Wingenfeld's obligatory cameo).

She's no abused spouse or wilting flower.

In fact, for all of its exploitative elements, all of the female characters are strong, empowered. They may be victims of circumstance, but they're not willing victims in any other way. It speaks to the writing, direction, and performances. We've all met people like the women (and, for the most part, the men) in this movie. The attack on Margaret is vicious and upsetting—Franco struggles to control her while Rochon as Margaret struggles in recognizable terror, displaying both fight and flight. D'Amato basically guts her with a Bowie knife that should have penetrated them both, and the look on Franco's face when the deed is done is one of utter horror. His tough guy bravado isn't enough to cope with the fact that he and his sidekick snuffed out a life in one of the most horrific ways possible. D'Amato's response to the act is that he can't even control what he's doing. Franco has to beg him to stop stabbing long after Margaret has died.

The behind-the-scenes stories are just as cringe-inducing as the film. The opening period prologue was shot in a one-room shack with no ventilation, in the middle of summer, with a fire burning just a few feet away from the actors. The humidity was so intense, all of the actors wear a sheen of sweat throughout the sequence. In several shots, Michael J. Thomas's burn make-up is visibly melting. On a low-budget shoot, the actors are asked to—and will—crawl through hell to get the picture made. No stunt doubles or trailers—though body doubles were employed when schedules prevented participation. During the stomach-churning climax, both Rochon and Wells held a mixture of fake blood and live insects in their mouths. For Wells, it was a challenge. For Rochon, well-known for her insect aversion, it was a nightmare that was only countered when Justin offered to shove a handful of meal worms into his own mouth (reminiscent of Spielberg's and Kate Capshaw's interaction during *Indiana Jones and the Temple of Doom* during that film's "bug scene"). Wells needed no such coaching. "I was hungry and craft services were horrible," Wells says, point blank. "No, I love doing anything for the project. Anything to get involved and be a real actress is really exciting to me. Aside from simulating sex, all of it I'm very enthusiastic about."[5]

The first production under the former E.I. Entertainment's[252] Shock-O-Rama label, shot on Betacam in 2002, *Skin Crawl* has, to modern eyes, a primitive film look to it, slightly

---

[252] Best known for its Seduction Cinema label (producing such disparate soft core parodies as *The Erotic Witch Project*, *Playmate of the Apes*, and *The Seduction of Misty Mundae*), E.I. rebranded itself as POP Cinema in the late 2000s. "Obviously, the sex is what pushes our movies," Wells explains. "But the actresses—me and Misty [Mundae], essentially—were really pushing to have more integrity and not be so exploited. And [president] Mike Raso really catered to us and accommodated us in a lot of ways. Because it was a bit of a sacrifice in terms of how they make their money. I came right at the cusp of that evolution. I did a couple, maybe two or three of the really overt parodies before they got more plot-driven." Sirens Vol. 2 No 7, 2006. P. 16

muddying the terrific lighting and camerawork of DP John P. Fedele (who also plays the killer, Franco). Because of the ultra-limited budget, the film spent almost five years in post-production as Piper layered in effects (his stop-motion demon conjured by the witches is just downright nifty), while he and Justin worked on the unusual structure that gives the film it's unique signature. The result, as I mentioned, is uneven and bumpy in parts, largely due to the repetition of key scenes, sometimes intact, sometimes broken with jump cuts, but the repetition is necessary to understand everyone's motivations. The story in *Skin Crawl* has an unusual depth and consideration for the people involved. It's no quick slasher/zombie cheapie knocked off in a weekend. For his first film, Justin wanted something that would last. Whether or not he was successful is up (as usual) to the individual viewer. I personally think it's an amazing achievement.[6]

Incidentally, I'd be remiss if I didn't mention the beautiful score created by Justin's and my old friend, Don Mike, who also scored Seduction Cinema's *Dr. Jekyll and Ms. Hyde*[7] (also starring Wells, who no longer works under that name[8]). It hits all the right tonalities for the scene and works extremely well to heighten the tension. For what was essentially made as a quickie to launch a label, *Skin Crawl* is a real melting pot of talent.

Chad Connelly at Movies Made Me Do It appreciated it the best from the critical point of view: "There's also some good scares to be found towards the end, and even though this was director Justin Wingenfeld's first film, it doesn't take a genius to see that the man knows how to set a scene for maximum effect. There's one particular shot that I especially enjoyed, and although I can't really explain it here for fear of spoilers, I felt that it was one of the better scenes that I've seen in quite some time. I can't say the same thing about every last scene in here, but again, this guy has the potential to make some damned good movies if this was any indication."[9]

Surprisingly, Wingenfeld has yet to produce a follow-up film. "I've been working on some ideas," he told me in 2016, "but I get so far into the script and get bored or frustrated that it's not going where I want to or I start thinking, 'Christ, how many times has this been done before?' But I'm really anxious to make another one. I just want to make the *right* one, you know?"

NOTES

[1] Gibron, Bill. "Review". 2007. DVD Talk, March 13. http://www.dvdtalk.com/reviews/26994/skin-crawl/

[2] Watt, Mike. 2006. "Eulogy for Julian Wells." Sirens of Cinema Vol. 2, No. 7. October. PP. 16, 18.

[3] Johnson, David. "Review". 2007. DVD Verdict. March 28th. http://www.dvdverdict.com/reviews/skincrawl.php

[4] Johnson, DVD Verdict. 2007.

[5] Watt, Mike. 2006. "Eulogy for Julian Wells." Sirens of Cinema Vol. 2, No. 7. October.

[6] I'm also beyond proud that *Skin Crawl* made its world debut at *Genghis Con*, a horror convention Amy and I ran for just two years in Pittsburgh.

[7] As well as many of my early films.

[8] ""Well, even after two or three [soft-core comedies] you get frustrated. I mean, I graduated from NYU Film School so... you know. It wasn't frustrating as much as it was humiliating. That's the word I'd use. [...] I was naive in the sense that I thought that anything that wasn't porn was noble and was going to assist me in my flight towards stardom. I didn't realize that it was actually sort of damaging. [...] No, no. It's *definitely* damaged my career. In fact, I just lost out on a TV show for the WB. They google me and see that I'm this b-queen, soft-core porn chick. I work under my real name, but Google is so sophisticated that it only takse a click of a mouse to put the two together. I'm not using 'Julian' anymore and I'm trying to avoid being naked--unless, you know, if it's something that really appeals to me. Again, speaking for myself, having graduated from NYU, I think I could have made much more of my career. But, I mean, nudity and erotica is very much frowned-upon [out here]. Especially because I would want to do comedy. So that's hard. I guess I'm not quite driven enough to really work that hard. In addition to how hard you have to work just to make it at all." Watt, Sirens No. 7. P. 18

[9] Connolly, Chad. "Review". 2007. The Movies Made Me Do It. http://www.moviesmademe.com/movie/review/1021

SKINNED DEEP (2004)

F/X artist Gabe Bartalos' debut feature film begins with real skin being really branded by a series of really hot instruments. For real. In terms of opening titles, the seared-in "SD" is a true attention-grabber. Moments later, while a muscular body builder flexes in front of some candles, the trap-jawed "Surgeon General" runs an old man off the road and proceeds to tear him several painful new ones. The remaining titles roll while unseen assailants destroy the man's car, while shattered glass and heated metal seem to melt and boil beneath pouring rain. The images are violent and unnerving and, under the pounding downpour, quite beautiful.

From there we meet the Rockwell family on their road trip vacation across the Rocky Mountains. If you've ever seen a horror movie, you know these people are ever-so doomed. Our suspicions are confirmed when they spot a sunglass-wearing state trooper standing guard over another wrecked auto. "Yep," the cop responds to Mr. Rockwell's query as to what did the damage. "Wild animal." Coyotes. Big fucking coyotes. Using tools. After a tire blows, a very nice old lady, speaking with a much more sinister tone than is appropriate, promises that she'll send help along to Mr. Rockwell and his family. "You people are so nice out here," he tells her menacing smile.

Nothing is going to end well, as we can plainly see. It's just a matter of how soon the bad is going to happen.

Before too long, we're down to a single member of the family, the sullen teenaged Tina, who likely never wanted to go on the vacation in the first place, just *knowing* that any car trip with her dim dad would end up with them all being killed and eaten. That's just part of the American Dream any more.

Part *Texas Chain Saw Massacre* and part *Nothing But Trouble* (1991), Bartalos' *Skinned Deep* is primarily a showcase for the gruesome, surreal, and often bloody special effects the man and his company specialized in for more than three decades. Really, that's why you'd pick up something like this in the first place, right? And off-kilter survival horror lives or dies—so to speak—on the backs of its craziest characters, and *Skinned Deep* offers genetically-manipulated maniacs in spades. The aforementioned Surgeon General aside, the backwoods murderfolk also include the diminutive Plates (Warwick Davis, barely suppressing his psychotic rage at first introduction), and the aptly-named Brain (Jay Dugré), whose oversized head is one giant pulsing organ. By the 20-minute mark, half of the family has been brutally slaughtered but even more mayhem is on the way. Will Tina be our Final Girl, surviving only to be betrothed to the childlike Brain ("It's 'Brian'!")? Or will Brain follow in the footsteps of the rest of his kin and reduce Tina to Tender Vittles? And—*Jesus Christ, where is The Creator's head??*

"You live in fear of a good laugh so as to not launch your dental work!"

Shot on 16mm over a series of nights and weekends between 1999 and 2001, Bartalos built the sets inside his Los Angeles shop, working on "day jobs"—like *Leprechaun 5* and *6* with his *Skinned Deep* star Warwick Davis—then working on his directorial debut during the downtime. "'At that point, the rules would go down," Bartalos told *Fangoria's* Marc

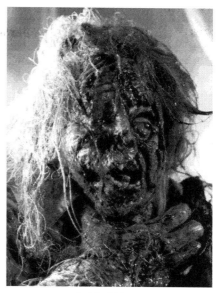

...And that'd be granny.
Photo courtesy Gabe Bartalos.

Shapiro. "Anybody who wanted to stay or bring a six-pack and work for a couple of hours was welcome. A lot of times, it was just me propping up a set and trying to get a wall up while teetering on a ladder. One night a friend of mine came in and was watching me, and he said, 'Gabe! What the fuck, let me come and help you.' We basically shot the film in waves. We'd shoot for 11 days, put the flats and sets aside, get back together and shoot for a couple of weeks, break apart and go back to our normal lives."'[1] And because of Bartalos' nice guy reputation, industry friends emerged from the woodwork to lend a hand to bring the director's vision to life.

"'I've met some awesome people through all my years in the business,' he says, 'and if they weren't available, more importantly, their stuff was. It was like, 'If you're shooting this weekend, take our dolly,' or 'Take all the rain gear you want, just get it back to us in the same condition.' People really responded to the fact that I was doing this on my own, and they felt it was a good cause.'"[2]

Incidentally, it's impossible to overstate the importance of Warwick Davis's support for *Skinned Deep*. As the film's only "name"—as the titular star of the *Leprechaun* series, but prior to his casting in the *Harry Potter* movies—Davis provided energy and high morale to the production. "'Each time I was in Los Angeles,' says Davis, who makes his home in Britain, 'it was a good time to do a couple of days on Gabe's film. But I was doing it on my days off from *Leprechaun*, when I really needed a day off. But I would do anything for Gabe, and I told him I wouldn't have done this for anyone else.'" Perhaps a bit of flattery was involved as well, as the role was specifically written with Davis in mind. "'Plates allowed me to go completely mad,' he says. 'There was no level that was too high. Gabe was like, 'Go with it and do whatever you want to do.' I liked the idea that I could just go utterly crazy.'"[3]

Skinned Deep's technical prowess excels over its budgetary limitations. The acting is the biggest let-down, with lead Karoline Brandt one of the worst offenders, looking only mildly inconvenienced that her entire family—including her brat younger brother—has been slaughtered before her eyes. Her sense of urgency to escape reminds one of someone looking for a spare phone charger. She barely reacts upon falling into a room decorated with rotting torsos and captured video of dad slaughter. Brandt's performance as Tina is the most consistent complaint leveled against the film. "The acting is what is to be expected in low budget horror, but not all of it is the actors fault. The dialogue is unnatural at points, and the character motivations are often boggling," wrote Steve Pattee for Horror Talk. "For instance, as our heroine tries to make her big escape from the house, she continually yells, 'Hello, is anybody there?' That is just the tip of the iceberg."[4] Playing "Marco Polo" with your captors doesn't strike me as the best survival instinct either.

Yet, before you start dredging up new horrors to visit upon Tina on your own, we're introduced to the film's heroes: a gang of elderly bikers, "The Ancient Ones", who know a thing or two about survival. Their members include the toothless "Shakes" (Allen Richard) and none-other than Forrest J. Ackerman (as member "Forry"), so suddenly our story seems to be in capable, if wrinkly hands.

Perhaps best-known for his bizarre and grotesque work on many of Frank Henenlotter's cinematic psychoses—*Frankenhooker, Basket Case 2 & 3, Brain Damage,* and *Bad Biology*—Bartalos' direction is strong on visual aplomb and gleeful sadism. The movie's biggest successes come during the stranger, quieter moments, such as when Granny alerts the family to the presence of new intruders, interrupting day-to-day activities like Plates polishing his porcelain namesake weapons, or the Surgeon casually strangling a cat. The sets are stuffed to the edges of the frame with odd production design—electronics and toys cannibalized for functional decoration, mingling with the bones of past victims. Little touches like Brain's ridiculous homemade Indian headdress add to the surrealism.

"I love working with Gabe," Henenlotter told *Shock 'till You Drop.* "When you know somebody, you trust them, it makes the collaboration a lot easier because I can talk to him in shorthand. When we create a creature, it's nice because we both feel authorship over it. When it's done, I honestly feel it's mine. He honestly feels it's his. And we're both right. It's really wonderful. [...] We spend a lot of time, but I tell Gabe what I want. He takes and turns that into 3D. He's the guy that spends all the time creating it and nurturing it and building it. Not me. And then I come in at the end and say well, we can have this or that, or it's perfect. That's all. He does the backbreaking work on it. [laughs] Some of his ideas are so radical and out there. He's one of the few people I encourage and say, 'surprise me. Go for it.' And we did! Some of the stuff like 'Twister' in *Basket Case 3* was a freak that I just couldn't believe I was seeing when I first saw it."[5]

Skinned Deep feels like Bartalos unleashed, without the boundaries of someone else's nightmares to recreate. Like the best of no-rules horror, *Skinned Deep* also has a punk sensibility that allows it to stand out. Take, for instance, the backroads gladiatorial match between pick-up truck and the family's tricked out Doom Mobile (with Tina strapped to the front *Road Warrior-*style).[253] Or, perhaps more appropriately, Brain's dream of being "just another face in the crowd", a freedom to run naked through Times Square—bringing to mind the guerrilla streaking scenes of both *Terror Firmer* and Henenlotter's first *Basket Case*—a sequence shot without permits and during rush hour.

"When I first cast actor Jay Dugré in the part of Brain, I gave him my whole "take" on the character. Misunderstood mutant with a sweet face, and he has to play the part straight in order for it to work. Jay understood and then I brought up the other tricky part about the part," Bartalos says, laughing at Dugré's future adventure. "He knew I wanted to created 'playful anarchy', no one really gets hurt and the bottom line is, it is for the good of all cinema. Shooting the scene was like a military operation. He sprang from a van once our Walkie-Talkies said it was crowded enough and sprinted down Forty-Third Street into a waiting sound blanket that dumped into a get-away pick-up truck. Now, I must say I use the word 'get-away' loosely because we did not get away. Undercover cops jumped Jay and promptly arrested him amidst my frantic pleas and lies of it just being a fraternity prank, etc! Luckily Peter Strietmann, the director of photography, was already en-route to our 'home base' safely with the precious footage. Jay was released fourteen hours later with no charges against him; just some strange looks from cops who still in the end did not realize that it was for a film. I think they thought he was some nut who liked to glue three-foot brain prosthetics on his head and let it all hang out

---

[253] One of the victims in this sequence being fellow effects artist "Big Al" Tuskes of Robert Kurtzman's Precinct 13 house.

for the thrill of Manhattan spectators!"[6]

"*Skinned Deep* is funny and inventive as hell," wrote Amanda Reyes for *Film Threat*. "Why Bartalos chose such an ambitious and original project as his debut remains a mystery, it's simply a bold turn for a first time director. The movie relies heavily on wacky special effects which Bartalos is the master of, but there's also a crisp and deranged sense of humor that connects with his weird creations. Some of the funniest moments involve Plates' bizarre soliloquies on life and of course, the Ancients battle to the death."[7]

For fans and lovers of low-budget horror, *Skinned Deep* is a crisp death-pursuit through the park, the 16mm footage beautifully saturated and the effort of all involved imbedded in the grain. For those raised on more polished fare, the criticism is expectedly harsher. So what you get out of *Skinned Deep* is what you bring into it.

"The cherished enamel, the porcelain, it's like a society," expounds Plates. "Every molecule an individual—like me! But, when you divide it, a structure takes shape. A circular vessel for distributing organic nourishment. We, like this plate, gain strength in numbers! We thrive in a herd environment. We feed off one another for a stronger society, aggressively growing in numbers, until one day—"

"What the fuck is wrong with you?"

Gabe Bartalos and "Shakes" (Allen Richard) Photo courtesy Gabe Bartalos.

NOTES

[1] Shapiro, Marc. "Skinned Deep." Fangoria Issue 242. April, 2004. P. 42

[2] Ibid. P. 41

[3] Ibid. p. 45

[4] Pattee, Steve. 2009. "Review". Horror Talk.com. April 28. http://www.horrortalk.com/reviews/movie-reviews/370-skinned-deep.html

[5] Rob G. 2010. "Exclusive Interview: Frank Henenlotter!" February 8. http://www.shocktillyoudrop.com/news/14024-exclusive-interview-frank-henenlotter/

[6] Slater, Jay. "Skinned Deep!" The Dark Side Magazine, Issue #108. pp. 25-26

[7] Reyes, Amanda. 2002. "Review". Film Threat.com. Review provided by the author as no archived version exists for the time being. Chris Gore is working to get *Film Threat* back up and running as of this writing.

SORORITY BABES IN THE SLIMEBALL BOWL-O-RAMA (1988)

In 2002, I was one of the head writers for Fred Clarke's *Femme Fatales Magazine* and we were working on an issue focusing on the 25th Anniversary of the "Scream Queen". At the time, there was some confusion as to which came first, *Nightmare Sisters* or the above-titled extravaganza. Mr. Fred Olen Ray confirmed that *Sisters* did indeed come first. Still, I wrote the following ode:

"Working with such directors as Fred Olen Ray and David DeCoteau, Brinke Stevens and her fellow Scream Queens, Linnea Quigley and Michelle Bauer, carved a niche for themselves, playing demon-possessed sex kittens and voluptuous virgins in low budget, low-calorie, eye- and mind-candy epics. The films themselves were a strange blend, too comical to be horror, to gory to be comedies, featuring enough skin to be sexy, but not enough to be considered soft-core, these Scream Queen films were a genre unto themselves, flooding the shelves of the home video rental stores that were spreading like wildfire in the early days of home VCRs.

Twenty-five years ago, the Scream Queen movie was born.

1987 saw the release of what may have been the first Scream Queen film. There is some speculation as to which came first, *Nightmare Sisters* or the wonderfully-named *Sorority Babes in the Slime-Ball Bowl-O-Rama*. Both were helmed under the watchful eye of David DeCoteau and both starred the pivotal sexy trio Brinke Stevens, Michelle Bauer and Linnea Quigley, and, historically, *Sorority Babes* was shot first, whether or not it showed up on the video-store shelves first or not is irrelevant. Because, for all intents and purposes, it is *Nightmare Sisters* that arguably stands as the very first Scream Queen film.

Yes, some may point to Fred Olen Ray's *Hollywood Chainsaw Hookers*, but that movie, shot in 1986, starred only Quigley and Bauer and was minus Stevens. And yes, the three appeared in *Sorority Babes*, but not on equal ground. In that film,

Bauer and Stevens were among the titular Sorority Babes, but Quigley was a low-level criminal breaking into the bowling alley setting.

So it is *Nightmare Sisters* that brought the three together for Scream Queen fans for generations to come.

Written by Kenneth J. (*Dr. Alien*) Hall, *Nightmare Sisters*, in typical goofy-horror fashion, involves three homely sorority girls, Melody, Marcie and Mickey (Quigley, Stevens and Bauer), who are magically transformed, thanks to a séance and a flea-market crystal ball, into beautiful and overtly sexual demons. Hilarity, nudity and bloody hi-jinx ensues. The highlight of the film: a bubble-bath shared by the three lovely ladies of no-budget horror. According to Bauer in Femme Fatales Number One: "We dubbed in the sound of balloons squeaking to simulate the sound of breast-soaping".

Also known as *Sorority Succubus Sisters* (these little gems go through a lot of name changes), this film set the stage and tone for "Scream Queen" movies from there on out, for the next ten years. The formula for a classic "Scream Queen" movie is ample amounts of nudity, simulated sex far tamer than today's so-called "soft core", small-to-medium amounts of blood, and plenty of silly black comedy that never seemed overly mean or cruel. The actors and filmmakers were having fun, and the fun transferred to the audience. These movies would never win awards, but that wasn't the goal. These movies were made during the early hey-days of home video, when fledgling Blockbusters and West Coast Videos were struggling to keep product on the shelves. It was a good time for independent filmmakers, and the last refuge for those who cut their teeth on the now-dying drive-in theater market.

The best way to get the movies into the hands of the consumers? Use the Scream Queen formula that was pioneered and best used by DeCoteau and Olen Ray. Often imitated, rarely replicated. And no, this isn't an advertisement.

In the later years, as the early nineties aged to the mid-nineties, irony and sarcasm bled into the humor, turning it blacker. As cynicism took hold of the new youth, they demanded their violence more graphic, their sex a little more intense. Simple—though ample—nudity was no longer enough. Once again, the prevailing American notion was that video violence was begetting real-life violence. Audiences were becoming deprived of blood in the mainstream, and no amount of *Scream* movies would bring back the beloved gore. Horror fans were forced to turn to home video for their bloody jollies. But the Scream Queen era—sex, silliness, decapitations—they were long gone."[1]

So that was that, more than fifteen years ago. At the time, the term "Scream Queen" was a contentious one, particularly within the low- to no-budget horror community. During the height of the mom 'n pop video store boom, every indie film featured a busty victim on its cover, touting so-and-so as the latest "scream queen". It got worse when models who hadn't even been in a movie yet started billing themselves as such. It got so aggravating that a very public internet backlash grew rapidly, prompting events like "Women in Horror Month" (February) and Amy Lynn Best and her partners Jen Whilden and Heidi Martinuzzi forming

Taffy (Brinke Stevens) and Lisa (Michelle Bauer).
Photo courtesy Full Moon Pictures

one of the arguably first women-in-horror websites, Pretty-Scary.com, where "Scream Queen" was a title that had to be earned and not self-applied.

"It's more than just crying and having ketchup thrown on you," said no-less an authority than Troma's Lloyd Kaufman. "You not only have to be attractive, but you also have to have a big brain. You have to be frightened, you have to be sad, you have to be romantic."[2]

The trouble was, the term was ubiquitous and easy to slap onto the description of any female character in a movie, regardless of whether or not she even screamed in the film. It was already lazy reviewer short-hand and as difficult to do away with as "your" vs. "you're". For most die-hard fans of '80s horror, there were only three legitimate "Scream Queens" as far as we were concerned: Quigley, Stevens, and Bauer.[254]

Directed by David DeCoteau, *Sorority Babes in the Slimeball Bowl-O-Rama* was my gateway into the world of '80s low-budget horror. Already familiar with Quigley from her iconic role as "Trash", the punk stripperess in *Return of the Living Dead*, her frequent co-stars were as-yet a mystery to me at the time. It wasn't until a terribly-edited, chopped-up version of *Sorority Babes* popped up on USA's *Up All Night*, hosted in this instance by Gilbert Gottfried, that I understood what I was missing.

In the '80s, where other guys had Sports Illustrated swimsuit models plastered all over their walls, I had Quigley posing with Gunnar Hansen in a *Fangoria* pull-out poster of *Hollywood Chainsaw Hookers*. I had a poster of Stevens that wound up as the cover of *Femme Fatales #1* (which, as I mentioned so no one will ever forget, I would later write for extensively)—an incredibly risqué image with Stevens completely naked (though hands are strategically placed) save for a pair of vampire fangs[255]. The poster scandalized my mother, but I hung it next to a

Vampirella painted by Frank Frazetta, so the "art" may have nullified the prurience. What made *Sorority Babes* unique to me, however, was that it's provocative poster was featured in an article run by the slick *Premiere* magazine, in an article about video store outrageousness. That something decried as "moronic" would pop up in something with Tom Cruise frequently featured on the cover, my attention was gained to say the least. First and foremost because its title was incredible. Next to *The Incredibly Strange Creatures Who Stopped Living to Become Mixed-Up Zombies, Sorority Babes in the Slimeball Bowl-O-Rama* was the *Citizen Kane* of wonderfully ridiculous titles. (My previous favorite up until that point had been Harlan Ellison's short story "The Wine Has Been Left Open Too Long and the Memory Has Gone Flat.")

Originally titled "The Imp", Charles Band and Full Moon wisely chose a more evocative

---

[254] A runner-up, or perhaps a precursor, that remains an exception to the above rule is Jamie Lee Curtis, the most famous "final girl" in modern horror history, thanks to her starring role in what became the horror template, John Carpenter's *Halloween* (1978). Though Curtis went through a phase where she didn't want to acknowledge her horror roots (I kind of set that date, not on the 1984 release of *Trading Places*, in which she crossed over into proper "mainstream" roles, but in 1996, whereupon her husband, Christopher Guest, inherited the title of Baron of Haden-Guest and became the Lady Haden-Guest, but is it fair to blame a change in career on ascension to aristocracy?), she seems to have come to terms with it over the last decade or so. In particular, she made her first (and supposedly last) convention appearance at the November, 2012, Horrorhound convention, where proceeds from her surprisingly-high $80 autograph fee went to Children's Hospital Los Angeles.

[255] Which would make for complicated therapy sessions later in life after I came to know Brinke and Linnea personally and professionally.

title. (Although truth be told, there's some confusion as to which title came first. I've always been under the impression that "The Imp" was the film's working title from Sergei Hasenecz's script.) In a large part, the title is the film's major selling-point. It tells you all you need to know about the movie: this is going to be "trash", as JoBlo's Jason Adams famously called it, "but enjoyable trash. […]Sometimes a great title is all you need. I don't know who wouldn't want to immediately watch a movie called *Sorority Babes in the Slimeball Bowl-O-Rama*, but it sure as hell isn't me. "[3] It's a classic take on "The Monkey's Paw"[256], in which wishes are granted but with terrible consequences.

The "meat" of the film actually occurs early on, in a cut-to-the-chase set-up where three nerdy college guys (*Bloody Movie* (aka *Terror Night*)'s John Stuart Wildman as "Keith", *Night of the Demons'* Hal Havins as "Jimmie", *The Attic Expeditions'* Andras Jones as "Calvin") sitting around thinking about sex, drinking beer, and watching a "succubus" movie, decide it would be more fun to spy on the Tri-Delta Sorority initiation happening across campus. "Last year, there was this girl with enormous boobs and Babs made her wear a bra filled with worms, then do deep push-ups!"

"Babs" (the late Robin Rochelle Stille), the lead sister (alongside *Necromancer's* Carla Baron as "Frankie" and *Lady Avenger's* Kathi O'Brecht as "Rhonda"), is a proud sadist with obvious aspirations to become a dominatrix, wields a paddle the size of a surfboard and puts it to work on the initiates, Lisa (Michelle Bauer—billed here as "Michelle McClellen") and Taffy (Brinke Stevens), the latter being more reluctant. "It's supposed to build character and a bond of sisterhood," explains Lisa. "I think it's institutionalized sadism," responds a more-accurate Taffy.

The guys spy on the girls. The guys get caught. As "punishment" for breaking and entering, they're forced to accompany the girls on the final part of the initiation: break into the local strip mall's bowling alley and steal a trophy from the case. Since Babs' father owns the mall, the stage is set for additional terror, failure, and "a more painful punishment!"

Unfortunately, the chosen trophy is a vessel imprisoning a centuries' old imp/genie/hottentot (a rubbery puppet voiced by Dukey Flyswatter[257]), who grants wishes that come with terrible consequences. (Told ya.) The girls are turned into nymphomaniac monsters. The guys are eaten, screwed to death, dismembered. A severed head is bowled. ("Ooh! Too bad! Gutter head!") Meanwhile, the king nerd, Calvin, discovers punk burglar Spyder (Linnea Quigley) robbing the joint, and the two team up in the hopes of surviving the night.

Spyder: "That is about the stupidest damn story I've ever heard."

That's the long and short of *Sorority Babes*. Bad jokes, sex, nudity, gore, a puppet spewing one-liners ("Monster in the back seat! Oldest trick in the book!"). We weren't aware of it at the time, but this would be the quintessential "Scream Queen" movie. If the gore or sex was minimized, *Sorority Babes* and its ilk would fit nicely with Roger Corman's drive-in entries. Yes, everyone is horny, but it never feels prurient. People are tortured and murdered, but not to the extent that the poor bastards in movies like *Mark of the Devil*

"The Imp" himself. (Voiced by Dukey Flyswatter)
Photo Copyright Full Moon Pictures

---

[256] Written by W. W. Jacobs, first published in England in 1902, in the collection *The Lady of the Barge*.

[257] AKA Michael Sonye.

suffer. The nudity is more of the "nudie cutie" variety—bouncy instead of sleazy. There was a really weird innocence about the "Scream Queen" films. No boundary-pushing; just the tried-and-true elements that brought in the rental bucks at the video stores.

For many of us of the *Femme Fatales* generation, to qualify as a "Scream Queen" movie, one of the three had to have a presence in the film. Which is why *Hollywood Chainsaw Hookers* is a "Scream Queen" movie (Michelle and Linnea), and *Night of the Demons* counts as "SQ" (Linnea), but *Assault of the Killer Bimbos* (1988) does not (despite David DeCoteau serving as a producer). "The late 1980's were incredibly successful for the 'Scream Queen' trio: me, Linnea, and Michelle," Brinke told Tony Brown. "We had such a great time working together, and traveling to talk-shows and conventions across the country. We were very supportive of one another, always sharing job leads and helping out one another. Nowadays, we've sort of scattered and moved on in different ways—but I'll never forget that exciting heyday."[4]

As has been proven time and again, "Scream Queen" movies are difficult to review because the standards that most films are held to don't really apply. They're not quite sexploitation, so you can't simply dismiss the thin stories that take a back-seat to the sex, because the sex in "SQ" movies are playful and avoid succumbing to "soft-core". They're not outrageously gory, despite some inventive effects (the lipstick-through-the-breast sequence with Linnea in *Night of the Demons* was certainly never offered before—and indeed wasn't even trumped in the inevitable 2009 remake), so they weren't "only" geared towards gorehounds. They're made on extremely low budgets, but manage to succeed in spite of no money, usually through inventiveness or playfulness with the form. The acting is never so much bad as stylized—not quite "over-the-top", but at a heightened awareness of absurdity. They simply defy all attempts to pigeon-hole them in any other category. They are "Scream Queen" movies: pretty girls, outrageous situations, ridiculous villains, Kayro blood. If ever movies were made "just to entertain", it would be these. And yet, reviewers try their damnedest to treat them like any other film that came down the pike. In fact, reviewers attempting to serious critiques can't even agree on what works and what doesn't:

"The 'acting' in *Sorority Babes* leaves much to be desired, and indeed some of director David DeCoteau's attempts at humour are marred by the thespians he had on hand. While those involved are a little too old for college, Bauer has long been my favourite scream queen, so I'll suffer inconsistent logic to get to check her out...er...enjoy her performances. Fans of Quigley may want to look elsewhere, as she remains clad throughout, but those who want to see a bit of Stevens or Bauer will get what they're after."[5]

Or: "Performance-wise, the entire cast are all very enjoyable in their respective roles, especially Linnea Quigley (*Night of the Demons*) in the role of SpYder [*sic*], a tough a nails delinquent. Another performance of substantial note is Michelle Bauer in the role of Lisa, one of the pledges that have been given the task of stealing a trophy from the blowing alley."[6]

And: "Brinke Stevens is the only 80's scream queen that was ever capable of pathos. Even in light-hearted romps like this, there's a palpable sadness to her characters. Taffy might be one of the saddest. When it's her turn for a wish, she asks to be prom queen. The imp outfits her in a lacy white dress. She spins around and around in it, deliriously happy. Later on, of course, the dress is revealed to be nothing more than tattered garbage bags, and poor Taffy is forced to fight demons dressed like a deranged hobo for the rest of the film."[7]

But: "My absolute favorite aspect beyond the Imp (who rightfully should be in local comedy clubs delivering zingers), is Linnea Quigley who is an entertaining heroine as the punker Spider who refuses to run and hide and is more intent on stopping the Imp and battling the super strong monsters. Her corny pep talks matched with her dated apparel makes for one banner heroine. I'm still trying to figure out why no one in this popular bowling alley never found the Imp before these saps. But don't try to think about it. Director DeCoteau features some really funny gags including bowling with a severed head, and one guy's wish for the girl of his dreams who is so aggressive she begins to inflict bodily pain on him. And for what it's worth, the film still has a very gritty and barebones quality about it that shines for anyone interested in re-visiting some eighties grade-A cheese. Hell, say what you want about this movie, but it's a proud place holder in my collection. It's trash, there's no arguing that, but in the end it's entertaining trash and one I can enjoy if I want to remember horror comedies that were much more prone to creativity and originality and not just completely reliant on shocking us in to submission with its cynicism. *Sorority Babes in the Slime Ball Bowl-O-Rama* is a guilty pleasure and one I intend to indulge in for years to come."[8]

Perhaps ironically, becoming world-renowned as "Scream Queens" was never part of the plan for any of the notorious "Trio". Stevens, for instance, as self-professed "nerd" in high school, studied Marine Biology at Scripps University, modeling on the side to pay for classes. After years being marginalized under the "SQ" title, she began to consider returning to the science field. "'When I was educated as a marine biologist, back in the late '70s, I worked on dolphin communications experiments. At that time, dolphin research was extremely unpopular because they were killing thousands of dolphins a day in tuna nets, and the navy was doing secret experiments with dolphins. Since then, dolphins have become extremely popular. Suddenly, doors are open that weren't open 20 years ago. I've been very tempted to go back to work with dolphins at Sea World, either here or in Orlando. I love doing animal behavior work. It's kind of an escape fantasy, and I haven't yet actually pursued it; perhaps when I retire.'"[9]

The "Scream Queen" phenomenon reached its apex in the late '80s when the mainstream media started to take notice. The aforementioned article in *Premiere* took a lot of underground horror fans by surprise, to say nothing of a 20/20 profile featuring Linnea gracing the family time airwaves. As the video market burgeoned, Quigley's name was indelibly tagged to low-budget commerce tailored for the medium [.] But by the time that she landed a spot on ABC's *20/20*, her phylum of film-formulaically link of promiscuous sex-was fading fast. Inept management had encouraged Quigley to approve quantity over quality. Her popularity floundering—adrift in a surfeit of nondescript splatter films Quigley tried to abdicate as "the country's #1 scream Queen." But it was too late. Still pigeonholed in a genre that's declared uncommercial, Quigley is hardly idle. As a representative for Aria Guitars, she makes public appearances. And drawing upon her earlier experience as one of The Skirts, a rock 'n' roll band, Quigley recently recorded nine songs for a CD cut in Philadelphia. [...] 'I loved the horror films, I didn't mind. I think that the press picked up on my legitimate interest and decided, 'Here is somebody who really enjoys this.' I never felt, 'Oh, I'm going to be typecast and do only cheesy movies.' I embraced it. "If I regret anything it's that, at the time, I didn't realize how much money my movies were making. I really should have asked for a lot more money. The people who made the movies financially profited—but I didn't,'" wrote Scapperotti.

"Quigley also grieves that the heirs to her matriarchal title have trivialized its former significance: "Everyone who had done a home movie or whatever, and wore little clothing at these conventions, were calling themselves scream queens and were going around selling things. Consequently, neither films nor conventions are paying like they used to pay. They would pay real good money to have us [authentic scream queens] appear, but, all of a sudden, these amateurs would pay their own way or do anything just to be there. That hurt people who were legitimately working. The people who put on the shows figured, 'Hey, as long as we have warm bodies here.' they stopped making the small budget films. Everybody with a Camcorder decided they could make movies, and a lot of really bad junk got out there and gutted the market. You can't just duplicate what a lot of talented people have done.'"[10]

"'The 'scream queen' thing really hurt us, and what we really wanted to do. I was trying to take on more mature roles, and get away from the bimbo kind of slaughterhouse thing. I wanted to do more comedy. I didn't want to get stuck in the 'murder! haunted house' genre or perpetually play the coed who gets slaughtered. I think the scream queen thing may have applied more back in the '80s, before there even was a term for it. We were all having a lot of fun doing the comedy-horrors. Then as we started to take our roles and our lives more seriously, career-wise, the scream queen thing came along. Some people, who somehow didn't realize that the phase so quickly came and went, just kept hanging on to it-even though 'scream queen' no longer applied. It died a long time before those people let it,'" Bauer told Dan Scapperotti. "In 1994, she threw in the towel 'That was the low point for me. I was getting offers for films I didn't want to do anymore. I was getting requests to be the 'boobs' or 'let's have a love scene.' It wasn't that I minded doing it, it was just that I was getting cheap offers and I really was frustrated. I was getting a bad attitude, and I didn't even want to work anymore. That was when I initially started to struggle with this retirement thing. Then when I did go into retirement, I took the time off but I thought, 'I still want to work, but I don't want to go out for the same stuff that I had been doing for so long.' Her frequent director, Fred Olen Ray, notes that when Bauer made a comeback in 1997, 'She started to pick and choose. Other girls who were in that 'scream queen' business are still trying to wring money out of it. They're hanging on to something that never amounted to much, even during its peak period.'"[11]

"Nobody really wanted the label [of Scream Queen]. It was the kiss of death—'Oh god, you don't want that. It limits you and it's not cool'. Everybody wanted to be thought of as a serious actress. Michelle and Brinke and I were doing these things, people would get down on us— 'Oh, you do *those* types of movies'. [But] we had fun—we became like a little family while doing these crazy movies. It wasn't cool to be a 'Scream Queen' at all. But then I did the *People* and *Premiere Magazines* and a lot of national TV shows and all of a sudden it became popular and everyone else wanted to do it too. I think [a Scream Queen] was suddenly the hip thing to be. I don't think a lot of them had ever watched the movies or got into the genre, it was just 'Hey, that's in, let's do it!'. That's still happening, actually—which is why I've avoided the conventions for so long. It got to be a joke. It was very weird. People were getting their wives for movies, girls were doing their own videos—it almost became a prostitution ring, women becoming 'Scream Queens'. Now, the more controversy you can generate, the higher your fee can be. Halle Berry! Five-hundred thousand dollars to show her breasts! Please! Why was that a major thing? That's the only reason people went to see [*Swordfish*]!" Linnea told me in 2001 for *Femme Fatales.* "I did get to a point where I would tell them 'if you want me to take off my top, you're paying me more money'. It sounds crude, but it was a truth. That was one of the reasons they were seeking me out, so why not? *Graduation Day* (1981)—the movie I did a loooong time ago—ugh! The reason I had gotten that part was the girl that was cast originally didn't want to take her top off. At that point it wasn't cool to do that. It was supposed to wreck your career to do that. It got to the point in the scene and she said 'I'm not gonna do it! I'm not gonna do it!' So they fired her and hired me. So in a lot of ways, I actually got started by doing something that everyone else thought was the wrong thing to do. It would be interesting to see where that girl is now."[12]

"Horror was the only genre you could jump into that was a director's medium, and you could also produce a film without name stars and still get it sold. It was a very small pool of talent back then, prior to the internet, so you would refer friends to friends. For example, I'd worked on a short film with Linnea Quigley and she referred me to Michelle Bauer. Then I was introduced to Brinke Stevens, and we all became fast friends and started working together. We would cast through a publication called *Dramalogue*, and if you enjoyed working with an actress, they'd be referred on to other directors like Fred Olen Ray," DeCoteau told Nathaniel Thompson. "In the mid-'80s there were only about six of us who were full-time B-movie directors in Los Angeles; at least, ones who were always in pre-production, full production, or post. We all got to know each other pretty well. It was myself, Fred Ray, Jim Wynorski, David Prior, and a couple of others. We were all working nonstop in L.A.; it was a very busy time. I had originally met Fred through his editor, Miriam Preissel, who edited *Creepozoids* and introduced me. I'd already seen articles on Fred in *Fangoria* so I was really pleased to meet him. I was a fan and still am!"[13]

"*Slimeball* was my first lead in anything and I loved it. The hours were dreadful. The accommodations lackluster, and the general attitude of the production team was one of mercenary cynicism. In that regard, not altogether different from the Nightmare production team. They just didn't seem to care if it was good. Speed and economy were the guiding motivations but the cast were funny (Hal Havins and Buck Flower), gorgeous (Michelle Bauer and Robin Stille), and legendary (Linnea and Brinke Stevens), and I was making $50 bucks a day to get chased around by zombies and eat free donuts. I was a happy boy," said Andras

Jones. "Linnea and I got to be pretty good buddies during the filming, and Brinke was always very sweet and encouraging. Michelle...well...what can I say? I was a healthy 18 year old hopped up on coffee and sugar. It's OK to have crushes on two B-movie goddesses at once right?"[14]

"Significantly, most of the people involved with Sorority are still working today, over 20 years later. Although he appears to be concentrating mostly on gay-themed films at this stage in his career, director David DeCoteau has a long and winding resume full of fun junk like this: *Dr. Alien* (1989), *Beach Babes from Beyond* (1993), *Creepozoids* (1987), and of course, *Nightmare Sisters* (1987). Linnea, Michelle, and Brinke are all still going strong: Brinke appeared in ten films in 2009 alone. Genre legend Buck Flower had a hell-for-leather run through the lower-rungs of the movie business, acting, writing, producing, and growling his way through hundreds of brain-boiling B & Z movies before his time finally ran out in 2004. Producer Charles Band is still a major figure in indie-film, and his Full Moon production company continues to crank out nutball opuses like the *Gingerdead Man* series. Soundtrack composer Guy Moon has racked up an armful of Emmys over the last two decades for his work in children's television[258]. Even the voice of the Imp, Dukey Flyswatter, managed to carve out a niche for himself. When he wasn't acting in cult-films like *Surf Nazis Must Die*, he was fronting shock-rockers Haunted Garage. A bonafide Hollywood legend, Dukey still pops up in odd places here and there, and is plotting out both a Haunted Garage resurrection and a stage play as we speak. Carla Baron joined the surprisingly lengthy list of former cult actresses turned (ahem) "psychics". Unfortunately, Robin Rochelle, a glamazonian, scene-gulping, b-goddess-in-the-making most remembered as the Final Girl in the original *Slumber Party Massacre*, committed suicide in 1996, after a long battle with alcoholism[259]. Sorry, I don't really know how to put a positive spin on that one."[15]

Femme Fatales writer Jason Paul Collum was one of the first to uncover this bit of news. While writing a retrospective for *Slumber Party Massacre*—a movie that introduced us to both Stevens and Stille, his search for "one elusive actress turned into something of an obsession for me. Several key players had simply retired from the business, but applying a tail to Robin Stille, who played the heroine in the 1982 original, always seemed futile yet tangible. The Screen Actors Guild listed the actress as a member; nevertheless, Stille's agent had no idea where she resided. Her former cast mates and directors said they had occasionally sighted her a year or two ago, but everyone could only generically conclude that Stille lived somewhere in Los Angeles. Then one actor shared a rumor: Stille had passed away. [...] Brinke Stevens, who co-starred with Stille in two movies, was a guest at a Chicago convention. Rhonda Baughman, a Stevens fan and poet, confirmed Stille's death in the conversation. Stevens was immediately enlightened to the facts [...] Robin Rochelle Stille took her life on February 9, 1996 in Burbank, CA. Her passing is doubly tragic: she left behind a family, and the industry she had strived so hard to impress never even knew she was gone. Stille may not have acknowledged herself as a celebrity, but a legion of fans didn't underestimate her work. The opening of Rhonda Baughman's book of poetry is prefaced with 'In Memory of Robin Stille'."[16]

As things are wont to do, the "Scream Queen"-type movie regained a resurgence over the last decade, largely thanks to the original principals revisiting their past sub-genre to play with the tropes that they themselves developed. DeCoteau, Stevens, Quigley, and Bauer first reunited in 2012 for *1313: Cougar Cult*, the description, according to IMDb: "Rufus, Darwin, and Coopersmith are three nerdy, but hunky young college students who score themselves a dream summer job working at a swanky mansion owned by wealthy and sexy middle-aged

---

[258] Including *The Fairly OddParents* and *The Grim Adventures of Billy & Mandy*.

[259] "Even some horror fans are hard-pressed to recognize her name. She went by a couple—Robin Rochelle as well as Robin Stille. That said, the Philadelphia born actress (11/24/61) came to Hollywood like so many others—seeking fame, but found only a taste of it. Tragically that quest ended when, supposedly disheartened by her lack of career success and/or fueled by drink, she took her own life in Burbank, California in 2/9/96 at the age of 35 and was laid to rest in Rose Hill Cemetery."—Keehnen, Owen. Celluloid Casket Case 1: Robin Rochelle." Racks and Razors.com. http://racksandrazors.com/robin.html

babes Clara, Victoria, and Edwina. However, the gals turn out to be a coven of deadly witches who transform into flesh-eating cougars who need fresh young man meat in order to live forever." This led to other sendups like *3 Scream Queens* (2014) and Charles Band's *Trophy Heads* (2014) in which the trio play variations of themselves.

(As Dr. Rhonda points out in the following chapter, Amy Lynn Best and I, through our Happy Cloud Pictures production company, produced our own "Scream Queens" movie in 2010, *Demon Divas and the Lanes of Damnation*. For years, Amy brought together dozens of actresses working in the horror industry and attempted to find a replacement for the "Scream Queen" moniker. "Demon Diva" was the one she liked best ("Spicy Sister" was another). The attempt was to reunite the Trio but scheduling conflicts prevented Quigley and Bauer from participating in our six-day marathon nightmare.)

As always, everything old is new again. In August, 2016, Full Moon released a beautifully remastered version of *Sorority Babes* on Blu-Ray, offering never-before-seen behind-the-scenes footage and outtakes. Today, just as then, the film's popularity seems like a surprise. Because of the title, the movie set a standard for outrageous direct-to-video marketing. Because of the sweetness of the leads, and the over-all playfulness of the sadistic fun, the movie is a staple for all genre video collectors. Say what you want about *Sorority Babes*—it's cheap, it's silly, it's this, it's that—it is its own thing: critic proof.

NOTES

[1] Watt, Michael. "Nightmare Sisters." *Femme Fatales* May 2002 Volume 11 Number 5/Volume 11 Number 6

[2] Arnold, Thomas K. 20007. "Three screams for these stars." USA Today. April 27.
http://usatoday30.usatoday.com/life/movies/news/2007-04-26-scream-queens_N.htm

[3] Adams, Jason. 2016. "AWFULLY GOOD: SORORITY BABES IN THE SLIMEBALL BOWL-O-RAMA + MORTAL KOMBAT 2." JoBlo.com. May 18. http://www.joblo.com/movie-news/awfully-good-sorority-babes-in-the-slimeball-bowl-o-rama-mortal-kombat-2-279

[4] Brown, Tony. 2001. "The Brinke Stevens Interview." The Old Hockstatter Place.
http://www.hockstatter.com/interviews/brinkeinterview.shtml

[5] Devon B. 2006. "Sorority Babes in the Slimeball Bowl-o-Rama (1988)" Digital Retribution.com. October 30, 2006.
http://www.digital-retribution.com/reviews/dvd/0537.php

[6] Den Boer, Michael. 2012. "Sorority Babes in the Slimeball Bowl-O-Rama." Ten Thousand Bullets.com. April 10.
http://10kbullets.com/reviews/s/sorority-babes-in-the-slimeball-bowl-o-rama/

[7] McIntyre, Ken. 2009. "Sorority Babes". Movies About Girls.com. May 23.
http://www.moviesaboutgirls.com/2009/05/sorority-babes-in-slimeball-bowl-o-rama.html

[8] Vasquez, Felix. 2010. "Sorority Babes in the Slimeball Bowl-O-Rama (1988)." Cinema Crazed.com. October 13.
http://cinema-crazed.com/blog/2010/10/13/sorority-babes-in-the-slimeball-bowl-o-rama-1988/

[9] Scapperotti, Dan. "Scream Queens The Originals: Brinke Stevens." *Femme Fatales*. Vol. 8 No 4. P. 18

[10] Scapperotti, Dan. "Scream Queens The Originals: Linnea Quigley." *Femme Fatales Magazine*. Vol. 8, No 4. P. 11

[11] Scapperotti, Dan. "Scream Queens The Originals: Michelle Bauer." *Femme Fatales Magazine*. Vol. 8, No 4. P. 18

[12] Watt, 2002

[13] Thompson, Nathaniel. "Bad Boys and Scream Queens: An Interview with David DeCoteau." Mondo-Digital.com.
http://www.mondo-digital.com/decoteautalk.html

[14] Brown, 2001.

[15] McIntyre, 2009.

[16] Collum, Jason Paul. 2000. "Cut Down: Abridged Bio of the Enigmatic Actress, Who Took Her Own Life at Age 35." Femme Fatales Vol. 9, No. 3. August 11. P. 14

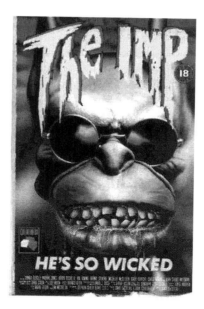

SORORITY BABES IN THE SLIMEBALL BOWL-O-RAMA (1988): TAKE TWO

By Dr. Rhonda Baughman

"In a bowling alley from Hell, there's only one way to score ..."

Real critics, as opposed to the grammatically-challenged internet generation of socially-awkward fan-fic writers, should be able to strip away personal bias and opinion to simply discuss and review why a film does or does not work. I'll do both in this epic review—be personal, then be objective. So, full disclosure: I have met and interviewed six cast members [260] from this film and befriended three of them[261] for over twenty years—and although each and

---

[260] Original Michelle Bauer interview for *Sirens of Cinema* magazine V.2, No. 14, 2008 'From Murder & Mayhem to Marathon Mom: My Interview of a Lifetime with Michelle Bauer', reprinted for *www.micro-shock.com* in 2009, and combined with a second interview, 'The Second Coming of Hollywood's Heart' alongside Brinke Stevens and Linnea Quigley interviews for Grindhouse Purgatory issue 4, Oct. 2014. The following are from *www.micro-shock.com*. 'Webcams and Hog Wings: My Dinner with Fred Olen Ray and Michelle Bauer', November 2012, 'Brinke Stevens on Halloween', Sept. 2009, 'Brinke Stevens on Quicksand', August 2009, interviews with Andras Jones 'Not Your Average Political Prettyboy', Jan. 2008 and 'Accidentally Initiated in 2012: A Book Review of *Accidental Initiations (in the Kabbalistic Tree of Olympia)*', Jan. 2012, Interview with Dukey Flyswatter (Michael Sonye) 'Hey You, in the Front Row—You Want a Wish?' Nov. 2012, 'Oysters with Dukey Flyswatter, December 2013, and 'An Acting Lesson with Hal Havins', December 2013. Havins and Flyswatter pieces reprinted in Grindhouse Purgatory Issue 6.

[261] The author of this piece has not officially located 'Sorority Babes' characters Rhonda and Frankie (Kathi OBrecht and Carla Baron, respectively) (BB), nor third nerd Keith (John Stuart Wildman). Brinke Stevens tells the author that she ran into him a few years ago, indicating he now worked behind the camera in some capacity. Director David DeCoteau has not responded to email requests for an interview. Veteran character actor Buck Flower (billed in the film as C.D. LaFleur) passed away in 2004. Dukey Flyswatter told this author they had kept in touch for many years up until Flower's death. And finally, the author was preparing to locate Robin Stille (who passed away in 1996 and was billed in 'Sorority Babes' as Robin Rochelle) for an interview when the author learned of her death in 1998. Although this information is readily available now, the author established personal contact with the early web hosts of imdb.com, who confirmed Stille's death. So, instead, Baughman would dedicate her book *Carnal Capers in Canton, OH Book II: Logging Logorrhea* to Stille. An overly excited UK fan would contact Baughman demanding personal and/or intimate knowledge of Stille the author, in fact, did not possess. Stille's family would later contact Baughman and offer a heartfelt 'thank you' for the book dedication and explain the family's reluctance to speak on the matter further. Journalist Jason Paul Collum, in *Femme Fatales* volume 9,

every one, both friends and interviewees, remains confused by my unwavering affection and fanatical devotion to this film, they all lovingly support it. In fact, *Sorority Babes'* writer Sergei Hasenecz told me of his own disbelief, the first time a fan gushed how fabulous the film really was … "I thought it was a joke," he tells me during an interview conducted for issue six *Grindhouse Purgatory* and this volume of *Movie Outlaw*.

It's no joke—that this film has obtained and maintained cult status[262] over the years for many reasons—and it still remains relevant—both well into the 21st century, and well over twenty years after it first debuted on the big screen[263] (4). Lead film nerd Calvin, star Andras Jones, would tell me this film was symbolic for me, in fact, the film is my very own "personal sync". And he would know[264] (5). So, when Jones claimed *Sorority Babes* was a sync film for me—he really wasn't kidding. And it goes back long before I would begin my decades of interaction with the film's cast.[265] (6)

---

issue 3, acknowledged the dedication as well. The UK fan, in a final note to Baughman, sent a photo of Stille's gravestone, also now readily available as an online image. Finally, the real name of the author of this piece, noting that there is a character named Rhonda in *Sorority Babes*, uses her real name to write—BUT decided to use a stage name when acting—she chose Rachelle Williams (changing the 'o' in Rochelle, from Robin Stille's billing to an 'a' and taking Williams from Wendy O., lead singer of the Plasmatics). Both Stille and Williams would commit suicide before Baughman could interview them—and this is how Baughman paid tribute. Journalist Jason Paul Collum, in *Femme Fatales* volume 9, issue 3, acknowledged the dedication as well.

(bb) *http://carlabaron.net/*—This may very well be her—now an "Internationally renowned psychic". In my birthday interview with scream queen Debra Lamb, I was fortunate enough to be on the receiving end of her psychic gift as well: 'Interview with a Lamb: Parts I and II', *http://dorkswithoutfaces.com/newmicroshock/interview-with-a-lamb-the-magic-of-scream-queen-debra-lamb-part-ii/* (2011 and 2013).

[262] *Sorority Babes* would eventually gain a more widespread cult following from those, this author included, who watched it on the USA Network's 'Up All Night' (*https://www.youtube.com/watch?v=jIAJftR-Hw*) with a particular sync for that video—host Rhonda Shear and I share the same name and the theme is 'education' (my current field). And, while using a restroom literally, to catch a breather during the bowling alley demon battle, a snippet of the dialogue between Linnea Quigley's Spider and Andras Jones' Calvin, can be heard as a sample in the Static-X song 'I'm With Stupid.'

[263] (May 30, 2015)—According to writer Sergei Hasenecz: "*Sorority Babes* did get a theatrical release, playing in downtown LA. One theater. A grindhouse called the Cameo, the glory days of which must have passed decades before. The Cameo usually showed triple-feature, third- and fourth-run Spanish language movies, but for one weekend, *Sorority Babes* premiered there. I went to see it with a friend of mine. Walking into the small lobby, you could smell a toilet which had overflowed. Fortunately, the odor hadn't reached the seating area. The sound system was a single speaker hanging from a nail above the screen. There were maybe a dozen people scattered about, all of them speaking Spanish and none of them paying much attention to anything being shown onscreen. A battered trailer for an old Cantinflas movie was playing: *Por mis pistolas* (1968). When *Sorority Babes* began, the audience chatted through it as well. No one seemed to be watching the movie until the scene where Michelle Bauer pulls off her top. And there was SILENCE. Every head had turned toward the screen, every eye fixed. Someone (I'm not making this up) whispered, 'Ay, chihuahua!' There was amazement in that voice, perhaps even a tone of reverence. Then the scene was over and they all went back to their conversations."

[264] A. *https://www.youtube.com/playlist?list=PLp0mEPvjqOmR_-a0nSm-Eit2m_TuBdmy0*

B. *http://g8ors.blogspot.com/2012/03/striking-balance-with-andras-jones.html*

[265] First contact with Brinke Stevens and Linnea Quigley occurred in 1989—when author was 10 years old. First personal meeting with both was in 1992 at the infamous Zombie Jamboree in Pittsburgh, PA. Author would establish internet contact with Andras Jones in 1997 and first meeting would occur at Theo's Java Club in Rock Island, IL for a solo concert performed by Jones. Brinke Stevens would drive the author to meet both Hal Havins and Dukey Flyswatter in Beverly Hills and Hollywood, respectively, in December 2013, for the author's first acting lesson as her alter ego with coach Havins and to dine at an oyster bar with food connoisseur Flyswatter. It would be the first time in over twenty years that Stevens would be reunited with her costars. Further syncs includes: A. Baughman, in a sixth grade spelling bee, held at a mall in Canton, OH would cut and style a tee (stolen from her father's drawer) to fashion into the style Quigley's Spider character wore in the film. Baughman had a very large cheering section and was too young to completely understand why—breasts did not really happen until after high school. Baughman would come in third place. B. Andras Jones would tour the US as a solo musician in the late '90s and in support, Baughman turned her mother's basement into a speakeasy/house concert venue aptly named The Taffy Pull—as homage to Brinke's death scene in *Sorority Babes* and Jones used the venue for a wildly successful performance in April 2001. C. Although I cannot verify the film being played on the TV that Jones watched in *Sorority Babes* is *Creepozoids'*, I do think the music is from the film, which in the end, would subliminally insert itself and lead to me interviewing *Creepozoids* star Ken Abraham,

I would stumble across the film in a local video store chain in Canton, Ohio—Videotime. My grandparents would drop me off and let me look around for hours, much in the same way some children would ask to go to the playground or the zoo. Eventually, I would be issued my own pink, laminated rental card—at 10 years old. I spent many hours of my formative years at Videotime, among the rows and high shelves of VHS, exploring the box cover art, eventually gravitating to the rolled and displayed posters, and badass small and large cardboard standees. I prayed the laminated tags for my favorite films were present for me to grab and hold in my sweaty little palms—that is, my favorite films generally had one copy, hence one tag to take to the rental counter.

And it was the box cover art that first drew me in—I came from a family of bowlers, and although the gene skipped me, I did enjoy lessons from my grandfather, Frank A. "Brooklyn" Baughman. The same man who drove me to Videotime each week, was a well-known and wildly respected Amateur Sports Hall of Fame inductee, and with bowling just one of his accomplishments, he bowled until he was 88, and followed the sport until his death in 2010. My mother and father were also both league bowlers, with the latter bowling several perfect games, making the local paper, and only bowing out after a major accident in 2014. I enjoyed watching the PBA on TV with my grandfather; those whispery announcers seemed so mysterious and exotic, as the pro bowlers would strut their form, going for the big money— and my grandfather never tired of explaining complicated lingo to me like Brooklyn, bagger, beak, tap, turkey, and top weight, to name a few. The same terms I would use in my 8th grade algebra class to score an 'A' and in high school during my budding career as a journalist for local paper, The Canton Repository, when I reviewed *Kingpin*. That same paper where my father would work and both he and his father would be featured for their bowling career highlights. Thus, an actual bowling joke in the film, which should have been lost on the younger me, was actually understood and found to be bloody hysterical.

Later, in 2007, Mike Watt, author of this book and owner of Happy Cloud Pictures would write and direct a feature called *Demon Divas in the Lanes of Damnation*[266] (AA), an homage to *Sorority Babes*; I jumped at the chance to have my alter ego, Rachelle Williams, act opposite screen sirens, make out in a hot tub, and run around in a bowling alley. I did not get paddled, but ultimately, Brinke Stevens' demon embodiment did rip out my bitchy bi character's spine onscreen. And even today, in 2015, as a college professor, I have a high-performing student who bowls both professionally and altruistically, teaching the sport to underprivileged children. My sync, indeed, runs deep with the elements of this film[267] (7).

The film itself contains thematic elements of both 'One Thousand and One Nights' and 'The Monkey's Paw', with C.D. LaFleur's[268] janitor characterization even going so far as to mention it: "Old King Soloman who bottled up all the genies, you know like you read about?" Director DeCoteau seemed a fan of the *Revenge of the Nerds*, certainly, if not also the classics involving fraternity/sorority hazings, and writer Hasenecz would agree: "The only change I was asked to make in the story was to add more nerd comedy at the beginning. David was stuck on the movie *Revenge of the Nerds*. He loved it. Again, it was a movie I hadn't seen, so David described to me what that movie was about, and I tried to go from there," he said.

---

http://dorkswithoutfaces.com/newmicroshock/dying-for-a-deadly-embrace-jerking-off-in-an-interview-with-ken-abraham/. D. Obviously, my name is Rhonda and a there is character in the movie of the same name. E. Many *Sorority Babes* characters repeatedly run past a claw machine in the bowling alley—the claw machine also played into a ridiculously large part of my childhood, with both my father and grandfather taking me to several venues, including a bowling alley, to play multiple machines in order to placate a younger me. F. The story told by janitor C.D. LaFleur, mentions the trouble with Uncle Impy "began 30 years ago, in March", which is the month of this author's birthday. G. If you Google 'Dave McCabe', you get the front man for the UK band The Zutons and a video on YouTube entitled 'Juniors 5th Birthday Bowling.' Seriously.

[266] *http://dorkswithoutfaces.com/newmicroshock/demon-divas-and-the-lanes-of-damnation/*

[267] Once you have identified your own sync, you'll understand.

[268] Aka George "Buck" Flower.

Finally, Imp voice actor Dukey Flyswatter, indicated to me, during our initial interview, and again over oysters, that he channeled *Little Shop of Horrors'* Audrey.

By now, the internet is awash in amateurs offering simplistic plot synopses for the film—all mentioning, to some degree; boobs, low-budget, magic, scream queens[269](8), bowling alley, frat nerds, sorority bitches, demons, unlucky pledges, paddling, crotchety janitors. Ask any red-blooded, American male (female, in this case) what *Sorority Babes* was about—and we might say *the trio*, who would unite in this film, as well as *Nightmare Sisters*, *The Trouble with Barry*, and *Cougar Cult*[270] (9). There are sites dedicated to *Babes'* censorship, specifically the UK/German releases, each missing about a minute of footage[271] (10). Moreover, the music has not had an official soundtrack release, and with other recent amazing offerings from vinyl vendors such as Death Waltz, Mondo, Waxwork Records, One Way Static, and Strange Disc Records, I am patiently waiting for the day my true vinyl love is released. In the meantime, I have actually ordered, from the UK, my Greg Stone LP—which contains the song featured during the opening credits[272] (11, 12).[273]

Even after all of the above, *Movie Outlaw* readers might be asking why this film *still* matters. Shame on you—but I will tell you. First, the film covers enough ground for a doctoral dissertation: from tropes (DD)[274], magazine mentions (EE)[275], title recognition (FF)[276]—to

---

[269] This author only acknowledges the term 'scream queen' in reference to Brinke Stevens, Linnea Quigley, and Michelle Bauer. Special consideration also given to Jamie Lee Curtis, Adrienne Barbeau, and Debra Lamb. This term does not refer to either my alter ego, or anyone born after 1978. The end.

[270] This author obtained her doctorate in 2008 and rarely bothers with non-academic sources, unless they are her own. And the ONLY excuse she has for updating Wikipedia—would be the Wiki for *Sorority Babes in the Slimeball Bowl-O-Rama*. Which she did—while writing this piece—when she noticed a fact needing updated. I.e. originally, the trio were in only two films (*Sorority Babes* and *Nightmare Sisters*), but now with *Cougar Cult* (2012) and *The Trouble with Barry* (2013), the number is now four.

[271] *http://www.movie-censorship.com/report.php?ID=341591* While the US version is uncut, trailers often lack Dukey Flyswatter's voice as the Imp- and instead, inserted some scratchy, synth robot voiceover. One DVD release contains trailer reels, but other than that, even the Cult Video DVD release is horribly lacking in extras or commentary.

[272] *http://musicrareobscure.blogspot.com/2013/04/greg-stone.html* "In 1987, Greg released the single "That's Where the Happy People Go/Here in the Darkness" which managed to peak at #34 on Billboard's Hot Dance Music/Club Play chart." The song was written by Bob Parr (E.T. the Extra-Terrestrial, performer: "Willie").

[273] Watch the credits for '*Sorority Babes*': Third Assistant Director: David McCabe, pseudonym for David DeCoteau and fictional demon raiser in *Sorority Babes*; Christopher Endicott went on to crew/sound/FX fantastic films like *Puppet Master II*, *Freaked*, *I Am Legend*, to mention only a handful; Craig Caton would go on to crew and offer FX to so many cult classics, such as *A Nightmare on Elm Street 4: The Dream Master* (also starring Andras Jones), *Tremors*, and *Solarbabies*, to name a few AND blockbusters like *Jurassic Park* and *Apollo 13*; Composer—Guy Moon, who began his career as a composer for *Creepozoids*, the same music featured in *Sorority Babes*, went on to Primetime Emmy nominations, ASCAP, Annie, and BMI awards, so really ... why is the *Sorority Babes* soundtrack not on vinyl? This author discovered Moon again while on the set of *Take Away Spirit* (CC) (*http://oneshotproductions.bizland.com/takeawayspiritthemovie/*) As-yet-unreleased Jess Franco film which will one day grace a volume of *Movie Outlaw*.) and watching Nickelodeon with the director's daughter. And with the success of Horrordecor.com, why are there not Uncle Impy plushies? And 'Sex', Zoom Zoom's memorable song in the film, used for Brinke and Michelle's "shower" scene—why is that band not on tour? I remember, at a very young age, I so loved the music to *Sorority Babes*, that I would call Camelot Music and ask if they had Guy Moon or Zoom in stock. I would inevitably get a 'What in God's name are you saying?' And then a dial tone. S'okay—I will win this fight. I won it with the song from *Maniac* I adored ('Goin to a Showdown' on Don Armando's 2nd Avenue Rhumba Band's 'Deputy of Love' album) and the EPIC *Slumber Party Massacre II* theme 'Hell's Cafe'—band of the same name, apparently, on the cd compilation 'Tales from the Edge: Volumes Nine and Ten', and I own these catchy tunes now, too—on vinyl and cd respectively.

[274]) *http://tvtropes.org/pmwiki/pmwiki.php/Main/BeCarefulWhatYouWishFor* and
http://tvtropes.org/pmwiki/pmwiki.php/Main/CantGetAwayWithNuthin and
http://tvtropes.org/pmwiki/pmwiki.php/Main/ThePunishment and
http://tvtropes.org/pmwiki/pmwiki.php/Main/PunishedWithUgly and
http://tvtropes.org/pmwiki/pmwiki.php/Main/CoolAndUnusualPunishment and
http://tvtropes.org/pmwiki/pmwiki.php/Main/SealedEvilInACan and

actual literary and educational arenas (GG)[277], and two additional lifelong fans (it's really not just me out here) weighed in:

"*Sorority Babes* feels almost like an adventure movie, like something you could create in your backyard as a child. But there are adult themes and vulgar language ... which come to thin in it were also present in my backyard. The deaths are lovably cartoony—this is when special effects were still just that ... special." (HH)[278]

"There's something 'raw' about the movie—it's so low-budget I feel like I am there on set. And coming into closer contact with my fuzzy childhood." (II)[279]

I agree with both fans above—and I can say that when I watched it, then and now, I walked away from this film happy—I'd had a good time—almost as if this adventure could have happened to me. In other words, I didn't walk away from this movie feeling cheated, or feeling like the world was doomed, or that humanity was a terrible thing. Furthermore, to the best of my cinematic knowledge, while not vase per se, is definitely rich in the B niche: The three lead females, and two of the nerds, as well as one janitor, and the Imp's voice actor—are seven consistent actors—that is, they have a style, technique, mark all their very own, and industry profiles of considerable weight. Even before I began looking these people up, to meet them, interview them, befriend them, I was in love with this movie. It's my comfort film, my celluloid binky. When it's on (how long is the film?), I have 80 minutes of fucking peace— which if you can find that anywhere in the world now, congratulations. What would make it *more* peaceful for me is if there was a proper DVD release, a complete Scream Factory style addition with many, many interviews, commentaries, and frankly, an Imp keychain.

The film opens with a black background and hot pink letters appearing to a funky, soulful tune 'Here in the Darkness'—which is both ominous and playful. I would see the same technique, although perhaps unintentionally, in the Ryan Gosling flick *Drive*—which opens the same way as *Sorority Babes*—hot pink lettering (although cursive and *Babes* is in late '80s caps) on a dark background, with a badass and memorable song playing as the credits flash.

Three fraternity dorks, two concerned with T&A, one concerned more with what's on the TV, drink, eat chips, banter, and venture out of the comfort of their man cave to a local sorority (which seems to be the same house used in *Linnea Quigley's Horror Workout*, probably

---

http://tvtropes.org/pmwiki/pmwiki.php/Main/WinToExit and

http://tvtropes.org/pmwiki/pmwiki.php/Funny/TrappedInTheCloset and

http://tvtropes.org/pmwiki/pmwiki.php/Main/ClosedCircle ... I have to stop here because I don't want to actually write the dissertation here. Yet.

Actually, one more trope: The gender-reverse *She's All That*:
http://tvtropes.org/pmwiki/pmwiki.php/Main/TheGlassesComeOff Glasses on = nerd. Glasses off = hottie. By the end of *Sorority Babes*, both Wildman and Jones emphasizes the trope a decade before *She's All That* would even come along, which would also usher in countless comedic skits and my own alter ego, Rachelle Williams. Unintentional irony, I'm sure—Jones and Wildman would both sport glasses that people now pay big bucks for at Warby Parker and EyeBuyDirect. ("Hey man, are those fucking glasses for real?"—Linnea Quigley to Andras Jones in *Sorority Babes*.

[275] Review from Variety—02/10/1988: "... [Michelle Bauer] is more than an eyeful and feisty Linnea Quigley makes an engagingly sarcastic and resourceful heroine..." *http://www.oldies.com/product-view/471250.html*

[276] Voted funniest title by Steve Friedman: *http://www.rogerebert.com/rogers-journal/readers-choice-as-funniest-movie-title-incredibly-strange*

[277] Literary studies could include: black magic, fantasy, magical realism, and *Sorority Babes* pops up in 'Educational Institutions in Horror Film: A History of Mad Professors, Student Bodies, and Final Exams' *https://books.google.com/books?id=r9K_BwAAQBAJ&dq=mall+used+in+sorority+babes&source=gbs_navlinks_s* (by Andrew Grunzke). Next, a review that wasn't *completely* repetitive—that does briefly address the film's camera work: *http://www.doomedmoviethon.com/reviews/144sororitybabesintheslimeballbowlorama.htm* , and finally, the fact you can STILL see the sorority house (used in other films, as well) from the street view on Google Maps—this is definitely a dissertation on privacy, or lack thereof, in the 21st century.

[278] Kyle Laudermilt, May 29, 2015

[279] Chris Grace, May 20, 2015

What you paid your admission to see. Photo courtesy Full Moon Pictures.

among others) and peep through a window at the paddling-hazing masochism on display before them—led by Tri Delta 'Felta Delta' Babs Peterson and her two lackeys, Rhonda and Frankie, both shallow and strangely worried about skin and hair throughout the entire film, even after they are turned into demons. Writer and director were able to use that imagery as social commentary that sadly still holds true today, probably even more so. Everyone here is obviously much older than traditional college pledges—which means everyone here can actually act, being able to draw from life experience and all. Everyone is attractive in a real, approachable, natural way—they possess personality and spunk—and again—they can act: they have screen presence, timing, and group chemistry—all items truly difficult to gather in one place at one time.

The nerds are caught peeking, now inside the damn house, and also paddled by Babs into a heap, crashing unashamedly onto the bathroom floor, where a naked Bauer and Stevens attempt to cover themselves. Stille's ritual-robed glee at using a very large, wooden *Animal House* paddle is truly scene-stealing. And although there are five other 'sisters' who enter this scene, we never see who they are and we never see them again. I want to know who else is in the robes and if there was some kind of scene cut here. Bauer and Stevens' pledge egos, Lisa and Taffy, will now be punished again by Babs—sentenced to break into a bowling alley (attached to a mall her 'daddy' owns) and now required to steal a bowling trophy. Everyone agrees, although not all happily. Writer and director tread a fine line here and never cross it— while Jones refers to Babs as "Madame DeSade", and her comrades insist she consider "prison work" we do get a glimpse that she indeed enjoys dishing out pain—the smile as she paddles, for example, but we never tread into any bullshit stereotype of the BDSM community as we know it now. It's playful and fun in this film, as it can be in real life, which is not how it's often viewed now.

Babs' plans of thwarting the actual theft are interrupted by Linnea's Spider character, as well as the Imp released from the bowling trophy once dropped by a nerd. The film's comedy itself is innocent: Jones' character vomits off-screen continuously: one beer, nerves, and fear all

L-R Linnea Quigley, John Stuart Wildman, Hal Havens, Michelle Bauer, Brinke Stevens, Andras Jones.
Photo copyright Full Moon Pictures.

play a role, everyone is actually running around in a bowling alley, bickering Odd Couple-style, such as the argument between Jimmy and Keith over who can pick a lock the best. But Buck Flower and Linnea Quigley are the true standouts here—as deaf old coot versus tough young sass, followed by Dukey Flyswatter's voice of the 'The Imp'—the original working title for this film. The dialogue is often campy and fun, and again quite tame as well compared to what is deemed comedic now.

And it works! Albeit vulgar in some spots—jokes like "have a nice trip, see you next fall" and "if I were any closer I'd be behind you" brought to mind classic, golden-age comedy: Henny Youngman, George C. Parker (KK) [280], Groucho Marx, pranks like Prince Albert silliness (LL) [281], which all pleasantly lead into more modern comedic dialogue, many of which are Linnea's lines. For example: 1. "It's too bad we had to kill her ... I really liked the outfit she had on." 2. "There's no pulse. Would a demon have a pulse?" 3. "That's really the most stupid damn story I've ever heard." Fantastic!

Foreshadowing is correctly employed in the film, as nerds and pledges meet Spider: "Oooo, jump back. Prom queens on the loose. Or is it high school hookers?" Lisa and Taffy would both fill these roles when wishes were granted, as an insatiable tart and prom queen wish-gone-wrong, respectively. Paddler Babs, who was jokingly called "Babs, the Dominatrix" and a "pain freak" by her sorority sisters, is later transformed into a demon dominatrix. And unlike most horror movies, camp or otherwise, there are actually two leads that sense something evil is afoot, and lazy CGI, torture porn, and gross-out-gore are NOT employed in the film, at all. The actual horror in this film is light and non-threatening. For example, the sorority sisters are punished for being naughty voyeurs and possessed as a demon lizard woman and a Bride of Frankenstein demon, ruining skin and hair as also foreshadowed back in the Tri Delta's house.

Shots of the, I suspect, fictitious Plaza Camino mall at night and the bowling alley are indeed ominous enough to move the film occasionally from camp to concern. And I could feel the claustrophobia from the janitor locked in a closet, and many can relate to the creep factor

---

[280] *http://en.wikipedia.org/wiki/George_C._Parker* the birth of "I've got a bridge to sell you", which Hal Havins can be heard saying in another film where, like *Sorority Babes*, he was both comedic and terrifying, *Night of the Demons* ("And if you believe that, I've got a real nifty bridge to sell you.")

[281] *http://www.heraldnet.com/article/20120405/LIVING03/704059960*

when Babs and her crew watch the pledges and geeks over a security camera—but when the biggest bowling trophy (made from balsawood, according to IMDB) is chosen and dropped, unleashing a jive-talking rubbery imp (that I want to own as much as I want a Bad Milo) (JJ)[282], and wishes are granted—people begin to die and magical shit gets real. In fact, the feelings of demonic struggling begin even before the demons ever actually arrive—who can't relate to that?

"A nasty lesson, for a nasty girl" says the Imp, at one point—specifically to lead bitch Babs. This is another running theme throughout the entire film: Bitchy girls get punished, only to meet up with and punish other bitchy girls, whereupon bitchy demons will then attempt to go after the baddest and bitchiest survivor of them all. Sociological magic realism? Cliques and social class and power struggle, young and old and REALLY old, all under the roof of one magically sealed mall—and the mall/bowling alley itself both status symbols and signs of a dying, dead, and bygone era. If this were a book series, I'd buy. If this were a class, I'd sign up. Or teach it. Whichever.

The movie is also cute, at times—romantically so. And not just the end, moped sputtering off at dawn. But the meet cute (MM)[283] scene between Jones and Quigley: "Hi, come here often?" said by a naive Jones to an obviously law-breaking Quigley: "Hey man, I'm robbing the fucking place. Do you understand?" This scene is mentioned again, later in the evening in a dark mall bathroom, as they seem to be astonished they're still alive—in a moment of levity amidst the demon rampaging. There's even the hint of a budding romance in this film that doesn't feel forced or melodramatic, and in fact, I can kind of relate to. Linnea's line: "How the fuck did I get stuck with you?" Perhaps writer and director met girls like this (and really, haven't we all! And if you haven't, well, then you might be one of bitchy girls referred to previously) and in their own Hollywood therapy, devised the perfect script for punishment and social commentary. The movie even has a happy ending. What recent horror movie can you think of that is goofy, contains a childlike excitement in its own execution, contains several really intense, really funny, really contagious acting moments, and there's still reason to celebrate at the end when someone likeable wins?

The actors in the film take it seriously. No one winks at the camera in this film, IF the Imp puppet *could* wink, he *might*, but he cannot and so he doesn't. The trio reigned supreme in the B world for a reason: they could own the screen. They weren't just sexy in three ways—they were also talented. Michelle Bauer feigns co-ed coquettish, dying-to-get-into-a-hip-sorority very well, before turning into a lingerie model built for sex, but really possessed the knowledge of how to command a comedic scene. Linnea Quigley, who it's been said more than once had great comedic timing ... proves it here. She doesn't have the slapstick of *Vice Academy* at her disposal, but instead she is snarky, sarcastic, and in a few scenes—intimidating. If you didn't know how sweet Linnea was, not aware of her humorous abilities, you'd back away from her character here. She's carrying a crowbar, robbing a mall, and wears her punk well: clothes, scowl, and attitude. She portrays a survivor, a real hardass coming around to human by the very end. The final scene, moped drive-off into the dawn for this unlikely duo, and even unlikelier couple, had that hint of romance and apocalypse in its light. And who could forget Brinke Stevens (NN)[284]—the woman can portray sultry upon waking—moves from quietly bitchy tag-a-long, to realizing the fulfillment of her dreams (queen of the prom) to fighting for her life before being torn in half (taffy-pulled, as it were). She is the peak of shallow wishers in the film, but her wish is saddled with regret—she really just wanted people to like her, to be noticed. Doesn't almost everyone?

SPECIAL THANKS: MW, KCL, Sergei Hasenecz, Ted Newsom, Chris Grace, Brinke, Linnea, Michelle, Dukey, Andras, and Hal.

---

[282] Milo is the butt puppet in the Duplass Brothers' indictment of corporate America, *Bad Milo*.

[283] *http://en.wikipedia.org/wiki/Meet_cute*

[284] *http://www.hockstatter.com/spm/cast.shtml* (Brief interview with Brinke, referring to SB filming)

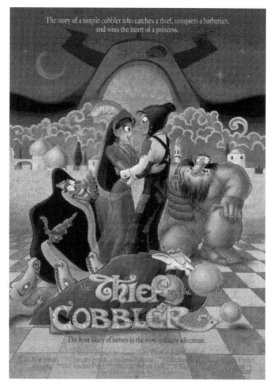

THE THIEF AND THE COBBLER (1993)

"It is written among the limitless constellations of the celestial heavens, and in the depths of the emerald seas, and upon every grain of sand in the vast deserts, that the world which we see is an outward and visible dream, of an inward and invisible reality ... Once upon a time there was a golden city. In the centre of the golden city, atop the tallest minaret, were three golden balls. The ancients had prophesied that if the three golden balls were ever taken away, harmony would yield to discord, and the city would fall to destruction and death. But... the mystics had also foretold that the city might be saved by the simplest soul with the smallest and simplest of things. In the city there dwelt a lowly shoemaker, who was known as Tack the Cobbler. Also in the city... existed a Thief, who shall be ... nameless."

One of the most notorious "lost" animated films in history, *The Thief and the Cobbler* is actually three stories: the primary central narrative; the tenacity of the film's creator, Richard Williams; and Garrett Gilchrist, the talented fan who worked tirelessly to rescue the movie from obscurity.

From a screenplay standpoint, there is very little "story" to be found in Richard Williams' gorgeously animated film. The central MacGuffin involves the titular thief going about his quest to rob the Golden City blind and stumbling upon the scheme to liberate the three protective globes from their spire upon the minaret roof. The unnamed Thief slithers along staircases, sidles around corners, slides up drainpipes, accompanied by a sly grin and an ever-present halo of flies buzzing around his head. During the course of his inevitably-thwarted burglaries, he encounters the beautiful Princess Yum-Yum, her sleepy father the King, the villainous Grand Vizier Zigzag, and the also-titular cobbler, Tack, so named for the shoe tacks he keeps in his mouth (which form his labial expressions, the heads of the tacks making up the dimples in his youthful face). The characters are defined by their desires: the Thief for the golden balls; Zigzag for the power that would come with the hand of the princess; the King for his desire for status quo; only Tack has no greater goal but for a simple happy existence, making him the ersatz hero of the story. Narrative thrust was never Williams' intent, but in the beautiful set pieces, the majority of them detailing the Thief's misadventures.

This is to say nothing of the supporting characters: from the intimidating King One Eye, to the wonderfully-loopy witch living inside a mountain comprised entirely of stone hands, to the gleefully grotesque and war-scarred desert-dwelling Brigands Yum-Yum conscripts into her private army. Even minor background characters are painstakingly designed—look fast during Zigzag's entrance—as a coalition of lackeys unroll a red carpet before and after his curling toes—and you'll see not only the Mullah Nasarddin (see below), but also Saddam Hussein! And for sheer brilliance, if you freeze-frame a section near the end where the Thief comes hurling towards the camera, you'll see that the ever-present flies buzzing around his head all share his face and robes! It's this deep attention to detail that make *The Thief...* such a dazzling visual treat.

Williams, a native of Toronto who had early aspirations to work for Disney as an animator, was put off by the business at an early age. Visiting the studio, Williams "overheard Disney himself talking to a reporter about his animated film about a spaniel, *Lady and the Tramp*," Williams told *Seventeen Magazine* in 1973. "He was doing a professional number on the reporter, describing how it would pull on your heartstrings when you thought Lady had savaged the baby, but she hadn't. The salesmanship appalled me because I was completely idealistic. He was doing his job, but I wondered why he had to do that. After all, he was Walt Disney."[285] The encounter put him off animation for years, turning his back on the industry to study and work as a "serious" painter throughout the '50s.

Returning to the industry in the '60s, with a self-produced short film titled *The Little Island*, Williams quickly became well-known for his whimsically-animated title sequences for such films as *What's New, Pussycat?* (1965), *Casino Royale* (1967), *The Return of the Pink Panther* (1975), *The Pink Panther Strikes Again* (1976), and the original title sequence for the bizarrely compelling train-wreck, *Can Heironymus Merkin Ever Forget Mercy Humppe and Find True Happiness?* (1969). At a time when animation was becoming less and less valuable to movie studios, with much of the "art" lost in favor of cheap shorts made for the TV market, much of the skill and artistry seemed to be dying. "As Williams attempted to improve his craft, the animation industry was struggling. "Back in the '60s, the design trend was such that people had forgotten how to animate properly," Garrett Gilchrist told Tested.com. "All this brilliant Disney knowledge that had given us *Snow White* and *Bambi* and *Fantasia*—they animated that stuff from life—they studied animals for *Bambi*, they studied dancers for *Snow White*...just got forgotten. By the '60s all these great animators of the '40s were getting old and working on crap."[1]

The prevailing wisdom in the industry at the time was that animation was television's domain. With the rising popularity of the Saturday Morning cartoon block, the "shortcut" was the rule of law. Limited, flat animation, geometry-based design—think the rectangular shapes of Hanna-Barbera characters like Yogi Bear. "Theatrical animation died out in the early 60s, for the most part. Thanks to [companies like] UPA, animation in the '50s trended more toward simpler flat shapes and heavy stylization. When animation started being produced for television in the 60s, everything had to be shortcuts. There wasn't the budget to do it right. The design trends in general, when Richard started out in animation, were like a flat '60s comic strip, like [Johnny Hart's] *B.C.* Outside of Disney nobody was really doing full animation," Garrett Gilchrist wrote to me in July of 2016.[2] "When Disney did these great films like *Fantasia*, they animated as an imitation of life. They studied animals for *Bambi*, they studied dancers for *Snow White*. Thirty, forty years later this knowledge was just getting forgotten. It wasn't being passed on to the younger generation. By the '60s all these great animators of the '40s were getting old and working on junk, to a much lower standard." Williams ignored the conventional wisdom and followed his heart and talent.

With a growing cache`, Williams illustrated Idries Shah's collection *The Exploits of the Incomparable Mulla Nasrudin*[286]. Based on the exploits of the title character, the 13th Century

---

[285] For those not in the business, a completion bond is an insurance policy that essentially takes over the production if deadlines or budgets are not met. They are not, inherently, evil.

[286] Sometimes spelled "Nasruddin" and who am I to fight with the Turks?

"philosopher-fool", whose "sideways" way of looking at things deflated conventional thinking and taught people to rethink how they saw the world, Shaw had translated and rewritten the classic stories. Shah and Williams embarked on a search for financing to produce short films based on the stories. "Potential investors saw greater potential in expanding the shorts into a feature, to be titled "The

Tack meets Zigzag. Screengrab copyright Miramax Films.

Majestic Fool." The complicated screenplay still had the feel of a series of shorts, or jokes, strung together into a film, without a strong narrative. Williams began animating the film in the late 60s, with comedian Kenneth Williams as the voice of many characters including a corrupt Vizier."

The collaboration was short-lived, partly because potential investors saw greater potential in expanding the shorts into a feature, which Shah rejected; partly because Shaw and his brother Omar wanted the largest share of profits from any finished film; and partly because the Shah family may or may not have been embezzling funds already raised.

Shah departed, along with Nasrudin, leaving Williams with some test animation and an underdeveloped "thief" character. With his then-wife Margaret French, Williams worked out a new script expanding the thief's role and returned to the drawing board, both literally and figuratively. The production evolved into a project holding various titles, including "The Cobbler, The Thief, and the Grand Vizir", "Once...", and "The Thief Who Never Gave Up," with Williams and a hand-picked team developing the story and animating vignettes.

Despite claims to the contrary, Williams was *not* working "without a full script or storyboards," as he toiled over the course of three decades. ("It's often said that Williams was working without a script or storyboards. This is untrue, and constantly repeated to make Williams look like a fool. At first, Williams used storyboards from the Nasrudin film and new voice acting from Vincent Price, Anthony Quayle and others to get started on the new film," Gilchrist wrote to me. "It's not clear when Margaret French's script *The Thief Who Never Gave Up* was completed, but it dates to sometime in the seventies. A draft from 1980 matches the "nearly-finished" 1992 film very closely, although with a lot of extra dialogue that Williams would cut. The scene and shot numbers of the 1980 draft also match the 1992 production. [...] Williams was now being secretive about the film, fearing that his ideas would be stolen. This led to rumors that he was working without storyboards, when really the ancient '60s and '70s storyboards were still good enough for him to keep plugging along with, just not good enough to show anyone else."[3]) The guidelines continued to evolve over the course of 30 years, as, you know, everything does, as Williams raised his standards, resulting in some work needed to be redone, years'-old animation scrapped and redrawn and repolished. Considered by most who met him to be an unqualified genius and an animation visionary, if perhaps difficult to work with at times due to these high standards, Williams was able to attract, building a team of talented animators that included Disney great Art Babbitt[287] (a man famous for once punching Walt Disney[288]), Chuck

---

[287] Babbitt was hired not only as an animator but as an animation "boot camp" instructor for the new animators who were used to working on projects with much lower standards. During this grueling period, artists would listen to Babbit's lectures in the morning, given animation assignments for the evening, and then worked ten-hour days on *The Thief...* "At his advanced age, Babbit mostly drew in stick figures, which Williams found fascinating. Williams had always hidden any deficiencies in his animation behind his skill as an artist. Having to animate stick figures and simple shapes, there was no hiding anything. However, when he looked at Babbit's animation in later years,

Jones' head of animation Ken Harris, and background designer Roy Naisbitt.

"Richard Williams was a brilliant artist but he wanted to be a great animator, and this film was his way to learn. He hired some of the greatest old guard animators—Art Babbitt, Ken Harris, Grim Natwick, Emery Hawkins—very late in their lives, to pass on their knowledge to a new generation before it was lost forever. Richard's studio helped train the great animators of the 80s and 90s, like Eric Goldberg and Andreas Deja, and helped make the Disney renaissance (*Aladdin, The Lion King*) possible. It's a hugely influential film, even though it's wound up as a footnote in history."[4]

Harris, in particular, was central to the development of the Thief. Working under Chuck Jones, Harris had expert comedic timing. As Gilchrist pointed out, "[Harris] complemented Dick perfectly because then Dick could go in and make the animation prettier, add the details and change the art style. The art style kept evolving. The lead characters of the cobbler and the princess weren't even added until the beginning of 1990."[5] A centerpiece of the film involves the Thief's increasingly desperate attempts to steal the balls from the minaret by pole vaulting towards the tower. First he stops short and falls backwards; another time, he misjudges his speed and sails through an open window—all the while being observed by Tack as he attempts to saw through the bars of his prison. Once he finally reaches the spire, the Thief gives the audience a smug Wile E. Coyote smile.[289] ("As if he hadn't spent the last 20 minutes failing," quips Garrett Gilchrist on his audio commentary.) This after getting trampled and hurled through the air during an exciting polo match.

Williams' vision for *The Thief* was clearly one for all audiences. While children would obviously respond to the familiar plot and the genial characters, the animators filled the background with adult jokes—"There are more than a few instances to suggest that Williams wanted to do a film more for adults than for children. After all, the chief of the One-Eyes doesn't sit on a throne, but rather on a group of women who are forced to pose in the shape of a throne! Later these women kill the One-Eye chief by throwing him off a cliff. There is a Benny Hill-like urination joke, and Zigzag will probably go down in cartoon history as the first villain who is eaten alive on screen."[6]

One magnificent sequence (which was likely one of the first to be jettisoned by the future producers) involved The Thief stealing jeweled back-scratchers from Yum-Yum while she bathed. Later, when the palace guards catch The Thief attempting to steal jewels from a clear jar, they take him to the square for capital punishment. Realizing he's about to have both hands severed, the terrified Thief quickly places the back scratchers in the stocks and reacts in horror when they're chopped. It isn't until he scurries through the cheering crowd and into the relative

---

Williams had to admit that little of it was useable. This was also true of the surreal, morphing work of Emery Hawkins, who animated the taffy monster in Raggedy Ann and a transformation sequence later deleted from The Thief. His work was fascinating to look at but the old animator was also clearly going senile. Babbitt's lectures about animation proved invaluable, however, and changed the game not only at Williams' studio but for animation in general, passing on the knowledge of the 30s and 40s to the animators who would build the 80s and 90s." Gilchrist, 7/24/2016.

[288] In 1941, Babbitt was one of a small number of well-paid Disney animators who joined their juniors on a well-publicized strike against the studio. During a picketing session, Disney confronted Babbitt and the two began to fight, with escalation only prevented by intervention by the other strikers. This earned Babbitt Uncle Walt's eternal animosity, resulting in the senior animator's subsequent firing and re-hiring, repeated several times during his remaining tenure. Babbitt subsequently sued Disney, taking the case all the way to the Supreme Court, where the justices ruled in his favor, granting him a handsome settlement, leading him to finally leave the studio to join UPA (United Productions of America).

[289] Working with Chuck Jones, Harris worked a Wile E. Coyote gag into *The Thief and the Cobbler*, incorporating the notorious "ACME Batman Costume" sequence from the short *Gee Whiz!* into the sequence in which The Thief attempts to fly to the top of a mountain comprised completely of stone hands (the home of a crazed witch). Harris virtually recreates the sequence complete with the opening homage to *Fantasia*'s "Night on Bald Mountain"—with the Thief strapping giant leaves to his arms and then soaring through the air, only to crash hard into the ground. (This is also one of the few instances where Jonathan Williams' one-take dialogue works in the Miramax version. His ad-libs during the steep ascent up the hand hills: "Two trees on an impossible-to-climb cliff. Perfect! I'd be dead if this cliff decided to applaud. Oh, these must be *palm* trees!")

safety of an alley does he reveal his own hands intact. (Now, consider that Disney would later acquiesce to complaints from Saudi Arabia that the line in *Aladdin's* opening song "Arabian Nights"—"Where they cut off your ears if they don't like your face,"—was culturally insensitive and changed it for home video release. The excision of this scene by latter producers from the body of *The Thief...* isn't at all surprising.

While working on the revamped *The Thief...*, Williams continued to work on commercials and title sequences for more films, including *The Return of the Pink Panther* (1975) and *The Pink Panther Strikes Again* (1976). In 1972, his animated adaptation of *A Christmas Carol* won an Academy Award. In 1977, Williams took over directorial duties for *Raggedy Ann & Andy: A Musical Adventure* (1977), after Abe Levitow died mid-production. The movie already suffered from budget and schedule problems, Williams clashed with the movie's producers, the animators worked from home in many instances due to the decentralized nature of the film, and ultimately Williams was removed from the movie, though he retained sole directorial credit.

"During the production of *Raggedy Ann*, Williams received a fair amount of publicity and in an interview with John Canemaker in the Feb. 1976 issue of *Millimeter*, he gave a hint about his vision for *T&C*. 'The Thief* is not following the Disney route. It's to my knowledge the first animated film with a real plot that locks together like a detective story at the end. It has no sentiment and the two main characters don't speak. It's like a silent movie with a lot of sound.'[290] A radical approach to be sure, but one must consider the animation scene at the time," wrote G. Michael Dobbs in *Animato!* "The Disney Studio was still floundering from the loss of its founder[291], and the animated films which had

The Thief slithers along. Screengrab copyright Miramax Films.

stirred the imagination of the critics and audiences were definitely not Disney. Williams' old boss George Dunning had directed *The Yellow Submarine* to acclaim and Ralph Bakshi's violent, profane and highly personal film *Heavy Traffic* hadn't just made money, it was accepted with a fair bit of hoopla into the collection of the Museum of Modern Art. This indeed was the time for yet another approach."[7]

Unfortunately, the *Raggedy Ann* experience was indicative of how the very elements that made Williams an exceptional creator also hindered the production on *The Thief...* Hoping to raise funds from overseas investors, Williams and the team threw themselves into finishing an amazing 10-minute battle sequence to show the money men, but two deadlines were missed. Workers arrived at the office one morning and were confronted with the simple message on the central board: "Didn't Get the Money."

Fortunes seemingly turned in the mid-80s, after Stephen Spielberg saw a Williams-produced ad for Fanta soda, featuring many famous Disney characters playing soccer against human kids. Mickey, Goofy, Donald and the group were rendered with shadowing that gave them the appearance that they were just as three-dimensional as the humans in the spot, and the depth was seen as something visually unique. Inspired, Spielberg hired Williams and his team to provide the animation for the landmark film, *Who Framed Roger Rabbit*. A commercial and critical success,

---

[290] Indeed, Tack is based on silent star Harry Langdon, while the Thief is cut from Buster Keaton cloth as, in Williams' words, "the ultimate sleepwalker."

[291] Walt Disney died December 15, 1966, due to complications from lung cancer.

Warner Brothers offered Williams the opportunity to finally complete his Arabian Night masterpiece, with the one catch being the studio's insistence on working with a Completion Bond Company.[292]

"*The Thief and the Cobbler*, [which] very few people have heard of, became the basis for *Aladdin*, for the [*Little*] *Mermaid*, for *The Lion King*, for that whole Disney renaissance, because the people Dick trained, he passed on that knowledge so that this new generation in the 70s could actually learn to animate Disney-quality stuff," Gilchrist said. "Dick doesn't get a lot of credit for that because of politics, I think. Dick was difficult to work with but brilliant. He was a perfectionist and really only interested in making this one film and wasn't really interested in *Roger Rabbit*...after the rabbit Disney offered him *Beauty and the Beast* at one point. He turned them down. He was only interested in this obsession that he'd been doing work on for about 25 years."[8]

"With *The Thief* he signed a contract with Warners that they could have the film taken away if it didn't meet a deadline, or didn't meet a certain budget. Dick didn't have a good business sense. He was good at finishing 90 percent of a film before going over budget, and believing his work would be so amazing that of course they'd give him a little leeway to finish the rest. And it never worked, because his standards were higher than anyone but Disney would budget for. *A Christmas Carol* was like that, *Raggedy Ann* and *Roger Rabbit* were like that. He figured they'd love *The Thief* so much that they'd give him a little more time and money. Instead Warners cut their losses."[9]

Eventually, and tragically, Williams and company came up against the realities of the completion bond. Attempting to buy some time by finally storyboarding the remaining sequences of the film—beautifully-rendered drawings that basically served as key frames for future animation—the film was taken out of Williams' hands. Sue Shakespeare of Creative Capers Entertainment attempted to fix some story problems with Williams, suggesting equally-legendary filmmaker Terry Gilliam be brought aboard for assistance. This was rejected by the Completion Bond Company, who brought in Fred Calvert to finish the movie. Calvert, another Disney veteran who left the studio following *101 Dalmatians* to work for various Saturday-morning cartoon companies, such as Format Films, Hanna-Barbera, *Sesame Street* via Children's Television Workshop, was brought in to make the film, in the Completion Bond Company's words, "commercially viable." Calvert was a notorious "cost-cutter" and found Williams' way of working wasteful. As his own company was failing, it would seem that Calvert saw an opportunity for advancement and set out—intentionally or otherwise—to undermine Williams, reporting that there had been no script for years, etc. Calvert told Dobbs for *Animato!*, "'We took it and re-structured it as best we could and brought in a couple of writers and went back into all of Richard Williams' work, some that he wasn't using and found it marvelous...we tried to use as much of his footage as possible.'

Of the footage Williams completed, Calvert claimed that he was only able to use about 50 percent of it, because of the repetitive nature of the scenes. 'We hated to see of all this beautiful animation hit the cutting room floor, but that was the only way we could make a story out of it. "One of the problems, there were a number of these situations...in the script, there might be two or three sentences describing the Thief going up a drain pipe. But what he animated on the screen was five minutes up and down that pipe which would ordinarily be five pages of script...These were the kind of imbalances that were happening. He was kind of Rube Goldberging his way through. I don't think he was able to step back and look at the whole thing as a story. [...] [He's] an incredible animator, though. Incredible. One of the biggest problems we had was trying our desperate best, where we had brand new footage, to come up to the level of quality that he had set," said Calvert."[10]

"Fred Calvert's involvement with the completion of the film is perhaps the most discreditable aspect of the story," wrote Williams's son, Alex, for *Animation World Magazine* in

---

[292] For those not in the business, a completion bond is an insurance policy that essentially takes over the production if deadlines or budgets are not met. They are not, inherently, evil.

1997. "Unable to appreciate the remarkable nature of the project he had inherited, he sent the inevitable song sequences to be completed in Korea by animators used to working on Saturday morning children's cartoons. That these sequences look grotesque when juxtaposed with Williams' original work should have come as no surprise. Fred Calvert's leading role in butchering *The Thief* has become perhaps his most infamous contribution to the medium."[11]

With virtually no budget, and less emotional investment in *The Thief*, Calvert employed two animation teams, one in Los Angeles and one in London, as well as an ink-and-paint service in Korea, and quickly restructured the film to better reflect the wishes of the studio. While Calvert has asserted that it "pained him" to jettison so much of Williams' animation, that he did so against his own wishes, but at the demands of the Completion Bond Company, Alex Williams disputes this. "My recollection of Fred Calvert's visits is that he was only too keen to take on the completion of the film. I clearly recall my father's astonished reaction when Calvert suggested, having been shown the painstaking and beautiful camerawork executed by the gifted [animator] John Leatherbarrow, that the film should be shot in Korea to save money. As we now know, Calvert was not only to shoot much of *The Thief* in Korea, but also to send large sections to be animated there. Such insensitivity to the quality of the film he was to inherit is the hallmark of his work."[12]

Though while it may be justifiable to cast Calvert as the villain in this situation, Alex Williams continued: "In any event, by taking on *The Thief* himself and convincing CBC that he could do justice to the movie, Calvert set in motion events which were to destroy the project. For that he must take responsibility and ultimately, blame. That said, there were plainly other villains. Jake Eberts, the producer whose weight in Hollywood set *The Thief* in motion, abandoned the project when Warners became jumpy. Betty Smith of CBC played a major role in removing what was left of Williams' cut. Calvert was thus in many ways a small player in a larger pool of sharks, who was unable to keep control of what he had inherited."[13]

For their part, some Warner Brothers' greatest misgivings had to do with Williams' nonconformist attitude towards "traditional" animation structure. To their eyes, the movie had no narrative through-line, no heroic showdown, and, worst of all, no catchy tunes. How was the film expected to keep the kiddies' attention with just dazzling visuals and engaging silent characters? Inconceivable! Their attitudes were further soured when, due to the delays, *The Thief* failed to beat Disney's *Aladdin* to theaters.

Aladdin was huge success, garnering acclaim, and many awards. Those in the know saw the liberties Disney had taken in appropriating Williams' designs—Jafar was a definite mix between 1940's *The Thief of Bagdad*'s Conrad Veidt and Zigzag; The Sultan was as much King Nod as it was Miles Malleson's Sultan.

"Watching both movies, it's impossible not to notice the striking similarities between *The Thief and the Cobbler* and *Aladdin*. 'Disney just stole it,' said [Philip Pepper, lead animator from 1990 through 1992]. 'It's as plain as the nose your face.' Many of the outfits, imagery, and character designs were very similar. Williams had been working on his movie for twenty years and dozens of animators had passed through and taken some ideas with them; it seemed only natural for the movie to blend into others. The studio recognized this natural thievery as a problem, but had no other option than to trudge forward."[14]

Kevin Schreck, whose documentary, *Persistence of Vision*, documents the whole tragic tale through archive film and new interviews with Williams' contemporaries due to the animator's refusal to participate, citing feelings still too-raw to revisit, says of the *Aladdin* similarities, "It's hard to say how much was deliberate theft, accidental inspiration, or mere coincidence," Schreck says of the likeness, allowing that it might be a combination of the three. All the same, a bad situation: "Whatever it is, it wasn't good for Williams."[15] There was great potential for garbled time-lines, making it appear that *The Thief…* had copied *Aladdin*, rather than the other way around. This proved to be true in the eyes of many fans and journalists at the time.

Where Williams had long-resisted the inclusion of musical numbers, Calvert and the studio had four songs inserted—two of them unremarkable, one ("The Brigands Ballad") irritating, and Princess Yum-Yum's intro a blatant rip-off of *The Little Mermaid*'s "Part of His World."

"But the film's executive producer, Jake Eberts, whose British-based company, Allied

Zigzag and Phido. This looks gorgeous in color. Screengrab copyright Miramax Films.

Filmmakers, invested $10 million in the project over nine years, said Miramax has done a 'fabulous job' taking the film to the big screen. 'It was significantly enhanced and changed by Miramax after Miramax stepped in and acquired the domestic [distribution] rights,' Eberts said. 'They made extremely good changes.' As for giving the cobbler and thief voices, Eberts said the original way did not work for two reasons. 'There wasn't a strong enough story line in and of itself that you could get the story through the actions and appearance of the cobbler,' Eberts said. "Secondly, the cobbler itself didn't have the kind of design that convey feeling. He didn't have enough characteristics in his face to convey full emotions. He also serves as the narrator.' Eberts, who said he still has great admiration for Richard Williams and his animation skills, nonetheless added that *Arabian Knight* is a classic case of art clashing with commerce. Williams' problem, Eberts said, was that 'he could never finish a scene.'"[16]

(So "fabulous" a job that in the ultimate pissing on Williams' leg, they took the first animated film shot in Cinemascope since *Lady and the Tramp*, and reduced it to a poorly-cropped pan-and-scan image.)

Once Calvert completed the film, the studio was confronted with some unavoidable facts, chiefly that the new animation was stiff and ugly when contrasted with Williams' smooth, almost life-like movement. As has been pointed out by animation experts, Williams drew "on ones"—twenty-four new drawings per second—where Calvert drew on twos, sometimes threes, resulting in images that were not only flat and jerky, but seemingly unfinished. Cutting their losses, Warner gave the film entirely over to The Completion Bond Company.

Things get even more convoluted at this point. *The Thief and the Cobbler* was finally released—dumped, more accurately—to theaters in Australia and South Africa in 1993 by Allied Filmmakers, under the title *The Princess and the Cobbler*. This version had the songs and the voices of Lively, Bobbi Page, Donald Pleasance (as Zigzag's pet vulture, Phido), and Clive Revill (replacing Anthony Quayle) as King Nod. Missing were great chunks of Williams' animation, including much of the magnificent 10-minute climactic battle.

In 1994, the Disney-owned Miramax picked up the rights to the now-orphaned movie, and further recut it. Adding further insult, Miramax's president, Harvey Weinstein, who never met a movie he didn't want to fuck with, cut the film further, recast the voices—Broderick, now, replacing Steve Lively as Tack; Jennifer Beals as an uninvolved Yum-Yum; Jonathan Winters doing a "Popeye" voice-over as the Thief's interior monologue—and further eliminated hunks of Williams' animation. Several cheap-shots against *Aladdin* were inserted into the dialogue—"Who needs a genie when you've got a tack?" asks Tack at one point. For the Thief's first line, Winters belts out "Good Morning, Arabia!", evoking both *Aladdin* and paying homage to that film's star (and Winters' friend) Robin Williams. This was apparently intentional to further "sell" the film as a cheap *Aladdin* rip-off.

As the L.A. Times reported, "'They decided, in their wisdom, to have them speaking,'

[Richard] Williams said. 'But it's very hard to have them speaking when their lips don't move. So you have them speaking in the bits they added, and in the other scenes they didn't animate, they put voices over the top. It looks ridiculous, but that didn't stop them.'

"'I never conceived of putting a voice on the thief,' Calvert said. 'That was a surprise to me. Whatever is wrong with the film, I'm sure someone will blame me for it.' "[17]

This version, *Arabian Knight*, was offered as a pan-and-scan DVD giveaway through General Foods cereals. For just the cost of a box of sugary-sawdust, you could get the cinematic equivalent for free!

"It is hard, looking at this Miramax video release, to find the spirit of the film as it was originally conceived. The character of The Thief was intended as a mute, a Chaplinesque primitive, subtle and understated. By stealing the three golden balls which protect the Golden City, he unwittingly creates havoc and destruction around him. Superimposed over these scenes is Jonathan Winters' voice, ceaselessly cracking pointless jokes like an unwanted barroom companion. It is as if those responsible for the completion of the film were terrified of silence, overlaying every quiet moment in the film with endless chatter. Matthew Broderick's narration strives to explain what does not need explaining, robbing the story of subtlety or surprises. The film condescends to the audience, insulting its intelligence," wrote Alex Williams. "There remains some beautiful animation in this fractured version of Richard Williams' epic; these include the opening sequence, where The Thief and The Cobbler get tangled up with each other and roll down the steps of the Cobbler's shop, interrupting Zigzag's march through the city, the chase through the palace through Escher-like optical illusions, and a little of the final war machine sequence. For those courageous enough to sit it out, I recommend watching with the sound turned off. Save for Vincent Price's brilliant valedictory performance as Zigzag, the evil Grand Vizier, all but a handful of the carefully selected original voice talents have been replaced with other, less suitable, actors. Even John Leatherbarrow's superb camerawork has been made to appear unremarkable, the once subtle colors now vulgar and garish. Finally, the substitution of Baghdad for the Golden City seems in extraordinarily bad taste for a film originally released shortly after the Gulf War."[18]

"*The Thief and the Cobbler* should have been the capstone achievement of one of Great Britain's finest animators. It was the last great hand-drawn animated film, and the final film of many of the greatest animators of the golden age: men whose careers stretched back to *Fantasia* and *Betty Boop*. As it went through iteration after iteration over its three decades of development (by my count, it had 10 different working titles over the years, some repeated), it served as a palimpsest and training ground for a new generation of animators. By the time a butchered version of the film finally limped into theaters, it was famous mostly as a financial and artistic debacle," wrote Matthew Dessem for The Dissolve. "For nearly 30 years, his obsession with creating the greatest animated film of all time kept him at the center of a maelstrom."[19]

At this point, *The Thief* could have vanished into obscurity if it weren't for a USC film school graduate named Garrett Gilchrist. Intrigued by Williams' tribulations as well as the near-legendary trials of bringing *The Thief* to life, Gilchrist found a copy of Williams' original workprint, which had been circulating online via animation buffs and collectors for years. Using the workprint as a guideline, Gilchrist reassembled the film, using additional footage from the *Princess and the…* laserdisc and the pan-and-scan DVD of *Arabian Knight*, attempting to recreate Williams' film and bring it closer to the filmmaker's original intentions. A task daunting in and of itself, Gilchrist threw himself into the project, in several instances reanimating by hand sections of the film, to eliminate Tack's speaking mouth in some cases, redrawing Yum-Yum's mouth in others to match her original dialogue, etc. Where no source material existed, Gilchrist employed Williams' storyboards to fill in gaps in the narrative. When former *Thief* animators caught wind of Gilchrist's project, they donated footage and artwork to his cause. The resulting "Recobbled Cut" was released for free on Gilchrist's website, and was celebrated by fans and Williams' devotees.[293] In 2015, Gilchrist returned to the editing deck again for "Recobbled Cut Mark IV",

---

[293] "My version of the film is the version that animation teachers are talking to their students about," Gilchrist said.

using cleaner HD footage from newer sources.[20]

("The 'Mark 3 Recobbled Cut' from 2008 used rare 35mm footage donated by an animator, allowing fans to finally see the 'War Machine' sequence in full and in high quality," Gilchrist wrote to me. "Interest in the film was so great that I went back to the editing deck for the 'Recobbled Cut Mark IV', spending two and a half unpaid years from 2010 to 2013 cleaning up newly-transferred HD footage by hand. I've said it's almost certainly the most complicated restoration of any film that's been independently attempted, and I'd love to work on an official restoration sometime if the rights could ever be worked out.")[21]

As Gilchrist wrote on his messageboard, "In 2006, at age twenty-four, I edited a restoration of the film combining the low-quality workprint with better quality DVD sources. I called it 'The Recobbled Cut.' Restoring such an obscure film, I assumed only a handful of people would be interested. Instead, 'The Recobbled Cut' has become something of a cult phenomenon, with viewers becoming captivated, as I was, by the tragic story of the film's demise, and then seeing it restored as intended, in the best quality available. Although often criticized for favoring animation style over the substance of story, the film is a masterpiece by any standard, on par with Disney's *Fantasia*, and considered by many to be one of the greatest animated films ever made—something you'd never know from watching the released versions."[22]

Thanks to Gilchrist's efforts, so much of Williams' animation is restored to the film, and, thus, the movie's visual gravitas. Returned are the sweeping helicopter shots approaching and retreating from the Golden City, as well as the "roller coaster" POV shots of the Thief plummeting through the One Eye's war machine. In these days of CGI extravaganzas where these types of first-person thrill ride sequences are *de rigeur*, the fact that these shots are all hand-drawn is nothing short of mind-boggling.

By his own admission, Gilchrist's "Recobbled Cut" is still not, technically, a "director's cut," primarily because Williams was never able to finish the film, though it probably goes without saying that this is the best way to see *The Thief and the Cobbler* today, probably coming as close to Williams' vision as humanly possible. Even still, he doesn't consider even the Mark IV version to be "complete", and continues to seek out lost footage from collectors. (One vexing sequence in particular remains elusive: seen during the end credits of Calvert's version, at one point in the film, the Thief straps springs to his feet and sails through the air. Utilizing multiple and stunning POV shots (possibly inspiring Bill Plympton's "Jumping" short), this "spring feet" sequence has yet to resurface in a clean enough copy. "I'm not sure what exactly still exists from the film," Gilchrist told Williams' son, Alex, in 2012. "When Richard was fired from the film, the Completion Bond Company took everything away, at least that they were aware of, and the animation houses in Korea tended to throw everything away as shots were 'completed.' Richard himself had never been a packrat and threw out older material all the time. I am not sure if he managed to keep or acquire a full 35mm copy of the film at any point. Princess and the Cobbler and Arabian Knight were not released in theaters in any serious way, so prints will be extremely scarce. When Miramax bought the film, apparently—according to Alex Williams, anyway—all the elements and artwork they intended to keep were stored in the Disney archives—a 'bunker in Burbank'."[23]

Yet, even with the admittedly uneven nature of "The Recobbled Cut", one would think that *The Thief and the Cobbler* would be vindicated. Unfortunately, not everyone is as enchanted with the film as its supporters. "From a visual standpoint, *The Thief and the Cobbler* is bold and innovative. Williams and his animation team created a riot of intricate and detailed sequences that have no precedent in animation history. The film's most remarkable sequence involved the title characters in a zany chase through the royal palace, which appears to be decorated in hypnotic black-and-white patterns—it is as if M.C. Escher and Mack Sennett joined forces for a chase to end all chases," wrote my colleague Phil Hall for *Film Threat*. "In watching the Gilchrist quasi-

---

"That's the power of the Internet, that some guy, some failed writer/artist/filmmaker in his apartment can actually make the definitive version of a film just because somebody's gotta. And it happened that that somebody oughta be me." Fenlon, Tested.com.

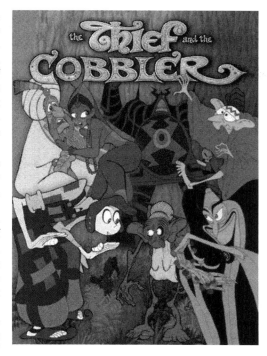

restoration and the unrestored Williams workprint, I can state that *The Thief and the Cobbler* is a masterwork of animation and a complete failure of storytelling. It is a brutal triumph of style and a bitter fiasco of substance. The real tragedy is not that Williams lost the ownership of his work, but that he was allowed by Warner Bros. to proceed without having responsible production controls in place."[24]

Just as was the case with Calvert, Warner Brothers, Miramax, and everyone else with an opinion about art vs. commerce, Gilchrist's efforts have been attacked as well. The cruelest comment I've run across I found on Tested.com: "I heard all this good stuff about this movie. [...] There is a reason Disney never restored this trash. Poor Garrett Gilchrist is stuck wasting his life trying to do what Williams can['t] be bothered to finish for good reason."[25]

Thus lies the crux of the matter: the masterwork of dozens of people is still not appreciated by many in the "general" populace. Another time-worn tradition of art dismissed by an uncaring audience. Sadly, and very unfortunately, Williams—who teaches an extensive animation curriculum today—refuses to even discuss his aborted child, and as of this writing has not seen the fruits of Gilchrist's devoted labor. "Richard is looking at his own workprint of the film only. And that's fine since the only 'finished' version of the film only ever existed in Dick Williams' head," Gilchrist told me via email. "'My Recobbled Cut' was intended for literally everyone else except Dick Williams. For everyone else, it's the version you watch so that it explains to you what the film's supposed to be."[26]

And therein lies the final tragedy. For any artist to have his life's work taken from him and bastardized by butchers is an incomprehensible nightmare. Without putting words in Williams' mouth, the pain must have been unimaginable. So it's understandable that he wouldn't want to watch any version of *The Thief*, it is to be hoped that he's at least aware of Gilchrist's admirable restoration, and that its existence brings the man a modicum of peace.[294]

"Generally when writing about this film, people focus many words on the debacle, and not enough on the artistry and on Richard's skill and vision and what's good about the unfinished film," Gilchrist wrote in his email to me. "Unfortunately, most people don't appreciate how difficult the process of animation is, or the artistry in what Williams was doing. Most people also understand the filmmaking process, and if something is unfinished they think it's bad. The meme persists that the film has no story, or that the story isn't worth mentioning. There is really a negative narrative about this film and I worked hard for seven-plus years to try to change that."[27]

The ultimate irony, however, is that *The Thief* was rejected by Disney, sold to Miramax, which was then bought by Disney, which is where *The Thief* legally resides. Though it's best not to get up too much hope that we'll ever see a completed film. Gilchrist gave us the closest thing.

---

[294] The way one might hope that Walter Murch's re-edit of *Touch of Evil* somehow touched Orson Welles beyond the grave

Screengrab copyright Miramax Films.

NOTES

1 Fenlon, Wesley. 2012. "Thieves, Cobblers, and Fan Edits: The 50-Year Odyssey of an Animated Masterpiece". Tested.com. January 13. http://www.tested.com/art/movies/44961-thieves-cobblers-and-fan-edits-the-50_year-odyssey-of-an-animated-masterpiece/

2 Gilchrist, Garrett. Personal Email exchange. July 24, 2016.

3 Ibid.

4 Williams, Alex. 1997. "The Thief and the Cobbler." Animation World Magazine

5 Ibid.

6 Dobbs, G. Michael. 1996. "An Arabian Knight-mare." Animato! #35. Archived https://groups.google.com/forum/#!msg/rec.arts.animation/3Ye9NZuQ1WM/n2iqyC8T_ecJ

7 Ibid.

8 Fenlon, Tested.com.

9 Gilchrist, 7/24/2016.

10 Dobbs, G. Michael. 1996. "An Arabian Knight-mare." Animato! #35.

11 Williams, Alex. 1997. "The Thief and the Cobbler." Animation World Magazine, Issue 1.12, March 1997. Archived http://www.awn.com/mag/issue1.12/articles/williams1.12.html

12 "Letters to the Editor." Animation World Magazine, Issue 2.1, April 1997 http://www.awn.com/mag/issue2.1/articles/letters2.1.html

13 Ibid

14 O'Connell, Rebecca. 2016. "13 Beautiful Facts About 'The Thief and the Cobbler'." Mental Floss.com. February 11. http://mentalfloss.com/article/74031/13-beautiful-facts-about-thief-and-cobbler

15 Heller, Steven. 2014. "The Greatest Animated Film That Never Was." The Atlantic. December 11. http://www.theatlantic.com/entertainment/archive/2014/12/the-greatest-animated-film-that-never-was/383640/

16 Ibid.

17 Welkos, Robert W. 1995. "How This 'Thief' Became a 'Knight'." L.A. Times. August 30. http://articles.latimes.com/1995-08-30/entertainment/ca-40326_1_richard-williams

18 Williams, Alex. 1997. "The Thief and the Cobbler." Animation World Magazine

19 Dessem, Matthew. 2014. "Animation's lost masterpiece." The Dissolve.com. June 5. https://thedissolve.com/features/movie-of-the-week/602-animations-lost-masterpiece/

20 http://youtube.com/thethiefarchive

21 Gilchrist, 7/24/2016.

22 http://orangecow.org/board/viewtopic.php?f=4&t=3

23 Williams, Alex. 2012. "The Thief & The Cobbler - The Recobbled Cut - Part 2". Flip Animation.blogspot.com. December 5. http://flipanimation.blogspot.com/2012/12/the-recobbled-cut-part-2.html

24 Hall, Phil. "The Bootleg Files 538: The Thief and the Cobbler." www.filmthreat.com/features/78188/#ixzz363bswaLt

25 Fenlon, Tested.com.

26 Personal email conversation. Sunday, July 24, 2016.

27 Ibid.

VIDEODROME (1982)

Unless you lived through it, it's difficult to emphasize just how important the VHS/Home Video revolution was for the budding cinephile. Arriving at the same time as cable TV, the in-home VCR changed the way society devoured entertainment. Prior to the advent of the VCR, those living in this dark period had to rely on "live" commercial-laden (or sometimes absorbed into) television programs, the occasional local station's afternoon ("matinee") or evening showing of whatever they could acquire for syndication (generally mutilated to accommodate more advertising), or re-releases of films that had done particularly well in the past. To give a more-recent example of these "re-releases", I can distinctly remember a special return to '70s and '80s cinemas by such movies as *Young Frankenstein, Gone with the Wind* and even *Star Wars*. These re-releases were big events in and of themselves and attracted audiences in droves, sometimes beating the original box office returns. Nowadays, a re-released film is generally confined to a repertory house, rather than a big box googolplex, targeting nostalgia and "buff" audiences.

By the '80s, VCRs had become as much a household staple as a television. They were clunky and expensive and heavy, the early models had a pop-up tray built into the top to receive the plastic cassette, others had enormous TV dials on the front to program a recording of a live television show. They were, at the time, miracles of modern technology. For the film aficionado, it meant nearly anything you wanted at the very time you wanted it. The hunger for both new and old entertainment meant that not only were Hollywood studios emptying their vaults onto video cassette, but were also producing low budget "straight-to-video" titles for greater consumption. When they ran out of respectable material, the film fanatic could turn to houses like Something Weird for true bizarro output from all over the world. On the other end of the spectrum, cheapjack houses like Goodtimes were snatching up public domain SF/horror cheapies and orphan television shows. Video stores—both the rising chains and the omnipresent "mom and pop" stores had overflowing shelves and lines that stretched out the door. Truly, these were glorious times.

As a result of all this new home technology, studios and artists hired copyright lawyers by the dozens. What were the ramifications, for example, of someone with two (!) VCRs renting a title, copying it, and then lending—or selling—the copy to third parties? Was this a fair use? How about if the copier *bought* the tape, at prices upwards of $100 per? Doesn't he then own that cassette, able to do with it as he will? This gave rise to electronic copy protection, like the proprietary Macrovision, which prevented a second VCR from receiving a clear, copyable signal. This, of course, opened the door wide open for pirates. In the effort to illegally copy videotapes in exchange for a quick buck, pirates then, as today, became technological wizards, able to override whatever stopgaps the studio techs could come up with.[295]

At the same time as the VHS boom, small television licenses were offered to local stations for broadcast on the lower UHF frequencies. This gave rise to the ever-parodied "public access" shows featuring amateurish lighting, single-set chat shows, "horror hosts", and paranoid rants from televangelists. (See *Wayne's World* or Weird Al's *UHF* if you're thus-far uninitiated). The allure of these lower frequencies mirrored the allure of the bizarre offerings from video stores: the chance to see something taboo, forbidden, fucking weird.

That's where *Videodrome* starts: the search for something fucking weird.

Max Renn (James Woods) runs the channel CIVIC-TV, a UHF station dedicated to softcore pornography and horror junk. His latest acquisition, *Samurai Dreams*, may do well for him, but cable is putting a dent in the softcore market. His partner, Harlan (Peter Dvorsky), scans satellite signals for the unique and different. Which is how he discovers a few precious minutes of "Videodrome", a plotless show set in a wet clay room, naked victims hanging from chains while their hooded captors torture and electrocute them. Max becomes instantly obsessed with the show and order Harlan to find more.

In the meantime, Max appears on a television talk show alongside radio host psychiatrist Nikki Brand (Debbie Harry), and the pop culture guru, Brian O'Blivion (Jack Creley), who only appears via closed circuit television. They debate the rise of violence and sex on television and Renn defends his feeding of the purile nature of his audience. O'Blivion's opinion is that television will soon supplant real life, with the cathode ray tube replacing experience. While O'Blivion o'bloviates, Renn asks Nikki out.

Back at Max's apartment, Nikki discovers his "Videodrome" tapes and becomes aroused, grilling him on "Videodrome"'s origins and how she could become a "contestant". A masochist, she first asks Max to "cut her, just a little" on her shoulder. When he refuses, she puts a cigarette out on her breast.

Revisiting the station, Max is informed that Harlan has located the source of the "Videodrome" signal. Instead of Malaysia as first expected, the surprise is that "Videodrome" is broadcast right out of Pittsburgh, PA. As Max continues to expose himself to the show, he begins to experience nightmares and then waking hallucinations. Then, after telling him of her intention to "audition" for the show, Nikki disappears. Becoming increasingly paranoid and anxious, Max takes to carrying a gun around his apartment. Sitting shirtless (save for a shoulder holster), Max discovers a rash on his abdomen that turns into a bloodless gash. Prodding it with the barrel of the gun, the gash sucks his hand in up to the wrist. He manages to pull away but the gun is now lost inside of him. On the TV, Nikki's face begs for a kiss. Crawling to the set, the screen bulges, rubberized, and Nikki's projected lips envelop his head.

Through Masha (Lynn Gorman), a softcore producer and friend, Max learns that not only is the "Videodrome" footage not faked, it's actually the "public face of a political movement,"

---

[295] In my day, Pirates were different from Bootleggers. Bootleggers, as I understand it, were the ones exploiting overseas copyright laws in order to copy films from overseas that were otherwise unavailable commercially in the U.S. or UK. It was thanks to the bootleggers that fans could devour "grey market" anime and Hong Kong action films, uncut Italian Gore, and the notorious Video Nasties. In the internet days, bootlegging and pirating seems to have merged. Torrents are the new bootlegs. Sites like the beleaguered Pirate Bay and Kickass Torrents cater to the "I need it now" crowd. Shadier underground operations like Cinemageddon are admission-only meccas for uncut films, European-only releases, and things that never made the transition from VHS to DVD. The members-only sites are your best bet to catch some of the films I discuss in these books. Not that I can legally condone this, of course. All I'm saying is, without bootlegging, I never would have been able to afford film school.

and that the mastermind behind it is none other than Brian O'Blivion. (Dun-dun-*duuuhhn!*) Heading to Pittsburgh, Max visits The Cathode Ray Mission, run by O'Blivion's daughter, Bianca (Sonja Smits), where the homeless are given food, shelter, and twenty-four hour exposure to television, fulfilling her father's mission to have television replace all aspects of waking life. She reveals to Max that her father is actually dead, the victim of a brain tumor, but had the foresight to record countless hours of video that would help maintain the illusion that he is still alive and kicking. Thousands upon thousands of tapes line the back walls of his office in the Mission. On one, O'Blivion lays out his belief that "the Videodrome" is the "socio-political battleground" upon which will be fought the war for the minds of humanity.

While O'Blivion was one of the creators of "Videodrome", he attempted to halt its use after discovering that his partners, including eyeglass magnate Barry Convex (Leslie Carlson) (who heads Spectacular Optical Corporation, a front for a weapons manufacturer), intends to use a signal implanted in the Videodrome broadcast to induce mind-altering tumors in the brains of those who view it. By loading the image with excessive sexual violence, Convex plans to "weed out" the malcontents of society. For only those who would willingly—gleefully—watch such drek would be susceptible. "Lowlifes" in Convex's opinion. Malcontents. Enemies of the state.

Convex inserts a mind-control video into Max's stomach slit which compels him to murder his colleagues at CIVIC-TV. He achieves this vicious goal by retrieving the gun lost inside of his torso. Withdrawing it from the slit, the gun seemingly merges its metal parts with the flesh of his hand, turning it into a bioweapon that fires bullets whose wounds erupt into cancerous growths. Before he can murder Bianca, she manages to reprogram him to fight against Convex and the Videodrome conspiracy. To defeat them completely, she tells Max that he must abandon the old flesh and transcend. She tells him, "Long live the New Flesh."

The son of a journalist father and a musician mother, Cronenberg studied biochemistry at the University of Toronto before transferring to the English department. Influenced by such filmmakers as Kenneth Anger and Canadian experimentalist Michael Snow[296], Cronenberg experimented with style and tone in early short 16mm films, *Transfer* (1966), *From the Drain* (1977), *Stereo* (1969) and the short feature *Crimes of the Future* (1970). He doesn't deny that his early medical education may have begun his fascination with the corruption of the body. "I did my dissection of foetal pigs and a few other things, because I started off in organic chemistry. I think I would've ended up being a cell biologist. And it was pretty gothic, that's true, and in fact it was the way the science was being taught that drove me out of the field of science. I felt that the students around me were so different from me and I ended up spending all my time hanging round with all the English language and philosophy students. So I can't say the University of Toronto led me to horror, but what it did do was lead me to cinema, though I never studied cinema. There was a student called David Secter who was making a movie called *Winter Kept Us Warm*, which starred some friends of mine. And it never occurred to me that you could make a movie. It was unlike someone growing up in LA where everybody's parents were in the business. In Toronto, no one's parents were in the movie business because there wasn't a movie business. So that was more influential in leading me to biological horror. I never thought of the biology

---

[296] Michael Snow's short film, *Wavelength*, a 45-minute dolly/zoom into a photograph on the wall, accompanied by a high-pitched tone that induces nausea, was a favorite selection of my instructors at Pittsburgh Filmmakers. As a result, I've banned it from my own classes.

part of it as horrific anyway. I thought that was all incredibly exciting, even dissecting the foetal pig, which if you shot that scene in a movie, it might be rather gross for people. To feel that you were really beginning to understand the form of life, how life came to be and exists, that was exciting. That's not horror to me, that's pure ecstasy actually."[1]

For decades, the filmmaker wrote and directed films unique to his psyche. The terms "Cronenberg-esque" and "body horror" were invented to describe his obsessive themes of malevolent disease, corruption of the human body, suppressed emotion bubbling forth as rage, murder, and sexual deviancy. He explored these themes in such films as *Shivers* (aka *They Came From Within*—sexual obsession driven by a biological parasite), *Rabid* (a plastic surgery recipient becomes a vampiric creature with a phallic, blood-draining appendage growing beneath her arm), *The Brood* (unorthodox psychology recommending developing fleshy physical manifestation of negative emotions that grow into murderous childlike monsters), and even his compelling remake of *The Fly* (in which a scientist's DNA is merged with the titular creature, causing grotesque physical transformation of human into insect). For my money, *Videodrome* is the culmination of the filmmaker's obsessions: sexual deviancy and violence exploited by unbridled pirate capitalists utilized by a utilitarian shadow contingency causing damage to the mental, the physical, and the perception of reality itself.

"Cronenberg's films, [...] explore new areas of horror that other directors would shrink from, if indeed they would ever even consider. Apocalyptic examinations of physical and psychological disintegration, Cronenberg's films resonate with contemporary life as it is inexorably evolving. And Cronenberg's key horror films [...] represent one of the most sustained records of artistic achievement since Hitchcock, Antonioni, Fellini, and Bergman in their prime," wrote Charles Derry. "Exploiting some of the issues raised in Susan Sontag's *Illness as Metaphor*[297], Cronenberg shows human beings whose bodies are transformed by disease or mutation into a more advanced, if psychologically traumatizing, state. The illness or mutated body becomes an other to be feared, as well as a metaphor for secret desires or social impulses. Ultimately, the body takes a revenge upon the individual, who often becomes alienated from and painfully imprisoned in his or her body. Cronenberg's films also show future apocalypse brought about by technology hailed as evolutionary. [...] Three other early Cronenberg films form a kind of trilogy of frightening body mutations. *The Brood*, directed by Cronenberg in 1979, deals with feminist-inspired hostility, especially that of women toward the physical reality of childbirth and the demands of child rearing. *The Brood* argues implicitly for the nonpropagation of the species by showing violent children—born from a sac outside the mother's body—who come to embody all the tensions and hostilities reposited in the nuclear family. Especially disturbing is the image of Samantha Eggar as Nola, bloodily tearing open her own fetal sac with her teeth. Another fascinating horror film, if not Cronenberg's most wholly successful, is *Videodrome* (1982), which predicts a sadomasochistic human future and contemplates our destruction as we lose our humanity and almost literally turn into videocassette recorders. Indeed, the image of a man growing a kind of deformed vaginal slit for a videocassette is especially repellent, balancing Cronenberg's earlier image, in *Rabid* (1977), of a woman growing a kind of deformed pineal set of jaws under her arm."[2]

"As an outsider Cronenberg is in many respects excellently placed to take a swipe at the eccentricities of Hollywood. He has lived in Toronto—the backdrop for many of his movies—his entire life[298]. [...] But Cronenberg is not a total outsider. Long ago, he was tapped up to see if he might direct *Return of the Jedi*,[299] and over the years he has had many involved, ultimately

---

[297] 1978, published by Farrar, Straus & Giroux.

[298] "Maps to the Stars is the first time he has actually filmed in Los Angeles; he spent five days there mostly, he says wryly, shooting palm trees." Lewis, Tim. 2014. "David Cronenberg: 'My imagination is not a place of horror'." The Guardian. September 14. https://www.theguardian.com/film/2014/sep/14/david-cronenberg-interview-my-imagination-not-a-place-of-horror

[299] Contrary to popular belief, Cronenberg received numerous offers to direct bigger budgeted movies, thanks only to the critical successes of his films. "Recently? *The Truman Show* and *Aliens 4* [sic], and in the early days things like *Witness*

doomed discussions with several of the major studios about making films, perhaps most intriguingly a spy caper with MGM starring Denzel Washington and Tom Cruise," wrote Tim Lewis for The Guardian in 2014. "'I'm 2,500 miles away from Hollywood and consider myself literally and figuratively halfway between Hollywood and Europe in terms of my cinema sensibility," says Cronenberg. "And being a Canadian, being outside the mainstream of America—as Marshall McLuhan used to say—allows you to have perceptions that you could not have otherwise. Like they say: 'A fish doesn't know what water is.' You have to be outside water to know what water is.'"[3]

In the early '80s, Cronenberg worked nearly exclusively in Canada, taking advantage of governmental tax credits to film his unusual horror/science-fiction allegories. When his tale of psychic terrorism, *Scanners*, became a box office sensation across North America, he was given virtually free-reign to let his cinematic imagination run wild. With *Videodrome*, he combined the all the puerile "marketable" elements of sensationalistic nudity and gore with the moral question of "who likes this shit?" asked *ad nauseum* by Reagan-era alarmists. This was the time of the Video Nasty panic spreading through the United Kingdom; in the United States, "Satanic Panic" was sweeping the nation. By approaching the gory effects-heavy horror genre from an intellectual standpoint, run through a post-noir narrative structure, Cronenberg attempted to explore "adult concerns" about violent entertainment without taking a moralistic stand on either side.

"['Videodrome' is] a torture and murder show, featuring guys in hoods torturing and electrocuting various victims. Renn figures he can broadcast the show free, because how will Brazil learn what Toronto is doing? He tries to learn more about the show and discovers what he's seen is real—Snuff TV—and it's being done for a very private clientele. I invented a sophisticated video underground—at least I hope I invented it—that exists in each country, expressing whatever is suppressed by that country's political and personal taboos," Cronenberg told Tim Lucas (the only journalist invited to visit the highly secretive set)[300]. "Cronenberg was quite willing to discuss what it is not: an attack on the television industry, 'I won't be surprised, but I'll be disappointed, if people read it that way,' he said. 'I think people who plug into the straightforward moral stance at the beginning of the film will find themselves utterly confused by the end of it. It's more subtle than that. People who have the simplistic outlook that says. 'TV is bad, it's rotting our minds,' won't understand. [...] Once again, I'm interested in the incredible way people alter their environment without knowing the consequences; you might consider that either foolhardy or courageous, *Videodrome* is about more than TV; it's about sex and violence *on* TV. People may approach it as some moral parable, but it's not specifically an attack on TV, as was *Network* [1976]. In public, Max Renn claims that televised sex and violence will help him survive in the cable business. But he's also *personally* fascinated with these things. So, the real question becomes: does democratic capitalism force him to 'do bad,' or is this an evil spawned by a private obsession?'"[4]

Certainly, Max Renn is no admirable protagonist. By casting his central character as a cynical producer whose livelihood depends on the insatiable appetites of his viewers, Cronenberg sets the baseline for his own audience. Who are we, he asks, we folks who devour the blood and gore and nihilism of slasher movies? In the '80s, we couldn't get enough of unstoppable murderers "hacking up young virgins"[301]. Was it the fascination with the new wave of realistic practical effects and their artists presenting dismemberment in the most realistic fashion ever seen? Or was it our bloodlust stirred in those dark theaters? Were we seeking catharsis or

---

and *Top Gun*. Oh, and *Flashdance*. [Producer] Dawn Steele, for some reason, kept bugging me to do *Flashdance*! And I kept saying 'No.' and 'You won't thank me! I would destroy this!' [...] The problem with doing a schlocky or big budget studio film is that it wouldn't actually be fun for me. It wouldn't be exciting. My rule of thumb is this: You're six months into it, you've got six months to go. It's February. It's winter. It's dark. Am I suicidal, or am I really excited and happy? And the answer with those projects would be, 'I'm suicidal.'" Contact Music.com

[300] Who collected his reportings for a marvelously detailed book, *Studies in the Horror Film: Videodrome*. China: Centipede Press. ISBN 1-933618-28-0.

[301] In the parlance of Peter Vincent (Roddy MacDowell) in *Fright Night* (1986, Dir. Tom Holland).

validation for our darkest natures? Honestly, we were better than Max's subscribers, weren't we? Sure, we were attracted to the exploitation, but then we went back to work then next day, resuming our roles as productive members of society.

"Cronenberg's sixth feature, released in 1983, just a few years into the home video revolution, ingeniously pairs the gross-out body horror of his earlier films with the techno-poetic musings of media guru (and fellow Torontonian) Marshall McLuhan. A droll, chilling riff on McLuhan's view of media as "extensions of man," *Videodrome* is a supremely trippy meditation on the transformative power of images, on the fraught relationship between what we watch and who we are," wrote Dennis Lim. "In its own elusive fashion, Videodrome addresses one of the hot-button issues of the culture wars: the effects on the viewer of exposure to violent imagery. The film revels in Max and Nikki's voyeuristic desires, even while apparently supporting the idea that graphic images can affect us in ways we don't immediately understand. Convex speaks in punitive terms of the decision to implant the brain-warping signal in debased pornographic material, but the point that it could have been embedded in any telecast echoes McLuhan's assertion that the medium is the message. The ambiguity in Cronenberg's films has led to charges of conservatism, but he is more a satirist than a moralist, and his films are above all philosophical. It's perhaps best to view the Videodrome virus as a technological variant on the epidemics of his earlier films, in which extravagantly repulsive diseases are reimagined as revolutionary agents of change. In both *They Came from Within* (aka *Shivers*, 1975) and *Rabid*, the plagues attack repression and bourgeois norms, ultimately purging bland, dehumanized communities. Whether or not Cronenberg is fully on the side of the infection, he gravitates toward characters who are poised to escape their corporeal prison or otherwise cast off the shackles of self, even if the emancipation eventually proves untenable."[5]

Cronenberg further muddies the waters by making Max's journey towards redemption a possible side-effect of brain damage—residual tumors induced by the low-grade radiation given off by Convex's virtual reality headgear, perhaps. Or else *Videodrome*'s malevolent sub-signal was genuine, affecting Max's brain chemistry. Either way, our anti-hero is not in his right mind for the majority of the film's running time. By the film's midway point, it's nearly impossible to tell if Max's reality has any corroboration to our own. Even the murders he commits under Convex's videotape—are they even real? If so, is he being controlled or has the stress finally snapped his mind? From a moral standpoint, Max's self-interests are rarely superseded by the concepts of "right" and "wrong". We get little indication that Max is bothered by the shit he shovels onto his audience, so perhaps his perceived manipulation by both Convex and Bianca is simply both sides of his own psyche at war with itself.

Even the people Max encounters could later be hallucinations. It's curious, for example, that Nikki Brand would be in the least bit attracted to the sleazy Renn. "Debbie, who portrays a psychologist /radio personality in the disturbing film about television and mind control, has given serious thought to the character she plays. 'Nikki was a little bit ambiguous,' says Debbie, 'she was mysterious. She did what she was hired to do. But what happened with the film was that it changed a lot in the editing, and the finished version is even more ambiguous than what we originally shot. As such, you never really know whether I'm actually a real person or in Jimmy's [co-star James Woods] mind or a video image. It could be interpreted on both levels; they tell him that I was never there, that I was just planted in his brain," she told *Starlog*'s Lisa Robinson. "As for TV and mind control, Debbie says, 'I think it is possible to project things from the TV. Obviously, there's a certain amount of mind control involved with TV, but I don't know if that could make you bio-mechanical. I was talking to Bob Marks, the astrologer, and he said that, since they've cracked the genetic code and they can clone, anything is possible. I do know that some people can't live without watching television. And,' she smiles, 'I always wondered if perhaps the moon landing was done in a studio.'"[6]

(Harry's presence in the film automatically gave *Videodrome* a punk authenticity, helping it establish a cult following long before the cyberpunks rediscovered it in the late '80s. "'[Don't] forget, I had done some sort of underground type movies before with Amos Poe[302],' she says, 'but yes, I guess this was my first 'real' movie. I found everyone working on it to be much slower, much straighter, than they are in rock and roll. It wasn't as depraved,'" said Harry. [...] 'I knew I had to make a transition with my audience,' she says, 'and at first, I thought I should establish a more easy, positive image than just jump into this. I was concerned about how I ended up in the movie, how masochistic I was to be, and what would happen to me physically. But after thinking about it, I just couldn't pass it up. It's too important a movie.'")[7]

In a lot of ways, this uncertainty is what makes *Videodrome* so compelling and endlessly watchable. Taken at face value, it's a surreal mystery with horrific overtones, replete with breathing, living plastic, proto-cyberpunk bioweaponry that cause internal tumors to burst through skull and tissue, and the inextricable symbiotic relationship between television radiation and the human body. But *Videodrome* doesn't exist on the surface. It's a movie whose subtext bubbles up unbidden, asking questions you may not want to answer, forcing you to question what it is that you're experiencing. In that way, a viewer can continually revisit *Videodrome* and see something different each time. As the viewer matures, so does his connection with the themes of the film.

"The bizarre and troubling mutations of body and machine manifest in Cronenberg movies[303] graphically illustrate the way he intentionally exteriorizes the body's functions of processing information, absorbing medication, and operating technology. Far from advocating repression, his films argue that the revolution begins at home—right in our central nervous systems and psyches," wrote Carrie Rickey in 1983. "In *Videodrome*, Cronenberg identi-fies power structures that are, essentially, invisible. While exalt-ing the awesome dynamics of the body—its sexual energy, its capacity for the extra-sensory, its suggestibility—he implies that the body is a transient state between individual existence and the creation of a "new flesh" for which the television screen is, literally, the retina of the mind's eye. In the trancelike, confounding universe of *Videodrome*, the only way to resist eradication is to trans-form oneself into pure electronic energy. [...] Centrally, *Videodrome* is about those who would control access to all broadcasting, who can unscramble all the scrambling devices, who can wash all the satellite dishes and incre-men-tally coerce all TV dropouts to tune in. Led by a benign-looking despot named Barry Convex, these cable totalitarians revel in the fact that they can search for and destroy their natural adversaries because thrill--seeking counterculturalists are easy marks for hidden signals beamed during more radical television entertainments. *Videodrome* is the 1984 blue-print contextualized. [...] Mystifying? *Videodrome* exalts technology while excoriating tech-nocracy, painting a dystopian picture. It is at once a baffling and entirely credible depiction: Cronenberg expresses what is usually repressed and makes visible those networks of power not seen by the naked eye. 'If you're a wishy-washy Canadian liberal,' sighed Cronenberg, 'who's the enemy? . . . I don't have a moral plan—I'm Canadian.'

"Yet there's a dazzling glimpse of Cronenberg's morality in *Videodrome*, the ultimate commitment to comprehending how the reality delivered by the media affects us figuratively—and literally. Videocassettes anthropomorphize—this was a decade before people talked about "virtual reality" but just before Cronenberg worked on a screenplay called *Total Recall*, which

---

[302] Amos Poe is considered to be one of the first true "punk" filmmakers, part of "The Remodernist" film movement, following the success of his film *The Blank Generation* (1976, co-directed with Ivan Kral), featuring early performance footage of Patti Smith, Richard Hell, The Talking Heads, and other members of the emerging New York punk scene. Harry worked with him in *The Foreigner* (1978).

[303] "You know, they talk about me as the inventor of body horror. But I've never thought of it as being horrific. Of course, you're being a showman, and if you're making a low-budget horror film—there were a lot of those around at the time—how do you get yourself noticed? Certainly I was in the world, and not an abstractionist. I was trying to make movies and continue to make movies. But there's the philosophical underpinning for all of it. If neurology is reality, that's an incredible theme—how to structure a narrative that will discuss that? Immediately you're into changing the body to change the reality, and that's what led me to all of those things like *Videodrome*." Wallace, Chris. 2014. "DAVID CRONENBERG." Interview Magazine. October 15. http://www.interviewmagazine.com/film/david-cronenberg/

became an Arnold Schwarzenegger blockbuster. TV reaches out to touch you—your body becomes the television apparatus. Early in the twentieth century, painter Paul Klee proposed that art was not the reproduction of reality but the invention of it. Cronenberg's revision of that is that art should identify reality. Then enlarge it."[8]

Highly anticipated to be a huge success—"Executive producer Victor Solnicki revealed that, regardless of *Videodrome*'s strong sexual and violent content, "soft" versions of several scenes were filmed. 'A TV version acts as an insurance policy on any picture costing more than $6 million,' said Solnicki. 'But the peculiar content doesn't concern us, commercially. Look at *A Clockwork Orange*. It was picture without a niche, but it had a classy and menacing advertising campaign and did beautifully at the box office. *Videodrome* has so many selling points, our publicity department has a wealth of materials on which to focus—it's a savagely satirical look at the media, it features outstanding actors, it's sexy, it has incredible special effects, and it has David himself. I feel David has great star potential. He'd be perfect for TV talk shows. When you compare this normal-looking man to his work, you have to fight an impulse to ask, 'What's a nice guy like you...?'"[9]—*Videodrome* was largely a critical failure, and definitely a financial one.

"Even Hitchcock liked to think of himself as a puppeteer who was manipulating the strings of his audience and making them jump. He liked to think he had that kind of control. I don't think that kind of control is possible beyond a very obvious kind of physical twitch when something jumps out of the corner of a frame. I also think the relationship I have with my audience is a lot more complex than what Hitchcock seemed to want his to be—although I think he had more going on under the surface as well," the director said in 1999. "But you can't control all of that. Anybody who comes tithe cinema is bringing they're whole sexual history, their literary history, their movie literacy, their culture, their language, their religion, whatever they've got. I can't possibly manipulate all of that, nor do I want to. I'm often surprised—I expect to be surprised—by my audience's reactions to things."[10]

Despite the efforts of critics at the time, *Videodrome* refuses to be boxed in as "splatter", cannot be dismissed as "puerile". Thanks in part to a provocative image of viscera pouring through the screen of a destroyed television (taken from the film's climax) that graced the cover of *Fangoria* #25, *Videodrome* was decried by critics as the apex of bad taste, a symbol for all that was wrong with the movie industry's corrupting influence on young minds. A brand new "Seduction of the Innocent" for the '80s. They needn't have bothered. Despite winning a number of science fiction-related awards, (including "Best Science-Fiction Film" at the 1984 Brussels International Festival of Fantasy Film where it tied for (wait for it) *Bloodbath at the House of Death!*), *Videodrome* left theaters almost as quickly as it arrived.

Following its theatrical demise, *Videodrome* (ironically?) found a new life on home video and cable, though it was often simply referred to as a "weird film", albeit sharing the title in good company with such offerings as *Visitor Q, El Topo, Jacob's Ladder,* and *Eraserhead*—all films with more going on than the sum of its visuals. While the film always had its supporters—chief among them *Video Watchdog* publisher Tim Lucas—it wasn't until it was adopted into the Criterion Collection that "serious" critics finally revisited the modern day Boschian nightmare.

Sometimes termed "prophetic," *Videodrome* is prescient in much the same way as its cyberpunk kin, William Gibson's 1984 novel *Neuromancer*. It grasped the cultural and existential implications of emerging technologies at an early stage, and its "sci-fi" extrapolations have come to seem less far-fetched as those technologies have extended their reach. We may not have developed video-ready orifices just yet, but *Videodrome* can only resonate more profoundly as our dependence on—and communion with—technology continues to reach unprecedented levels and as the gratification promised by virtual worlds becomes ever more immediate. There is also the matter of content. Lightweight cameras and Internet video have made it easier than ever before to capture and disseminate footage of real sex and real death. In the early twenty-first century, extreme imagery is not something that might drift into your living room in the middle of the night from a wayward cable broadcast—often enough it's on CNN, and for anyone with an Internet connection, the hard stuff is just a couple of clicks away."

For my part, *Videodrome* latched onto my psyche at a too-early age and refused to leave. Though I was too young to parse the underpinning cultural discussion, its surreal visual themes

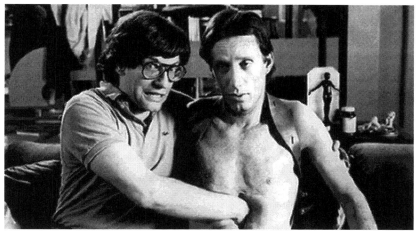

Source Unknown. This Image is pirated.

haunted me well into adulthood. Today it's a film that I find myself revisiting more than any other movie. Each time I watch and I think I have a grasp of its nature, something slips away and leaves me with questions I hadn't had previously. This is why I assert that *Videodrome* becomes a different movie upon each viewing, depending solely on where your head and heart is when you watch. To paraphrase Heraclitus[11], one can never dive twice into *Videodrome*, for it is never the same movie, and you are not the same person.

"My imagination is not full of horrors at all. This is the misunderstanding of what my movies are. First of all, I think all my movies are funny. Not everything in them is funny, but they are full of humour. And second, it's not really my imagination. Anybody looking at the news on the internet or in a newspaper, there's horror there every day—compared with that, my imagination is a wonderful playground! So I don't feel that my imagination is a place of horror at all."[12]

NOTES

[1] Lewis, Tim. 2014. "David Cronenberg: 'My imagination is not a place of horror'." The Guardian. September 14. https://www.theguardian.com/film/2014/sep/14/david-cronenberg-interview-my-imagination-not-a-place-of-horror

[2] Derry, Charles. "Dark dreams 2.0 : A Psychological History Of The Modern Horror Film From The 1950s To The 21st Century." McFarland & Company, Inc., Publishers 2009. PP. 330-333

[3] Lewis, 2014.

[4] Lucas, Tim. 1982. "Videodrome." *Cinefanatastique.* Vol. 12, No 2/ No. 3. April. P. 5

[5] Lim, Dennis, "Videodrome." Chapter from "The B List : The National Society Of Film Critics On The Low-Budget Beauties, Genre-Bending Mavericks, And Cult Classics We Love." edited by David Sterritt and John Anderson. 2008 Published by Da Capo Press. PP 184

[6] Robinson, Lisa. 1984. "Deborah Harry." *Best of Starlog.* No. V. O'Quinn Studios. P. 40

[7] Ibid

[8] Rickey, Carrie. 1983. "Videodrome: Make Mine Cronenberg." The Village Voice. January. Archived at: https://www.criterion.com/current/posts/337-videodrome-make-mine-cronenberg

[9] Lucas, 1982.

[10] Bison, Brave. "David Cronenberg Interview". Contact Music.com http://www.contactmusic.com/david-cronenberg/cronenberg

[11] Heraclitus of Ephesus (c. 535 – c. 475 BCE) was a pre-Socratic Greek philosopher, he was called "The Obscure" and the "Weeping Philosopher". *Panta chōrei kai ouden menei kai dis es ton auton potamon ouk an embaies…* "Everything changes and nothing remains still … and … you cannot step twice into the same stream." https://en.wikipedia.org/wiki/Heraclitus

[12] Lewis, 2014.

VIVA MAX! (1969)

"All persons mentioned in this story are completely fictitious except for: Davy Crockett, Col. William B. Travis, James Bowie, John Wayne, and Richard Widmark."

Okay, here's a movie whose absence on DVD is borderline criminal. Based on a book by world-renowned journalist Jim Leher[305], directed by TV vet Jerry Paris (replacing Arthur Hiller, and Telly Savalas bowing out of the title role, after a long delay in which the production moved from MGM to Commonwealth United, a division of CBS), starring the most marvelous character actors since *It's a Mad, Mad, Mad, Mad World*—Peter Ustinov, John Astin, Keenan Wynn, Kenneth Mars AND Jonathan Winters (to say nothing of Paul Sand, Alice Ghostly, Harry Morgan, Gino Conforti, and Larry Hankin)—and a wonderfully Quixotic story about a lovesick Mexican general who leads less than 100 soldiers across the border to re-take the Alamo. Hell, with all the rhetoric coming from politicians today shouting to build a Trump wall to keep out illegal immigrants, this gentle satire feels even more relevant today than it was in '69. So where the hell is the remastered DVD? I ask to the various On Demand services out there (Warner Archive, I'm looking at you!).

Border Guard: "Do you intend to attempt to overthrow the government of the United States of America?"

General Maximilian Rodrigues De Santos: "With less than a hundred men?"

---

[304] Lovely poster painted by MAD Magazine impresario Jack Davis (RIP 7/27/2016)

[305] Jim Lehrer sold the rights to the book for about $45,000. It was to come from the amount of money the producer would raise for the film's entire production budget rather than from Hollywood's elusive "net profits." Reportedly, Lehrer used the money to quit his newspaper job and head to Washington, DC to try to land a TV anchor gig. He undoubtedly succeeded with public television's The MacNeil/Lehrer News Hour, which morphed into The News Hour with Jim Lehrer and then the PBS News Hour." Lisanti, Tom. 2016. "Viva Pamela! An Excerpt from Pamela Tiffin: Hollywood To Rome, 1961-1974". March 2nd. http://sixtiescinema.com/2016/03/02/viva-pamela-an-excerpt-from-pamela-tiffin-hollywood-to-rome-1961-1967/

Border Guard: "Yes or no, General?"

General: (Looks sad.) "No."

Under the auspice of marching in a parade in Laredo ("It is somebody's birthday," the General informs the Border Guard. The Border Guard replies, "It's Washington's Birthday." General: "Yes, that's it."), General Maximilian Rodrigues De Santos mounts his giant white horse and leads a small platoon of disgruntled soldiers into Texas. His men don't respect him even a little, but thanks to the loyalty of his beloved Sergeant Valdez (the transcendently perfect John Astin), the General is oblivious of this. In fact, Valdez threatens every man that he will shoot them "in a very bad place" if they do not obey. So struggling under musical instruments and unloaded guns, the Lil' Militia That Could regretfully stomps into America.

General: "I want everything that was said [written] down in case we don't survive."

Valdez: "But General, how could we not survive a parade?"

You see, in point of fact, General De Santos intends to re-occupy The Alamo, to follow in the footsteps of Mexican hero General Santa Ana, and prove to his beloved Maria Consuelo that he is, indeed, a great leader.

> **General:** "A friend of mine, a woman, she told me the men do not respect me. She said they would not follow me even into a whorehouse!"
>
> **Valdez:** "She is wrong, senõr. The men *would* follow you into a whorehouse."

While Valdez scolds the parade from ogling a billboard for "Maidenform Brassieres", they are all nearly killed by a Buick driven by a typical unhappy Midwestern family. Commandeering the vehicle, DeSantos and Romero (who used to drive a cab in Guadalajara and should be able to do so in Texas) also commandeer their ridiculous clothes—with DeSanto in an incredibly ill-fitting suit, Hawaiian shirt, and straw chapeau—the two drive out to the Alamo to stake out its defenses. There they, and we, are given a tour of the famous battle site. Also while there, the General encounters Paula Whitland (Pamela Tiffen), who sells postcards by day, and is a student radical by night. (As Lisanti wrote, "Commenting on her character, Pamela said, "It's a marvelously funny role. I play this girl who could have been yesterday's cheerleader or baton twirler, but today she is a go-go political science major, an activist who loves to use big words like 'absolutism' or 'totalitarian.' She might never have been out of San Antonio yet you know that she cares for the world.")[1]

Returning to his men, DeSantos mounts his horse (after Romero drives the car into a creek) and leads his men into town. Almost immediately, an old lady backs into Romero, wrecking his bass drum and spraining his ankle. DeSantos hijacks a bus and orders the driver to take Romero to the Alamo. The driver argues that he isn't going there. Fortunately, a helpful passenger informs him that he could drop Romero off at the next stop and he could transfer. A groaning Romero accepts this compromise.

Racing against the clock now, the General and his men manage to seize the building just before closing (5:00), taking the workers (including Paula) prisoner. The local Sherriff thinks the occupation is a college prank. Gradually, the surrounding populace realizes that the General is completely serious. So on guard against disrespect, DeSantos refuses to speak to anyone beneath the rank of general. Unfortunately, the closest General San Antonio has on hand is General Billy Joe Hallson (Winters) (who missed World War II because he was installing fluorescent lights at Fort Hawkins) who runs the local furniture store. Reaching General Lacomber (Keenan Wynn) on the phone, DeSantos is further insulted when the military honcho tells him "Mexico isn't exactly the Soviet Union, after all" and tells him that if the Army leaves in peace, the U.S. military will look the other way.

Meanwhile, local fussbudget Hattie (Alice Ghostly) contacts her nephew, Dr. Sam Gillison (the ever-outrageous Kenneth Mars), and gives him the goods on what she perceives is a Communist China plot masquerading as a Mexican invasion. Gillison heads an anti-Communist militia, and he leads his own rag-tag band of miscreants to win back the Alamo. All through this, Paula believes that DeSantos could be an updated Che Guevara and bring real change to the political atmosphere. Until, well, he turns out to be less Guevara and more... well, DeSantos. While we, the audience, are just hoping everyone makes it out alive. The odds are pretty good— neither side is carrying ammunition!

Thanks to the Internet and its culture of "satire sites" generating blatant fiction in order to score "clicks" for its advertisers, the actual idea of satire has been beaten and thrown into a wayside ditch. The best satire—*Network, The Front Page, Brazil*—skewers cultural and social norms, usually by portraying those in power as weak-minded, indecisive, and worshippers of the CYA protocol. Middling satire "punches down", beating up on those who are eagerly ushering society into a large, nihilistic ditch. Middling Satire, like *Ideocracy,* attacks the common man for not aspiring to something greater. Middling Satire is often harsher towards the "average" or "below average" intelligence of the populace who can't be trusted to make their own decisions because, like the uber-rich, will only do something if it personally benefits their own preconceived beliefs. It punches down on those who are anti-intelligence, pro inequality, pro dogma of any religion but especially the dominant Christian culture, etc. Middling Satire is often an indictment of society as a whole, an anchor dragging down progress.

This all largely stems from the "gentle" Roman satirist, Horace (65–8 BCE), whose satire reminded us that we're all in this together, yet we're always looking for an external fall guy, someone we can point to and say "it's his fault, not mine", and how disingenuous this attitude is. This attitude, of course, prevails to this day. Look at our current crop of politicians providing the easy answers to the angry populace: "It's not your fault you're broke and hungry—and it's not *our fault* either for stealing your money. It's obviously the fault of the Mexicans/Jews/Homosexuals/Hottentots!" This justifies the bigoted anger of the dis-enfranchised. And when in doubt, misdirection always works best.

Politician A: "I think we should have a discussion about gun control."

Politician B: "He's trying to deny your 2nd Amendment Rights! Get him!"

Viva Max! is possibly the gentlest of satires because it's not saying anyone is particularly wrong, but their actions are borne out of feelings that are as far from altruistic as you can get. DeSantos doesn't really want to be a great general, has no real beef with America, he just wants his girlfriend to respect him. So if he conquers America, maybe she will. Valdez loves De Santos—he's Sancho Panza to De Santos' deluded Don Quixote—and he'll do anything to prevent the buffoon from further humiliation. Hattie and Gillison are staunch Americans who are terrified by the notion of Communists running this country, though it's obvious they have no real understanding of Communism or its followers. They've just been told that "Communism = Bad" since the 1930s. They're protecting their American ideals. Pamela is doing the same but from a "leftist, Pinko" point of view. She wants De Santos to be a figurehead for her imaginary revolution. The Sherriff just wants to go home and go to bed, but he can't because he has a museum full of whack-jobs throwing off order all William-Nillium. Everyone in the film is about as harmless as they come, but can't see beyond their own preconceived notions of equality, order, and what's "acceptable" in "modern" society. That was more or less Leher's point of the book, as well as his screenplay (written with Elliott Baker) for *Viva Max!* Among the messages of the book and film are "Relax. Not everything is as bad as it seems." As well as "Never attribute to evil that which can explained as incompetence."

Ironically—or perhaps not so—in trying to get these messages to the screen, the production of *Viva Max!* met with some incredible push-back from the Daughters of the Republic of Texas, the more-or-less official protectors of The Alamo. They didn't appreciate the script's tone or the idea that a group of Mexicans and Texans—both painted as equally doltish— would be running rampant inside their great fortress and possibly damaging the historical contents. "Along with other historical groups, staged multiple protests in attempts to prevent filming at The Alamo. They claimed that the film was "desecrating the memory" of The Alamo. One particularly contentious moment was when the production actually flew the Mexican flag over the Alamo for a scene, causing the many Mexican American extras to cheer."[2]

As journalist Gilbert Garcia wrote, "One of my favorite recent purchases is the April 25, 1969, issue of *Life* magazine. (Newsstand price: 40 cents!) Its cover depicts the student unrest then unfolding on the Harvard campus, but my favorite article in the issue is Puro San Antonio: A Gary Cartwright piece about the obsessive campaign by the Daughters of the Republic of Texas to block the Alamo Plaza production of the Peter Ustinov comedy *Viva Max*," which he called "a profoundly silly comedy about a Mexican general who tries to impress the woman who dumped him by leading 87 followers across the border to recapture the Alamo. But the DRT, led by then-President Mrs. William Lawrence Scarborough, from Corpus Christi, quickly flew into counterattack mode. Scarborough stubbornly ignored the advice of two attorneys—both of whom resigned on her—and tried to get a court injunction to shut down the movie, which she described (based purely on the Jim Lehrer novel from which it derived) as a 'mockery and desecration of our heroes who died for us at the Alamo.'

"Scarborough vented about a scene in which Ustinov's character 'takes the pretty little blond girl (actress Pamela Tiffin) to the hothouse and seduces her.' When she was assured that the scene was not even remotely raunchy, Scarborough shot back: 'Why can't they make a nice movie like John Wayne?'

"The DRT failed to halt the filming and lost the PR battle, with enthusiastic locals signing on as extras (including 40 people who answered a call for "local bigots" to play a right-wing militia that charges the scene of the siege) and forming crowds around Alamo Plaza to watch the movie being made. […] As for the *Viva Max* flap, the best line came from Ustinov, who said, "It's come as a complete surprise to me that the cradle of Texas liberty still has babies in it."[3]

While the producers were able to get a good many exterior shots of the famed building[306]— DRT members wanted to cover the shrine in a large black cloth. "Ultimately," wrote Garcia, "they settled for covering the gate with black plastic."—the filmmakers were forced to film within the walls of a replica set of the Alamo in Bracketville, Texas, in addition to interior scenes shot in Cinecittà in Rome (where Tiffin had already scheduled another film shoot; moving the production was the only way to complete her scenes in time). Nationalism at its finest: protest the depicted absurdity of Nationalism.

While *Viva Max!* is still relatively tame and largely family-friendly, is "offensiveness" is debatable. It is true that Ustinov and the majority of the Army were played by non-Mexicans, each giving their character an accent worthy of Speedy Gonzales, and this may make Mexican-Americans and, especially, Liberal Americans a few squirmy moments, it's done in caricature, not particularly meant as stereotype. (I have my suspicions that this manner of political incorrectness is what has kept it off of modern home media, along the same lines as Disney's embargo of *Song of the South*). It isn't an indictment of Mexicans or Americans in particular, it is a shot at the values of both cultures, especially the military of both, and the American fetishism of The Alamo. It takes its jabs at xenophobia on both sides, and at unyielding Patriotism even in the face of contradictory evidence. Both sides are buffoonish and stubborn; neither will admit fault. Even after its resolution, bureaucracy still scuttles the peaceful resolutions. And if that isn't an indictment of the modern political environment, nothing is.

While the script is riddled with strange geographical plot holes—showing up at the border, DeSantos informs the guards that they are heading for Laredo, which is about 100 yards from the main checkpoint at this time in history; in another instance, DeSantos and Romero manage to commute 280 miles—Laredo to San Antonio—in a couple of hours, and the army traverses that distance on foot in record-breaking time—it's undeniably amusing at its worst, hilarious at its best. This is due to the wonderful performances of the actors. Paris, a television fixture, shoots everything with a TV pace, as a result, the editing is choppy and the pace is very uneven. The photography is perfunctory if not particularly stylish (though this is difficult to judge thanks to the sole VHS-to-Bootleg-DVD print I was able to run down).

"In general, he was a perfect, 'smile, you're on camera' TV director, but not a good film director is the best I can say. He had no idea how to work with actors—particularly talented ones, which he had in *Viva Max*," actor Larry Hankin told Lisanti. "All Jerry wanted was to be liked—toxically so. He wasn't a storyteller. He was an excellent traffic manager, which is perfect for sitcom directing and he was obviously great at that."[4]

---

[306] Which, as we learned from *Pee Wee's Big Adventure*, does *not* have a basement.

Ustinov and Winters. Image copyright Commonwealth United Entertainment. All Rights Reserved

Eldon Quick agreed, noting that Paris would let the cast improvise as much as they wanted, but without much direction. "This may have effected Jonathan Winters most of all. His ad-libs and improvisations were truly hilarious. The cast and crew would fall down laughing in rehearsals. When the camera was rolling, Jonathan would try to repeat what he had done in rehearsal and because it was no longer spontaneous it just fell flat. Jerry should have filmed the rehearsals and let the camera run empty for the take. If only the humor that was in the script had made it to the screen."[5]

However, there is one sequence during DeSantos' and our tour of the monument, where the fabled battle is re-enacted through sound design and optical zooms, giving us the dizziness of a battle without having a bunch of re-enactors go through the motions in an extravagant, wasteful, visually-interesting set-piece. (This sequence, tied to the tour, is narrated by an unidentified woman that NY Times critic Vincent Canby described as "a pretty, middle-aged lady, whose name I don't know but who is, briefly, very funny as an Alamo tourist guide. She looks—and sounds—very much like one of Texas's best-known citizens."[6]) I kid. It's actually an interesting sequence obviously borne of problem-solving. Because, hey, it cost the production a bucketload to move the shoot to Italy.

NOTES

[1] Lisanti, Tom. 2016. Quoting from Marika Aba, "Pamela Tiffin—American Sex Queen in Exile," Los Angeles Times, July 6, 1969.

[2] The Father Emil Wesselsky Collection - Viva Max! (1969). http://www.texasarchive.org/library/index.php/2012_01110

[3] Garcia, Gilbert. 2013. "DRT's rejection of Van de Putte recalls 'Viva Max' flap." Express News. October 5. http://www.expressnews.com/news/news_columnists/gilbert_garcia/article/DRT-s-rejection-of-Van-de- Putte-recalls-Viva-4872417.php

[4] Larry Hankin, Email interview with Tom Lisantis, Sept. 18, 2013. Lisanti, Tom. 2016. "Viva Pamela! An Excerpt from Pamela Tiffin: Hollywood To Rome, 1961-1974". March 2nd. http://sixtiescinema.com/2016/03/02/viva-pamela-an-excerpt-from-pamela-tiffin-hollywood-to-rome-1961-1967/

[5] Eldon Quick, Email interview with Tom Lisanti, Sept. 13, 2013.

[6] Canby, Vincent. 1970. "Screen: 'Viva Max' and the History of the Alamo:Peter Ustinov Stars in Music Hall Comedy Jerry Paris Is Director of 24-Hour Siege." New York Times, January 23. http://www.nytimes.com/movie/review?res=9A02EFD91F39EF34BC4B51DFB766838B669EDE

Marcello Mastroianni
Sydne Rome

What?

a film by Roman Polanski

WHAT? (1972)

(a.k.a. CHE?, DIARY OF FORBIDDEN DREAMS)

Before we get started, I want to get something out of the way, lest I'm accused of being a Polanski apologist. I am not. I find the man reprehensible. The artist, however, is among those I most admire. It's an ethical contradiction that many film addicts shamefully share. The only explanation we can give of the difference between Polanski and, say, Victor Salva, is "Because…*Chinatown*!" It isn't enough and we all know it. But *Chinatown* (1974) still stands as one of the greatest movies ever made. So rather than leap back into the imbroglio, I'll present the facts as they happened:

In 1969, Polanski's new bride, actress Sharon Tate, and unborn son were viciously murdered by Tex Watson and the Charles Manson "Family". Polanski had the world's sympathy during the notorious ensuing investigation and trial.

In the years following, he threw himself back into his work, writing and directing *Macbeth* (1971), *What?* (1973), *Chinatown* (1974), and the third part of what has been called his "Apartment Trilogy" (which include *Repulsion* and *Rosemary's Baby*), *The Tenant* (1976). Then in 1977 he destroyed all feelings of goodwill he'd accumulated when he drugged and raped 13-year-old Samantha Gailey, lured to Jack Nicholson's Los Angeles home under the pretense of a photoshoot

"In March 1977, film director Roman Polanski was arrested and charged in Los Angeles with five offenses against Samantha Gailey, a 13-year-old girl—rape by use of drugs, perversion, sodomy, lewd and lascivious act upon a child under 14, and furnishing a controlled substance to a minor. At his arraignment Polanski pleaded not guilty to all charges, but later accepted a plea bargain whose terms included dismissal of the five initial charges in exchange for a guilty plea to the lesser charge of engaging in unlawful sexual intercourse.

"Polanski underwent a court-ordered psychiatric evaluation, and a report was submitted to the court recommending probation. However, upon learning that he was likely to face imprisonment and deportation, Polanski fled to France in February 1978, hours before he was to be formally sentenced. Since then Polanski has mostly lived in France and has avoided visiting countries likely to extradite him to the United States."[1]

Though the statute of limitations on pedophilia in America remains at a madden three years thanks to influence by the "beleaguered" Catholic Church[307], Polanski has never returned to the U.S. for fear of incarceration. In Europe, he's been largely "forgiven", for lack of a better word, and has enjoyed an inconsistent career of critical highs and lows. If you're among the fans of his films, cognitive dissonance is essential.

In 2009, Gailey finally begged the world to stop his pursuit for her own sake. "Los Angeles authorities seeking to imprison fugitive film director Roman Polanski may face a new obstacle in the 32-year-old case: The victim wants no part in it. [...] In a court filing today, Gailey said she has been besieged by nearly 500 calls from news media since Polanski's arrest. She lives in Hawaii and long ago publicly identified herself as the victim and forgave Polanski, but said she and her family have to contend with pressure when he is in the news. She said she is being stalked by journalists from international news organisations and has received interview requests from Oprah Winfrey and CNN's Larry King.

"The pursuit has caused her to have health-related issues," the filing states. "The pursuit has caused her performance at her job to be interfered with and has caused the understandable displeasure of her employer and the real possibility that Samantha could lose her job."

In the filing she asks the court to dismiss the case and ends with: "Leave her alone."

[...] The Los Angeles county district attorney's office considers Polanski a convicted felon and a fugitive, and began tracking him immediately after he fled."[2]

And this is where I leave Polanski the man. I have no use for him.

In 1972, Polanski wrote and directed *What?*, a capricious, surreal romp detailing the sexual misadventures of a naïve and wide-eyed hippy waif named Nancy (Sydne Rome). We first meet her in the back of a car filled with men who picked her up hitch-hiking through Italy. They ask her if she's been molested on her travels. "No," she responds. "Everyone I've met has been really nice."

Immediately, the driver pulls over and the man drag her out of the car to rape her. One of the three is so anxious that, after he crushes his own eye glasses, mistakes one of his buddies for her and accidentally sodomizes him. (Which might be the "joke" in this sequence.) Escaping with only her diary and the tattered clothes on her back, she flees via gondola elevator to a lavish villa by the ocean. Once there, she meets Alex (Marcello Mastroianni), a self-confessed "former pimp" and deranged heir to the villa. Intrigued, she agrees to meet him, covertly, of course, as Alex has no wish to be interfered with by the American ping-pong obsessed hooligans renting an apartment upstairs. Once alone, he dresses in a tiger costume, hands her a whip, and demands she "tame" him.

Her trysts with Alex are usually interrupted by the other inhabitants of the villa, including Joseph (Hugh Griffith), the millionaire who may be the owner, and Mosquito (Polanski), so-named because he "stings with his big stinger", also known as a harpoon. Over the course of the two or three days she spends there, Nancy scribbles away in her diary as she attempts to make

---

[307] The tensions are being played out in courtrooms and state legislatures, where the Church is using its legal and political clout to oppose bills that would extend the statute of limitations for victims of child sex abuse. A statute of limitations forbids prosecutors or plaintiffs from taking legal action after a certain number of years.

The pontiff has vowed to root out "the scourge" of sex abuse from the Roman Catholic Church, and this year created a Vatican tribunal to judge clergy accused of such crimes. But U.S. victims' advocates contend the biggest obstacle they face in giving victims more time to report abuse remains the Church itself, and want the pope to change that stance. The U.S. church has already been dealt a heavy financial blow by settlement payments and other costs totaling around $3 billion, which has forced it to sell off assets and cut costs.

"It is the bishops who have blocked any kind of meaningful reform," said Marci Hamilton, a professor at the Cardozo School of Law in New York who studies statutes of limitations.

[...] "The pope has virtually limitless powers," said David Clohessy, executive director of the Survivors Network of Abuse by Priests, who was sexually abused by a priest as a child. "He could sack, and should sack, literally dozens of bishops tomorrow and if he does that, that's what will make a difference. That's the missing piece."

Scott Malone; Additional reporting by Philip Pullella in Vatican City; editing by Stuart Grudgings, 2015. Reuters. Business Insider, Sep. 10. http://www.businessinsider.com/r-as-pope-visit-nears-us-sex-victims-say-church-remains-obstacle-to-justice-2015-9

sense of her exploits. Succumbing to sleep, she usually awakes to find herself being assaulted in some way—a slumbering man's head in her crotch; Mosquito having stolen her clothes, etc. At one point, for no reason, a laborer paints her left leg blue.

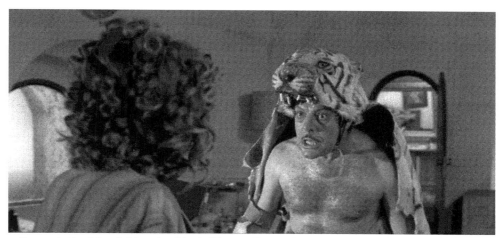

Rome and Alex (Marcello Mastroianni) in the "Tame me!" scene. Photo courtesy Severin Films. All Rights Reserved.

Near the end, it's alluded that Alex and the other residents are actually patients, and the villa is a high-end asylum. It's not clear if this is true, or another of Alex's fantasies. It is, after all, mentioned after he digs up a buried chest filled with Italian military regalia. Donning it there on the beach, he then handcuffs Nancy's wrists to her ankles, bends her over, beats her with a switch while demanding she "Confess!" And she does, curled in a ball on the sand and moaning "I love you! I love you!" as he disrobes, his coat covering her face.

As with most fever-dream fairy tales, Nancy can only escape the madness once she chooses to. Until then, she is at the whim of each stranger, the victim of each strange encounter. Yet she never loses her wide-eyed innocence. In the service of the story, no matter what she suffers, Nancy remains pure and unsullied, at least in spirit, having broadened her sexual horizons. When she finally bids the madhouse adieu, she's learned little, but neither have we.

Long-unseen in its intended form, *What?*—both its existence and it's legendary status—is as much the fault of producer Carlo Ponti as it is Polanski's, offering both the production money and his own private villa as the film's setting. Upon seeing the finished film, he allegedly asked the outraged question that became the film's title: "What?"

"In its original version, it looked like the work of a madman, of a crazed cinematic genius off the deep end. Ponti, in desperation, had all of Polanski's outtakes printed up (outtakes are versions of a shot that the director decides not to use.) With the aid of skilled editors, Ponti attempted to substitute various outtakes in an attempt to construct a film that resembled, well, a film. No luck. When Polanski makes a bad movie, he does it with a certain thoroughness. Even the shots he didn't use were bad," wrote Roger Ebert in a scathing review. "There's probably a level of competence beneath which bad directors cannot fall. No matter how dreary their imaginations, how stupid their material, how inept their actors, how illiterate their scripts, they've got to come up with something that can at least be advertised as a motion picture, released and forgotten. But a talented director is another matter. If he's made several good films, chances are that sooner or later someone will give him the money to make a supremely bad one. I wonder how much Carlo Ponti gave Roman Polanski to make *Diary of Forbidden Dreams*. Ten cents would have been excessive. [...] This is a movie so incredibly bad that I ask you to ponder the following facts. Even though (a) it stars Marcello Mastroianni, Hugh Griffith and Polanski himself, and (b) provides us with almost 90 minutes during which the attractive Sydne Rome wears little more than a table napkin, and (c) is almost exclusively concerned with that surefire box office winner, sex, it (d) was completed in 1973 and has not been released until now because almost every distributor who saw it fled the screening room in horror, clutching at his wallet."[3]

The famed Italian film mogul was a strange individual himself. In an attempt to establish a film industry in Milan in 1940, Ponti produced a film for Mario Soldati, *Piccolo Mondo Antico*, a story of family tragedy starring Alida Valli, in her first major role. Because the film dealt with "the Italian struggle against the Austrians for the inclusion of northeastern Italy into the Kingdom of Italy during the Risorgimento"[4], and was also successful, Ponti was briefly imprisoned by Italian Fascists for "undermining" relations with Nazi Germany.

While judging a beauty contest in 1950, Ponti met a young woman named Sofia Lazzaro. So taken with her, he immediately cast her in a number of features, while his friend and head of production at Titanus Pictures, Goffredo Lombardo, changed Ms. Lazzaro's name to "Loren." In 1958, Ponti was forced to flee Italy under bigamy charges, as divorce was still illegal in that country, and he'd married Ms. Loren while still legally married to his first wife, Giuliana Fiastri. Sofia Loren was subsequently charged with "concubinage". They also both faced excommunication from the Church and the whole mess wouldn't be resolved until they became French citizens in the late '60s.

Sydne Rome as "Nancy". Photo Courtesy Severin Films. All Rights Reserved.

He was the subject of two unsuccessful kidnapping attacks in the '70s. As a result of their conviction of evading Italian taxes, Ponti's vast art collection was seized and liquidated. During all of this, he managed to produce some of the greatest classics of cinematic history including *Contempt* (1963), *Doctor Zhivago* (1965), *Blowup* (1966), *The Firemen's Ball* (1967), and *Flesh for Frankenstein* (1973).

Because of the breathtaking beauty of his Amalfi villa, *What?* is almost tearful to watch. The lush, rolling beach, the crystal-blue ocean, that bleached-white stone structure—plus the startlingly attractive Rome—makes every scene a feast for the eyes. For the brain, not so much. With a script that was at least partially improvised and only marginally finished, the actors seem to be having a good time. (And why shouldn't they? They're in Italy, for fuck's sake!) But the further down the metaphorical rabbit hole one goes, the more uncomfortable *What?* becomes.

In addressing the beach scene, Nathan Rabin wrote, "This makes no more or less sense than anything else in the film; random shit just happens. Only a hopeless square would look for meaning in Polanski's leaden freak-fest. As in *Candy*[308], the humor, such as it is, stems from the surreal incongruity between the protagonist's guileless innocence and unshakable belief in the innate goodness of humanity, and the amorality, perversity, and sexual rapaciousness of everyone

---

[308] 1968 sex farce directed by Christian Marquand, screenplay by Buck Henry, adapting the 1958 novel by Terry Southern and Mason Hoffenberg.

she encounters. With *What?*, Polanski seems to have forgotten everything he knew about filmmaking. Lazily improvised scenes linger on endlessly, with little regard for pacing, shape, or rhythm. What? is a self-indulgent mess masquerading as a trippy free-for-all. It's a dream, all right, and like most dreams, it's of interest only to the dreamer. This is Polanski's long, strange, kinky, insufferable trip all the way. What? isn't just a cinephile endurance test; it's a waste of a beautiful villa and a naked woman."[5]

While it's never a good idea to view a film outside of the context in which it was made, there are many sections of *What?* that should have been inexcusable in the '60s, but were instead viewed as comedy. Nancy's constant escape from attempted—and successful!—rape is played for laughs, as a trope common to European sex romps. In the context of such films, rape is little more than "reluctant sex". But the "meat", so to speak, of the sex comedy is, of course, the sex, and the U.S. wasn't immune to it either. At the risk of making a ludicrous parallel, how many of us cheered when Gilbert (Robert Carradine) removed his ersatz Darth Vader mask in *Revenge of the Nerds* (1984) and revealed to a post-coital Betty Childs (Julie Montgomery) that he was not, in fact, her boyfriend Stan Gable (Ted McGinley), but she had just made love to an abhorrent nerd? I'd say, safely, most of us. And cheered even more loudly when she proclaimed, breathless and orgasmic, "I can't believe I'm in love with a nerd." For the sex comedy, rape—sorry, "reluctant sex"—is a crime unless orgasm is achieved and, thus, some sort of philosophical enlightenment. This is the attitude that pervades scene after scene in *What?* In light of Polanski's indefensible real-life crime, it's impossible to evade the feeling of misogyny rampant through the film.

Rome, defending the film on Severin's sumptuous Blu-Ray edition, explains that Nancy is the "Little Annie Fanny" character, evoking Harvey Kurtzman's and Will Elder's creation for *Playboy*, in which the titular (pun intended) heroine often finds herself undressed and at the mercy of unwanted advances, okay with sex but always in danger when her physique enflames the libidos of weirdoes around her. She argues that the film is closer in nature to its international title, *Diary of Forbidden Dreams*, in which all of Nancy's adventures are little more than erotic fantasies, safe from any "real world" danger. Indeed, despite Rome's fluctuating states of undress, there's no on-screen sex, only the build-up, only the foreplay. Often, it seems, Nancy is just "going with the flow". If sex results, so be it. That's the freewheelin' '70s nature. Yet, something unwholesome bubbles up simply due to the nature of the man behind the camera (and occasionally in front of it). The more you know about Polanski, the more you tend to read into his films, finding horrific subtext in every scene.

For years, various versions of *What?* floated around the grey markets, running time bouncing between 80 and 100 minutes, and for once, the editing wasn't about censorship but a search for something coherent and, dare we say it, *marketable*. But even Alice's adventures started beneath a real world tree, beside a real-world stream, before the Wonderland rabbit makes its first appearance. In *What?*, we receive no such grounding. At the same time, we're submitted to madness, but no internal logic. Because Nancy is foreign even to the viewer—how many of us watching are beautiful, self-sufficient libertine Americans wandering the Italian countryside seeking sexual adventure?—even she is a poor surrogate for entry into Polanski's weird world. The story is as empty as the photography is beautiful. *What?* is best when it's a travelogue, occasionally interrupted by preambles to the eventual villa-wide outbreak of syphilis.

"While [Rome's] additional comments make *What?* sound like it was a lot more fun to make than it is to watch, she is somewhat naïve when she says nothing about the film has dated. It may not look old fashioned, as she rightly argues, but it is certainly a film of its era," wrote Jeremy Carr for *Studies in Cinema*. "*What?* was a success in Italy, less so throughout the rest of Europe, and was a bomb in the United States. It failed to even garner much interest when it was re-cut, re-titled (*Roman Polanski's Diary of Forbidden Dreams*), and re-released in an exploitative attempt to cash in on Polanski's rape case. This goofy romp may have better production values and a better director than most of its kind, but there is little to distinguish it as something exceptional. If one tries hard enough, one could perhaps find Polanski parallels in the film's initial situation of a stranger in a strange land (*The Tenant*, 1976) where a foreign language creates communication barriers (*Frantic*, 1988). Or, one could make the case that this singular setting serves the purpose of intimidating confinement (*Repulsion*, 1965, and *Rosemary's Baby*, 1968). But really, *What?* is simply not the type of film one expects from a director as talented as Roman Polanski. At best, it is for a curious few or a devoted Polanski completist (the only reason I've now seen it twice)."[6]

Remarkably, enjoyment of *What?* might come down to what Vincent Canby—of all people—wrote about the film in the New York Times. For the critic who hated everything, *What?* touched something close to his brain's pleasure center, and he manages to defend the indefensible in the exact way so many film fans fail to articulate, this writer included: "*What?*, which opened yesterday at the Coronet Theater is a male chauvinist pig sort of comedy. It is not consistently inspired in its lunacy, but it is so totally without redeeming social value that it should be protected and, from time to time, cherished, as when a grumpy maid attempts to clear the air of flies and mistakes and aerosol can of shaving cream for Fly-Tox. Anarchic comedy is a form that continues to challenge Polanski even though neither he nor his script collaborator, Gerard Brach succeeded in their earlier *Cul-de-Sac* or *The Fearless Vampire Killers*. Perhaps, like verse drama, it's become one of those things that need only to be attempted to succeed in partial measure. It can be fun to watch the try. Occasionally Polanski and Brach seem to want to introduce a system of surreal disorder to the girl's adventures in the villa, but I doubt that they really much care beyond presenting us with an Alice trying to comprehend an X-rated Wonderand. [...] The girl, the villa and the performances are beautiful enough to bridge those sequences when the film, like its heroine, seems searching for explanations that will never be found."[7]

What contemporary critics seem to be saying is that enjoyment of *What?* probably doesn't make you a bad person, as long as you realize that what you're watching is something naughty and fanciful. Modern critics are arguing that enjoying any Polanski doesn't necessarily translate into the viewer being a woman-hating rape-apologist either, so long as you're constantly separating the art from the artists. It's a lot to ask of the casual viewer. But then again, the casual viewer isn't likely to pick up *What?* in the first place.

NOTES

[1] https://en.wikipedia.org/wiki/Roman_Polanski_sexual_abuse_case

[2] Nasaw, Daniel, 2009. "Roman Polanski's victim asks court to drop charges against director." The Guardian October 26.

[3] Ebert, Roger. 1976. "Diary Of Forbidden Dreams." Chicago Sun-Times. September 21.
  http://www.rogerebert.com/reviews/diary-of-forbidden-dreams-1976

[4] "Movie Producer Carlo Ponti Dies". Kansas City Star. 2007-01-10. Retrieved 2007-01-14.

[5] Rabin, Nathan. 2009. "Polanski-tastic Sick-Fuck Case File #149: What?". The A.V. Club. October 28.
  http://www.avclub.com/article/polanski-tastic-sick-fuck-case-file-149-iwhati-34678

[6] Carr, Jeremy. 2016. "What?" Studies in Cinema. May. http://studiesincinema.blogspot.com/2016/05/what-written-by-gerard-brach-roman.html

[7] Canby, Vincent. 1973. "Film: X-Rated Polanski: What?' Shows a Lot of Sydne Rome The Cast." New York Times.
  October 4. http://www.nytimes.com/movie/review?res=9C02EEDB1F30E63ABC4C53DFB6678388669EDE

WORLD ON A WIRE (1973)

Q: In your opinion, what effect can films have on society? What can a filmmaker do for society?

RWF: He can do a lot. Entertain. Tell stories in such a way that the moviegoer is entertained and afterwards is no stupider; he can make various things clear to him or make him want to get various things straight for himself, he can express fears. For others. If no one does that, we'd withdraw into the kind of silence in which sooner or later you become a moron. Film can give the moviegoer the courage to continue expressing things, taking a position on them, and making it known. I do feel that film as a medium can be effective in all sorts of ways. And it's always a means of entertainment, and should remain that, too. Like literature, which is also supposed to be fun, or music, quite aside from the effect it can have.

Q: If you were to do an interview with yourself, what further questions would you have?

RWF: I don't have any other questions, I don't know. This was your interview, after all. [1]

Professor Vollmer (Adrian Hoven), technical director of the Institute for Cybernetics and Future Science ("Institut für Kybernetik und Zukunftsforschung, IKZ"), where a supercomputer runs a simulation program, in which an artificial world inhabited by over 9,000 "identity units" living as virtual human beings (yet unaware that their world is a simulation), was on the verge of an incredible discovery when he dies under mysterious circumstances. Later, Günther Lause (Ivan Desny), the security adviser of the institute vanishes under equally mysterious circumstances. Into this mess enters Dr. Fred Stiller (Klaus Löwitsch), successor to Prof. Vollmner, becoming the inheritor of the project and its seemingly-unrelated tragic incidents. His attempts to pick up where the good Professor left off leads Stiller to one roadblock after another. Despite having met with Lause himself, Stiller can't get a single IKZ employee to admit the security adviser ever existed. No one has a single memory of the missing man.

Stiller discovers that his colleague, Fritz Walfang (Günter Lamprecht), who recently deleted one of the simulated identities after the unit attempted suicide. Walfang explains that the deletion was necessary to stabilize the simulation. Further, Stiller realizes later that Walfang is somehow "inhabited" by a unit from the simulation, a "contact" called Einstein. Einstein was the only unit aware that it was a simulation, the realization being necessary to keep the simulated world working sufficiently. Somehow, while Walfang communicated with the simulation, Einstein was able to swap its consciousness for that of the scientist. He tells Stiller that the real world he perceives is nothing more than a higher-level simulation, and that they are all being controlled by scientists "one level above".

With the existential crisis weighing heavily on his sanity, Stiller discovers that his new-found knowledge has made him a target of the now-vulnerable IKZ. He's framed for Vollmer's murder and must go on the run to find this simulation's contact unit who turns out to be Eva (Mascha Rabben), Vollmer's daughter and Stiller's former lover. She tells him that his identity is actually based on the upper level's "real" Fred Stiller, who is now running the upper level's program with an iron fist. The only possible escape for Stiller would be to switch consciousness with his "real world" counterpart. But can this be possible with the entirety of the simulation actively trying to kill him?

There doesn't seem to be a lot of love for Rainer Werner Fassbinder these days, which is a damn shame. One of the more influential German directors of the '60s and '70s, Fassbinder had a wicked eye for both composition and satire. A self-styled "unpleasant" human being, Fassbinder's films reflected his dissatisfaction with the world in general, and the people who reside in it in particular. Politically and sexually outspoken at a period in Europe where those things were unacceptable, Fassbinder's films focused on human beings in seemingly-rational situations behaving in irrational ways, only to reveal midway through that the situations were just as untenable as the people battling their way out. Usually bleak, his satires have a sense of hopelessness to them, as if there really were no way out, that acceptance is the rational solution, but the protagonists would rather die than go with the proverbial flow.

"Rainer Werner Fassbinder was a filmmaker prolific to the point of being a workaholic. From 1969 to 1982 he directed over 40 productions, most of them feature films, a few TV specials and one huge 931-minute TV mini-series *Berlin Alexanderplatz* (1979-80). More remarkable than this perhaps is that these films were nearly all written or adapted for the screen by Fassbinder himself. He was also art director on most of the early films, editor or co-editor on a lot of them (often credited as Franz Walsh), and he acted in nine of his own films as well as for other directors. On top of this, he occasionally performed many other roles such as cinematographer and producer on a small number of them. His films tackle a wide variety of topics and, to be frank, range from the astounding to the amateur. They give an incisive picture of post-war Germany, at first through ironic and nearly plotless deconstructions/pastiches of Hollywood genre cinema with a formally experimental and astute provocative political edge, yet they remain relevant to urban life in contemporary times and human relationships. Some of the films (especially the ones centering on a group rather than a single victim figure) are also endowed with a decidedly dark and sardonic sense of humour," wrote Joe Ruffel for *Senses of Cinema*. "Though his films were often very compassionate studies of outsiders unwanted by society for reasons beyond their control, he was publicly notorious for being a difficult man, and deliberately cultivated an image of being a rather dislikeable figure. If his work displays a deep understanding of the bitter power struggles of those apparently in love it is because he practised those cruel games himself, not just in his relationships but also in the stock company of actors that clung to him (although to be fair it does seem that his closest associates were weak people with a penchant for masochism and backstabbing). However, a self-awareness of his own torturous personality is also the source of his undeniable genius. […] Fassbinder made no bones about the fact that he was an oppressor and had compassion for both victims and victimisers (often one and the same). In this light, his work is both a unique personal catharsis and a break from the crude moralising of directors who look down on the fiends they create for dramatic purpose (many of his most monstrous creations are self-portraits). His work, inspired by his own feelings of rejection and alienation as left-leaning and overweight bi-sexual in the repressive new 'economic miracle' of West Germany, was forever willing to tackle difficult subject matter such

Kurt Raab as "Mark Holm" in a shot exemplifying Fassbinder's use of mirrors throughout World on a Wire. Image copyright Janus Films. All Rights Reserved.

as terrorism, racial tension, alienation, class exploitation (on the political left as well as right), trans-sexuality and masochism in a provocative but non-sensationalist manner."[2]

"In the seventies the moribund West German film industry, essentially dead since the most important filmmakers of the thirties fled Hitler, was reborn as the New German Cinema. A young generation of directors became famous around the world. Their names included Volker Schlondorff, Werner Herzog, Wim Wenders, Alexander Kluge, Margarethe von Trotta—but none more famous than Rainer Werner Fassbinder. He became a familiar figure at the world's film festivals, always roughly dressed in jeans and leather jackets, always with a drink and a cigarette," wrote Roger Ebert in 1983. "It seemed almost a paradox that he went to so many festivals, because once he was there he refused interviews, rejected praise and responded rudely to compliments. Still, he went; [Swiss filmmaker David] Schmid says it was because he could not stand to be alone. The bad boy image was in contrast with a remarkable body of work. Films poured from Fassbinder's imagination, and he made more of them in less time than any other major director in history, usually about deliberately uncommercial subjects. [...] Those subjects often included eerie projections of his own final years. In *The Bitter Tears of Petra von Kant* (1972), an alcoholic lesbian isolates herself in her room and lives on the floor with a gin bottle after being rejected by her lover. In *Merchant of the Four Seasons* (1972), a fruit peddler, insecure and cuckolded, deliberately drinks himself to death. In *Fox and His Friends* (1975), a simple-minded young homosexual wins the lottery, becomes the lover of the owner of a bankrupt factory, is taken for all of his money, and finally dies alone in an underground station, In *Ali: Fear Eats the Soul* (1974), a Moroccan immigrant, desperately lonely, marries a cleaning woman twenty-five years older than he is, and then collapses of an ulcer."[3]

Originally aired as a two-part miniseries on German TEV, *World on a Wire* (*Welt am Draht*) was based on American author Daniel F. Galouye's 1964 novel *Simulacron-3*, and it's not too difficult to see why the subject matter would have attracted the iconoclastic filmmaker. Rife with paranoia—both justified and seemingly irrational—the film's protagonist, Stiller, begins the story convinced he's real. He "knows" that the people he interacts with are real. His world *exists*. Until he receives the shock that it might not. Not at all. And it's quite obvious that, like Galouye, Fassbinder wants Stiller's existential quandary to dribble off the screen and over the viewer. Though the danger Stiller finds himself in is quite genuine—that he could be literally and completely deleted—may not be as literal in what we think of as "the real world" (depending on what your spiritual beliefs may be), it raises that age-old question in the backs of our minds (one that's gained traction over the last 20 years or so, with the advancements made in virtual reality): is our reality a simulation? Do we exist, or are we some higher level's virtual entertainment.

At the risk of triteness, look at the popular computer game, *The Sims*. Published by Electronic Arts, Will Wright, the game's creator, allegedly developed the game following a fire that engulfed his own home. Set about rebuilding, he was inspired to create a satire of consumer culture, a world populated by gibberish-speaking humanoids who interact in ways both set by the player and by the game. Time passes differently in the virtual *Sims* world, and one can't help but wonder what the little characters are doing when the player is not playing. We're told, by the game, that they go to work, interact on the edges of the screen, swim, play, eat, fuck. Who's to say that while we're playing *The Sims*, some higher level beings are playing *us*?

"It may come as a bit of a shock to modern viewers who think of this concept as relatively new—having perhaps first encountered it in the 'cyberpunk' novels of the 1980s or in films from *Tron* (1982) to *The Matrix* (1999)—to realise that it has actually been around for four decades. Perhaps modern viewers inevitably link computer games with VR, assuming the two arrived simultaneously, but writers such as Ray Bradbury, Stanislaw Lem, Philip K Dick and Daniel F Galouye, who penned the novel that *World on a Wire* is based on, had already been developing the concept in the 1950s and 60s. For the sake of confining this argument to 'virtual reality' as we define it today, I won't go back as far as Plato and his cave."[4]

The tragedy of *World on a Wire* is that Stiller's existential paranoia is proven to him to be absolutely justified and there's nothing he can do about it. How do you escape existence? (Well, there is a back door in this particular situation, but it's a longshot, and there are an awful lot of his fellow simulations who'd prefer he didn't "ascend".)

"The compulsion for truth, one might say, drives many to madness. Society's thirst for justice, its significant valuation of objects of authenticity, true love, one's real family—these tropes endlessly pepper the canon of cinema with accompanying melodramatic performances of the human condition in urgent, desperate malfunction," wrote Chris Rusak. "The work of German director Rainer Werner Fassbinder distinguishably ranks amongst his peers as beautiful, capable depictions of the conditions for and unraveling of emotional implosion. His work concomitantly disassembles the human ontological structure and the societal structures generally assumed to provide the cohesion necessary for fortifying our being in order to undertake honest living. Two of Fassbinder's particularly dense and complex movies, *Welt am Draht* [English: *World on a Wire*] (1973) and *In einem Jahr mit dreizehn Munden* [English: *In a Year with 13 Moons*] (1978), exemplify how he integrates anti-familist themes through reversals of identities, often by mirroring his own personal history onto characters and frequently through transposition of traditional societal archetypes, as a means to underscore how truth victimizes the self. Moreover, he hopes to reveal to his viewers the absurdity and fallibility of identity given the precariousness inherent in truth judgments, something he accomplishes through attentive aesthetic construction, visual metaphor, and reliance on moral and metaphysical philosophy."[5]

A product of dysfunctional familial upbringing, much has been made of Fassbinder's consideration of his cast and crew as a "surrogate family". He was outspokenly "anti-family"—meaning one of biological origins—but yearned to surround himself with those he found a kinship. In this way, the director is also creating his own reality, not just the fabrication for the benefit of the film being made, but also the world the participants will inhabit during the course of production. In this regard, Fassbinder was almost always "the father" of the film and its creators (i.e. "his children"). Rusak expounds: "In his essay *World on a Wire: The Hall of Mirrors*, critic Ed Halter looks these questions in the eye, noting the film's confrontation with 'the relationship of illusion to identity'. After pointing out the film's reliance on both visual reflectivity and metaphysical philosophy, Halter states that Fassbinder achieved more than just a slick production with its flashy aesthetic, rather he used the film as a meditation on a facet of his own identity, that of a filmmaker. Like a computer which synthesizes alternate worlds, the director, too, creates a 'virtual reality'."[6]

For instance, after revealing to Franz Hahn (Wolfgang Schenck) that the world around them is a simulation, Hahn "kills" himself, and Stiller is instantly branded—and pursued—as a murderer. In reality, the Hahn element is simply deleted by the Simulcrom, but the other inhabitants of the world are unaware of their nonexistence, nor that Stiller himself is an identity unit. How can bits of information "murder" each other? Yet in this world, the perceived murder/suicide is quite real. It's all perception. If we were to learn, without a doubt, that there was no "God", how would our society collapse? Quickly? Or with resistance, resentment, and denial? What does this theory of simulated reality say about the existence of Free Will? Is Stiller a product of his upbringing or his programming? Are his actions his own or pre-programmed? Is Stiller "free" when the programmer is AFK?[309]

"The socially insignificant and the typically unseen actually play a much more important role for Fassbinder than just thematics, and interestingly enough his sole science fiction work, *Welt*, demonstrates how he continually brings the oft-overlooked into view. *Welt* tells the story of the Simulacron 1 machine, a supercomputer that allows its users to construct, enter, and experience alternate worlds that seemingly exist on digital circuitry. The machine thus incites examination of ontology and identity for those who, in real human life, use and, in (real?) digital life, are birthed of it. *Welt*'s protagonist, Fred Stiller, at the film's midpoint, discovers his digital unrealness and spends the final half of the movie trying to exit the multiple layers of the Simulacron and "go up" to reach the summit of "true life"," wrote Rusak. "In order to set up this later subjective consternation, Welt is constructed as a world of mirrors and their myriad indications. Quickly, it becomes apparent that almost every scene in the film contains at least one object that displays a reflection, often now glaring out from the margins of otherwise plain sight —not just quotidian mirrors, but pristine glass surfaces, intricate work-desk tchotchkes, high-polish chromed furniture, chic Lucite sculptures, shiny marble, and even faintly still waters. Banal objects become outstanding monuments. Everything is meant to be recognized. Such fine detail to *mise en scène*, coupled with an obsessive attention for cinematographic structuring through precisely calculated angles of framing, according blocking of actors, and multiple-point lighting, all craft a kaleidoscopic aesthetic, the conditions for multiplicative imagery. Early dialogue also reinforces this optical geometry. 'You are nothing more,' belts out the Simulacron's first victim of murderous termination shortly before his death, 'than the image others have made of you.'"[7]

It isn't a stretch to say that the majority of shots in *World on a Wire* contain mirrors, with characters constantly reflected back at themselves and other viewers. Reflections are foreshadowing as well as a sort of silent Greek Chorus, observing the action, reflecting the action, but never generating or betraying what is being reflected. This is all the reality Stiller gets and he's largely blind to the symbology. All he can trust is what he sees, but if everything he sees is optically reversed, where then does he place his trust? At the film's midway point, the mirror becomes as much a mocking antagonist as those identity units hounding him—ostensibly for murder but, in a greater context, for "heresy". Blasphemy. "There is no God but Simulcrom 1."

Stiller, here, is Neo the Chosen One from *The Matrix*. Only he can't fly and has no greater purpose. For Stiller to transcend his world, he must somehow escape, change minds with one of the higher programmers. He's no messiah, in this case. He's only a victim of enlightenment.

"Fassbinder made *World on a Wire* immediately after his art-film breakthrough, Effi Briest, and, abetted by many of his regular actors, the 27-year-old filmmaker seemed eager to re-establish his punk bona fides. As wildly ambitious as it is cinephilic, *World on a Wire* mixes the pop art effrontery of Godard's *Alphaville* with the cyber-phobic metaphysics of Kubrick's *2001* (to name the two movies most bluntly referenced) while remaining wholly Fassbinderian in its insolently lugubrious ironies. Less characteristic, if equally deadpan, are the choreographed action sequence—notably the lurking crane that threatens to dump a load of debris on the movie's angst-ridden protagonist (Klaus Löwitsch)," wrote J. Hoberman, reviewing the film's first U.S. revival at the Museum of Modern Art in 2010. "A power-elite conspiracy yarn played out on two levels of reality—virtual and real, both suffused with free-floating paranoia—*World on a Wire* hardly lacks for narrative. But its meaning is largely delivered via an economical yet stylish *mise-en-*

---

[309] In gamer's parlance: "Away From Keyboard."

scène. This is corporate hell—the blandly futuristic, neon-lit look leans heavily on molded plastic furniture and ubiquitous TV monitors. (That the men are uniformly dressed in power suits and the women as Barbies may remind some of *Mad Men*.) Strategically placed mirrors suggest the character's illusory or divided nature, while the alienated performances—alternately declamatory and uninflected—as well as Fassbinder's Warholian deployment of actors stolidly hanging out in frame, encourage the thought that the real world, too, is rife with 'identity units.'"[8]

If some of this seems familiar, and not because of *The Matrix* and its impact crater on pop culture, Galouye's novel was adapted again in 1999 by Josef Rusnak and Ravel Centeno-Rodriguez as *The Thirteenth Floor*, starring Craig Bierko and Vincent D'Onofrio. Produced by Roland Emmerich (with Ute Emmerich and Marco Weber), *The Thirteenth Floor* makes it explicit from the beginning that the multiple simulated worlds are distinct, with the "simulated" level imitating 1940s Los Angeles. In a large way, this undercuts both the mystery central to the plot as well as the essential philosophical nature of the novel and *World on a Wire*. The existential twist is something we can see coming because every scene in the latter film telegraphs its every move, typically mistrusting the audience to follow along. It also shoehorns multiple action set-pieces to amplify the "science opera" modern audiences are supposed to prefer. Where *World on a Wire* has you questioning your existence, *The Thirteenth Floor* has you questioning only your cinematic choices.

"While certain aspects of *World on a Wire* were designed to create a world that seemed unusual at the time—such as shooting many scenes in the shopping malls and newly built developments of Paris, which were unfamiliar to viewers in 1970s Germany—there are continuing tropes from Fassbinder's own oeuvre that mark it out as simply his style of filmmaking. For example, the idiosyncratic sound design and overtly 'theatrical' performances from some of the cast and extras do create the feeling of a world inhabited by 'the other', when viewed in isolation and without having seen many of the director's other films. Ironically, it's these idiosyncrasies that give the series a science fiction feeling, rather than his conscious efforts to shoot in 'alien' locations. From a current perspective, all 1970s European architecture seems broadly similar, and this is both a blessing and a curse to filmmakers who want to create a futuristic world by seeking out the modern locations of their time. Michael Winterbottom's use of a global architectural collage in *Code 46* and Jean-Luc Godard's choice of brutalist architecture in *Alphaville* (1965) to create a Paris of the future have quickly dated (Fassbinder was a fan of Godard and acknowledges his debt to *Alphaville* by giving Eddie Constantine a cameo in *World on a Wire*)," wrote Alex Fitch for Electric Sheep Magazine. "Viewing *World on a Wire* in May 2010 is a strangely appropriate experience. Despite its age, the film still seems fresh, and this combination is unsettling to modern viewers. Although a little slow overall—in part due to the fact that it was conceived as two two-hour-long parts with commercials, which makes the first episode seem padded—it is continuously engaging, intriguing and suitably strange, thanks to the performances and the director's use of disorientating camera angles as well as shots framed with mirrors reflecting other mirrors. As an early example of a genre, it's interesting to note that it has almost exactly the same ending as the final episode of *Lost* (and as the co-creators of *Lost*[310], who wrote that episode, are refusing to give any more interviews on the subject, I guess we'll never find out if they're fans of Fassbinder)."[9]

While Fassbinder plays with some of his favorite themes in *World on a Wire*, it was largely uncontroversial upon release, far less so than *The Bitter Tears of Petra von Kant*, for example, for which he was accused of misogyny[311], or his final film, the homosexual revenge thriller *Querelle* (1982)[10], or his absurdist anti-family "comedy", *Satansbraten* (1976), or even his masterpiece, the

---

[310] ABC Series, 2004-2007, created by Jeffrey Lieber, J. J. Abrams, and Damon Lindelof.

[311] "Somehow it's really idiotic to always have to be saying "I'm not a misogynist, I'm not an anti-Semite." This is where I think this misogynist business comes from: I take women more seriously than most directors do. To me women aren't just there to get men going; they don't have that role as object. In general, that's an attitude in the movies that I despise. And I simply show that women are forced more than men to use some pretty revolting methods to escape from this role as object." *Performing Arts Journal*, Vol. 14, No. 2.

sprawling 1980 miniseries, *Berlin Alexanderplatz*, all of which are much angrier and sardonic than the thoughtful *Wert*.

If much of his life was made difficult due in a large part to his own penchant for self-torture, Fassbinder's death was no different. "Late on the night of June 9, 1982, the West German film director Rainer Werner Fassbinder made a telephone call from Munich to Paris to tell his best friend he had flushed all his drugs down the toilet—everything except for one last line of cocaine. The next morning, Fassbinder was found dead in his room, a cold cigarette between his fingers, a videotape machine still playing. The most famous, notorious and prolific modern German filmmaker was dead at thirty-six. To those who knew him well, the death was not a surprise, Fassbinder had been on a collision course with drugs. He had long been a heavy drinker and user of drugs, but in the final two years of his life cocaine came to rule him completely, and he became reclusive and paranoid, a stranger to his friends."[11]

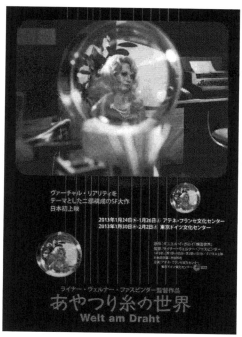

For decades, *World on a Wire* went unseen in the United States, unavailable on home video in any format in any part of the world for decades. Following the premiere of its restored, 205-minute glory on Turner Classic Movies, the film was picked up for DVD released by the Criterion Collection, where it can still be had for a quite reasonable price.

NOTES

[1] "I've Changed along with the Characters in My Films": An Interview with Rainer Werner." *Performing Arts Journal*, Vol. 14, No. 2 (May, 1992), pp. 23 Published by: Performing Arts Journal, Inc. http://www.jstor.org/stable/3245627

[2] Ruffell, Joe. 2002. "Rainer Werner Fassbinder." Great Directors Issue 20 Issue 20. May. http://sensesofcinema.com/2002/great-directors/fassbinder/

[3] Ebert, Roger. 1983. "daniel schmid: the fleeting days and eternal nights of r.w. Fassbinder." Chicago Sun-Times. August 31. http://www.rogerebert.com/interviews/daniel-schmid-the-fleeting-days-and-eternal-nights-of-rw-fassbinder

[4] Fitch, Alex. 2010. "World on a Wire." Electric Sheep Magazine. June 11. http://www.electricsheepmagazine.co.uk/features/2010/06/11/worldonawire/

[5] Rusak, Chris. 2015. "Rainer Werner Fassbinder and the Dishonest Direction of Life." Chris Rusak.com. March 16. http://text.chrisrusak.com/fassbinder-dishonest-direction-life/

[6] Ibid.

[7] Rusak, 2015.

[8] J. Hoberman. 2010. "Fassbinder's Sci-Fi World On A Wire At MOMA." Village Voice. April 13. http://www.villagevoice.com/film/fassbinders-sci-fi-world-on-a-wire-at-moma-6420484

[9] Fitch, 2010.

[10] Based on Jean Genet's novel *Querelle de Brest*, this would be Fassbinder's final film. Indeed, Fassbinder died before the film's release. The film was dedicated to his lover of a decade, El Hedi ben Salem, the star of his film, *Ali: Fear Eats the Soul* (1974), who committed suicide while in police custody in 1977. A fact Fassbinder remained unaware of until 1982.

[11] Ebert, 1983.

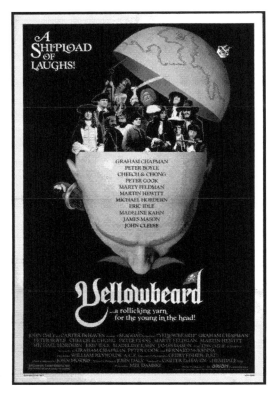

YELLOWBEARD (1983)

The history of piracy is rife with great beards. Edward Teach, he dreaded Blackbeard. Redbeard—a pirate so dreaded (much more than Blackbeard) that he was actually two *different* pirates from the Ottoman Empire—Oruç Reis, and Hayreddin Barbarossa. Then there was Bluebeard—not really a pirate, but no less tough on the ladies. None of them, though, could hold a candle to the even-more-dreaded-than-the-others-combined: Captain Yellowbeard! The scourge of all seven seas and a dozen more tributaries. Yellowbeard! His very name has caused spontaneous trouser-soiling world-wide. Yellowbeard! Who would feed you your own body parts to once again feel the rage in his nethers! Yellowbeard! A man so dangerous, so scurrilous, he could only be justifiably convicted of tax evasion!

We first meet Yellowbeard and his scurvy crew as they plunder the Spanish ship helmed by El Nebuloso (Tommy Chong) and his lackey, El Secundo (Cheech Marin). After frightening half the crew into submission, the vicious bastard absconds with the loot, managing to mangle his Bosun, Mr. Moon (Peter Boyle) out of the cruelty of his heart. Sometime later, we learn that Yellowbeard has cunningly buried his treasure on a remote island, shortly before his incarceration for the above cardinal sin of hiding wealth from her Royal Majesty.

While toiling away in St. Victim's Prison for the Criminally Naughty, constantly pestered by Mr. Gilbert (the late great Marty Feldman) regarding the whereabouts of the treasure, Yellowbeard (Graham Chapman) receives a surprise visit from his former conquest and possible legally-married wife, Mrs. Betty Beard (Madeline Kahn).

"What? You again?"

"I haven't seen you in fifteen years."

"Well, what is it this time?"

"Remember the last time I saw you and we were having that cuddle?"

"I was *raping* you, if that's what you mean."

"Well, half-rape, half-cuddle. Anyway, I'm here to tell you that you're the proud father of a bouncing 20-year-old boy named Dan."

But Yellowbeard has no time for sentiment. He's about to be released and, soon, reunited with his beloved treasure. Except that Commander Clement (Eric Idle), head of Her Majesty's Secret Service (so don't go blabbing about), has a cunning plan to relieve the dread pirate of his ill-gotten booty (ill-booten gotty?) by increasing Yellowbeard's sentence. "You see," he explains. "You see, twenty years ago, no one was expected to live in jail for twenty years." So her Majesty Queen Anne (played by Peter Bull[312] in grotesque drag) has graciously granted a sentence of an additional 140 years.

Responding as expected, Yellow-beard almost immediately escapes.

Following closely—but not too closely—Clement and his second, Mansell (*The Young Ones'* Nigel Planer), pursue Yellowbeard to Mrs. Beard's public house, wherein he'd hidden his vital map. Betty, taking advantage of an angle when she sees one, had the map destroyed, but not before tattooing it on the crown of young Dan's head. Dan, now a serious student, lives a comfortable life with his other possible father, the often-

Damski and Chapman. Photo courtesy Mel Damski

besotted Lord Lambourn (Peter Cook). Refusing to kill Lord Lambourn, and thus discounted as useless by his other, more ruthless father, Dan offers the idea that he could join Yellowbeard on a legitimate quest for the treasure, hiring a ship and crew for the adventure. Unfortunately, Dan, Lambourn, and Dr. Gilpin (Michael Hordern[313]) are almost immediately shanghaied to serve the strict-but-mostly-unfair Captain Hughes (James Mason). Fortunately, Yellowbeard stows aboard, hiding in a pig pen and accosting the various women snuck aboard in disguise (particularly Captain Hughes' officer of discipline, "Mr. Prostitute" (Greta Blackburn[314])).

Unbeknownst to Dan, several of Yellowbeard's former scurrilous crew have also joined, including the now hook-handed Mr. Moon. With Gilbert, Moon orchestrates a mutiny and elects Dan as the new Captain. They are almost immediately beset upon by Clement aboard The Lady Edith, and thus a modestly-budgeted ship battle commences. Sometime later, the island is reached. To the surprise of no one, it is El Nebuloso who has declared himself ruler of the island, and he will stop at nothing to defend his treasure. "Nothing", so long as he doesn't have to work too hard. Violence ensues. As the good Captain Y says, "I'll kill anyone who gets in the way of me killin' anyone!"

Like so many of our favorite *Movie Outlaw* entries, *Yellowbeard* has a long and complicated history behind it. Originally conceived as a vehicle for notorious *The Who* drummer, Keith Moon. Moon, Chapman, Cook, Bernard McKenna, and a variety of others who claimed to have been there at the time, met at a pub and Moon paid them $1,000 to write him a "mad movie" to star in. After explaining to Moon that he couldn't play Superman, or Batman, or Spider-Man, or a host of other copyrighted characters, they began to play with the concept of a gritty, funny pirate film in which Moon could really let loose.

When financing proved difficult, Chapman conceived of *The Odd Job* (1978), in which Moon would portray a little lunatic who offers to provide hitman services for the depressed

---

[312] Possibly reprising his role as the Duchess in 1972's *Alice's Adventures in Wonderland. Yellowbeard* was his final film role.

[313] "Captain Bules Martin" in *The Bed Sitting Room* (1969). See Fervid Filmmaking

[314] Best-known to Americans as the naked prostitute almost murdered by Jonathan Banks in *48 Hrs* (1982)

Chapman. But Moon, going through alcohol withdrawal at the time in a renewed bid to get sober, couldn't pass a studio-mandated screen test, so the role went to the "only OK" David Jason. Work returned on *Yellowbeard*. Then Moon did the unthinkable: the indestructible man up and died.

Moon's death was particularly hard on "The Gay Python", and he returned to *Yellowbeard* with an obsessive's tenacity, determined to bring the film to life and pay tribute to his departed friend, even if that meant assuming the leading role of the vicious buccaneer. Between 1979 and 1982, the production went through numerous changes of location and scope. As time wore on, actors were cast then let go or quit, while the American financiers became concerned that the film was "too British". At one point, Adam Ant was set to play Young Dan, but quit early on over the length of the pre-production. Sting was then courted, but, again, "too British", and was replaced by Martin Hewitt, inspiring the question that haunts us to this day, namely: "Who?" According to *Yellowbeard: Hijinks on the High Seas*, even Hewitt was against being cast. "Sting should have had my part. For crying out loud, I would have hired Sting over me any day.")[1]

On the flip side of that, Warner Brothers turned down Harry Nilsson's offer to write original songs for the film because he was too much of an alcoholic to be trusted. That was their story and they stuck to it. However, notes the Python group "The Daily Llama": "Another Nilsson song, 'Men at Sea,' was recorded uniquely for *Group Madness: The Making of Yellowbeard*[315] and can be heard during the end-credits of the documentary film. This song is dedicated to Marty Feldman."[2]

Eventually, the cast was rounded out by a cavalcade of very funny people representing multiple "groups" of popular comedians. Idle, Chapman, and John Cleese (as "Blind Pew") representing the Monty Python camp; Feldman, Kahn, and Boyle repping for the Mel Brooks family; Cook, Hordern, and Spike Milligan (cameoing as yet another Butler) representing the pre-Python Brit coalition; Cheech and Chong representing the American stoner set; plus James Mason and David Bowie[316] representing the "What the Hell?" side of casting. To oversee the predictable madness, the producing studio, Hemdale Film Corporation, hired first-time feature film director Mel Damski.

Up to *Yellowbeard*, Damski's career was primarily centered in television, having directed a number of TV movies and, most notably, the *Mary Tyler Moore Show* spin-off series *Lou Grant* (1977-1979) starring Ed Asner (for which he was nominated for an Emmy). "It was starting to dawn on me why they hired an inexperienced director with no movie credits to direct this picture," Damski wrote in 2012. With Chapman calling him at all hours to "discuss" how he wanted the next day's scenes to be shot. "I asked the producer and he admitted that Graham had wanted to direct the picture himself but the studio said no. They needed someone who they

---

[315] "And then there's *Group Madness*..., the irreverent documentary film which shows some of the behind-the-scenes antics of the *Yellowbeard* cast. 'Shooting the documentary was the easiest and most enjoyable experience I've ever had in the film business," recalls [director Michael Mileham]. The group followed the *Yellowbeard* cast and crew from Rye to Herfordshire, England and later to Zihuatanejo, Mexico, some 130 miles north of Acapulco. 'Once I had convinced the production staff of *Yellowbeard* that my crew and I had to be housed with the cast, my film was as good as made.' The documentary features each of the principal cast members in turn, including the Pythons and director Mel Damski. [...] *Group Madness* was later syndicated to 75 television stations in the United States upon the release of *Yellowbeard* in 1983. The film was shown only once on television, pre-empting *Saturday Night Live*, and hasn't aired since then." http://www.dailyllama.com/news/1995/llama012.html Once a very difficult documentary to obtain and not terribly informative, though fun to see the performers squirm in front of the camera (Feldman repeatedly runs away; Kenneth Mars becomes intentionally incoherent until the cameraman cuts away), it can now be streamed on Amazon.

[316] In an oft-quoted tale, Bowie was actually vacationing in Barbados, lounging on a beach when he saw a Spanish Galleon sail by. Intrigued, he followed the ship to the film camp and was offered the cameo role of a sailor masquerading as a shark to intimidate a keel-hauled Mrs. Beard. The following day, Bowie stole a company vehicle and took some of the stars on a joyride. A wreck left Hewitt with a broken foot. "We were shut down for a week, prisoners in paradise, waiting for the two lead actors to recover from their wounds so we could resume shooting. Bowie, unscathed, would sit at the pool all day long and avoid making eye contact with me." Damski, Mel. 2012. "Yellowbeard – Part Two." La Conner Weekly News. July 11. Archived at http://www.ifmelranthezoo.com/2012/07/11/yellowbeard-part-two/

Director Mel Damski with Mary Feldman. Not depicted: the rest of the guy on the left.
Photo courtesy Mel Damski.

could trust to get the work done and they thought a television director would have the discipline to keep things moving along. They also knew a big time filmmaker like Richard Lester or Stanley Donen would be unlikely to allow Chapman to basically function as a co-director. The challenges were starting to mount up and I realized that I wasn't in Kansas anymore. I had lived a somewhat sheltered life and was surrounded by nice, talented mentors on shows like *Lou Grant* and *M*A*S*H*."[3]

Damski encountered push-back from the more-established stars almost from the get-go. When presenting his notes to the film's writers—Chapman and Cook (Bernard McKenna had moved on at this point[317])—the derision was unsubtle, to say the least. "When I got to London and attempted to give the writers notes from myself and from the studio, Peter Cook openly mocked me. He was already a legend in England because of *Derek and Clive*, his comedy act with Dudley Moore, as well as movies like *Bedazzled* and the Broadway show *Beyond the Fringe*.[318] He was certainly wondering who does this kid think he is. And he was always drunk, so his attacks on me were pretty cruel and pretty funny to everyone else in the room but me. I called Mike Medavoy, the head of the studio back in Hollywood, and told him what was happening and he said "You're the director—do what you think has to be done!" [...] I took the challenge and told Graham Chapman, no stranger to alcohol himself, that Peter Cook would have to go, not only as a writer but as Lord Lambourn, the character he was to play in the movie. There was no way I was going to be able to actually direct the movie with Peter constantly questioning my decisions and having fun at my expense. Graham had been pre-med school at Cambridge, where he had

---

[317] "'Bernard and I spent a long time in Los Angeles writing It-possibly because we were *in* Los Angeles. The lifestyle there is rather distracting-great fun, but it didn't really suit two lads from England who were supposed to get down to work!' The pair eventually completed a script in which Yellowbeard was only a historical figure. The story occurred 20 years after his pirate days, and centered on his son. A re-wrIte brought *Yellowbeard* firmly into the plotllne. Then, McKenna dropped out, leaving Chapman in search of another writing partner. 'I was trying to decide on the person I would *most* like to write with in the entire world, and thought of Peter Cook," Chapman says of Dudley Moore's former comedy partner who starred in *Beyond the Fringe* and *The Two of Us*. "In my view, he's one of the funniest men in the world. So, I said 'Please!' He said 'Yes!' 'And we spent a month re-writing, working six days a week, making a new character of Yellowbeard. After that, it was a matter of eliminating the lunacy that was just *too far* out-which I did with David Sherlock." Johnson, Kim. 1983. "Yellowbeard." *Mediascene* Prevue 53, Volume 2 Number 13, September / October. P 64.

[318] Apropos of nothing but trivia, a billboard for the show is featured prominently during the climax of the 2016 *Ghostbusters* reboot.

met Cleese, and he administered an injection of Antabuse to Peter. Antabuse is a Clockwork Orange drug that alcoholics could take if they wanted or needed to go cold turkey. After the injection, if you even took a sniff of alcohol, you would get incredibly sick and vomit. The result was amazing. Peter continued to be funny—in fact, he made me laugh more than any of those comic geniuses—and he was totally supportive of me and we bonded and hung out together after work probably because I was a teetotaler and he knew he wouldn't even think of it in my presence."[4]

"I feel like the conductor of an all-star orchestra," Damski admitted to Stephen Farber. "All these actors are used to doing solos. They come in with new ideas all the time. I have to say no a lot, and sometimes I'm saying no to very funny things that just happen to be extraneous to the plot or inconsistent with the character."[5]

Moviemaking presents odd challenges beyond just getting the fucking thing in the can. The film's primary set, the HMS Bounty, on loan from its anchored retirement north of Acapulco in Zlhuantenejo Bay, originally built for 1960's *Mutiny on the Bounty*, had been adapted to be motor driven for the Mel Gibson remake of *The Bounty*. As a result, during *Yellowbeard*, the sails were often billowing in the opposite direction and had to be lacquered in place. It also served triple duty as Captain Hughes' ship, "to El Nebuloso's Spanish galleon to the French frigate of Commander Clement (Idle). More than half of the filming took place on the craft. Each day, the cast and crew—sometimes numbering over 100—were ferried out and crowded aboard. Despite the discomfort, the unit avoided a mutiny."[6] To Farber, Damski said, "We've gone from English efficiency to Mexican chaos. For example, we had a whole box of 18th-century weapons sent from England, and it's been sitting here in customs for eight weeks. We've had to use the same two pistols in every scene because that's all we had. Many other things have gone wrong. Fortunately, my television background helped me in being able to work quickly and shoot around problems. I'm used to improvising."[7]

El Nebuloso's island was largely uninhabited, forcing the Mexican government to rough-hew a serviceable road from one end of the beach to the other. On December 2, 1982, Marty Feldman, who had been suffering from back pain—which the entire cast and crew believed to have been caused by his insistence on doing his own stunts throughout production (often defying Damski's orders not to[319], but simply flinging himself into the air as soon as the cameras rolled)—succumbed to heart failure and died in his hotel room. "Please come quickly," he called down to John Tomiczek (the film's associate producer and Graham Chapman's adopted son and business manager), "I'm dying."

"When we finally got back to shooting at the studio in Mexico City, I was told to call the producer, Carter DeHaven, immediately. There were no cell phones in those days, so I left the set, went into a nearby office and called Carter. He told me that Marty was found dead in his hotel room. In shock, somehow I finished the scene I was shooting without saying a word to anyone else. When I got back to the hotel, Marty's body was still in his room, awaiting an ambulance that was called hours earlier when he was still alive. He had lots of pain pills and some illegal substances in his room and I watched as one of our production assistants flushed them down the toilet, not wanting to add scandal to tragedy. That night, I went from hotel room to hotel room to inform Marty's close friends and colleagues that he had passed. These were people who had worked with Marty for twenty years and each one of them broke down as I sat there trying to make sense of the unfathomable."[8]

"Chapman, a friend of Feldman's for more than 20 years, says the saucer-eyed comedian

---

[319] "While we were shooting on the coast, our art department was busy building sets at Churubusco Studios in Mexico City. We had shot a scene at Pinewood Studios in London on a prison set, and in the scene, Marty Feldman's character climbs over a wall and lands on the other side on his back. Marty wanted to do his own fall. I was young but I wasn't stupid and so I said he couldn't. His stunt double would do the wide shot of the fall, and Marty could just roll into the close-up on the ground. Marty set an apple box next to the camera and jumped into the air and landed hard on his back before I realized what was happening. We got the shot and moved on." Damski, Mel. 2012. "Yellowbeard – Part Two." La Conner Weekly News. July 11. Archived at www.ifmelranthezoo.com/2012/07/11/yellowbeard-part-two/

gave no indication of illness before his fatal heart attack. 'He seemed to be in good condition at the beginning," Chapman recalls, "though he did dislocate his coccyx during a stunt in the middle of filming. I thought he was a bit on edge, smoking about 80 cigarettes a day, but there was nothing apparently wrong with him, no 'Goodness me, he's on his way *out!*' The only anxious moment was when he was *not* acting, something typical of Marty. He was very much the old Marty, having a very happy time performing. Even an hour *before* the heart attack, he was in the lobby, joking and laughing'."[9]

"But it was the *News of the World* that screamed the headline: 'Blunder killed Marty'. It reported that Marty lay dying for one and a half hours before the doctor and ambulance successfully battled through the heavy traffic in the roads surrounding the Mexico City hotel. John Tomiczek was quoted as saying that: 'They told me they had got stuck in traffic and couldn't get there any faster. When they finally did arrive, Marty was too far gone even to move. God knows what might have happened if they had managed to get him to a hospital. They did what they could in the room and I just sat there crying and watching the heart monitor machine. Then came that awful moment when it just stopped bleeping:' He had given Marty oxygen but it had not helped. 'I could see him just sinking before my eyes,' he said. It was Tomiczek who rang [Marty's wife] Lauretta in Los Angeles to relate the last, tender message to her: 'They were personal messages between a man and his wife'[.]"[10]

"When Marty died, it seemed ridiculous to me," wrote Terry Jones. "That's not to be frivolous. It seemed ridiculous. He wasn't much older than me. Certainly less than 10 years. How could he die so young? Forty-eight. Madness. Graham died in 1989, also at the age of 48. Equally insane. Apparently, Marty's wife, Lauretta, went to her grave convincing herself that Marty was still in Mexico City, filming one last scene for *Yellowbeard*."[11]

Marty had completed the bulk of his role, save for the ending. "We had to resolve Marty's character in the movie, so I constructed a scene in which he falls to his death into a pool of acid. I shot it with a very good stunt double, but if you watch the movie, you can see that I had to avoid any close-ups. Ironic that Marty wanted to do his own stunts yet a stunt man doubled him for his final death scene."[12]

When released in 1983, thousands flocked to avoid *Yellowbeard*. Because of contractual stipulations, Orion couldn't market the film as either a Python film or a Cheech & Chong joint, so it was sold under the auspices of truth: it was a rousing all-star adventure, rife with absurdist comedy. But the "pirate" aspect of it proved to be the killer. Sometime after Burt Lancaster's *The Crimson Pirate* in 1952, the pirate movie had fallen out of fashion, as proven by the disastrous box office returns of things like *Swashbuckler* (1976), *Roman Polanski's Pirates*, *The Pirates of Penzance*, and *The Pirate Movie*. Not to mention *Nate & Hayes* or *Cutthroat Island*. In fact, not until Disney hired Johnny Depp to play Captain Jack Sparrow in *Pirates of the Caribbean* was the pirate genre finally re-legitimized (and even that franchise delivered diminishing returns). So *Yellowbeard*'s failure didn't come as too much as a surprise. "The pirate genre flourished for several decades but fell out of favor in the 1950's. After that, adventure films were more likely to be set in the future than in the past; the buccaneer hero took up residence in outer space,"[13] wrote Stephen Farber, but how was he to know just how awful his prediction would become, once *Ice Pirates* hit screens a year later.

"Monty Python has already done its pirate satire. The prologue of *Monty Python's Meaning of Life*,[320] which was one of the best parts of the film, involved that funny fantasy in which deskbound insurance clerks turn their ancient building into a galleon and set sail against the enemy skyscrapers. It was funny, it was quick, it was original. None of those statements apply to *Yellowbeard*," wrote Roger Ebert. "I guess there's a built-in danger with satires of old movie genres like the pirate movie. Once you've got everybody in costume and equipped them with a sword, a mustache and some handy clichés, there's the temptation to think they're funny. Not true. You've got to go ahead and write characters and create a plot that leads from laugh to laugh.

---

[320] "*The Crimson Permanent Assurance*" short film directed by Terry Gilliam, in which an office building full of chartered accountants sail the "chartered accountant-*sea*" lay siege to other corporations.

The sight of movie stars looking ridiculous is not, in itself, funny—or the Academy Awards would be a laff riot. *Yellowbeard* seems almost to have exhausted itself with its casting. This movie contains half the population of most of the movie comedies of the last decade. Anybody, in short, who is anybody is in this movie. I wonder if they had most of their laughs during the coffee breaks. The movie itself is a chaotic mess, in which herds of actors rush from one side of the screen to the other, waving their swords, making threats, and looking lost. The plot involves the most evil pirate of all time, but as Graham Chapman plays Yellowbeard, he never seems truly evil or even very mean—and with that anchor gone, the whole plot's meaningless."[14]

Not everyone hated it, mind you. The L.A. Times generously declared "There are many moments of hilarity here." Lawrence Van Gelder mentioned in his NY Times, "Their writing offers an occasional chuckle." Still, it wasn't much to write home about, apparently.

"When they tested the concept of "pirate comedy", the results were dismal. The pirate movie was a thing of the past and it was difficult to lampoon a genre that was unfamiliar to young audiences," wrote Damski. "I went to one of my favorite movie theaters at New York's Lincoln Center. I stood outside waiting for the crowds to show up but they never did. I felt like I was actually deflating on the sidewalk at Columbus Circle. The theater was less than half full, and there were a lot of chuckles but the movie didn't ever seem to fully captivate the audience. Not surprisingly, the same was true across the country. *Yellowbeard* landed with a thud. Box office-wise it was a shipwreck. The movie opened well in Australia, but everywhere else, it opened soft and didn't stick around for long. I was getting lots of meetings before the movie opened, just in case I was the new kid on the block with a hit movie under my belt. But the buzz was killed, there were no follow up meetings, and I was wounded but happy to be working back in television. [...] Still, I can't help but think what could have been. My goal was to be the American Francois Truffaut. He made wonderful small personal movies such as *400 Blows* and Jules and Jim and ethnographic movies such as *Wild Child*. [...] Which brings us back to my chance meeting with John Cleese in the security line at the airport. I turned to him and said 'John, Mel Damski, we did *Yellowbeard* together.' John nodded in recognition. 'I finally got to see that movie on late night television', he said. 'Impenetrable!' It was obvious from his facial expression that he didn't mean it as a compliment."[15]

In point of fact, on in interview on the DVD for his film *Clockwise*, Cleese described *Yellowbeard* as "One of the six worst films made in the history of the world"[321]. His shipmate Idle doesn't agree. "*Munchausen* was probably the worst," he said in The Independent, but referring to difficult shoots, rather than the quality of the films. "*Grail* was pretty tough. Being crucified in *Brian* wasn't easy either. No, I know you didn't exactly mean that... but making movies is making life experiences—and sometimes, the best times can be on the worst movies and vice versa, e.g. *Yellowbeard*, which I wouldn't have missed for the world."[16]

"*Yellowbeard* all but wrote its own scathing reviews. For starters, it contains perhaps the greatest concentration of rape-based humor in film history. If I had to describe its comedy using a single, made-up, incredibly offensive adjective, that word would be "rapey." Unsurprisingly, not too many critics risked looking sexist and emotionally stunted by going against the tide and standing up for the film's use of rape and murder as go-to gags. Yet despite the abundance of rape, murder, and gratuitous profanity, the film was inexplicably rated PG. The producers must have bribed the ratings board with rum and hookers. Unfortunately, viewers couldn't be bribed quite so easily," wrote The A.V. Club's Nathan Rabin. "*Yellowbeard* is uncompromising in its darkness. It's a measure of the film's warped conviction and refreshing dearth of sentimentality that its only heartwarming moment comes from Hewitt ostensibly murdering Chapman in cold blood. Then, and only then, does Chapman see his son as a proper pirate instead of a book-learning fancy lad."[17]

While it's one thing to condemn a movie made thirty-some years ago for its outdated non-P.C. humor, the rape jokes in *Yellowbeard* do wear a bit thin, even though they're made by the film's ostensible anti-hero. Yellowbeard isn't one to admire, obviously, and he isn't exactly

---

[321] "But I was happy to do it. Particularly after he called me, pleading." As usual, it's difficult to tell if Cleese is kidding.

redeemed at the end by his son's love. "Us Yellowbeards are never more dangerous than when we're dead!" he proclaims, unrepentantly evil even after the end. More curiously, however, is that as vicious as the titular character is, the film drags when he's absent. The entire section aboard The Lady Edith, with Yellowbeard "hiding" in a pig sty, lacks his bombast. Hewitt and his obligatory love interest Nelkin aren't terribly interesting either. Your best bet, during these sequences, is to watch Cook in the background, subtly reacting to everything around him as if he'd just suddenly sobered up and hadn't the faintest clue where he was. I won't make a joke here; some of the best people in the world are alcoholics and god knows *Yellowbeard* had its share.

"Still, *Yellowbeard* is hardly intended as piercing social commentary. It attacks the pirate genre with a mad comedic thrust. The story stirs memories of many other adventure films: A group of greedy characters fight to discover the buried treasure secreted on an

island in the Spanish Main. All the familiar elements of the genre are here: the battles at sea, plunder and pillage on land, torture in the brig. But the mayhem is perpetrated by a choice collection of British and American loons. [...] Despite the cast of comedians, all of the filmmakers insist that *Yellowbeard* is not a burlesque in the style of *Airplane* or *Blazing Saddles*. 'There are elements of parody,' says Graham Chapman, one of the writers as well as the star, 'but this is not really a spoof of the genre. It has a story that, although ludicrous, hopefully sweeps you along with it. The characters are slightly larger-than-life but not incredible." Bernard McKenna, the co-writer, concurs: 'It's a celebration of the genre, but done in a comedic way.' The director, Mel Damski, says that he spent a lot of time looking at Richard Lester's film of *The Three Musketeers*, hoping to reproduce its mixture of adventure and comedy," wrote Farber. "Warner Bros. bought the script of *Yellowbeard* a few years ago, then dropped the project because they considered it 'too British,' according to Mr. McKenna. The success of *Life of Brian* and *Time Bandits* made British humor more commercial, and Orion revived the project. In casting the movie, however, the producer, Carter De Haven, wanted to broaden its appeal for American audiences. 'I got the cast I wanted,' he says. 'All the actors are integral. They are not just playing cameo roles.' It was Mike Medavoy, the executive vice president of Orion, who suggested adding Cheech and Chong, in the roles of a sadistic Spanish ruler and his servile henchmen. Now the question is whether the American and

British styles of humor will mesh in the finished film. Peter Boyle comments on one of the basic differences: 'The English like wordplay, whereas I look for physical action and physical humor.' Before arriving on location, Bernard McKenna spent several months editing segments of *Saturday Night Live* for British television, and he had an opportunity to reflect on the differences between American and British humor. 'I found American humor less subtle than ours,' he says. 'It's slightly louder even in volume. But I enjoyed its bravery of attack, which our comedy doesn't always have. I think *Yellowbeard* is more in the British style. Even the American actors are underplaying.'"[18]

With all of this gloom and doom from the reviewers, their ire was premature. As with all cult films, it took a while for *Yellowbeard* to find its cult. I can barely count the number of times I've heard folks walking around muttering, "Stagger, stagger, roll, stagger..." (Referring to the device Yellowbeard uses to find his treasure on the beach—wounded and exhausted, he could barely do "ten paces west, three paces North of that interesting rock", now could he? And while 'tis true that the film was a bit of a catastrophe, box-office-wise, it hardly hurt the careers of those involved. Damski, for example, was nominated for a pair of Emmys—for "Outstanding Directing In A Drama Series", *Lou Grant* (1979) and *American Dream* (1981)—as well as an Oscar nod for Best Documentary Short Subject for the film *Still Kicking: The Fabulous Palm Springs Follies* (1998, which he shared with co-director Andrea Blaugrund). In fact, as we were first discussing this chapter, Damski was in Vancouver directing *Love on a Limb* with Marilu Henner. So *he's* still together.

But, yes, so many of the great men and women of *Yellowbeard* are gone now, and it almost seems strange to believe that they didn't take "comedy" with them. Peter Cook died January 9, 1995; Michael Hordern, the same year; Madeline Kahn left us December 3, 1999; we lost Peter Boyle December 12, 2006. While not dead, Idle has spent the last decade doing his own plundering, mining *Holy Grail* and *Life of Brian* for past gold and burying it beneath cheap laughs and strained musical numbers for Broadway, specifically *Spamalot* and *Not the Messiah*. And he had the nerve to accuse Cleese of doing anything for a buck.[322]

Disowning the film, Cheech and Chong reportedly only did *Yellowbeard* as a "favor" for Orion, a trial-run for their remake of *The Corsican Brothers*, which met its own box office demise the following year. Feldman, for his part, was delighted to work on the movie. "Some movies you do for money," he said, "and some you do for joy. This one is for love. I really did it to hang out with a lot of friends. I've always liked being part of an ensemble. When I was a child, my fantasy was to be Peter Lorre, not Humphrey Bogart. Even in my dreams I played supporting parts."[19]

"*Yellowbeard*, of course, has got Graham and John; there was always the Python connection. But it's not good at all; it was a very hit-and-miss piece," wrote occasional Python producer John Goldstone. "It's kind of representative of Graham in many ways, a rather hit-and-miss kind of career, and person. I man, sweet and lovely, but he needed very much the support of everybody else (particularly John) in creating what he did. He was individually inspired with some of the ideas that he had, but it needed to be contained."[20]

Peter Boyle and Marty Feldman.
Photo courtesty Mel Damski.

We lost Graham Chapman in October, 1989, but his presence remains (like Feldman, whose autobiography was discovered in his attic in 2014) through his *Monty Python* work, his own writings, like *Looks Like Another Brown Trouser Job* and *A Liar's Autobiography*, brought to the screen in animated form by Bill Jones, Jeff Simpson, and Ben Timlett. In fact, Chapman is nearly ubiquitous now (so where is our remastered DVD of *The Odd Job?*), a fact he'd probably find amusing.

"Chapman was one of the first celebrities ever to come out publically, doing so on an English talk show. When a member of the audience wrote to the show to point out that homosexuality was against the teachings of the Bible, Eric

---

[322] "John Cleese has said in several interviews that he felt this was the worst movie in which he ever appeared. He's always claimed that he only did it as a favor to Chapman, who was the driving force behind the film. It may have also been for the money, as fellow Python Eric Idle has famously maintained that Cleese would do anything for money, once offering him a Pound if he would shut up, which Cleese took."
www.threemoviebuffs.com/review/yellowbeard

Idle responded 'we've found out who it is and we've taken him out and had him killed.' Chapman lived for two decades with his partner David Sherlock, and was a vocal supporter of LGBT rights. Chapman and Sherlock later adopted a son, John Tomiczek. Chapman died on October 4, 1989 after suffering from complications from tonsil cancer and secondary spinal cancer. David Sherlock and fellow Pythons Michael Palin and John Cleese were at his bedside when he died, and Terry Jones and Peter Cook had visited earlier that day. Chapman died on the eve of the 20th anniversary of the first broadcast of *Flying Circus*, which Terry Jones called 'the worst case of party-pooping in all history'. The Pythons chose not to attend Chapman's funeral in order to give his family privacy and protection against a media craze, but they sent a wreath in the shape of the Python foot with the message: "To Graham from the other Pythons. Stop us if we're getting too silly." Since his death, members of Monty Python have rejected the possibility of a Python revival except to say: 'We would only do a reunion if Chapman came back from the dead. So we're negotiating with his agent.'"[21]

As far as *Yellowbeard* went, Chapman had no complaints. He made it for a friend, with friends, and died surrounded by friends. Not a bad way to live or die, come to think of it. "It was a great experience to live out a childhood dream. One needs to think a bit about *Yellowbeard*, but, fortunately, not too deeply. I think Marty described the film best as 'a rollicking comic yarn for the young in head.' That's quite a fair summary."[22]

NOTES

[1] Chapman, Graham. "Yellowbeard: Hijinks on the High Seas." New York : Carroll & Graf, 2005.

[2] ten Cate, Hans. 1995. INTERESTING FACTS ABOUT "YELLOWBEARD". Python Daily Llama. Thursday, 21.http://www.dailyllama.com/news/1995/llama013.html

[3] Damski, Mel. 2012. "Yellowbeard – Part One." La Conner Weekly News. July 4. Archived at http://www.ifmelranthezoo.com/2012/07/04/yellowbeard-part-one/

[4] Ibid.

[5] Farber, Stephen. 1983. "Ahoy! Just Over The Horizon, A Fleet Of Pirate Movies." New York Times. January 9. http://www.nytimes.com/1983/01/09/movies/ahoy-just-over-the-horizon-a-fleet-of-pirate-movies.html

[6] Johnson, Kim. 1983. "Yellowbeard." Mediascene Prevue 53, Volume 2 Number 13, September / October. P 62.

[7] Farber, 1983.

[8] Damski, Mel. 2012. "Yellowbeard – Part Two." La Conner Weekly News. July 11. Archived at http://www.ifmelranthezoo.com/2012/07/11/yellowbeard-part-two/

[9] Johnson, Kim. 1983. "Yellowbeard." Mediascene Prevue 53, Volume 2 Number 13, September / October. P 77

[10] Ross, Robert. "Marty Feldman: The Biography of a Comedy Legend." Titan Books; 2011. P.294.

[11] Jones, Terry. 2016. "Marty Feldman: The best there ever was." The Jewish Chronicle Online. January 21. http://www.thejc.com/arts/theatre/152612/marty-feldman-the-best-there-ever-was

[12] Damski, Mel. 2012. "Yellowbeard – Part Two."

[13] Farber, Stephen. 1983. "Ahoy! Just Over The Horizon, A Fleet Of Pirate Movies." New York Times. January 9. http://www.nytimes.com/1983/01/09/movies/ahoy-just-over-the-horizon-a-fleet-of-pirate-movies.html

[14] Ebert, Roger. 1983. "Yellowbeard." Chicago Sun-Times. June 24. http://www.rogerebert.com/reviews/yellowbeard-1983

[15] Damski, Mel. 2012. "Yellowbeard – Part Two."

[16] No author cited. 1999. "You ask the questions Such as: Eric Idle, do you always look on the bright side of life? And what does 'ni' mean?" The Independent. October 5. http://www.independent.co.uk/news/people/profiles/you-ask-the-questions-739095.html

[17] Rabin, Nathan. 2008. "My Year Of Flops Case File #113, Ask The A.V. Club Crossover Edition: Yellowbeard." The A.V. Club. July 9. http://www.avclub.com/article/my-year-of-flops-case-file-113-ask-ithe-av-clubi-c-2375

[18] Rabin, 1983.

[19] Ibid

[20] Morgan, David. "Monty Python Speaks!" London. Fourth Estate Limited. 1999. P 198

[21] Karen, 2013. "January 8: Today's Birthday in Comedy: Graham Chapman." Notes on the Road. January 8. http://www.notesontheroad.com/Today-s-Birthday-in-Comedy-Graham-Chapman.html

[22] Johnson, 1983. P 77

INDEX

FILMS COVERED IN PAST VOLUMES
Key: *Fervid Filmmaking (FF), Movie Outlaw (MO), Movie Outalw Rides Again (MORA)*

Les Aventures Extraordinaires D'adèle Blanc-Sec (2010) (MO)

The Adventures of Mark Twain (1985) (MORA)

Alatriste (2008) (MO)

All About Evil (2010) (FF)

All Through the Night (1941) (MO)

Angel (1984) (MORA)

Anguish (1987) (FF)

Animal Room (1995) (FF)

The Atrocity Circle (2005) (MORA)

The Baby of Mâcon (1993) (FF)

Backtrack (1990) (MORA)

Banned (1989) (FF)

The Bed Sitting Room (1969) (FF)

The Big Fix (1978) (MO)

Bitch Slap (2009) (FF)

Blood on the Moon (1948) (MO)

The Blood Shed (2007) (FF)

Blue Collar (1978) (MORA)

Brain Dead (1990) (MO)

Brain Donors (1992) (MO)

The Brave (1997) (MO)

The Boneyard (1991) (FF)

Breakout (1975) (MORA)

Britannia Hospital (1982) (MO)

Brute Force (1947) (MO)

Buddy Buddy (1981) (MORA)

Buried (2010) (MORA)

Butcher, Baker, Nightmare Maker (1980) (MO)

Café Flesh (1982) (MORA)

Cannibal Girls (1973) (MO)

Cast a Deadly Spell (1991) (FF)

Chatterbox (1977) (MORA)

Child's play (1972) (MORA)

Coonskin (1975) (FF)

The Cotton Club (1984) (MORA)

Crazy Moon (1987) (MORA)

Dangerous Encounters of the First Kind (1980) (MORA)

The Dark Backward (1991) (MO)

Dark Blood (1993) (MORA)

Dead Heat (1988) (MORA)

Deadgirl (2009) (MO)

Deadwood Park (2007) (FF)

Dear Mr. Gacy (2010) (MO)

Death Watch (1980) (FF)

Doc Savage: The Man of Bronze (1975) (MO)

Don's Plum (2001) (MO)

Dr. Caligari (1989) (FF)

Dr. Cook's Garden (1971) (MO)

Dreamchild (1985) (MORA)

Drones (2010) (MO)

The Dueling Accountant (2008) (FF)

Dust Devil (1993) (MORA)

Dust Up (2012) (MO)

Dynamite Chicken (1971) (FF)

Eddie Presley (1992) (MO)

Electric Dreams (1984) (MORA)

Escape from Tomorrow (2013) (MO)

Fantasy Mission Force (1982) (MO)

Fast-Walking (1982) (MO)

Fearless Frank (1967) (FF)

Fedora (1978) (MO)

Felidae (1994) (MO)

Figures in a Landscape (1970) (MO)

Film Noir (2007) (MORA)

The Final Programme (1973) (FF)

The Final Terror (1983) (MORA)

Folks at Red Wolf Inn (1972) (MO)

Forbidden Zone (1980) (FF)

Frankenhooker (1990) (MORA)

The Front (1976) (MORA)

Gambit (1966) (MO)

Get Crazy (1983) (FF)

The Ghastly Love of Johnny X (2013) (MO)

Ghost in the Noonday Sun (1973) (MO)

The Girl Hunters (1962) (MO)

G-Men from Hell (2000) (FF)

Gospel According To Vic (1986) (MO)

Grendel Grendel Grendel (1981) (MO)

Hammett (1982) (MO)

Harry in Your Pocket (1973) (MO)

Head (1968) (FF)

Head Office (1986) (MORA)

Hell Fire (2012) (MO)

Hey, Stop Stabbing Me! (2003) (FF)

Hickey & Boggs (1972) (MO)

His Kind of Woman (1951) (FF)

Hisss (2010) (MO)

Holiday Affair (1949) (MO)

House of Bad (2013) (MO)

I Bought a Vampire Motorcycle (1990) (MO)

I Sell the Dead (2009) (FF)

The Imaginarium of Doctor Parnassus (2010) (MO)

Impure Thoughts (1985) (MORA)

Insignificance (1985) (MO)

Invasion (1999) (MO)

Jane White Is Sick and Twisted (2002) (MORA)

Je T'aime, Je T'aime (1968) (FF)

Jubilee (1977) (FF)

Kafka (1991) (MO)

Killer Joe (2012) (MORA)

Killer Tongue (1996) (MO)

King of the Ants (2003) (MORA)

The Land of College Prophets (2005) (FF)

Last Exit to Brooklyn (1989) (MO)

The Last Hard Men (1976) (MO)

The Last of Sheila (1973) (FF)

Last Summer (1969) (MO)

The Legend of the Lone Ranger (1981)

Lethal Force (2006) (FF)

Life and Death of a Porno Gang (2009) (MO)

Little Big Horn (1951) (MORA)

The List of Adrian Messenger (1963) (MO)

Lo (2009) (MO)

The Lone Ranger (2013) (MORA)

Lone Star (1996) (MORA)

Looker (1981) (MORA)

Le Magnifique (1973) (FF)

Man Facing Southeast (1986) (MO)

Marat / Sade (1967) (MORA)

Mark of the Beast (2012) (MORA)

Massacre at Central High (1976) (MORA)

Meet the Feebles (1989) (MORA)

Meet the Hollowheads (1989) (FF)

Murder By Decree (1979) (MO)

The Madwoman of Chaillot (1969) (MORA)

The Magic Christian (1969) (MORA)

The Maltese Bippy (1969) (MORA)

The Maltese Falcon (1931) (MORA)

The Man Who Wasn't There (1983) (MORA)

The Mutilation Man (1998) (FF)

Night of the Strangler (1972) (MO)

Nightbreed (1990) (MORA)

Nightwing (1979) (MORA)

The Ninth Configuration (1980) (MO)

Nothing Lasts Forever (1984) (FF)

O. C. And Stiggs (1987) (FF)

Oblivion (1994) (FF)

The Odd Job (1978) (MO)

Open Season (1974) (MO)

Operation Midnight Climax (2002) (FF)

Original Sins (1995) (MO)

The Outfit (1973) (MORA)

Parasomnia (2008) (FF)

Penn & Teller Get Killed (1989) (MORA)

Phantom of the Paradise (1974) (MORA)

The Phynx (1970) (MO)

Pom Pom and Hot Hot (1992) (MORA)

Possession (1981)

Pretty Maids All In a Row (1971) (MO)

Prime Cut (1972) (MORA)

The Prodigy (2004) (FF)

The Projectionist (1971) (FF)

Psychos in Love (1987) (FF)

Puckoon (2002) (FF)

The Rage (2007) (MORA)

Raw Meat (1972) (MORA)

Razorback (1984) (MORA)

The Redsin Tower (2005) (MORA)

Rented Lips…A Tale of Two Scripts (1988) (FF)

Repo! The Genetic Opera (2008) (FF)

The Return of Captain Invincible (1983) (FF)

The Rise and Rise of Michael Rimmer (1970) (MORA)

Rolling Thunder (1977) (MORA)

Rosencrantz and Guildenstern Are Dead (1990) (MORA)

The Ruling Class (1971) (MO)

Santa Sangre (1989) (FF)

Satan Met A Lady (1936) (MORA)

Satan Was a Lady (2001) (FF)

Saturn 3 (1980) (MORA)

Schizopolis (1996) (FF)

Scream and Scream Again (1970)

Screaming Mimi (1958) (MORA)

The Seven-Per-Cent Solution (1976) (MORA)

Sex Machine (2005) (FF)

Shadey (1985) (FF)

Shanks (1974) (FF)

Shockheaded (2002) (FF)

Sixteen Tongues (1990) (FF)

Skidoo (1968) (FF)

Son of Dracula (1974) (FF)

Sonny Boy (1989) (FF)

Southland Tales (2007) (MO)

Spike of Bensonhurst (1988) (MORA)

The Spirit (1987) (MO)

The Spirit (2008) (MO)

Straight To Hell (1987) (FF)

The Stunt Man (1980) (MORA)

Success (1980) (FF)

Survival of the Dead (2010) (FF)

The Sword Bearer (2010) (MORA)

Sword of the Valiant (1984) (MORA)

Tank Girl (1995) (MORA)

Teen Ape vs. the Nazi Monster Apocalypse (2009) (FF)

Thursday (1998) (MO)

Tideland (2005) (FF)

A Time for Killing (1967) (MO)

The Traveling Executioner (1970) (MO)

Treasure of the Four Crowns (1983) (MORA)

Triangle (2009) (MO)

Tromeo and Juliet (1996) (FF)

Trouble in Mind (1985) (FF)

Twice Upon a Time (1983) (FF)

Volere Volare (1991) (MO)

The Way of the Gun (2000) (MO)

Who Do I Gotta Kill? (1992) (MO)

Winter Kills (1979) (MO)

Withnail & I (1987) (MORA)

The World's Greatest Sinner (1962) (FF)

The Wrath of God (1972) (MORA)

Xtro (1983) (FF)

The Zero Theorem (2014) (MORA)

ALL HAIL CINEMAGOG!
(Art by Ryan Hose)

74232681R00197

Made in the USA
Middletown, DE
22 May 2018